Personnel Management in Government

PUBLIC ADMINISTRATION AND PUBLIC POLICY

A Comprehensive Publication Program

Executive Editor

JACK RABIN
Professor of Public Administration and Public Policy
School of Public Affairs
The Capital College
The Pennsylvania State University—Harrisburg
Middletown, Pennsylvania

1. *Public Administration as a Developing Discipline* (in two parts), Robert T. Golembiewski
2. *Comparative National Policies on Health Care*, Milton I. Roemer, M.D.
3. *Exclusionary Injustice: The Problem of Illegally Obtained Evidence*, Steven R. Schlesinger
4. *Personnel Management in Government: Politics and Process*, Jay M. Shafritz, Walter L. Balk, Albert C. Hyde, and David H. Rosenbloom
5. *Organization Development in Public Administration* (in two parts), edited by Robert T. Golembiewski and William B. Eddy
6. *Public Administration: A Comparative Perspective, Second Edition, Revised and Expanded*, Ferrel Heady
7. *Approaches to Planned Change* (in two parts), Robert T. Golembiewski
8. *Program Evaluation at HEW* (in three parts), edited by James G. Abert
9. *The States and the Metropolis*, Patricia S. Florestano and Vincent L. Marando
10. *Personnel Management in Government: Politics and Process, Second Edition, Revised and Expanded*, Jay M. Shafritz, Albert C. Hyde, and David H. Rosenbloom
11. *Changing Bureaucracies: Understanding the Organization Before Selecting the Approach*, William A. Medina
12. *Handbook on Public Budgeting and Financial Management*, edited by Jack Rabin and Thomas D. Lynch
13. *Encyclopedia of Policy Studies*, edited by Stuart S. Nagel
14. *Public Administration and Law: Bench v. Bureau in the United States*, David H. Rosenbloom
15. *Handbook on Public Personnel Administration and Labor Relations*, edited by Jack Rabin, Thomas Vocino, W. Bartley Hildreth, and Gerald J. Miller
16. *Public Budgeting and Finance: Behavioral, Theoretical, and Technical Perspectives, Third Edition*, edited by Robert T. Golembiewski and Jack Rabin

17. *Organizational Behavior and Public Management*, Debra W. Stewart and G. David Garson

18. *The Politics of Terrorism: Second Edition, Revised and Expanded,* edited by Michael Stohl

19. *Handbook of Organization Management*, edited by William B. Eddy

20. *Organization Theory and Management*, edited by Thomas D. Lynch

21. *Labor Relations in the Public Sector*, Richard C. Kearney

22. *Politics and Administration: Woodrow Wilson and American Public Administration*, edited by Jack Rabin and James S. Bowman

23. *Making and Managing Policy: Formulation, Analysis, Evaluation*, edited by G. Ronald Gilbert

24. *Public Administration: A Comparative Perspective, Third Edition, Revised*, Ferrel Heady

25. *Decision Making in the Public Sector*, edited by Lloyd G. Nigro

26. *Managing Administration*, edited by Jack Rabin, Samuel Humes, and Brian S. Morgan

27. *Public Personnel Update*, edited by Michael Cohen and Robert T. Golembiewski

28. *State and Local Government Administration*, edited by Jack Rabin and Don Dodd

29. *Public Administration: A Bibliographic Guide to the Literature*, Howard E. McCurdy

30. *Personnel Management in Government: Politics and Process, Third Edition, Revised and Expanded*, Jay M. Shafritz, Albert C. Hyde, and David H. Rosenbloom

31. *Handbook of Information Resource Management*, edited by Jack Rabin and Edward M. Jackowski

32. *Public Administration in Developed Democracies: A Comparative Study*, edited by Donald C. Rowat

33. *The Politics of Terrorism: Third Edition, Revised and Expanded*, edited by Michael Stohl

34. *Handbook on Human Services Administration*, edited by Jack Rabin and Marcia B. Steinhauer

35. *Handbook of Public Administration*, edited by Jack Rabin, W. Bartley Hildreth, and Gerald J. Miller

36. *Ethics for Bureaucrats: An Essay on Law and Values, Second Edition, Revised and Expanded*, John A. Rohr

37. *The Guide to the Foundations of Public Administration*, Daniel W. Martin

38. *Handbook of Strategic Management*, edited by Jack Rabin, Gerald J. Miller, and W. Bartley Hildreth

39. *Terrorism and Emergency Management: Policy and Administration*, William L. Waugh, Jr.

40. *Organizational Behavior and Public Management: Second Edition, Revised and Expanded*, Michael L. Vasu, Debra W. Stewart, and G. David Garson

41. *Handbook of Comparative and Development Public Administration*, edited by Ali Farazmand

42. *Public Administration: A Comparative Perspective, Fourth Edition*, Ferrel Heady

43. *Government Financial Management Theory*, Gerald J. Miller

44. *Personnel Management in Government: Politics and Process, Fourth Edition, Revised and Expanded*, Jay M. Shafritz, Norma M. Riccucci, David H. Rosenbloom, and Albert C. Hyde
45. *Public Productivity Handbook*, edited by Marc Holzer
46. *Handbook of Public Budgeting*, edited by Jack Rabin
47. *Labor Relations in the Public Sector: Second Edition, Revised and Expanded*, Richard C. Kearney
48. *Handbook of Organizational Consultation*, edited by Robert T. Golembiewski
49. *Handbook of Court Administration and Management*, edited by Steven W. Hays and Cole Blease Graham, Jr.
50. *Handbook of Comparative Public Budgeting and Financial Management*, edited by Thomas D. Lynch and Lawrence L. Martin
51. *Handbook of Organizational Behavior*, edited by Robert T. Golembiewski
52. *Handbook of Administrative Ethics,* edited by Terry L. Cooper
53. *Encyclopedia of Policy Studies: Second Edition, Revised and Expanded,* edited by Stuart S. Nagel
54. *Handbook of Regulation and Administrative Law,* edited by David H. Rosenbloom and Richard D. Schwartz
55. *Handbook of Bureaucracy,* edited by Ali Farazmand
56. *Handbook of Public Sector Labor Relations*, edited by Jack Rabin, Thomas Vocino, W. Bartley Hildreth, and Gerald J. Miller
57. *Practical Public Management*, Robert T. Golembiewski
58. *Handbook of Public Personnel Administration*, edited by Jack Rabin, Thomas Vocino, W. Bartley Hildreth, and Gerald J. Miller
59. *Public Administration: A Comparative Perspective, Fifth Edition*, Ferrel Heady
60. *Handbook of Debt Management*, edited by Gerald J. Miller
61. *Public Administration and Law: Second Edition*, David H. Rosenbloom and Rosemary O'Leary
62. *Handbook of Local Government Administration*, edited by John J. Gargan
63. *Handbook of Administrative Communication*, edited by James L. Garnett and Alexander Kouzmin
64. *Public Budgeting and Finance: Fourth Edition, Revised and Expanded*, edited by Robert T. Golembiewski and Jack Rabin
65. *Handbook of Public Administration: Second Edition*, edited by Jack Rabin, W. Bartley Hildreth, and Gerald J. Miller
66. *Handbook of Organization Theory and Management: The Philosophical Approach*, edited by Thomas D. Lynch and Todd J. Dicker
67. *Handbook of Public Finance*, edited by Fred Thompson and Mark T. Green
68. *Organizational Behavior and Public Management: Third Edition, Revised and Expanded*, Michael L. Vasu, Debra W. Stewart, and G. David Garson
69. *Handbook of Economic Development*, edited by Kuotsai Tom Liou
70. *Handbook of Health Administration and Policy*, edited by Anne Osborne Kilpatrick and James A. Johnson
71. *Handbook of Research Methods in Public Administration*, edited by Gerald J. Miller and Marcia L. Whicker
72. *Handbook on Taxation*, edited by W. Bartley Hildreth and James A. . Richardson

73. *Handbook of Comparative Public Administration in the Asia-Pacific Basin*, edited by Hoi-kwok Wong and Hon S. Chan

74. *Handbook of Global Environmental Policy and Administration,* edited by Dennis L. Soden and Brent S. Steel

75. *Handbook of State Government Administration,* edited by John J. Gargan

76. *Handbook of Global Legal Policy,* edited by Stuart S. Nagel

77. *Handbook of Public Information Systems,* edited by G. David Garson

78. *Handbook of Global Economic Policy,* edited by Stuart S. Nagel

79. *Handbook of Strategic Management: Second Edition, Revised and Expanded,* edited by Jack Rabin, Gerald J. Miller, and W. Bartley Hildreth

80. *Handbook of Global International Policy,* edited by Stuart S. Nagel

81. *Handbook of Organizational Consultation: Second Edition, Revised and Expanded,* edited by Robert T. Golembiewski

82. *Handbook of Global Political Policy,* edited by Stuart S. Nagel

83. *Handbook of Global Technology Policy,* edited by Stuart S. Nagel

84. *Handbook of Criminal Justice Administration,* edited by Toni DuPont-Morales, Michael K. Hooper, and Judy H. Schmidt

85. *Labor Relations in the Public Sector: Third Edition,* edited by Richard C. Kearney

86. *Handbook of Administrative Ethics: Second Edition, Revised and Expanded,* edited by Terry L. Cooper

87. *Handbook of Organizational Behavior: Second Edition, Revised and Expanded,* edited by Robert T. Golembiewski

88. *Handbook of Global Social Policy,* edited by Stuart S. Nagel and Amy Robb

89. *Public Administration: A Comparative Perspective, Sixth Edition,* Ferrel Heady

90. *Handbook of Public Quality Management,* edited by Ronald J. Stupak and Peter M. Leitner

91. *Handbook of Public Management Practice and Reform,* edited by Kuotsai Tom Liou

92. *Personnel Management in Government: Politics and Process, Fifth Edition,* Jay M. Shafritz, Norma M. Riccucci, David H. Rosenbloom, Katherine C. Naff, and Albert C. Hyde

Additional Volumes in Preparation

Handbook of Crisis and Emergency Management, edited by Ali Farazmand

Handbook of Comparative and Development Public Administration: Second Edition, Revised and Expanded, edited by Ali Farazmand

Handbook of Monetary and Fiscal Policy, edited by Jack Rabin and Glenn L. Stevens

Financial Planning and Management in Public Organizations, Alan Walter Steiss and Chukwuemeka O. C. Nwagwu

Handbook of Developmental Policy Studies, edited by Stuart S. Nagel

Handbook of International Health Care Systems, edited by Khi V. Thai, Edward T. Wimberley, and Sharon M. McManus

Annals of Public Administration

1. *Public Administration: History and Theory in Contemporary Perspective*, edited by Joseph A. Uveges, Jr.
2. *Public Administration Education in Transition*, edited by Thomas Vocino and Richard Heimovics
3. *Centenary Issues of the Pendleton Act of 1883*, edited by David H. Rosenbloom with the assistance of Mark A. Emmert
4. *Intergovernmental Relations in the 1980s*, edited by Richard H. Leach
5. *Criminal Justice Administration: Linking Practice and Research*, edited by William A. Jones, Jr.

Personnel Management in Government

Politics and Process

Fifth Edition

Jay M. Shafritz
University of Pittsburgh
Pittsburgh, Pennsylvania

David H. Rosenbloom
American University
Washington, D.C.

Norma M. Riccucci
State University of New York
Albany, New York

Katherine C. Naff
San Francisco State University
San Francisco, California

Albert C. Hyde
The Brookings Institution
Washington, D.C.

MARCEL DEKKER, INC.   NEW YORK • BASEL

The fourth edition was published as *Personnel Management in Government: Politics and Process, Fourth Edition, Revised and Expanded,* by Jay M. Shafritz, Norma M. Riccucci, David H. Rosenbloom, and Albert C. Hyde.

ISBN: 0-8247-0504-1

This book is printed on acid-free paper.

Headquarters
Marcel Dekker, Inc.
270 Madison Avenue, New York, NY 10016
tel: 212-696-9000; fax: 212-685-4540

Eastern Hemisphere Distribution
Marcel Dekker AG
Hutgasse 4, Postfach 812, CH-4001 Basel, Switzerland
tel: 41-61-261-8482; fax: 41-61-261-8896

World Wide Web
http://www.dekker.com

The publisher offers discounts on this book when ordered in bulk quantities. For more information, write to Special Sales/Professional Marketing at the headquarters address above.

Preface

More than 20 years have passed since the first edition of this book appeared. In 1978, public sector personnel management seemed complex but still quite straightforward. The first edition was fewer than 300 pages with a fairly simplistic structure. We began with an extensive historical section explaining the political context of personnel, which we felt had been largely ignored by the standard personnel textbooks of the time—indeed, we felt that was perhaps the most important reason for us to write a new textbook. Our history section was followed by one on the functions of personnel and separate sections on employee rights and labor relations. Our inclusion of a separate chapter on equal employment opportunity, one of the first public personnel texts to do so, seemed almost radical at the time. Finally, we tried to integrate personnel into the major management movement (what some now call a fad) of the era—productivity improvement— so we concluded with several chapters on how personnel supported productivity efforts in government. That also seemed radical back in the late 1970s.

So much is different today. Ironically, we wrote in our fourth edition that "while history does not change much, almost everything else about personnel management in government does." That certainly seemed apparent back in 1990—the economy was yet again in recession, state and local governments were playing cutback management déjà vu, scrambling to cover massive budget short-falls, while the federal government was forecasting slow growth with budget deficits for decades to come. Government had no concept of the Internet, broad-band, or e-commerce, much less the new economy or globalization. The big management issue was whether to emulate Japan, then the most successful economy in the world, and adopt quality management. For the fifth edition it should be noted that it is history now that is changing rapidly and that governments at all levels are facing tremendous challenges to be competitive and relevant. For public personnel management, the line from Tomasi's classic novel, *The Leopard*, seems most appropriate: "If we want things to stay as they are, things will really have to change."

All the more reason for a new fifth edition addressing how the environment has changed and assessing both how far we have come in public personnel management and how far we have to go. For this edition, there are now five coauthors. Katherine C. Naff, formerly with the U.S. Merit Systems Protection Board and now at San Francisco State University, has joined us.

The textbook itself has been redesigned but structurally looks very much like our first edition. We've kept the opening prologues but extended the range of material they encompass. There's much more state and local analysis as, not surprisingly, that's where much of the action in public personnel management has been in the 1990s, and this promises to be even more true in the 21st century. The chapter on equal employment opportunity is now its own section with an additional new chapter on diversity. The labor relations section remains but includes a new chapter on employee relations. Having predicted wrongly for four editions about which management fad would forever solve our performance problems in government, the productivity section has been replaced with a single chapter on the legacy of quality and reengineering. But more than anything, we've tried to keep the focus on the future. After all, the value of public personnel management is primarily about solving the "people" problems of tomorrow's government organizations.

As with each edition, we remain solely responsible for the content that follows. We would be pleased to hear from any reader regarding our perspectives or positions, or your thoughts on any of the issues presented in the text. With email and all the other communications advances of today, there's no reason not to.

Jay M. Shafritz	jays@pitt.edu
David H. Rosenbloom	rbloom@american.edu
Norma M. Riccucci	nriccucci@sunyalbany.edu
Katherine C. Naff	kcnaff@sfsu.edu
Albert C. Hyde	ahyde@brookings.edu

Acknowledgments

All totaled, well over a hundred people were acknowledged in the first four editions of *Personnel Management in Government*. Many of them were helpful colleagues at the universities where we were teaching, who shared with us their expertise and encouragement. Many more were our students, who provided us with insights about what was and wasn't in our textbook and even occasionally showed us in their research papers their assessment of what was new and, perhaps more importantly, what was really old and boring. For the purpose of trying to keep this section from resembling a phone directory, we simply extend thanks again to all our aforementioned colleagues and students for their help in the past.

There is a third group of individuals we have also listed in previous editions who have aided immeasurably in making this textbook what it is: the many personnel professionals in the federal government and in state and local agencies, who have shared with us their best practices and lessons learned in leading change. There are also our colleagues in two professional associations—SPALR (the Section on Personnel and Labor Relations of the American Society for Public Administration) and IPMA (the International Personnel Management Association)—who have greatly assisted us in the past.

We would be remiss, however, if we did not give special thanks to two organizations and their exceptional staff who have made special contributions to our study of public personnel. The first is the U.S. Merit System's Protection Board Office of Policy Evaluation, directed by John Palguta, which has continued to provide some of the most insightful and best-researched studies of federal personnel policies and surveys of the federal public service. The other is the National Academy of Public Administration's Center for Human Resources Management, led by Frank Cipolla, whose research reports on federal reforms have been invaluable.

For this fifth edition, we add some new names to our list of debts. For this edition, we are especially indebted to:

Carolyn Ban, University of Pittsburgh
John Crum, U.S. Merit Systems Protection Board
Randy Hamilton, Institute for Government Studies, University of California at Berkeley
Joel Kassiola, San Francisco State University
Tom Novotny, Publisher of *The Public Manager*
Steve Ott, University of Utah
Ray Pomerleau, San Francisco State University
Frank Scott, San Francisco State University
Genie Stowers, San Francisco State University
Robert Tobias, The American University
Andrew Wasilisian, U.S. Office of Personnel Management

Stephanie Hyde of Cox Communications helped convert the entire manuscript from paper to electronic files. Alexis Katz of HR Consulting managed the archive.

Finally, our thanks to Paige Force and her colleagues at Marcel Dekker, Inc.—for her patience and all their many helpful efforts in putting this fifth edition on your bookshelf.

Contents

Preface   iii
Acknowledgments   v
Introduction: Why This Book?   xiii

**Part I   The History and Environment of Public Personnel
           Management**

1. The First Century of Civil Service Reform   1

   *Prologue: President Garfield's Assassination and the Origins
        of the Merit System*   1
   A Historical Perspective: Enter the Spoils System   2
   The Motivation for Civil Service Reform   6
   The Impetus for Reform   8
   The Pendleton Act   13
   The Development of the Central Personnel Agency   15
   State and Local Institutional Arrangements: A History
        in Parallel   33
   Civil Service Reform and the Decline of the Commission
        Format   37
   A Summary Note on the Merits of Reform   39
   Bibliography   40

2. Civil Service Reform in the Postreform Era (1979 to 2000)   45

    Prologue: The Death of the Merit System in Georgia   45
    The Aftermath of the Civil Service Reform Act of 1978   48
    Overture for Postreform: The Volcker Commission   53
    The First Movement: The Clinton Administration "Transition"   57
    The Second Movement: The NPR and Federal Workforce
        Restructuring   60
    The Third Movement: Reinvention of OPM   67
    An Unfinished Symphony: Civil Service Reform in the
        Second Term   72
    Civil Service Reform at the State and Local Level   77
    Appendix: 1999 Civil Service Improvements   82
    Bibliography   91

3. The Legal Framework of Public Personnel Management   93

    Prologue: Elrod *v.* Burns *(1976)*   93
    Comparing the Legal and Managerial Frameworks
        of Government   96
    Merit Principles and Civil Service   97
    The Constitutional Law of Public Employment   106
    The Individualized Rights Approach   109
    The Public Service Model   110
    Conclusion: Know Your Law   128
    Bibliography   128

Part II   The Processes of Human Resources Management

4. Human Resources Planning   131

    Prologue: Where Have All the Firefighters Gone?   131
    The Environment for Human Resources Planning   134
    Human Resources Planning in an Era of Downsizing   139
    A Historical Overview of Human Resources Planning   147
    Workforce Planning   149
    Forecasting Human Resources Supply   153
    Forecasting Organizational Demands   156
    Strategic Human Resources Planning—Future Prospects   164
    Bibliography   168

5. Classification and Compensation   171

    Prologue: Transforming Waiting Rooms into Museums   171
    Why Classification—Why Not Staffing in Public Sector
        Organizations?   176

The Evolution of Position Classification: *The Ascendancy
    of Scientific Management* 177
After the War: ''The Triumph of Technique Over Purpose'' 183
The 1970s and the Behavioralist Critique 185
The System Response: Factor Evaluation in the 1970s 188
The Reform Initiative of the 1990s—Broadbanding? 197
Classification in the States 202
Pay Administration in Government 206
Federal Pay Reform: 1990 208
State and Local Compensation Developments 212
Pay Issues of Another Kind: Living Wages 215
Bibliography 217

6. Recruitment and Selection 221

Prologue: A Michigan Executive Recruitment Experience 221
The Legal Environment of Public Sector Selection:
    From *Griggs* to *Adarand* 224
The Development (and Decline) of the Uniform Guidelines 230
The Importance of Public Employment 236
Personal Rank Versus Position Rank 241
Essentials of the Employment Process 242
Examinations and Validation 246
A Federal Case History from PACE to ACWA to Other 251
Human Capital in Government: The Next Frontier 256
Bibliography 260

7. Performance Appraisal 265

*Prologue: 360-Degree Appraisal: Rising Star or Wreck on the
    Performance Appraisal Highway?* 265
The Problem of Performance Appraisal 267
The Traditional Approach to Performance Appraisal 273
Changing the System: The Behavioral Focus 277
The History of Merit Pay 281
Some State Government Perspectives on Merit Pay 287
Other Alternatives: Assessment Centers and Assessments
    of Multisource Appraisals 293
Bibliography 298

8. Training and Development 301

*Prologue: The Future of Training in the New Era
    of Knowledge Management* 301

The Evolution of Training and Development   304
Training and Personnel Relationships   306
Methods of Training: The Design Issue   310
Career Development and the Employee   313
On Planning Training: The Strategy Issue   321
On Assessing Training: The Evaluation Issue   325
Training and Development and Technology: The Issue
    of Choice   331
Bibliography   332

9. Quality Management and Reengineering   335

Prologue: TQM and The Invisible Man   335
Quality Management: Back to the Future   337
The Advent of TQM   341
The 1990s: The "Demise" of TQM and the BPR Challenge   345
Understanding Reengineering (and Quality) as Change
    Management   350
Quality on the Edge   356
The Gulf Between the Quality Haves and Have Nots   361
Appendix: Can Your Personnel Management Policies
    and Quality Management Premises Coexist?   363
Bibliography   372

Part III   Equal Opportunity and Diversity in Government

10. Equal Employment Opportunity and Affirmative Action   375

Prologue: From Bakke *to* Hopwood   375
The Difference Between Equal Employment Opportunity
    and Affirmative Action   378
Abuses of the Past   378
The Development of EEO   383
The Organization of EEO   390
The Managerial Aspects of Affirmative Action   393
Comparable Worth and Pay Equity   408
The Female–Male Pay Gap: Causes and Cures   411
Legal and Judicial Developments   412
Additional EEO Concerns   413
The Future of EEO and Affirmative Action   415
Bibliography   416

11. Diversity in the Workforce   421

     Prologue: A Success Story in Seattle, Washington   421
     The Challenge of Ensuring Equal Opportunities   423
     The Nature of Unequal Treatment in Today's Workplace   431
     Strategies for Greater Inclusion   439
     Who Is Responsible?   453
     Epilogue: "Proving" Discrimination   454
     Bibliography   455

Part IV   Unions and Employee Relations in Government

12. Labor–Management Relations   461

     *Prologue: The Brave New World of Labor–Management
          Partnerships*   461
     "An Unauthorized History" of the Origins of Federal Labor–
          Management Partnership   463
     The Development of Collective Bargaining in the Public Sector   466
     Modifications for the Public Sector   470
     Adjusting the Model   473
     A Loss of Coherence   474
     Dysfunction   475
     Early History   476
     Early Change   481
     The Federal Program Matures   482
     Labor–Management Partnerships   487
     Why Employees Unionize   488
     State and Local Arrangements   491
     Supervisors   496
     Organizing and Unit Determination   496
     The Scope of Bargaining   498
     Impasse Resolution   499
     Strikes   503
     Conclusion   510
     Appendix: Glossary of Federal Sector Labor–Management
          Relations Terms   510
     Bibliography   528

13. Employee Relations   531

     Prologue: Are Public Sector Employees at Risk?   531
     Defining Employee Relations   535

Formal Dispute Resolution Mechanisms   535
Job Safety and Health   543
Employee Assistance Programs   553
Bibliography   557

Index   *561*

Introduction: Why This Book?

The statement "public personnel management is a rapidly changing occupation" is an understatement. In late 1999, the U.S. Office of Personnel Management (OPM) released a study assessing how the federal human resources profession had changed in the 1990s. It reported that by 1991 the personnel function in the federal government had reached a 30-year high in the number of full-time employed professionals working as "personnelists." In all fairness, personnel wasn't the only management function that had grown rapidly—OPM noted that the 49% growth in full-time employees in personnel since 1969 compared to an 89% increase in budget occupations and 70% in procurement.

Although no similar evidence was presented for state and local governments, there is some broad-based support that state and local trends have generally followed federal trends. Personnel was increasing in governments at all levels for two major reasons: first, because over time there were more public employees, and second, and more importantly, because the role of personnel management in government had broadened. Beginning in the 1970s, the combined pressures of court decisions challenging the validity of personnel actions from examinations to compensation decisions and new and expanded roles for labor relations, equal opportunity, and employee development meant more personnel work to do. As just one illustration: in 1969, before the advent of formal equal employment opportunity (EEO) programs and labor relations programs within federal personnel, there were no specialty EEO or labor relations specialists; by 1991 they numbered more than 3500.

As the reader will learn in Chapter 2, one of the major targets of the Clinton administration's effort to improve government performance was focused on re-

TABLE 1   The State of the Personnel Profession in the Federal Government—
1969 to 1998

Human resources occupational specialties in the federal government (professional positions)	1969	1991	1998	1990s Percentage change
Staffing	3,485	3,547	2,009	−43%
Classification	2,470	2,079	868	−58%
Employee relations	1,236	2,154	1,530	−29%
Labor relations	0	1,113	1,002	−10%
Employee development	1,800	2,737	1,890	−31%
EEO	0	2,451	2,622	+7%
Personnel generalists	8,024	11,287	10,986	−3%
Totals	17,015	22,917	18,305	−20%

Source: OPM/Federal Human Resource Employment Trends, September 1999.

ducing the number of government employees. A key part of that effort targeted "administrative occupations," which they argued had grown disproportionately compared to overall growth of employees in the executive branch. In terms of numbers, this was certainly true—although little credit was given to the expanding roles concept. At any rate, the growth of the federal personnel occupation is now history. Since 1991, human resources (HR) (as the personnel occupation series is known) in the federal government has dropped by 17.5% (including support functions). Indeed, in each of the core professional groups within HR, except for EEO, there has been significant decline.

For those contemplating a career in personnel management, at least in the federal arena, your career prospects are best if you specialize in EEO (now the largest HR specialty) and worst in position classification (which is now approaching endangered-species designation levels). Another approach is to avoid trying to specialize in any one personnel area and become a personnel generalist. In the 1990s generalist positions declined by just 3% compared to an average decline rate of nearly 30% among the specialty areas.

There is some good news in this federal report on the state of the personnel occupation. While there are fewer HR professionals, grade levels are increasing. In 1991, 30% of HR professionals were at the GS-13 grade level (base pay just over $60,000), which in 1998 increased to 34%. For those worried about the glass ceiling, since 1989 the percentage of women in HR has risen from 60% to 71%, and minority representation in HR has doubled over the past two decades. Minorities account for 37% of the HR workforce and just over 70% of the EEO specialty. Furthermore, there is a strong record of advancement of women in HR. At the top three grade levels below executive service (GS-13 to GS-15), women now occupy 63% of GS-13 positions, 52% of GS-14 positions, and 47% of GS-15 positions.

Public personnel management, of course, is caught in the same strong currents of change as are all governments. Governments at every level are being challenged to produce greater results, use fewer resources in the process, and at the same time pursue new strategies and employ new technologies to be innovative, customer-responsive, and highly accountable. State and local governments, and now even some federal agencies, are facing a new arena—often referred to as "competitive government"—in which public employees are being challenged to compete with outside contractors over who will produce services. In some cases, the outside contractors are other public agencies who want to provide administrative services, from travel and payroll to computer support and personnel. Here is an interesting example: the U.S. Merit Systems Protection Board—which is charged with oversight of the merit system, administering the public service appeals process, and assessing the state of public service—has outsourced its personnel function to a contractor, namely, the U.S. Department of Agriculture's Animal Plant Health Inspection Service.

Rapidly accelerating change does not mean that politics is any less important than before. The public personnel process has always been a political process; frankly, that is what makes it so interesting as an area of study. But the political nature of personnel does not mean that personnel management or governments can ignore the new realities of the 21st century. Bolstered by the longest-running economic expansion in the past half century, governments in the United States at all levels have entered into a new era of budget surpluses, with increasing citizen expectations for services and solutions but declining levels of trust and confidence in government's ability to perform and accomplish its missions. Public personnel management faces the same dilemma, but here the critics are internal—public agency executives and managers. They want assurances that the human resources department can attract, select, develop, and retain the next generation of the public service while working closely with its union partners, and escape its past reputation for being bureaucratic, regulatory, and non–value added. They will no longer accept the premise that it is better (i.e., safer) to be part of the central personnel system. If personnel cannot deliver timely results, agency executives will pursue creating their own personnel systems, contracting out or automating the core human resources functions, and effectively taking charge of their own personnel fortunes.

Not so long ago, a major American business periodical ran a cover article on human resources in the future, with the creative title basically asking: "HR—why not just blow it up?" That is not an isolated thought. This is the crux of an ongoing debate in any number of articles that have appeared in the business journals demanding new philosophies, new roles, new technologies, and massive, radical change. One leading business scholar, Dave Ulrich at the University of

Michigan, in a 1998 article in the *Harvard Business Review* cited HR as "often ineffective, incompetent, and costly, and in a phrase—it is value sapping."

Will governments abolish their personnel departments and seek other remedies? Perhaps not yet, but the need for change is real. It is our hope that this fifth edition will contribute to the discussion of what is and what is not working among the basic elements of public personnel practice, and what the political possibilities are for change and the most probable concerns of tomorrow. Our past editions were largely dedicated to individuals preparing for careers in public management and specifically for those seeking to specialize in personnel. Personnel, now human resources management (perhaps human and intellectual capital in the coming decade), is so vital that it must be mastered by everyone who seeks to be a manager or a leader. Similarly, we recognize that careers in the public service are also different—that many readers will work in and out of government, spending time in the public, private, and even nonprofit sectors. Distinctions among sectors, and even organizational boundaries, will blur and be subject to constant change. But one thing will always be paramount—finding ways to maximize employee involvement and commitment to government agencies and the public service, and reciprocally shaping how government organizations reward, develop, and engage all of its workforce. That is the real essence of how human resources becomes human resources management in government.

Lastly, a word about the style of the book is in order. As in past editions, there are no footnotes in the text. If a work is referred to in a chapter or a quote extracted, the full citation will be found in that chapter's bibliography. Tables, figures, and our ubiquitous shaded boxes include their own source note. We've tried to maintain a balance so that the main body of the text is reasonably comprehensive, but other perspectives and aspects are presented throughout each chapter. Public personnel management has its own vocabulary or jargon; thus, several chapters include a glossary of terms. Each chapter begins with a prologue, backtracks to provide some historical or political context, and proceeds to some assessment of core issues and challenges. We confess that the bibliographies at the end of each chapter have gotten longer. This is partly a result of the growing body of literature and information sources in personnel management and partly a reluctance to leave out many of our favorite "historical" sources used in previous editions. As always, we welcome your comments and suggestions.

Personnel Management in Government

1

The First Century of Civil Service Reform

PROLOGUE: PRESIDENT GARFIELD'S ASSASSINATION AND THE ORIGINS OF THE MERIT SYSTEM

Just as it was the assassination of President John F. Kennedy in 1963 that fostered the congressional climate essential for the passage of his previously thwarted domestic legislative goals, it was the 1881 assassination of President James A. Garfield—who was elected the year before on a platform that called for complete and radical civil service reform—that created the climate necessary for the passage of the nation's first significant reform measure—the Pendleton Act of 1883. Hollywood could hardly have written a scenario that was more conducive to reform. Garfield was not shot by a mere political fanatic or run-of-the-mill deranged mind. His assassin, Charles Guiteau, was a disappointed office seeker.

Knowing that the vice president, Chester A. Arthur, was such a thorough spoilsman that he was removed from his post as head of the New York Customhouse by President Hayes for notorious partisan abuses, Guiteau approached Garfield at a Washington railroad station on July 2, 1881 and shot him with a pistol. The first wound in the arm was minor; the second in the back proved fatal. Almost immediately captured, Guiteau explained his action by asserting, "I am a stalwart and Arthur is president now." Obviously, Guiteau felt that Arthur would be more receptive to his petitions for office than Garfield had been. Although Guiteau

1

was plainly insane, many reasonable people thought that his insanity differed only in degree from that of many political leaders of the period.

Although popular sympathy for civil service reform was certainly in the air, it was an idea whose time had by no means come. Guiteau's bitter act changed the political climate precipitously, however. The reformers, who took a moralistic tone to begin with, were suddenly able to equate the spoils system with murder. This the public took to heart. Garfield was a martyr to the spoils system. Sympathy for Garfield, who dramatically took more than two months to die as he lingered on in pain, was equated with support for reform. With Garfield's death on September 19, 1881, the press turned its attention to Guiteau's sensational trial, in which the defendant, a lawyer, sought to defend himself, and the prosecution introduced into evidence a portion of the deceased martyr's vertebra. Guiteau was found guilty and hanged on June 30, 1882.

On January 16, 1883, President Arthur signed the Pendleton Act into law, creating the U.S. Civil Service Commission. Civil service reform did not result quite as dramatically from Garfield's martyrdom as may appear, however. The Pendleton Act hardly provided the framework of a modern merit system, and its passage, although aided by Garfield's death, was predominantly a reflection of the political trends of the time.

A HISTORICAL PERSPECTIVE: ENTER THE SPOILS SYSTEM

Just as an individual's life cannot be properly appreciated without reviewing the time of childhood and youth, the modern import of a social movement, in this case civil service reform, cannot be appreciated without reviewing the hopes of its founders, the environment that molded it, and its evolution over time.

Although a civil service has long been a feature of government, a career civil service based upon merit had until the twentieth century been a historical novelty. Such corps have popped in and out of history since the days of ancient China, but merit systems in the modern sense had to await the advent of industrialization and the modern nation-state. Prussia, one of the constituent states of what was to become modern Germany, was the first modern nation to institute a merit system. It was this German civil service that inspired Max Weber's famous "ideal-type" bureaucratic model that is the point of departure for many present-day discussions of bureaucratic theory. Weber, a scholar of prodigious output, is considered in consequence to be one of the principal founders of the academic discipline of public administration. Prussia began its merit system in the mid-eighteenth century. France followed the Prussian model shortly after the revolution of 1789. After developing a professionalized civil service for India in the 1830s, Great Britain adopted the concept for itself in the 1850s. The United States was among the last of the major industrialized nations to inaugurate a civil service based on merit.

American civil service reform is generally dated from the post-Civil War period, but the political roots of the reform effort go back much earlier—to the beginning of the republic. John Adams tended to maintain the appointments of George Washington, but Thomas Jefferson was the first president who had to face the problem of a philosophically hostile bureaucracy. While sorely pressed by his supporters to remove Federalist officeholders and replace them with Republican partisans, Jefferson was determined not to remove officials for political reasons alone. Jefferson rather courageously maintained that only ''malconduct is a just ground of removal: mere difference of political opinion is not.'' With occasional defections from this principle, even by Jefferson himself, this policy was the norm rather than the exception down through the administration of Andrew Jackson.

Andrew Jackson has been blamed for inventing the spoils system. High school students were once taught that upon becoming president he shouted ''to the victor belong the spoils,'' and replaced every federal employee with one of his less competent friends, but the truth is much more subtle. Far from firing everybody, Jackson continued with the appointing practices established by his predecessors. The federal service prior to Jackson's administration was a stable, long-tenured corps of officials decidedly elitist in character and remarkably barren of corruption. Jackson for the most part continued with this tradition in practice. He turned out of office about as many appointees as had Jefferson. During his eight years in office (1829–1837) removals are generally estimated to have been less than 20%. As for that famous phrase ''to the victor belong the spoils,'' it was neither uttered by Jackson nor recorded at all until the latter part of Jackson's first term as president. The famous phrase maker was Senator William L. Marcy of New York, who, in an 1832 debate with Senator Henry Clay of Kentucky, stated that the politicians of the United States ''see nothing wrong in the rule, that to the victor belong the spoils of the enemy.'' Marcy was to get his comeuppance years later when as secretary of state under President Pierce he futilely sought to establish the rudiments of a career system for clerks in the State Department.

President Jackson's rhetoric on the nature of public service was far more influential than his administrative example. While there was general agreement at the time that the civil service represented a high degree of competence and integrity, there was also widespread resentment that such appointments still tended to go to members of families of social standing at a time when universal white male suffrage had finally become a reality. To a large degree Jackson's constituency was made up of the previously disenfranchised and their sympathizers. In this context Jackson's rhetorical attack upon what had become an elitist

President Jackson's Spoils Doctrine Was Eloquently Stated in His Message to Congress of December 8, 1829

There are, perhaps, few men who can for any great length of time enjoy office and power without being more or less under the influence of feelings unfavorable to the faithful discharge of their public duties. Their integrity may be proof against improper considerations immediately addressed to themselves, but they are apt to acquire a habit of looking with indifference upon the public interests and of tolerating conduct from which an unpracticed man would revolt. Office is considered as a species of property, and government rather as a means of promoting individual interests than as an instrument created solely for the service of the people. Corruption in some and in others a perversion of correct feelings and principles divert government from its legitimate ends and make it an engine for the support of the few at the expense of the many. The duties of all public officers are, or at least admit of being made, so plain and simple that men of intelligence may readily qualify themselves for their performance; and I cannot but believe that more is lost by the long continuance of men in office than is generally to be gained by their experience. . . .

In a country where offices are created solely for the benefit of the people, no one man has any more intrinsic right to official station than another. Offices were not established to give support to particular men at the public expense. No individual wrong is, therefore, done by removal, since either appointment to nor continuance in office is matter of right. The incumbent became an officer with a view to public benefits, and when these require his removal they are not to be sacrificed to private interests. It is the people, and they alone, who have a right to complain when a bad officer is substituted for a good one. He who is removed has the same means of obtaining a living that are enjoyed by the millions who never held office.

and inbred civil service was well justified. In his most famous statement on the character of public office Jackson asserted that the duties of public office are "so plain and simple that men of intelligence may readily qualify themselves for their performance; and I cannot but believe that more is lost by the long continuance of men in office than is generally to be gained by their experience."

In claiming that all men, especially the newly enfranchised who did so much to elect him, should have an equal opportunity for public office, Jackson played to his plebian constituency and put the patrician civil service on notice that it had no natural monopoly on public office. Jackson's concept of rotation

An Excerpt from the Henry Clay–William L. Marcy Senate Debates of 1832 During Which the Spoils Systems Was So Famously Defended

Mr. Clay: It is a detestable system, drawn from the worst periods of the Roman republic: and if it were to be perpetuated; if the offices, honors, and dignities of the people were to be put up to a scramble, to be decided by the result of every Presidential election, our Government and institutions, becoming intolerable, would finally end in a depotism as inexorable as that at Constantinople. . . .

Mr. Marcy: It may be, sir, that the politicians of the United States are not so fastidious as some gentlemen are, as to disclosing the principles on which they act. They boldly preach what they practice. When they are contending for victory, they avow their intention of enjoying the fruits of it. If they are defeated, they expect to retire from office. If they are successful, they claim, as a matter of right, the advantages of success. They see nothing wrong in the rule, that to the victor belong the spoils of the enemy. . . .

I have good reasons, very good reasons, for believing that it is the gentleman's rule of conduct to take care of his friends when he is in power. It requires not the foresight of a prophet to predict that, if he shall come into power, he will take care of his friends, and, if he does, I can assure him I shall not complain; nor shall I be in the least surprised if he imitates the example which he now so emphatically denounces.

in office was basically conceived as a sincere measure of reform. As such it was enthusiastically supported by contemporary reformers. While Jackson's personal indulgence in spoils was more limited than commonly thought, he nevertheless established the intellectual and political rationale for the unmitigated spoils system that was to follow. Of course, Jackson's spoils doctrine would hardly have taken as it did were it not for the fact that the country was well prepared to accept it. Indeed, much of the venality of the spoils process was in full flower in state and local governments a full generation before it crept into federal office.

The spoils system flourished under Jackson's successors. The doctrine of rotation of office progressively prevailed over the earlier notion of stability in office. Presidents even began turning out of office appointees of previous presidents of the same party. President Millard Fillmore had dissident Whigs turned out in favor of "real" Whigs. When James Buchanan, a Democrat, succeeded Franklin Pierce, also a Democrat, it was announced that no incumbents appointed by Pierce would be retained. This development led William Marcy to remark "they have it that I am the author of the office seeker's doctrine, that 'to the victor belong the spoils,' but I certainly should never recommend the policy of pillaging my own camp."

As president, Abraham Lincoln followed the example of his predecessors and was an unabashed supporter and skillful user of the spoils system; his highly partisan exploitation of federal patronage was a great aid to the war effort. Paradoxically, while the spoils system reached its zenith under Lincoln, its decline may also be dated from his administration, for Lincoln refused to accede to the hitherto observed principle of quadrennial rotation after his reelection in 1864. This was the first significant setback that the principle of rotation had received since Jackson laid out its theoretical justifications. Through the height of the spoils period, however, there existed what some historians have called a "career service." Many clerks had continuous tenure all through this period, retaining their positions through competence, custom, and neutrality.

THE MOTIVATION FOR CIVIL SERVICE REFORM

It should come as no surprise then that public personnel management seems to be continually in state of change or transition. It was ever so. When the first textbook, Mosher and Kingsley's *Public Personnel Administration*, was published on this subject in 1936, the authors were able to state with great justification that "thorough-going reform of personnel administration is long overdue." This statement is equally true today, but with a crucial difference. While the early reform efforts concentrated upon creating institutions, the thrust of present-day efforts is centered upon reforming institutions. It is a vexing philosophical question as to which reform effort is the more difficult undertaking.

The chronology of civil service reform is easily delineated. A variety of specific events and documents have provided a convenient framework for analysis. The motivations of those who led the reform movement have remained a clouded issue, however, lending themselves to considerable speculation. Historians tend to agree that the leaders of the reform movement represented a socioeconomic class that was both out of power and decidedly antagonistic to those elements of society who were in power. In simplistic terms it was the WASP (white Anglo-Saxon Protestant) patricians versus the ethnic plebeians. The social upheaval that accompanied the Civil War left in its wake what Richard Hofstadter has described as a displaced class of old gentry, professional men, and the civic leaders of an earlier time. This displacement, this alienation, did much to establish the "ins" versus the "outs" pattern of the politics of reform. Because the reformers blamed the professional politicians for their own political impotence, they struck at the source of its strength—the spoils system. President Grant inadvertently accelerated the demand for reform when, upon obtaining office, he not only excluded from patronage appointments the old gentry, but denied office to the editors of influential newspapers and journals. This was in contrast to Lincoln's policy of courting the press by bestowing lavish patronage upon them. As a result, the press of both parties started speaking out more strongly than ever before in favor of reform.

As the American economy expanded during the last half of the nineteenth century, the orientation of the business community became less and less focused on parochial interests bounded by the neighborhood and more and more oriented toward urban, regional, and international markets. Economic determinists could well argue that the death knell of the spoils system was sounded when the ineptness of government began to hamper the expansion of business. It is noteworthy in this respect that the federal government made some efforts to institute merit system concepts in both the New York Post Office and the New York Customhouse several years before the passage of the Pendleton Act. Such reform measures, limited as they were, were a direct result of pressure from a business community that had grown increasingly intolerant of ineptness in the postal service and extortion by the customs service.

Depending upon one's point of view, the advent of modern merit systems is an economic, political, or moral development. Economic historians would maintain that the demands of industrial expansion—a dependable postal service, a viable transportation network, and so on—necessitated a government service based upon merit. Political analysts could argue rather persuasively that it was the demands of an expanded suffrage and democratic rhetoric that sought to replace favoritism with merit. Both economic and political considerations are so intertwined that it is impossible to say which factor is the exact foundation of the merit system. The moral impetus behind reform is even more difficult to define. As moral impulses tend to hide economic and political motives, the weight of moral concern that is undiluted by other considerations is impossible to measure. Nevertheless, the cosmetic effect of moral overtones was of significant aid to the civil service reform movement in the United States because it accentuated the social legitimacy of the reform proposals.

With the ever-present impetus of achieving maximum public service for minimum tax dollars, even business leaders were quite comfortable in supporting civil service reform. Support for reform was just one of a variety of strategies employed by business interests to have power pass from the politicos to themselves. The political parties of the time were almost totally dependent for a financial base upon assessments made on the wages of their members in public office. The party faithful had long been expected to kick back a percentage of their salary in order to retain their positions. A good portion of the Pendleton Act is devoted to forbidding this and other related methods of extortion. With the decline of patronage the parties had to seek out new funding sources. Business interests were more than willing to assume this new financial burden and its concomitant influence.

Career and Patronage Side by Side

During the first forty years of the Republic . . . there was no legislation dealing with appointments, examinations, promotions, removals, or any other familiar aspects of a personnel system except that establishing pay rates for clerks and officers. There was nevertheless a genuine career system based strictly on custom and on the deference that one gentlemen owed to another. Men became clerks in their early years and remained clerks often in the same office, until they died. . . . The country started its history with a career system that stood intact and unchallenged for the first forty years. It was the model to which the country has been steadily returning, with modern improvements ever since 1883. Contrary to almost universal opinion, this system did not disappear with the inauguration of Andrew Jackson in 1829. Jackson advocated and introduced the idea of rotation, for reasons which in 1829 commanded respect. But he rotated during his first administration not more than 20 percent of the federal employees and probably less. In his second term he rotated none.

Without pursuing the record of succeeding administrations, it may be said that from 1829 to 1861 and later, the career system continued alongside the patronage system. Heads of departments found that it was absolutely necessary to have in the key positions of middle-management men who knew their business, were familiar with the laws and regulations, and could protect them against mistakes.

Source: White, Leonard D. "Centennial Anniversary," *Public Personnel Review*, vol. 14 (January 1953), p. 6. Reprinted by permission of the International Personnel Management Association, 1850 K Street, N.W., Suite 870, Washington, D.C. 20006.

THE IMPETUS FOR REFORM

It was congressional disenchantment with the policies of President Andrew Johnson that instigated the first comprehensive and highly publicized proposals for a merit system based upon competitive examinations. Congressman Thomas A. Jenckes, a Republican of Rhode Island, sponsored several bills to curb the patronage power of the president by foisting a merit system upon him. Jenckes's proposals—which borrowed heavily from the British model—were worthy in and of themselves; but they were obviously inspired, at least initially, by antipathy to President Johnson. While Jenckes's 1865 proposals advocated a civil service commission appointed by the president, a growing hostility toward President Johnson certainly motivated the strikingly novel feature of his 1868 proposals—

"to furnish employment for the Vice-President by making him the head of a new department—that of the civil service." This was a thinly disguised effort to take patronage out of the hands of a president whose appointments tended to antagonize the Congress. Once Johnson was out of office, Jenckes reverted to his original proposal for a presidentially appointed commission to administer a civil service merit system. The Jenckes proposals, however, having to compete for public attention with Andrew Johnson's impeachment trial and the forthcoming Republican national convention, made little impact. Johnson's impeachment was occasioned by his violation of the Tenure of Office Act of 1867. Many of the opinion leaders of the time, including the *Nation* and the *New York Times* praised the act as a sincere measure of reform that would bring stability to government service. Indeed, one can argue that the nation's first impeachment controversy can be viewed as a struggle between the executive branch and the legislative branch for the control of patronage. (What historians will say in the future about the causes of our second impeachment experience between President Clinton and the Republican-dominated Congress in 1999 is another story.) The Jenckes proposal to have the vice president serve as a buffer between the president and the Congress does not seem so outlandish considering the time frame.

While the various reform proposals that Jenckes put forth during the Johnson administration owed their origins to mixed motives on the congressman's part, they nevertheless did serve as an important rallying point for reform agitation. The movers and shakers of the budding reform movement as well as many of the important newspapers and journals of the day gave the Jenckes proposals considerable attention and concomitant publicity. The civil service reform movement that eventually led to the Pendleton Act did not exist in 1866. Jenckes's initial reform proposals of 1865 and 1866 were literally ignored by the press and other national opinion leaders, yet within five years the reform movements had mobilized to the extent that the president of the United States, Ulysses S. Grant, recommended civil service legislation to the Congress in 1870 and obtained it, at least in the form of a short rider, in 1871. Jenckes deserves considerable credit for this mobilization of opinion and attention, however, possibly because he did not pay enough attention to his own patronage garden, Jenckes was defeated for re-election in 1870 and thereupon retired from public life.

In 1859, Ulysses S. Grant, as a private citizen, sought an appointment as a county engineer in Missouri and was denied it because he lacked the requisite political sponsorship. This may have inspired Grant's support for civil service reform when he became president. It is one of the cruelties of one-dimensional popular history that the first administration to make a large-scale effort at civil service reform should be most noted for its spoils system excesses. Reform, fleeting as it was, was achieved not after the careful and lengthy deliberations of the legislature, but mainly through the parliamentary skill of its proponents. On the last day of the legislative session of the Forty-first Congress in 1871, Senator

Lyman Trumbull of Illinois attached to an otherwise unrelated appropriations bill a rider that authorized the president to make rules and regulations for the civil service. Surprisingly, the total bill was approved by both houses. Although Grant supported the measure, historians tend to argue that the bill passed not so much because of Grant's influence but because of an awakening public opinion that had been coalescing for several years around the Jenckes proposals. Contributing to this arousal were the recent exposés of Boss Tweed's operations in New York City and other journalistic ferment. The rider itself was only one sentence long and did not formally require the president to do anything. It certainly would not have passed had it been thought to be anything more than a symbolic sop to the reformers. The rider essentially authorized the president "to prescribe such rules and regulations for the admission of persons into the civil service of the United States as will best promote the efficiency thereof, and ascertain the fitness of each candidate."

To the surprise of almost everyone, Grant proceeded to appoint a civil service commission shortly thereafter. He authorized the commission to establish and implement appropriate rules and regulations. The commission required

The Patrician Reformer

To the patrician reformer, the ideal government tended to be one by men like himself. They, he was sure, would treat all problems with no urge for self-aggrandizement and would mete out to each group a disinterested justice.

In seeking his ideal government, the patrician reformer frequently gave special emphasis to the establishment of a civil-service system. The "chief evil" of the day, explained Charles Bonaparte, a Marylander who had inherited a lofty family name and more than a million dollars' worth of real estate, was "the alliance between industrialists and a political class which thinks like industrialists. . . ." These politicians would be replaced by "gentlemen . . . who need nothing and want nothing from government except the satisfaction of using their talents," or at least by "sober, industrious . . . middle class persons who have taken over . . . the proper standards of conduct." The argument of Bonaparte was common in the literature of patrician reform. The whole civil-service movement, as the patrician Theodore Roosevelt later remarked, was decidedly one "from above downwards."

Source: Goldman, Eric F. *Rendezvous with Destiny: A History of Modern American Reform.* New York: Knopf, 1965, pp. 18–19.

boards of examiners in each department who worked under the commission's general supervision. All things considered, a viable program existed during 1872 and 1873. Several thousand persons were examined, and several hundred were actually appointed, but once the Congress realized that Grant was serious about reform and intent upon cutting into its patronage powers, the program was terminated. Congress simply refused to appropriate funds for the work of the commission. Although the president formally abolished his commission in 1875, the enabling legislation, the short rider of 1871, remains law to this day.

Although the first federal Civil Service Commission was short-lived, the experiment served as an important object lesson for later reform measures and established presidential prerogatives that are now taken for granted. For the first time the president was given unchallengeable authority over federal government personnel. The reform measures implied by the rider went far beyond the control of personnel. By authorizing the president to in effect provide himself with staff assistance, the rider of 1871 marks the beginning of the presidency's rise to the actual leadership of the federal administrative apparatus. It was by the authority of this rider as well as the later Pendleton Act that the president issued executive orders and rules concerning the civil service.

The policies that this first Civil Service Commission promulgated still haunt merit systems to this day. The word *haunt* in this instance seems exceedingly appropriate, for it is the dead hand of the past that all too often prevents the public service from achieving its full potential. An analysis of the terminology and concepts developed by Grant's commission shows that many of the provisions that are taken for granted today in merit systems at all jurisdictional levels were first developed in 1871. It was this commission that first instituted the ''rule of three''; that adopted the policy of restricting lateral entry and making initial appointments only at the entrance level; and that mandated that promotion within the service should be decided by competitive examinations limited to those already in the agency. Ironically, this last measure, which is still in widespread use today, especially among state and local municipal police and fire departments, was found by the commission upon trial to be an unsuitable method to determine promotions. All of the above-mentioned measures were appropriate innovations at the time, but they have not aged well. Although the federal service is not generally confined by these particular constants upon management, many state and local jurisdictions have chafed under these and similarly antiquated practices. Not only are they locked into such practices by legal mandates, tradition, and inertia, but public employee unions, finding that such procedures that give a decided advantage to seniority over merit are to the advantage of their members, remain insistent that such provisions remain.

With the demise of the Grant commission, reform took only a few halting steps until the Arthur administration. Rutherford B. Hayes, who succeeded Grant, was personally in favor of reform, but with a Congress hostile to it, he did not

Corruption in Perspective

The typical historian has been too loose in applying the term "corruption." Specifically, he labels a politically partisan civil service corrupt rather than inefficient; he equates the spoils system with corruption when honest spoilsmen far outnumber dishonest ones; he pronounces Gilded Age politicians guilty of corruption for associating with corruptionists even while attacking guilty by association in his own day.

One apparent reason why the historian has exaggerated the corruption of the Gilded Age is his desire to enliven lectures and writings. All the world loves a scandal, and the historian is loathe to abandon the pleasure of dispensing "vicarious sin." More basically, the historian dislikes the dominant forces in the Gilded Age. The historian is usually liberal, more often than not a Democrat. He is typically hostile to big business, an advocate of government regulation, of strong executive leadership, and of a civil service staffed by experts. The post-Civil War era stands for all the historian opposes. It was an era of Republicanism, of big business domination, of few and ineffectual attempts at government regulation, of weak executives, and of an essentially nonprofessional civil service. The historian naturally dwells upon the shortcomings of the period, particularly on the failures of Ulysses S. Grant, whose political career both personifies all the historian abhors and symbolizes Gilded Age politics.

Another reason the historian has exaggerated corruption in this period is the bias of his sources. The most articulate individuals in this age were its severest critics.

Source: Hoogenboom, Ari. "Spoilsmen and Reformers: Civil Service Reform and Public Morality," in H. Wayne Morgan (ed.), *The Gilded Age: A Reappraisal*. Syracuse, N.Y.: Syracuse University Press, 1963, p. 71.

press the matter beyond issuing an executive order requiring competitive examinations for the notoriously corrupt New York Customhouse and for parts of the New York Post Office. It was during the time of the Hayes administration that the various civil service reform associations were established, however. The first of these was the New York Civil Service Reform Association, formed in 1877. By 1880 a variety of other cities had also organized associations. The National Civil Service Reform League was formed at that time "to facilitate the correspondence and the united action of the Civil-Service Reform Associations." These associations were to be a potent force in the fight for reform over the coming decades. It was the New York association that in 1880 drafted a reform program that was to be submitted to Congress for consideration. Meanwhile, Senator George H. Pendleton, a Democrat from Ohio, had independently (and unbeknown to the association) introduced a version of one of Jenckes's old proposals in the Senate. When the association learned of this, it convinced the senator to replace his own bill with the one written by the association. The "second" Pendleton bill, written by the New York Civil Service Reform Association, was thus submitted to the Senate during 1881. Two years later it would become law.

There is no doubt that civil service reform would have come about without the 1881 assassination of President James A. Garfield. There is also no doubt that the assassination helped. While Garfield's assassination was certainly instrumental in creating the appropriate climate for the passage of "An Act to regulate and improve the Civil Service of the United States," popularly known as the Pendleton Act after Senator Pendleton, historians maintain that the Republican reversals during the midterm elections of 1882 had the more immediate effect on enactment. Civil service reform had been the deciding issue in a number of congressional contests. The state that harbored the greatest excesses of the spoils system, New York, even elected as governor the reform-minded mayor of Buffalo, Grover Cleveland. When President Arthur signed the Pendleton Act into law on January 16, 1883, and created the United States Civil Service Commission, it was thus essentially a gesture by reluctant politicians to assuage public opinion and the reform elements.

THE PENDLETON ACT

The Pendleton Act of 1883, or "An Act to Regulate and Improve the Civil Service of the United States," became a remarkably durable piece of legislation. Within it was the framework for personnel management that was at the heart of the federal civil service system until 1979. The act created a civil service commission as the personnel management arm of the president. While it was termed a commission, the U.S. Civil Service Commission (CSC) was by no means independent. It was an executive agency that for all practical purposes was subject to the administrative discretion of the president. Its three bipartisan commissioners served at the pleasure of the president. The act gave legislative legitimacy to many of the procedures developed by the earlier unsuccessful civil service commission during the Grant administration. Written into the act were requirements for open competitive examinations, probationary periods, and protection from political pressures. While the personnel program was to remain decentralized and in the control of the departments, the commission was authorized to supervise the conduct of examinations and make investigations to determine the degree of departmental enforcement of its rules. Of tremendous significance was the authority given to the president to extend merit system coverage to federal employees by executive order. Historically, the authority to extend also carried with it the authority to retract. Both Presidents McKinley and Eisenhower had occasion to remove positions from merit coverage by executive order. The Supreme Court's decision in *Rutan* v. *Republican Party of Illinois* (1990), however, makes patronage an unconstitutional basis for personnel actions affecting most public employees.

The Pendleton Act was hardly a total victory for the reformers. It only covered about 10% of the federal service. Actually, the reformers were not at all anxious for near-universal merit system coverage. They well recognized the problems of creating the appropriate administrative machinery and were concerned that the reform program would be overburdened and subject to failure if complete reform were attempted all at once. With the ensuing years federal employees would be more and more brought under the jurisdiction of the CSC or of other federal merit systems, such as those of the Foreign Service and the Tennessee Valley Authority. One hundred years later, when President Reagan took office in 1981, only about 7,000 of approximately 3 million federal positions were specifically designated as potential patronage positions.

Why the Pendleton Act Passed!

The outlook for the Republican party in 1884 was not promising; members of that party were filled with apprehension and the Democrats with anticipation. The "outs" were nearly in and the "ins" were nearly out. Yet the lameduck session of the Forty-seventh Congress had been elected in 1882 and was very much Republican. The congressional "outs," or at least those who very shortly would be "outs," were in a majority and controlled the presidency. It would be advantageous for Republicans to make permanent the tenure of their office holding friends while supporting the reform their constituents so obviously desired. Accordingly, the Republican senators met in caucus to discuss the Pendleton bill. Pending amendments were considered, and those offered by Republicans were generally approved. No vote was taken and nothing was done to bind senators to a particular course, but it was understood that all Republican senators with one or two exceptions would vote for the Pendleton bill. Republicans supported the bill for two reasons: they could pose as reformers in 1884 and win back lost support, and they could "freeze" Republicans in office behind civil service rules if the Democrats would win the election.

Source: Hoogenboom, Ari. *Outlawing the Spoils: A History of the Civil Service Reform Movement, 1865–1883*. Urbana, Ill.: University of Illinois Press, 1961, pp. 236–237.

American presidents during the reform period typically entered office taking full advantage of their patronage prerogatives and left office with extensions of the merit system to their credit. This was the case with every president from Arthur to Wilson. Merit system coverage went from 10% in 1884 to over 70% by the end of World War I. Generally, lame duck presidents being succeeded by someone of a different party would blanket in large numbers of employees in order to reduce the amount of patronage available to the opposition party. One of the ironies of civil service reform brought about by such blanketing is that such initial reforms have a tendency to benefit those who may be the least meritorious.

Presidents undoubtedly had mixed motives concerning their last-minute extensions of the merit system. While they sincerely wished to deny to their successors the patronage prerogatives that they enjoyed, many had become truly disillusioned by their experiences with spoils and possibly repentant of their excesses. The definitive statement on the disillusioning aspects of political patronage is credited to President William Howard Taft, who was moved to conclude that whenever he made a patronage appointment, he created "nine enemies and one ingrate." Actually, this quip is generally attributed to all sophisticated dispensers of patronage from Thomas Jefferson to Louis XIV. The American presidency has produced only two memorable patronage jokes besides many of the appointees themselves. In addition to President Taft's remark, which seems to have been often borrowed by many a latter-day, lesser politico, there is the story of Abraham Lincoln, who, while lying prostrate in the White House with an attack of smallpox, said to his attendants: "Tell all the office seekers to come in at once, for now I have something I can give to all of them."

THE DEVELOPMENT OF THE CENTRAL PERSONNEL AGENCY

As with many questions in public administration, the issue of how the overall public personnel function should be organized has been plagued by an attempt to realize several incompatible values at once. Foremost among these values have been those of "merit" or neutral competence; executive leadership, political accountability, and managerial flexibility; and representativeness. The main problem of the structural organization and policy thrusts of central personnel agencies has been that maximizing some of these values requires arrangements ill suited for the achievement of others. Achieving neutral competence thus requires the creation of a relatively independent agency to help insulate public employees from the partisan demands of political executives. The same structural arrangement will tend to frustrate executive leadership and the ability of political executives to manage their agencies, however. To facilitate executive leadership, on the other hand, the central personnel agency should be an adjunct of the president, governor, mayor or city manager, or other chief executive. Similarly, maximizing the value of representativeness may require a serious reassessment of traditional merit concepts and examinations, and the placement of personnel functions having an impact on equal employment opportunity in an equal employment or human rights agency. So doing, however, will also complicate the possibilities of achieving a high degree of executive leadership and neutral competence as traditionally conceived. Matters are further confused by the rise of public sector collective bargaining, which emphasizes employee—employer codetermination of personnel policy and the creation of independent public sector labor relations authorities.

The desire to simultaneously maximize these incompatible values accounts for many of the problematic aspects of the organization of the central personnel function. Arrangements satisfying some values inevitably raise complaints that others are being inadequately achieved. As the emphasis shifts from one value to another in conjunction with changing political coalitions and different perceptions of what is required in the public sector, structural changes also take place, yet since the process of public personnel reform is somewhat cyclical, no set of arrangements will be immutable. Figure 1.1 shows a typical organization for a central personnel office.

Phase I—Policing

In the years immediately following the creation of the U.S. Civil Service Commission, its main role was that of policing. While this was certainly not its sole purpose, the commission was overwhelmingly concerned with preventing patronage encroachments by spoilspersons and in depoliticizing the federal service. "Good" public personnel administration amounted to efficiently and effectively filling the ranks of the competitive service in a nonpartisan fashion. By the early 1900s this approach was viewed with less and less favor. The reformers had rationalized their wider political objectives in terms of efficiency, but depoliticization and selection through primitive open competitive exams failed to yield this result. In addition, the quest for greater efficiency became increasingly important as the government began taking on more complex tasks and as the regulatory policies it was pursuing began to penetrate the society and economy more deeply. Indeed, almost from the very moment that the reform movement achieved its fundamental success, clearer minds recognized its limitations in this regard. As early as 1887, in his famous essay "The Study of Administration," Woodrow Wilson wrote that "we must regard civil service reform in its present stages as but a prelude to a fuller administrative reform."

Phase II—Scientific Management

During the second and third decades of the twentieth century it was widely believed that a panacea for all administrative ills had been developed. A number

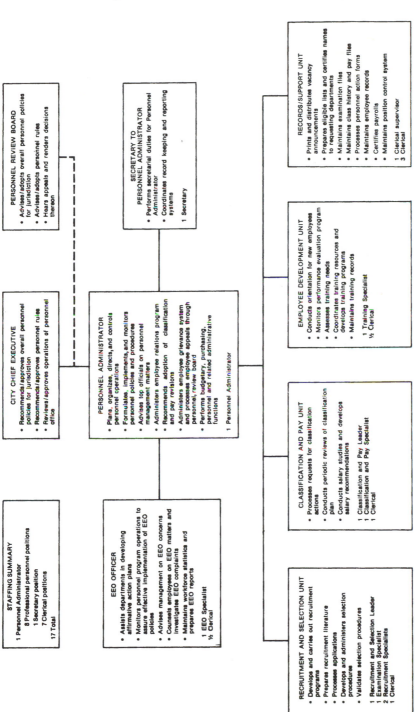

FIGURE 1.1 Organization of a central personnel office to serve a city of 4,000 employees. *Source: U.S. Civil Service Commission, Bureau of Intergovernmental Programs. Organizing the Personnel Function: A Guide for Local Government Managers. Washington, D.C.: USCSC, April 1978, p. 15.*

The Curse of Civil Service Reform

The civil service law is the biggest fraud of the age. It is the curse of the nation. There can't be no real patriotism while it lasts. How are you goin' to interest our young men in the country if you have no offices to give them when they work for their party? Just look at things in this city today. There are ten thousand good offices, but we can't get at more than a few hundred of them. How are we going' to provide for the thousands of men who worked for the Tammany ticket? It can't be done. These men were full of patriotism a short time ago. They expected to be servin' their city, but when we tell them that we can't place them, do you think their patriotism is goin' to last? Not much. They say: "What's the use of workin' for your country anyhow? There's nothin' in the game." And what can they do? I don't know, but I'll tell you what I do know. I know more than one young man in past years who worked for the ticket and was just overflowin' with patriotism, but when he was knocked out by the civil service humbug he got to hate his country and became an Anarchist.

This ain't no exaggeration. I have good reason for sayin' most of the Anarchists in this city today are men who ran up against civil service examinations. Isn't it enough to make a man sour on his country when he wants to serve it and won't be allowed unless he answers a lot of fool questions about the number of cubic inches of water in the Atlantic and the quality of sand in the Sahara desert? There was once a bright young man in my district who tackled one of these examinations. The next I heard of him he had settled down in Herr Most's saloon smokin' and drinkin' beer and talkin' socialism all day. Before that time he had never drank anything but whisky. I knew what was comin' when a young Irishman drops whisky and takes to beer and long pipes in a German saloon. That young man is today one of the wildest Anarchists in town. And just to think! He might be a patriot but for that cussed civil service.

Source: From Riordon, William L. *Plunkitt of Tammany Hall*. New York: Dutton, 1963, pp. 11–12. Reprinted by permission of E. P. Dutton & Co.

---

of empirical observations, techniques, moral values, and premises concerning economics were loosely connected to form the "scientific management movement." At the center of its development was the thinking of Frederick Taylor, who believed that management had a responsibility to determine "scientifically" how each and every task, both large and small, could be performed in the "one best way" by each worker. This would presumably yield far greater efficiency than the ad hoc techniques that had traditionally been developed and used by workers. Productivity would be further increased by adopting pay plans that were closely related to individual output. Were the whole world organized in this fashion, abundance and harmony would reign supreme. The thrust of these thoughts was to turn the individual employee into an appendage of an organizational machine, rather than to adapt organizational arrangements to individual talents and idiosyncrasies.

In government, the concerns of scientific management were translated into an attempt at developing a more scientific personnel administration. The notions that there was one best way of doing a job and that one type of person could perform best in any given kind of position required the development of scientifically derived standards and the standardization of positions. Consequently, position classification moved to the core of public personnel administration. The content of the job or a group of similar jobs became the element upon which almost all else was based, thus more concern was devoted to ensuring that examinations were related to job requirements rather than just to depoliticization as in the earlier period. The public service increasingly began to revolve around positions rather than people, and the rank was securely vested in the former rather than in the latter. The philosophic essence of this approach was written into law with the enactment of the Classification Act of 1923.

Phase III—Centralization

Until the 1930s the commission remained primarily an examining agency. Indeed, until that time position classification, efficiency ratings, and retirement programs were separately administered elsewhere. Other aspects of personnel administration, including training, promotion, transfer, health and safety, employee relations, and working conditions, were subject to almost no central direction or influence. The absence of coordination and responsibility inherent in this situation was increasingly deplored, and in 1931 the commission called for the integration ''in one administrative body of all Federal agencies which have to do with personnel in the civil service.'' In the following three years, the commission was given authority for position classification, efficiency ratings, and retirement administration. This did much to make it more of a genuine central personnel agency, but its role was still far from complete in this regard. Moreover, most of its functions were cast in a negative vein. Having policed the spoilsperson in the past, the commission now found itself applying rather restrictive regulations to bureau chiefs and other federal employees, many of whom were themselves under the merit system. In addition, it performed its functions in a centralized fashion, which often presented difficulties in serving the managerial needs of various agencies. So negative was the commission's role and image that an analysis associated with the 1937 President's Committee on Administrative Management con-

Theodore Roosevelt As Civil Service Commissioner

Although he professed still to be enjoying his work as Civil Service Commissioner, and to "get on beautifully with the President," an increasing restlessness through the spring and summer of 1894 is palpable in his correspondence. It would be needlessly repetitive to describe the battles he fought for reform under Cleveland, for they were essentially the same as those he fought under Harrison. "As far as my work is concerned," he grumbled, "the two Administrations are much of a muchness." There were the same "mean, sneaky little acts of petty spoilsmongering" in government; the same looting of Federal offices across the nation, which Roosevelt combated with his usual weapons of publicity and aggressive investigation; the same pleas for extra funds and extra staff ("we are now, in all, five thousand papers behind"); the same fiery reports and five-thousand-word letters bombarding members of Congress; the same obstinate lobbying at the White House for extensions of the classified service; the same compulsive attacks upon porcine opponents, such as Assistant Secretary of State Josiah P. Quincy, hunting for patronage "as a pig hunts truffles," and Secretary of the Interior Hoke Smith, "with his twinkling little green pig's eyes."

All this, of course, meant that Roosevelt was having fun.

Source: Morris, Edmund. *The Rise of Theodore Roosevelt*. New York: Coward, McCann & Geoghegan, 1979, p. 472. (Footnotes omitted.)

cluded that "many friends of the Commission . . . feel that the more constructive types of personnel activity cannot be carried effectively by an agency which necessarily must give so much attention to the enforcement of restrictive statutes." The commission's "policing" role was proving incompatible with the "friendly cooperation" required by the more positive aspects of centralized personnel administration. This realization heralded a new era in federal personnel administration.

Phase IV—The Decentralization of Personnel Operations

Toward the close of President Franklin Roosevelt's first term it became increasingly clear that governmental administration was in a state of disarray. Agencies had overlapping and even contradictory functions, and controlling the "headless fourth branch" of government presented great difficulty. Roosevelt appointed the President's Committee on Administrative Management, chaired by Louis Brownlow, to study the administrative organization of the executive branch and

---

Whose Merit? How Much?

The late Henry Aronson, who spent some 30 years developing and enforcing merit system standards for state agencies, used to tell this story: In the late '30s a certain Southern state paid little attention to the federal merit requirements newly established for grant-in-aid programs. Persuasion and threats accomplished nothing, and finally Uncle Sam began action to ''cut off the water''—as politically unthinkable an action then as now. The governor of the state sent an assistant to see Aronson, who gave him the full sales business on merit system principles. When Henry paused, the emissary said, ''Well, Mr. Aronson, the guv'nor—he b'lieves in the merit system—he just b'lieves that his friends have more merit than his enemies.''

Source: Stanley, David T. ''Whose Merit? How Much?'' *Public Administration Review*, vol. 34 (September–October 1974), p. 425.

---

to make recommendations for its improvement. The most important of these led to the creation of the Executive Office of the President, but the committee also had a profound effect on thinking about public personnel administration. Believing that ''personnel administration lies at the very core of administrative management,'' and that ''to set it apart or to organize it in a manner unsuited to serve the needs of the Chief Executive and the executive establishments is to render it impotent and ineffective,'' the committee sought the establishment of a whole new institutional framework for this function. Because the committee found the civil service commission to be generally unresponsive to the needs of agency management, it recommended that the commission be replaced by a civil service administration, headed by a single administrator appointed by and responsible to the president. A seven-member civil service board would be appointed ''to act as a watchdog of the merit system and to represent the public interest.'' Although these recommendations were not then enacted into law, they would be similar to reforms implemented in 1979. In any event, decentralized personnel administration eventually became the order of the day. During 1938 President Roosevelt issued an executive order that required each agency to establish a division of personnel supervision and management.

The federal bureaucracy underwent a tremendous expansion during World War II. Recognizing that the growth of the federal service made centralized personnel administration largely a thing of the past, a 1947 executive order by President Truman accordingly stressed decentralization. The president declared that ''personnel management is a primary responsibility of the head of each agency, and his officials who are responsible for the economical and efficient conduct of the work.'' Under the order, agency heads and their designated subordinates were expected to plan, organize, coordinate, and control all personnel management programs in the agency. They were assigned the responsibility of ensuring that personnel management was effective and efficient. Moreover, the order required that ''authority for the conduct of personnel matters within each agency should be delegated to the extent compatible with provisions of law and economical and efficient administration to those officials responsible for planning, directing and supervising the work of others.'' As a result of this approach, which was also written into the Classification Act of 1949, agencies are currently responsible for position classification, evaluation, promotion, a good deal of recruitment efforts, and a host of other personnel functions. All of the major studies of the federal bureaucracy, including the Brownlow Committee and the First and Second Hoover Commissions, have strongly endorsed the decentralized approach to public personnel management. Yet decentralization has also had some costs, both in terms of weakening the merit system, as in the Nixon years, and in creating something of an identity and image ''crisis'' for the CSC.

Phase V—The Demise of the Civil Service Commission

It is not surprising that the transition from the role of policing the federal personnel system to that of ''serving'' agency management placed considerable strains upon the CSC. What becomes of a regulatory agency that acts as a servant for the group it was originally established to regulate? The transition turned what was once an image crisis into an identity crisis. Criticism came from many quarters. Some found the CSC too responsive to special interests. Marver Bernstein observed that the ''Commission's role with respect to veteran's preference and similar provisions is not merely that of policeman [sic]; it is also an agency at the service of a clientele group.'' Its image was one of an agency engaged in ''hemming in the line operator with restrictive rules governing job classification, appointment, promotion, transfer, salary change, and dismissal of employees.'' Others, such as Louis Gawthrop, were critical of the commission because it ''consistently resisted major innovations in the federal career process.'' Supervisors at virtually all levels were troubled by its inspection (later called ''evaluation'') activities, which sometimes pointed out the shortcomings of agency personnel policy and agitated rank-and-file employees. Conversely, and somewhat ironically, still others, including Ralph Nader, criticized the commission for failing to use its authority. With regard to its activities in the area of equal employment opportunity (EEO), Nader had observed that there was no doubt whatsoever concerning the adequacy of the commission's authority to do its job. ''It has ample authority, leverage, and disciplinary powers vis-á-vis other federal agencies, but it has been reluctant to use these tools.''

Decentralization

Another common reform theme is the decentralization of certain functions normally performed by a central personnel agency. Such actions are designed to place more decision-making authority in the hands of line managers, commensurate with their accountability to the public. The functions may include recruiting, examining, and position classification, with the central personnel agency usually retaining responsibility for the preparation of interagency class specifications and examination material, and postauditing personnel actions relating to the decentralized functions.

The 1979 Merit System Standards specifically permit such decentralization as long as post audit procedures are maintained by a central personnel agency with effective enforcement authority to correct improper actions made by line agencies. In other words, a line agency with delegated authority to perform such personnel actions can assume responsibility for meeting the requirements of the Standards without the central personnel agency surrendering all of its accountability. For example, the central personnel agency may delegate to operating agencies responsibility for allocating individual positions to classes while retaining the specification writing function centrally and conducting post audits of the agency classification actions. Also, examinations could be decentralized in a similar fashion. Decentralization of position classification in the Federal Government has long been a necessary practice. It would be difficult to imagine position classifiers traveling from one central location, or even from ten regional locations, to classify jobs all over the country and even the world. However, the development and maintenance of classification standards, which is the basis for the allocation of positions in the agencies, is accomplished by the central office.

Source: U.S. Office of Personnel Management. *Personnel Management Reform*, vol. 1, no. 1 (September 1979), pp. 2–3.

In an effort to overcome its poor image and to find a new role after the decentralization of the 1940s, the commission tried to serve the needs of a diversity of groups, many of which have conflicting interests and some of which favor a substantial weakening of the merit system. It thus sought to serve the needs of Congress and the president and management and labor, as well as veterans, women, and other protected-class groups seeking recourse from discriminatory treatment. It tried to stress ''merit,'' executive leadership, and representativeness all at once, to the possible detriment of each of these values. No wonder one former chair of the Commission lamented ''What is the role of the Civil Service

Commission in these fast-changing times? . . . Why do we exist? What is our identity? What is our purpose? Whom do we represent?''

On a formal level, these questions could be answered by enumerating the commission's functions as a central personnel agency.

1. To recommend legislation
2. To encourage departments and agencies to improve their personnel management
3. To promulgate governmentwide personnel policies and standards under the law
4. To develop personnel programs
5. To centrally operate certain personnel services
6. To provide technical assistance to agencies
7. To evaluate the effectiveness of personnel management in the agencies
8. To adjudicate employee appeals
9. To secure compliance with civil service laws and merit principles

Such a response was unsatisfactory, however, because it failed to indicate in whose interest and to what ends these functions should be performed; nor was the commission able to clarify these matters.

Ultimately, by 1978 the commission had been so racked by its conflicting roles, attempts to achieve mutually incompatible values, and its participation in the scandalous breaches of the merit system during the Watergate years that despite its long history it was reorganized out of existence by the Civil Service Reform Act of 1978. Already in 1976, presidential candidate Jimmy Carter promised the American people that if elected he would reform the federal civil service system that had been suffering so publicly from a variety of scandals concerned with both the probity of the officials managing the system and the competence of the system in general. On October 13, 1978, President Jimmy Carter signed into law the Civil Service Reform Act of 1978, which provided for the dissolution of the U.S. Civil Service Commission as of January 1, 1979. This act was only the most recent culmination of a long history and tradition of reform, however.

Phase VI—Reform

The 1978 Civil Service Reform Act constituted a sweeping attempt to change the nature of the federal personnel administration that had existed since the passage of the Pendleton Act of 1883. The demands for widespread reforms had been growing since the 1930s. The Brownlow committee in 1937 asserted that the CSC seemed to have outlived its usefulness. The agency's general disarray during the early 1970s seemed to be additional evidence of its inadequacy. As bureaucratic power had grown during the post-New Deal era, the value of executive leadership took on added importance. By the 1970s it had become clear that the conventional strategies of strengthening the executive office of the president and providing the president with more power vis-á-vis the federal bureaucracy, such as reorganizational authority, still left the president and his political executives with insufficient managerial clout. Indeed, the expansion of the Executive Office of the President turned out to have distinct liabilities of its own. From a political perspective, however, leaders of the Carter civil service reform effort continued to be concerned that "every new administration feels the negative aspects of the bureaucracy's pressure for continuity. New policy makers arrive with mandates for change and find that though they can change structures and appearances, it is very difficult to make dramatic changes in direction." In their view, the prevailing institutional arrangements for federal personnel administration stressed neutral competence in the form of rigidity and the protection of federal employees to such an extent that the concerns of executive leadership had been almost totally eclipsed.

Indeed, during the campaign to win support for the proposed reforms, the Carter administration constantly exposed the horrors of prevailing federal personnel administration. Among these were such issues as the following:

> An award of about $5,000 in back pay to a postal worker who was fired for shooting a colleague in the stomach in a Manhattan post office
> A 21-month paperwork maze to fire an $8,000-a-year Department of Commerce employee who consistently failed to show up for work without valid reasons
> The existence of numerous $40,000- and $50,000-a-year employees who literally were "do-nothings"
> The rating of 98% of all white-collar employees as "satisfactory" at a time when public confidence in the bureaucracy was very low and numerous major and minor scandals were being exposed
> The firing of only 226 out of a total 2,800,000 civilian employee workforce for inefficiency during 1977

Summing up the case against prevailing federal personnel administration, President Carter said, "There is not enough merit in the merit system. There is inadequate motivation because we have too few rewards for excellence and too few penalties for unsatisfactory work."

In addition, the CSC had been under attack from civil rights groups and others interested in greater employment of African Americans, Latinos, and women in the federal service. At the beginning of the decade of the 1970s, efforts were made to divest the commission of the federal EEO program and place the program in the Equal Employment Opportunity Commission (EEOC). The commission had thus managed to lose the support of elements pursuing the values of executive leadership and representativeness. The commission and the federal personnel system were also criticized by some public employee labor unions who complained that the scope of collective bargaining in the federal service was too

What Are the Merit System Principles?

The Civil Service Reform Act of 1978 put into law the nine basic merit principles that should govern all personnel practices in the federal government and defined prohibited practices. The principles and prohibitions as follows.

Personnel Practices and Actions in the Federal Government Require

- Recruitment from all segments of society, and selection and advancement on the basis of ability, knowledge, and skills, under fair and open competition
- Fair and equitable treatment in all personnel management matters, without regard to politics, race, color, religion, national origin, sex, marital status, age, or handicapping condition, and with proper regard for individual privacy and constitutional rights
- Equal pay for work of equal value, considering both national and local rates paid by private employers, with incentives and recognition for excellent performance
- High standards of integrity, conduct, and concern for the public interest
- Efficient and effective use of the federal workforce
- Retention of employees who perform well, correcting the performance of those whose work is inadequate, and separation of those who cannot or will not meet required standards
- Improved performance through effective education and training
- Protection of employees from arbitrary action, personal favoritism, or political coercion
- Protection of employees against reprisal for lawful disclosures of information

limited and that the labor relations process was overwhelmingly dominated by management interests.

In combination, these forces generated enough support in the presidency and Congress to bring about the following major changes in federal personnel management.

The CSC was replaced by the following major changes:

An office of personnel management (OPM) headed by a director appointed by the president with the advice and consent of the Senate for a four-year term, a deputy director, and up to five assistant directors. (See Figure 1.2.) The OPM has authority for the positive managerial functions that previously were vested in the commission. Among these are responsibilities for human resources management, evaluations, and enforcement of federal personnel laws and regulations. The OPM is an independent agency that is intended to work closely with the president and be the president's arm for managing the personnel aspects of the federal bureaucracy.

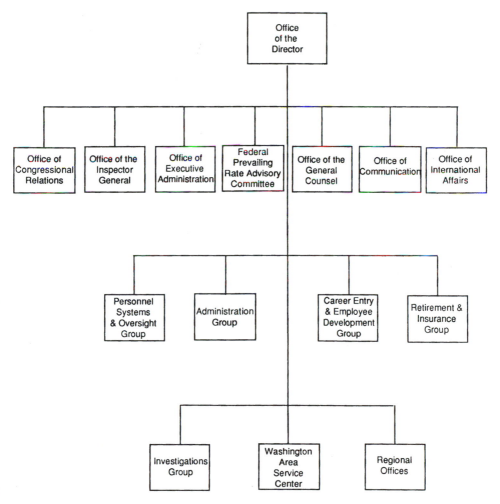

FIGURE 1.2 OPM organization chart, May 1990. *Source*: OPM.

The Merit Systems Protection Board (MSPB), headed by a chair and two additional members holding seven-year nonrenewable terms, constitutes a "watchdog" of the federal merit system. (See Figure 1.3.) The bipartisan MSPB, whose members cannot be removed except for cause, received the commission's appeals functions. The MSPB also has general oversight functions and the authority to review OPM rules and regulations. In addition, when the reform act was first passed, the Office of Special Counsel (OSC) was created as a semi-independent body within the MSPB. The special counsel holds a five-year term of office and is removable only for cause. This official is responsible for investigating allegations of prohibited personnel practices, including such areas as political activity, "whistleblowing," discrimination, and arbitrary or capricious withholding of information sought under the Freedom of Informa-

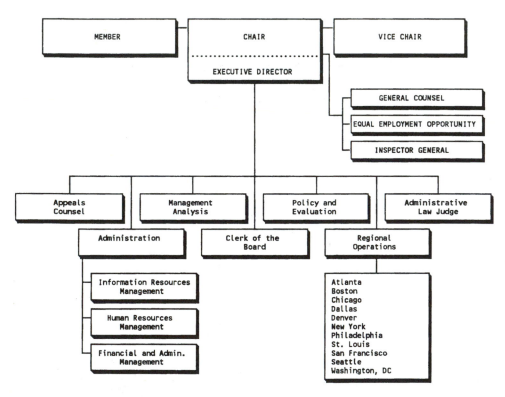

FIGURE 1.3 U.S. Merit Systems Protection Board organization chart. *Source*: U.S. Merit Systems Protection Board. *Organization and Functions Manual*. Washington, D.C.: USMSPB, 1990.

tion Act. The special counsel can bring charges against federal employees before the MSPB.

The Federal Labor Relations Council was replaced by the more independent and less managerially based Federal Labor Relations Authority (FLRA). (See Figure 1.4.) This agency has general oversight and regulatory authority for the conduct of labor relations in the federal service.

Although not part of the Civil Service Reform Act itself, the federal EEO program was assigned to the EEOC. The intent is to create independent enforcement of EEO regulations, as opposed to the previous practice of allowing the central personnel agency to sit in judgment of its own regulations in the face of allegations that they are discriminatory.

In addition, other major systems changes were enacted, including the following:

The top of the general schedule (GS) career structure, the ''supergrades,'' was largely converted into a senior executive service (SES). This change, which was prompted by the desire for managerial flexibility and executive leadership, facilitates the transfer of senior executive servants from position to position and from agency to agency. SES members can also be removed from the SES for unsatisfactory performance without meaningful appeal. At least 45% of all positions in the SES will be reserved for career officials, and no more than 10% of all SES employees can be political appointees. In order to assure a measure of continuity and to protect career senior executive servants, they cannot be involuntarily reassigned within 120 days of the appointment of a new agency head or new noncareer supervisor.

A merit pay system was adopted for grades GS-13 to GS-15. Under this system managers may reward effective and efficient employees for their performance without having to promote them to a higher salary step or grade. Related to this was a bonus system authorized for SES members and a cash awards system created to reward any federal employee for superior accomplishment and cost savings.

A number of other reform elements include the modification of veterans preference, the creation of research and demonstration authority, and the sanctioning of whistleblowing that exposes violations of law or mismanagement, gross waste of funds, abuse of authority, or substantial and specific dangers to public health or safety. In addition, the creation and utilization of agency performance appraisal systems was mandated.

This was the essence of the Civil Service Reform Act of 1978. There were other features, including provisions for demonstration projects under which personnel

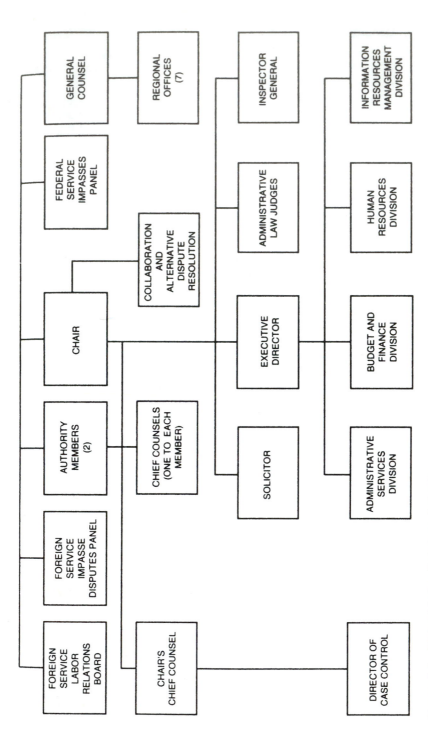

Figure 1.4 Federal Labor Relations Authority.

systems rules could be suspended and experiments with classification, compensation, and performance management—indeed, all the personnel functions attempted. In Chapter 2, an assessment of the postreform era, the impacts of various other administrative reform efforts (most notably the National Performance Review effort in the Clinton administration), and new proposals for reform will be discussed, but the story of civil service reform is incomplete without examining developments that occurred over the same period in the arena of state and local government.

Officials and Employees Who Are Authorized to Take Personnel Actions Are Prohibited from

- Discriminating against any employee or applicant
- Soliciting or considering any recommendation on a person who requests or is being considered for a personnel action unless the material is an evaluation of the person's work performance, ability, aptitude, or general qualifications, or character, loyalty, and suitability
- Using official authority to coerce political actions, to require political contributions, or to retaliate for refusal to do these things
- Willfully deceiving or obstructing an individual as to his or her right to compete for federal employment
- Influencing anyone to withdraw from competition, whether to improve or worsen the prospects of any applicant
- Granting any special preferential treatment or advantage not authorized by law to a job applicant or employee
- Appointing, employing, promoting, or advancing relatives in their agencies
- Taking or failing to take a personnel action as a reprisal against employees who exercise their appeal rights; refuse to engage in political activity; or lawfully disclose violations of law, rule, or regulation; or mismanagement, gross waste of funds, abuse of authority, or a substantial and specific danger to public health or safety
- Taking or failing to take any other personnel action violating a law, rule, or regulation directly related to merit system principles.

Source: U.S. Civil Service Commission, *Introducing the Civil Service Reform Act.* Washington, D.C.: U.S. Government Printing Office, November 1978, p. 2.

What Is the Whistleblower Protection Act (WPA) of 1989?

The WPA is a federal statute that amended the Civil Service Reform Act (CSRA) to enhance protections against reprisal for employees disclosing wrongdoings in the federal government. The WPA made some of the following changes to the CSRA:

- The OSC is no longer a part of the MSPB; instead, the OSC is now an independent agency within the executive branch.
- A showing of reprisal no longer requires proof that a supervisor had a specific intent to retaliate against a whistleblower. It is enough that a personnel action was taken ''because of'' a protected whistleblower disclosure.
- Employees alleging that a personnel action was taken because of whistleblowing have a new ''individual right of action'' (IRA) before the MSPB, with appeal rights to federal court. Before employees may exercise this right, they must first seek assistance from the OSC. Attorney fees and other costs are available to employees who prevail before the MSPB or the courts.
- A threat to take or not take a personnel action because of whistleblowing or the exercise of a lawful appeal right is a prohibited personnel practice.
- Employees who file an IRA, or any appeal in which it is alleged that a personnel action was because of whistleblowing, can request a stay of a personnel action from the MSPB.
- Agency heads may grant a preference in transfers or reassignments when the MSPB finds that an employee has been a victim of a personnel action because of whistleblowing.
- The taking of an adverse personnel action because of a refusal by an employee to obey an order that would require the employee to violate a law is clearly defined as a prohibited personnel practice.

Source: *A Report to Congress from the Office of Special Counsel*. Washington, D.C.: USOSC, 1989, pp. 17–18.

STATE AND LOCAL INSTITUTIONAL ARRANGEMENTS: A HISTORY IN PARALLEL

Influenced by the example of the 1883 Pendleton Act, state and local jurisdictions began to institute civil service commissions, but this was a very slow process. While New York State adopted a merit system that same year and Massachusetts did so during the following year, it would be more than 20 years before another state did so in 1905. By 1935 only 12 states had formally instituted merit systems. These early efforts weren't all successes—Connecticut had its first civil service law repealed, while Kansas kept its statute as law but refused to vote appropriations for it—nor were these laws necessarily effective even when kept on the books. For example, New York State, which had the most stringent prohibitions against political assessments on the salaries of public employees since 1883, had widespread ''voluntary'' contributions to the party at least through the 1930s. Indeed, a special probe in Onondaga County (Syracuse) in the late 1970s alleged the widespread practice of political assessment.

Perhaps the most striking difference in public personnel management found among different jurisdictional levels in the United States is that the merit system and the commission form of administering it have been far less successful in state and local governments than at the federal level. The reasons for this have been largely political. Although national politicians once relied dearly upon patronage for securing and maintaining their positions, the federal government never fell under the control of a unified political machine. At most it was dominated by a coalition of state and local political ''bosses.'' At the state and local levels, however, another picture was once common. While less important in recent decades, political machines once ruled supreme at these levels, especially in local politics. Even where this was not the case, the spoils tradition was often strong. Consequently, with some exceptions, until the post-World War II period, the politics of patronage was largely able to forestall the adoption of effective merit-oriented reforms.

While some cities, including New York, Albany, Buffalo, Syracuse, Chicago, Evanston, and Seattle, introduced merit systems during the 1880s and 1890s, the vast number of local jurisdictions were left untouched by the first wave of civil service reform. During the progressive era of the early 1900s, when corruption and ''bossism'' were among the prime targets of muckrakers and reform politicians, progress was also made in many cities, including Los Angeles, San Francisco, Pittsburgh, Cincinnati, Cleveland, St. Louis, and Baltimore. Overall, only 65 cities had created civil service commissions by 1900. By 1930 that number had risen to 250. As of the mid-1980s, less than 12% of cities with populations exceeding 50,000 lacked merit systems, and only about 60% of all state employees were formally under merit systems.

Of course, statistics concerning merit system coverage are inherently deceptive. While such figures may be numerically accurate, often they merely indicate that merit systems are "on the books," not that they exist in practice. The surveys of merit system coverage that are annually undertaken by a variety of good-government groups are typically administered by mailed questionnaires. These statistics are by no means ascertained by empirical investigation. Consequently, while the arithmetic of these surveys may be impeccable, the resulting summaries frequently belie the true extent of merit system coverage. Remember, Chicago has an excellent merit system on the books, yet it has managed to retain a reputation for years as being a city with patronage abuses. Even attempts to minimize the use of patronage simply led to its manifestation in other forms. Court-imposed orders, for example, curtailed the late Mayor Washington's direct power over patronage hiring in the mid- to late 1980s in Chicago, but he was very skillful and effective in awarding city contracts on a patronage basis. In this sense, he retained indirect control over jobs in the city. Ultimately, even systematic legal efforts to eliminate patronage abuses have not ended the doling out of government largesse based on partisan politics.

Subnational jurisdictions followed the federal merit system example in many respects: bipartisan civil service commissions became common, examining methods and related administrative detail were frequently similar, and prohibitions concerning political assessments and other varieties of interference were legally binding many years before a general pattern of compliance appeared. In some areas, such as position classification programs and retirement provisions, a variety of local jurisdictions were many years ahead of the federal service. At the local level however, the pattern of reform that evolved contained a crucial difference—the civil service commission was made administratively and presumably politically independent of the jurisdiction's chief executive officer. The commission format was mandated by political, not administrative, considerations. Then, as now, the illogic of divorcing the control of personnel from programmatic authority was recognized; nevertheless, the more immediate goal of defeating the influences of spoils was paramount, and thus the rationale for the commission device was quite reasonable. Not only would it be independent from the party-controlled government, but its three- or five-part membership would be in a better position to resist political pressures than could any single administrator. Appellate functions, especially, are better undertaken by a tribunal than by a solitary judge. Not insignificantly, a commission provides a political safety valve by making room for special-interest representation, such as racial, religious, or employee groups.

It wasn't very long before the rationale for the independent commission was seriously challenged. As the city manager movement developed early in this century, managers—nonpartisan reform-type managers at that—found themselves burdened with the same kinds of restrictions upon their authority over personnel that had been designed to thwart the spoilsperson. These managers thus asserted that the original reason for establishing an independent personnel agency—namely, lack of confidence in the appointing authority—did not exist with regard to them. They felt quite reasonably that the personnel function should be integrated with the other administrative functions under the executive. While this line of reasoning made considerable headway where the city manager concept was firmly entrenched, it had little applicability for most of the larger cities, in which the merit system provisions implemented only a few years earlier had degenerated into a sham. This was achieved by the dual process of appointing persons unsympathetic to merit system ideals as civil service commissioners and by restricting the work of the commission by denying adequate appropriations. In response to such "starve'em out" tactics, many jurisdictions later enacted ordinances providing that a fixed percentage of each year's budget would be for the administration of the merit system.

Despite these rather inauspicious beginnings, the merit system gradually took a firm hold in most sizable public jurisdictions. All cities with a population of over 250,000 have some provisions for a municipal civil service system. The smaller the number of employees in a jurisdiction, the less likely it is to have a merit system. Two basic factors have accounted for the continued growth of merit systems at the state and local levels. First, as the scope and nature of state and local employment changed it was almost inevitable that patronage appointees would have to give way to those with greater technical training and an interest in public service careers. It should be remembered in this context that even in the federal government at its worst the spoils system never substantially abused positions requiring technical skills. To some extent, then, the complex functions of government, rather than the ideas of civil service reformers, have led to the relative demise of spoils practices.

At this same time, the federal government had thrown its weight in favor of the development of forceful merit systems at the state and local levels. Beginning in the 1930s, it adopted a variety of measures to coerce or induce states to use merit procedures where federal funding is involved. Federal standards for this purpose were issued in 1939 and revised in 1948 and 1971. The most important step in this process was the enactment of the Intergovernmental Personnel Act of 1970 (IPA). The act declared that "since numerous governmental activities administered by the State and local governments are related to national purpose and are financed in part by Federal funds, a national interest exists in a high caliber public service in State and local governments." First, the federal CSC and now OPM were charged with developing elaborate standards for merit systems and were given the authority to allocate grants for improving state and local personnel systems. In addition, the act made possible the temporary interchange of personnel between jurisdictions, allowed the use of federal training facilities for state and local government employees, and created a mechanism for the col-

The Statutory Basis for Merit Systems

An effective merit personnel system starts with a clear mandate in law. The statutory provisions can be fairly short and general or quite detailed. Too much detail in a law, especially of a procedural nature, can stand in the way of progress because laws are difficult to change when change is needed. On the other hand, too little detail, especially where rights and obligations are concerned, can cause problems of interpretation and also open the way to circumventing the purpose of a merit system.

It is desirable to keep the statutory language as general and flexible as possible, leaving most details to be spelled out in administrative rules and regulations authorized by the statute.

a.   State Constitutions or Local Charters

The basic authority for a merit system is often found in a State constitution or local charter adopted by the vote of the people. The constitutional or charter provision is usually in the form of a broad statement expressing the will of the people that their government be staffed by persons who are selected on the basis of merit. Some State constitutions and local charters, however, go into more detail and contain provisions for the appointment and terms of office of the Civil Service Commissioners, the appointment of the Personnel Director, the powers and duties of these officials, and requirements for reporting on the activities of the merit system organization.

b.   State Statutes or Local Ordinances and Resolutions

State statutes and local ordinances generally contain considerably more detail than is found in the constitutions or charters. They may either be based on a constitutional or charter provision or enacted independently of the legislative body.

The merit system organization and the major functions of the central administering body will usually be spelled out in the statute. Generally, the statute will direct a specified agency or person to issue the necessary rules and regulations which have the effect of law, and the necessary administrative procedures to carry out the provisions of the statute.

Other statutory provisions will cover such matters as pay, retirement, labor relations, conflicts of interest, and other essential components of a modern public personnel system.

If all the major components of the merit personnel system are not covered in one basic public personnel statute but, instead, are covered in several different statutes, it is desirable to codify all such provisions in one public personnel title of the State statutory code or comparable local instrument.

c. Civil Service or Personnel Rules and Regulations

Detailed provisions for operating a merit system are generally found in the rules and regulations issued by the central personnel agency or other designated agent of the jurisdiction, whether a civil service commission, a personnel board, or a personnel director. The rulemaking and regulatory authority is usually set out in the statute.

Source: U.S. Civil Service Commission, *Guide to a More Effective Public Service . . . The Legal Framework*. Washington, D.C.: Bureau of Intergovernmental Personnel Programs, August 1974, pp. 5–6.

lection, coordination, and dissemination of information of public personnel administration. Few provisions of the IPA are in force today, however, since the act was virtually gutted under the Reagan administration's program of "new federalism."

CIVIL SERVICE REFORM AND THE DECLINE OF THE COMMISSION FORMAT

Ironically, at the same time that the federal government has been pressuring state and local governments to adopt and strengthen merit systems, the commission form of administering them was on the wane for reasons similar to the abolition of the commission format at the federal level. Put simply, independent, structurally, and politically isolated personnel agencies of a regulatory nature were having great difficulty in serving the needs of elected executives and public managers. They became viewed as obstacles to efficiency and effectiveness and seen as often unduly influenced by pressure groups.

Ever since the 1930s efforts have been made to bring public personnel administration into greater harmony with public management in general. At state and local levels this was often attempted through the appointment of a single personnel director as the head of a central personnel agency that is clearly located within the executive chain of command. In some cases, a citizens' "oversight" group without rule-making authority complements this approach. Jean J. Couturier, a former executive director of the National Civil Service League, noted that by the mid-1970s about "half the large governments in the U.S. had abandoned the commission form of government for personnel management." Such changes in institutional arrangements do not necessarily militate against the maintenance of merit systems. Indeed, many of their supporters believe that personnel divi-

The Malek Manual

When Fred Malek was the chief of the Nixon administration's White House personnel office he occasioned the drafting of the *Federal Political Personnel Manual*, popularly known as the Malek manual. As Frank J. Thompson has suggested, "the Malek manual is to personnel administration what Machiavelli's *The Prince* is the broader field of political science." Malek's infamous manual did not specifically advocate the violation of any law; rather, it encouraged the systematic and widespread abuse of the spirit of the federal merit system. In fairness, it must be added that the Nixon administration did nothing in this regard that was not done in earlier administrations. The Nixon Republicans were simply more comprehensive—more ambitious—in their abuse of the merit concept. They felt that their friends, their fellow Republicans, had more merit than strangers with like qualifications but differing affiliations. The nonpartisan processes of appointments based upon merit were merely an administrative inconvenience that could be overcome by mastering the minutiae of the civil service regulations. The politicos were out to beat the careerists at their own game. They nearly won!

The best way to appreciate the usefulness of the Malek manual is to read an excerpt:

Let us assume that you have a career opening in your Department's personnel office for a Staff Recruitment Officer. Sitting in front of you is your college roommate from Stanford University in California who was born and raised in San Francisco. He received his law degree from Boalt Hall at the University of California. While studying for the bar he worked at an advertising agency handling newspaper accounts. He also worked as a reporter on the college newspaper. Your personnel experts judge that he could receive an eligibility rating for a GS-11.

The first thing you do is tear up the old job description that goes with that job. You then have a new one written, to be classified as GS-11, describing the duties of that specific Staff Recruitment Officer as directed toward the recruitment of recent law graduates for entry level attorney positions, entry level public information officers for the creative arts and college news liaison sections of your public information shop, and to be responsible for general recruiting for entry level candidates on the West Coast. You follow that by listing your selective criteria as follows: Education: BA and LLB, stating that the candidate should have extensive experience and knowledge by reason of employment or residence on the West Coast. Candidate should have attended or be familiar with law schools, and institutions of higher education, preferably on the West Coast. The candidate should also possess some knowledge by reasons of education or experience of the fields of college journalism, advertising, and law.

> You then trot this candidate's Application for Federal Employment over to the Civil Service Commission, and shortly thereafter he receives an eligibility rating for a GS-11. Your personnel office then sends over the job descriptions (GS-11) along with the selective criteria which was based on the duties of the job description. When the moment arrives for the panel to "spin the register" you insure that your personnel office sends over two "friendly" bureaucrats. The register is then spun and your candidate will certainly be among the only three who even meet the selective criteria, much less be rated by your two "friendly" panel members as among the "highest qualified" that meet the selection criteria. In short, you write the job description and selective criteria around your candidate's Form 171.
>
> There is no merit in the merit system!

sions or departments rather than commissions should serve to strengthen merit procedures.

One of the more significant influences on current thinking about civil service reform was the National Civil Service League's model public personnel administration law, which was first promulgated in 1970. The organization that wrote the actual text of the Pendleton Act in the 1880s, creating the U.S. CSC, was by the 1970s recommending the abolition of commission formats for public personnel management. The league would replace civil service commissions with a tripartite structure consisting of (1) a personnel division headed by a director of cabinet rank whose task would be to serve the needs of effective management; (2) some form of ombudsperson to provide recourse for employees—a role that conceivably could be fulfilled by a labor relations board; and (3) a citizen's advisory board to represent the public interest. In 1895 Chicago became one of the first American cities to create a civil service commission. In 1976 it became the first major city to abolish its civil service commission in favor of reforms espoused by the model law of the National Civil Service League.

A SUMMARY NOTE ON THE MERITS OF REFORM

The development of satisfactory institutional arrangements for the formulation and implementation of public personnel policy presents several complexities and difficulties that cannot be readily resolved. At the heart of the overall problem is the diversity of roles played by central personnel agencies and the tension among several of them. Originally the central personnel agency as we now know it in the United States was created to carry out the purposes of civil service reform. While some of these institutions have done admirably in this regard, the merit system in and of itself has been of limited efficiency in contributing to the development of highly effective and efficient public bureaucracies. While the merit system has gone far to recruit better people for public employment, it has seldom helped a chief executive to maximize the potential of his or her organization. The reasonable suggestion, incorporated in the federal Civil Service Reform Act of 1978, that the personnel system should be subordinated to the control of a chief executive, can result in undesirable politicization.

It is important for public managers and students of public personnel administration to confront this matter. All too often they have echoed the view that efficiency is the number 1 axiom of administration without considering whether or not it is fully compatible with democracy, fairness, and apolitical public services. Improvements in the institutional arrangements involved in public personnel administration can certainly be made, but those searching for simplistic structural solutions to the overall problem are likely to be disappointed. Deep-seated and intractable social and political problems cannot be resolved with organizational cosmetics. The tension between society's desire for depoliticized, merit-oriented public services and its interest in enabling its elected representatives to effectuate their policies is likely to make the nature of institutional arrangements for public personnel administration subject to constant re-evaluation and modification well into the new century.

BIBLIOGRAPHY

Aron, Cindy S. *Ladies and Gentlemen of the Civil Service*. New York: Oxford University Press, 1987.

Aronson, Albert H. "State and Local Personnel Administration," In *Biography of an Ideal*, edited by the U.S. Civil Service Commission, Washington, D.C.: U.S. Government Printing Office, 1974.

Aronson, Sidney H. *Status and Kinship in the Higher Civil Service*. Cambridge: Harvard University Press, 1964.

Ban, Carolyn and Norma M. Riccucci, eds. *Public Personnel Management: Current Concerns, Future Challenges*. White Plains, N.Y.: Longman Press, 1991; See in particular Ban's "The Navy Demonstration Project."

Banfield, Edward C. and James Q. Wilson. *City Politics*. New York: Vintage, 1963.

Bellone, Carl J. "Structural vs. Behavioral Change: The Civil Service Reform Act of 1978," *Review of Public Personnel Administration* (spring 1982).

Bernstein, Marver. *The Job of the Federal Executive*. Washington, D.C.: Brookings Institution, 1958.

Bussey, Ellen M., ed. *Federal Civil Service Law and Procedures*, 2nd ed. Washington, D.C.: Bureau of National Affairs, 1990.

Campbell, Alan K. "Civil Service Reform: A New Commitment," *Public Administration Review*, vol. 38 (March–April 1978).

Carpenter, William S. *The Unfinished Business of Civil Service Reform*. Princeton, N.J.: Princeton University Press, 1952.

Cook, Charles. *Biography of an Ideal: The Diamond Anniversary History of the Federal Civil Service*. Washington, D.C.: U.S. Government Printing Office, 1959.

Couturier, Jean J. "The Quiet Revolution in Public Personnel Laws," *Public Personnel Management* (May–June 1976).

Crenson, Matthew A. *The Federal Machine: Beginnings of Bureaucracy in Jacksonian America*. Baltimore: Johns Hopkins University Press, 1975.

Dalby, Michael T. and Michael S. Werthman, eds. *Bureaucracy in Historical Perspective*. Glenview, Ill.: Scott, Foresman, 1971.

Dresang, Dennis L. *Public Personnel Management and Public Policy*. White Plains, N.Y.: Longman Press, 1991.

Eriksson, Erik M. "The Federal Civil Service Under President Jackson," *Mississippi Valley Historical Review*, vol. 13 (March 1927).

Fish, Carl R. *The Civil Service and the Patronage*. New York: Russell & Russell, 1904, 1963.

Freedman, Anne. "Doing Battle with the Patronage Army: Politics, Courts, and Personnel Administration in Chicago," *Public Administration Review*, vol. 48 (September/October 1988).

Gawthrop, Louis. *Bureaucratic Behavior in the Executive Branch*. New York: Free Press, 1969.

Golembiewski, Robert T. and Michael Cohen, eds. *People in Public Service: A Reader in Public Personnel Administration*, 2nd ed. Itasca, Ill.: F. E. Peacock Publishers, 1976.

Hall, Chester. "The United States Civil Service Commission," *Public Personnel Review*, vol. 28 (October 1967).

Hampton, Robert. "The Basic Question," *Civil Service Journal*, vol. 13 (January–March 1973).

Heclo, Hugh. *A Government of Strangers: Executive Politics in Washington*. Washington, D.C.: Brookings Institution, 1977.

Hofstadter, Richard. *The Age of Reform*. New York: Vantage, 1955.

Hoogenboom, Ari. *Outlawing the Spoils: A History of the Civil Service Reform Movement, 1865–1883*. Urbana, Ill.: University of Illinois Press, 1961.

Ingraham, Patricia W. and David H. Rosenbloom. "Symposium on the Civil Service Reform Act of 1978," *Policy Studies Journal*, vol. 17 (winter 1988–1989).

Ingraham, Patricia W. and Carolyn Ban, eds. *Legislating Bureaucratic Change: The Civil Service Reform Act of 1978*. Albany, N.Y.: State University of New York Press, 1984.

Josephson, Matthew. *The Politicos, 1865–1896*. New York: Harcourt, Brace, 1938.

Kaufman, Herbert. "Emerging Conflicts in the Doctrines of Public Administration," *American Political Science Review*, vol. 50 (December 1956).

Knudsen, Steven, Larry Jakus, and Maida Metz. "The Civil Service Reform Act of 1978," *Public Personnel Management*, 8 (May–June 1979). For an official OPM response to this article, see Campbell, Alan K. "Letter to the Editor," *Public Personnel Management*, vol. 8 (September–October 1979).

Kramer, Kenneth W. "Seeds of Success and Failure: Policy Development and Implementation of the 1978 Civil Service Reform Act," *Review of Public Personnel Administration* (spring 1982).

Lee, Robert D. Jr. *Public Personnel Systems*, 2nd ed. Rockville, Md.: Aspen Publishers, 1987.

McBain, Howard L. *DeWitt Clinton and the Origin of the Spoils System in New York.* New York: AMS Press, 1967.

Meriam, Lewis. *Personnel Administration in the Federal Government.* Washington, D.C.: Brookings Institution, 1937.

Meriam, Lewis. *Public Personnel Problems: From the Standpoint of the Operating Officer.* Washington, D.C.: Brookings Institution, 1938.

Mosher, Frederick C. *Democracy and the Public Service*, 2nd ed. New York: Oxford University Press, 1982.

Mosher, William E. and J. Donald Kingsley. *Public Personnel Administration.* New York: Harper & Bros., 1936.

Murphy, Lionel V. "The First Federal Civil Service Commission, 1871–1875," *Public Personnel Review*, vol. 3 (October 1942).

Patten, Thomas H. Jr. *Classics of Personnel Management.* Oak Park, Ill.: Moore, 1979.

Patten, Thomas H. Jr. "Where Was the Commission?" *Good Government* (spring 1975).

Pearce, Jone L. and James L. Perry, "Federal Merit Pay: A Longitudinal Analysis," *Public Administration Review*, vol. 43 (July/August 1983).

Perry, James L., Beth Ann Petrakis, and Theodore K. Miller. "Federal Merit Pay, Round II: An Analysis of the Performance Management and Recognition System," *Public Administration Review*, vol. 49 (January/February 1989).

Rosen, Bernard. *The Merit System in the United States Civil Service.* Monograph for the Committee on Post Office and Civil Service of the House of Representatives. Washington, D.C.: U.S. Government Printing Office, 94th Cong., 1st sess., December 23, 1975.

Rosenbloom, David H. *Federal Service and the Constitution.* Ithaca, N.Y.: Cornell University Press, 1971.

Rosenthal, Harvey. "In Defense of Central Control of Public Personnel Policy," *Public Personnel Review*, vol. 28 (October 1967).

Rutan v. Republican Party of Illinois, 58 *Law Week* 4872 (1990).

Sayre, Wallace. "The Triumph of Techniques Over Purpose," *Public Administration Review*, vol. 8 (spring 1948).

Seidman, Harold and Robert Gilmour. *Politics, Position, and Power: The Dynamics of Federal Organization*, 4th ed. New York: Oxford University Press, 1986.

Shafritz, Jay M. *Public Personnel Management: The Heritage of Civil Service Reform.* New York: Praeger, 1975.

Sorauf, Frank J. "The Silent Revolution in Patronage," *Public Administration Review* (winter 1960).

Stahl, O. Glenn. *Public Personnel Administration*, 7th ed. New York: Harper & Row, 1976.

Stewart, Frank M. *The National Civil Service Reform League: History, Activities, and Problems.* Austin, Tex.: University of Texas, 1929.

Tolchin, Martin and Susan Tolchin. *To the Victor: Political Patronage from the Clubhouse to the White House*. New York: Random House, 1971.

Van Riper, Paul P. *History of the United States Civil Service*. Evanston, Ill.: Row, Peterson, 1958.

Weber, Max. *From Max Weber: Essays in Sociology*, translated and edited by H. H. Gerth and C. W. Mills, New York: Oxford University Press, 1958.

Wilson, Woodrow. "The Study of Administration," *Political Science Quarterly*, vol. 55 (December 1941); originally published in 1887.

White, Leonard D. *The Federalists*. New York: Macmillan, 1948.

White, Leonard D. *The Jeffersonians*. New York: Macmillan, 1951.

White, Leonard D. *The Jacksonians*. New York: Macmillan, 1954.

White, Leonard D. *The Republican Era*. New York: Macmillan, 1958.

U.S. President's Committee on Administrative Management. *Report of the Committee with Studies of the Administrative Management in the Federal Government*. Washington, D.C.: U.S. Government Printing Office, 1937.

2

Civil Service Reform in the Postreform Era (1979 to 2000)

PROLOGUE: THE DEATH OF THE MERIT SYSTEM IN GEORGIA

The August 1997 cover story ("Who Needs Civil Service?") for *Governing* magazine (see Figure 2.1) tells the tale of Georgia state law SB 635. Passed in 1996, it is in the words of *Governing*, "the most dramatic civil service experiment in recent times anywhere in America." Under the terms of the law, the civil service rights of all Georgia employees hired after July 1, 1996, can be summed up in one word: *zero*.

What's happening here? The essence of Georgia's legislative action removes the extraconstitutional legal protections for civil service employment for all new job hires. Georgia's ending of civil service was prompted by beliefs that the central system, which was designed to regulate and protect civil servants from political abuse, had in fact become a system of regulatory abuse and protectionism. Then-governor Zell Miller promised in his 1996 state of the state address that he would totally revise the state merit system, which had gone from being a solution when created in 1943 to being a problem. The central system was taking up to two months to fill job vacancies, and because of massive paperwork and a lengthy appeals process between 12 to 18 months to dismiss a poorly performing employee.

FIGURE 2.1   Cover of *Governing* magazine (August 1997).

Miller was a very popular governor with strong views on how to make the state workforce more responsive and more productive. In his first years as governor he reacted to the recession of 1990–1991 with a major reduction in force, resulting in the laying off of several thousand state employees. He created a commission on effectiveness and economy in government that was highly critical of centralized bureaucratic processes and pushed for market-based reforms and expanded outsourcing to produce competition within agencies.

Governor Miller's next step was to push for an overhaul of the pay-for-performance that which was begun in 1992. Installed in 1996, GeorgiaGain rated all employees on a four-point scale. Any employee rated at the low point (did not meet performance requirements level) would receive no annual pay increase, while the second through fourth points received greater percentages of pay increases. GeorgiaGain was still problematic in that less than 1% of the state's more than 64,000 employees actually received a "did not meet" rating.

A more radical and final solution to deinvent civil service then unfolded. The governor's 1996 plan called for "unclassifying all vacant positions," and any new employee hired after July 1, 1996, would become an "at-will" employee after he or she they completed the standard one-year probationary period. Over time, as those employees in the protected civil service retire or leave their positions, all positions will thus become part of the nonprotected service.

Politically, Georgia was able to accomplish this rather daunting feat because of a number of factors. In one analysis Stephen Condrey has noted that Georgia is a strong right-to-work state with weak public unions that have very limited collective bargaining rights. Another factor was the extent to which many of Georgia's top agency managers were exempt from the state merit system and had moved their agency workforce to become "excepted service." As Condrey summarizes, "clearly, the state bureaucratic leadership sought to break from a system that would not or could not reform itself."

How does Georgia's new noncivil service system work? Basically, there is a major delegation of power and control from a market-based statewide pay and classification system to one in which agencies set pay grades and minimum job qualifications for their "agency-unique jobs." The agencies now control recruiting and qualifying applicants for selection, and with at-will employee status, the agencies can establish and follow more rapid firing processes as long as they afford due process and don't discriminate.

Of course, the Georgia Merit System still exists and now seeks to become a new strategic partner, with each public agency assisting in advising on hiring and selection processes and still administering statewide benefit programs. Georgia's central personnel services have moved from a regulatory focus to a service-provision focus. Georgia will still provide base services centering on the statewide data information system, payroll, and some testing services. The state will also offer customized services and consulting on a fee-for-service basis for personnel systems assistance for such services as salary survey, position classification, and training programs.

The new system is really the triumph of "decentralized personnel authority," and the numbers of "unclassified personnel" are rising quickly. By 1998, the state had reached 34% unclassified, up from 17% in 1994. The Georgia Merit System deputy commissioner, Robert Stephens, cites studies estimating that by 2006, "90% of the state's workforce could be at will." As Georgia moves to that date when the majority of the state workforce is unclassified, we will be able to contrast how total decentralization truly works.

In the interim, Georgia's great experiment is attracting considerable attention. New York State, historically one of the bastions of the civil service tradition, has launched a number of reforms and had its own article in *Governing* recently, entitled "Untangling Albany." The article by Jonathan Walters concludes that "Viewed realistically, all New York has really done is start to pull even with other relatively advanced states. But considering New York's dead-last status in the state civil service world just three years ago, the list of recent accomplishments there borders on the unbelievable." The changes in New York seem modest by Georgia standards; most of the "reforms" are in the category of internal improvements or "streamlining" the way personnel does business. There is more flexibility in hiring because the lists of potential candidates for job hiring are larger and deeper thanks to more assertive recruitment and faster examination efforts. Likewise in staffing practices, more flexibility has been created by broadening position classifications and decreasing job titles along with lowering restrictions on work assignments and lateral transfers across agencies. Even the unions are in agreement that New York's reform efforts have brought about positive change in many areas.

For personnelists, perhaps the real lesson of Georgia is that there's nothing like one good example of total destruction to promote change and innovation. As the management consulting expression goes, "show them death, and they'll accept injury and necessity to move forward."

THE AFTERMATH OF THE CIVIL SERVICE REFORM ACT OF 1978

The early years of the Civil Service Reform Act (CSRA) were marked by much turbulence. A primary reason for this can be attributed to the Carter administration's support for a long-term implementation process, whereby agencies were given several years to develop and implement the various new programs (e.g., merit pay and performance appraisal) called for by the act. This strategy proved to be detrimental to many of the act's components. As critics of reform have pointed out, the nature of the American political system, which tends toward instability and is primarily focused on short-term results, is opposed to any long-term implementation strategy.

Although theoretically sensible, the long-term strategy was particularly inept in view of the politics of the CSRA. There was much support for many of the parts of the reform, but no comprehensive vision of public personnel policy was discernable. Careerists could thus favor the Merit Systems Protection Board (MSPB); organized labor; the labor relations program; management and political executives; the merit pay and SES provisions; and protected-class persons and civil rights advocates and greater involvement of the Equal Employment Opportunity Council (EEOC) in federal personnel policies. Each of these interests sought to strengthen itself through the reform, but very few members of the reform coalition cared much about how the *whole package* would work. This was the politics of coalition building at its best and the prospects for successful implementation at their worst.

In addition, the act's emphasis on decentralization resulted in a number of managerial abuses as well as errors. Compounding these problems were the political realities associated with the election of Ronald Reagan, whose emphasis on political control of the federal bureaucracy rather than personnel management became a driving force behind the reform efforts.

Within a decade, nearing the end of the Reagan administration, the major reforms of the civil service reform effort had a very mixed track record. As the following review suggests, they both succeeded and failed in reforming the federal system of personnel management.

> 1. *On replacing the Civil Service Commission with a new structure (i.e., Office of Personnel Management [OPM], MSPB, and Office of Special Counsel [OSC]).* The OPM itself produced very mixed results. It was initially successful in working toward its original goals of "improved federal management, stronger executive direction, and modernized personnel management." It emphasized, as was intended by the act, the value of *managing* human resources. Soon, however, rather than being a management tool for the president, OPM had become an "instrument of political persuasion." In the words of OPM's second director Donald Devine, who was appointed by Reagan, "the skill and technical expertise of the career service must be utilized, but it must be utilized under the direct authority and personal supervision of the political leader who has the moral authority flowing from the people through an election." Under Devine, OPM virtually lost its management orientation and became a political instrument of the executive branch to assert and manage the values and partisan ideology of the president.
>
> Subsequent directors, Constance Horner and Constance Newman (under President Bush), worked hard to shift OPM back toward its intended managerial focus. Both Horner and Newman devoted great effort to the systems and mechanics of federal personnel, especially in leading efforts to reform position classification and modernize pay systems. They fought successfully to keep the central system intact against increasing attempts by agencies to create their own civil service systems or what is called "excepted service."
>
> The MSPB, while successful in establishing itself as an adjudicator of appeals brought by federal employees, suffered from a perception that its decisions were biased toward management. This perception stemmed in part from MSPB's decisions against appeals by air traffic

controllers, who walked off their jobs in 1981 over a labor dispute with the federal government. Still, over time MSPB's decisions on employee appeals have largely favored management, by about a 4-to-1 margin. It should be pointed out that the courts have generally upheld MSPB decisions upon appeal. In 1998, the courts reaffirmed MSPB decisions in over 90% of the cases.

In more recent years, the MSPB would undertake and publish a variety of important studies on the federal personnel system. It also issued reports evaluating aspects of OPM's performance and conducted regular surveys of federal employee perceptions on a range of merit system issues as well as overall morale and attitudes within the federal public service.

The OSC, at least in its first 10 years of operation, was not very successful in fulfilling its role as protector of merit principles. This was due to a number of factors, including understaffing and skepticism on the part of federal employees and their unions as to the executive's actual commitment to a watchdog agency. Indeed, the powers of the special counsel were initially limited, especially in terms of its ability to protect whistle-blowers from retaliation by federal employers.

Some of these problems were addressed by the passage of the Whistleblower Protection Act (WPA) of 1989, which converted the OSC into an independent agency within the executive branch. The OSC ultimately became completely separate and apart from the MSPB, and the powers of the special counsel have been enhanced, particularly in the area of protecting whistle-blowers from punitive, retaliatory actions by federal agencies.

2. *On the changes in Federal Labor Relations.*   The Federal Labor Relations Authority (FLRA) has been relatively efficient and "even-handed" in addressing and resolving labor–management problems and disputes. In its first decade, however, the FLRA has been largely unsuccessful in gaining judicial deference. Its rulings and decisions were overturned at a much higher rate by the courts than they have been upheld. Moreover, in several opinions the courts issued harsh criticisms of the FLRA for its inconsistent and illogical decisions.

3. *On the reorganization of federal equal opportunity.*   As noted earlier, civil service reform included a reorganization of EEO. Initially this helped EEO efforts insofar as oversight of the federal EEO program was transferred to the independent EEOC. In fact, the EEOC was successful in abolishing a major obstacle to the achievement of EEO goals—the Professional and Administrative Careers Exam (PACE). The PACE was a so-called merit exam, of which the CSC was an ardent defender. Such exams tend to have an adverse effect on EEO

efforts, and so the EEOC has been more opposed to their use than the CSC.

Despite the relative success of this institutional reorganization, however, the federal government's EEO program, which goes well beyond the scope of the civil service reform efforts, has not been wholly satisfactory. The federal service is more socially diverse today, but it is white women more than any other persons or groups who have made the most progress. African Americans and Latinos continue to lag behind, particularly in terms of holding jobs at the upper levels of the federal government. Nevertheless, the CSRA does make it federal policy to eliminate the "underrepresentation" of EEO target groups.

4. *On creating a senior management cadre (the Senior Executive Service).*   Perhaps the most disappointing aspect of the CSRA has been the Senior Executive Service (SES), which got off to a poor start. SESers charged that they were being subjected to illegitimate political pressures and many resigned or retired. In fact, by 1985 over half of the original SES cadre had left office. Still, the total number in the SES would grow from approximately 7000 in 1980 to over 8000 in 1990. Relatively few SESers moved from agency to agency, however, which has frustrated realization of the ideal of developing top-level federal managers who are familiar with a broad range of policy areas and management issues. Within a decade it would be clear that most employers of the SES stayed within their own agencies. A study by Toni Marzotto of interagency and intra-agency mobility rates of the SES found that interagency transfers had dropped from 2% in 1980 to 1% in 1992 and intra-agency transfers had declined form 15% in 1980 to 11%. Marzotto concluded that the lack of movement indicated that SES "may be a haven for home grown technocrats rather than the 'go anywhere-lead anything' generalists managers imagined in the original reform."

Pay also lagged, causing further disaffection among SESers. Alan K. "Scotty" Campbell, OPM's first director and the individual generally credited with being the inventor of CSRA, acknowledged in a 1995 symposium that SES policies had to be revised to include mandatory rotation, better training and development, and pay commensurate with performance. In accepting that the reality of the SES had not lived up to its potential, he made the following observation about the compensation issue: "Experience in the private sector has shown that compensation bonus opportunities depend mostly on the performance of the total corporation. But we have not figured out how to measure the performance of the federal government. Incentive pay should not occur until performance can be measured, and it should be relevant to the goals of the overall organization. There needs to be a balance between focusing on the goals of your agency and the goals of government."

Overall, the SES leaves open to question whether a personnel system based on narrow position classifications and intense specialization in professional fields and policy areas can produce a flexible corps at the top that can bring a broad vision of the public interest to bear on the formulation and design of public policy.

5. *On the concept of pay for performance or merit pay.* The original merit pay system for grades GS-13 to GS-15 quickly proved to be "demoralizing and counterproductive." Its biggest failure has been its inability to meet its primary goal: improving the performance of federal managers by establishing a link between pay and performance. To redress this problem, a new system was created in 1984—the Performance Management Recognition System. It, too, however, was ineffective in linking reward structures to the performance of federal workers. Prevailing practice in government was to either rotate awards among workers each year or reduce the amount of pay increases by pooling bonuses or limiting award money to inconsequential levels.

The federal government remains committed to the assumption that pay for performance will work, but the underlying politics of personnel simply have not supported this premise. Such a linkage may be possible only in an ideal sense in cases in which politics are "separate" from administration. Interestingly, the public personnel community was generally willing to challenge this flawed pay-for-performance principle behind closed doors, but unwilling to admit publicly that the "emperor is wearing no clothes." Further complicating the merit pay issue was the growing pay gap between what federal workers were being paid and their private sector counterparts. To argue about 3 to 5% variable pay bonuses when federal pay was lagging private sector pay by 15% to 25% depending upon how you count benefits was almost disingenuous.

6. *On other reforms, most notably experimentation.* Other reforms incorporated in the CSRA have also met with mixed results. One of the most touted reform elements was Title VI of the act, which called for the development of research and demonstration projects to explore new and improved approaches to federal personnel management. The demonstration provisions in particular would allow federal agencies to suspend civil service law under certain circumstances in order to improve the quality of such personnel functions as recruitment, hiring, performance appraisal, and classification and pay.

The research provisions of the reform act were quickly gutted when Donald Devine was appointed to head the OPM. Devine, aggressively pursuing and fostering Reagan's posture of economic austerity, drastically cut existing research efforts and also abolished the Research Management Division, which had been created by Campbell to oversee the research provisions mandated by the CSRA.

The demonstration provisions also ran into funding problems. The few demonstrations that were funded were proven to be relatively effective, however. For example, the Navy's China Lake demonstration, which was one of the largest and most ambitious projects, provided line managers with the flexibility needed to hire and retain high-quality employees and created new systems for classification called broadbanding. Other demonstration projects at such agencies as the Federal Aviation Administration and the National Institute of Standards and Technology (formerly the National Bureau of Standards) were equally successful. The problem was leveraging results or converting the lessons learned on the demonstration projects into general legislation or system permission for any agency to apply proven demonstration project formulas. Demonstration projects became most notable for thick evaluation reports that filled bookcases, but weren't implemented into action.

Such mixed results left public personnelists—both advocates and critics—in a quandary. Should they push for another round of systemwide, broad-brush reforms, or should they simply address specific reform problems and try to improve upon or in some cases actually implement the provisions and spirit of civil service reform—to in effect, paraphrasing Campbell, make the reality of civil service reform live up to its promise? Given an increasingly badly divided Congress and presidency and major budget uncertainties, the latter seemed the more appropriate course of action.

OVERTURE FOR POSTREFORM: THE VOLCKER COMMISSION

In 1987, in the waning years of the Reagan administration, a national commission was formed in Washington to study what it termed a "quiet crisis." The National Commission on the Public Service became a 36-member body under the chairpersonship of former Federal Reserve Board Chair Paul A. Volcker. The commission's task was to assess the problem of the poor quality of the image of the federal government and its impact on recruitment and retention. In its preface it stated: "Simply put, too many of the best of the nation's senior executives are ready to leave government, and not enough of its most talented people are willing to join. This erosion in the attractiveness of public service at all levels—most specifically in the federal civil service—undermines the ability of government to respond effectively to the needs and aspirations of the American people, and ultimately damages the democratic process itself."

The commission, which included former president Ford, former vice president Mondale, congressional representatives, and a who's who of prominent Americans in public and private life, was the very model of bipartisanship. It formed five task forces to examine all aspects of the personnel problem in government and came up with a range of recommendations, all designed to deal with three core themes: leadership, talent, and performance. Within each of these core themes, the commission created five goals and specific recommendations within each goal area.

It's fair to say that if one viewed the sum of the parts of the Volcker commission's 1989 report, they really required major systems reform, but the commission's report was almost conciliatory in defining required actions for the OPM and laying blame for the current set of problems. The report began with an explanation for the current set of conditions that sounded more like an apology than analysis: "The OPM is undoubtedly often blamed for problems beyond its control. Its mission would stretch the capabilities of the strongest agency. Its clientele is huge, and its staff and funding limited. Most important, it continues to be encumbered by operating responsibilities that limit its ability to set policy; not only does OPM operate an extensive federal training program; but it must oversee countless personnel decisions that could be easily decentralized to the departments and agencies."

Regarding what OPM should do to cope with such an untenable set of management conditions, the report continued: "The OPM was created in 1978 to provide efficient, responsive personnel leadership on behalf of the President. Although OPM has never fully realized this potential, the need for such an agency remains . . . The Commission believes that the President and Congress should take additional steps to restructure OPM, first by strengthening its technical expertise, then by decentralizing unnecessary operating responsibilities and revitalizing its staff."

The report then recommended that OPM be allowed to concentrate on the following five major duties:

1. Providing policy guidance on personnel standards and practices
2. Overseeing implementation of those standards and practices
3. Providing technical support for departments and agencies that need help
4. Undertaking research on ways to enhance government productivity and performance
5. Anticipating future trends in government

Finally, the commission took a parting shot at the "political OPM" and urged that the number of politically appointed managers within OPM be drastically reduced.

The Volcker Commission's Recommendations for "Rebuilding the Public Service"

First, Presidents, their chief lieutenants, and Congress must articulate early and often the necessary and honorable role that public servants play in the democratic process, at the same time making clear they will demand the highest standards of ethics and performance possible from those who hold the public trust.

Second, cabinet officers and agency heads should be given greater flexibility to administer their organizations, including greater freedom to hire and fire personnel, provided there are appropriate review procedures within the Administration and oversight from Congress.

Third, the President should highlight the important role of the Office of Personnel Management (OPM) by establishing and maintaining contact with its Director and by ensuring participation by the Director in cabinet level discussions on human resource management issues.

Fourth, the growth in recent years in the number of presidential appointees, whether those subject to Senate confirmation, noncareer senior executives, or personal and confidential assistants, should be curtailed.

Fifth, the President and Congress must ensure that federal managers receive the added training they will need to perform effectively.

Sixth, the nation should recognize the importance of civic education as a part of social studies and history in the nation's primary and secondary school curricula.

Seventh, America should take advantage of the natural idealism of its youth by expanding and encouraging national volunteer service.

Eighth, the President and Congress should establish a Presidential Public Service Scholarship Program targeted to 1,000 college or college-bound students each year, with careful attention to the recruitment of minority students.

Ninth, the President should work with Congress to give high priority to restoring the depleted purchasing power of executive, judicial, and legislative salaries.

Tenth, if Congress is unable to act on its own salaries, the Commission recommends that the President make separate recommendations for judges and top level executives and that the Congress promptly act upon them.

Eleventh, the President and the Congress should give a higher budget priority to civil service pay in the General Schedule pay system.

Twelfth, the President and Congress should establish a permanent independent advisory council, composed of members from the public and private sector, both to monitor the ongoing state of the public service and to make such recommendations for improvements as they think desirable.

Source: Reprinted from the *Report of the National Commission on the Public Service*. Washington, D.C., 1989.

Ironically, little of the Volcker commission's systems prescriptions would be heeded. Instead, the Bush administration and Congress focused on the centerpiece of the Volcker commission's recommendations—pay reform. This was hardly a surprise, since three of the commission's twelve major proposals (see box) dealt with compensation. A year later, the first and basically only major reform that would come out of the Volcker commission emerged as the Federal Pay Comparability Act of 1990, which set up mechanisms to close the pay gap

What Is "Excepted Service?"

The dominant method for determining pay in the federal service over the years has been through the general schedule. Agencies within the general schedule are subject to Title 5 of the U.S. Code on Government Organization and Employees.

Some agencies are exempted from Title V provisions, especially for the purpose of being able to set up their own methods for determining white-collar pay. Employees under these non-Title V pay programs are called "excepted service." The agency in this instance has the ability to set its own pay structure and classification and qualification standards, and set up methods for additional compensation, such as incentive awards, and even recruitment and retention bonuses.

By 1996, there were over 123 organizations in the federal government with some excepted-service employees. The U.S. Postal Service is the largest organization, comprising over 60% of all the excepted-service employees, but most of the other federal organizations are typically smaller, such as the U.S. courts, State Department, Tennessee Valley Authority, Congressional Budget Office, and the Federal Reserve.

In the latter part of the 1990s, the trend toward excepted service accelerated. The FAA became the first larger organization to become excepted in the mid-1990s when the Congress added a rider to its appropriations bill giving it new personnel and procurement responsibilities. Likewise, the IRS received authority for some of its employees (especially its senior executives) in 1998. The FBI and other law enforcement agencies and the Department of Defense (DOD) are pressing for exemption form Title V.

The General Accounting Office in a recent profile report on the excepted versus competitive service has noted that in 1988, the percentage of excepted service was at 44% and by 1998 had reach 49%. It projects that should DOD and other agencies seeking exemptions be granted, that the excepted service would reach as high as 75% of the total civilian federal work-force.

between the public and private sectors and create a new concept of locality pay that could take into account regional differences in the cost of living and salary competition.

Some have criticized the Volcker commission's effort by saying that once the pay reforms were institutionalized there was no incentive to work on the harder issues of fixing merit pay, changing classification systems, or dealing with political control of the system. Perhaps if the reforms had been linked, there might have been some motivation to deal with a wider range of issues, but personnel reforms should not be taken out of context. Nineteen-ninety was also the year of the new Budget Enforcement Act, the culmination of a major budget and tax confrontation between President Bush, the Democratic Congressional majority, and the emerging power of the Republican minority in the House led by Newt Gingrich.

Seen in the context of a major recession affecting the U.S. economy and an escalating budget deficit, it should also be mentioned that this recession hit state and local governments very hard, causing significant layoffs and reduction-in-force actions. Budget issues dominated much of the political agenda in the midterm of the Bush administration, forcing other less vital issues off the stage. President Bush was ultimately forced to retract his famous "read my lips—no new taxes" pledge in a $500 billion budget deal designed to put new caps on federal spending and lower the deficit. This was the same president whose popularity ratings had hit 90% after the Gulf War, which had caused a number of the better-known Democratic candidates to decide to pass on the 1992 elections.

One who didn't was then-governor Bill Clinton of Arkansas, who in the span of two short years would win the election and put his own stamp on public and personnel management reform in the 1990s.

THE FIRST MOVEMENT: THE CLINTON ADMINISTRATION "TRANSITION"

Candidate Clinton had a reasonable and almost modest campaign goal in the area of federal personnel reform. In his speeches he hit upon the ideas of quality management, employee participation, and new uses of technology and innovation to offer the following campaign promise—his administration would not only improve the way government does business but would also reduce the number of federal employees by 100,000 over four years. That might not seem like much, given a workforce of nearly 2 million, depending upon what branches and organizations are included, but Clinton successfully argued that despite all the budget and tax hawkishness of the Reagan–Bush years, federal workforce numbers had continued to rise. As a self-proclaimed new-style Democrat, he claimed his administration would accomplish something basic that previous Republican administrations had not.

Indeed, when the Clinton–Gore transition teams were organized in late November, the week after the election victory, one of the first documents distributed to each team was a composite list of Clinton–Gore campaign promises. To the members of the OPM transition team (which in the interest of full disclosure included two of this textbooks' co-authors and the current director of OPM, who then was working for one of the federal unions) there at the top of the campaign promises list was: reduce federal workforce by 100,000 employees.

The transition team process is an interesting phenomenon which may or may not have considerable influence on policy and management agendas of an incoming chief executive. In President Clinton's case, the teams started at a major disadvantage because they were started so late in November. Although candidate Clinton enjoyed the lead in the polls throughout the campaign, he balked at appearing overconfident by having to announce that he had already formed his transition teams, so he had only a handful of staffers working on the transition strategy, and most of the transition teams wouldn't get started until the first week of December.

This essentially left these teams of eight to 12 members from very diverse backgrounds (congressional staffers, public and private sector executives, subject matter policy and legal experts, academicians, and of course a few key campaign staffers) only a few weeks to conduct reviews of existing departmental policies, identify critical looming legislative issues, review budgets and personnel levels, interview unit heads and key staff, and of course address all those campaign promises. There was one final expectation—that the heads of the transition teams might be candidates for the agency or department they were reviewing. While that was the expectation in the case of the OPM transition team, the team leader opted to become deputy secretary at Health and Human Services (HHS), leaving the administration to find another (ultimately James King) at a later date than originally envisioned.

The OPM transition team focused on a very different set of issues than the Volcker commission's agenda. They recommended that the new director of OPM prepare a limited but highly prioritized agenda for the first year. The following four key issues were to be the thrusts:

1. Reducing the size of the federal workforce
2. Implementing federal pay reform
3. Improving family leave and the federal government's reputation as a model employer
4. Implementing federal health care benefits reform

The transition team urged that reductions in the size of the federal workforce be coupled with progress on federal pay reform. Regarding the number one issue, *reducing the size of the federal workforce*, it noted that including the entire civilian workforce would make the goal easily achievable, since this number totals over 3.1 million (or 2.3 million if the postal service is excluded). The assumption was that the goal should relate to the general schedule employees, which then included 1,532,683 employees, according to the March 1992 Federal Civilian Workforce Statistics report. Of this total, Department of Defense employees include 651,710, compared to 880,973 non-Defense executive branch employees.

The transition team noted the following:

> The federal workforce had grown, but only very slowly over the previous decade. From 1982 to 1992, total growth was only 9.9% (or under 140,000 employees), or an *annual rate of just under 1%*. To put this into context, cutting the workforce by 100,000 over four years would represent an annual rate of decrease of 1.6%.
>
> Federal workforce growth had also been sharply affected by the Defense build-up of the mid- to late 1980s and subsequent Department of Defense (DOD) downsizing effort. The DOD workforce levels were still 7.9% higher in 1992 than 1982, but in 1992 Defense growth was below the executive branch average and falling. Up until 1990, Defense averaged a 1.4% annual increase in its workforce compared to a non-Defense executive branch average of .5%. It would be expected that a sizeable proportion of the workforce cuts, perhaps as much as 75%, would come from Defense, which would have significant political ramifications.
>
> Federal agency experiences varied considerably in terms of workforce growth. Some agencies increased by 20% or more during the Reagan era, while others had experienced significant staffing cuts, averaging 10%. A breakout of ''winners and losers'' is revealed in Table 2.1.
>
> There was also a major change in the grade composition of the federal workforce. Driven by the combined impacts of increased automation and a major pay gap (variously estimated at between 20% and 30%), agencies ''traded'' lower-grade positions (GS-1 to GS-5) for significant expansion in the higher grades (GS-12 to GS-15). In 1982, the lower grades (GS-1 to GS-6) accounted for the largest slice of the general schedule grades (39%). By 1992, the largest slice was GS-11 to GS-13 at 37.7%, compared to 30% for GS-1 to GS-6.

TABLE 2.1 Change in General Schedule
Employees from 1982 to 1992

Justice	+68%	HUD	7.8%
State	+57%	HHS	−9.6%
Treasury	+39%	Education	−12.5%
Transportation	+19%	Labor	−13.1%

Source: Federal civilian workforce statistics (1982–1992), OPM.

In its final analysis, the transition team argued that all of the above factors did not mean that a reduction of 100,000 employees in the general schedule was impractical, but it strongly urged avoiding traditional cutback strategies that would do more harm than good. In the words of the transition team:

> Imposing a hiring freeze would be an especially poor tactic. It would harm those agencies already decimated by twelve years of disproportionate staffing change while not requiring those agencies who have experienced the most growth to review their expansions. The ''over-grading'' patterns might also be further exacerbated by a hiring freeze—prompting agencies to escalate promotions as a reward for those who must contend with increased workloads caused by a freeze.
>
> Holding the line on staffing replacement by implementing an across-the-board percentage of attrition replacement policy would be likewise biased. It would disadvantage losing agencies more and provide little incentive to re-examine staffing levels and grade escalation. Reduction-in-force (RIF) as a strategy would be equally impotent in these areas and also generate considerable distrust within the workforce and between the labor relations representatives. RIF might also severely impact on minority and female representation numbers in federal agencies at a time when percentages of minorities and women at upper levels are being challenged (glass ceiling) as part of the federal government's commitment to workforce diversity.

Easy advice to provide perhaps, but harder to live by. The Clinton administration actually chose another route entirely to accomplish its still evolving personnel policy objectives. The transition team members went back to their universities, law practices, and executive jobs. The president announced in March the creation of a governmentwide task force under the direction of the Vice President Gore to be known as the National Performance Review.

THE SECOND MOVEMENT: THE NPR AND FEDERAL WORKFORCE RESTRUCTURING

> The people demand and deserve an active government on their side. But they don't want a government that wastes money, a government that costs more and does less. They voted for change. They wanted a literal revolution in the way government operates, and now, you and I must deliver.
>
> *Remarks of President Bill Clinton to the Cabinet, February 10, 1993*

Management reform in the federal government is neither a new idea nor a novel metaphor. Indeed, depending upon which historian or administrative expert one consults, there were no fewer than 10 major reform initiatives in the last century alone, beginning with the Taft Commission in 1910, which produced the first blueprints for a federal executive budget, to the Clinton administration's National Performance Review (NPR), which also goes under the label of reinvention. When one reads these reports proposing new visions for government reform—whether the date is 1910, 1937, 1949, 1972, 1982, or 1993—they share one thing. All began with an assumption that government as typified by the American federal government was broken, fragmented, badly organized, and incapable of performing at a level acceptable to the public.

On September 7, 1993, the Clinton administration unveiled its report on how federal government operations and management practices must be radically changed to bring government into the twentieth century. The study was the culmination of a six-month comprehensive review and assessment by a special task force led by Vice President Al Gore. The report, *From Red Tape to Results: Creating a Government That Works Better & Costs Less*, is a 168-page document containing 380 major recommendations. In addition to this report, there were a series of subreports that examined various agencies and management areas. Two of the subreports dealt directly with civil service issues—one entitled *The Office of Personnel Management* and the other *Reinventing Human Resources Management*.

Given the comprehensiveness of the NPR, it is important to look briefly at the "process" of the reform effort and the "principles" that guided the reformers. Much of the guiding philosophy for the NPR came from the management book *Reinventing Government*, by columnist David Osborne and consultant and former city manager Ted Gaebler. Prominent on the back cover of this 1992 bestseller was an endorsement by then Arkansas governor Bill Clinton: "Those of us who want to revitalize government in the 1990's are going to have to reinvent it. This book gives us the blueprint."

Osborne and Gaebler's *Reinventing Government* decried the bankruptcy of bureaucracy and heralded entrepreneurialism as the solution to transforming government. Using primarily examples of innovative practices and experiments in state and local governments their book called for a series of radical changes in the public sector, which, according to Osborne and Gaebler, had to seek to restructure itself by vigorously pursuing a "new form of governance." Each of the main chapters in *Reinventing Government* outlined a prescriptive dimension to the nature of the change intended: "Community-Owned Government through Empowerment," "Competitive," "Mission Driven," "Results-Oriented," "Customer Focused," "Enterprising," "Anticipatory," "Decentralized," and "Market-Oriented."

The root of Osborne and Gaebler's prescription was entrepreneurialism. The authors explained that the original idea of entrepreneur goes beyond the business risk taking normally associated with the private sector. Entrepreneurial government follows a broader model that "uses resources in new ways to max-imize productivity and effectiveness." Osborne summarized the importance of this philosophy in testimony before the U.S. Senate a week after the NPR had been launched:

> We must restructure the basic incentives that drive public managers, public employees, and elected officials. Our federal bureaucracies grow so large and so sluggish not because those who work for them want it that way, but because the basic incentives operating on those bureaucra-cies literally demand it be that way. For example, most public programs are monopolies whose customers cannot go elsewhere for a better deal. Most are funded according to their inputs—how much children qualify, how many families are poor enough—rather than their outcomes or re-sults. Most are considered important not because they achieve tremen-dous results but because they spend tremendous sums of money. Their managers earn greater stature and higher pay not because they have dem-onstrated superior performance, but because they have built up a larger bureaucracy. . . . With such incentives embedded within all our major control systems—our budget system, our personnel system, our reward system—is it any wonder that we get bureaucratic behavior rather than entrepreneurial behavior?

The NPR was, of course, no copy of the blueprint offered by *Reinventing Government*, but the guiding influence of *Reinventing Government* is unmistak-able from the introductory chapter, which touts "creating entrepreneurial organi-zations" as "the solution" to the massive emphasis on deregulating federal man-agement control systems (e.g., budget, personnel, procurement, and support and information services).

The NPR was basically an internal reform process, primarily because it was staffed by a large group of federal employees who made up the bulk of the task force. This was in sharp contrast to the last major executive reform effort under Reagan in 1982, the Grace commission, headed by outsider business execu-tive J. Peter Grace. The vice president served as an active chair, and approxi-mately 200 federal employees were either detailed or given part-time assignments to the project team under an assistant secretary of defense as project director. In terms of consulting expertise, David Osborne was the major adviser, and he was joined by several state government executives, most notably from Texas and Ohio, who had worked on similar governmentwide performance reviews.

A crosscutting structure, similar to the organizational format used for the transition team, was used to organize the effort. The transition team had various teams within clusters; some reviewed specific agencies while others examined larger policy domains that cut across all agencies. The NPR used 11 crosscutting work groups called ''systems reinvention teams,'' and 22 agency-specific work groups called ''redesign teams.'' System reinvention teams included work groups focusing on budget, personnel, and information governmental systems and work groups examining generic management aspects, such as organizational structures, program designs, regulatory systems, or environmental impact management. The final report included numerous recommendations for each of these various teams, along with other more generic management-improvement categories.

On the other side, obviously, 22 agency-specific teams couldn't cover the 100 plus federal organizational units within the executive branch. To accomplish this review, NPR commissioned 14 redesign teams for the cabinet-level agencies and seven teams for the largest and most important independent agencies. A final team covered the remaining smallest agencies. While the three ''management control'' agencies, the Office of Management and Budget, the OPM, and the General Services Agency, were assessed by three of the crosscutting systems reinvention teams, a separate report on each the management agencies was prepared in addition to their ''systems'' report, thus the smaller volume on reinventing OPM and a much larger report, *Reinventing Human Resources Management*, came about.

Finally, in terms of process, it is important to note that the NPR assumed that the agency redesign teams would remain. In fact, these teams were to evolve into department ''reinvention teams'' that would push for continuous improvements and innovations.

As always, the trick is making reform happen and having the reality live up to the promise. Although in 1993 the Clinton administration was working with a Democratically controlled Congress, there was little inclination among Democratic congressional leaders to put any parts of the NPR into fast-track legislation. The Congress had already passed another $500 billion major tax increase and budget bill by the thinnest of margins and was at loggerheads over the growing complexity and page counts of the health care reform bill. Key congressional leaders saw no real priorities among the NPR's myriad recommendations. Besides, during the NPR's review process, the vice president had said on several occasions that the NPR was keeping its distance from the Congress, and NPR would be focused on management and policy issues it was in control of.

It was thus left to a series of executive orders and presidential memorandums to detail the reforms embodied in the reinvention revolution. For starters, a presidential memorandum entitled ''Streamlining the Bureaucracy'' was issued on September 11, detailing requirements to cut the federal workforce by 12%. The *NPR*, in the spirit of the first principle—to make do with less—called for $108 billion in budget savings over five years led by a reduction in the federal workforce of 252,000 workers. Also included in the memorandum were explicit directions that workforce reductions were not to come solely out of lower-grade positions and that agencies were to move to increasing the supervisory span of controls (i.e., the average ratio of subordinates under a supervisor) from 1 to 8 to 1 to 15.

Two other executive orders followed on September 14; one requiring a 50% reduction in internal management regulations and the other articulating approaches for creating a customer service strategy. The latter contains provisions for customer service standards and customer survey feedback efforts. On October 1, a presidential memorandum entitled "Implementing Management Reform in the Executive Reform" was issued, creating the position of chief operating officer directly responsible for "reforming the agency's management practices by incorporating the principles of the National Performance Review into day-to-day management." It also established the President's Management Council, consisting of the chief operating officers from all 14 cabinet-level agencies (including EPA) and select central management agency representatives.

Last and perhaps most important came federal labor relations. Executive Order 12871, also issued on October 1, 1993, created a national partnership council to join federal management and public unions in implementing NPR reforms. As will be seen, this step may ultimately have the most far-reaching effect of all in affecting management change and reform.

Of course the focus following the flurry of NPR-based executive orders and presidential memorandums was on the size of the workforce reductions. What was once a campaign pledge to cut the size of government by 100,000 workers had now reached 252,000 and was growing. The most interesting question was where that number came from. Various stories emerged. One account from unnamed sources within the NPR project indicated that the number was half of the rough estimate made of the number of planned supervisory reductions and excess administrative positions. Another indicated that 250,000 was about the size of the workforce that would be needed to staff the administration's new health care management agency when health care reform passed. In the final analysis, critics would charge that no serious staffing analysis had been undertaken to determine what the number should be and therefore NPR would be hard-pressed to avoid charges that it was just pushing downsizing in disguise.

To reduce the federal workforce by 12% when attrition levels in the federal government had fallen to their lowest levels in 20 years would require incentives. The NPR itself noted that "voluntary early retirements had declined from 17 in the mid 80s to 4% in 1992, while regular optional retirements had declined from 36% to 23%." To meet a target that was nearly three times what the transition team had considered would require financial payments authorized by Congress, so with congressional concurrence the administration passed the Federal Workforce Restructuring Act of 1994, which created buyouts for employees willing to leave the federal service either by early retirement or separation.

Reinventing Human Resource Management—The NPR Recommendations

HRM01   *Create a flexible and responsive hiring system.* Authorize agencies to establish their own recruitment and examining programs. Abolish centralized registers and standard application forms. Allow federal departments and agencies to determine that recruitment shortages exist and directly hire candidates without ranking. Reduce the types of competitive service appointments to three. Abolish the time-in-grade requirements.

HRM02   *Reform the general schedule classification and basic pay system.* Remove all grade-level classification criteria from the law. Provide agencies with flexibility to establish broadbanding systems built upon the general schedule framework.

HRM03   *Authorize agencies to develop programs for improvement of individual and organizational performance.* Authorize agencies to design their own performance management programs that define and measure success based on each agency's unique needs.

HRM04   *Authorized agencies to develop incentive award and bonus systems to improve individual and organizational performance.* Authorize Agencies to develop their own incentive award and bonus systems. Encourage agencies to establish productivity gainsharing programs to support their reinvention and change efforts.

HRM05   *Strengthen systems to support management in dealing with poor performers.* Develop a culture of performance that provides supervisors with the skills, knowledge, and support they need to deal with poor performers, and hold supervisors accountable for effectively managing their human resources. Reduce by half the time needed to terminate federal employees for cause.

HRM06   *Clearly define the objective of training as the improvement of individual and organizational performance; make training more market-driven.* Reduce restrictions on training to allow managers to focus on organizational mission and to take advantage of the available training marketplace.

HRM07   *Enhance programs to provide family-friendly work-places.*   Implement family-friendly workplace practices (flextime, flexiplace, job sharing, telecommuting) while ensuring accountability for customer service. Provide telecommunications and administrative support necessary for employees participating in flexiplace and tele-commuting work arrangements. Expand the authority to establish and fund dependent care programs. Allow employees to use sick leave to care for dependents. Allow employees who leave and then re-enter federal service to be given credit for prior sick leave balances.

HRM08   *Improve processes and procedures established to provide workplace due process for employees.*   Eliminate jurisdictional overlaps. All agencies should establish alternative dispute resolution methods and options for the informal disposition of employment disputes.

HRM09   *Improve accountability for equal opportunity goals and accomplishments.*   Charge all federal agency heads with the responsibility for ensuring equal opportunity and increasing representation of qualified women, minorities, and persons with disabilities into all levels and job categories, including middle and senior management positions.

HRM10   *Improve interagency collaboration and cross-training for human resource professionals.*   Establish an interagency equal employment opportunity and affirmative employment steering group under the joint chair of the Equal Employment Opportunity Commission and the Office of Personnel Management. Require appropriate cross-training for human resource management professionals.

HRM11   *Strengthen the senior executive service so that it becomes a key element in the governmentwide culture change effort.*   Create and reinforce a corporate perspective within the Senior Executive Service that supports governmentwide culture change. Promote a corporate succession planning model to use to select and develop senior staff. Enhance voluntary mobility within and between agencies for top senior executive positions in government.

HRM12   *Eliminate excessive red tape and automate functions and information.* Phase out the entire 10,000-page *Federal Personnel Manual* (FPM) and all agency implementing directives by December 1994. Replace the FPM and agency directives with automated personnel processes, electronic decision support systems, and "manuals" tailored to user needs.

HRM13   *Form labor–management partnerships for success.* Identify labor–management partnerships as a goal of the executive branch and establish the National Partnership Council.

HRM14   *Provide incentives to encourage voluntary separations.* Provide departments and agencies with the authority to offer separation pay. Decentralize the authority to approve early retirement. Authorize departments and agencies to fund job search activities and retraining of employees scheduled to be displaced. Limit annual leave accumulation by senior executives to 240 hours.

Armed with buyout authority, OPM and other agencies got down to the business of reducing the size of the federal workforce and pursuing other objectives in reinventing human resources management. Political situations can be notoriously unstable, however. By the fall of 1994, the Democrats had lost their control of both houses of Congress in one of the most spectacular political upsets of the century. President Clinton would now face a very different political opponent, and the path lying in front of the NPR was infinitely more complicated. Of course, the Republican majority in Congress was more than pleased with the planned reductions of the federal workforce; everything else would be up for renegotiation.

THE THIRD MOVEMENT: REINVENTION OF OPM

Facing a very different political situation, the Clinton administration changed parts of its NPR agenda. A strong legislative agenda was successfully pursued in the arena of procurement reform, in which there was a strong bipartisan group of agency heads, congressional committee members, and business leaders. The agenda of internal reinvention was pursued in the areas of budget and personnel, where there was no such support. Specifically in the case of federal personnel reform, OPM was reinvented rather than human resources management.

Buyouts and the Federal Workforce Restructuring Act of 1994

SEC. 3 VOLUNTARY SEPARATION INCENTIVES

(b) AUTHORITY
   (1) IN GENERAL—In order to avoid or minimize the need for involuntary separations due to a reduction in force, reorganization, transfer of function, or other similar action, and subject to paragraph (2), the head of an agency may pay, or authorize payment of, voluntary separation incentive payments to agency employees—
      (A) if any component of the agency;
      (B) in any occupation;
      (C) in any geographic location; or
      (D) on any basis of any combination of factors under subparagraphs (A) through (C).
   (2) CONDITION—
      (A) IN GENERAL—In order to receive an incentive payment, an employee must separate from service with the agency (whether by retirement or resignation) before April 1, 1995
      (B) EXCEPTION—An employee who does not separate from service before the date specified in subparagraph (A) shall be ineligible for an incentive payment under this section unless—
         (i)   the agency head determines that, in order to ensure the performance of the agency's mission, it is necessary to delay such employee's separation; and
         (ii) the employee separates after completing any additional period of service required (but not later than March 31, 1997).
(c) AMOUNT AND TREATMENT OF PAYMENTS—A voluntary separation incentive payment—
   (1) shall be paid in a lump sum after the employee's separation;
   (2) shall be equal to the lesser of
      (A) an amount equal to the amount the employee would be entitled to receive under section 5595(c) of title 5, United States Code, if the employee were entitled to payment under such section; or
      (B) $25,000
   (3) shall not be a basis for payment, and shall not be included in the computation, or any other type of Government benefit;

> (4) shall not be taken into account in determining the amount of any severance pay to which an employee may be entitled under section 5595 of title 5, United States Code, based on any other separation; and
>
> (5) shall be paid from appropriations or funds available for the payment of the basic pay of the employee
>
> (d) EFFECT OF SUBSEQUENT EMPLOYMENT WITH THE GOVERNMENT—
>
> (1) IN GENERAL—An employee who has received a voluntary separation incentive payment under this section and accepts employment with the Government of the United States within 5 years after the date of the separation on which the payment is based shall be required to repay the entire amount of the incentive payment to the agency that paid the incentive payment.

In 1993, at the start of the Clinton administration, OPM consisted of over 6100 employees with an administrative budget of nearly half a billion. It had major field offices, training centers, and other operations throughout the United States. Whereas the Volcker commission had commiserated with OPM and recommended change, the NPR based much of its report on a highly critical 1989 General Accounting Office (GAO) study that had concluded ''The government is not well postured to meet future challenges, in part due to lack of effective OPM leadership.'' This critical viewpoint was shared by the newly appointed OPM director, James King, who set out to make OPM a model agency of NPR tenets and to put OPM back into a strong leadership role.

The NPR's report on OPM had the following three key recommendations:

1. Strengthen OPM's leadership role in transforming federal human resources management systems. Clearly defining OPM's policy, service, leadership role in addressing human resources problems and delegating operational work to the agencies.

2. Redefine and Restructure OPM's Functional Responsibilities To Foster A Customer Orientation. Restructure and rightsize OPM to enhance and reflect its commitment to addressing its customer's needs.

3. Change the Culture of OPM to empower its staff and increase its Customer Orientation. Use interagency groups to involve OPM's external stakeholders in changing federal human resource systems. Improve OPM's policy-making process through experimental use of negotiated

rulemaking and broaden the customer focus of OPM and agency personnel specialists.

The NPR report added some other provisions. First, it expected staff reductions to exceed 12% over the next five years. Second, it noted that the majority of its recommended actions fell in the category of "agency heads can do themselves." The OPM was going to be a model agency and OPM director King was ready to lead the charge.

Four years later, OPM had reduced its staff by nearly half, to under 3000. It had created the federal government's first employee stock ownership plan, moving its entire investigations group of over 700 employees out of OPM into the private sector. In terms of streamlining, it led all federal agencies in terms of reductions of supervisors (53%, compared to the 20% federal average), reduction in headquarters staff (65%, compared to the 14% federal average), and management control positions (41%, compared to the 9% federal average).

In terms of structure, the base of OPM is radically different from what was created out of CSRA. The staff offices—general counsel, communications, inspector general, congressional relations, and federal prevailing rate advisory committee—are essentially the same. Now the core divisions are workforce compensation and performance, executive resources, employment service, workforce relations, merit systems oversight and effectiveness, human resources, and EEO. Basically, only retirement and insurance is the same. (Compare Figure 2.2 to Figure 1.2 in Chapter 1.) It has also made a number of efforts to reduce regulations and even eliminated its own federal personnel manual as a symbol of the new era of delegation of power to agencies.

Summing up the reinvention of OPM in his last year as director, James King made the following remarks at a speech at the Brookings Institution in March 1997:

> The Government of the Future must hire the right people with the right skills, quickly, easily, and fairly. To that end, OPM has delegated hiring to the Agencies. They are free to carry out their own hiring or hire us to do it for them. If they want to contract with us, they know we have experts on designing tests, and on rating and ranking and assessing qualifications. They also know that our work will be in strict accordance with merit principles. To speed the hiring process, we got rid of the overly complicated Standard Form 171 which for decades has helped drive people away form federal jobs. Today, in most cases, you can simply submit a resume . . .
>
> To the maximum degree possible we want to shift accountability to the agencies themselves. We believe that most agencies want to do the right thing, but may need a little training or encouragement from time to time.

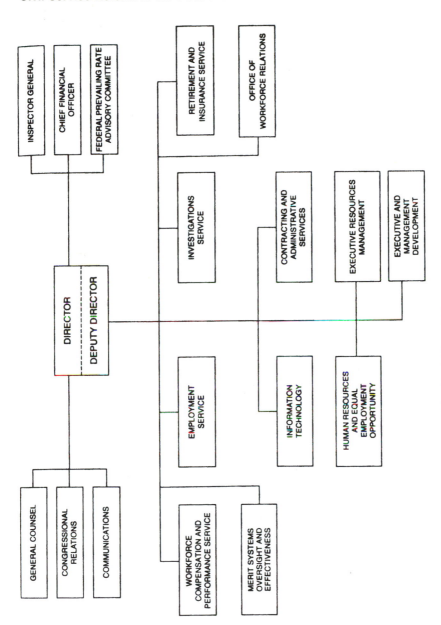

FIGURE 2.2 Organization chart for 1999, U.S. Office of Personnel Management.

Critics of the reinvented and vastly slimmed down OPM have assessed the changes put in place and still been unhappy. A 1996 Brookings study griped: "But while the Clinton Administration has worked hard to shed pieces of OPM's work, it has yet to redefine what its core mission ought to be . . . it has yet to move from what it ought not to be doing to what is should do."

Perhaps the harshest criticism of all came from the Congress after a series of hearings held by the House Committee on Government Reform and Oversight in late 1995. The committee's majority report first branded the entire NPR effort as an "ad hoc and episodic approach to management." Then it denounced the failure to establish "a solid empirical rationale" for reducing over 250,000 federal jobs, no matter how warranted, the carving out of OPM, which it felt seriously impaired its capacity to provide leadership, and the poor use of buyouts, which resulted in the loss of some of the federal government's most talented personnel, and the retention of many poor performers. The committee went as far to conclude that a new office of federal management was needed that "would combine the management functions of the OMB, the residual policy and oversight functions of the Office of Personnel Management, and the policy functions from the General Services Administration into an entity separate from but equal in stature to the remaining Office of the Budget."

The political fortunes of the newly triumphant Republican party were rapidly changing, however. From a position of remarkable unity and strength in their first 100 days, they ultimately would overplay their hand in a major budget showdown with the Clinton administration. Shutting down the federal government and assuming that the public wouldn't care badly backfired on the Republican Party. The presidential campaign of 1996 would find the Republicans on the defensive regarding their plans to reform government. It would be the Clinton administration trumpeting its record of using the NPR to reduce the workforce and improve efficiency as part of its campaign. Clinton would announce in his 1996 state of the union address that "the era of big government is over." The Democrats would show tables and charts illustrating the dramatic reduction in the federal budget deficit and in the federal workforce.

AN UNFINISHED SYMPHONY: CIVIL SERVICE REFORM IN THE SECOND TERM

The Clinton administration's efforts to reform the federal personnel service were not limited to just reinventing OPM. Beginning in 1994, the administration put together a number of legislative proposals that would address the themes and recommendations from the NPR's reinventing human resources document. (See box.) By May of 1995, OPM was circulating a draft civil service reform bill called the Federal Human Resource Management Reinvention Act of 1995. Its six titles dealt with the redesign of OPM, provisions to decentralize the hiring system, major changes to performance management that covered provisions on incentive awards and dealing with poor performers, new provisions on demonstration projects and alternative personnel systems, classification reform that would create criteria for broadbanding, and labor law reform language that would codify labor–management partnerships.

This time it would be the unions that voiced the loudest objections. In a three-page letter written on May 24, 1995, to the senior policy advisor to the vice president, Elaine Kamarck, the heads of the four major federal unions opened with the following: ''We would like to express our grave concerns about the Administration's draft Civil Service Reform Bill. While we recognize this is only a draft which we expect is still open to improvement, we felt compelled to register our ardent opposition to the bill as now written. Simply put, we would be forced to publicly oppose this bill in the strongest possible terms should it be sent to Congress for action.''

Speaking to the core of their disappointment the union heads noted the following:

> Earlier recommendations from the NPR and the National Partnership Council sought to strike a careful balance between the need for decentralization and increased managerial flexibility with the equally important goal of increased employee involvement in the design and implementation of new human resource systems. Regrettably the careful balance has been lost in the reform bill. In its place are variations of the same tired and unacceptable mix of centralized OPM control and unreviewable agency decision making. In our view, turning authority and flexibility over to OPM and agency managers without any of the checks and balances provided by collective bargaining is a recipe for abuse.

In various forms, the Clinton administration and OPM have been revising and negotiating proposals for new legislation ever since. Stymied on overall legislation, the next thrust focused on reforms involving the SES. The Clinton administration sought especially to revise the regulations on the SES performance appraisal systems. In keeping with its idea of creating performance-based organizations (PBOs), it wanted to be able to pay substantial bonuses to senior managers who led their agencies to meet agreed-upon performance targets.

Of course the problem with linking SES reforms to PBOs was getting the Congress to pass legislation to create them. The PBO concept was heavily used in Britain, Australia, and New Zealand as part of their new public management agenda in the 1990s. The British took many of their public agencies that provided direct services to the public, created a policy board that remained in the government, and chartered the PBO as a quasi-independent nonprofit organization. The CEO of the agency had very relaxed personnel and budget rules, could choose

What Is a Performance-Based Organization?

A PBO is a discrete management unit with strong incentives to manage for results. It has three characteristics. First, it commits to accountability for results by having clear objectives, specific measurable goals, customer service standards, and targets for improved performance. In exchange, it can be granted managerial flexibilities to achieve these aims and goals in areas such as personnel, procurement, financing, and real property.

Second, to ensure a management focus, primary responsibility for policy making is separated from program operations and remains in the domain of the Department under the control of political appointees. Program operations are retained in the PBO. While this division of responsibilities will not always be distinct, the managers of the PBO will continue to operate within the structure of the organization's present Department to ensure communication between the policy formulation and operation functions. Separating policy decisions affecting those operations from daily activities creates strong incentives within the PBO to manage for results by committing to clear objectives, specific measurable goals, customer service standards, and targets for improved performance.

And third, a PBO is led by a Chief Operating Officer (COO) hire for a fixed term based on a demonstrated track record of effective management, as distinguished from policy expertise. The COO might come from the private sector or from the ranks of the civil service. The COO position should provide the balance between the problems associated with short-term tenures of most political appointees, yet without the problems associated with permanent career tenure. The COO would sign an annual performance agreement with the Secretary; and his or her compensation and tenure would be tied to the organization's performance. The Secretary may reappoint the COO to subsequent terms, if he or she has met organizational and individual performance goals.

Not all government functions may be suited to become a Performance-Based Organization. Agencies or functions that do not have clear, measurable results should be excluded. For example, the foreign policy and planning functions in the State Department or the Office of Science and Technology may not be appropriate candidates. Similarly, functions that develop regulatory policy may not be appropriate candidates.

Source: National Partnership for Reinventing Government. "Performance-Based Organizations Draft Conversion Guide," July 1999.

and reward the management team, and stay "in business" as long as he or she met the performance targets established for the chartered agency. Performance-based organizations were a much harder sell in the United States. After more than six years of debating the merits of the concept, only one has been created—a part of the Department of Education that administers student loans called the Higher Education Loan Authority.

The OPM finally submitted a separate but comprehensive proposal for SES reform in 1998 called the *Proposed Framework for Improving the Senior Executive Service.* (See Figure 2.3.) Newly confirmed OPM director Janice Lachance announced a major overhaul plan that would divide the SES into roughly two halves, or SES corps. One group—the senior executive corps (SEC)—would be the CEO types, the generalist leaders who would be expected to produce results. The second group, essentially the technocrats, would be called the senior professional corps and consist of the senior scientists and professionals who would stay in place in their agencies.

In a major departure from current practice, senior executives would be required to be mobile, taking on different leadership roles from agency to agency. Mobility would be required for advancement within the SEC, and executives would have three-year contracts. The definition of who would be an executive would be limited to those who direct organizational units or programs, supervise employees as opposed to personal assistants, and have direct responsibility for organizational goals and objectives. In return, reward levels would be increased,

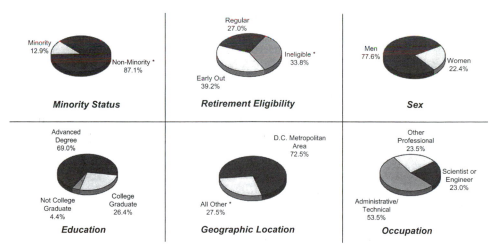

* Data shown are **excluded** from the source table.

FIGURE 2.3 Senior Executive Service member profile as of September 1998 (Adapted from Laurent 1998.)

beginning with the delinking of senior executive and congressional pay and raising annual bonus levels to 30% of base pay. Of course there were a number of provisions to make removal on the grounds of performance easier, but the reaction to the proposal made the union presidents' rejection of the 1995 civil service reform proposals look mild.

Anne Laurent, an associate editor of *Government Executive*, wrote in a cover story subtitled "Executives in Lather Over Plans to Change Senior Executive Services," that the real crux of the debate is "an argument about the best method for developing leaders. While OPM favors a market model, relying on incentives for individuals and agencies to use the new core qualifications and encourage mobility, others favor more deliberate management of the executive corps." In this case, others meant the Senior Executive Association (SEA), which is a professional association consisting of many SESs and which was dead set against these reforms. The SEA had also been a loud and frequent critic of many of the NPR reform efforts from the beginning. The proposal quickly went nowhere.

In January 1999 Vice President Gore announced one more attempt for a legislative initiative to "improve the performance management systems of the federal workforce and to encourage a culture of high performance and labor/management collaboration." Interestingly, this effort was renamed "civil service improvement." The core areas are proposals permitting flexible pay systems, new evaluation formats for senior executives, and new hiring options through OPM to promote alternative selection procedures. Gore noted clearly that the proposals would provide principles that would then be used as a framework for change subject to mutual agreement with federal labor unions. Gore stressed that civil service improvement was an essential "part of our rejuvenated partnership" with labor.

Newly appointed OPM director Lachance also addressed the proposals in a January speech quoting *Hamlet* that this was all about "the insolence of office." Lachance drew a crucial distinction between "two primary and competitive schools of thought" regarding federal civil service organization—"strong centralization" versus "maximum flexibility." Lachance desired for OPM to have the best of both schools. The OPM advocated flexibility primarily around pay and performance systems suited to agency tastes followed with wide latitude for staffing and development, but insisted on maintaining consistency in three areas: the federal government should remain one single employer, it should promote government values in merits systems oversight and open recruitment, and it should maintain OPM's leadership role in human resources management.

The actual proposals were distributed as a discussion paper entitled "1999 Civil Service Improvements." The outline of the approximately 40 plus proposed changes is summarized in the appendix of this chapter, showing the range and scope of what constitutes Civil Service Reform in the last year of the 1990s, but there is no indication that the 1999 Civil Service Improvements Act will get any further than the HRM Reinvention Act of 1995. By mid year the proposal was hopelessly bogged down, primarily by the unions who essentially wanted no part of the improvement package until they saw the partnership executive order of 1993 enforced regarding the expansion of bargaining.

The 1999 Civil Service Improvement Act was destined to mark the end of six long years of intense activity in workforce reform on both fronts—with very little progress on either increasing the scope of bargaining under partnership or rewriting significant portions of the CSRA. This administrative and legislative history of civil service reform for the 1990s will show only fragments of results—compensation reform in 1990, downsizing legislation in 1994, and a few appropriation riders enabling agencies to create their own personnel systems, in part by moving to excepted service (FAA and the IRS most notably). The long-awaited promise of broad civil service reform will have to wait until a new Congress and a new administration are in place, but given the history of federal civil service reform and the nearly 100 years it took to get from the Pendleton Act of 1883 to the Civil Service Reform Act of 1978, public sector personnelists have learned to be patient.

CIVIL SERVICE REFORM AT THE STATE AND LOCAL LEVEL

The example of Georgia reminds the personnel field that anything can happen, especially in the American political system. It is appropriate to conclude this chapter on reform in the postreform era with an assessment of progress made at the state and local level, especially among state governments.

Initially, reform was measured in terms of state actions to follow the federal civil service reform model from 1978. The OPM devoted a section to its first-year report on civil service reform to state government events. It reported

> That 32 of the 50 states were pursuing civil service reforms
> That 13 states had established or were considering creating an SES
> That 15 states were creating merit pay systems
> That 17 states were reforming their performance appraisal systems
> That 9 states were decentralizing their personnel functions
> That 8 states were reforming their labor relations programs and establishing protections for whistle-blowers

It would be misleading, however, to say that the 1980s were a period of severe discontent with the public service and personnel management in the state and local sector. What the 1980s were was the continuation of a period of strong growth. By 1990, state and local government employment (full-time and part-time) had reached over 15,250,000 million—an increase of almost 50% in 20 years, as Table 2 discusses.

Education was a major reason for growth, especially in higher education, in which college enrollments increased by over 60% in the period from 1970 to 1990. Even when the American economy hit a major recession in 1990 and there were a number of layoffs in state and local governments, the overall pattern of growth continued as state and local governments increased. (Note: State government employment would actually begin to slow to 5% growth levels after 1993, reaching 4,582,000 employees in 1999. Local governments continued to increase at a rate of 10%, reaching 12,501,000 employees in 1999.)

It should therefore not come as a surprise that the reinvention idea that would dominate federal civil service reform thinking emerged in a very different light at the state and local level. Along the lines of the Volcker commission, the states would create their own version of public service commissions to explore ways to improve state and local government performance. In 1991, the National Commission on the State and Local Public Service was formed under the chairpersonship of former Mississippi governor William Winter. Its 27 members would include former governors, legislators, academics, media people, and state and local executives. The Winter commission, as it was usually called, issued a report in 1993 entitled ''Hard Truths and Tough Choices: An Agenda for State and Local Reform.''

Unlike the reinvention agenda being pursued by the Clinton administration, the Winter commission focused on the idea of revitalization. In this case revitalization meant strengthen executive leadership, flatten government, and dismantle the regulatory dimension of bureaucratic processes. In the personnel arena, they

TABLE 2.2 Public Employment by Type of Government

Type of government	1960	1970	1980	1990
State	1,592	2,755	3,753	4,503
County	725	1,229	1,853	2,167
Municipalities	1,692	2,244	2,561	2,642
Townships		330	394	418
School districts	1,919	3,316	4,270	4,950
Special districts	581	275	484	585
Total	6,387	10,149	13,315	15,263
S&L employees per 100,000	356	495	585	614

Source: Report of the National Commission on the State and Local Public Service, 1993.

subtitled their recommendations ''End Civil Service Paralysis,'' noting that what had been invented a century ago with the best of intentions had created personnel systems in hiring and retention, classification and pay, and training and development that were so rule-bound and complicated that merit was ''often the last value served.''

Civil service reform, à la the Winter commission, would be based on a decentralized model that would enable agencies to take charge of selection, staffing, and pay decisions affording them more flexibility, speed, and simplicity. Once these systems were effectively in the hands of the agencies, the central personnel office should, they advised, learn to operate a consultant to help make better decisions and improve agency processes.

The Winter Commission's report targeted classifications systems, specifically noting that most states had too many pay levels and far too many job classification titles. In a refreshingly candid admission, the report noted ''The best available research suggests that pay-for-performance in the public sector has been a disappointment and that states and localities should be exceedingly cautious about overselling what are likely to be small performance bonuses allocated through a cumbersome and potentially political process.'' Taking one last shot at the regulatory nature of the civil service system, the report admonished: ''The fairness of the civil service hiring and promotional process can best be measured by the quality of the people hired and the work they perform, not by the number of steps in the process, the amount of paperwork involved, or the rigidity of the policies.''

What has followed in the wake of the Winter commission's report is a mixed emphasis on systems decentralization, process modernization, and streamlining of practices. Indeed, there is really no dominant model for reform at the state and local levels. States are following one model or a hybrid of models of civil service reform that can be loosely defined on the following continuum:

Point 1	Point 2	Point 3	Point 4
Modernization and streamlining functions	Decentralization and delegation authority	Retrenchment and reduction of civil service protections	Termination (phase out civil service)

Point 1—Modernizing civil service systems and processes; streamlining hiring, classification, pay, rewards, and appraisal functions to reduce delays, complexity, and paperwork

Point 2—Decentralizing and delegating personnel functions to agency

> managers so that managers have more control over employee selection,
> compensation, appraisal, and so on, and more flexibility; fewer levels of
> approval
> Point 3—Retrenchment of central control by reducing the scope of civil
> service protections so that employee staffing, dismissals, transfers, or
> length of contracts are easier and faster to accomplish for agencies
> Point 4—Termination or abolishing civil service so that new hires are ex-
> cluded from the system (e.g., Georgia) and after time each agency has
> its own excepted employees

Having discussed in the prologue the efforts of Georgia and New York, which
represent the farthest extremes of state reform efforts, it is useful to examine
another state's effort, which is more characteristic of a middle ground effort at
civil service reform, somewhere between points 2 and 3 on our reform continuum.
In 1993, South Carolina became one of the very first states to pass civil service
reform legislation in the 1990s. According to an article by Steven Hayes and
Shawn Whitney, the State Government Accountability Act of 1993 represented
an attempt by the state's new political leadership to create personnel reforms
that would provide increased flexibility and decentralization of several personnel
functions, primarily in staffing. The law set up new arrangements for agency
managers to control performance-based salary adjustments and group productivity incentives, as well as cash incentive awards for individuals, scheduling innovations to support job-sharing and flextime programs, extension of probationary
periods from six months to a year for new hires, and major extensions of supervisory authority in reassignment, transfer, reclassification, and promotion that
would no longer be subject to higher-level review outside the agency.

About the only thing seemingly missing would be hiring, but as Hays and
Whitney point out, "The state had long followed the practice of permitting agencies (at least those outside of the federally mandated merit system) to fill their
own vacancies without reliance on a central job register. Once viewed as an
invitation to abuse, this practice is now (ironically) perceived as progressive personnel management."

Four years after passage, the South Carolina reforms have a rather odd
track record. In the analysis provided by Hays and Whitney using an extensive
survey of state agencies, less than half of the agencies seem to have actually
changed their staffing practices. While directors from the 78 different state agencies surveyed were mostly in favor of the stated purpose of civil service reforms,
they mostly had acted to ensure that the reform act's provisions were being "implemented aggressively."

A wide range of factors, many of them political, can be explored in this
discussion of the slow pace of change in South Carolina. Resistance from the
"usual suspects," in this case middle managers, always seems to be a factor.

Lack of resources is another force, since the state did not make much available in terms of extra funding to drive changes. There was also fallout from several shake-ups of state agencies in which the top officials of several organizations were replaced en masse, which certainly affected the overall managerial climate for pushing reform. Hayes and Whitney give a table of lessons learned that provides a fitting closing on both South Carolina's reform experience and what federal civil service reformers from the Volcker commission to the NPR have learned about the difference between making reform happen and making reform work.

Lessons Learned in South Carolina's Reinvention Experience

---

* Inertia and defensiveness are likely to make initial progress slower and more variable than might otherwise be anticipated.
* Reform will not be self-executing; successful implementation requires a considerable amount of groundwork, including the creation of policies and procedures within agencies, the establishment of evaluation criteria, and the education of affected workers.
* Enabling legislation should include sufficient guidelines and standards (hammers) to ensure agency compliance on a regularized schedule.
* The central personnel office has an important role to play in the reform effort; diffusion of reform can be expedited by providing agencies with clear and concise explanations of specific reform initiatives and implementation guidelines.
* A systematic means of information sharing between and among agencies will foster experimentation and promote program acceptance.
* Initiatives that require the direct expenditure of money must be funded by the legislature if they are to have their intended effect.

Source: Hayes and Whitney 1997; 340.

APPENDIX: 1999 Civil Service Improvements

What	Why	How
I. Pay for Performance		
A. Results-oriented performance management; "We need a workforce that will be held accountable for real results."— REGO VP speech	• The government's employee performance management system should shifts its focus away from an existing emphasis on individual process inputs to achieving results, to improvement, and to group performance. • The performance management system should support options like linking executive and manager pay to a balanced set of measures (e.g., balanced scorecard). • These changes permit further options for more direct pay for performance initiatives, designed by agencies and tailored to their needs • The 1998 NPR employee survey results suggest that employees need more clarity about how good performance is defined. • There was consensus that SES recertification has not achieved its intended purpose, and stakeholders preferred to strengthen the annual performance appraisal as a more effective way of assessing executive performance • Regulations would be streamlined to support this change	In Chapter 43, "Performance Appraisal" • Change title to "Performance Management" to emphasize full range of performance management—planning, developing, assessing, and rewarding—as opposed to an individual performance appraisal. • Permit a greater variety of performance assessments, particularly for linking performance to pay. • Create specific requirement to establish goals and objectives at individual, group, and/organizational level, consistent with planning methods such as GPRA, to support performance improvement and accountability. • Retain appropriate OPM oversight and control. • Abolish SES recertification because it duplicates current statutory provisions for assessing individual and organizational performance, and focus on more effective methods of supporting performance improvement and accountability.

B. Dealing with poor performers; "Help managers deal with poor performers." —REGO Proceedings

- Although, as our poor performers study shows, managers do address poor performers and there are fewer poor performers than thought by many, perceptions persist, and we know that managers need continuing support and tools such as OPM's CD-ROM and booklet.

- The system must retain individual accountability under Merit Principle #6 which says only employees who meet required standards should be retained. These changes recognize that managers need increased confidence in the creditability of the performance system if we are going to push for them to more actively address performance issues.

- These changes make it easier to manage the good employees (largest group) and also easier to manage the process for dealing with poor performers (small group).

- This change also puts into law our recent regulatory change to eliminate repeated improvement periods on the same element (the "roller coaster" employee).

- Our changes are designed to support a performance management system that works best for all employees, and that shifts the focus to better supervisor—employee dialogue for performance improvement.

In Chapter 43, "Performance Appraisal"

- Require that agencies address unacceptable performance.

- Further improve process for actions when taken (e.g., clarify use of retention standard at start of opportunity period as basis for appealable action).

- Establish a clear, 1-year period during which a second failure to meet a retention standard can be basis for removal without another opportunity to improve.

- Make changes consistent with other pay-for-performance changes (e.g., under broadbanding, allow an option to reduce pay within a band).

- Maintain the requirement for a performance improvement period, if agency continues to use Chapter 43 as the basis for the action about poor performance.

- Maintain employee appeal rights, under any system.

APPENDIX: Continued

What	Why	How
C. Performance-driven pay adjustments; "Permit flexible pay systems so pay can be more performance-oriented."—REGO Proceedings 1. Broadbanding systems	• Government experience with broadbanding has effectively demonstrated that adjustments to individual employees' pay can be more directly linked to performance than the existing system of within-grade step increases. • The key element to establishing more performance-oriented adjustments is the use of "open range"; i.e., no fixed steps for pay progression. • In addition, broadbanding supports streamlined career-oriented classification.	In Chapter 51, "Classification" • Establish a new authority to establish broadbanding systems, within the general schedule. • Broadbanding structure to include the following parameters: linked to minimum/maximum pay rates for GS grades; work within a band must be of similar level of difficulty, and responsibility, involuntary movement to a lower band is considered an appealable action; OPM to regulate number of grades in a band.
2. Open range general schedule	• Agencies should have the option to consider alternative to longevity-based WIGI's, without necessarily moving to broadbanding.	In Chapter 53, "Pay Rates and Systems" • Create options to establish alternative, performance-oriented, pay progression schemes for general schedule positions. • See pay administration features described under Broadbanding above.

D. Results-driven awards; "A portion of [manager's] pay determined by how well they do their jobs and meet the people's needs."—REGO VP speech

- Even though agencies have access to significant flexibilities now, they need to do more to apply modern compensation practices and link results achievement to lump sum payments, particularly for managers.
- Bonuses are an effective way to focus on group performance; e.g., as defined and measured using a balanced scorecard approach.
- Current aggregate compensation limits hamper agencies' ability to use flexibilities provided by the 105th Congress that raised the amount of SES Rank Awards and enlarged SES performance award funding pool limits in order to fully compensate executives for excellent performance.

E. Complementary pay system changes

- The pay system should be clear and understandable to employees.
- Situations should be reduced where employees receive windfalls or losses that are inequitable due to system constraints and that are not performance related.
- Government overtime practices should be consistent with private sector overtime practices.
- Conforming changes, including final PMRS termination, are necessary to enhance readiness for new performance-oriented pay system.

In Chapter 45, "Incentive Awards"

- Give agencies more flexibility to pay larger cash awards, without external approval; set award limits using indexed values.
- Provide an explicit authority for group incentive plans.
- Retain the authority for awards and add reference to informal recognition awards (but no nonmonetary awards).

In Chapter 53 "Pay Rates and Systems"

- Raise the aggregate compensation limitation for employees paid at rates of basic pay above the general schedule to an amount equal to the vice president's rate of basic pay.
- Establish in Chapter 53 an equitable "highest applicable rate" principle to govern pay setting when employees move between systems or geographic areas.
- Amend overtime provisions in Chapter 55 for FLSA-exempt employees to fix overtime pay cap problems.
- Amend Chapter 53 to cover promotions between systems.
- End grade retention but enhance pay retention features.
- End the use of the GM pay plan designators.
- Make necessary conforming changes elsewhere.

APPENDIX: Continued

What	Why	How
II. Staffing flexibilities		
A. Improved hiring and retention alternatives; "Provide agencies with flexible policies for hiring and retaining a high-quality workforce."—REGO		
B. Proceedings		
1. Category ranking	• Government experience shows this is an effective tool for identifying well-qualified candidates while protecting veterans' preference. • Agencies need other options for making merit-based competitive selections, while preserving veterans preference. • Agencies need more choices among equally qualified applicants, including veterans, to best fill individual positions. • Current practices described in law no longer match conditions for which they were designed (i.e., many applicants for unspecified jobs and central registers).	• In Chapter 33, "Examination, Selection, and Placement," authorize agencies to use an alternative ranking and selection procedure (like Agriculture demonstration). • Applicants are divided into quality groups based on maximum qualifications and job-related criteria. • Veteran's preference within each quality group is absolute. • Selections are made from the highest-ranking category.
2. Shortage and critical needs hiring authority	• Agencies need tools to respond quickly to critical hiring needs (e.g., CFO occupations). • Competing employers are able to make offers to high-quality candidates in shortage and critical need occupations before agencies can.	• Add authority for shortage and critical needs hiring to Chapter 33. • OPM, with agency consultation, will predefine criteria for shortage and critical needs. • Authority will be used under OPM oversight. • Note: New authority does not apply to occupations/grades covered by the Luevano decree.

3. Career intern program

- Agencies need alternate selection procedures for hiring high-quality entry-level employees for selected occupations; e.g., Accountants.

- Establish programs through executive order.
- Model program after the Presidential Management Intern (PMI) or other similar programs.
- Note: Executive order would not apply to occupations/grades covered by the Luevano consent decree.

4. Intra-agency details

- Documentation requirements for inter-agency vs. intra-agency details are inconsistent

- Amend Chapter 33 to strike the requirement to document intra-agency details.

5. Market-sensitive recruitment and retention flexibilities

- Existing pay authorities designed to address changing labor market conditions for recruiting and retaining need further flexibility.
- Stakeholders cite annual leave accrual as one of the disincentives for attracting high quality executives from the private sector.

- Create further flexibility in Chapter 57, "Travel, Transportation, and Subsistence," for designing and delivering recruitment, relocation, and retention payments; e.g., better options for service agreements, paying lump sums, higher ceilings.
- For broadbanding and open range pay systems, create in Chapter 53 a "staffing supplement" to be used in lieu of special rates for categories of employees; use an improved special rate authority for rest of general schedule.
- Amend Chapter 63, "Leave," to give SES members an 8-hour annual leave accrual on appointment and provide annual leave credits as a recruitment tool for agency use on a selected basis as a hiring incentive.

APPENDIX: Continued

What	Why	How
6. Training flexibilities	• In today's competitive employment market, agencies need more tools to recruit, develop and retain a high-quality workforce. • Training flexibilities would also be useful in workforce restructuring and reshaping.	• Amend Chapter 41, "Training," to remove the prohibition against an agency paying costs associated with an academic degree. • Add language to Chapter 41 to authorize an agency to pay for training that leads to licensure or certification.
7. Complementary changes in statutory structure	• With delegation of examining authority and to support merit-based staffing, it is particularly important to have a clean, accessible statutory structure for agency use.	• Update and reorganize Chapter 31, "Authority for Employment," and Chapter 33 to improve their accessibility and ease of use.
C. Workforce reshaping and re-structuring; "Agencies . . . will require management tools to restructure their workforces and achieve greater efficiencies." —FY 2000 budget	• Agencies need tools to deal with current and future changes in mission, funding, etc. • Fairness to employees at the same time remains a value to be preserved. • Available tools should allow for ongoing consolidations, agency restructuring, and some additional downsizing, using voluntary tools that are more cost-effective, preserve diversity gains, and maintain employee morale and productivity. • The government should be seen as an employer who values its employees and treats them with concern even under downsizing/restructuring conditions. • Career transition approaches should encourage employees to apply for jobs for which interested and well qualified.	• Establish buyout authority through 9/30/2001. • Amend early out authority to permanently fix Torres. • Authorize nonreimbursable "tryout details" inside and outside government for surplus employees. • Authorize paying relocation costs for surplus employees who separate voluntarily • Establish statutory responsibility to provide career transition assistance. • Authorize agencies to share interagency training costs. • Authorize payments to nonfederal employers for retraining costs. • Amend regulations to make the re-employment priority lists (RPLs) application-based.

III. Improved HR roles and relationships

A. Model employer

- As the largest employer in the country, the government should continue to set the standard for effective benefits design and administration.
- Introduce national policy initiatives at the federal level.
- Fixes specific inequities (e.g., FE Benefits Act).

Separate legislation
- FEHB Children's Equity Act (H.R.)
- Long-Term Care Insurance (H.R. 110)
- Support federal child care facilities (H.R.)
- FE Benefits Act (H.R.)

B. Improved labor–management relations; "the right kind of partnerships between labor and management."—REGO VP speech

- Successful reinvention of government will continue to require effective relations between workers and managers. Government experience with cooperative arrangements, such as labor–management partnerships, has been positive, but more support and emphasis are needed.

In Chapter 71, "Labor–Management Relations"
- Emphasize ADR and authorize additional dispute resolution approaches as alternatives to statutory procedures.
- Create permanent structures to support improved methods for effective labor–management relations (permanent NPC, require agency councils, FACA exemption).
- Authorize means of bargaining above the individual bargaining unit level.
- In either Chapter 71 or elsewhere, define means of union involvement; e.g., via written agreements or expanded score of bargaining.

APPENDIX: Continued

What	Why	How
C. OPM leadership role	• OPM's redefined role is to provide leadership and help ensure that all executive branch agencies manage their human resources effectively within the core values of merit principles. • Automation leadership will facilitate movement of electronic HR data across government, and will ensure consistency and accuracy of the applications of HR programs/processes federal governmentwide. • As HRM authority continues to be deregulated and decentralized the executive branch must have the ability to obtain workforce information from, and review the effectiveness of, all agency HRM programs. • Current demonstration project law is much too restrictive and cumbersome, which discourages experimentation with innovative HRM approaches. • OPM and agencies need a method to implement tested, successful HRM flexibilities without seeking legislation.	Amend Chapter 11, "Office of Personnel Management," to • Clarify OPM role and responsibilities in statute, including leadership role in HR automation. • Authorize OPM to collect workforce information throughout the executive branch. • Authorize OPM to review the effectiveness of HRM programs throughout the executive branch. Note: *Issue Executive Order on HR < accountability.* Amend Chapter 47, "Personnel Research Program and Demonstration Projects," to • Streamline, expand, and improve OPM's authority to conduct demonstration projects. • Authorize agencies to establish alternative personnel systems, with OPM approval.

Source: U.S. Office of Personnel Management, 1999.

BIBLIOGRAPHY

Ban, Carolyn and Norma M. Riccucci, eds. *Public Personnel Management: Current Concerns, Future Challenges*, 2nd ed. White Plains, N.Y.: Longman, 1997.

Behn, Robert D. "Ending Civil Service As We Know It," *Governing* (November 1996).

Condrey, Stephen. "Reinventing State Civil Service Systems: The Georgia Experience," American Society for Public Administration 1998 National Conference, Philadelphia, PA, 1998.

Figura, Susannah Z. "Muscling In," *Government Executive* (June 1999).

Gore, Al. "Reinvention's Next Steps: Governing in a Balanced Budget World," speech March 4, 1996; see NPR home page—http://www.npr.gov.

Government Operations Cluster. *Office of Personnel Management: Presidential Transition Book*. December 1992.

Hayes, Steven and Shawn B. Whitney. "Reinventing the Personnel Function: Lessons Learned from a Hope-Filled: Beginning in One State," *American Review of Public Administration*, vol. 27, no. 4, pp. 324–342 (December 1997).

Ingraham, Patricia W. and David H. Rosenbloom. *The Promise and Paradox of Civil Service Reform*. Pittsburgh: University of Pittsburgh Press, 1992.

Ingraham, Patricia W. *The Foundation of Merit*. Baltimore: Johns Hopkins University Press, 1995.

Johnson, Ronald N. and Gary D. Libecap. *The Federal Civil Service System and the Problem of Bureaucracy*. Chicago: University of Chicago Press, 1994.

Kettl, Donald et al. *Civil Service Reform: Building a Government That Works*. Washington, D.C.: Brookings Institution, 1996.

King, James B. "Government of the Future: A Personnel Perspective," *The Public Manager*, vol. 26, no. 2, pp. 21–23 (summer 1997).

Lachance, Janice. "The Future of the Public Service," speech; see http://www.opm.gov/speeches/1999/aspa.htm.

Laurent, Anne. "New Improved SES," *Government Executive* (June 1998).

Light, Paul. *Thickening Government*. The Brookings Institution, 1995.

Maranto, Robert. "Thinking the Unthinkable in Public Administration: A Case for Spoils in the Federal Bureaucracy," *Administration & Society*, vol. 29, no. 6 (January 1998).

Marzotto, Toni. "Whither the Generalist Manager: Reinventing the Senior Executive Service," American Political Science Association National Conference, Washington, D.C., 1993.

Miller, Zell. "1996 State of the State Address," Atlanta, January 1996; see http://gnsun1.ganet.state.ga.us.

Mosher, Frederick C. *Democracy and the Public Service*, 2nd ed. New York: Oxford University Press, 1982.

National Partnership for Reinventing Government. *Performance-Based Organizations: A Conversion Guide*. Washington, D.C., July 1999; see http://www.npr.gov for latest version.

National Performance Review. *The Best Kept Secrets In Government*. Washington, D.C., September 1996.

National Performance Review. *Creating a Government That Works Better & Costs Less.* Washington, D.C., September 1993.

National Performance Review. *Reinventing Human Resources Management.* Washington, D.C., November 1993.

National Performance Review. *Reinventing Office of Personnel Management.* Washington, D.C., November 1993.

Report of the National Commission on the Public Service (Volcker Commission). Washington, D.C., 1989.

Report of the National Commission on the State and Local Public Service (Winter Commission); reprinted in Thompson, Frank, ed. *Revitalizing State and Local Public Service.* San Francisco: Jossey-Bass, 1993.

Shafritz, Jay M. *Public Personnel Management: The Heritage of Civil Service Reform.* New York: Praeger, 1975.

Stephens, Robert L. "An Examination of Georgia's Civil Service Reform," American Society for Public Administration 1999 National Conference.

Sturdivant, John N. and Robert Tobias. Letter to Elaine Kamarck, Senior Policy Advisor to the Vice President of the United States, May 24, 1995.

U.S. General Accounting Office. *The Excepted Service: A Research Profile.* May 1997; see http:/www.gao.gov.

U.S. House of Representatives, Committee on Government Reform & Oversight. *Making Government Work: Fulfilling the Mandate for Change.* December 21, 1995.

U.S. Office of Personnel Management. "Progress in Strengthening the Senior Executive Service," Washington, D.C.: Office of the Director; October 1996.

U.S. Office of Personnel Management. *Proposed Framework for Improving the Senior Executive Service.* Washington, D.C., March 16, 1998.

U.S. Office of Personnel Management. *Civil Service Reform: A Report on the First Year.* Washington, D.C., January 1980.

Van Wart, Montgomery. "Commentary: Is Making Any Fundamental Change in the Civil Service Dangerous?" *Review of Public Personnel Administration*, vol 19, no. 1, pp. 71–78 (winter 1999).

Walters, Jonathan. "Albany Unbound," *Governing* (December 1998).

Walters, Jonathan. "Who Needs Civil Service," *Governing* (August 1997).

White House Personnel Office. "Malek Manual." U.S. Senate, Select Committee on Presidential Campaign Activities, Executive Session Hearings, Watergate and Related Activities: Use of Incumbency—Responsiveness Program, Book 19, 93rd Cong., 2nd sess. Washington, D.C.: U.S. Government Printing Office, 1974.

3

The Legal Framework of Public Personnel Management

PROLOGUE: *ELROD* V. *BURNS* (1976)

The use of public jobs for political patronage in America is a practice almost as old as the American political experience itself. In colonial days, the British used patronage widely and often abusively; the creation of sinecures and the sale of public office were a central aspect of colonial public administration. Indeed, so incensed were the Americans with these practices that in the Declaration of Independence they included the complaint that King George III had "erected a multitude of new offices, and sent hither swarms of officers to harass our people, and eat out their substance." By the time the spoils system rolled into full swing in the 1840s, however, patronage could be considered as American as apple pie. As President Jackson pointed out, rotation in office is a democratic principle, and one that makes the public service accountable to the electorate; nor can it be doubted that among the lasting benefits of patronage has been the creation of a strong two-party political system. The use of political patronage for democratic ends was a major aspect of American political development. It is not surprising, therefore, that despite the efforts of civil service reformers to eradicate patronage practices at all levels of government, some jurisdictions managed to hold on to hallowed traditions, but what the reformers missed, the Supreme Court took care of in *Elrod* v. *Burns*—a case that well illustrates the law-bound quality of contemporary public personnel administration.

The facts of the case were rather straightforward and reminiscent of events that have taken place throughout the history of the nation. In December 1970, the sheriff of Cook County (Chicago), Illinois, a Republican, was replaced by Richard Elrod, a Democrat. Elrod, along with "boss" Richard J. Daley, the Democratic organization of Cook County, and the Democratic Central Committee of Cook County, adhered to the time-honored practice—employed by his Republican predecessor as well—of replacing all noncivil service employees of his office who were unable to win the approval of the Democratic Party with new appointees. John Burns and other "deposed" Republican employees brought suit on the grounds that their First and Fourteenth Amendment rights had been abridged by their dismissals. This complaint was somewhat remarkable because they had received their jobs in the same general way as the Democrats who replaced them.

The Supreme Court held that the dismissals were unconstitutional, but its members could not fully agree on precisely why. Justice Brennan announced the judgment of the Court in an opinion joined by Justices White and Marshall. While recognizing that "patronage practice is not new to American politics," Brennan also maintained that "the cost of the practice of patronage is the restraint it places on freedoms of belief and association." In order to justify these costs, in his view, the government had to demonstrate some compelling logic for using patronage: "In short, if conditioning the retention of public employment on the employee's support of the in-party is to survive constitutional challenge, it must further some vital government end by a means that is least restrictive of freedom of belief and association in achieving that end, and the benefit gained must outweigh the loss of constitutionally protected rights."

What possible justifications might exist? First, patronage might help to ensure effective government and the efficiency of public employees. Those workers holding the same political views as the head of a governmental agency might work harder toward implementing official policy. To this argument, Brennan's terse reply was, "We are not persuaded." Clearly, the history of patronage indicates that it breeds inefficiency, corruption, and ineffective administration.

Second, patronage might yield greater political accountability. Brennan was quick to point out, however, that this objective could be accomplished by limiting patronage to policy-making positions, which was not the situation back in Cook County.

Third, patronage might be necessary for the maintenance of strong political parties and thus for the democratic process as well. Although this line of thought has substantial force—political parties were weakened by civil service reform, and voter participation began dropping at the same time that patronage was being limited—Brennan did not believe that the elimination of the practice being challenged specifically would "bring about the demise of party politics."

In Brennan's view, therefore, although the ends associated with arguments in favor of patronage were laudable, the means themselves were unsatisfactory because they abridged public employees' rights too severely. Consequently, Brennan thought that patronage dismissals violated the First and the Fourteenth Amendments.

Justices Stewart and Blackmun concurred in a much narrower opinion: "The single substantive question involved in this case is whether a nonpolicy making, nonconfidential government employee can be discharged from a job that he is satisfactorily performing upon the sole ground of his political beliefs. I agree with the Court that he cannot."

Chief Justice Burger dissented. He argued that a state's right to use a patronage system was protected by the Tenth Amendment. This would be especially true in cases which the state, as in the case of Illinois, "pointedly decided that roughly half of the Sheriff's staff shall be made up of tenured career personnel and the balance left exclusively to the choice of the elected head of the department."

The chief justice, along with Justice Rehnquist, also joined in a wide-ranging dissent by Justice Powell. According to Powell, "History and long prevailing practice across the country support the view that patronage hiring practices make a sufficiently substantial contribution to the practical functioning of our democratic system to support their relatively modest intrusion on First Amendment interests. The judgment today unnecessarily constitutionalizes another element of American life—an element certainly not without its faults but one which generations have accepted on balance as having merit."

The Supreme Court holding in *Elrod* was strengthened by its action in *Branti* v. *Finkel* (1980). The case involved the patronage dismissals of assistant public defenders in Rockland County, New York. In finding the removals to be unconstitutional, a majority of the Supreme Court expanded the *Elrod* ruling by holding that "the ultimate inquiry is not whether the label 'policymaker' or 'confidential' fits a particular position; rather, the question is whether the hiring authority can demonstrate that party affiliation is an appropriate requirement for effective performance of the public office involved."

Elrod and *Branti* went a long way toward making patronage *dismissals* unconstitutional, but what about making other personnel actions, such as hiring, promotion, transfer, or "dead-ending," based on partisanship? In 1990, a full decade after the *Branti* decision, a slim majority of the Supreme Court ruled in *Rutan* v. *Republican Party of Illinois* that "unless . . . patronage practices are narrowly tailored to further vital government interests, we must conclude that they impermissibly encroach on First Amendment freedoms." Practically speaking, then, partisan intrusion into public personnel administration should become a thing of the past and the merit orientation of most contemporary public personnel should be strengthened considerably.

There are at least two lessons public personnelists should draw from these cases. First and most specifically, the use of patronage will be constitutional only if it can be demonstrated that partisan affiliation is strongly related to effective job performance. Second and more generally, the role of the judiciary in contemporary public personnel management cannot be overlooked. Here "a practice as old as the Republic," as Justice Powell put it, was found to be unconstitutional as the result of evolving judicial concepts and perspectives. If something as traditional as patronage can now be found to violate the Constitution, certainly other aspects of public personnel administration are also vulnerable. Constitutional law is ever changing; public personnel managers must remain abreast of it lest they find themselves on the losing side.

COMPARING THE LEGAL AND MANAGERIAL FRAMEWORKS OF GOVERNMENT

American public personnel administration is generally considered to be primarily a managerial endeavor. Its overall purpose is to manage human resources in the manner that gives the public the greatest cost-effectiveness for their tax dollars. Public personnel management takes place within an elaborate legal framework, however. Because the resources are *human*, we very much care about how they are treated. We recognize that they must be protected against maltreatment, discrimination, and victimization by personnel systems, other public employees, or political officials. Just as employee Burns in the prologue to this chapter has a constitutional right to freedom of belief and association, all public employees have broad statutory and constitutional rights to fair treatment, privacy, and equal protection. The fact that public personnel management is regulated directly by constitutional law sets it apart from private sector practices, where only the Thirteenth Amendment's prohibition against slavery applies.

In the title of one of her books, Carolyn Ban, a public personnel scholar, asks *How Do Public Managers Manage?* She finds that many are "creative copers," who are reasonably successful in negotiating the personnel and other constraints they face, but that other managers are more prone to failure and demoralization because they fail to understand the rulebound systems in which they operate. If anyone ever doubted it, Ban's work leaves no doubt that a knowledge of the law is preferable to ignorance when it comes to public management.

This chapter provides a general overview of the statutory and constitutional framework for public personnel management in the United States. It is not intended to provide a detailed legal analysis of the entire law of public employment. That would take several volumes, especially if attention were devoted to differences among the states, localities, and more than 80,000 other governments that operate in the United States. It will, however, convey the basic legal requirements and principles within which a great deal of American public personnel management takes place.

MERIT PRINCIPLES AND CIVIL SERVICE

Ever since the Civil Service Act of 1882 (the Pendleton act) went into effect, the ideal for public personnel management in the United States has been a merit system. At first the principles were rudimentary; the main idea was that workers should be hired based on their ability to do the job rather than according to their political support for the president or members of Congress. In principle, though without significant legal protection, it was expected that they would retain those jobs as long as their performance was satisfactory.

That left plenty of room for arbitrary or discriminatory treatment. There was plenty of it, too. Minorities and women were excluded from the vast majority of positions. Racial segregation extending to cafeterias, drinking fountains, and restrooms was rife in some agencies and government facilities. Federal law allowed lower pay for women doing the *same* work as men. Anybody could be dismissed for almost any reason other than partisan politics without much procedure, if management claimed it would promote the efficiency of the service. Abuses were manifold and over the years since the 1880s, many statutes and regulations have been adopted precisely to guard against them.

When public managers and reinventers complain that public personnel management is overregulated, they may be correct. The rules may have become so complex and encompassing that cost-effective public personnel management is difficult, but unlike statutes that are enacted to serve special interests, such as loopholes in the tax code, they were adopted to prevent undesirable or abusive treatment of government workers. Perhaps some of this abuse would no longer occur, but some, including sexual harassment, most certainly would. That is why public personnel management's legal framework tends to endure.

Today the federal merit system principles, which are codified in Title 5 of the U.S. Code, provide an elaborate framework for federal personnel management. Their main provisions are as follows:

1. *Recruitment should be from among qualified individuals from appropriate sources in an endeavor to achieve a workforce from all segments of society; and, selection and advancement should be determined solely on the basis of relative ability, knowledge, and skills, after fair and open competition which assures that all receive equal opportunity.* This legal mouthful is largely drawn from the Civil Service Reform Act of 1978. Several points should be emphasized. The policy that the federal workforce should be drawn from all segments

of society is sometimes referred to as "representative bureaucracy," especially in academic writing. It is based on two assumptions of fundamental importance to contemporary public personnel management. First, a socially representative workforce is a check against discrimination based on factors such as race, ethnicity, or gender. If people from all segments of society are in federal jobs—especially at all levels—in rough proportion to their numbers in the workforce generally, it is evidence of nondiscrimination. It also creates a dynamic that makes it harder to discriminate. An "old boys network" is difficult to operate when lots of employees at the decision-making table are not old boys.

Second, representative bureaucracy contends that a civil service that is socially representative is more likely to be representative in a policy sense as well. To the extent that public employees are involved in policy formulation, social diversity brings a wider variety of perspectives to bear on issues and choices.

In the 1960s, when representative bureaucracy began to have a real impact on public personnel theory and policy, there was a great deal of skepticism about the existence of a relationship between administrators' social backgrounds and their policy preferences on the job. Today, however, this aspect of representative bureaucracy is widely accepted in government and supported by several empirical studies.

The idea that selection and advancement should be based on relative ability, knowledge, and skills—that is, "achievement" factors—is also important. Historically, many civil services, including the federal service in the eighteenth and most of the nineteenth centuries, were selected largely on the basis of "ascriptive" qualities. Family, politics, and personal connections were at least as important as a relative ability to do the job.

The requirement of fair and open competition means among other things that individuals should not be preselected for federal jobs, that tests and other screening devices should be job-related, and that they should be administered in a nondiscriminatory fashion. This does not necessarily mean everybody should be treated identically, regardless of circumstances. Equal opportunity may sometimes require affirmative steps to help members of groups historically subject to discrimination to compete on an equal footing. Veterans have historically received a variety of preferences in federal personnel. Following the federal welfare reform legislation of 1996, federal agencies were expected to make special efforts to hire and train those coming off the welfare roles.

Fair competition also means that the screening devices, such as personnel exams, will be valid in the sense that they measure qualities related to job performance. This has presented a great deal of difficulty over the past two decades or so. It often turns out to be very difficult to show a strong relationship between individuals' scores on an exam and their performance on the job. For one thing, it is often very difficult to measure performance. For another, those hired or promoted often have similar scores. Where an exam is not valid *and* proves to be a barrier to equal opportunity, it will be highly vulnerable to legal challenge.

2. *All employees and applicants for employment should receive fair and equitable treatment in all aspects of personnel management without regard to political affiliation, race, color, religion, national origin, sex, marital status, age, or handicapping condition, and with proper regard for their privacy and constitutional rights.* This set of principles adds specificity to the requirements discussed above. It identifies certain factors, including race or handicapping condition, that are an *illegal* basis for taking any action that will be unfair or inequitable. Whereas some arbitrary personnel decisions are perhaps inevitable, any such action based on one of these prohibited factors is clearly illegal and subject to appeal or other legal redress.

   The admonition to protect privacy and constitutional rights is also important. Historically, up until the 1950s and 1960s, public employees in the United States did not really have any clear privacy or constitutional rights in the context of their employment. Many public managers and personnelists initially criticized the federal courts for "interfering" in personnel when they began declaring procedural due process, First Amendment, and equal protection rights for public employees in the 1950s and afterward. Some still do, but failure to respect employees' constitutional rights is now a violation of basic merit system principles. In practice, this principle accepts the federal courts as partners in public personnel management.

3. *Equal pay should be provided for work of equal value, with appropriate consideration of both national and local rates paid by employers in the private sector, and appropriate incentives and recognition should be provided for excellence in performance.* Again, the underlying value is fairness. Federal employees should be paid at fair rates of compensation, despite the temptation to ask them to sacrifice when government budgets are tight. Men and women, blacks and whites, and so on should be paid at equal rates for work of equal value. The historic tendency to downgrade pay in occupations primarily per-

formed by women, such as traditional nursing, is inappropriate. Paying men more than women in the same jobs is positively prohibited.

Nevertheless, equal pay does not preclude *merit pay*. Pay for performance is a legitimate managerial practice, as long as it is fairly administered.

4. *All employees should maintain high standards of integrity, conduct, and concern for the public interest.* Federal employment is a public trust and employees have legal obligations to act accordingly. This puts a variety of ethical and legal demands on them. Public employees must act with integrity, of course, but also avoid the appearance of impropriety. They are expected to subordinate their private interests to the public interest should a conflict arise. In practice, this may require limitations on their nonwork and postemployment activities, as well as disclosure of assets and other matters that are usually regarded as private or personal. FBI background checks continue to inquire about morality, substance or alcohol abuse, loyalty to the nation, and whether or not there is something about the individual's behavior that might make him or her vulnerable to blackmail.

5. *The federal workforce should be used efficiently and effectively.* This principal is so obvious that one may wonder why it is mentioned at all. The reason is simple. In the past, especially under the spoils system, federal workers were often used for partisan rather than governmental purposes. Some of them had no government work at all. Featherbedding, ''cooping'' (sleeping on the job), and make-work still characterize the public service in some places and rip off the taxpayer.

6. *Employees should be retained on the basis of the adequacy of their performance, inadequate performance should be corrected, and employees should be separated who cannot or will not improve their performance to meet required standards.* The Civil Service Act of 1883 prohibited partisan dismissals, but provided no other specific job protection for covered federal employees. In 1912, the Lloyd–LaFollette Act closed this ''backdoor'' a bit by limiting dismissals of federal civil service employees to such causes as would promote the efficiency of the service. It required that the employee be informed of the reasons for his or her dismissal, but had no other procedural safeguards. The Veterans Preference Act of 1944 allowed those eligible for veteran preference to appeal some adverse actions. Eventually this provision was made more elaborate and extended to the vast majority of federal civilian employees. Today, even in the absence of statutory restrictions, constitutional law limits the reasons and proce-

dures that can be used for dismissing public employees (as discussed further on in this chapter).

Civil service job protection has been subject to a great deal of criticism for demotivating employees, protecting poor performers and nonperformers, and hampering good management, but the basic principle is clear—dismissals should be performance-based, rather than allowed for arbitrary, capricious, or discriminatory reasons. Nobody should be dismissed from the federal service simply because the supervisor does not like one of his or her personal qualities. It would be impossible to empower employees or even expect them to invest in their jobs under such circumstances.

Although few would disagree with the core principal that dismissals should be performance-based, applying procedural safeguards to ensure that this is the case has been difficult. Many of the civil service reformers in the 1880s warned against establishing dismissal by ''lawsuits,'' but how can we be sure a dismissal is for poor performance without some procedural checks? Of course, once an employee can contest his or her dismissal, the supervisor has to be ready to document the alleged poor performance (and maybe even show that it was the real cause, not a pretext for firing the employee).

That is one reason why contemporary merit principles favor trying to correct the unsatisfactory performance before dismissing the employee. It may be more cost-effective, and it is certainly more humane. As the reinventers point out, it is also highly desirable to revisit dismissal procedures in an effort to simplify them and reduce their cost without sacrificing fairness.

7. *Employees should be provided effective education and training in cases in which such education and training would result in better organizational and individual performance.* This principle requires the government to invest in its employees. It is premised on the existence of a career system in which an agency's first obligation is to obtain the skills, knowledge, and abilities it needs by developing the human resources available within its own workforce. Such an obligation makes the civil service attractive to employees who want to improve their human capital, but adhering to the principle can be difficult, especially when employees are likely to take their new skills to the private sector for better pay and working conditions or when the agency can obtain what it needs at lower cost by contracting out the work.

8. *Employees should be: (A) protected against arbitrary action, personal favoritism, or coercion for partisan political purposes, and (B)*

prohibited from using their official authority or influence for the pur-
pose of interfering with or affecting the result of an election or a
nomination for election. This is the principle of political neutrality.
Federal employees are in the service of the nation as a whole, not the
political party in power. There should be a bright line separating partisan politics from federal administration. Members of the public have
a right to expect fair treatment from agencies such as Social Security,
IRS, or the EPA regardless of whether they are Democrats, Republicans, or members of any other legal political party. Political appointees can determine policy, insofar as they have the legal discretion to do so, but they cannot try to involve employees in partisan
matters, including campaign funding and elections.

Since the Hatch Act reform of 1993, most federal employees can
voluntarily engage in partisan campaign activity, but they cannot use
their official authority as part of that effort. Soliciting money for partisan campaigns in federal workplaces has been strictly prohibited since
1883 (as Vice President Al Gore learned in *1996*, when it was revealed that he was raising campaign funds via telephone from the
White House).

9. *Employees should be protected against reprisal for the lawful disclo-*
    sure of information which the employees reasonably believe evi-
    dences: (A) a violation of any law, rule, or regulation, or (B) misman-
    agement, gross waste of funds, and abuse of authority or a substantial
    and specific danger to public health or safety. This is the whistle-
    blower protection principle. The Civil Service Reform Act of 1978
    and subsequent legislation afford specific procedural protection to
    whistle-blowers through the Office of Special Counsel and the Merit
    Systems Protection Board. The whistle-blower protection provision
    aims at a change in organizational cultures, rather than being the sin
    of going outside the agency (a dread form of insubordination), appro-
    priate whistle-blowing is recognized as a public virtue.

10. Additional practices specifically prohibited by the Civil Service Re-
    form Act of 1978 include: *discrimination based on marital status;*
    using information other than personal knowledge or materials in the
    employee's or applicant's record when making a personnel decision
    (e.g., acting on a political recommendation); obstruction of the right
    to compete for employment; exercising influence to secure an advan-
    tage for one candidate over another (e.g., ''wiring'' or undercutting
    competition); nepotism; reprisal for exercising appeal rights; and
    making an adverse judgment about an employee based on private
    conduct that does not affect the individual or the organization's per-
    formance. These principles are encompassing. Each has a statutory

base. They create rights in the workplace that are necessarily accompanied by procedural protections. When an employee challenges an action covered by merit principles, the burden of persuasion is often on the agency to show that no statute or regulation was violated. Taken together these principles place a great deal of public personnel management in a comprehensive legal framework. If they encumber management, that is actually one of their purposes. The challenge is to manage effectively within them and/or to reformulate them in the interests of flexibility and simplicity.

The principles and rules just reviewed are more than the tip of the iceberg when it comes to public personnel management's legal framework, but there are many more components to it. These also must be considered if public managers are to manage effectively.

Civil Rights and Equal Opportunity Law

The civil rights and equal opportunity law applicable to the public sector is elaborate. Discrimination based on race, color, religion, national origin, or sex is prohibited in most public and private sector employment by the Civil Rights Act of 1964, as amended, broadened, and strengthened by the Equal Employment Opportunity Act of 1972 (EEO act). The prohibitions are comprehensive in their application to almost all facets of public personnel management: recruitment, selection, promotion, training, retention, discipline, allocation of assignments, and related actions. Nondiscrimination based on sex includes sexual harassment. Both "quid pro quo" sexual demands and "hostile work environments" based on sexual remarks, jokes, taunting, and so forth are prohibited.

As is often the case, enforcement has lagged behind legal principle. Many jurisdictions are still struggling to achieve the nondiscrimination and harassment-free workplaces mandated by these statutes. The Civil Rights Act of 1991 provided new tools in the struggle. One of its purposes is to eliminate the "glass ceiling" effect in both public and private employment. The glass ceiling is essentially an invisible barrier to the advancement of women and minorities into the top levels of organizations. Its composition is hard to pin down because it is largely based on culture and ingrained practices as opposed to specific personnel rule or procedures. The act calls on the federal Equal Employment Opportunity Commission to help break glass ceilings where they exist. Other provisions of the 1991 act charge the Department of Labor with promoting the elimination of pay disparities based on sex. They also make it easier to sue discriminatory employers and recover damages for intentional discrimination.

These statues are augmented by the Equal Pay Act (1963), the Age Discrimination in Employment Act (1967), the Rehabilitation Act (1973), which protects the employment interests of handicapped persons, and the Americans with Disa-

bilities Act of 1990, which prohibits discrimination in most nonfederal employment against persons with disabilities (including recovery from drug or alcohol
abuse). Several of the acts mentioned have been amended and strengthened since
they were first enacted. Equal opportunity will be discussed in detail in later
chapters.

Ethics Law

As the fourth merit principle discussed above implies, public employees are often
subject to comprehensive ethics requirements. These typically cover matters as

Gifts, including hospitality, from outside sources
Gifts between employees
Conflicts of interest
Impartiality in performance of official duties
Moonlighting and postemployment activity
Misuse of employment
Outside activities

Elaborate legal systems for ethics may rely on an independent agency for
enforcement. For instance, the Federal Office of Government Ethics was established in 1978 within the Office of Personnel Management and then made independent in 1989. It employs about 80 people to draft and enforce rules as well
as to provide guidance, training, and education about federal ethics requirements.
(As important as public sector ethics are, during the federal government's shut-
down for want of a budget in November 1995, the Office of Government Ethics
was partly closed as nonessential!)

Labor Relations

Labor relations and collective bargaining are another area of public personnel
practice that is subject to comprehensive legal regulation. Statutes define who
may bargain with whom over what, when, how disputes will be resolved, and
much more. Because the present chapter focuses primarily on restrictions on public personnel management, here it is necessary only to mention that there are
long lists of unfair labor practices that are prohibited in many jurisdictions.

Enforcement

By now there can be no doubt that the public personnel management's legal
framework is elaborate—often so encompassing that enforcement becomes difficult. Several approaches are typically used. First, administrative adjudicatory
systems are usually used to deal with discipline, dismissal, other adverse actions,

complaints of discrimination, and unfair labor practices. Second, although these vary widely, there is often an opportunity to appeal an action within the agency and then to an outside administrative body such as a civil service commission, equal opportunity office, or public employment relations board (primarily for labor disputes). Third, after exhausting their administrative appeals, or reasonably trying to do so, employees may be able to take their cases to state or federal court. Later chapters will say more about adjudicatory systems and legal remedies, but just to provide something of their legalistic flavor, it is worth a few lines on the federal procedures for adverse actions and performance-based actions.

Adverse actions are disciplinary steps taken against an employee for misconduct. If the penalty is dismissal, suspension for more than 14 days, reduction in pay or grade, or disciplinary furlough, the employee must be given advance written notice of the charge and an opportunity to respond. The employee may be represented by counsel and is entitled to see all of the information on which the charge is based.

Performance-based disciplinary actions may be taken against an employee who fails to meet established standards in a critical element of his or her job. Again the employee is entitled to advance notice. He or she can contest the finding of unacceptable performance to the supervisor involved. Again, counsel may render assistance. The employee must also be given an opportunity to correct the deficiency before disciplinary action takes effect.

In either case, the employee can appeal to the Merit Systems Protection Board (MSPB). Where discipline is for misconduct, the agency involved has the burden to show by a preponderance of the evidence that the conduct at issue adversely affected performance and that the purpose of the action is to promote the efficiency of the service. In performance-based actions, the agency need only show that its decision is backed by substantial evidence and that the action was procedurally correct. (A preponderance of the evidence means the decision is more likely correct than incorrect. Substantial evidence is evidence sufficient to make a decision reasonable.)

By now the reader should be rather sympathetic to Ban's question, with emphasis: how *do* public managers manage? There is a whole additional side to public personnel's legal framework, however, the Constitution. As the rest of this chapter will show, constitutional law also broadly regulates public employment practices. In many respects it is even more comprehensive than statutory law because it applies nationwide. Some of its elements are also more complex. The greatest problem it poses for public managers, however, is that, unlike statutes, it is the product of adjudication. One cannot pick up a rulebook and read it; rather, one has to read and distill a large number of cases or rely on casebooks compiled by others to discern its meaning and applicability. As with statutory law, only an overall outline focusing on core principles can be presented here.

THE CONSTITUTIONAL LAW OF PUBLIC EMPLOYMENT

Historically, there have been three distinct phases in the Constitution's applicability to public personnel management. The first phase was the longest, lasting from the adoption of the Constitution in 1789 to the 1950s. It treated the public employment relationship as very similar to the private employment relationship; that is, largely unregulated by the Constitution. Employment in both sectors was considered to be at the "will" of the employer, who, insofar as the Constitution was concerned, could hire and fire employees for virtually any reason whatsoever, or for no reason at all. This approach made the spoils system possible and ironically also set forth the first constitutional justifications for prohibiting public employees from taking an active part in partisan politics. For the sake of convenience, this approach can be called the "private sector model."

In terms of constitutional interpretation, the private sector model was sustained by what became known as the doctrine of privilege. Under this approach it was generally accepted that since there was no constitutional right to public employment, it was a privilege to hold a government job. Moreover, because such employment was voluntary rather than compulsory, public employees had few rights that could not be legitimately abridged by the government in its role as employer. The logic behind this position is still best conveyed by Justice Holmes's often quoted statement that "the petitioner may have a constitutional right to talk politics, but he has no constitutional right to be a policeman." Under this approach, public personnel management was free to place virtually any conditions it saw fit upon public employment, and the judiciary played almost no role in this policy area.

The doctrine of privilege and the private sector model contained a certain logic, but they also had substantial defects. Most important, as the size of public employment increased to the point to which about 16% of the workforce held public jobs, it became evident that the rights of a substantial proportion of the population could be abridged by governments in their roles as employers—and abridge these rights they did! During the late 1940s and early 1950s, governments at all levels developed "loyalty-security" regulations to protect themselves against subversive employees, but one's definition of *subversive* tended to vary with one's politics and geographic location. Consequently, some federal employees were charged with such dangerous activities as favoring peace and freedom, being critical of the American Legion and public power projects, being related to someone who might have had procommunist leanings, having "communist literature" and "communist art" in their houses, living with members of the opposite sex to whom they weren't married, learning Russian, and favoring racial integration. Some employees were even asked whether they regularly read the *New York Times*, attended church, or had intelligent, clever friends and associates.

THE BILL OF RIGHTS

Amendment I

Congress shall make no law respecting an establishment of religion, or prohibiting the free exercise thereof; or abridging the freedom of speech, or of the press, or the right of the people peaceably to assemble, and to petition the Government for a redress of grievances.

Amendment II

A well regulated Militia, being necessary to the security of a free State, the right of the people to keep and bear Arms, shall not be infringed.

Amendment III

No Soldier shall, in time of peace be quartered in any house, without the consent of the Owner, nor in time of war, but in a manner to be prescribed by law.

Amendment IV

The right of the people to be secure in their persons, houses, papers, and effects, against unreasonable searches and seizures, shall not be violated, and no Warrants shall issue, but upon probable cause, supported by Oath or affirmation, and particularly describing the place to be searched, and the persons or things to be seized.

Amendment V

No person shall be held to answer for a capital, or otherwise infamous crime, unless on a presentment or indictment of a Grand Jury, except in cases arising in the land or naval forces, or in the Militia, when in actual service in time of War or public danger; nor shall any person be subject for the same offence to be twice put in jeopardy of life or limb, nor shall be compelled in any criminal case to be a witness against himself, nor be deprived of life, liberty, or property, without due process of law; nor shall private property be taken for public use without just compensation.

Amendment VI

In all criminal prosecutions, the accused shall enjoy the right to a speedy and public trial, by an impartial jury of the State and district wherein the crime shall have been committed; which district shall have been previously ascertained by law, and to be informed of the nature and cause of the accusation; to be confronted with the witnesses against him; to have compulsory process for obtaining witnesses in his favor, and to have the assistance of counsel for his defense.

Amendment VII

In Suits at common law, where the value in controversy shall exceed twenty dollars, the right of trial by jury shall be preserved, and no fact tried by a jury shall be otherwise re-examined in any Court of the United States, than according to the rules of the common law.

Amendment VIII

Excessive bail shall not be required, nor excessive fines imposed, nor cruel and unusual punishments inflicted.

Amendment IX

The enumeration in the Constitution of certain rights shall not be construed to deny or disparage others retained by the people.

Amendment X

The powers not delegated to the United States by the Constitution, nor prohibited by it to the States, are reserved to the States respectively, or to the people.

Note: The first ten amendments (Bill of Rights) were ratified effective December 15, 1791.

Questions of this nature placed severe strains upon the federal employee's First Amendment and privacy rights. The abuses did not stop there, however; federal servants were also subject to coercion that infringed upon their right of liberty under the Fifth Amendment. Not only were they required to attend lectures and films on such topics as racial integration and the cold war, but in 1966 Senator Ervin observed that there was "outright coercion and intimidation of employees to buy everything from savings bonds to electric light bulbs for playgrounds."

At a time in which public employment was rapidly growing, many feared that such governmental power over this segment of the population could pose a threat to democracy. Not only were the rights of a substantial number of citizens abridged, but concerted coercion could also turn them into a significant political force. Perceptive observers recognized that governments could also limit the rights of other citizens receiving other privileges, and in the modern administrative state this could have included everyone who receives welfare benefits, social security, government contracts, passports, and even driver's licenses. Clearly the doctrine of privilege was ill-suited to the modern administrative state in democratic regimes, and its demise was not limited to the realm of public employment.

THE INDIVIDUALIZED RIGHTS APPROACH

Beginning in the 1950s, the federal judiciary became more sensitive to the threats to individual rights posed by the private sector model and the doctrine of privilege in its broad application. Several Supreme Court justices urged that the public employment relationship be controlled by the Constitution's guarantees and that an individual not be required to sacrifice his or her constitutional rights as a condition of becoming a public employee. Public employees, like other citizens, had constitutional rights that were inviolable—even in the context of the employment relationship.

At first these views were voiced mostly in dissent, but by the early 1970s, the doctrine of privilege had been completely discarded by the judiciary. Replacing the doctrine of privilege with one that is more balanced, does not promote undue judicial intervention in public personnel management, and enables public managers and employees to understand their respective rights and obligations has nevertheless been difficult. Just as the doctrine of privilege was doomed by its simplicity in an age of complex public administration, a general judicial inclination to treat the constitutional rights of public employees as essentially the same as those of other citizens proved inadequate.

Initially the doctrine of privilege was replaced by the doctrine of substantial interest. It held that whenever there was a "substantial interest," such as the individual's reputation, the employee, facing possible dismissal, had a right to a procedure to determine whether legitimate grounds for the removal really existed. This procedure would generally consist of a hearing of some sort, perhaps including the rights of confrontation and cross-examination. The doctrine of substantial interest gave public employees considerable constitutional rights, but it did not serve the needs of either the judiciary or public personnel managers very well. Indeed, it led to an ever-increasing number of cases involving the public employee's constitutional position and to great perplexity over what actually constituted a substantial interest.

As the Supreme Court wrestled with the perplexities involved in the constitutional aspects of public employment and as its membership changed during the Nixon and Ford administrations, another approach developed. This involved the assessment of each and every case on its own merits and the avoidance of the development of a broad constitutional doctrine specifying the general outlines of the constitutional rights of public employees. Good examples occurred in the area of mandatory maternity leaves, where the Supreme Court held that these could not commence without an individualized determination of a woman's physical capability to continue at her public sector job (except very late in the normal term of a pregnancy), and in the area of barriers to the public employment of aliens, where the Court held that they could be banned from some jobs but not others.

The "individualized" approach multiplied the practical deficiencies of the doctrine of substantial interest and is best attributed to the Supreme Court's inability to develop a dominant coalition among its members on public employment issues. As might be expected, the approach encouraged further litigation and made public personnel management more difficult by requiring the individual treatment of individual employees. While the doctrine of privilege afforded public employees virtually no constitutional protection, at least it was clear. The individualized rights approach afforded them expansive constitutional rights, but it lacked clarity. Beginning in the mid-1970s and crystallizing in the 1980s, the Supreme Court formulated the current model for determining public employees' constitutional rights.

THE PUBLIC SERVICE MODEL

The public service model seeks to balance the sometimes competing concerns of the government as employer, the interests of public employees in retaining constitutional protections, and the public's interest in the way its affairs are run by public administrators. As Justice O'Connor pointed out in *Waters* v. *Churchill* (1994), the key to the balancing is that "the government's interest in achieving its goals as effectively and efficiently as possible is elevated from a relatively subordinate interest when it acts as a sovereign [dealing with ordinary citizens] to a significant one when it acts as employer." Nevertheless, its interests are not synonymous with those of the public at large, which has a strong reason to want public employees to speak out about the operation of their agencies and to blow the whistle when appropriate.

Freedom of Expression: Nonpartisan Speech

The Supreme Court's current approach to public employees' constitutional rights to nonpartisan speech was mapped out in *Rankin* v. *McPherson* (1987). The case involved the dismissal of a deputy county constable who, after hearing of an assassination attempt on President Reagan, said to a fellow employee in the constable's office, "Shoot, if they go for him again, I hope they get him." Another employee overheard the remark and reported it to Constable Rankin. Rankin discussed the matter with Ms. McPherson and then fired her. In turn, she sued for reinstatement, back pay, costs, fees, and other equitable relief.

In a somewhat surprising 5 to 4 decision, a majority of the Supreme Court held that McPherson's dismissal was unconstitutional in violation of her rights to freedom of speech. In so doing, the majority set forth the general constitutional framework for determining whether public employees' nonpartisan remarks are constitutionally protected. The Court built upon earlier cases, *Pickering* v. *Board of Education* (1968) and *Connick* v. *Meyers* (1983), in noting that the key consideration is to strike a balance between the interests of the governmental employer in promoting efficiency and those of the employee as a citizen commenting on matters of public concern. Consequently, the threshold question is whether an employee's remarks can be considered to address a matter of public concern. This is an important element in the public service model because it is assumed that public employees often have information about public policies and the operation of the government that can help to inform the electorate. If remarks are not of public concern, the public should have little interest in them.

If an employee's speech is on a matter of public concern, then "in performing the balancing, the statement will not be considered in a vacuum; the manner, time, and place of the employee's expression are relevant, as is the context in which the dispute arose." Among the factors of special pertinence are "whether the statement impairs discipline by superiors or harmony among co-workers, has a detrimental impact on close working relationships for which personal loyalty and confidence are necessary, or impedes the performance of the speaker's duties or interferes with the regular operation of the enterprise."

In applying this framework specifically to McPherson's comment, the Court found that her remark was of public concern because it was part of a larger conversation regarding Reagan's policies. It was also constitutionally protected since "[t]he burden of caution employees bear with respect to the words they speak will vary with the extent of authority and public accountability the employee's role entails. Where, as here, an employee serves no confidential, policymaking, or public contact role, the danger to the agency's successful function from that employee's private speech is minimal." Consequently, "at some point," for an employee such as McPherson, such statements "are so removed from the effective function of the public employer" that they cannot constitutionally be the basis for dismissal.

The Rankin approach affords considerable protection to public employees' right to freedom of nonpartisan expression. As with many aspects of constitutional law, however, it can require public personnelists and employees to exercise subtle judgment. First, how can one always be sure whether a remark such as McPherson's is on a matter of public concern? The dissenting justices offered little encouragement here because, unlike the majority, they concluded that the remark did *not* meet the threshold test of being on a matter of public concern. Second, if one concludes that a remark does meet the threshold test, it is still necessary to strike the correct balance. Here again, the dissenting four justices disagreed with the majority five. Clearly the most tenable approach for public personnelists is to employ the Court's general framework and follow the constitutional law closely in this area. As the federal district courts apply the Supreme

Personnel Managers Beware!

The material in this chapter is hardly academic. A local governmental public personnel manager who violates the federal constitutional or statutory rights of employees or applicants may be held personally liable for monetary damages awarded as a result of a civil suit against him or her. Several U.S. Supreme Court decisions eroded the traditional immunity of public administrators from such liability. In general, the state and local personnel administrator would not be immune from suit if his or her conduct violated ''clearly established statutory or constitutional rights of which a reasonable person would have known.'' Monetary damages assessed against such a personnelist may be intended to compensate the individual illegally or unconstitutionally treated, and in some cases they may be punitive as well. In the latter instance damages would go beyond making the wronged individual ''whole''; they would be intended to punish the personnelist and serve as a deterrent against breaches of individual rights in the future. Municipalities can also be sued if their personnel policies violate federally protected statutory or constitutional rights. They are liable if such violations actually occurred regardless of what the city should ''know'' about the status of such rights. Punitive damages cannot be awarded against municipalities in cases of this type.

When dealing with current employees, federal personnelists appear to be exempt from such liabilities because Congress provided an alternative remedy by creating an elaborate adverse action appeals system. States are not subject to suits of this kind in federal court. Public personnelists at all levels of government who exercise adjudicatory roles are absolutely immune from such suits. A sticky issue for state and local personnelists is figuring out what they *reasonably* should know about individuals' rights, with the federal courts determining what's reasonable. A good place to start is by considering the constitutional values inherent in the cases and approaches discussed in this chapter.

For further information, see Rosenbloom, David H. and Rosemary O'Leary. *Public Administration and Law*, 2nd ed. New York: Marcel Dekker, 1997; and Rosenbloom, David H. and James D. Carroll. *Toward Constitutional Competence*. Englewood Cliffs, N.J.: Prentice-Hall, 1997.

Court's approach to differing situations, the extent of public employees' rights to freedom on nonpartisan expression will be delineated further.

In the meantime, it can be reported that a public employee's remarks on a matter of public concern made in a private conversation with a supervisor are subject to the kind of balancing considerations articulated in the *Rankin* case, but that according to the *Rankin* majority, "a purely private statement on a matter of public concern will rarely, if ever, justify discharge of a public employee." Public employees' constitutional rights to freedom of expression on matters of public concern have been held to encompass private communication with a supervisor, the filing of lawsuits, and "symbolic speech"—specifically, police officers removing the American flag from their uniforms to protest racial discrimination in the police force. These protections apply not only to personnel actions involving dismissal, but also to refusals to hire, demotions, transfers, refusals to promote, letters of reprimand, and reprisals in the form of reductions in force. They apply to probationary as well as to permanent employees. Despite the breadth of these protections, prepublication clearance agreements in the area of national security are currently considered valid and can create an obstacle to informing the electorate about the performance of agencies such as the CIA.

Finally, it should be mentioned that when there is a dispute as to what the employee may actually have said, the public manager must take reasonable steps to ascertain when the remarks were. This does not require elaborate procedures, only reasonable ones.

Political Neutrality

Political activity by public employees has presented a persistent concern in the United States. The notion of political neutrality was first introduced by President Jefferson when he issued a circular declaring that the federal employee was expected not to attempt to influence the votes of others or to take part in electioneering, "that being deemed inconsistent with the spirit of the Constitution and his duties to it." It was not until the introduction of civil service reform in the 1880s, however, that restrictions on the political activities of public employees became common and effective. The undesirable aspects of a partisan and politically active public service were made evident by the spoils system. Public employees, either through their own volition or as a result of coercion, were deeply engaged in partisan politics. Sometimes, although drawing their salaries from the public treasury, they performed no public functions at all, only partisan ones. Administration became partisan, employees were forced to vote for the party in office, their salaries were "taxed" (assessed) by the parties, and the corruption and personnel turnover associated with partisanship became serious problems.

Depoliticization of the public service was crucial to the objectives of civil service reform, and the spoils system gave the reformers plenty of arguments in favor of it. Regulations intended to assure the partisan neutrality of the federal service were issued shortly after the enactment of the Civil Service Act of 1883. It was not until 1907, however, that political neutrality became an important feature of the federal service. In that year President Theodore Roosevelt changed the civil service rules to forbid employees in the competitive service from taking an active part in political management or in political campaigns. The rule explicitly allowed such employees to express privately their opinions on all political subjects. The Civil Service Commission (CSC) was charged with enforcing this provision, but by the commission's own admission, it was impossible to provide a complete list of the activities in which an employee could not engage. Consequently, decisions have been largely made on a case-by-case basis, and by 1940 a kind of case law had developed in over 3,000 rulings.

In 1939 matters were complicated by the passage of the first Hatch act. It extended the coverage of political activity restrictions to almost all federal employees, whether in the competitive service or not. The impetus for this legislation came primarily from a decrease in the proportion of federal employees who were in the competitive service. This was a direct result of the creation of several New Deal agencies that were placed outside the merit system. Senator Hatch, a Democrat from New Mexico, had worked for several years to have legislation enacted that would prevent federal employees from being active in political conventions. He feared that their involvement and direction by politicians could lead to the development of a giant national political machine.

From the perspective of public personnel management, the Hatch act created some confusion. It allowed federal employees to express their views freely on all political subjects rather than only in private. It also, however, proclaimed that the act was intended to prohibit the same activities that the CSC considered illegitimate under the 1907 regulations, which allowed only private expression. The second Hatch act (1940) extended these regulations to positions in state employment having federal financing and allowed public employees to express their opinions on ''candidates'' as well as political subjects, but not as part of a political campaign.

The constitutionality of these regulations was first upheld by the Supreme Court in *United Public Workers* v. *Mitchell* (1947). The court was divided 4 to 3. The majority adopted the private sector model of the employment relationship. It held that the ordinary constitutional rights of federal employees could be abridged by Congress in the interest of increasing or maintaining the efficiency of the federal service. The minority, on the other hand, could find nothing special about public employees that justified placing such limitations upon them. The Supreme Court reaffirmed its decision in *Mitchell in Civil Service Commission* v. *National Association of Letter Carriers* (1973). The Court reasoned that despite some ambiguities, an ordinary person using ordinary common sense could ascertain and comply with the regulations involved. It also argued that its decision did nothing more than to confirm the judgment of history that political neutrality was a desirable or even essential feature of public employment in the United States.

The Supreme Court's decision, of course, does nothing to prevent Congress from modifying or abandoning the restrictions on political activity. After losing in court, public employee unions and other opponents of political neutrality turned their attention increasingly in the legislative direction. It took two decades, but in 1993 the first Hatch Act was reformed to allow most federal employees to engage in a wide variety of campaign activities, including distributing literature, making phone calls, stuffing envelopes, giving speeches, and holding offices in political parties. Soliciting funds is still strictly regulated. The reforms did not extend to the Senior Executive Service, administrative law judges, several law enforcement positions, and agencies with defense, intelligence, or other missions that could be compromised by overt partisan displays, such as the MSPB and the Federal Election Commission.

Several state and local governments use political neutrality regulations in one form or another. Under the Supreme Court's decisions in the *National Association of Letter Carriers* case, they are highly likely to be constitutional unless they are very poorly drafted or arbitrary in their application.

Freedom of Association

The public employee's freedom of association was broadly guaranteed for the first time by the Supreme Court in *Shelton* v. *Tucker* (1960). Subsequent cases have upheld the public employee's right to join a labor union and even to have membership in subversive organizations or organizations with illegal ends as long as they do not personally support or participate in such activities. In the 1970s, however, the thorny problem of a public employee's right *not* to joint organizations came to the fore.

As we saw in the prologue, in *Elrod* v. *Burns* five Supreme Court justices agreed that rank-and-file public employees could not be compelled to join or support political parties on pain of dismissal. In *Abood* v. *Detroit Board of Education* (1977), the Court was confronted with an "agency shop" arrangement "whereby every employee represented by a union—even though not a union member—must pay to the union, as a condition of employment, a service fee equal in amount to union dues." The Court reasoned that such arrangements are common in private employment and can be considered a fundamental aspect of collective bargaining. Although when applied in the public sector it interferes with the civil servant's freedom of association, "such interference as exists is constitutionally justified by the legislative assessment of the important contribution of the union shop to the system of labor relations."

Agency shop arrangements are coercive, but they are a price often paid in the hope of establishing stable labor relations. While the Court was willing to accept this, it opposed the practice of forcing employees to pay for the union's spending of funds "for the expression of political views, on behalf of political candidates, or towards the advancement of other ideological causes not germane to its duties as collective bargaining representative." In other words, public employees can be compelled to pay for a union's collective bargaining activities, but not its general political and social endeavors. This right was strengthened substantially by the Supreme Court's holding in *Chicago Teachers Union* v. *Hudson* (1986), that "the constitutional requirements for the Union's collection of agency fees include an adequate explanation of the basis for the fee, a reasonably prompt opportunity to challenge the amount of the fee before an impartial decisionmaker, and an escrow for the amounts reasonably in dispute while such challenges are pending." Both the *Abood* and *Chicago Teachers Union* decisions fit the public service model in that they seek to assure that public employees will not be coerced to join and unreasonably support unions, but rather will remain free to identify primarily with their governmental employer if they so choose.

Liberty

As noted earlier, over the years there has been a tendency for governments to place a variety of restrictions upon the personal liberty of their employees. Since the 1970s, the Supreme Court handed down several important decisions in this area.

In *Cleveland Board of Education* v. *LaFleur* and *Cohen* v. *Chesterfield County School Board*, argued and decided together in 1974, the Court addressed the issue of mandatory pregnancy leaves. The policies being challenged were particularly arbitrary and harsh by requiring leaves to commence early in the term of a pregnancy while at the same time serving no rational purpose. Indeed, Justice Powell expressed the opinion that the policies were aimed at preventing schoolchildren from gazing upon pregnant teachers. Teachers were also banned from returning to their jobs until three months after the birth of their children. The Court found such policies to be unconstitutional. It did so, however, not on the basis of a violation of equal protection of the laws, but rather on the grounds that "by acting to penalize the pregnant teacher for deciding to bear a child, overly restrictive maternity leave regulations can constitute a heavy burden on the exercise of . . . protected freedoms." The Court held that with the exception of a regulation forcing the employee to go on leave a few weeks prior to the expected date of the birth of her child, regulations based on elapsed time rather than on the individual's capability to continue at her job were constitutionally unacceptable.

The constitutionality of grooming regulations for male police officers was at issue in *Kelley* v. *Johnson* (1976). The regulations included such requirements as "sideburns will not extend below the lowest part of the exterior ear opening, will be of even width (not flared), and will end with a clean-shaven horizontal line." Although a lower court reasoned that "choice of personal appearance is an ingredient of an individual's personal liberty," the Supreme Court found no constitutional infirmity in the regulations. In fact, it placed the burden of proof on the employees, challenging them to "demonstrate that there is no rational connection between the regulation . . . and the promotion of safety of persons and property." The Court went on to reason that since such regulations make police more identifiable and may contribute to an esprit de corps, they cannot be considered irrational. Such logic, of course, is peculiar to say the least. It's difficult to imagine how sideburns and the like could possibly obscure the uniforms and badges police wear to facilitate identification; and since it was the president of the local Patrolmen's Benevolent Association who, in his official capacity, was challenging the regulation, it is difficult to imagine how it could have enhanced morale. What explains the Court's decision, then, is primarily its desire

---

Foley v. *Connelie* 435 U.S. 291 (1978)

Facts—The plaintiffs, in a class action, charged that a State statute which limited the appointment of state troopers to applicants who are U.S. citizens violated the Equal Protection Clause of the 14th amendment. A three judge District Court held that the statute was constitutional.

Issue—Can a State constitutionally limit its State Troopers to citizens?

Discussion—The Supreme Court held that citizenship may be a relevant qualification for fulfilling important nonelective positions held by officials who participate directly in the formulation, execution, or review of broad public policy. The Court held that a State need only show some rational relationship between the interest sought to be protected and the limiting classification. Inasmuch as police officers are clothed with authority to exercise an almost infinite variety of discretionary powers which can seriously affect individuals, citizenship bears a rational relationship to the demands of the particular position, and States may limit the performance of such responsibility to citizens.

Source: U.S. Office of Personnel Management. *Equal Employment Opportunity Court Cases*. (Washington, D.C.: U.S. Government Printing Office, September 1979) p. 37.

to avoid public personnel management issues of limited importance that can be dealt with in other forums, including lobbying and collective bargaining.

In a more or less related fashion, in *McCarthy* v. *Philadelphia Civil Service Commission* (1976), the Supreme Court upheld the constitutionality of residency requirements for municipal employees in the face of a challenge to them on the grounds that they unconstitutionally abridge the individual's liberty. In the Court's view, the case, which involved a firefighter, established a "bona fide continuing residence requirement" of constitutional acceptability. It did not provide a comprehensive explanation of this position, but residency requirements are very common and seem not to pose constitutional issues.

A recurrent question involves the circumstances under which off-duty conduct can be the basis for unfavorable public personnel actions. For instance, when, if ever, can failure to pay debts or taxes, sexual solicitation, illegal possession of a controlled substance, or child abuse be a basis for dismissal, suspension, or other disciplinary action? Unfortunately for public personnel managers and employees, the law is unsettled. The MSPB relies on a "nexus" test that requires the agency to show a link between the conduct and the efficiency of the service. If the conduct involved is highly egregious, such as sex crimes, armed robbery, or murder, it permits the agency to make the assumption that such a nexus exists. The Circuit Court for the Federal Circuit, which hears appeals from the MSPB, has subscribed to this approach.

In applying its nexus test, the MSPB recommends managers consider the "Douglas factors" (after a 1981 case).

> The seriousness of the offense and the strength of the nexus
> The nature of the employee's job, including level, supervisory responsibility, public contacts, and prominence
> The employee's past performance
> The consistency of the proposed discipline with other cases
> The notoriety involved
> The likelihood of rehabilitation
> Mitigating circumstances

These factors are eminently sensible, but other judicial circuits and the Supreme Court have yet to weigh in clearly on the issue. In *United States* v. *National Treasury Employees Union* (1995), the Supreme Court placed a heavy nexus burden on federal ethics rules that sought to ban off-the-job constitutionally protected expressive activity. By contrast, though, the Supreme Court of Florida has upheld the legality, under its state constitution, of a local governmental rule that prohibits the public employment of persons who smoke, even if only in their own homes. The purpose of the regulation is to reduce the government's health insurance costs. Consequently, there is a nexus in the aggregate, but will refusing to employ people who live with smokers or overdo junk food be next? Clearly, the relationship between off-duty conduct and public personnel management will bear watching over the next several years.

Equal Protection

Following enactment of the Civil Rights Act of 1964, the constitutional law regarding public employees' equal protection rights became complex and uncertain. New questions arose. Do personnel exams that have a disparate negative impact on the employment interest of African Americans violate equal protection? Is affirmative action in the public sector constitutional? Under what circumstances?

These questions remain relevant, but over the past several decades the Supreme Court has worked out a much clearer framework for dealing with them. The key to equal protection analysis is whether or not a law, regulation, rule, policy, or government practice explicitly or implicitly classifies people. If there is no classification, there is no equal protection issue. The mere fact that law or public policy, such as taxation, has different impacts on different social groups does not trigger equal protection concerns. There must be some intent to treat categories of persons differently; that is, some discriminatory purpose must be present, though it need not be overt.

If there is a classification, then its basis becomes all-important. Classifications based on age, residency, wealth, and similar factors that are not immutable trigger a "rational basis" test. This typically puts the burden on the challenger to show that he or she is not rationally related to the achievement of a legitimate governmental purpose. The courts exercise ordinary scrutiny when reviewing such challenges and tend to be highly deferential toward the government's claims.

By contrast, classifications based on race, ethnicity, and, for nonfederal governments, alienage, face much tougher constitutional hurdles. They are considered "suspect" in the sense that they are deemed likely to violate equal protection. Because they are typically aimed at minorities who have difficulty protecting themselves through the nation's majoritarian political processes, the courts exercise "strict scrutiny" to ensure that they meet constitutional requirements. Those requirements are that they serve a compelling governmental interest and are "narrowly tailored." The burden of persuasion is on the government and the courts are not deferential.

At present, under the Supreme Court's decision in *United States* v. *Paradise* (1987), *City of Richmond* v. *Croson* (1989), and *Adarand Constructors* v. *Pena* (1995), it may be that suspect classifications in public personnel will serve a sufficiently compelling interest only as a remedy for past proven unconstitutional discrimination by the specific agency involved. Promoting workforce diversity, equal opportunity, or representativeness, at least as a general rule, are not currently compelling governmental interests.

Narrow tailoring includes the following five factors:

1. The efficacy of alternative remedies
2. The planned duration of the remedy
3. The relationship between the percentage of minority group members in the relevant population or workforce
4. The availability of waiver provisions (e.g., if the plan is waived because there are no qualified minority applicants)
5. The effect of the remedy upon ''innocent'' third parties

The last factor requires some explanation. In a philosophical sense American racism has been such a historical force that there may be no ''innocent'' third parties. The Supreme Court has something more tangible in mind, however. To date narrow tailoring is not violated by allocating training or promotions based on race (to overcome past discrimination by the organization involved). The innocent third parties merely lose some opportunity. By contrast, firing or laying off whites as a part of a remedy is considered too serious a disruption of their lives to clear the narrow tailoring threshold.

Gender-based classifications face an intermediate test. They must be substantially related to the achievement of important governmental objectives, and the government must provide an ''exceedingly persuasive justification'' for them. Ironically, under this test, it is easier to justify affirmative action for women than for African Americans. It also makes any public personnel management practice that promotes occupational segregation or pay differentials based on sex vulnerable to constitutional challenge.

Who Are the ''Innocent'' Individuals in Race and Gender Discrimination Cases?

Writing the dissenting opinion in *Martin* v. *Wilks* (1989), Justice Stevens said that the ''white respondents in this case are not responsible for [the] history of discrimination [in this country], but they are nevertheless beneficiaries of the discriminatory practices that the litigation was designed to correct. Any remedy that seeks to create employment conditions that would have [been] obtained if there had been no violations of law will necessarily have an adverse impact on whites, who must now share their job and promotion opportunities with blacks. Just as white employees in the past were innocent beneficiaries of illegal discriminatory practices, so is it inevitable that some of the same white employees will be innocent victims who must share some of the burdens resulting from the redress of the past wrongs.''

The Right to a Hearing

The Constitution protects citizens against governmental denial of ''life, liberty, or property, without due process of law.'' A technical definition of due process is problematic, but generally it is taken to mean ''fundamental procedural fairness.'' In public personnel management the issues raised by the due process clause are (1) under what conditions the Constitution requires that discipline be accompanied by hearings and (2) what protections must be afforded to public employees at such hearings.

In *Board of Regents* v. *Roth* (1972), the Supreme Court established the principle that although there is no general constitutional right to a hearing, one might be constitutionally required in individual instances. This would be true under any one of the following four conditions:

1. Where the removal or nonrenewal was in retaliation for the exercise of constitutional rights such as freedom of speech or association
2. Where the adverse action impaired the individual's reputation
3. Perhaps not fully distinguishable from the above, where a dismissal or nonrenewal placed stigma or other disability upon the employee that foreclosed his or her freedom to take advantage of other employment opportunities
4. Where one had a property right or interest in the position, as in the case of tenured or contracted public employees

Roth changed the playing field for public personnel management. Today an employee's constitutional right to procedural due process must be evaluated on a multidimensional basis. The basic structure of procedural due process requires balancing three factors: (1) consideration of the employee's interests, (2) the risk of an erroneous deprivation of those interests through the procedures used, and the probable value of other procedures in reducing that risk, and (3) the government's interests, including cost-efficiency. In weighing these factors, attention must be paid to such factors as the nature of the charge, the type and level of the position, the age of the individual, and the employee's prospects for employment elsewhere. Under these circumstances, it is evident that each case is largely a separate one. The best rule for public personnel management would be to (1) avoid giving reasons for adverse actions, insofar as possible, despite the obvious costs of such an approach in terms of employee morale and the possibilities for arbitrary decisions; (2) communicate the reason to the employee in strict privacy; or (3) hold a hearing in each and every case, whether required by statute and regardless of the expense involved.

The first two options were legitimized by the Supreme Court's decision in *Bishop* v. *Wood* (1976). It held that at least in the case of an employee *without* legal job protection, ''in the absence of any claim that the public employer was motivated by a desire to curtail or penalize the exercise of an employee's constitutionally protected rights, we must presume that official action was regular and, if erroneous, can best be corrected in other ways. The Due Process Clause . . . is not a guarantee against incorrect or ill-advised personnel decisions.'' Furthermore, in *Codd* v. *Velger* (1977), the Supreme Court held that hearings need not be held in any event if the employee is not challenging ''the substantial truth of the material'' upon which a dismissal or other adverse action is based. Whatever the merits of this as constitutional law, its desirability as public personnel policy is questionable and consequently public personnel managers may opt to hold hearings even where they are not constitutionally required.

In *Cleveland Board of Education* v. *Loudermill* (1985), the Supreme Court *required* the third approach, that of holding a hearing for dismissals whenever the public employee has a property interest in his job or her job. The property interest can be conferred by a statute or regulation prohibiting dismissal except for ''cause.'' In the Court's words, ''The essential requirements of due process . . . are notice and an opportunity to respond. The opportunity to present reasons, either in person or in writing, why proposed action should not be taken is a fundamental due process requirement. . . . The tenured public employee is entitled to oral or written notice of the charges against him, an explanation of the employer's evidence, and an opportunity to present his side of the story.'' In addition, such an employee will generally be entitled to a more elaborate posttermination hearing.

The procedural due process balance may tip against the employee on the issue of whether or not hearings must be held prior to suspensions, however. In *Gilbert* v. *Homar* (1997), the Supreme Court reasoned that the government's interest outweighed the employee's, at least in the case of a law enforcement officer charged with a felony. The Court distinguished suspensions from dismissals on the basis that: ''So long as a suspended employee receives a sufficiently prompt post-suspension hearing, the lost income is relatively insubstantial, and fringe benefits such as health and life insurance are often not affected at all.'' It also noted that since the employee had been arrested and charged with illegal drug possession there were reasonable grounds for the suspension. Aside from the specific legal holding, the decision illustrates that the law is still developing a quarter century after the *Roth* case.

Sometimes a public employee will be dismissed or disciplined for a number of reasons, only some of which are constitutionally impermissible. For instance, an employee whose performance is poor enough to warrant dismissal may make some derogatory public comments about the agency for which he or she works. The comments may prompt dismissal proceedings, but they may also be constitutionally protected. Under the prevailing case, *Mt. Healthy City School District Board of Education* v. *Doyle* (1977), in such circumstances the governmental employer would have to show ''by a preponderance of the evidence that it would have reached the same decision . . . even in the absence of the protected conduct.'' This rule fits the public service model well; on the one hand, public employees cannot immunize themselves from legitimate adverse actions by exercising constitutionally protected rights; while on the other, agencies must meet a heavy burden of persuasion when they take an action against employees that might be in retaliation for the exercise of such rights. Under the Supreme Court's ruling in *LaChance* v *Erickson* (1998), however, employees can be disciplined for lying to agencies about conduct under investigation.

Fourth Amendment Privacy

The constitutional privacy rights of public employees currently constitute an area of considerable interest. The Fourth and Fourteenth Amendments protect individuals against *unreasonable* governmental searches and seizures. In the course of a normal day's work, a supervisor might enter an employee's workspace to retrieve a file, manual, or similar item. The supervisor might take the item off the top of the employee's desk, perhaps from a desk drawer, or even from an open briefcase, but a supervisor might also look through an employee's desk, filing cabinet, or briefcase in search of evidence of poor performance, illegal activity, or controlled substances. How should the constitutional right to privacy be framed in the context of public employment? Here, too, the public service model provides for a balancing among the interests of the employee, the employer, and the public.

A divided Supreme Court wrestled with establishing such a balance in *O'Connor* v. *Ortega* (1987). The case involved the search of a doctor's office at a state hospital and the seizure of its contents, which included such personal items as a Valentine's card, a photograph, and a book of poetry sent to him by a former resident physician. Although all the members of the Supreme Court agreed that public employees such as Dr. Ortega have rights under the Fourth Amendment that can restrain administrative searches in the workplace, they disagreed on the scope of these rights. The plurality opinion written by Justice O'Connor reasoned that "individuals do not lose Fourth Amendment rights merely because they work for the government instead of a private employer," but the legitimacy of administrative searches depended on two factors. First is the threshold issue of whether or not the employee has a reasonable expectation of privacy in the circumstances involved. The issue of such an expectation, in turn, breaks down into two elements: (1) if the employee actually had an expectation of privacy, and (2) it was one that society was prepared to accept as reasonable. In O'Connor's view, "given the great variety of work environments in the public sector, the question of whether an employee has a reasonable expectation of privacy must be addressed on a case-by-case basis." Again, until the case law develops further, many personnelists will face a judgment call when trying to determine whether or not an employee has such an expectation.

Second, according to the plurality, even if the employee did have such an expectation, an administrative search would be constitutionally permissible if the government could show that "both the inception and the scope of the intrusion . . . [were] reasonable." Justice O'Connor argued that a reasonableness test was more appropriate than a requirement that the government have a warrant or probable cause.

Justice Blackmun dissented in an opinion joined by Justices Brennan, Marshall, and Stevens. They agreed that the further "development of a jurisprudence in this area might well require a case-by-case approach." The dissenters argued, however, that the plurality was far too quick to substitute a reasonableness standard for that of warrants or probable cause. Justice Scalia, by contrast, concurred, but agonized little over what standard should be employed: "searches to retrieve work-related materials or to investigate violations of workplace rules—searches of the sort that are regarded as reasonable and normal in the private-employer context—do not violate the Fourth Amendment."

Although the *O'Connor* case places a framework on thinking about public employee's constitutional rights to privacy in the workplace, it is neither definitive nor comprehensive. The courts have more recently been laboring over perhaps the major privacy issues in the public sector today—mandatory testing of public employees for drug use and AIDS.

The Supreme Court has not settled the question of testing public employee for the AIDS virus. The public service model would point to the same kind of balancing that takes place for drug testing: the employee's interests, the government's interests, and the public interest. The balance will vary with the circumstances. For instance, in a leading lower court case, *Glover v. Eastern Nebraska Community Office of Retardation* (1989), a state agency providing services to mentally retarded persons required an employee who has direct contact with agency clients to undergo testing for AIDS and hepatitis B viruses. The agency justified such testing on the grounds that is sought to protect the safety of the developmentally disabled persons it served as well as all employees of the agency.

The U.S. Court of Appeals for the Eighth Circuit ruled that mandatory testing for AIDS and hepatitis B violated the employees' Fourth Amendment rights against unreasonable searches and seizures, because the agency's interest in protecting the safety of its clients did not outweigh the privacy rights of its employees. The court said that the agency's "articulated interest in requiring testing does not constitutionally justify requiring employees to submit to a test for the purpose of protecting the clients from an infected employee."

Also important to the court in *Glover* was the potential for disease transmission. Here, the court said that "the risk of transmission of the AIDS virus from staff to client, assuming a staff member is infected with [the AIDS virus] . . . is extremely low, approaching zero. The medical evidence is undisputed that the disease is not contracted by casual contact. The risk of transmission of the disease to clients as a result of a client biting or scratching a staff member, and potentially drawing blood, is extraordinarily low, also approaching zero.''

Finally, the courts are more lenient with pre-employment drug and AIDS testing, as well as other routine medical screening, providing that the procedures involved in the collection of urine or blood samples are not overly obtrusive. In *Fowler* v. *New York City Department of Sanitation* (1989), the federal district court reasoned that pre-employment physical examinations, including urinalysis, are ''simply too familiar a feature of the job market on all levels to permit anyone to claim an objectively based expectation of privacy in what such analysis might disclose.'' It is important to remember, though, that these cases address administrative searches and concerns, not law enforcement efforts to apprehend those engaged in criminal conduct. In the latter situation, warrants or probable cause are required, rather than reasonableness.

The Right to Disobey

Among the constitutional rights now held by public employees is a right to refuse to engage in an unconstitutional act. This nascent right grows out of the liability that public servants may face if they violate the constitutional rights of individuals upon whom they act in their official capacities, including their subordinates. In *Harley* v. *Schuylkill County* (1979), a federal district court confronted the situation of a prison guard who was dismissed because he refused to take an action that would have violated an inmate's Eighth Amendment rights, which prohibit cruel and unusual punishment. After noting that the guard ''would have been liable for a deprivation of [the inmate's] constitutional rights if he had proceeded to obey the order given to him,'' the judge reasoned that ''the *duty* to refrain from acting in a manner which would deprive another of constitutional rights is a duty created and imposed by the constitution itself. It is logical to believe that the concurrent right [to refuse to act unconstitutionally] is also one which is created and secured by the constitution. Therefore, we hold that the right to refuse to perform an unconstitutional act is a right 'secured by the Constitution.'''

It is unlikely that many public administrators will face situations in which asserting a constitutional right to disobey will be appropriate. Successfully refusing to disobey, however, may require that the employee (1) sincerely believe that the order is unconstitutional, and (2) be correct in claiming that the proposed action is, in fact, unconstitutional.

Privatization

Following Justice Powell in the *Elrod* case discussed in the prologue, it is not too much to say that public personnel management has now been thoroughly constitutionalized. In one way or another, constitutional law affects it from hiring

The Use of Polygraph Tests for Pre-Employment Screening

The U.S. District Court for the Southern District of Texas in *Woodland* v. *City of Houston* (1990) found unconstitutional a polygraph test that inquired about

1. The applicant's religion, religious practices, or lack of them.
2. The applicant's consensual sexual activity, except to the extent that the act was unlawful in the jurisdiction where it took place and involved a minor and occurred within three years of the screening.
3. Extramarital sex.
4. Crimes committed as a child, except to the extent they involved a felony or a physical injury or a sexual assault in the jurisdiction within which they occurred, or the applicant was tried and convicted for them as an adult.
5. The use of marijuana, except to the extent that it was used unlawfully by the applicant in the jurisdiction where it was used within the six months preceding the screening process. Illegal use of marijuana cannot be used to disqualify an applicant unless similar level offenses are similarly used as disqualifications (e.g., traffic, drinking or hunting violations).
6. Adult criminal behavior, except to the extent that the applicant committed a felony, a sexual assault, theft, a Class A misdemeanor, or caused serious injury.
7. Theft, unless it involved at least $25 and occurred within the 12 months before the screening process or there have been four thefts within the three years preceding the screening process.
8. Membership in organizations, except to the extent that the applicant is currently or, within the previous five years, has been an active member of an organization which advocates violent, unlawful acts.
9. Drug use, unless the questions are about the applicant's illegal use of uppers, downers, steroids, or cocaine in the last 12 months; or hallucinogens within five years; or heroin within 12 months and more than one use in five years.

to firing and in between. Constitutionalization sometimes raises costs and almost always reduces managerial flexibility. It is one of the reasons that governments often seek to have their work performed by private contractors. In the 1990s, however, the Supreme Court added a significant catch—the Constitution is relevant to privatization. Private parties now have constitutional rights in their contractual relations with government, government cannot avoid its constitutional obligations by contracting out, and if contractors become "state actors," they are more vulnerable to suits than are public employees. Although these developments are tangential to public personnel, they deserve brief review because they very well may affect contracting decisions in the future.

Essentially, the Supreme Court extended free speech rights similar to those enjoyed by public employees to private parties having contractual or other commercial dealings with governments. In *O'Hare Truck* v. *City of Northlake* (1996), the Court was clear that government cannot circumvent its Fist Amendment obligations by contracting out: "Recognizing the distinction [between public employees and persons under contract] in these circumstances would invite manipulation by government, which could avoid constitutional liability simply by attaching different labels to particular jobs." Like probationary public employees such as McPherson, who have no job protection, private parties retain substantive constitutional rights in their economic relationship with the government: "Government officials may indeed terminate at-will relationships, unmodified by any legal constraints, without case; but it does not follow that this discretion can be exercised to impose conditions on expressing, or not expressing, specific political views."

In *West* v. *Atkins* (1988) and *Lebron* v. *National Railroad Passenger Corporation* (1995), the Court made it abundantly clear that governments cannot shed their constitutional responsibilities to clients or customers by privatizing. In *West* the Court explained: "The fact that the State employed [Dr. Atkins] pursuant to a contractual arrangement that did not generate the same benefits or obligations applicable to other 'state employees' does not alter the analysis . . . Contracting out prison medical care does not relieve the State of its constitutional duty to provide medical treatment to those in its custody." In *Lebron* the Court admonished that government cannot circumvent the Constitution by corporatizing its operations: "It surely cannot be that government, state, or federal, is able to evade the most solemn obligations imposed in the Constitution by simply resorting to the corporate form." *Lebron* strongly suggests that constitutional law will not treat personnel management in government corporations or performance-based organizations (PBOs) much differently than in conventional government agencies.

When private parties become "state actors"—that is "governmental" actors—they are potentially liable for violations of individuals' constitutional rights. This typically occurs when the private party is engaged in a public function, such as criminal corrections, or is organizationally indistinct from a government agency. Public employees have "qualified immunity" in such suits. They cannot be sued unless they violate clearly established constitutional rights of which a reasonable person would have known. (Refer back to box.) In *Richardson v. McKnight* (1997), the Supreme Court refused to extend qualified immunity to private prison guards, and by implication to other private state actors as well. Its decision, based on the absence of any common law tradition of immunity for private parties in these circumstances, makes it easier to sue private guards than public ones. It is predicted to make privatization more expensive for both the government and the contractor.

In sum, if the Court continues on its current track, there will be more blurring of the public from a constitutional point of view. The putative advantages of contracting out will fade, and government may be more apt to rely on its own employees to perform its functions.

CONCLUSION: KNOW YOUR LAW

Public personnel management has a highly developed legal framework. It is comprehensively regulated by statute and by constitutional law. It is a given that public managers in personnel and other areas are obliged to comply with legal requirements. This requires keeping abreast of new legal developments, including constitutional law decisions. Agency counsel or other legal specialists can provide an invaluable service by alerting public personnelists and other public managers to changing statutory requirements and court decisions.

It is also a given, as Ban found in *How Do Public Managers Manage?*, that compliance may at times be at odds with mission. Public management is about serving customers and performing functions cost-effectively—no matter, law is part of the job. As Ban emphasizes, it is not part of the job that can be left to lawyers. Public managers will manage better when they personally know and understand the legal frameworks in which they operate. They need to internalize law and blend it into their administrative decisions and actions.

This chapter provides a start. The overview of personnel's legal framework it presents should be applied to much of the material in the chapters that follow. Although some of these chapters emphasize management and other concerns, the legal framework is related to virtually everything public personnelists do. We will elaborate on the framework itself in other chapters throughout the text and especially in Parts III and IV, which deal with EEO, employee relations, and labor–management relations.

BIBLIOGRAPHY

Ban, Carolyn. *How Do Public Managers Manage?* San Francisco: Jossey-Bass, 1995.
"Developments in the Law—Public Employment," *Harvard Law Review*, vol. 97 (May 1984), pp. 1611–1800.

Riccucci, Norma M. "Drug Testing in the Public Sector: A Legal Analysis," *The American Review of Public Administration* (June 1990).

Roberts, Robert N. and Marion T. Doss. "The Constitutional Privacy Rights of Public Employees," *International Journal of Public Administration*, vol. 14 (May 1991).

Rosenbloom, David H. *Federal Service and the Constitution.* Ithaca, N.Y.: Cornell University Press, 1971.

Rosenbloom, David H. and James D. Carroll. "Public Personnel Administration and the Law," in Jack Rabin, Thomas Vocino, W. B. Hildreth, and Gerald Miller (eds.), *Handbook of Public Personnel Administration.* New York: Marcel Dekker, 1994.

Thompson, Frank J., Norma M. Riccucci, and Carolyn Ban. "Biological Testing and Personnel Policy: Drugs and the Federal Workplace," in Carolyn Ban and Norma M. Riccucci (eds.), *Public Personnel Management: Current Concerns, Future Challenges.* White Plains, N.Y.: Longman Press, 1991.

Thompson, Frank J. "Drug Testing in the Federal Workplace: An Instrumental and Symbolic Assessment," *Public Administration Review*, vol. 51 (November/December 1991).

CASES

Abood v. *Detroit Board of Education*, 430 U.S. 209 (1977).

Adarand Constructors v. *Pena* 115 S. Ct. 2097 (1995).

AFSCME v. *Woodward*, 406 F.2d. 137 (1969).

Bishop v. *Wood*, 426 U.S. 341 (1976).

Board of Regents v. *Roth*, 408 U.S. 564 (1972).

Branti v. *Finkel*, 445 U.S. 506 (1980).

Chicago Teachers Union v. *Hudson*, 475 U.S. 292 (1986).

City of Richmond v. *Croson*, 478 U.S. 1016 (1989).

Civil Service Commission v. *NALC*, 413 U.S. 548 (1973).

Cleveland Board of Education v. *La Fleur*, 414 U.S. 632 (1974).

Cleveland Board of Education v. *Loudermill*, 470 U.S. 532 (1985).

Codd v. *Velger*, 429 U.S. 624 (1977).

Cohen v. *Chesterfield County School Board*, 414 U.S. 632 (1974).

Connick v. *Meyers*, 461 U.S. 138 (1983).

Elrod v. *Burns*, 427 U.S. 347 (1976).

Fowler v. *New York City Department of Sanitation*, 704 F. Supp. 1264 (1989).

Fraternal Order of Police v. *City of Philadelphia*, 812 F.2d. 105 (1987).

Gilbert v. *Homer*, No. 96-651 (1997).

Glover v. *Eastern Nebraska Community Office of Retardation*, 867 F. 2d. 461 (8th Cir. 1989), *cert. denied*, 110 S.Ct. 321 (1989).

Harley v. *Schuylkill County*, 476 F. Supp. 191 (1979).

Kelley v. *Johnson*, 425 U.S. 238 (1976).

LaChance v. *Erickson*, No. 96-1395 (1998).

Lebron v. *National Railroad Passenger Corporation*, 115 S. Ct. 961 (1995).

McAuliffe v. *New Bedford*, 155 Mass. 216 (1982).

McCarthy v. *Philadelphia CSC*, 424 U.S. 645 (1976).

Mt. Healthy City School District Bd. of Education v. *Doyle*, 429 U.S. 274 (1977).

National Treasury Employees Union v. *Von Raab*, 489 U.S. 656 (1989).

O'Connor v. *Ortega*, 480 U.S. 709 (1987).

O'Hare Truck v. *City of Northlake*, 116 S. Ct. 2353 (1996).

Personnel Administrator v. *Feeney*, 422 U.S. 256 (1979).

Pickering v. *Board of Education*, 391 U.S. 563 (1968).

Rankin v. *McPherson*, 483 U.S. 378(1987).

Richardson v. *McKnight*, 138 L. Ed. 2d 540 (1997).

Rutan v. *Republican Party of Illinois*, 497 U.S. 62 (1990).

Shelton v. *Tucker*, 364 U.S. 479 (1960).

Snepp v. *U.S.*, 444 U.S. 507 (1980).

Sugarman v. *Dougall*, 413 U.S. 634 (1973).

Thorne v. *City of El Segundo*, 726 F. 2d. 459 (1983).

United Public Workers v. *Mitchell*, 330 U.S. 75 (1947).

United States v. *National Treasury Employees Union*, 130 L.Ed. 2d 964 (1995).

United States v. *Paradise*, 480 U.S. 149 (1987).

Waters v. *Churchill*, 511 U.S. 661 (1994).

Washington v. *Davis*, 426 U.S. 229 (1976).

West v. *Atkins*, 487 U.S. 42 (1988).

Wygant v. *Jackson Bd. of Education*, 476 U.S. 267 (1986).

4

Human Resources Planning

PROLOGUE: WHERE HAVE ALL THE FIREFIGHTERS GONE?

Few responsibilities of government are as compelling as that of the federal land management agencies and their protection of the millions of acres of forests, grasslands, and other natural habitats in the United States. The most dramatic threat to these acres and the communities that live around such federal lands are wildfires. In a typical fire year, somewhere between 75,000 to 100,000 fires will consume over 2 million acres of land. Typically, the vast majority (over 90%) of these fires are small, consuming less than 10 acres, and successfully contained by local forces within an area, but in a catastrophic fire those few fires that escape can be devastating. In 1994, one of the worst fire years on record, 34 lives were lost and nearly $1 billion was spent by large-scale interagency fire suppression efforts.

Deteriorating natural ecosystems and the potential impacts of global warming are only one dimension that has made fighting wildfire more complicated. Over the past five years, there has been a growing concern over what is commonly called the shrinking firefighter workforce. A 1999 General Accounting Office (GAO) report, *Federal Wildfire Activities*, cited as a significant problem a declining fire-fighting workforce because of attrition and competing work demands. It noted first that the fire-fighting workforce "is getting older and nearing retirement age which could result in a lack of qualified individuals to fill critical fire management positions.'' It also cited a number of problems that are decreasing the number of employees who ''become qualified to fight fire as a collateral duty.'' Factors such as other primary job duties, family and dual career issues, and low overtime pay rates were mentioned as lowering the rates of qualification and adversely affecting the willingness to serve.

The GAO was only reinforcing what previous reports in the Forest Service and the four primary Department of the Interior (DOI) agencies responsible for wildland fire management have been noting for some time about strategic planning for the fire-fighting workforce. A key contextual dimension to the problem has been the ongoing ''streamlining efforts'' (or downsizing) of the federal government. For example; the four DOI agencies who play a part in fire management experienced changes in full-time employees (FTE) numbers between 1993 and 1998 (Table 4.1).

The Forest Service itself, the largest employer of the five agencies primarily involved in fire, has dropped from a 1993 level of just over 35,000 permanent employees to just under 29,000. The Forest Service also hires an additional 15,000 temporary employees as seasonal hires, and this number can vary from year to year. The problem is that even as the number of workers dedicated to fire fighting has remained stable or moderately increased because of the new emphasis on hazardous fuels reduction programs, any increase comes out of a larger overall decrease in the total workforce.

A National Fire and Aviation Management Workforce needs analysis report of July 1997 concluded that a ''lack of available and qualified fire personnel is critically hampering management of large fire situations and impeding progress in prescribed fire activities.'' This report echoes concerns raised among all the agencies involved in wildland fire fighting and reflects three major issues. The first is that a major portion of the current workforce is aging and will retire soon, under the provisions of the federal firefighter retirement system. (Federal firefighters, like some parts of the military, can take advantage of an earlier retirement eligibility age; i.e., 50.) There is also concern that some personnel will

TABLE 4.1

Full-time employees (FTE)	FY 1993	FY 1998	Change
Department of the Interior (total)	77,937	65,728	−11,178
Bureau of Land Management	11,287	9,892	−1,495
Fish & Wildlife Service	7,664	7,770	+6
Bureau of Indian Affairs	12,741	9,600	−3,141
National Park Service	19,574	19,421	−153

retire as soon as they are eligible, to take advantage of better work opportunities in terms of pay and benefits either for other partners or contractors.

A second issue is the length of the current training cycle. A recent study of federal wildland fire qualifications revealed the lengthy development process involving training and experience for just the 11 common firefighter positions (the four first line supervisory position titles, the four fire project specialist position titles, and the three fire program manager position titles). The GAO report estimated the combined training and experience cycle at 17 to 22 years in order to function successfully as a Type II incident commander and between 20 to 25 years for Type I levels. Of course these are positions at the apex of the firefighter force, but the point remains that the qualification cycle is so lengthy that it works against efforts to inspire the next generation of firefighters to begin development.

The third and last major issue is the point of availability of the general workforce—what is often called the militia—alluded to earlier. The Forest Service has stated a goal repeatedly since 1995 that 75% of its workforce should be certified or qualified to fight fires. This is actually tracked in each region of the country on a separate "red card" system that counts who is currently qualified and details their training and experience in fire. A recent count of the regions for the Forest Service shows the percentage well below 75% and declining. Of course even if this number were stable, it is not a measure of availability. The Forest Service does not require all of its employees to become qualified to fight fires; it only specifies that each employee should fulfill roles and responsibilities during fire emergencies. Studies done in several of the Forest Service regions and Department of the Interior agencies shows less willingness on the part of employees to take national fire assignments, to be away from their families and job responsibilities for more than 14 days, and to be able to take the time to take training and assume other fire roles because of increased workloads at their home base.

This is a new human resources (HR) planning environment for public managers. In this case, it cuts across agency lines, involves different kinds of workforce issues, and cannot be solved by simply hiring more people or contracting out. How do the five agencies plan for ensuring a firefighting workforce for the next five years that will be capable of handling fire operations and other emergency responses (i.e., preparing for immediate future) and build a new workforce concept that will be the foundation for the next generation (i.e., investing for the long-term future)? The issues are not trivial. Over 35% of the current qualified fire-fighting workforce will be eligible for retirement in the next five years. The training cycle for replacements is long and extensive, and there is a growing issue of decreasing numbers, availability, and interest in fire-fighting work. Finally, there is one additional complicating factor. New employees who come into the Forest Service or DOI agencies must be under the age of 35 to start in the fire qualification program. In 1998 and 1999, only 40% of the new hires coming into the Forest Service were under the age of 35, and less than 25% were under 30.

THE ENVIRONMENT FOR HUMAN RESOURCES PLANNING

All organizations face considerable problems regarding the use of their human resources. In public organizations, which are service- and information-oriented, employees tend to be the most significant resource. Personnel-related costs generally constitute between 50 and 70% or more of an operating budget, so the need for planning in this area is particularly acute. In the 1970s and 1980s the primary incentive for such planning was directly related to two factors: the amount of change or turnover in personnel and the levels of expense that personnel involve as a majority resource item. Governments at all levels closely tracked the numbers of accessions (i.e., new or renewed hiring of employees) and separations (i.e., the numbers of resigned, discharged, retired, or disabled employees who left). The latter separations became increasingly more important in the 1990s when governments confronted the economic recession of the early 1990s and the subsequent downsizing movement that engulfed first the private sector and then government in the 1990s.

When confronting poor economic and business conditions, the automatic response of any organization is to stop hiring and look for ways to accelerate attrition. Public sector organizations, given their long-standing commitment to sustaining a professional career service and the influence of their public sector unions, will by definition seek to manage unexpected short-term and even more predictable longer-term economic imbalances by shrinking the workforce through attrition. Of course the effectiveness of this strategy depends upon many factors—the turnover rate in the organization, the development time factor for replacement workers, and the level of change or continuity in the organization's mission and what work skills are needed to accomplish the mission. Each of these factors can be positive or negative, and each can produce very dynamic interactions in terms of solving problems or creating them.

In terms of turnover rates, most governments have relatively low attrition—or what is called voluntary separation rates—than the private sector. (See Table 4.2) Taking the federal government as a primary example, its total separation rate actually declined in the 1990s. Whereas in the mid-1980s it averaged under 20% annual total separation rates, that figure had decreased to just under 12% in 1998. This trend may seem rather remarkable, considering the overall decline in the number of federal civilian employees during the 1990s. On the plus side, governments can look at these lower attrition rates. (Many private sector corporations routinely experience 20 to 25% annual turnover rates and in some industries would proclaim that anything under 18% as very good.) On the negative side, if a government organization needed to make a major shift in mission or change

TABLE 4.2 Saratoga Institute's
1999 Study of Turnover by
Industry Sector

Retail	69%
Consumer products	33%
Banking	27%
Services	27%
Medical devices	22%
Telecommunications	21%
Manufacturing	20%
AVERAGE	20%
Hospitals/health care	19%
Metals/mining	16%
Semiconductors	15%
Insurance	15%
Pharmaceuticals	15%
Government	13%
Utilities	8%
Aerospace	7%

Source: *New York Times* (April 12,
2000).

in work roles or skill sets, this lower attrition rate is not going to make a fast solution possible.

The second factor, the development rate of new hires, impacts in other ways. Again using the federal government, its number of accessions and new hires has slowed dramatically from what was between 600,000 to 700,000 in the mid-1980s to under 300,000 in 1998. Since the federal government is shedding jobs and has reduced its workforce throughout the Clinton administration, this would seemingly be an example of managing a substantial workforce reduction through attrition. The complicating factor is that the jobs and the required job skills (i.e., the time to develop them) are not necessarily the same. Over the past 20 years there has been a major shift in the grade levels of federal jobs upwards. New hires are on average older and going into jobs of higher levels, which require more development time.

This leads directly into the third factor—changing organizational mission and workforce roles. Public organizations are not just facing turnover and replacement pressures, they must adjust for different roles and different occupations. A recent graph in a local northern California newspaper (Figure 4.1) depicts this in a different way. It shows growing federal and state of California jobs and declining occupations in the 1990s. Secretaries and clerk-typists are decreasing

Growing government jobs

The 10 fastest growing occupations in the federal and state governments, according to records for 1992 and 1997 maintained by the U.S. Office of Personnel Management

Federal jobs

Occupation	1992	1997	Increase
1. Transportation specialist	1,994	7,390	5,396
2. Medical officer	37,694	42,398	4,704
3. General inspection, investigation	5,618	9,766 ·	4,148
4. Social ansurance administration	22,881	26,483	3,602
5. General claims examining	759 ·	4,157	3,398
6. Correctional officer	9,225	12,601	3,376
7. Border patrol agent	4,026	6,819	2,793
8. Foreign affairs	1,140	3,874	2,734
9. Compliance inspection and support	4,298	6,974	2,676
10. General business and industry ˙	17,695	20,303	2,608

State of California jobs

Occupation	1992	1997	Increase
1. Border patrol agent	1,259	2,555	1,296
2.General education and training	132	1,194	1,062
3. General inspection, investigation & comp.	632	1,426	794
4. Compliance inspection and support	562	1,114	552
5. Transportation specialist	181	651	470
6. OFC automation clerical and assistance	1,365	1,796	431
7. Transportation clerk and assistant	195	536	341
8. General claims examining	35	319	284
9. General business and industry	1,303	1,534	231
10. Environmental engineering	483	708	225

FIGURE 4.1   Fastest growing and declining federal and state of California jobs.

dramatically, while a variety of new jobs from border patrol agents to inspection and other technology-related fields are increasing. Organizations have to examine carefully what kinds of skills they are going to need and what kinds of jobs they are going to create in order to employ these skills. Contracting is another major factor in this, as government organizations rethink what they're going to do and who they're going to hire and contract with to accomplish their work.

Organizations must still view their personnel resources as their most significant category of investment, requiring considerable effort, time, and cost to recruit, select, evaluate, train, and staff effectively. Generally, more highly trained and experienced employees will achieve greater levels of productivity, so the development of (meaning the investment of resources in) employees seems a rational long-range decision. The actual investment in terms of imparted skills and maturity of judgment remains inside the individual, however, who may or may not stay within the organization. The individual employee's attitude about the organization's investment or lack of investment in his or her development will naturally affect present levels of both productivity and commitment to the

Declining government jobs

The 10 most rapidly declining occupations in the federal and state governments, according to records for the federal payroll in 1992 and 1997 maintained by the U.S. Office of Personnel Management

Federal jobs

Occupation	1992	1997	Decrease
1. Secretary	100,432	65,443	-34,989
2. Clerk-typist	22,383	3,898	-18,485
3. Electronics technician	19,398	10,953	-8,445
4. Supply clerical and technician	25,028	17,223	-7,805
5. Materials handler	23,148	15,470	-7,678
6. Railroad retirement claims examiner	7,627	265	-7,362
7. Mail and file	21,594	14,650	-6,944
8. Engineering technician	25,257	18,437	-6,820
9. Miscellaneous clerk	79,562	73,262	-6,300
10. Electronics engineering	29,887	23,684	-6,203

State of California jobs

Occupation	1992	1997	Decrease
1. Secretary	7,603	4,400	-3,203
2. Clerk-typist	2,139	382	-1,757
3. Materials handler	3,415	2,088	-1,327
4. Electronics mechanic	2,335	1,055	-1,280
5. Forestry technician	5,106	3,873	-1,233
6. Electronics technician	3,314	2,117	-1,197
7. Quality assurance	2,334	1,139	-1,195
8. Engineering technician	3,323	2,156	-1,167
9. Electonics engineering	5,409	4,291	-1,118
10. Electrician	1,494	552	-942

SOURCE: Scripps Howard News Service

FIGURE 4.1 Continued

organization. As expensive as personnel is, the cost of turnover, replacement, and redevelopment adds on even more.

What does it cost to replace an employee? Of course, the answer varies with the organization. In his book *Costing Human Resources*, Wayne Cascio developed a now standard format complete with formulas to calculate the costs of turnover. (See Table 4.3.) Cascio calculated turnover costs at about 12 to 15% of the compensation levels being recruited against. Since there's little reason to doubt that the higher the salary level being recruited for the higher the proportionate cost of filling the vacancy, this cost formula is a rather disturbing validation of what personnel managers have known intuitively for years. It is expensive to replace personnel—and the expense is even greater if the wrong choice is made. That wrong choice can be made in two ways—hiring the wrong person for the job or hiring a person for a wrong job that your organization doesn't need or may have to eliminate in the future.

TABLE 4.3   Measuring the Costs of Personnel Replacement

Separation costs	Replacement costs	Training costs
1 Exit interview costs 2 Administrative costs to separate employee 3 Separation pay 4 Unemployment taxes (if applicable)	5 Advertising and recruiting communication costs 6 Pre-employment and ad- ministrative costs 7 Entrance interview costs 8 Staff and organizational meetings and reviews 9 Medical examinations, se- curity clearances, refer- ences file checks 10 Administrative costs and functions to place indi- vidual into employee status—payroll, fringe, and all insurance cov- erage	11 Informational and orienta- tion literature 12 Formal training and orien- tation costs 13 On-the-job instruction (breaking in) 14 Other job training pro- grams (technology, other job skills)

Source: Adapted in part from Cascio, Wayne F. *Costing Human Resources*. Boston: Kent, 1982.

Although the need for HR planning seems obvious, translating that need into a specific planning program is a more difficult matter. The same questions that plague planning in general must be addressed here. Who should do the planning for the organization—top management or lower operating levels? Should planning be long-range or short-range, formal or informal, proactive or reactive, "blue sky" or realistic? How often should plans be updated? What planning techniques should be used? How and by whom will the planning be evaluated?

Different answers to these questions do not mean that any one planning approach will be better than another. This depends upon the size, complexity, and needs of the organization and the amount of uncertainty involved. There is a difference in techniques between what might be termed strategic planning (or planning that *integrates* management strategies based on some anticipation of needs) and adaptive learning, however, (the formation of management strategies based on an *incremental* approach of observing and evaluating dissatisfaction with current performance). While both strategic planning and adaptive learning can lead to change, only a strategic planning approach can be categorized as a *planned change approach*. Effective HR planning as a strategic planning approach must involve a systematic process of analyzing external conditions and organizational needs *and* delineating management strategies and tactics to make responsive changes.

This is not an easy assignment. The arrival of a new century affords personnel managers a unique perspective to reflect on the increasing difficulty for HR planning, and unlike the assumption of the 1980s that all the challenges were on the demand side (new technology, new organizational arrangements), or of the 1990s that all the major challenges were on the supply side (shortage of highly trained workers and increasingly older workforce), personnel managers must balance both supply and demand in an environment in which the organization's mission and work processes are undergoing rapid change. How should governments respond to the demands of the new E-business/E-government environment? Indeed, this new century with its accelerating rates of change has even caused a revolution in thinking about planning. Managers are being urged to think more about strategies for the future in time frames of 12 to 15 months as opposed to traditional time spans of five to 10 years. In the dynamic and highly complex labor markets of the twenty-first century, in which public sector jurisdictions will be increasingly hard-pressed to compete, public sector organizations will have to take HR planning very seriously indeed.

HUMAN RESOURCES PLANNING IN AN ERA OF DOWNSIZING

Governments at all levels have faced budget constraints and fiscal shortages that have seemed at times to be quite unpredictable. In the 1980s, personnel offices added new scenarios (and vocabulary) to their HR planning efforts, such as "planning for retrenchment," "management through attrition," and "cutback management." Cutback management in the 1980s emphasized first stretching the organization's workforce by eliminating overtime, using hiring freezes, and leaving vacancies unfilled. If that proved inadequate to meet necessary budget reductions, the organization went to more drastic measures using furloughs, reductions in force, and other personnel budget-reduction techniques. By the mid-1990s, however, cutback management had been replaced by competitive government. Even though government executives and political leaders would talk about having to resort to the meat axe (i.e., cutting all agency budgets by a percentage across the board) or the necessity to "flatten bureaucracy" or "rightsize government," government saw diminution of the very work it was asked to do. While the mantra of reinvention (i.e., "works better, costs less") dominated the management rhetoric of the 1990s, government's workload increased.

Guidelines for Responsible Restructuring from the U.S. Department of Labor

Even though there is no one, [sic] right way to restructure, following the guidelines below has yielded good results for companies and their workforces.

1. Articulate a vision of what you want your organization to achieve.
2. Establish a corporate culture that views people as assets to be developed rather than as costs to be cut.
3. Be clear about your short- and long-range objectives; e.g., to cut costs (short-range) and to improve customer service and shareholder value through more effective use of assets (long-range).
4. Establish an alternative menu of options for reaching the short- and long-range objectives.
5. Get the people who will have to live with the changes involved in making them; provide opportunities for input at all levels.
6. Communicate, communicate, communicate! Share as much information as possible about prospective changes with those who will be affected by them.
7. Recognize that employees are unlikely to contribute creative, ingenious ways to cut costs if they think their own employment security will be jeopardized as a result.
8. If cutting costs by cutting people is inevitable, establish a set of priorities for doing so (e.g., outside contractors and temporaries are laid off first) and stick to it. Show by word and deed that full-time, value-adding employees will be the last to go.
9. If employees must be let go, provide as much advance notice as possible, treat them with dignity and respect, and provide assistance (financial, counseling) to help them find new jobs.
10. Consider retraining and redeploying surplus workers to promote their employment security and self-reliance and to protect your human resources investment.
11. Give surviving employees a reason to stay. Explain what new opportunities will be available to them.
12. View restructuring as part of a process of continual improvement—with subgoals and measurable check points over time—rather than as a one-time event.

What did all this mean? First of all, it would be unfair to either credit or blame the Clinton administration for having initiated a new round of reform that would lead to downsizing or competitive government. Many of the driving forces for organizational change had already been created in the states and cities. Reform mayors and governors across the country led new efforts to make their governments leaner, more decentralized, and by their definition, more innovative. Typical of the competitive government leaders were Stephen Goldsmith, the mayor of Indianapolis, who was quoted as saying, ''We have the most comprehensive competition and competitiveness effort of any major city or maybe any governmental entity on the United States. We are trying to create a marketplace for municipal services.'' Massachusetts governor William Weld noted that ''Entrepreneurial government is discovering what the private sector has known all along. When private vendors compete for the state's business, quality goes up and costs go down.''

Competitive government does not automatically mean downsizing or reducing the size of the workforce, nor does it mean outright privatization of a government service or program. The concept is designed to ensure that when government performs a service or produces a product that is not ''inherently governmental'' that there will be a competition between potential providers to determine who will produce that good or service. That potential provider list can include government personnel. At the federal level , there was a long and hard debate about what that definition means. The GAO defines ''inherently governmental'' as any activity ''so intimately related to the public interest that it must be done by federal employees. These functions include those activities that require either the exercise of discretion in applying government authority or the making of value judgements in making decisions for the government.''

For the federal government, competitive government is driven by, Office of Management and Budget (OMB) circular A-76, which requires government agencies to review their activities, define those that are commercial (i.e., not inherently government), and make provisions for competing those activities. Circular A-76 has driven much of the organizational and workforce restructuring that has come from the drawdown of the Defense Department in the 1990s, as the military closed bases around the world and converted much of its support structure to commercial contracts following the end of the cold war. Congress also passed the Federal Activities Inventory Reform Act (FAIR), which provides an annual list of all agency commercial activities and goes further by designating which full-time employee positions are performing potentially commercial activities. This could potentially have a major impact on the shape of the federal workforce. The 1999 inventory identified over 900,000 federal FTE (53% of the federal civilian workforce, excluding the Postal Service) as potentially commercial.

It is at the state and local level, however, that competitive government has perhaps had the most impact. Some cities and states have created competition councils to set up rules and processes for competing public versus private contractors for what were formerly exclusively government services. It will be interesting to see how public–private competition plays out in the next decade. In a revealing study of four major American cities and two countries, Lawrence Martin shows that anyone who assumed that the private sector would completely dominate public–private competition may want to rethink that notion (Table 4.4) shows the numbers of competitions from six entities. The percentage of competitions won by public employees indicates that except for Australia, public sector employees do quite well in the business end of competitive government.

The issue of downsizing remains. Some critics have claimed that reinvention and competitive government are just pseudonyms for downsizing. It certainly is true that downsizing makes headlines. Even the *New York Times*, normally not prone to trying to cash in on a "management fad gone bad," couldn't resist taking several special reports from 1996 and turning them into a best-selling "instant book" entitled *The Downsizing of America*. The back cover proclaimed that the "startling and depressing headlines" were on to something that since 1979 had led to "43 million jobs vanishing." While the *Times* admitted that many new jobs had been created, it warned that "increasingly the jobs that are disappearing are those of higher-paid, white collar workers, and many of the new jobs pay much less than those they replaced." The *Times* was not the only media source to trumpet the dangers of downsizing. Others had cover articles ranging from "Corporate Killers" to "Is Your Job Safe?"

In retrospect, most analysts now see that round of downsizing in the 1990s as not being nearly as bad as the headlines made it out to be. This statement doesn't mean that downsizing didn't have terrible effects on people in public and private organizations. What some have called management by amputation created extraordinary stress and negative effects on morale. Indeed, one study by the

TABLE 4.4 Public–Private Competitions

Government entity	Number of competitions	Percentage won by public employees
Charlotte, N.C.	34	70.5%
Indianapolis, Ind.	60	72%
Philadelphia, Pa.	32	12.5%
Phoenix, Ariz.	56	39.3%
United Kingdom	3500	75%
Australia	1515	1.5%

Source: Adopted from Martin, L. *Public-Private Competition.*
Review of Public Personnel Administration, (winter 1999).

American Management Association found the following among major American corporations that underwent downsizing between 1989 and 1994: operating profits increased in 50% and stayed constant in 30%, worker productivity increased in 35% and stayed constant in 35%, but employee morale declined in 86% of the firms undergoing downsizing.

The economic statistics during the 1980s and 1990s don't really support the political hysteria, however. Throughout the two decades, there was a moderate increase in the rate of job displacement, which closely followed the economic performance of the country as a whole. In the two recessions (1981–1983 and 1991 and 1993), the job displacement rate was 12.8% and 13.4%, respectively. During the 1983–1985 recovery and the 1993–1995 recovery, the job displacement rate was 10.4% and 11%, respectively. As for other claims about lower-paying jobs and replacement jobs, the numbers are also not as bad as claimed. In the 1981–1983 recession, 59% of displaced workers found another job, compared to 67% in the 1991–1993 recession. There was a rather constant average wage reduction of 14% during the recession periods. Of course in the current economic climate, with the lowest levels of unemployment in nearly 25 years, the demand for workers has drastically lowered wage reduction, and job replacements lags.

One other factor needs to be mentioned. What was new in the 1991–1993 recession was the effect on middle-aged, educated, white males. In contrast to the 1980 recessions, the job displacement rate on males aged 45 to 55 was 14% compared to 10% and 15% among males 55 to 65 compared to 11% in the 1980s. The 1990s downsizing impact was felt much more acutely by old technology workers, supervisors and middle managers, and administrative workers. Underneath all the job changes were major movements toward new technology platforms, more use of teams and elimination of supervisory positions, and simplification of administrative systems, many of them viewed as costly overhead functions (which in many cases they were).

A balanced assessment of downsizing requires that it be viewed in context. The 1990s were the transition period to what we now call "the new economy." This was a period of major restructuring led by new technologies, new concepts of work processes, and a new perspective on how knowledge workers were going to dominate this new economic landscape. When downsizing or whatever it was called was tied to a restructuring effort, it could lead to systematic, positive change. When it was simply tied to workforce reduction or work redesign efforts, it normally led to failure. In the private sector, this meant either repeating cycles of downsizing or being merged with another company and resulting in more job reductions. Kim Cameron, who has done the most seminal work on the positives and negatives of downsizing, uses an interesting continuum chart (see Table 4.5) to show the differences between ineffective and effective repositioning. His main point is simply that downsizing as headcount reduction creates a vicious cycle

Downsizing's Unintended Consequences (from the National Academy of Public Administration)

In many cases, changes in basic work processes did not occur when downsizing was taking place. This meant there were fewer workers to do the same amount of work to the same specifications. It is not surprising that the remaining workers were overworked and stressed. What is surprising is that their employers had no idea this would happen. A major reason for this inaccurate assessment is that many top managers are internally driven, self-motivated, and accustomed to change. Many of their subordinates are externally driven and find comfort in routine. As a result, managers often believed that if they dealt with the organizational issues of restructuring, employees would immediately adapt. This was not the case.

The inaccurate but prevailing attitude concerning employee reaction to downsizing was found in a review of more than 500 articles on the topic and interviews with twenty-five senior executives affected by downsizing conducted by Dr. Wayne Cascio of the University of Colorado. He found that management often regards employees as '' 'units of production,' costs to be cut, rather than as assets to be developed. This is a 'plug-in' mentality—that is, like a machine, plug it in when you need it, unplug it when it is no longer needed. Unlike machines, however, employees have values, aspirations, beliefs—and memories.'' This lack of understanding led many organizations to ignore or downplay the effects that downsizing would have on remaining employees.

Losses Due to "Management by Amputation"

A vital fact to consider when organizations contemplate downsizing is that they are more than buildings and equipment; organizations are living organisms. For every action there is an opposite and equal reaction. When organizations downsize, or ''amputate'' part of the workforce, this opposite reaction is a phenomenon called ''survivors' syndrome,'' a generic term for a set of attitudes, feelings, and perceptions occurring in employees who remain in an organization following downsizing.

> In his book *Healing the Wounds: Overcoming the Trauma of Layoffs and Revitalizing Downsized Organizations*, David Noer, Vice President for Training and Education for the Center for Creative Leadership, states that the most common symptoms of survivors' syndrome are anger, fear, insecurity, uncertainty, frustration, resentment, sadness, depression, guilt, unfairness, betrayal, and distrust. This cluster of symptoms results in reduced risk-taking, lowered productivity, unquenchable thirst for information, survivor blaming, and denial.

Managers often did not understand the overwhelming impact downsizing would have on employees, nor did they understand that its effects would be felt for years to come.

- A Wyatt Company survey of over 500 companies that downsized found survivors' syndrome can last for two years.
- David Noer reports that five years after their company downsized, employees were still feeling stress, fatigue, decreased motivation, sadness, depression, insecurity, anxiety, fear, a sense of unfairness, anger, resignation, and numbness.

Simply put, frightened people are not productive. As a result, downsizing can cut productivity instead of improving it. One reason for this negative outcome is that survivors often try, consciously or subconsciously, to "balance" a situation they regard as unfair by demanding more from their employer, such as pay increases, promotions, and awards, or by giving their employer less by producing less, working shorter hours, or producing lower quality products.

TABLE 4.5   Cameron's Downsizing Strategies

	Workforce reduction	Work redesign	Systematic
Focus	Reduce head-count	Redesign jobs, levels, units	Change the culture
Eliminate	People	Work	Standard operating procedures
Implementation time	Quick	Moderate	Long-term payoffs
Payoff Target	Short-term	Moderate term	Short-term savings
Inhibits	Long-term adaptability	Quick payback	Involve everyone
Examples	Attrition	Combine functions	Simplify (re-engineer) everything
	Layoffs	Merge units	Bottom-up change
	Early retirement	Redesign jobs	Target hidden costs
	Buyout packages	Eliminate layers	

**Interview with Robert Reich (former U.S. Secretary of Labor)
Has Downsizing Gone Too Far?**

Q. Do we have a new social contract in America between workers and
management? Is the old social contract breaking down?
A. There used to be—thirty years ago, forty years ago—an implicit social
contract, and although it was never written down, it was understood. It was
enforced partly by unions—when 35 percent of the wage force was unionized, that was not an insignificant enforcer—but also by public norms. That
social contract said that if the company was doing better and better, workers
could be reasonably assured that they would have their jobs and also that
they would see better wages and better benefits. That old social contract has
come apart. Now we have the spectre of companies doing better and better,
and yet some companies—not all, by any means—but some companies are
pushing wages down, pushing benefits down, abandoning communities,
breaking all of those implicit contractual terms.
Q. Will it correct itself without some kind of government encouragement?
A. The first role of government in terms of corporate responsibility is to
act as a kind of cheerleader. Use the bully pulpit. Use jawboning. Bringing
the spotlight of public opinion to bear on the companies that are doing it
right and occasionally the companies that are doing it wrong. The optimistic
view is that gradually companies will see the light, that they will understand
that the only way they can really make money over the long term is if they
treat their employees as assets, if they invest in their training, if they bring
them in as partners, if they value them, and also if they value the communities
that they live in, because after all, employees and communities are where
their customer is ultimately coming from. Good will is very important to the
bottom line. Now that's the optimistic view. The pessimistic view is that
even over the long term, companies may not fully do what is in the interest
of society because investments in employees and investments in communities
will never be fully returnable to just the shareholders. There is also a societal
stake in all of this. And the true pessimist would say we're never going to
get companies to take the long-term view anyway.
Q. And where do you stand on that spectrum between optimist and pessimist?
A. On Mondays and Wednesdays and Fridays, I'm very optimistic. The
other days, cautiously pessimistic.

Source: Challenge, July–August 1996. Copyright 1996 by M. E. Sharpe, Inc.

of more downsizing. To be effective so that it happens once in a systematic change requires a different set of strategies.

Done for all the right reasons, downsizing still must contend with the tremendous impact it has on the workforce. Study after study shows that managers, whether they are corporate or government, underestimate the impacts on the workforce, whether it is measured in terms of morale, stress, decreased feelings of loyalty, or potential workplace violence. The U.S. Department of Labor has offered guidelines for what they call responsible restructuring that apply to both public and private sector organizations. The former secretary of labor, Robert Reich, has gone a step further. In 1996, near the end of his tenure in the cabinet, he argued that downsizing has changed the social contract between workers and management and that the new century will be marked by a new level of anxiety and lack of trust between organizations and workers.

A HISTORICAL OVERVIEW OF HUMAN RESOURCES PLANNING

A long-standing problem with the term *human resources planning* or *workforce planning* is definitional. Simply put, it means different things to different people. There is no universally accepted definition of what workforce planning is or consensus on what activities should be associated with it. Organizations claiming that they do workforce planning appear to use a wide variety of methods to approach their own unique problems.

Although workforce planning seems to emulate a formalized strategy for response to current and anticipated problems, many of its definitions bear little resemblance to each other, either in terms of substance or methodology. James Walker defines HR planning as ''the process of analyzing an organization's human resources needs under changing conditions and developing the activities necessary to satisfy these needs.'' Such a definition sees HR planning as more than a simple personnel function—one that involves the entire management process. This is vastly different from the older concepts of labor force or workforce planning. It is important, however, that one realize that the confusion over what earlier versions of workforce planning were and what HR planning is hides a very significant development—in fact, a true evolution in substance and methodology.

Historically, workforce planning was, and of course still remains, an integral part of numerous public and private programs whose objective is to affect the labor market in order to improve the employment status and welfare of individuals. These goals of the Full Employment Act of 1946 are reflected in training and development programs for economically disadvantaged groups, the aging, the disabled, and others. The programs are primarily designed to further the use, development, and retention of individuals as members of the labor force. As such, the programs have a macro focus in that they deal with the aggregate labor force of the nation or region.

Labor force planning efforts undertaken by organizations also reflect the concern for balancing supply and demand; that is, at the organizational level, planning involves managing the organization's assets. At the "economy" level, however, planning involves managing the nation's assets. The distinction is apt— planning in both cases involves projecting and managing the supply and demand of HR, only at different levels. This is not a trivial issue. Perhaps the most contentious issue involving labor force planning today concerns computer programmers and high-tech workers. Corporations and by extension governments must grapple with how many computer programmers are needed to meet the demands of the information technology sector. Some argue that the supply of degreed workers coming from American universities is woefully inadequate and the number of work visas for workers from abroad must be dramatically raised. The counter-argument, of course, is that corporations and governments need to create more education programs and retraining programs for older workers, and new technical training programs for minorities who are not well represented among the nation's information technology (IT) workforce. This is never an easy debate.

What exactly do HR planning levels involve, however? Both are concerned with future demand aspects; that is, what the requirements for the future workforce will be. At the macro level this means projecting what skills will be in demand to service the economy. At the micro level, this entails projecting specific requirements for the workforce of the organization or what quantities and qualities of personnel will be needed to carry out organizational objectives. Both levels are concerned also with future supply aspects. At the macro level this means that projections must be made on what the national labor force will consist of in terms of future skills, both surpluses and deficits. For the micro level, the organization must forecast what its future workforce will consist of as well as evaluate its competitive position in order to decide what quantities and qualities of personnel it can encourage to enter the organization as replacements.

Although there is a certain symmetry in terms of the supply-and-demand aspects for labor force planning at both levels, the methodologies involved in the processes are quite dissimilar. The objectives involved are also different in that an organization's workforce policy may be efficient when viewed from its own perspective, but quite dysfunctional to the national economy. For example, an organization may fire X number of employees (whose skills are in surplus nationally) and hire X number of new employees (whose skills are in deficit nationally). A macro-oriented workforce decision might have called for retraining some of the old employees about to be displaced. From the organization's vantage point, however, the training cost and the delay involved may have rendered that option inefficient.

WORKFORCE PLANNING

The late 1960s and early 1970s saw the first real advancements in HR planning at the organizational level. The planning tools available to management multiplied considerably. Major technical advancements in computers, information systems theory, and modeling and simulation methodologies were applied in such a way to the problems of supply and demand that a new second generation of workforce planning was created. These related to either of the following two planning elements:

> *Organizational requirements planning*—The projection and analysis by organizational management of the categories and quantities of job skills needed to implement organizational programs
>
> *Workforce planning*—The projection and analysis of the quantities of each category of current workers' skills that will be available to the organization in future periods

Each element has, of course, numerous components and processes. Workforce skills planning, probably the more advanced element, involves techniques that focus on the following three separate exercises:

1. *Attrition projections*—Forecasting the impact of changes in the quantity of specific categories within the workforce because of separations, especially retirements, since these workers usually represent the deepest part of the organization's knowledge base
2. *Adjustment projections*—Forecasting the impact of changes in the current workforce involving those employees who change some aspect of their status (functional skills, preference, employment categories, grade levels, and so on)
3. *Current recruitment projections*—Forecasting the impact of current recruitment efforts and special policy programs (such as minority recruitment, lateral entries, or special highly skilled functional categories)

The logic of workforce skills planning requires that the above components reflect all of the possibilities of the status changes that an employee can undergo in the organization. In essence, there are four such possibilities of situational change.

1. Employees can enter the organization (new hires).
2. Employees may leave the organization (separation).
3. Employees can change their grade level (be advanced or demoted).
4. Employees can change their skill characteristics (change job skills, change positions, change employment status, etc.).

The use of some type of model combining the forecasts for both requirements and skills planning would provide the basic components for constructing an organizational plan for recruitment purposes.

Methodologies for determining attrition, adjustments, and recruitment projections are integral parts of the overall planning effort involved in producing some type of workforce plan that indicates what the future workforce will look like given current assumptions. Workforce planning also recognizes that the time dimension would vary the focus of various forecasting efforts. Forecasts were expected to vary between short-range periods (now considered to be between one and two years) and intermediate and long-range periods (from two to 10 years and beyond).

Organizational requirements planning is a far more abstract process in that the needs of future programs are obviously more difficult to predict and are more subjective. Despite the advent of some fairly sophisticated modeling and forecasting techniques, the available methodologies for this are not universally accepted or employed. In the private sector, forecasts for organizational needs are usually based on sales and market forecasts by various unit managers. Since control is generally more internalized, decentralized, and less dependent upon outside review channels, these forecasts have a better chance of being realistic. Of course the growth assumptions that dominated the thinking on workforce planning also changed over much of the 1990s. First, in the era of downsizing, private sector organizations have had to readjust many of their forecasts. Many of the forecasts were significantly impacted by mergers and corporate restructuring that required a degree of rapid response well beyond what attrition would provide.

Paradoxically, organizations in the public sector seemed to have even less control over their future plans. When reinvention and competitive government pressures mounted in the 1990s, public sector organizations were now confronting major questions about whether they would be producing the service directly or hiring a contractor (who often would be hiring their former employees as part of the contract package) to produce the service.

Forecasting continuous workforce demand or future program requirements has always been a difficult process in the public sector milieu. A common approach was to link such forecasting to the budgeting cycle, but the inherent instability of public sector budgets usually prevented this approach from being effective. The adoption of Delphi techniques or decision analysis forecasting represent processes was an initial attempt to overcome this problem. In essence, these processes purport to "qualify" and weigh the various forecasts being made in order to increase the probability that the most accurate projections are given appropriate emphasis by the organization. These techniques are characteristic of this second generation of workforce planning. Justifications for this genre generally focus on its supply-and-demand balancing aspect, the purpose being to ensure that the organization has the right types of people in the right positions at the right times.

Second generation workforce planning techniques were widely employed in the public sector throughout the 1980s and 1990s, albeit with varying success. Indeed, one can still find numerous employment and trends reports for the federal government and larger state governments that are by-products of the computerized information systems developed in this generation that provided summary data by occupation on employment, labor turnover, job vacancies, and wage categories and pay levels. By the 1990s these reports were augmented with new reports on diversity showing how representative the public workforce was generally, by specific departments and position level. For a excellent example of what these reports can offer, one can download the entire current *Fact Book* of the OPM and see a wide array of current data on all aspects of the federal workforce.

While second generation workforce planning systems were not universal, advances in computer technology brought down the costs and accessibility of workforce data dramatically. At first, the larger an organization was (by employment size), the more likely it would have some kind of workforce planning system. This soon changed to a norm that the more dependent the budget was on personnel and highly qualified workskills, the more imperative a proactive HR planning process was for the organization. By the late 1990s workforce planning systems were easily accessible to any moderately sized HR department. The acceleration of computing power was such that even the Defense Department's workforce forecasting systems could be run from a modest HR department's network system.

This does not mean that the analysis will be any easier. The case can be made that there is now a third generation of HR planning emerging. This third generation will be based on a very different set of planning assumptions. Obviously, when political and economic circumstances change as dramatically as international events did in the 1990s, the forecasting emphasis must change. Focusing on this new economy in the private sector, the expectation is that corporations will plan with 12- to 15-month cycles. A popular expression often heard in the IT sector is "In three months, we'll be a different company." Speed and change are the requisites for survival in an economy that sees only the difference between "the quick and the dead."

How should public sector organizations plan under these new assumptions? For now, most public sector organizations expect little real growth in overall employee population, but nearly all foresee radical changes in the job compositions of personnel working in government. There will be fewer blue-collar jobs, but increases in service workloads. The Bureau of Labor Statistics (BLS) predicts very stable and decreasing rates of growth for government. For the federal government, there was an increase of .5% in employment between 1986 and 1996 but this growth is projected to decline to .3% from 1996 to 2006. For state governments, BLS sees a rate of growth of 1.9% from 1986 to 1996, declining to .9% from 1996 to 2006. Both the federal and state projected rates of growth for 2006 are well below the national projected average of 1.3%.

Within these parameters the new workforce planning focus will shift to internal change and reprogramming. It is focusing on occupational shifts, such as predicting the impacts on technology and automation on the workforce. Computer technology is one of the most dramatic examples of how workforce planning is adjusting. Most public sector organizations have gone to computers and automation to be more productive. In some cases, agencies have proposed IT modernization programs that were ''guaranteed'': to reduce budget costs because reductions in the workforce were built into the modernization program as the savings necessary to finance the effort. As expected, initially the biggest effects were in administrative, clerical, and office services. Using the federal government as an example, the effects were initially quite modest. In the age of mainframe computers (1970s) there was a 4% increase in the administrative clerical occupational categories. By the 1980s and the age of personal computing, clerical levels had declined by over 10%. That reduction really exploded in the 1990s, the age of networks. Federal secretarial and clerical jobs decreased by 35% and 75%, respectively. Now in the twenty-first century, in the age of the Internet, the total of remaining federal secretarial and clerical jobs is at such a low number that they constitute less than 5% of the federal workforce.

Obviously, we will have much fewer secretaries and clerical workers in government. The bigger question is what job skill sets we will need. How many computer programmers? How many budget analysts and contract managers? This is why workforce planning systems will always be an important information source to managers. As a system, it requires a variety of ongoing judgments at various managerial levels as to what anticipated needs (either pluses or minuses) will be (organizational requirements planning). In addition, the system contains components that provide for current accountability and the projection of changes to the current workforce. This is a system that can answer the following questions, which are particularly important as we move into the twenty-first century:

1. What is the current status of the organizational workforce (e.g., how many persons, and with what types of skills will they leave or transfer)?
2. Where will current plans take the organization X months or Y years hence—what will this mean in terms of workforce requirements (e.g., what are the impacts of technology and changes in occupational needs caused by changing workloads)?
3. Where will the current workforce be in terms of skills X months or Y years hence given current policies (e.g., is the aging of the workforce being considered)?

4. What changes must be made now to bring the future workforce into balance with anticipated needs (e.g., what will recruitment and training priorities be)?

5. What will be the impact of interim or short-range personnel policies (whether they be buyouts, RIFs [reduction-in-force], furloughs, and hiring freeze policies or recruitment bonuses, relocation, retention bonuses, etc.) on current and longer-range supply and retention of personnel?

At this point it is necessary to focus with more detail on the supply-and-demand aspects of HR planning.

FORECASTING HUMAN RESOURCES SUPPLY

A variety of techniques have been employed in attempting to forecast what a current organizational workforce will resemble X years hence. The key to such exercises has been to predict the turnover rate for the organization; that is, the numbers and kinds of employees who will leave the organization for various reasons, whether voluntary retirement, medical or disability retirement, death, leave without pay, or resignation. The initial techniques used reflected the fact that for the most part the turnover that was available to organizations was not very comprehensive. Typically, various modes of trend analysis would be utilized to calculate three-to-five-year averages in the number of separations by category. This average could then be recalculated each year and would form the projection for the coming year. (In forecasting methodology, this updating of the mean is known as establishing a ''moving average.'') Still, this method is much like calculating tomorrow's weather based solely on the weather of the previous week; unless the organization is a very stable one, the method is not very satisfactory.

Methods of statistical analysis offer numerous ways to go beyond the limited applicability of the historical approach. For example, simple five-year means can be replaced with a weighted mean based on the different sizes of the workforce categories; a trend line analysis might be used when the more recent years are especially significant in calculating expected attrition.

Considerable research and analysis has also been expended in pursuit of other methods to forecast turnover. If the variables that influenced turnover could be identified, it has been argued, then forecasting might be relatively simple to predict. For example, one type of analysis would attempt to focus on motivational factors and the organizational environment and project the impact of these influences—whether positive or negative—on the number of resignations, retirements, and so forth that could be expected. Historical ranges would be constructed for past years for each turnover category, and depending upon the organization's analysis of its expected environmental factors, a forecast could be made of how many employees would probably leave.

The most common method of identifying the causal factors of turnover has been some type of exit interview. Such interviews attempt to discover the reasons for quitting or leaving at that particular time. Several problems can be encountered, however, rendering this approach for forecasting turnover fruitless. First, employees do not often relate their real reasons for leaving, particularly if they are concerned about future references. There is no incentive for them to be frank or honest since they are terminating their association with the organization. Second and more important, however, is that the number of possible factors for leaving can be so numerous and involved that meaningful analysis is virtually hopeless. For example, a simplistic psychological test for workers' preferences developed by Tomkins and Horn identified 655 basic factors and combinations of factors that were potential influences on the decision to leave a job.

Of course there are exceptions, in which the use of exit interviews or in this case exit surveys can provide important information, especially for public personnel policy. In 1989, the U.S. Merit Systems Protection Board (MSPB) developed an exit survey that was sent to over 2,800 federal employees who had separated from government that year. This broad-based survey attempted to identify what factors most influenced the decision to leave. The MSPB listed 46 different factors and asked the survey respondents to rank those that were most critical in making their decision. Not surprisingly, given all the press about the adverse effects of the federal pay gap (at that point it purportedly lagged private sector compensation rates by over 25%), compensation and advancement reasons were top-ranked (28% of the surveys), but most survey respondents cited multiple reasons for leaving, and the MSPB's report concluded that different groups of federal employees (varying by age, grade, sex, location, and performance rating) had different rankings of reasons, the policy implication thus being that corrective strategies to reduce turnover must focus specifically on each category of employee to be the most effective.

For distinct organizations, the recognition that turnover or attrition rates should be based on the characteristics of the workforce itself represented a major step in the development of workforce planning skills. This concept means that depending on such characteristics as sex, age, and length of service, the choices made by individuals will exhibit probabilistic frequency patterns. The logic of this approach is based in part on the fact that retirements and resignations constitute the primary withdrawal categories from the workforce. In addition, most resignations will occur early (with short time of service), and retirements will be blocked out over a very specific time span (the years of retirement eligibility).

The forecast process involves the use of matrices for various occupational groups or work units which correlate age by length of time of service. Table 4.6 takes an entire workforce group as an example. In this hypothetical case, the more than 15,000 federal personnel in the Department of Interior who are certified as fire fighters are spread out by age and years of service. One can see both the

TABLE 4.6 A Transitional Matrix for Estimating Internal Movement of Human Resources

Age/years of service	Under 5	6 to 10	11 to 20	20 to 30	Over 30	Totals
Under 20	206	0	0	0	0	206
20–24	1430	158	0	0	0	1589
25–29	1304	651	217	0	0	2173
30–34	874	874	437	0	0	2185
35–39	472	708	944	236	0	2360
40–44	2523	504	1008	756	0	2521
45–49	368	245	1102	735	0	2451
50–54	77	115	192	999	153	1538
55–59	0	37	54	366	152	610
Over 60	0	0	13	122	136	272

Source: Adapted from Gordon L. Nielsen and Allan Young (1980), Manpower Planning: A Markov Chain Application, in *Strategic Human Resources Planning*, George Biles and Stevan Holmberg (editors).

retirement zone, where employees are coming up on retirement eligibility, and a resignation zone where employees are most prone to leave because they are younger with less time in service and less investment in the organization. Following the age/years of service matrix is a calculated set of transitional probabilities (Table 4.7). These probabilities are estimates of what percentage will depart each year in that age and service category whether because of resignation, retirement, disability, termination, and even death. By tracking separation rates over time, organizations can calculate their own transitional probability factors or they can rely on general actuarial tables for the rates of change. It should be noted that separation rates vary significantly by sex, so for larger calculations like the example in Table 4.7, it would be important to have separate tables for males and females.

The turnover for any given cell of the matrix (Table 4.6) is calculated by multiplying the number of employees in that cell by the transitional probability factor. For example, if the organization has 999 employees coming up on their first year of retirement eligibility (i.e., over 50 years old and minimum of 20 years of service), you would be able to estimate that 249 would leave upon reaching their first year. As Table 4.6 illustrates (remember that transitional probabilities cited in this example are hypothetical) attrition can be projected for each category. Further applications of what is called markov chain forecasting can be used to age the workforce, evaluate the impacts of promotions, and even assess what the workforce will look like in five years, ten years, or even a generation

TABLE 4.7 Transitional Probabilities of Separation (Combined Resignation/Termination/Retirement/Disability)

Age/years of service	Under 5	6 to 10	11 to 20	20 to 30	Over 30	Projected separations
Under 20	.5	N/A.	N/A.	N/A.	N/A.	103
20–24	.2	.1	N/A.	N/A.	N/A.	302
25–29	.1	.075	.05	N/A.	N/A.	190
30–34	.075	.125	.05	N/A.	N/A.	197
35–39	.05	.025	.01	.005	N/A.	52
40–44	.1	.065	.05	.025	N/A.	127
45–49	.125	.075	.01	.001	N/A.	76
50–54	.15	.175	.2	.25	.5	360
55–59	N/A.	.2	.1	.4	.75	274
Over 60	N/A.	N/A.	.3	.5	1.0	201

Source: Adapted from Gordon L. Nielsen and Allan Young (1980), Manpower Planning: A Markov Chain Application, in *Strategic Human Resources Planning*, George Biles and Stevan Holmberg (editors).

given current personnel policies. Of course, to do this type of organizational supply forecasting effectively, organizations must have accurate databases on their workforce which today should include data on separations, hiring, training, and advancement.

FORECASTING ORGANIZATIONAL DEMANDS

A very different set of problems is encountered in predicting organizational requirements over time. The problem with demand forecasting is that the emphasis is usually on the incremental portion of change. Forecasting consists of making predictions based upon the observed regularities of the past. The supply models just discussed certainly use this premise as their base, but forecasting must also allow for certain changes, whether technological, organizational, or policy-oriented, which disrupt the progression of the observable regularity of the past. Such disruptions are the primary concern of demand forecasting. If demand forecasting is to be accurate, qualitative information must somehow be obtained from those closest to the decision. Supply forecasting, on the other hand, has gained—with the advent of computerized personnel information systems—a much more accessible and quantifiable database.

One approach to forecasting organizational demand for HR is to incorporate the HR concept into organizational planning. Essentially, as the organization's long-range planning and budgetary processes occur, they must include specific references to future personnel requirements. It remains to be determined how an organization can integrate information from management at the top policy, operational, and personnel levels (if, indeed, all levels are involved) into one coherent HR plan. Delphi techniques were among the first methodologies developed to date in terms of piecing together various opinions to arrive at a future consensus. Delphi techniques involve asking various individuals or groups for their opinions and weighting their responses with some factor that considers their relative importance or influence on the situation, their expertise, their past forecasting accuracy, and so on. When all the opinions are weighted and aggregated, a calculation can be obtained as to the likely probability of a future situation. The Delphi technique can also reroute results through the same individuals or groups as a further check, this time weighting responses with their intensity of belief.

The OPM's decision analysis forecasting technique is an excellent application of the Delphi concept. Developed in the 1970s specifically for HR planning at the executive level, it utilizes decision analysis network theory to set up planning considerations in the form of decision trees. The technique develops staffing requirements by

1. "Decomposing" each HR planning problem into relevant factors
2. Quantifying subjective preferences and probability judgments for each problem factor
3. Combining the available data plus these quantified judgments into a table of predictions

A strength of the Delphi technique is that it outlines future outcomes. This in itself is a major advantage in forecasting organizational demand for HR. The organization is compelled to recognize and delineate alternatives and plan out each option in terms of HR requirements. Unfortunately, this technique also recognizes the real difficulty in charting out the future in times of great uncertainty. The best that can be hoped for is that possible paths can be charted out in advance as an aid to rational decision making, thus increasing the possibility that future choices will be informed ones.

New conceptual advances in workforce planning will mean that while current planning techniques involved in predicting future workforce requirements and skill levels are important, present practice simply does not go far enough. Human resources planning (see Figure 4.2) must be expanded by bringing planning methodology to the various strategies that an organization must employ if it is to manage the interaction of its future needs and resources. Perhaps the planning methodology that best encapsulates this dimension is the use of scenario planning.

In 1991, Peter Schwartz caught the attention of management thinkers when he published his book *The Art of the Long View*. Schwartz made public, if you

The Delphi Technique: A Hypothetical Example

The figure below presents a hypothetical decision tree designed to predict the probability of an increase in staffing for an agency that is considering a new training office. The question of the new staff seems to hinge on whether or not the organization's budget is to be cut. In the example, the group of organizational influentials consists of 20 individuals who "vote" on one of four outcomes, but the final outcome shows that 16 of 20 voters believe the training office will be established anyway. This Delphi exercise concludes that the probability of new training being established is .8—and the organization would do well to begin plans for staffing this new office.

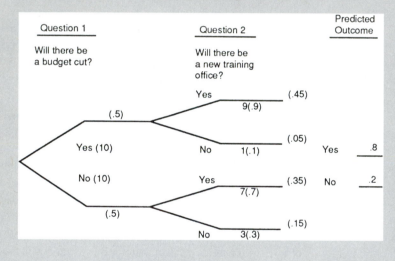

will, a number of corporate stories (both successes and failures), in which corporate planning had relied upon a technique that forecasted a number of alternative futures in an effort to cope with the increasing complexity in the global business and political environment. Some of the more famous scenario planning events were the Shell Oil Corporation's development of scenarios that accurately predicted the 1973 global oil crises and the prediction of the end of the cold war and the breakup of the former Soviet Union.

The former event (both the accuracy of the forecast and how it affected Shell's corporate behavior) has been the subject of extensive controversy. Schwartz's contribution in the early 1990s was to describe scenario planning as

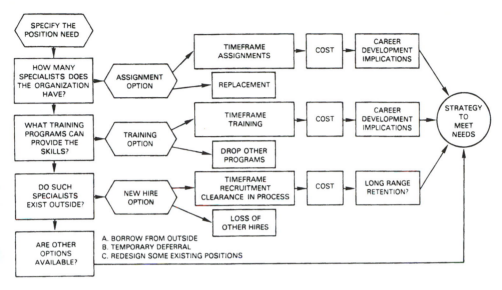

FIGURE 4.2   The human resources planning approach.

an art form that might still help prepare an organization for the breakup of the former Soviet Union, the end of apartheid, or even different views of the world of work in an Internet-dominated economy. Still, as the 1990s became dominated by strategic management as the central organizing logic for planning and resource allocation, it was not surprising that scenario planning failed to catch on. While a few saw scenario building as an interesting tool for the strategist, the majority of management experts saw scenarios as creating more problems than they solved. Some, such as Henry Mintzberg, attacked the basic assumption of scenarios—that they were assuming "if you can not predict the future, then by speculating upon a variety of them, you might just hit upon the right one." Others saw major problems with an organization taking them seriously, from determining how many contingency plans it should develop to changing behavior.

The value of scenario planning began to change with the emerging interest in strategic thinking and the explosive rates of change experienced with the first wave of major Internet applications. Wrapped up in the accelerating change levels of the business environment, major shifts in technology and communications, and the new importance of "innovation," managers starting looking at the future differently. The first casualty of what Gary Hamel and others called the strategy revolution was conventional management, and any form of planning that simply projected the future based on present capabilities and operations. Hamel charged that senior managers must "invite new voices into the strategy-making process, encourage new perspectives, start new conversations that span organizational boundaries, synthesize unconventional options into a point of view about organizational directions."

That prescription fit scenario planning quite well as a planning process— it begins with the question "what if" and then explores what are called PEST projections (political, economic, social, technological factors) for change. Scenarios detail a different set of future conditions, policy and program options and impacts, and explores different responses from stakeholders, partners, and competitors. Once the scenarios are developed, the organization has to refine what its "response" to that scenario will be. From an HR planning perspective this would mean delineating the following:

Organizational response	Human capital strategy
Change in vision/mission	Change in workforce scope (size and skill mix)
Change in programs/activities	Change in compensation and recruitment
Change in organizational structures	Change in training and development

Once a set of scenarios has been developed, management assesses the formal scenarios to better understand the dynamics of their environment. In addition to determining what seems likely and where the greatest uncertainties are, analysts can see more clearly what they know and what they don't. Scenario planning also entails a vigorous analysis of the different scenarios, probability estimation and review of risk, and evaluation of policy, program, and resource allocation change recommendations. "Contingency strategies" can be developed to respond to changing environmental conditions or necessary course alterations if desired. Once developed, scenario planning helps refine the organization's long-term vision as it tracks actual events and outcomes.

The EPA has been conducting some scenario-planning work as part of its ongoing policy and research efforts, which are presented next. From EPA's standpoint, they chose the impacts of E-commerce and developed four scenarios to show how the workforce might be affected. Naturally, EPA's interest is in such things as energy conservation and traffic patterns, all of which have major impacts on pollution levels. They are still instructive for HR management offices thinking through where and how people will work in 2020 as well as how many and what kinds of workers will be in the workforce.

Scenario 1: Remote Controls (Assumes High-Level Growth in E-Commerce, Telecommuting, and Public Concern About the Environment)

In this scenario, the growth in E-commerce is extremely high. It would be very difficult for a person to function normally in society without access. Voting, work, and commercial transactions are all done online. In this world, telecommuting is more the norm than the exception, and public concern about the environment is at an unprecedented level in opinion polls. The year is 2020, and the world is reaping the benefits of the technological revolution. The explosive growth of E-commerce is beyond anyone's expectations, giving rise to an entrepreneurial virtual economy. Global businesses invest in state-of-the-art technology to deliver services and products cheaper and faster, thereby satisfying customer demand for instant gratification. In addition, the evolution of global corporations and international finances have been instrumental in the dissolution of trade barriers. The de-emphasis on the importance of international borders further facilitates free trade.

Retail stores and wholesalers have all but disappeared as Websites employ fully interactive, 3-D, and customization technology (3-D body images that match an individual's physical dimensions), simulating an in-store experience. Consumers have found this mode of shopping both convenient and very compelling. The creation of a government watchdog cybercrime unit within the FBI to both investigate claims of fraud and to police commercial cybertransactions has bolstered consumer confidence and trust in E-commerce. Removal of regulatory barriers to E-commerce (e.g., third party encryption keys registration) gives rise to the dawn of the "Me II" decade—a credit card is all that is needed to start up a business. These upstart companies proliferate at a staggering rate and can be run by individuals working exclusively at home. Relatively unencumbered access to equity and venture capital affords even those who are undereducated the opportunity to enter competitively the digital marketplace—and succeed.

The elderly population is also reaping the benefits of this booming economy. Some retirees have gone on to start new businesses and continue to be healthy and productive contributors to society. As the business of the day is all about technology, telecommuting has flourished. High-tech employers have attracted workers by offering subsidized housing units that are wired to the workplace through smart technology (e.g., retinal, voice, or fingerprint scanning security systems, smart appliances, and virtual-vacation simulators). Quality of life issues, such as long commutes and long hours away from home and family, take precedence over climbing the corporate ladder. Those with "portable work" choose to live a more balanced lifestyle, maintaining an equilibrium between work and leisure time. With the 24-hour connection to the office, however, some still work long hours.

Scenario 2: Let the Environment Beware! (Assumes a High Level of E-Commerce Usage and Telecommuting and Low Public Environmental Awareness)

Over the next 15 years, E-commerce grows at a robust and quite unexpectedly high rate. Business transactions on the World Wide Web exceed by an order of magnitude the wildest expectations of Internet analysts and E-commerce promoters. Anticipated problems associated with bandwidth availability and the unscrupulous use of the Internet never materialize. Anticipating problems with Internet privacy and security, Congress in 2002 passes legislation effectively resolving such issues. The legislation includes a permanent ban in the application of any form of taxation on Internet commerce. Coupled with the explosion in Internet commerce, telecommuting accelerates to a point where 70% of those employed in the United States conduct business from offices located in their homes. High-speed communications through fiberoptic links to cable and telephone networks and improved visual communications technology create at-home environments in which those telecommuting feel as if they are in the same room with their colleagues or customers.

At the same time, the environmental movement seemed to have faltered. Human health and environmental improvement in the last 30 years of the twentieth century was the high point of the environmental movement in the United States. Even the eco-conscious countries of Western Europe seemed to have lost their interest in environmental protection after the formal creation of the United States of Europe in 2007. Burgeoning growth in environmental commerce has spurred the advancement of formerly third-world countries at growth rates in excess of 10% per year early in the twenty-first century, but with little associated environmental protection technology or practices being employed.

The EPA, a pioneering government force in the use of the Internet, has essentially become a nonplayer in Internet information delivery. Environmental regulation, compliance, and enforcement are passe, as virtually all private sector organizations self-certify their environmental compliance under ISO 14078. High-growth countries have simply refused to comply with either mandatory or voluntary compliance standards, resulting in increased emissions and releases that cross national borders and regional boundaries. Fully half of the individuals telecommuting do so because environmental pollution has manifested itself in an immune system dysfunction that is best addressed by individuals remaining in controlled environments in their homes.

Scenario 3: Small Change (Assumes Midlevel Growth in E-Commerce, Telecommuting, and Public Concern About the Environment)

In 2020, E-commerce has expanded to include approximately 30% of retail sales, primarily associated with services and products that can be provided electronically (tickets, books, music, banking, tax preparation), consumer electronics, and automobiles. Approximately 20% of workers work in their homes. The percentage of the public that ranks environmental issues as "of highest concern" has increased by approximately 50%. The early promise of E-commerce has been only partially fulfilled. Rising fuel prices drove up the cost of home delivery, driving down demand for low-cost retail goods through E-commerce, and retailers were successful in lobbying Congress to impose sales taxes and other protective regulations that raised entry barriers for small (home) businesses.

Trade barriers stifled another source of E-business, international E-commerce in retail goods. High-cost items that entail substantial customization and inventory costs continue to be a growth area. Telecommuting never really took off—only service jobs that entailed piecework (e.g., writing software, preparation of tax returns) moved to the home, and those workers were largely independent contractors for larger firms that provide training and advertising. Other service jobs either require physical presence (e.g., restaurants), or could not forego face-to-face contact with customers, peers, supervisors, and direct reports. An aging, more affluent, and better-educated populace shows higher and more sophisticated concern about environmental quality, particularly in the face of a 30% increase in global population. This has been tempered by the failure of past environmental horror stories to materialize.

Scenario 4: Environment! (Assumes a High Level of E-Commerce Usage, Telecommuting, and High Public Environmental Awareness)

E-commerce follows the same pattern as shown in Scenario 2 (see first paragraph of Scenario 2).

The private sector has expanded weather.com to environment.com and delivers information on global, national, and environmental information 24 hours per day, custom designed to a user's specifications. Such information is much in demand by the public; the Website is accessed 20 million times a day. The private sector has gone 95% green (determined by a supercomputer software program analyzing the 37-factors database at each private sector site). Each site pays $500,000 per year to be part of this "green country" program and touts its environmental ethic using electronic "cookies" sent daily to more than 150 million Internet users who have specifically asked to receive the information.

From an increased emphasis on E-commerce and telecommuting, the 20th century institutions of commercial retailing and concentrations of businesses in city centers crumble to a fraction of what they were 30 years ago. Environmental awareness and the desire to preserve environmental resources causes a ground swell of public support for more national reserves that limit human access and can be enjoyed through on-line virtual reality experiences. Inner cities are recognized as a resource that needs to be redeveloped, and increased emphasis is placed on urban living for the social, cultural, and economic benefits that it conveys. Anticipated problems with the cost of delivery of E-commerce purchases and associated waste management is more than offset by the reduction in use of individual transportation for shopping, working, and the development and commercialization of a new system that delivers purchases "packaging free."

With telecommuting and E-commerce operating on a 24-hour basis, human productivity is substantially increased, thereby reducing the number of hours per week an individual actually spends working. This increases both individual and family time spent in "at-home virtual reality chambers" that provide a broad array of sensual experiences. While city centers flourish as rediscovered communities, the growth in suburban sprawl decreases, and past sprawl issues are resolved at local levels by an environmentally aware public. Those seeking a more rural life move to small villages in appealing areas, causing local growth at times to exceed 15% per year. Such a situation is successfully handled, however, by urban planners working remotely with local decision makers. World-friendly growth strategies are developed for these high-growth communities using a virtual tool box of sophisticated planning tools and software that stresses economic, environmental, and social sustainability.

Scenario planning is not likely to be the next big fad in management thinking. This technique was around for most of the 1990s and seems finally to have sufficient management literature behind it that any good strategic planner or strategic thinker can examine some samples and see where it might be appropriate. It will be very useful for any organization that expects great levels of change, along with the unexpected. Alas, for those organizations that don't see that the future is going to be very different from the current situation, it would be a waste of time.

STRATEGIC HUMAN RESOURCES PLANNING—FUTURE PROSPECTS

Logic certainly suggests that HR planning will become an even more significant decision-making process in the future. Unless workforce planning as a discipline continues to grow, however, it may fall into the same disrepute as economic forecasting and political forecasting have. As the workforce gets older, the demographic aspects to HR planning will be important to a point. The numbers of retirees are significant, but as the workforce is dominated more by employees who think differently about what a career means and who expect to work for different organizations, retention, recruitment, and training may all take on very different meanings.

To be of value, HR planning will have to develop in two directions: establishing new planning methodologies and broadening the scope of planning and strategy efforts. Some of these new directions will likely include linking interactive functions of personnel management, considering individual reactions and preferences, charting new forms of organizations, work teams, and alliances, and developing new types of information. It is worth commenting on each of these new developments.

For some time, the complexity and interrelatedness of personnel decisions has been recognized. Placements, training, intake selections, promotions, and separations all impact on each other and present alternative routes for organizations to meet HR needs. Human resources planning approaches in the future will be increasingly concerned with mapping and costing out these various components within the personnel management process. That will include new concepts of learning paths, careers, and compensation methods.

Perhaps the most sensitive area of concern for HR planning will be in considering the individual. That organizations can no longer get by without recognizing an individual's needs and desires is becoming obvious. Human resources planning will need to consider the preferences of individual employees, and that will not be as easy as it once was. Downsizing and the very poor way many organizations handled major structural realignments in the 1990s has negatively impacted the trust of individuals in organizations generally. Some have even argued that many younger professionals now think of a career as a series of five years of work in different organizations with the full expectation of switching industry sectors. The norm in many private sector firms is a signing bonus for recruitment, and that may soon be a tool offered by governments.

Other HR professionals see HR planning as having to come to grips with a new breed of employee. A Florida-based HR firm conducted a survey in 1996 of "new full-time workers" going into the workforce. Their findings indicate that loyalty is defined differently and it has little to do with memories of downsizing and/or insensitive treatment in the past. Quoting the concluding statement in an article in the *Journal of Business Strategy*

> We're calling these people the "new loyalists" or the emerging workers. For this group, which we think makes up 20% of the workforce and which will grow to 40% (in the next decade) loyalty isn't based on tenure. This group would throw their 10 year pin in the trash can. What they'd prefer is to be sent to England so they can learn about working in a new culture, or they'd like to work in a different department so they can add a new skill to their resume. They're not looking for a long-term commitment. Instead their loyalty is generated by an opportunity to learn, to grow, and to become autonomous. And they are just as likely to be 55 year old middle managers as freshly minted MBA's.

Finally, HR planning techniques must be concerned with rapidly changing organizational structures and informational linkages. As computer technology and increased communications capabilities make possible more decentralized working environments, and as project teams, process teams, and telecommuting

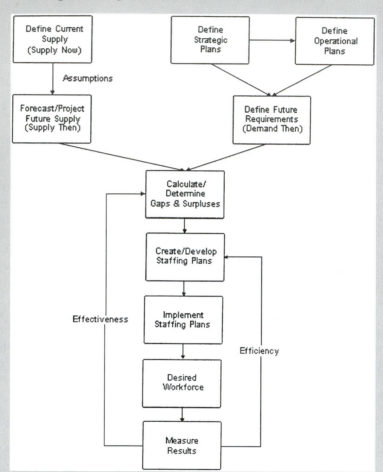

A Strategic Staffing Model from the State of Minnesota

It is highly recommended that a process to identify critical strategic and operational issues be established prior to implementing a strategic staffing approach. It is also important to note that one of the strengths of strategic staffing lies in its ability to adapt to an individual agency's strategic and operational planning processes.

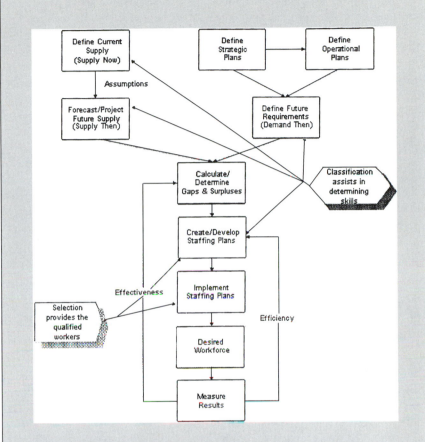

Linkages to Other Processes

- The strategic staffing process identifies the staffing requirements to meet the organizational goals.
- The classification process assists in determining the workforce's skills.
- Selection provides the qualified workers.

become the norm, HR planning may be applied in whole new areas. For starters, there may be major shifts in the content of work and the skills required. We are long since past the rather interesting projections made in the 1980s on how computerized knowledge systems would change both professional work and even the nature of professional judgment. It was predicted that over time professionals would spend far less time memorizing, gathering information, analyzing, and reasoning, and far more time in the areas of intuition and perception. The information revolution has changed all of that and much more. Analysts now speak of a new renaissance that will dramatically alter all aspects of business, work, home, and of course government.

There is already a growing literature on how technology and change will impact work structures for the twenty-first century. The premise that knowledge workers will dominate the work environment is largely accepted. Joseph Mosca has argued that these changes will lead to a complete restructuring of jobs. In his view, the restructured job will be aligned along the following dimensions:

1. Employees at all levels make decisions on a daily basis that once were primarily the responsibility of managers.
2. Employees will have complete access to organizational information that was once reserved for managers.
3. Employees will be trained to understand organizational business issues and be expected to respond to them.
4. Employees will be stakeholders in the organization.

Underwriting the advent of new jobs in the future will be the development of knowledge management, which may actually be the management fad that dominates the first decade of the twenty-first century for very obvious reasons. It certainly will resonate with those emerging workers or those knowledge workers in the restructured jobs mentioned above. How people work together, collaborate, share information and exchange knowledge, and operate in what is called a community of practice is all about a new vision of work in a new economy. That is the emerging environment HR planning must operate in and public sector organizations must learn to compete in.

BIBLIOGRAPHY

Baird, Lloyd, I. Meshoulam, and G. DeGive. "Meshing Human Resources Planning with Strategic Business Planning," *Personnel*, vol. 60, no. 5 (September–October 1983).

Blakely, Robert T. "Markov Models and Manpower Planning," *Industrial Management Review*, vol. 11, no. 2 (winter 1970).

Cameron, Kim S. "Strategies for Successful Organizational Downsizing," *Human Resources Management*, vol. 33, no. 2 (1991), pp. 189–211.

—"*Downsizing, Quality, and Performance*," in Robert Cole ed., *The Death and Life of the American Quality Movement*. New York: Oxford University Press, 1995, pp. 93–111.

Burack, Elmer H. and Robert D. Smith. *Personnel Management: A Human Resource System Approach*. New York: John Wiley, 1982.

Cascio, Wayne F. *Costing Human Resources: The Financial Impact of Behavior in Organizations*. Boston: Kent, 1982.

Clark, Harry L. and Dona Thurston. *Planning Your Staffing Needs*. Washington, D.C.: U.S. Government Printing Office, 1977.

Franklin, Daniel. "Downsizing: Is It Aimed at the Right Targets?" *Washington Monthly* (November 1994), pp. 22–27.

Franklin, James C. "Employment Outlook 1996–2006: Industry Output and Employment Projections to 2006," *Monthly Labor Review* (November 1997), pp. 39–57.

Gillespie, Jackson E., Wayne E. Leininger, and Harvey Kahalas. "A Human Resource Planning and Valuation Model," *Academy of Management Journal*, vol. 19, no. 4 (December 1976).

Greco, JoAnn. "America's Changing Workforce," *Journal of Business Strategy* (March–April 1998), pp. 43–46.

Hamel, Gary and C. K. Prahalhad. *Competing for the Future*. Cambridge: Harvard Business School Press, 1994.

Heneman, Herbert G. III and Marcus Sandver. "Markov Analysis in Human Resource Administration: Applications and Limitations," *Academy of Management Review*, vol. 2, no. 4 (October 1977).

Johnston, William B. *Workforce 2000: Work and Workers for the 21st Century*. Indianapolis: Hudson Institute, 1987.

Judy, Richard W. and Carol D'Amico. *Workforce 2020: Work and Workers in the 21st Century*. Indianapolis: Hudson Institute, 1997.

Light, Paul C. *The True Size of Government*. Washington, D.C.: Brookings Institution Press, 1999.

Martin, Lawrence L. "Public-Private Competition: A Public Employee Alternative to Privatization," *Review of Public Personnel Administration*, pp. 59–70.

Mills, D. Quinn. "Human Resources in the 1980's," *Harvard Business Review*, vol. 51, no. 4 (July–August 1970).

Mintzberg, Henry and Joseph Lampel. "Reflecting on the Strategy Process," *Sloan Management Review*, vol. 40, no. 3 (1999), pp. 21–30.

Mishel, Lawrence and Ruy A. Teixeira. *The Myth of the Coming Labor Shortage*. Washington, D.C.: Economic Policy Institute, 1991.

Mosca, Joseph A. "The Restructuring of Jobs for the Year 2000," *Public Personnel Management*, vol. 26, no. 1 (spring 1997), pp. 43–59.

National Academy of Public Administration. *Effective Downsizing: A Compendium of Lessons Learned for Government Organizations*. Washington, D.C., 1995.

National Academy of Public Administration. *Downsizing the Federal Workforce: Effects and Alternatives*. Washington, D.C., 1997.

National Academy of Public Administration. *Remembering the Future: Applying Foresight Techniques to Research Planning at EPA*. Washington, D.C., 1999.

National Performance Review. *Serving the American Public: Best Practices in Downsizing*. September 1997.

Naff, Katherine and Paul Vin Rijn. "The Next Generation: Why They Are Leaving," *Bureaucrat* (summer 1990).

Niehaus, Richard J. *Computer-Assisted Human Resources Planning.* New York: Wiley-Interscience, 1979.

Noer, David. *Healing the Wounds: Overcoming the Trauma of Layoffs and Revitalizing Downsized Organizations.* San Francisco: Jossey-Bass, 1993.

Perry, Lee T. "Key Human Resource Strategies in an Organizational Downturn," *Human Resource Management,* vol. 23, no. 1 (spring 1984).

Randall, Douglas. "Consumer Strategies for the Internet: Four Scenarios," *Long Range Planning,* vol. 30, no. 2 (1997), pp. 157–168.

Reich, Robert. Has Downsizing Gone Too Far?" *Challenge* (July–August 1996), pp. 4–10.

Ringland, Gill. *Scenario Planning: Managing for the Future.* Chichester: John Wiley, 1998.

Schwartz, Peter. *The Art of the Long View.* New York: Currency Doubleday, 1996.

Schein, Edgar H. "Increasing Organizational Effectiveness Through Better Human Resources Planning and Development," *Sloan Management Review* (fall 1977).

Shoemaker, Paul J. H. "Scenario Planning: A Tool for Strategic Thinking," *Sloan Management Review* (winter 1995), pp. 25–40.

Silvestri, George T. "Employment Outlook 1996–2006: Occupational Employment Projections to 2006," *Monthly Labor Review* (November 1997) pp. 58–82.

Stein, Howard. "Death Imagery and the Experience of Organizational Downsizing or, Is Your Name on Schindler's List," *Administration & Society* (May 1997), pp. 222–247.

U.S. Department of Labor. *Guide to Responsible Restructuring.* Washington, D.C.: U.S. Government Printing Office, 1995.

U.S. General Accounting Office. *Federal Workforce: A Framework for Studying Its Quality Over Time.* Washington, D.C., 1988.

U.S. General Accounting Office. *Federal Downsizing: The Costs and Savings of Buyouts Versus Reductions-in-Force.* Washington, D.C., May 1996.

U.S. General Accounting Office. *Federal Wildfire Activities.* Washington, D.C., 1999.

U.S. General Accounting Office. *The Changing Workforce: Demographic Issues Facing the Federal Government.* 1992.

U.S. General Accounting Office. *Transforming the Civil Service: Building the Workforce of the Future.* Washington, D.C., December 1995.

U.S. Merit Systems Protection Board & U.S. Office of Personnel Management. *A Report on the Conference on Workforce Quality Assessment.* Washington, D.C., 1989.

U.S. Merit Systems Protection Board. *Evolving Workforce Demographics: Federal Agency Action & Reaction.* Washington, D.C., 1993.

U.S. Merit Systems Protection Board. *Why Are Employees Leaving the Federal Government?* Washington, D.C., 1990.

U.S. Merit Systems Protection Board. *Who Is Leaving the Federal Government?* Washington, D.C., 1989.

U.S. Office of Personnel Management. *Civil Service 2000.* Washington, D.C., 1988.

Walker, James W. *Human Resources Planning.* New York: McGraw-Hill, 1980.

5

Classification and Compensation

PROLOGUE: TRANSFORMING WAITING ROOMS INTO MUSEUMS

Back in the early 1990s, the New York regional benefits office of the Veterans Benefits Administration was a typical small federal field organization with a very large mission. Approximately 250 employees worked to provide over 1.2 million veterans in 31 counties surrounding New York City with a range of services from insurance, education, and housing programs to pension benefits and burial allowances. New York was like any other federal benefits office—workloads were increasing, cycle time to complete claims processing was growing longer, and staff morale was sinking. Some initial work improvement efforts as part of a total quality management effort were launched, but most saw this as nibbling around the edges.

In 1993, a strong, highly charismatic director led New York in a series of sweeping fundamental changes. New York went from a hierarchical organization with an assembly line claims-processing system to an entirely different structure. It changed how work was done, how veterans received service, and most of all, changed the human resources management approach to the workforce. New York converted to self-directed work teams, moving quickly from having a 50-person prototype team in 1993 to reorganizing the entire claims-processing organization (about 200, or 80% of the entire regional office). These teams took complete control of what New York called end-to-end ownership of every claim they handled. The claims process was redesigned and simplified, with the 17 different jobs that were involved in claims reduced to three. As for the old organizational structure with seven functional divisions and several layers of hierarchy, including 47 supervisors, it was flattened to 10 teams with 11 supervisors and 14 coaches supported by a small support division—a human resources group.

New York regional benefits has become a well-documented success story. Within two years, it had reduced processing time by half, and more important, it had reduced backlog from 23,000 claims in 1993 to 11,000 by 1995 and under 8,000 by 1997. The average time spent waiting for personnel interviews had declined from 20 minutes to three minutes. Phone responsiveness had improved from 16% of veterans getting through on their first attempt at calling to 96%. The office received Vice President Gore's first Hammer Award [an award given thorough the auspices of the National Performance Review (NPR) to recognize excellence in reinvention]. It was made an NPR reinvention laboratory, received numerous other awards, and became a role model for innovative practices in teams, but underneath this team's reinvention success story is a major public sector human resources staffing case study. For all of the success of New York's radical change effort, it was grounded in a series of human resources management innovations that merit greater examination.

Organizations don't get to teams by fiat. New York did the requisite process-reengineering steps in the early 1990s that redesigned the claims work process, but the heavy lifting in this process involved changing the staffing, classification, and compensation systems. Teams could work because New York recast the old job structures dramatically. (See Table 5.1.) Taking the adjudication process, they converted the old job structures on the left of Table 5.1 to the new structure on the right.

How did New York get to this new job structure? It began by collapsing the number of job families and position descriptions. For example, the five clerk positions (i.e., file, claims, correspondence, development, and burial) listed in Table 5.1 were collapsed into the position of case technician. Then the grade level of the new case technician position was increased so that most clerks were receiving some form of salary increase going into the technician position. The case manager position was developed similarly. For teams to work, New York modified its classification system to have more employees classified at equal levels in fewer job families, effectively creating a broadbanding model.

Next it needed to develop an interim compensation guide and skills-development system. The problem was that there were very narrow job descriptions that restricted skill development. Sitting down with the union, New York developed a transition system that listed core skills, skill blocks, and combinations of skill blocks that had to be demonstrated for employees to obtain the new

TABLE 5.1 New York Regional Office—Old Structure
vs. New Teams

Old adjudication job structure	New team structure
Adjudication officer	Division chief
Assistant adjudication officer	Assistant division chief
Section chief	Coach
Unit chief	Case manager
Files supervisor	Case technician
Claims control supervisor	
Rating specialist	
Senior claims examiner	
Claims examiner	
Claims control clerk	
Development clerk	
Correspondence clerk	
Burial clerk	
File clerk	
Searcher	

and higher-graded case technician and case manager positions. This idea of skill-based pay involved 25 core skills in the schema shown in Table 5.2.

Each of the letters from B1 to B25 in Table 5.2 entails a specific set of work skills. For example, B1 involves 12 specific work activities from the ability to identify a compensation claim to handling folders and filing them in numerical order. Taking B25 at the highest end of the scale involves the ability to handle claims for special monthly compensation, including ratings involving the issue of grant or denial for different types of claims involving multiple issues or alleging clear and unmistakable error.

TABLE 5.2 New York Regional Office Skill-Based Pay Framework

Clerical skills	Adjudication skills	Authorization skills	Counselor skills	Rating skills
B1	B5	B11	B14	B19
B2	B6	B12	B15	B20
B3	B7	B13	B16	B21
B4	B8		B16A	B22
	B9		B17	B23
	B10		B18	B24
				B25

Once skills are identified, compensation levels that provide a salary range tied to the number of skill blocks an employee possesses are added. Aligning skill sets to compensation levels can be complex, as shown in Table 5.3, with Levels 4 through 10 and 12 being for both the case technician and case manager team positions. (Of course all of the salary ranges below were in 1995 pay levels and would be adjusted annually for cost-of-living increases, etc.) Still, Table 5.3 completes the picture of how New York aligned its job and salary structure to support its new team concept.

What New York was transforming was a reward system in which pay was based on the position held and an individual's time in grade to a skills-based system in which base pay was determined by skills (certified by the organization)

TABLE 5.3 New York Regional Office Compensation and Skill-Base Alignment

Compensation levels	Skill requirements	Skill-block combinations
Level 4 ($20,062–$25,075)	Case technician	Two of four clerical skill blocks
Level 5 ($21,823–$27,432)	Case technician	Four of four clerical skill blocks
Level 7 ($25,488–$32,530)	Case manager	Two adjudication + two counselor + four clerical (*B-18 required)
Level 9 ($30,612–$39,793)	Case manager	Three adjudication + three counselor + four clerical
Level 10 ($33,712–$43,825)	Three case manager (CM) skill sets	Four clerical + four adjudication + four counselor
		Four adjudication OR three adjudication + two clerical OR two adjudication + four clerical
		Four counselor OR three counselor + two clerical OR two counselor + four clerical OR two counselor + two clerical + three rating
Level 11 ($37,039–$48,153)	Six case managers skill sets	Not provided
Level 12 ($45,239–$57,708)	Case manager (all backgrounds, 2)	Six adjudication + 3 authorization + four clerical
		Six counselor + all seven rating

and a variable amount that would be paid based on organizational achievements. This final step—plans for using a results-based team award or bonus-led New York to go the Office of Personnel Management (OPM) and apply for status as a demonstration project so that it could develop its own approach to variable pay. New York felt that employees would work together in teams if some portion of their salary was tied to team performance. New York's variable pay plan approach involved creating a score card on all teams' performance and passing out incentive awards to each team based on its performance.

Additional funds were provided to coaches to give incentive awards to individuals who had made special contributions, and funds were also provided to each team to distribute to its team members for teamwork. Concerned that awards might lead to inappropriate team competition and potential cutthroat behaviors, the total amount of money available for awards increased with the number of teams who reached their performance goals.

Now, five years after the full inception of teams at the New York office, the question can be asked—is it still working? The fact that teams are still in place and still the dominant way work is performed in New York is in itself a measure of success. This does not mean that there haven't been problems adjusting to all the changes and discovering new problems arising out of a team-based work environment. The labor–management partnership has been a key factor of success, but that does not mean that the union hasn't opposed key aspects of change. One example has been the union's strong opposition to peer rankings by employees. Another lesson learned was on the size of the teams and the alignment of the coaches. Initially the teams were smaller, on the order of eight to 10 employees, with as many coaches as there were teams. In 1998 New York went to eight teams so that teams could be larger and have more people assigned to each team and thus more work-scheduling flexibility. Eight operating coaches—one for each team—were kept, but the city went to five technical consulting coaches to support all the teams in such areas as business or interpersonal skills as well as training in technical skills. Competitive behavior within and among teams is a new issue and has to be dealt with.

Still, this remarkable effort highlights new possibilities for government workplaces everywhere. Perhaps the biggest lesson to be learned is that organizations must rethink their use of teams. For decades organizations have used various forms of teams to solve organizational problems, but if teams are the norm in terms of the way in which the organization does work, it then becomes the organization's role to learn to support teams (culture, training, rewards, etc.). This role would include redesigning the space and technology the team uses to do its work. Indeed, it was the space redesign issue that inspired the prologue title. When the New York regional office redesigned its offices to support team-based work, it converted much of the large space formerly set aside for the reception area and waiting room into a small museum. Of course, there's a problem now with the average waiting time reduced to minimal levels; veterans will have to come to their appointments early to have the chance to walk through the exhibit space.

WHY CLASSIFICATION—WHY NOT STAFFING IN PUBLIC SECTOR ORGANIZATIONS?

It would seem that job structures, position classification, compensation linkages, and rewards systems would be the essence of staffing, which is defined broadly as the various organizational and management processes used to identify, structure, and evaluate work assignments for individuals and groups within organizations and to integrate as effectively as possible individual and organizational needs. Historically, staffing has always been central to public administration, but a closer look reveals that even in POSDCORB, the acronym coined by Gulick and Urwick in the late 1930s in their classic statement on the science of administration, there is both an *O* for organizing—which they defined as the "formal structure of authority through which work subdivisions are arranged"—and an *S* for staffing—which they saw as "the whole personnel function of bringing in and training the staff." Why, one might ask, does this distinction exist?

Public administration theorists have argued for decades about the dichotomies between politics and administration in managing governments. One might make a persuasive case that there has always existed an organizing and staffing dichotomy in public personnel administration; that is, classification that has been obsessed with organizing has come to view itself as a distinctly separate domain within (and sometimes independent from) personnel management. It has focused almost exclusively on such considerations as work subdivisions and let personnel management concern itself with recruitment, placement, training, and so on. Classification has enforced much of this dichotomy by its long-time admonition to "focus on the job, not the person."

Whether this view of organizing can hold in the new century is another matter. Change in organizations today is enormous and accelerating. The nature of work has changed dramatically and will change even more rapidly. Actual work content and methods, because of new technology and informational processes, are very different today in many organizations and promise to be radically different in the new era of the Internet economy. Even our understanding of why work is important and what work means to individuals and organizations has changed. Changing organizations, employees, and work have placed increasing pressures on classification, especially to be more flexible, dynamic, and holistic. These pressures are not likely to lessen. On the other hand, classification has shown remarkable resilience in staying its course. Many of the major "reforms" such as broadbanding, skill-based pay, gainsharing, and now team-based work systems confidently predicted a decade (in some cases two decades) ago that classification systems and methods would have be revolutionized or consigned to the trash can; rather, it is the reform efforts that have failed like minor coup attempts while classification still stands, largely unchanged.

THE EVOLUTION OF POSITION CLASSIFICATION: *THE ASCENDANCY OF SCIENTIFIC MANAGEMENT*

In the beginning, salaries of public employees were individually determined by legislative statute or by departmental administrators. Consequently, the first modern position classification plans were intended to remedy conditions of excessive political and personal favoritism in determining the duties and pay of public employees. It wasn't until 1902 that the federal government began to give serious consideration to the establishment of a classification program. In its annual report, the U.S. Civil Service Commission first urged positions to be classified ''on the basis of duties performed and to make compensation uniform for work of the same kind.'' Although Presidents Theodore Roosevelt and William Howard Taft were openly sympathetic to the installation of such a program, the Congress was not so inclined until 1912, when it authorized the Civil Service Commission to establish a division (later bureau) of efficiency to develop a system of efficiency ratings on the premise that standard salaries should be adopted for similar kinds of work.

Despite the federal government's ambivalence toward position classification during this time period, there was considerable reform activity at the state and local levels. In 1912 Chicago became the first jurisdiction to implement a position classification program. Later in the same year, Illinois was the first state to do so. Within the next two decades position classification plans were implemented by many of the largest state and local jurisdictions and certainly by all the progressive ones.

In 1919 the Congress created the Congressional Joint Commission on Reclassification of Salaries. The commission's report, issued in 1920, announced that ''equal pay for equal work as a standard for employment does not prevail in the U.S. Civil Service.'' The commission maintained that it was the lack of a comprehensive position classification plan that caused so many gross inequities in pay and concomitant problems of organizational structure, morale, excessive turnover, and inefficiency. Because the commission was mandated to propose remedies for the problems it encountered, the commission's staff developed a comprehensive classification system that evaluated positions according to duties, qualifications, and responsibilities.

The basic principles were codified in *The Classification Act of 1923*, which set up the method for job standardization, drew up grade levels and salary levels for each grade, created five services to group occupational categories, and established the Personnel Classification Board (later abolished in 1932 and transferred

The Language of Position Classification

Job evaluation.   A broad term meaning any approach, method, or process that distinguishes among jobs for the purpose of establishing rates of pay.

Job analysis.   The process of gathering and assessing facts about jobs in order to determine their proper classification. Any of several techniques may be used for job analysis so long as the technique is objective and accurately identifies and measures all significant aspects of jobs. The results of a thorough job analysis provide input into recruitment, selection, and training programs in addition to the classification process.

Factors.   These are aspects of a job such as nature of supervision received or exercised, guidelines available, complexity of the work, impact of decisions, relationships with others, mental demands and working conditions. These dimensions of a job are used for purposes of evaluation.

Factors are used in both "whole job" and factor point approaches to position classification. The "whole job" approach, however, does not define each factor and degree in advance nor does it use numerical points to weight each factor. In contrast, factor point systems evaluate each factor separately and give each one a numerical value according to how strongly the factor is represented in the job. The points for all of the factors are added to arrive at the total amount for the job, which determines its classification.

Position.   Any combination of duties and responsibilities, assigned by competent authority, to be performed by one person. A position may be full or part-time, temporary or permanent, filled or vacant; it is distinguished from an employee who may at any time be assigned to it.

Positions are fundamental units of classification just as they are the smallest elements within the organization structure. The emphasis on the position as the unit of evaluation is a significant concept. It focuses attention on what is done rather than on who performs it and thus avoids the subjective judgments that are inevitably associated with evaluating people. The concept also underscores another fundamental of position classification—that management ultimately controls the classification of positions by approving the assignment of specific duties and responsibilities to be performed.

Job.   Any combination of duties and responsibilities to be performed by one or more employees that is identical in all significant respects so that a single descriptive word or title can be used to identify the work and employees can be readily transferred from one position to another without noticeable interruption of performance. Examples include the jobs of trash collectors, hoseman, voucher clerk, urban planner, etc., all of which may be performed by one or more employees.

Class.   A "class" is a grouping of positions for which the duties, responsibilities and qualification requirements and conditions of employment are sufficiently alike to justify the same treatment with respect to pay, selection, and other personnel processes. At times, the terms "jobs" and "class" may be used interchangeably though "class" is a broader concept, normally encompassing more than one job.

Classes generally are defined as broadly as is feasible so long as the test of similarity in treatment is met. This contributes to efficient and cost effective management by reducing the number of categories for which it is necessary to separately recruit, examine, certify, train and establish pay levels. Nevertheless, there are always cases where a narrowly defined class must be established for a few or even a single position because different personnel procedures must be used.

Class series. Class series can be likened to occupational career ladders. They usually begin with an entry level which contains positions to be filled by persons with the basic preparation necessary to enter the occupation. Beyond the entry level, class series ordinarily progress through commonly identified levels in the field of work in this fashion:

> Experienced level—jobs that are typically performed by persons who have acquired a good knowledge of the field and are able to perform a wide range of tasks typical of the occupation; frequently termed the "journey" level.
>
> Advanced level—positions usually performed only by persons with considerable experience who are able to handle the most difficult and complex work in the field; frequently termed the "expert" level.
>
> Supervisory and administrative levels as necessary.

Class series indicate the normal lines of promotion within a field of work. By dividing the field into commonly identified levels they permit the recruitment and induction into the service of persons at commonly identified stages in their career development from outside the service. Hence, the formation of class series requires a good knowledge of the common patterns of career development that characterize occupations.

Occupational group. This represents the largest grouping of occupations (classes) that can be feasibly related for purposes of recruitment, selection, transfer, promotion and training. It also provides a fundamental category for the application of compensation policies.

The position, class, class series, and occupational group are the basic categories of a system of position classification. Together, they comprise a classification plan which is an orderly grouping of all positions in the organization according to kind of work and level of difficulty and responsibility.

Source: U.S. Office of Personnel Management. *Position Classification: A Guide for City and County Managers.* Washington, D.C.: U.S. Government Printing Office, November 1979, pp. 3–5.

to the Civil Service Commission) as the central classifying authority. The 1923
act was a major precedent or foundation for practically all position classification
systems at the state, local, and national levels. The principles that were promulgated were very much reflective of the scientific management movement, which
was very influential at that time, so it is hardly surprising that their implied view
of the individual worker was that of a human interchangeable machine part.

The principles established in 1920 were as follows:

1. That *positions* and *not individuals* should be classified
2. That the duties and responsibilities pertaining to a position constitute
   the outstanding characteristics that distinguish it from—or mark its
   similarity to—other positions
3. That qualifications with respect to the education, experience, knowledge, and skill necessary for the performance of certain duties are determined by the nature of those duties, therefore the qualifications for
   a position are important factors in the determination of the classification of the position
4. That the individual characteristics of an employee occupying a position
   should have no bearing on the classification of the position
5. That persons holding positions in the same class should be considered
   equally qualified for any other position in that class.

In the two decades after the 1920 report, a period of extensive classification
activity occurred. Cities, counties, states, and federal government agencies conducted surveys of their positions and completed studies of how positions related
individuals to organizations as part of the classification system. As the practice
diversified, there was a perceived need to review position classification and
appraise the state of the art. In 1937, the Civil Service Assembly sponsored
such an effort, which resulted in the formulation of a committee on position
classification and pay plans in the public service, which was under the direction
of Ismar Baruch. Baruch, who was chief of the U.S. Civil Service Commission's
Division of Classification, was ideally placed as a director to see that the best
"expertise" was available to produce the report and to ensure that the report
would be used.

Published in 1942, the resulting volume was over 400 pages, and was a
unique document. It was the authoritative source on position classification, and
its use by practicing classifiers compared with the ministry's use of the Bible.
The Baruch report, as it was called, was the definitive statement of the theory
and applied practice of position classification for the 1940s and 1950s. The report
covered all the pertinent aspects of the practice, beginning with the role of personnel administration, and extending to the fundamental concepts and definitions to
applications, methods, legal authority, development, installation, and maintenance. Although it is difficult to summarize the Baruch report in a few paragraphs,

the basic concepts can be briefly identified. First, the meaning of position classification must be considered, perhaps best stated just as the Baruch report defined it.

> Reduced to its simplest terms, classification of positions means the process of finding out, by obtaining the facts and analyzing them, what different kinds or "classes" of positions, calling for different treatment in personnel processes, there are in the service; it further includes making a systematic record of the classes found and of the particular positions found to be of each class. The duties and responsibilities of the positions are the basis upon which classes are determined and the individual positions assigned or "allocated" to their appropriate classes.
>
> When every position has been allocated to its appropriate class, each class will consist of all positions, regardless of departmental location, that are sufficiently alike in duties and responsibilities to be called by the same descriptive title, to be accorded the same pay scale under like conditions, and to require substantially the same qualifications on the part of the incumbents.

An important footnote to the above mentions the problem of excluding personal bias. The report adds: "This is an objective, impersonal basis. Allocations of positions to classes are based on the essential characteristics of the work performed in each position, and not on the education, experience, background, efficiency, or ability that the incumbent employees at the time may happen to possess or lack."

With this purpose clearly stated, the report defines a position as: "a group of current duties and responsibilities, assigned or delegated by competent authority, requiring the full-time or part-time employment of one person."

Under this definition a position consists of assignment of duties and delegation of responsibilities. It comes into existence through the action of management or another controlling authority, proceeding through supervisory operating officials who formally or informally specify work for individuals to do and delegate responsibilities for them to exercise. Each position was to be specified separately through completion of a "position description" or some form of joint statement by the employee and the supervisor of what the work duties and responsibilities were. This definition was further amplified by the recognition that position duties and responsibilities are changing and that position classification must stay tuned to these changes. These changes had to be organizationally inspired and mandated, however, as opposed to being based on employee interest. In one classic paragraph, the Baruch report reviews how to deal with the problem of matching the employee to the job, in this case referring to a Phi Beta Kappa working as a janitor.

To be sure, in the cases we have just mentioned there may be an administrative error in matching employee to his job. Position classification serves a very important function in bringing such administrative errors into focus. It displays the facts about the actual duties and responsibilities of the position to which the employee is assigned. If, in the interests of the employee or of the department, that assignment can be made more effective, it is a matter for correction, not through position classification, but through placement procedures. Another common reason for falling into an unconscious attempt to classify the employee rather than the position is failure to distinguish between the duties and responsibilities an employee performs or exercises and the relative degree of efficiency or effectiveness with which he carries them out.

The Baruch report saw positions as individual units or microstructures within larger designations, which are referred to as classes, and further states that "a class of positions constitutes a group of positions which, irrespective of the particular operating units in which they are located, are, in respect to their duties and responsibilities, sufficiently alike for purposes of personnel administration. In a position-classification plan, the class is the fundamental unit."

In effect, then, the class was the aggregate concept that provided the method for vertical and horizontal comparisons. Vertical comparisons were made inside each class and attempted to distinguish between higher and lower levels of work. Horizontal comparisons were made between job classes in order to relate each class to each other within the organization. Once these comparisons were made and documented, along with a set of procedures for updating the comparisons, the plan for position classification was completed and could be put into effect.

All of the above concepts hinge on a final set of analytical factors that are the basis for comparisons of positions and classes of positions. These units of analysis obviously varied, depending on the kinds of positions involved, but the Baruch report also discussed in depth how they may be used for measurement purposes. The following four general areas were to be used:

Difficulty and complexity of duties
Nonsupervisory responsibilities
Supervisory and administrative responsibilities
Qualification standards

The Baruch report in essence summarized the basis of the traditional position classification system that emerged out of the application of scientific management to personnel management. Baruch himself, writing in 1937 in a monograph entitled "Facts and Fallacies in Position Classification," added an important caveat. He wrote that "a duties classification plan is not an end in itself but a tool or device for accomplishing the many and varied ends of personnel administration."

It was a prophetic insight, because traditional classification was very much the backbone of the traditional concept of public personnel management. In the aftermath of the Second World War, when public administration was confronting a different and more political environment, a different genre of public personnel management began to emerge. This new environment would focus considerable criticism on position classification.

AFTER THE WAR: "THE TRIUMPH OF TECHNIQUE OVER PURPOSE"

By the Second World War, there were substantial new pressures on the federal classification system. The sheer increase in the number of positions and the resulting deluge of classification actions work as governments grew made the idea of one central classifying authority impossible. Increasing numbers of white collar jobs were presenting problems in classifying for a system that was predominantly based on blue collar jobs. The result was a major revision of the system in the Classification Act of 1949.

The 1949 act created the general schedule (GS) pay plan with 18 grade categories to cover white collar workers. Blue collar workers were grouped into a craft, protective, and custodial (CPC) pay plan. Later amendments in 1954 would change the CPC pay schedule to a wage grade system in which blue collar workers were linked to local prevailing rates. Finally, the Classification Act of 1949 specified classification standards (i.e., detailed statements of job duties and qualifications for each grade level). The resulting framework was virtually permanent. Indeed, a 1989 report by the U.S. Merit Systems Protection Board noted: "These grade level criteria have come to be viewed as if they were 'cast in stone' since they have only had one minor modification in the last 40 years."

The changes brought about by the 1949 act lessened some of the administrative difficulties but did not abate managerial pressures. The most constant complaint about classification procedures was that the system placed primary emphasis on the position rather than on the qualifications and abilities of an individual incumbent. This situation, critics maintained, generated dysfunctional activities in order to compensate for the inflexibility of the classification system. As long as organizational structures tried to maintain the principle established by the 1920 *Report of the Congressional Joint Commission on Reclassification of Salaries*, namely, that "the individual characteristics of an employee occupying a position," administrators, recognizing the futility of maintaining such a principle, would compensate via administrative finesse—that is, "fudging the system."

What the Baruch report provided was an irrefutable set of theories and principles for classifiers. Practice, however, was another matter. Classification practices were widely resisted by managers who ridiculed what they viewed as a rigid and static set of standards administered by unreasonable "classifiers." In part the problem was a lack of standards for classification actions and insufficient authority by classifiers to ensure conformity to rules and procedures. Classifications in the federal government, as Van Riper notes, "continued all through the war [World War II] to remain a major bone of administrative contention between the [Civil Service] Commission and nearly all government agencies."

The problem, in a nutshell, was the felt need on the part of most government agencies to upgrade position levels in order to increase pay and prestige as a means of retaining employees in a highly competitive environment. Classification on the other hand, was concerned about the lack of control and potential abuse that such agency demands represented. While agencies complained about nonresponsive, inflexible classification actions, classifiers rebutted with charges of "unwarranted grade escalation" or "grade creep."

The grade escalation controversy became the pivotal point in the deterioration of the traditional classification practice. Despite the passage of the new classification act in 1949, which remedied (at least legally) some of the older problems of insufficient standards, lack of authority, and inadequate audit procedures, criticism was unabated. Van Riper's history quotes an experienced practitioner: "the Civil Service Commission is sacrificing quality for mass production, and is forcing standards on the agencies that are technically invalid for many reasons, and that in style and content are so ambiguous and incomplete as to leave the classifier in the same state of uncertainty that existed before they were issued."

Despite the unhappiness of the agencies, the Civil Service Commission began to press its claims against grade escalation. In 1963, the Bureau of Programs and Standards released a research report, *The Nature and Meaning of Grade Escalation Under the Classification Act*, which conceded that public sector grade escalation was "a sign of the times that would continue." Further, it should be expected because of the rapidly changing composition of the government workforce, which was shifting significantly from low-level routine work to higher-level professional/technical work. The report also indicated that this trend was prevalent in private industry, which was also experiencing escalation.

The report took a much harder line in its view of the causes, noting

1. *Some of the causes are basically good.*
   a. Growth in research and development activities that contribute to our national security and that result in breakthroughs in the fight against disease.
   b. Better service or greater protection for the public (e.g., improvement in air traffic control).
2. *Other causes are clearly bad.*
   a. Reorganization specifically for the purpose of raising grades by spreading higher-level duties thinly among a larger number of positions.

    b. Establishment of more organizational units than are really necessary in order to get more high-level supervisory jobs.

    c. Inflated position descriptions.

    d. Deliberate misclassification of jobs for purposes of adjusting to outside pay pressures.

3. *Still other causes cannot be clearly labeled as good or bad.*

    a. Decisions to establish a new organizational segment or to set up a new staff position, where the soundness of management judgment cannot be determined ahead of time.

    b. Management action to delegate decision-making authority on cases (e.g., claims or appeals to more positions in order to cut processing time; soundness of such management action often is not determinable in advance).

The causes of overstaffing and misclassification have not changed over the years:

1. Poor management practices, resulting in excess personnel, improper distribution of assignments, poor utilization, etc.

2. Disregard of classification standards for recruiting advantages, for pirating purposes, or for empire building

In 1964, Seymour S. Berlin of the U.S. Civil Service Commission wrote an article attempting to reconcile the manager's and the classifier's stands on grade escalation. Berlin argued that the ultimate responsibility for this unwarranted grade escalation belonged to the manager, and that classification of jobs "is the result of management decisions which occur long before the position classifier takes his formal action. The classification of the job is all but final after the manager decides what duties are to be performed, how the position will relate to other jobs etc." Berlin spared neither classifiers, whom he felt regarded classification as an end in itself, nor managers, who in their attempts to beat the system were evading their responsibilities.

THE 1970s AND THE BEHAVIORALIST CRITIQUE

Berlin's conclusion was basically that the classification system as it stood was sound; it simply was not being adhered to, but in the 1970s a new critique emerged that was prepared to take on the theory itself. The behavioralists, as this group of then young scholars and practitionier critics was referred to, drew a different conclusion about the deterioration of the practice of classification. Leading off the critique was Shafritz's 1973 work, *Position Classification: A Behavioral Analysis for the Public Service*, which argued that traditional classification practices were "obsolete."

The critique began by noting that the scientific management-oriented principals of traditional classification were counterproductive for more highly skilled, knowledge-oriented employees, and for highly flexible organizational structures with different relationships between managers and workers. The advent of public sector unions was another development that changed the basis for classification, but the crux of the behavorial critique (and hence the reason for its name) was that classification ignored the behavioral implications of organization. This complex argument was based on the premise, as one leading behavorialist argued that: "A long-recognized behavioral tenet holds that, 'when formal organizations come into operation, they create and require informal organizations.' Thus position classifications, being an integral part of the formal bureaucratic structure would create informal organizational structures to compensate for the deficiencies of the formal structure. The behavorial critique advocated a new theory of classification for the coming postbureaucratic era that could deal with new forms of workers and organizations. The new theories of behavioral science would radically change the role of personnel from its largely accounting and policing functional mentality to more of an internal consulting team specializing in the motivation and optimal utilization of human resources.

The behavioral critique drew support from a variety of sources. Jay F. Atwood, a personnel practitioner with the state of California, argued the case for applying behavioral science principles to actual techniques of position classification. New dimensions to classification would be required, he argued, to understand positions in which "the sum of the total positions is greater than the sum of its individual tasks. Thus, we need to use 'position synthesis' rather than 'job analysis' to understand how the position and its particular incumbent relate in a multi-faceted organizational environment." Atwood's breakthroughs in methods called for (1) using broader position/organizational data; (2) examining critical factors in individual-position relationships; and (3) applying behavior science/ organizational dynamics to position classification.

Another part of the behavioral critique was provided by Frank J. Thompson's influential study of personnel policies and politics in Oakland which examined the political dimension. Thompson stated that the study of classification had focused too much on who wins and who loses and not enough on the dynamics of the process. To begin with, he indicated that there are four categories of classification systems, which are subdivided according to complexity (the relative number of classes existing) and precision (how specifically class labels describe work duties). His categories were as follows:

  I.   Focused—very precise labels, few classes
 II.   Differentiated—very precise labels, but many classes
III.   Elemental—imprecise labels, but few classes
 IV.   Blurred—imprecise labels and many classes

The Position Classifier's Dilemma

Position classifiers may fall into two extreme profiles. One resembles the zealous police officer who tickets anyone, whether garbage collector or mayor. The other profile resembles a philanthropist, a person who approves all requests for grade and salary increases automatically. The first profile requires a combative personality. The zealot must constantly be prepared to fight to ensure that the official standards, and her interpretation of them, prevail. The zealot proclaims a high ethical and moral purpose. She feels personally responsible for the taxpayer's money, and treats the official standards as Holy Writ. The zealot is a fundamentalist.

The second profile possesses a personality that is resigned to bureaucratic "reality." He curries favor with superiors and employees alike. To disappoint no one is his motto. As the fundamentalist seeks her reward in another world, the philanthropist obtains his pleasure in this world. The philanthropist's generosity makes him an object of love and attention. His vested interest is in serving others, creating good will, and earning a special place in the hearts and minds of his benefactors.

While some position classifiers may actually fall neatly into these two profiles, most probably do not. People do, however, tend to develop habit patterns, and these patterns may enable any individual classifier to gravitate predominantly toward either the zealot or the philanthropist profile. Most position classifiers are sensitive to the prevailing winds in their respective agencies. They learn to sense what is expected of them by their superiors, and they adapt.

Source: Adapted from Monroe, Michael L., "The Position Classifier's Dilemma," *Bureaucrat*, vol. 4 (July 1975), pp. 205–206. (Changes have been made in gender terminology.)

While speculative, Thompson's categories were very provocative. He examined how these different categories (perhaps a better word is conditions) of classification practices might impact recruitment, pay, productivity, advancement, affirmative action, and other personnel practices. He concluded: "Classification is, then, replete with political implications. Regrettably, we know relatively little about such politics. What are the dynamics which lead some agencies to opt for one kind of classification over another? What characterizes bureaucratic politics when some seek to enlarge jobs in a government agency? What relationship in fact exists between classification and government productivity? Well documented answers to these and other questions are extremely scarce."

The behavioral critique set off a revolt. Classification had to reform itself and incorporate into its reform new modes of responsiveness. Unfortunately, the forces of reform were already at work. They rushed to prescribe new cures for more effective practices, rightly calculating that a pound of responsiveness might head off an ounce of true reform.

THE SYSTEM RESPONSE: FACTOR EVALUATION IN THE 1970s

Already in 1967 the House Committee on Post Office and Civil Service had decided that "a comprehensive review should be made of all classification and ranking systems in the federal service." Thereupon a comprehensive survey of federal classification practices was undertaken by the Subcommittee on Position Classification. The subcommittee's report was a detailed indictment of current practices. It found that

1. Although job evaluation and ranking should provide the basis for good personnel management, many believed it was not doing so.
2. Classification and ranking systems had not been adapted to, maintained, or administered to meet the rapidly changing needs of the federal government.
3. Classification was not generally used as a management tool. Many officials commented that the only function of classification in their organization was a basis for fixing pay.

These findings were serious enough that they led to the passing of the Job Evaluation Policy Act of 1970. This act asserted that it was the sense of the Congress that there be a coordinated classification system for all civilian positions and that the U.S. Civil Service Commission should exercise general supervision and control over it. The Civil Service Commission was authorized to establish a planning unit that would submit its final report within two years and then cease to exist. This unit became known as the Job Evaluation and Pay Review Task Force. The final report of the task force, released in January 1972, was popularly known as the Oliver report, after the task force director, Philip M. Oliver. The Oliver report declared the federal government's classification and ranking systems obsolete.

The task force recommended a new job evaluation system. The new system was field-tested and revised. Finally, in December 1975, the Civil Service Commission approved the implementation, over a five-year period, of the factor evaluation system for nonsupervisory positions. The factor evaluation (or factor comparison) system was designed to be accurate and flexible, yet simple and relatively inexpensive. Even more important, however, it hoped to secure the active involvement of operating management, thus helping to reduce the "them or us" mentality that was usually associated with traditional control-oriented classification methods.

Actually, the federal government's use of a factor evaluation system was seen by some as a return to the classification practices of the 1920s, such as the first factor comparison system installed by Eugene J. Benge at the Philadelphia Transit Company in 1926. The factor comparison system was basically a hybrid of traditional position classification systems; but the differences are significant. In the case of traditional classifications, different combinations of factors were used for different positions; the factor evaluation system uses the same factors for all positions. In the case of traditional classifications grade levels were ascertained by the weight and eloquence of narrative descriptions; the factor evaluation system determined grade levels by comparing positions directly to one another. In short, the factor evaluation system sought to take traditional classification concepts a step further into rationality.

Obviously, the main ingredient of a factor evaluation system is the factor—any of the various key elements individually examined in the evaluation process. Although there are an infinite number of specific factors that pertain to differing jobs, the factors themselves are usually categorized within the following five groupings:

1. *Job requirements*—The knowledge, skills, and abilities needed to perform the duties of a specific job
2. *Difficulty of work*—The complexity or intricacy of the work and the associated mental demands of the job
3. *Responsibility*—The freedom of action required by a job and the impact of the work performed upon the organizational mission
4. *Personal relationships*—The importance of interpersonal relationships to the success of mission accomplishment
5. *Other factors*—Specific job-oriented elements that should be considered in the evaluation process—for example, physical demands, working conditions, accountability, number of workers directed

Once the factors of a position have been identified, it can be ranked; that is, the factors of one position can be compared to another. Such a factor comparison can have only three outcomes. Any given factor must be higher than, lower than, or equal to the factor of another position. When positions are ranked by factors, all of the factors of each position are compared and an overall ranking is achieved.

The crucial focus of a factor comparison system is the benchmark—a specific job at a specific point within an array of evaluations. Each series of choices based on ranking one position as compared to another results in a composite or total of the choices. When assigned numerical values, these yield a score that assigns position X and position Y to specific points within an array of evaluations. Each time such determinations are made, they add to the array, thereby increasing the number of benchmarks. Each addition to the number of benchmarks facilitates arriving at the ranking choices for other jobs not yet evaluated.

Finally, when all of the jobs within an organization have been evaluated, they all become benchmarks. Once this has been achieved, all the positions within an organization would have, in effect, been compared to each other; each would have found its place in the classification and pay plans because it was found to rank higher than, lower than, or equal to its neighboring positions.

In adapting general factor evaluation for the federal government, the system was based on the following nine factors:

1. *Knowledge required by the position*—This factor measures the nature and extent of information or facts that the worker must understand to do acceptable work (e.g., steps, procedures, practices, rules, policies, theory, principles, and concepts) and the nature and extent of the skills and abilities necessary to apply this knowledge.

2. *Supervisory controls*—This factor covers the nature and extent of direct or indirect controls exercised by the supervisor, the employee's responsibility, and the review of completed work. Controls are exercised by the supervisor in the way assignments are made, instructions are given to the employee, priorities and deadlines are set, and objectives and boundaries are defined. Responsibility of the employee depends upon the extent to which the employee is expected to develop the sequence and timing of various aspects of the work, to modify or recommend modification of instructions, and to participate in establishing priorities and defining objectives. The degree of review of completed work depends upon the nature and extent of the review—for example, a close and detailed review of each phase of the assignment, a detailed review of the finished assignment, a spot check of finished work for accuracy, or a review only for adherence to policy.

3. *Guidelines*—This factor covers the nature of the guidelines and the judgment needed to apply these guidelines. Jobs vary in the specificity, applicability, and availability of guidelines for performance of assignments. Consequently, the constraints and judgmental demands placed upon employees also vary. For example, the existence of specific instructions, procedures, and policies may limit the opportunity of the employee to make or recommend decisions or actions; however, in the absence of procedures or under broadly stated objectives, the employee may use considerable judgment in researching literature and developing new methods.

4. *Complexity*—This factor covers the nature and variety of tasks, steps, processes, methods, or activities in the work performed, and the degree to which the employee must vary the work, discern interrelationships and deviations, or develop new techniques, criteria, or information. At the low end of the scale, the work involves few clear-cut and directly related tasks or functions.

5. *Scope and effect*—This factor covers the purpose of the assignment and the effect of work products both within and outside the organization. At the lower end of the scale, the purpose is to perform specific routine operations that have little impact beyond the immediate organizational unit. At the high end of the scale, the purpose is to plan, develop, and carry out vital administrative or scientific programs that are essential to the missions of the agency or affect large numbers of people on a long-term or continuing basis.

6. *Personal contacts*—This factor includes face-to-face contacts and telephone and radio dialogue with persons not in the supervisory chain. The nature of contacts ranges from those with other employees in the immediate work unit to contacts with high-ranking officials outside the agency. In between are many variations.

7. *Purpose of contacts*—The contacts covered by this factor range from the factual exchanges of information to situations involving significant or controversial issues and differing viewpoints, goals, or objectives.

8. *Physical demands*—This factor covers the requirements and physical demands placed on the employee by work assignment. This includes physical characteristics and abilities (e.g., specific agility and dexterity requirements) and the physical exertion involved in the work (e.g., climbing, lifting, pushing, balancing, stooping, kneeling, crouching, crawling, or reaching). To some extent the frequency or intensity of physical exertion must also be considered; for example, a job requiring prolonged standing involves more physical exertion than a job requiring intermittent standing.

9. *Work environment*—This factor considers the risks, discomforts, or unpleasantness that may be imposed upon employees by various physical surroundings or job situations.

It is important that factor ranking be viewed in a comparative perspective. Philip Oliver, the principal architect of the method, argued that the system was essentially a recompilation of existing methods in the private and public sectors. Table 5.4 illustrates the four major categories of job evaluation plans, in which factor comparison can be seen as a blend of the ranking and point-rating methods. Of course its application on a scale as large as the federal government or many state and municipal governments was a major development in itself.

TABLE 5.4 Typology of Job Evaluation Plans for Classification Methods

Category of method	Concept	Best applications
Ranking method	Rank order each position by value using some form of collective judgment. Positions evaluated as whole units.	Small organizations where all positions are common knowledge.
Classification method (traditional)	Sort positions into grades/classes using predetermined standards or descriptions to ascertain grade levels. Positions evaluated as whole units.	Stable, large organizations (traditional) where outside control is significant (especially if legislature is involved).
Point-rating method	Uniform set of job factors are chosen as the basis for establishing the value of the job. Positions are then rated in terms of degrees on each factor with points assigned for each degree. Position evaluated as a cumulative score from its components.	Used extensively in private industry where flexibility is important and different perspectives are involved in determining value of positions/jobs.
Factor comparison method	Combines aspects of ranking and point ranking. Predetermined selection of factors, weights for the factors, and key jobs (benchmark positions). Positions are then scored on each factor compared to benchmark positions. Position is then evaluated as cumulative score.	Most suitable for large, dynamic public sector organizations where extensive employee/supervisory involvement and interaction are critical for acceptance.

Source: Adapted in part from Milkey, R. F. "Job Evaluation After 50 Years," *Public Personnel Review* (January 1960).

To cement the significance of factor ranking and other more sophisticated methods, an effort was made to replace the standard reference work, the Baruch report. Harold Suskin edited a comprehensive volume in 1977 that provided illustrations of the new methods of job evaluation, overviewed pay administration and legal issues, and surveyed applications and new developments portending change. Suskin himself wrote the descriptive chapter on factor ranking and explained the advantages as follows:

> All major job characteristics must be weighed under the factor ranking approach. Strengths and weaknesses of a job must be recognized and quantified. The classifier's judgment on each factor is placed squarely on the record for all to see. This eliminates much of the mysticism commonly associated with classification decisions.
>
> Job evaluation is a subjective decisionmaking process. The classification method involves a review of the job as a whole, as well as a single subjective judgment concerning the appropriate grade, skill level, or pay range. If that decision over-credits or under-credits the job as a whole, the job is placed in the wrong grade, skill level, or pay range. Factor ranking involves a series of subjective decisions (i.e., a decision concerning each factor). Errors tend to offset one another, and the end product is likely to be more valid. Numerous psychological studies have indicated that a series of subjective judgments usually produce more valid results than does a single subjective judgment.

Although Suskin recognized that there would be disadvantages, these were generally categorized as being problems of implementation that would inevitably occur when any jurisdiction switched from a more subjective method to a much more objective, mechanically oriented process.

One should understand what was really at variance, however. Table 5.5 gives an abridged version of an old Civil Service Commission exhibit used in educating administrators about the differences among job evaluation systems. As Table 5.5 shows, the informational factors are not that different. What was most different was the method used by the classifiers in making the classification decisions.

Few critics were consequently surprised when the factor evaluation system proved not to be major surgery but only a Band-Aid for the wounds of the federal classification system and the pressing need for pay reform. It offered better and more efficient methods, but it could not address the deterioration of the entire classification system. By the early 1980s this was all too apparent, as the trend to reallocate positions upward (frequently referred to as ''grade escalation'' or ''grade creep'') continued unabated. In a 1983 federal survey, the OPM (the replacement for old U.S. Civil Service Commission) calculated that at least 14% of jobs are misclassified or overgraded.

TABLE 5.5 Comparison of Job Evaluation Systems (Nonsupervisory Positions)

Characteristics	Federal wage system	Traditional position classification system (1940s)	Factor evaluation system (1970s)
Occupations	Trades and labor	Clerical, technical, administrative, and professional	Clerical, technical, administrative, and professional
Pay basis	Hourly rates (area wage surveys)	Per-annum rates—national general schedule	Per-annum rates—national general schedule
Factors used in evaluating positions	1. Skill and knowledge 2. Responsibility (includes supervisory controls, guidelines, scope, and effort) 3. Physical effort 4. Working conditions	1. Qualifications 2. Supervision received 3. Guidelines 4. Originality 5. Nature and variety of work 6. Recommendations, decisions, etc. 7. Nature of person-to-person work relationships (physical demands and hazardous work environment as important in particular occupations)	1. Knowledge required 2. Supervisory controls 3. Guidelines 4. Complexity 5. Scope and effect 6. General contacts 7. Purpose of contacts 8. Physical demands 9. Work environment
Standards	Same factors used consistently in narrative descriptions of grade levels	Various combinations of factors—mostly narrative descriptions of grade levels: some quantitative and factor format standards	Some factors used consistently in benchmarks and factor-level descriptions (each factor level carries a point value)
Application	Positions graded to highest level reflected in regular, recurring duties	Positions graded to highest level compared to standards	Positions graded by totaling points and converting to grade—all regular, recurring work considered

Note: The traditional position classification system typically covers supervisory positions as well as nonsupervisory positions. Because this table compares systems for nonsupervisory positions, "nature and extent of supervision over work of other employees" is not included under "Factors Used."

Job Evaluation and Class and Comp Systems

Job evaluation has been defined in a number of different ways. Today, it is mainly seen as the overall process by which organizations develop "job worth" hierarchies, and it is through job evaluation that formal classification and compensation (class and comp) systems in both public and private sectors are set. The antiquated job evaluation techniques that continue to underlie most class and comp systems result in, among other things, pay disparities between women and men; and between whites and people of color.

A number of states, particularly in the 1980s, became more and more concerned with these pay disparities. As such, many began to reevaluate their class and comp systems in order to, as the New York State Center for Women in Government has stated, "determine whether assumptions about the value of jobs and the assignment of job titles to salary grades have been distorted by the sex or race of the typical job incumbent." Studies have shown that such "distortions" are widespread, thus giving way to job evaluation systems that are more equitable in orientation and outcome.

Source: New York State Center for Women in Government. *Comparable Worth Study.* Albany, N.Y.: October 1985.

In August of the same year, OPM issued a moratorium of the issuance of classification standards. This was a remarkable admission on the part of OPM as it in effect refused to put more resources into creating and updating standards when the system clearly needed total repair. The question was which path to take—should classification be "modernized" or should reform follow a totally new path—one that would incorporate a new vision for both classification as an organizational function and a personnel process?

The moratorium lasted until 1986, when OPM announced new initiatives to move toward more flexible and simplified standards. A major thrust of this movement was to experiment with "multioccupation classification guides" that were designed to be more general and compare similar work across different occupational categories to avoid being overly specialized or narrow. Finally, new initiatives promised—again—more delegation of authority to agencies and more flexibility for managers.

Classification reform had to take a back seat to pay reform, however. In the 1980s, severe pay pressures were greatly distorting the classification system. As federal wages, especially for white collar occupations, fell behind private sector wages by 10 to 15% and then 20% by the end of the decade, federal

	1986	1990	1994	1996	1998	% change '86 - '98
Total GS and Related	**1,592,696**	**1,655,562**	**1,587,069**	**1,482,644**	**1,427,870**	**-10.3%**
GS 1	5,590	4,649	2,931	2,966	3,141	**-43.8%**
GS 2	18,255	11,282	7,182	6,060	6,672	**-63.5%**
GS 3	83,960	56,946	38,919	29,286	27,490	**-67.3%**
GS 4	174,989	155,252	112,406	85,079	74,397	**-57.5%**
GS 1 - 4	**282,794**	**228,129**	**161,438**	**123,391**	**111,700**	**-60.5%**
GS 5	209,664	206,425	174,651	153,574	134,473	**-35.9%**
GS 6	98,840	108,943	110,708	103,066	95,974	**-2.9%**
GS 7	149,669	155,887	148,224	141,705	142,377	**-4.9%**
GS 8	33,172	34,878	43,878	43,652	44,134	**33.0%**
GS 5 - 8	**491,345**	**506,133**	**477,461**	**441,997**	**416,958**	**-15.1%**
GS 9	168,498	170,821	148,263	138,369	132,763	**-21.2%**
GS 10	31,249	31,024	16,693	17,301	17,531	**-43.9%**
GS 11	199,363	222,726	217,145	198,314	191,585	**-3.9%**
GS 12	190,882	223,636	250,646	245,527	232,898	**22.0%**
GS 9 - 12	**589,992**	**648,207**	**632,747**	**599,511**	**574,777**	**-2.6%**
GS 13	122,816	145,918	169,698	174,908	179,597	**46.2%**
GS 14	66,642	81,226	93,010	90,250	91,746	**37.7%**
GS 15	39,107	45,949	52,445	52,287	53,092	**35.8%**
GS 13 - 15	**228,565**	**273,093**	**315,153**	**317,445**	**324,435**	**41.9%**

Source: Affirmative Employment Statistics; Office of Workforce Information.

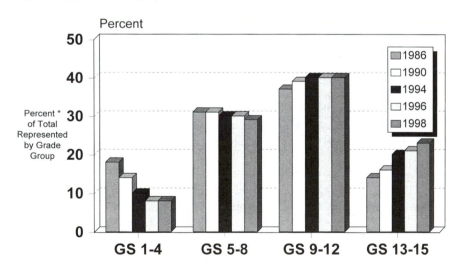

* Base data used to calculate percents are **excluded** from this report.

FIGURE 5.1   Executive branch employment by General Schedule (GS) and related grades (1986–1998).

managers inflated the grades of jobs as their surest response to increase pay. The result was a major change in the grade composition of the federal workforce. Driven also by the impacts of increased automation, agencies "traded" lower-grade positions at levels GS-1 to GS-8 for significant expansion in the upper grades (GS-13 to GS-15). In 1982, the lower grades (GS1–GS-8) accounted for just over half (50.5%) of the GS grades. By 1998, the lower grades had dropped to below 35% while the ranks GS-13 to GS-15 had increased by 40% and now constituted nearly 25% of the GS. (See Figure 5.1.)

The OPM's conscious effort to defer any significant change in classification reform led to growing unrest among agencies who wanted out of the centralized federal pay system anyway. Already in the early 1980s, the research and demonstration authority under Title VI of the Civil Service Reform Act had been invoked to sponsor several major experiments with broadbanding, and OPM began lobbying for passage of a new "civil service simplification act" that would have let agencies adapt grade banding as an option as long as there were linkage points back to the central system.

The pressure to seriously consider grade or broadbanding led to the commission of a major study by the National Academy of Public Administration (NAPA), which released its report in July 1991, just after OPM was able to secure passage of pay reform. Within the classification community, there was acceptance that the state of progressive deterioration since the 1980s had taken too large a toll. Personnelists were ready for a job classification system that would be completely "redesigned, retooled, and recalibrated."

THE REFORM INITIATIVE OF THE 1990s— BROADBANDING?

Change comes from experimentation, and when the Civil Service Reform Act was put together in 1978, the reformers envisioned a series of special projects to develop such innovations. Title VI authorized demonstration projects in which existing civil service rules would be waived and new systems developed and evaluated. In 1980 one of the most ambitious demonstration projects ever undertaken was begun at the Naval Weapons Center in China Lake, California, and the Naval Ocean Systems Center in San Diego. In the mid-1980s a parallel effort was initiated at McClellan Air Force Base in a union environment. A third experiment involving classification reform was undertaken by the National Institute of Standards and Technology.

What made these particular demonstration projects so different was their reliance on a unique and more flexible classification system that aggregated separate grade levels into broader categories or pay bands. These demonstration projects thus created a different compensation scheme. In the case of China Lake, a performance appraisal system tied compensation to performance levels. At

McClellan (called PacerShare), individual performance appraisals were replaced completely with a productivity gain-sharing system.

The advantage of broad- or pay banding came from combining grade levels and simplifying occupational categories. In fact, broadbanding was not an original idea developed just for the demonstration projects. In a 1968 report, *Job Evaluation and Ranking in the Federal Government*, the idea of grade reduction was proposed as a solution to problems of rigidity and arbitrariness. It was felt that fewer overall grades with broader ranges within grade levels would provide more flexibility and authority for managers. Using the China Lake project as an example (see Figure 5.2), the following steps were taken:

> Five career paths were created covering separate major occupational groups, assuring that employees in comparable jobs would get comparable pay evaluations.
> Each career path was divided into pay bands that combined at least two GS grades, giving each pay band a salary range of at least 50% (by

Career Group	General Schedule Grade Levels & Organizational Pay Band Groups					
Scientists Engineers Senior Staff	GS	1-4	5-8	9-11	12-13	14-15	16-18
	PB	A	I	II	III	IV	V

Technicians	GS	1-4	5-8	9-10	11-12
	PB	A	I	II	III

Technical Specialists	GS	1-4	5-7	8-10	11-12
	PB	A	I	II	III

Administrative Specialists	GS	1-4	5-8	9-10	11-12
	PB	A	I	II	III

General	GS	1-4	5-8	9-10	11-12
	PB	A	I	II	III

Administrative & General Support	GS	1-3	4-5	6-7	8-9	10-11
	PB	A	I	I	III	IV

FIGURE 5.2 Broad-band China Lake.

comparison, the maximum range within a single GS grade is less than 30%).

Finally, individuals are paid at least the minimum pay rate in their pay band with increases tied to either performance levels or some other type of incentive plan.

The broadbanding component of the demonstration projects was widely hailed as the next generation of classification. The first requirement was that the resulting system be budget-neutral (i.e., that it not increase salary costs).

In addition to determining the cost and budget impacts, there were other problems relating to pay comparability and performance appraisal. Critics contended that the drive to simplification would hinder comparisons between specific jobs, making salary surveys more complex and blurring distinctions about job values within organizations. Others were worried about the increased pressure on performance appraisal practices. (Broadbanding shifts the classification focus from specific positions to more emphasis on an individual's performance within a broader pay band as determined by the manager.) Some even questioned whether or not the government's appraisal tools and processes were up to the demands of a system using broad pay bands. Of course the counterargument was made that the above freedom, flexibility, and increased managerial discretion is precisely the goal of this potential innovation that links classification and compensation systems.

In the case of cost, the China Lake evaluations conclude that revised personnel practices that rely on broadbanding for classification, appraisal, and pay were quite workable. Both OPM and General Accounting Office (GAO) advised caution in drawing general conclusions, however, because of other mitigating factors and external events. Initially OPM noted that overall salary costs increased 6% more for the demonstration sites than for the control sites. Not surprisingly, attitudinal surveys showed higher pay satisfaction among most employees at the demonstration sites and a greater sense of "connectedness between pay and performance." A later OPM study revealed that pay banding at China Lake did not have a dissimilar effect on salary costs as pay levels at the control sites caught up to demonstration project levels.

This question about increased salary costs is important in gauging the potential of broadbanding. The intent behind the demonstration projects was to prove it is budget-neutral, that it can work without increasing costs, or that it would produce benefits that outweigh the costs. Probably most of the federal personnel community believes that pay banding would increase overall salary costs and overtime, as the U.S. Merit Systems Protection Board (MSPB) noted in its 1989 review of OPM's Classification and Qualification Systems: "Over a longer time span, the Board is still inclined to believe that pay banding will increase overall salary costs, all other things being equal. Of course, even if pay

banding does increase costs, it may still be a valuable enhancement to the classification system.''

This is an old problem, however, and one can only ask whether or not it
really matters. On the last page of his now classic critique, Shafritz noted in
1973: ''It has been found that savings are realized when the central budget agency
removes personnel ceilings, while retaining budgetary ceilings.'' Why not then
extend the same timeless rule back to classification and compensation levels
within organizations? There is certainly some irony in the fact that to do so would
be to essentially return to the personnel practice of over a century ago, in which
lump-sum appropriations for salaries were the rule and organizational heads had
the authorization to set salaries within budgetary ceilings. One might instead
conclude that that prospect is precisely what classification has fought against for
over a century and understand its reluctance to follow it as a path for reform.

The 1991 report by NAPA on broadbanding moved the discussion to a full-
scale debate between classification supporters who defend the framework of the
system and want ''modernization,'' and classification critics who want reform
through ''radical change.'' Frank P. Cipolla, the head of NAPA's Center on Human Resources Management, argued the case quite forcefully.

> We need to fix the classification system *first*. It doesn't matter whether
> we adopt the NAPA broad banding model intact or whether we go to
> some other flexible system. The important thing is that we move away
> from the position-based approach to managing work and performance
> to one that focuses on the individual as a *contributor* to the work of the
> *team* or an organization. If we don't move in this direction we'll only
> be swimming up the TQM stream, treading water at best. In any case,
> we don't need pigeon-holing and unnecessary grade levels at a time
> when we are trying to flatten organizational structures and expand career
> broadening opportunities for employees.
>
> The current system pre-empts managers from fully exercising their
> responsibilities for managing work. Those who want to be accountable
> can't be because personnelists run the system. Those who don't want
> to be accountable can hide behind the barriers and restrictions of the
> current system and blame the Personnelists. Too many Personnelists
> aren't ready for a new system because they can't bring themselves to
> relinquish the control the current system gives them. They rationalize
> by saying cynically that managers aren't ready, that it would take too
> much time to train them, and that going to a more flexible system run
> by managers necessarily would drive up costs. No matter which side of
> the fence you are on, as a minimum we ought to agree that line managers
> should be calling the shot on what shape a new classification system
> ought to take. . . .

As things stand now, it may well be two decades before the federal government decides to move in this direction. Why can't we be in the front wave for a change? Dragging a system which has its origins in the 19th century into the 21st century hardly seems in the public interest.

The issue of broadbanding was put to a working group of the Interagency Advisory Group of Personnel Directors. This working group was established by OPM to develop final recommendations for system changes in classification, performance management, and pay-for-performance. Its report (entitled ''Framework of Policy and Program Initiatives for Performance Management and Position Classification'') issued in June 1992 to the director of OPM, argued that the basic structure of the classification system is adequate and that reform should concentrate on ''simplification, automation, and redefinition of the roles of classifiers and managers.'' While the document did accept using ''alternative classification'' systems, such as grade banding, these would be approved on an ''exception basis for occupations or organizational entities that can not accommodate to the general system.''

A simple reading of the ''framework'' document shows the reticent to radically change. It begins: ''For most of the work performed in the Federal civil service, the current classification framework of Title 5, USC, is adequate to achieve fundamental federal human resources goals such as equal pay for equal work and structuring work to accomplish missions. There are cases, however, where alternative structures may be needed to address unique circumstances.'' A vision statement follows that summarizes the direction of ''modernization'' as a destination point for the progress of classification over three-quarters of a century. To advocates who have long extolled the need for redefining roles, simplifying standards, automating the system, and providing more training for managers, surely this was seen as demonstrable proof of how far classification has come. To critics who were committed to reengineering the system, ''informating'' the function, and devolving the process back into line management, this only validated how little real change would occur.

To say that a final decision was not made on a new course for federal classification would be unfair. Provisions were included in nearly all of the civil service reform legislative proposals drawn up and circulated throughout the Clinton administration. The thrust of the proposals was to allow any agency that wanted to pursue some form of broadbanding to be able to do so. Indeed, had that legislation been passed, the New York regional veterans office could have taken its proposal for skill-based pay for its teams directly to its own personnel office as opposed to having to obtain demonstration project status, but for all the effort after a decade, there is neither new civil service reform legislation nor comprehensive reform of the federal classification system.

CLASSIFICATION IN THE STATES

How has classification fared among state and local governments? There are some interesting reforms underway. The city of Charlotte, North Carolina, has adopted a broadbanding approach. The state of Washington has its own unique version of broadbanding called the Washington Management System, which applies to the approximately 32,000 managers and supervisors in the state government (approximately 137,000 employees). Washington's broadbanding approach allows each state agency to handle its own recruitment and hiring of managers and then classify them into one of four management bands. Each management band has a minimum and maximum salary level, allowing the agencies to then adjust actual pay within the bands (Table 5.6).

The management bands themselves look like any series of grade levels within an executive service, but the fairly wide salary range provides considerable flexibility. Each agency is asked to place the individual into an appropriate band based on points coming from a managerial job value assessment chart that reflects decision-making environment, policy impact, and scope of accountability and control. There are no step rates (i.e., salary increases based on length of service).

There are other experiments underway with different models of broadbanding or skill-based pay (à la the New York regional office of the Veterans Benefits Administration). The state of Virginia has been using a variation of skill-based pay since 1995 in its transportation department. The pilot project involved only maintenance workers in a system with 32 steps within the salary band. Salary progression was dependent upon maintaining critical skills and taking training to acquire new skills. The system also had a productivity performance-based lump-sum bonus component.

As intriguing as some of these experiments and new models are, there is certainly no broad-scale reform effort in classification underway at the state and local levels. Data at the state level shows, predictably, that change is occurring

TABLE 5.6 Washington Management
Service—Pay Bands for Managers
(July 1999)

Band	Minimum salary	Maximum salary
I	$34,000	$56,300
II	$44,000	$69,500
III	$56,700	$85,000
IV	$70,000	$101,900

in classification, but the states are going in many different directions, as Table 5.7 illustrates. Table 5.7 shows the numbers of job classifications in each of the 50 states over the last 15 years, using 1986, 1991, and 1998 as data points. To give a fuller picture of the state of classification in the states, the change in the number of state employees from 1993 to 1998 is also included. (The year 1993 was chosen because it is past the 1991–1992 recession, which affected most states severely.)

If one sorts through Table 5.7, there are a few trends, which might be summarized as follows:

The states vary as "employers" in size, from Wyoming with 13,000 state employees, to California, with over 418,000. Using 75,000 employees as a divider, there are 26 larger states with more than 75,000 employees and 24 with fewer.

Of the 26 large states, 16 have decreased their numbers of job classifications, five have trimmed classifications by under 10%, and 11 have decreased job classifications by more than 10%.

Within the 26 large states, however, 10 have actually increased their job classifications, five by less than 10%, and five by more than 10%.

Among the 24 smaller states, 19 have decreased job classifications—10 by under 10%, and 9 by more than 10%. The smallest group comprises the five small states that have increased their job classifications—only one by less than 10% to four over 10%.

As for hiring, a recent *Governing* article—"The Myth of the Meat-Axe"— put it succinctly. Only seven of the 50 states have decreased state roles since 1993. While the numbers of new state employees overall is only 5% nationally (compared to a 10% employment increase at the local government level), state governments have been in a modest growth mode for most of the 1990s.

In terms of classification, it would seem that there is somewhat of a general trend toward fewer job classifications. Thirty-five of the 50 states have simplified, streamlined, or slimmed down the number of job classifications, compared to 15 that have increased. The trends in the 1990s were a perfect reverse reflection of the late 1980s, however. Between 1986 and 1991, 35 of the states increased their job classification numbers. Behind the trend numbers are surely intriguing stories, such as West Virginia, which more than doubled its classification from the late 1980s to 2000 and cut back to 750 in 1998. Finally, there is the state that increased the most in terms of classification—Georgia—which of course is the state highlighted in Chapter 2 as leading its own civil service reform effort in a very different direction.

TABLE 5.7 Job Classifications by State Government (1986–1998)

	Number of job classifications			Change		Number of state employees		
	1986	1991	1998	1986–1991	1991–1998	1993	1998	Change
Alabama	1340	1600	1400	19%	−13%	94000	95000	1%
Alaska	1000	1050	1500	5%	43%	21000	21000	0%
Arizona	1450	1500	1400	3%	−7%	52000	75000	31%
Arkansas	2100	1900	1854	−10%	−2%	52000	59000	12%
California	4400	4324	4500	−2%	4%	390000	418000	7%
Colorado	1600	1348	951	−16%	−29%	64000	69000	7%
Connecticut	2500	2600	2600	4%	0%	63000	59000	−7%
Delaware	1100	1434	1400	30%	−2%	24000	27000	11%
Florida	1651	1596	1537	−3%	−4%	179000	197000	9%
Georgia	1500	1570	2355	5%	50%	137000	153000	10%
Hawaii	1605	1660	1600	3%	−4%	66000	68000	3%
Idaho	1100	1550	1400	41%	−10%	23000	24000	4%
Illinois	1620	1680	1011	4%	−40%	148000	153000	3%
Indiana	1525	1500	1300	−2%	−13%	96000	93000	−3%
Iowa	1116	1250	812	12%	−35%	57000	57000	0%
Kansas	1200	1142	750	−5%	−34%			12%
Kentucky	1442	1614	1750	12%	8%	81000	85000	5%
Louisiana	3764	3800	2800	1%	−26%	103000	109000	6%
Maine	1497	1500	1100	0%	−27%	24000	23000	−4%
Maryland	3000	3000	2000	0%	−33%	94000	95000	1%
Massachusetts	1000	1150	1100	15%	−4%	97000	98000	1%
Michigan	1766	2700	1500	53%	−44%	148000	152000	3%
Minnesota	1600	2140	2269	34%	6%	80000	83000	4%

Mississippi	1700	2053	2400	21%	17%	57000	59000	3%
Missouri	1080	1100	1300	2%	18%	89000	100000	11%
Montana	1500	1350	1500	-10%	11%	19000	21000	10%
Nebraska	1300	1300	1500	0%	15%	37000	47000	21%
Nevada	1200	1300	1300	8%	0%	21000	26000	19%
New Hampshire	1470	1490	1100	1%	-26%	18000	19000	5%
New Jersey	6500	6400	8000	-2%	25%	126000	130000	3%
New Mexico	800	1200	1200	50%	0%	54000	58000	7%
New York	7300	7300	5075	0%	-30%	267000	247000	-8%
North Carolina	3012	3500	3500	16%	0%	148000	163000	9%
North Dakota	960	1075	1000	12%	-7%	19000	17000	-12%
Ohio	1832	1804	2500	-2%	39%	156000	158000	1%
Oklahoma	1136	1418	1462	25%	3%	73000	76000	4%
Oregon	1185	1100	780	-7%	-29%	64000	60000	-7%
Pennsylvania	2700	2782	3000	3%	8%	144000	137000	-5%
Rhode Island	1500	1500	1400	0%	-7%	21000	18000	-17%
South Carolina	2400	2318	500	-3%	-78%	102000	105000	3%
South Dakota	579	551	551	-5%	0%	17000	16000	-6%
Tennessee	1451	2258	1800	56%	-20%	88000	89000	1%
Texas	1288	1339	790	4%	-41%	296000	314000	6%
Utah	2100	2500	2300	19%	-8%	48000	56000	14%
Vermont	1063	1280	1300	20%	2%	14000	14000	0%
Virginia	2100	1888	1800	-10%	-5%	136000	129000	-5%
Washington	2400	2100	1600	-13%	-24%	126000	137000	8%
West Virginia	950	2000	750	111%	-63%	40000	41000	2%
Wisconsin	2011	2000	2800	-1%	40%	88000	94000	6%
Wyoming	1375	774	550	-44%	-29%	14000	13000	-8%
United States						4372000	4582000	5%

PAY ADMINISTRATION IN GOVERNMENT

Pay reform has been a problem in government for decades, primarily due to political issues. While the federal government will serve as the primary example, the issues are equally complex in state and local governments. What makes it so complex and so political is that compensation levels for public employees are linked to pay levels of politically elected or appointed officeholders (the president, legislators, and even judges).

The beginning seems simple enough. As previously discussed, back in 1949 the Classification Act established the single GS with 18 grade levels. The top rate of pay was $14,000, which was set up for a very small group of senior executives. Salaries for cabinet heads were set above the top of the scale, at $22,500. Some agencies were exempted from the GS (e.g., the CIA). A few others, such as the Federal Reserve and some other authorities, were given their own pay authority, but by and large most agencies were tied to the general classification system, for which Congress would pass periodic legislation to update pay levels. Pay issues were primarily about white collar workers; the idea of paying blue collar workers wages that were based on prevailing wage rates of local private sector counterparts had long been established.

Up to the 1950s the problems were numerous, in part because of congressional reluctance to approve pay increases for higher grade levels and the difficulty in relating pay adjustments across different pay systems. It was the Salary Reform Act of 1962 that first required the president to submit an annual report to Congress evaluating federal wage rates against the private sector's. This report established basic salary surveys by agencies and required a recommendation by the president for an annual salary adjustment. Of course, congressional action was required to approve the request. Further complicating the political requirements of getting Congress to legislate, there was an 18-month lag built into the process from the first survey actions to implementation. These problems led to minor corrections in the Federal Salary Act of 1967 and a major revision in the 1970 Federal Pay Comparability Act.

The Federal Pay Comparability Act of 1970 codified the principle that federal pay rates would be comparable to private sector wage rates for similar work. More important, it created separate mechanisms to make pay adjustments. A primary organ with responsibility for wages called the pay agent was created, consisting of the directors of the Office of Management and Budget (OMB), OPM, and the Labor Department (the secretary of labor actually being added by amendment in 1977). The Advisory Committee on Federal Pay was also established to get recommendations from the public. Finally, the Federal Employees Pay Council, representing labor unions and employee organizations, was created.

Section 5305(c)(1) of the act, however, added a subtle but major change. It stipulated that "If, because of national emergency or economic conditions affecting the general welfare, the President should, in any year, consider it inappropriate to make the pay adjustment required . . . he shall prepare and transmit to the Congress before September of that year such alternative plan with respect to a pay adjustment as he considers appropriate.''

Finally, the act provided for a legislative veto provision stating that if either house of Congress vetoed the president's alternative pay plan the pay recommendation provided for in the pay agent's and advisory committee's annual report would be approved instead. Despite the best intentions, it was thus the 1970 Pay Comparability Act that created an almost 30% pay gap that would exist between federal and private sector wages. Since the Carter administration, the annual adjustment has been basically the president's alternate pay plan because of one excuse or another that decries economic necessity to ward off further inflation, counteract the deficit, or whatever the current economic fad term is for American economic problems. For almost two decades, the Congress seldom overrode the president's alternative pay plan.

This began to take on special meaning in the 1990s because of the increasing significance of the public sector pay gap. Under the direction of Paul A. Volcker, the National Commission on the Public Service in 1989 issued its report, *Leadership for America*, calling for desperately needed public service revitalization and urging a significant salary increase for the federal civil service. As mentioned, this was not a sudden development. The OPM had previously concluded in its 1988 report, *Civil Service 2000*, that "federal compensation is increasingly noncompetitive . . . public esteem for civil servants has been declining and the prestige of government jobs has been falling . . . [and] low pay and low prestige have been exacerbated by outdated management practices and needless aggravations." The GAO conducted numerous surveys of federal agencies and reported major recruitment and retention problems, especially in geographic areas with higher costs of living.

Returning to the federal government's response to its 1990 pay crises, the Volcker commission had gone on record indicating that by the end of the 1980s the gap between federal and private sector wages had reached canyon proportions of over 25%. In fact, the pay gap in 1990 was estimated at 30% by the report of the Advisory Committee on Federal Pay, but other salary surveys contended that the gap was smaller. Others reiterated the timeworn argument that other factors must be considered. Although the same white collar occupations tend to pay more money in the private sector, salary surveys can't take into account the enhanced job security that most federal workers enjoy (or thought they were enjoying before the Clinton administration's arrival).

The most telling statistic tied to any pay gap issue, however, is the question of pace. Typically in an election year, federal employees would receive a solid increase. (Indeed, in 1988 they received a 4.1% increase, the largest increase of the decade.) The overall trend for the decade, however, revealed that federal white collar salary increases were not even keeping pace with inflation. Studies indicated that from 1970 to 1990, federal employees had lost on the average nearly 20% of their purchasing power.

The pay gap was further exacerbated by cost-of-living differentials in different parts of the country. With a few exceptions, federal government salaries were the same no matter what part of the country the employee worked and resided in, so in New York City or San Francisco (where living costs are high), salaries were declared '' noncompetitive,'' compared to cities such as Atlanta or Pittsburgh (where living costs are lower). Pay reform in the 1990s had to deal ''locality pay'' to offset regional cost-of-living differences.

There is a larger question regarding the quality of the workforce that makes this history of federal pay reform efforts in 1990 very relevant. Simply stated, do pay and performance evaluation policies negatively impact who stays and who leaves the federal workforce? This incredibly complex and difficult question has been tackled by a number of studies. The Congressional Budget Office (CBO) weighed in first in a 1986 study, concluding that quit rates were not extensive when compared to other organizations and that the greatest turnover was with clerical workers. The CBO explored briefly the problem of who was leaving the public service. Their conclusion was that a ''healthy pattern'' existed in that there was no ''disproportionate turnover'' among higher-rated managers.

In 1988, the MSPB examined the quality retention issue in two reports. Its studies showed more support for the ''desirable pattern'' as it concluded that the ratio (26%) of employees who had been rated unsatisfactory leaving government compared favorably to that (6%) of employees given an outstanding rating who had left. In retrospect, using performance evaluation ratings as a marker for quality seems suspect. Subsequent efforts, notably Greg Lewis's analytical work in the early 1990s, used education and work experience levels and found no statistically significant decline in the quality of those leaving the federal workforce. Philip Crewson has analyzed federal, state, and local turnover using qualification test scores and confirmed the federal pattern—that among younger employees (under 40), there is ''no evidence to support the conclusion that the federal government is losing its most capable employees,'' but state and local were, in some cases among managers, in others among lower-graded support positions. Crewson also points out another interesting pattern—that almost 25% of all government separations were to take other public sector positions. Despite the lack of subsequent studies supporting the negative effects of compensation on workforce quality, however, a political consensus had emerged to move forward on federal pay reform.

FEDERAL PAY REFORM: 1990

Pay reform legislation was hammered out in congressional conference in the fall of 1990, producing the Federal Pay Reform Act of 1990. The act focused its greatest impacts on new linkages to local private sector wage rates, or *locality pay*. This emphasis was perhaps the most important feature of pay reform at this time because it seemed to be the only way to stave off pressure for splintering the GS system. If agencies can't get relief to pay their personnel wages that are competitive in high-cost areas, their only course of action is to push for their own separate special pay systems. Some federal agencies, such as the Defense Department, Justice, and NASA, were pushing strenuously for their own systems. Locality pay, it was argued, would enable agencies to recruit and retain qualified personnel at prevailing local wage rates.

To close the pay gap, the legislation called for 5% raises across the board for 1992, 1993, and 1994. In 1994, surveys of high-cost areas showed the remaining gap, and extra salary raises will be paid to workers in those areas that close the gap by 20%. These extra increases would be paid until the year 2003 at a rate of 10% of the remaining gap. To handle critical local situations, the president was authorized to extend immediate salary increases of 8%. Special provisions for federal law enforcement officials amounting to 4 to 16% salary increases for high-cost areas were also included in 1992. There were also provisions to substantially alter the pay system for administrative law judges.

Interestingly, the cost of these salary increases was not guaranteed. Initially about $3.6 billion was budgeted by the Bush administration over the subsequent five years (which was roughly 3% of the total annual federal payroll costs, but only half of what would be needed to cover the necessary salary increases). Departments and agencies were supposed to provide the other half by reducing turnover and managing other payroll costs. Finally, the sums targeted for this pay reform package only extended for five years, leaving future congressional and administration leaders to determine where the funding would come from after 1995.

Looking back in 1990 at a slow but still growing federal civilian workforce of approximately 2.2 million employees, suspicions about how this could work seem well founded. The Clinton administration tried to derail locality pay completely in its first rounds of implementation and even canceled a 2.2% inflation-tied general salary increase In 1994, David Hornestay wrote a scathing indictment of the reformed federal pay system in a cover article in *Government Executive* entitled ''Tear It Down,'' with the byline ''The monolithic fed pay system has long since exhausted its flexibility, forfeited its integrity, and outlived its usefulness.'' Hornestay again pointed out the futility of having public pay rates set by political leaders feuding over budget issues. Of course a major part of the pay problem is that congressional salaries are tied to executive salaries, so when Congress refuses to increase its pay, as it did through out the mid-1990s, this limits the pay of senior executives.

By 1996, however, with a civilian federal workforce trimmed to under 1.9 million, wholesale changes occurring within the workforce in terms of contracting, and inflation reduced to its lowest levels in almost a quarter century,

TABLE 5.8 General Schedule and Senior Executive Service Locality Annual Pay Rates (2000)

	Washington–Baltimore	Atlanta	Boston	Chicago	Houston	Los Angeles	New York	San Francisco
GS-1*	15,125	14,923	15,357	15,464	15,921	15,640	15,547	15,952
GS-2	17,005	16,789	17,266	17,386	17,900	17,584	17,479	17,935
GS-3	18,555	18,318	18,839	18,970	19,532	19,186	19,702	19,569
GS-4	20,829	20,563	21,148	21,295	21,925	21,537	21,409	21,967
GS-5	23,304	23,007	23,661	23,825	24,531	24,097	23,954	24,578
GS-6	25,976	25,645	26,374	26,557	27,343	26,859	26,700	27,395
GS-7	28,866	28,498	29,308	29,511	30,385	29,848	29,670	30,443
GS-8	31,968	31,561	32,458	32,683	33,651	33,056	32,859	33,715
GS-9	35,310	34,860	35,851	36,100	37,169	36,512	36,295	37,240
GS-10	38,885	38,389	39,481	39,755	40,932	40,208	39,969	41,010
GS-11	42,724	42,179	43,378	43,680	44,972	44,177	43,915	45,059
GS-12	51,204	50,552	51,989	52,350	53,900	52,946	52,632	54,003
GS-13	60,890	60,114	61,823	62,253	64,095	62,962	62,674	64,218
GS-14	71,954	71,037	73,056	73,564	75,742	74,402	73,960	75,887
GS-15	84,638	83,559	85,934	86,532	89,093	87,518	86,998	89,264
SES-1	115,970	114,335	117,585	118,402	121,907	119,751	119,040	122,141
SES-2	121,430	119,718	123,121	123,977	127,646	125,389	124,644	127,891
SES-3	127,000	125,209	128,767	129,663	130,200	130,200	130,200	130,200
SES-4	130,200	130,200	130,200	130,200	130,200	130,200	130,200	130,200
SES-5	130,200	130,200	130,200	130,200	130,200	130,200	130,200	130,200
SES-6	130,200	130,200	130,200	130,200	130,200	130,200	130,200	130,200

Note: GS-1 through GS-15 are at step 1 levels.

TABLE 5.9   Toward New Pay Models for the Public Sector—
Changing Compensation Beliefs

Traditional beliefs	New pay beliefs
We have good relationships with our employees and try to be diligent in avoiding problems. We feel we have a good workforce.	Every employee is expected to contribute. The compensation system was designed and is managed as an incentive for employees to use their capabilities to achieve our goals.
Compensation is an HR system. We look to the HR specialists to manage the program and payroll increases.	Compensation is seen as a management system, with HR serving as a consultant to help managers make pay decisions.
It is important to maintain consistency in salary management.	Management flexibility is an overarching program goal.
Employees need to know we are paying them fairly, but we see no reason to involve them when we redesign our pay programs.	Whenever we redesign a pay program we look to managers and employees in the business unit for their input to ensure that the changes are accepted and meet their operational needs.
Pay increases are based primarily on tenure.	Pay increases are based primarily on individual performance and competence.
We rely on a proven job evaluation system to ensure that pay is equitable.	Pay levels reflect the value of the person as dictated by the labor market and individual capabilities.
Our base pay program is based on internal equity principles.	Our program is aligned with prevailing labor market pay rates.
Our program is consistent with widely used program design principles. Leading employers rely on the same salary management practices.	Our program is based on our business needs, our values, and the way work is organized and managed in each business unit. It was designed to fit our organization.
Virtually all of our employees are good people and earn their pay. Salary increases reward them for their continued efforts.	Our managers are expected to identify the best contributors and to make sure pay differentials reflect their contribution.
Our budget for salary increases depends on several factors, but primarily what we can afford.	We rely on variable pay plans to tie rewards to the achievement of our organizational goals and to our ability to pay.

Source: Adapted from Risher, Howard. "Are Public Employees Ready for a New Pay Program?" *Public Personnel Management*, vol. 28, no. 3 (Fall 1999), p. 340.

the issue of pay reform receded in importance. Other federal agencies, notably the FAA and the IRS, were able to gain exemptions from the GS. The IRS was given the authority to bring in a specific number of ''external'' senior executives who would be eligible for substantial bonuses if they met the terms of their performance contracts. The idea of having a separate executive core is not new; NASA has always had the ability to set aside a number of executive positions outside its classification system. It is the executive bonus system that will likely draw the most attention.

Locality pay has already been implemented, as Table 5.8, which shows select 2000 federal salary ranges, attests. There are now 30 different regional locality areas, along with Washington and a ''rest of the country'' average. Locality pay, as anticipated, has produced a modest wage spread that reflects regional cost-of-living indices and salary competition factors. As one might expect, cities such as San Francisco and New York have higher salaries than Washington and the rest of the country, but there are always interesting anomalies. Houston has the second highest salary ranges, not because Houston has higher costs of living but because of salary competition. (In a 1999 survey of professional occupations across the country, Houston was the only city in which government employees ranked in the top 10 highest-paid professions.)

The full implementation of locality pay does not mean that federal pay problems have come to an end; rather, the pressure has been shifting to entirely new pay models. Skill-based pay and broadbanding reflect some of the effort to find new approaches, but more fundamental change is being called for. Howard Risher, one of the leading advocates for new pay models and compensation strategies, has argued that a new set of beliefs will have to be recognized if public sector pay is going to be keep pace (Table 5.9).

STATE AND LOCAL COMPENSATION DEVELOPMENTS

Of course public pay crises and problems are not limited just to the federal civil service; state and local governments and nonprofit organizations have also faced increasing competition, both in the current conditions of low unemployment and because of other legal and budgetary constraints. They also suffered with the onset of the 1990–1991 recession. Perhaps more significantly, the fiscal situation of many states and cities has always been more subject to a feast or famine cycle. In 2000, most states and local governments are flush with budget surpluses. Some are pursuing tax cuts. Others, such as California, which has a statute requiring rebates to be paid to the taxpayers if the budget surplus is too large, will look to refunds. Many will remember, however, the difficult times in the early 1980s followed by surpluses in many states and cities in the mid-1980s until 1990 brought in a major crunch that had states and cities running in the red, raising taxes, and cutting personnel costs either through layoffs or hiring freezes. Many state and local governments mishandled their fiscal crises and undermined their credibility with their workforces and unions.

In 1990, *Governing* magazine concluded in an article on the state and local compensation gap, "[t]he core issue is quality. As the needs of government grow more complex, the public sector is drawn into competition with private industry for skilled people: engineers, nurses, computer specialists and able managers." Those words are a fitting prologue for the human capital problem facing all governments as they seek to find innovative ways to make their compensation systems competitive and yet remain fiscally conservative.

A superb example of one innovative approach from the early 1990s aptly summarizes this dilemma. The city of San Diego reorganized its information technology (IT) division as a nonprofit organization. This was done in large part to be able to set competitive salaries to attract and hold the computer and information systems talent it needed for the city, but not to the point of distorting the total wage system for the rest of city employees. Yesterday's innovation may be viewed rather differently in the future, however. In the early 1990s, the city of San Diego contemplated "insourcing" technology work from the county and surrounding governments. Skip forward to 2000—the county of San Diego is now the engine of growth in this fast-growing suburban metroplex and has just awarded an information management technology contract to the private sector for over $.5 billion dollars (more than 40% of the county's operating budget). As the county goes its own way, the future competitiveness of the city's nonprofit IT department will surely be tested.

As for how competitive state and local governments are in terms of compensation, the debate is likely to continue. In 1996, economists with the Bureau of Labor Statistics released a report comparing state and local pay with private sector (nonfarm) pay. Their major findings were mixed and highly unlikely to satisfy either advocates or critics. Briefly, they found the following:

> At the low end of the scale, state and local governments paid better than private industry.
>
> Among white collar jobs, the private sector usually paid better.
>
> State and local government pay lagged far behind that for professional and administrative jobs.
>
> Pay patterns were mixed for technical, clerical, and blue-collar employees.
>
> Occupations with workers in lower-paying jobs were better paid in government.
>
> Occupations with workers in higher-paying jobs were more likely to be paid in the private sector.

These findings reflected 1993 salary data. (See Figure 5.3.) Today's labor market is different, as has been discussed. Increasingly, corporate America is moving away from its pattern of providing moderate salary increases slightly above infla-

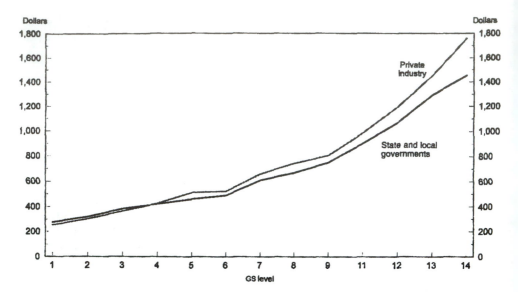

FIGURE 5.3 Average weekly pay in state and local governments and in private industry, by federal General Schedule (GS) grade level in 1993. (From Miller 1996.)

tion levels (mainly 3% to 5%). Indeed, one of the remarkable features of this new economy is its low inflation rates in the face of low unemployment levels and wage pressures. Even the Federal Reserve Board concluded in one of its periodic studies that the private sector's use of variable pay (i.e., bonus and flexible benefit packages) has been a major contributing factor in keeping wage increases down and deterring inflation.

What does this mean in terms of competition for governments? On the benefit side, government has long had an edge because it provided a top benefit package. In fact, some of the packages awarded government employees through collective bargaining have resulted in some cities having two-tiered benefit systems. In a two-tiered system, employees hired after a certain date aren't eligible for the more generous package granted first-tier employees. Likewise, in some cities, certain occupational groups, such as fire and police, often have a more lucrative benefit package than other city employees. Recent benefit offerings by the private sector, however, are cutting into the public sector's advantage. Corporations are now offering flexible benefits packages with such choices as flexible working hours, telecommuting from home, elder care and child care programs, fitness centers and wellness programs, and access to on-site medical care.

What may be more troubling to public sector employers is variable compensation. A study of major U.S. corporations in 1999 indicated a 16% increase nationally in bonuses and stock options. Among IT employees and other highly-sought-after technical workers, substantial signing bonuses (and a recruitment bonus for an employee finding a new hire) are almost a rule. All of this points toward a new era of performance-related, organizational results-driven bonus systems. For governments, going to skill-based pay systems and some form of group-derived bonus, as radical as they appear, may be only a small step in the new world of work for the twenty-first century.

PAY ISSUES OF ANOTHER KIND: LIVING WAGES

It would be inappropriate to conclude this chapter on classification and compensation without discussing another related and highly controversial aspect of compensation, namely the living wage. Specifically, this refers to the nearly 30 cities in the United States that have passed ordinances requiring contractors working for the city to pay higher wages to their employees who live in the city. (See Table 5.10.) In 2000 San Francisco was in the middle of such a debate as it considered requiring its contractors to pay their employees a living wage of $14.50 an hour. This would be in contrast to the current California minimum wage of $5.75 an hour and the U.S. minimum wage of $5.15.

Why require contractors or anyone for that matter to pay more than the minimum wage? The idea was initially debated and passed in Baltimore in 1994. There a coalition of religious leaders, unions, and community groups led a movement that passed a $7.70 hourly wage requirement for any business doing contract work with the city of Baltimore. A key argument was simple economics—that the minimum wage was inadequate given the higher costs of living in the city. Advocates also point out that over the last 20 years, the current national minimum wage has not kept pace with inflation. The 1979 minimum wage of $2.90 an hour would, properly adjusted for inflation in 1999 be more than $2 an hour higher, at $6.92.

By 2000, 28 city and county governments had passed such ordinances, ranging from Santa Clara County, currently with the highest living wage of $10.00, to Milwaukee with the lowest, at $6.05. Two cities—New York and Gary, Indiana—set the living wage equivalent to the prevailing industry wage in the city. There are two basic variations of these living wage ordinances, which complicates comparisons somewhat. Some cities have a two-tiered system, one lower wage for companies that provide health benefits and a second for those that don't. A second variation involves who is affected by living wages. Some cities simply require all companies that are contractors to the city to pay the city's hourly wage requirement. Others use another approach that also re-

TABLE 5.10 Cities and Counties That Had Living Wage
Ordinances as of 1999

Baltimore	$7.70
Boston	$8.23
Chicago	$7.60
Cook County, IL	$7.60
Dane County, WS	$8.03
Des Moines	$9.00
Detroit	$8.35/$10.43[a]
Duluth	$6.50/$7.25[a]
Durham, NC	$8.25
Gary, IN	Prevailing industry wage
Hayward, CA	$8.00/$9.25
Hudson County, NJ	$7.73
Jersey City, NJ	$7.50 + $2,000/year benefits
Los Angeles	$7.39/$8.64
Madison, WI	$7.91
Milwaukee	$6.05
Minneapolis	$8.47
Multnomah County, OR	$9.00
New Haven, CT	$8.03
New York	Prevailing industry wage
Oakland	$8.00/$9.25
Pasadena, CA	$7.25/$8.50
Portland, OR	$7.75
San Antonio	$9.27
San Jose, CA	$9.50/$10.75[a]
Santa Clara County, CA	$10.00
St. Paul, MN	$8.47
Federal minimum wage	$5.15

[a] Indicates two-tiered system (with and without health benefits).

quires all businesses that are recipients of city subsidies, grants, or tax breaks to
comply.

Some contend that the need for cities to pass living wage ordinances would
not be necessary if the Congress would regularly pass minimum wage legislation,
but while political parties squabble, cities are increasingly likely to act. In terms
of impact, they will be quick to point out that even paying $7.00 an hour would
just barely bring those employees to current national poverty levels. As large and
small business contemplate doing business in our nation's cities, the difficulty
of finding and keeping employees in lower-wage jobs (usually these are lower-

paid service workers) is being recognized as a major problem. Living wages may even become a welcomed new economic reality.

BIBLIOGRAPHY

Abosch, Kenan S. and Janice S. Hand. *Broadbanding Design, Approaches and Practices.* American Compensation Association, 1994.

Atwood, Jay F. "Position Synthesis: A Behavioral Approach to Position Classification," *Public Personnel Review*, vol. 32 (April 1971).

Balkan, David B. and Luis R. Gomez-Mejia. "Toward a Contingency Theory of Compensation Strategy," *Strategic Management Journal* (March–April 1987).

Ban, Carolyn. "The Navy Demonstration Project: An Experiment in Experimentation," in Carolyn Ban and Norma M. Riccucci (eds.), *Public Personnel Management: Current Concerns, Future Challenges.* White Plains, N.Y.: Longman Press, 1991.

Baruch, Ismar. *Position Classification in the Public Service.* Chicago: Public Personnel Association, 1941, 1965.

Bergmann, Thomas J. and Kenneth P. DeMeuse. "Diagnosing Whether an Organization is Truly Ready to Empower Work Teams: A Case Study," *Human Resource Planning*, vol. 19, no. 1 (1996), pp. 38–47.

Blank, Rebecca M. "An Analysis of Worker's Choice Between Employment in the Public and Private Sectors," *Industrial and Labor Relations Review* (January 1985).

Braddick, Carol A, Michael B. Jones, and Paul M. Shafer. "A Look at Broadbanding in Practice," *Journal of Compensation and Benefits* (July–August 1992).

Boston Federal Executive Board. *Competing for the Future: A Report on the Effects of Federal Pay Policy on Public Service.* Boston, March 1989.

Crewson, Philip. "Are the Best and Brightest Fleeing Public Sector Employment?" *Public Productivity and Management Review*, vol. 20, no. 4 (June 1997), pp. 363–371.

Cummings, Thomas G. and S. Srivastva. *Management of Work.* Kent, Ohio: Kent State University Press, 1977.

Davis, Louis E. and James C. Taylor. *Design of Jobs.* Santa Monica, Calif.: Goodyear, 1979.

DeSanto, John F. "Higher Pay for Good Performance: The Average Grade Approach," *Public Personnel Management*, vol. 9, no. 4 (1980).

Duggan, Martin L. "The Bottom Line on Federal Pay," *Labor Law Review* (January 1985).

Epperson, Lawrence L. "The Dynamics of Factor Comparison/Point Evaluation," *Public Personnel Management*, vol. 4 (January–February 1975).

Fogel, Walter and David Lewis. "Wage Determination in the Public Sector," *Industrial and Labor Relations Review*, vol. 27 (April 1974).

Fredlund, Robert F. "Criteria for Selecting a Wage System," *Public Personnel Management*, vol. 4 (September–October 1976).

Ganschinietz, Bill and Stephen McConomy. "Trends in Job Evaluation Practices of State Personnel Systems," *Public Personnel Management*, vol. 12, no. 1 (spring 1983).

Ghropade, Jai and Thomas J. Atchison. "The Concept of Job Analysis: A Review and Some Suggestions," *Public Personnel Management*, vol. 9, no. 3 (1980).

Gilbert, G. Ronald and Ardel Nelson. "The Pacer Share Demonstration Project: Implications for Organizational Management and Performance Evaluation," *Public Personnel Management* (summer 1989).

Government Employee Relations Report. *Reforming the Federal Pay System: Special Report* (December 1989). Washington, D.C.

Greenough, William C. and Francis P. King. *Pension Plans and Public Policy*. New York: Columbia University Press, 1976.

Hackman, Richard and Greg R. Oldham. *Work Redesign*. Reading, Mass.: Addison-Wesley, 1980.

Holley, Lyn Meridew. "Pay Reform and Job Classification," *The Bureaucrat* (spring 1990).

Holley, Lyn Meridew. "Job Classification: The Support System for Personnel Decision Making," in Howard Risher and Charles H. Fay (eds.), *New Strategies for Public Pay: Rethinking Government Compensation Programs*. San Francisco: Jossey-Bass, 1997, pp. 76–97.

Hornestay, David. "Tear It Down," *Government Executive* (March 1994), pp. 14–21.

Ippolito, Richard A. "Why Federal Workers Don't Quit," *Journal of Human Resources* (spring 1987).

Jensen, Ollie A. "An Analysis of Confusions and Misconceptions Surrounding Job Analysis, Job Evaluation, Position Classification, Employee Selection, and Content Validity," *Public Personnel Management*, vol. 7 (July–August 1978).

Lewis, Gregory B. "Turnover and the Quiet Crises in the Public Sector," *Public Administration Review*, vol. 51, no. 3 (May–June 1991), pp. 145–155.

Lust, John and Charles Fay. "The Impact of Compensation and Benefits on Employee Quit Rates," *Compensation and Benefits Management* (summer 1989).

Mankin, Don, Susan G. Cohen, and Tora K. Bikson. *Teams & Technology*. Boston: Harvard Business School Press, 1996.

McCarthy, Eugene M. *The Congress and the Civil Service: A History of Federal Compensation and Classification*. background paper for National Commission on the Public Service, 1989. Washington, D.C.

Miller, Michael. "The Public–Private Debate: What Do the Data Show?" *U.S. Monthly Labor Review* (May 1996).

Mohrman, Susan A., Susan G. Cohen, and Allan M. Mohrman. *Designing Team Based Organizations: New Forms for Knowledge Work*. San Francisco: Jossey-Bass, 1995.

Naff, Katherine C. and Raymond Pomerleau. "Productivity Gainsharing: A Federal Sector Case Study," *Public Personnel Management* (winter 1988).

National Academy of Public Administration. *Modernizing Federal Classification: Operational Broad-Banding Systems Alternatives*. 1995.

National (Volcker) Commission for the Public Service. *Leadership for America*. Washington, D.C.: 1989.

Oliver, Philip M. "Modernizing a State Job Evaluation and Pay Plan," *Public Personnel Management*, vol. 5 (May–June 1976).

Penner, Maurice. "How Job-Based Classification Systems Promote Organizational Effectiveness," *Public Personnel Management*, vol. 12, no. 3 (fall 1983).

Perlman, Kenneth. "Job Families: A Review and Discussion of Their Implications for Personnel Selection," *Psychological Bulletin*, vol. 80, no. 1 (January 1980).

Remsay, Arch S. "The New Factor Evaluation System of Position Classification," *Civil Service Journal*, vol. 16 (January–March 1976).

Report on Job Evaluation and Ranking in the Federal Government. Committee on Post Office and Civil Service, Subcommittee on Position Classification, 91st Cong., 1st Session, House Report no. 91–28. Washington, D.C., February 27, 1969.

Risher, Howard. "Are Public Employees Ready for a New Pay Program?" *Public Personnel Management*, vol. 28, no. 3 (fall 1999), p. 340.

Risher, Howard and Charles H. Fay, eds. *New Strategies for Public Pay: Rethinking Government Compensation Programs.* San Francisco: Jossey-Bass, 1997.

Sayre, Wallace S. "The Triumph of Techniques Over Purpose," *Public Administration Review* (spring 1948).

Shafritz, Jay M. *Position Classification: A Behavioral Analysis for the Public Service.* New York: Praeger, 1973.

Shareef, Reginald. "A Midterm Case Study Assessment of Skill-Based Pay in the Virginia Department of Transportation," *Review of Public Personnel Administration* (winter 1998), pp. 5–22.

Shay, Brigitte and Howard Risher. "Grade Banding: The Model for Future Salary Programs," *Public Personnel Management* (summer 1994), pp. 187–199.

Siegel, Gilbert B. "Compensation, Benefits and Work Schedules," *Public Personnel Management* (summer 1989).

Siegel, Gilbert B. *Public Employee Compensation and Its Role in Public Sector Strategic Management.* New York: Quorum Books, 1992.

Smith, Russ. "Job Redesign in the Public Sector," *Review of Public Personnel Administration*, vol. 2, no. 1 (fall 1981).

Suskin, Harold, ed. *Job Evaluation and Pay Administration in the Public Sector.* Chicago: International Personnel Management Association, 1977.

Thompson, Frank J. "Classification as Politics," in R. T. Golembiewski and M. Cohen, (eds.), *People in the Public Service.* Itasca, Ill.: Peacock, 1976.

U.S. Civil Service Commission. *A Report on Study of Position Classification Accuracy in Executive Branch Occupations Under the General Schedule.* Washington, D.C.: 1978.

U.S. Congressional Budget Office (CBO). *Employee Turnover in the Federal Government: A Special Study.* February 1986.

U.S. General Accounting Office (GAO). *Federal Workforce: Pay, Recruitment, and Retention of Federal Employees.* February 1987.

———. *Federal Workforce: Pay, Recruitment, and Retention of Federal Employees.* September 1990.

U.S. General Accounting Office (GAO). *Locality Pay for Federal Employees.* June 1989.

———. *Federal Pay: Comparisons with the Private Sector by Job and Locality.* May 1990.

———. *Federal White-Collar Employee Salary Reform.* March 1990.

U.S. Merit Systems Protection Board (MSPB). *OPM's Classification and Qualification Systems: A Renewed Emphasis, A Changing Perspective.* November 1989.

U.S. Office of Personnel Management (OPM). *Integrated Salary and Benefits: Programs for State and Local Government*. Washington, D.C.: U.S. Government Printing Office, November 1979.

————. *The Classifiers' Handbook*. Washington, D.C.: U.S. Government Printing Office, November 1991. (Subsequent revisions can be found on OPM's website—www. opm.gov.)

————. *Federal White-Collar Pay System: Report on a Market-Sensitive Study*. Washington, D.C.: August 1989.

White, Robert D. "Position Analysis and Characterization," *Review of Public Personnel Administration*, vol. 4, no. 2 (spring 1984).

Winn, Russ. "A Comparison of Internal and External Factors Affecting Voluntary Turnover," *Review of Public Personnel Management* (fall 1984).

Witt, Elder. "Are Our Governments Paying What It Takes to Keep the Best and the Brightest?" *Governing* (December 1988).

6

Recruitment and Selection

PROLOGUE: A MICHIGAN EXECUTIVE
RECRUITMENT EXPERIENCE

Occasionally one gets an inside view of what an organizational process looks from an unlikely source. John Kost was the CIO (chief information officer) for the state of Michigan and later deputy director of the Department of Management and Budget for Procurement and Information Technology. In 1996, after he had left the state, he authored a report for the Brookings Center for Public Management, reviewing some of the major changes in the state of Michigan in the period from 1992 to 1996. His "experience" with civil service executive recruitment is recounted in the following report excerpt.

> One would assume that since the process of hiring a contractor to perform the work of the state is so difficult, the process of hiring internal staff to do the work is commensurably easier. One would be mistaken. To ensure fairness, the commission relies heavily on formal testing to determine candidate qualification. For some positions, tests are administered infrequently, making it extraordinarily difficult to hire fresh talent. For senior management positions, the examination for entrance into the classified executive service is an exercise in understanding bureaucratic behavior, with no emphasis on the substance of the position for which a person might be hired.

The perils and merits of this process are illustrated by what occurred in 1993 as the state sought to hire a new state purchasing director.
The incumbent had announced his retirement in early 1993. By April
of 1993 notice of the position had been posted in Michigan newspapers
and the *Wall Street Journal*. There were more than 250 applicants for
the position. The applicant pool was screened down to the top 30 candidates, from whom additional information was sought. Of these, 20 were
invited to take the classified executive examination.

One needs to actually participate in such an examination to understand its true import. Before being locked in a room, a candidate is
handed a scenario describing the problem to be solved, an organization
chart, and a pencil. The scenario is typically as follows:

*It's Saturday afternoon and you've just learned you must be out
of town for the entire next week. Your in-basket is jammed full of issues
and requests. Your phone and E-mail are inoperable (smoke signals are
apparently still allowed). You must handwrite instructions for everything
you need to do on that Saturday afternoon to ensure that everything in
your in-basket gets dealt with in your absence. Using the blank sheets
of papers, your test is to write memos to your subordinates with appropriate instructions.*

One must understand that some of what is in the in-basket is non-
sense that all but the least effective executives would have dealt with
by firing their subordinates years ago. But the most pressing matters at
hand involve issues of process within the bureaucracy.

Having completed the memos, a candidate is then brought before
an inquisition board consisting of current or retired government executives who question his every action and motive. The makeup of this
board biases the test in favor of those who understand government bureaucracy (and are able to articulate it) and against those who do not
understand it or rely on more creative management practices (especially
those who have worked in the private sector).

In 1993 the range of applicants for the position of purchasing director included the purchasing directors from several large banks, and
from many large and successful manufacturing firms and, of course, a
large number of current and former state employees who had already
passed the test. Those who had not taken the test but had survived the
screening process (that is, the private-sector applicants) were required
to come to Lansing (at their own expense) and take the test. Not surprisingly, several refused to come at their own expense. But, more surprising (at least to the naive executives who were trying to fill those
positions), several of the private-sector executives failed the test. (In
part to understand it better, I took the test. Although it may be an in-

dictment of my own thought process, I did pass the test with flying colors.)

After the testing process, the pool of candidates was narrowed to four; one private-sector candidate who was well qualified for the position, and three state employees who had passed the test and were on the civil service register but who barely met the minimum qualifications. There are many other subprocesses involved in the recruitment process that are too cumbersome to enumerate here. Suffice it to say that there were other intervening events that made it impossible to make an offer to the one viable private-sector candidate before he had accepted a position elsewhere.

Thus, with only three barely acceptable candidates, the candidate pool needed to be expanded. The machinations of filling this position took until June 1994, sixteen months after the previous director had announced his retirement. Between the time the pool was reduced to four and the final candidate was successfully hired (from the private sector), many parts of the process were changed. Once the commission became aware of the broad variance in qualifications between those on the register (barely qualified or completely unqualified for this important position) and the private sector candidates who were not allowed to be interviewed, they realized they needed to act to avoid a calamity.

The commission approved the creation of an alternative selection process, which allowed for recruitment and selection of candidates without the classified executive examination. If an agency wishes to hire at the senior executive level, it need only file a selection plan (in advance) that describes the process to be followed. The commission staff reviews the process to ensure fairness and the involvement of "protected classes" (protected classes include women, minorities, and the handicapped) but largely stays out of the way of the selection and recruitment effort.

The earlier process for selecting a purchasing director also demonstrated the huge amounts of time and energy that one or more department directors or deputy directors must put into filling such positions. To optimize the time of these executives, the commission also gave approval to the use of a private-sector headhunter to help recruit and screen applicants for key senior management positions. Some governments (notably Washington State) use internal executive recruiters. A few hire private headhunters. In April 1996, the state of Michigan awarded a master contract to two private headhunter firms to assist in recruiting and selecting people to fill all senior management positions in state government. This service is available on request, and agencies are encouraged, though not required, to use it.

In filling positions such as purchasing director, computing and telecommunications director, and other key administrative positions, the difficulty of finding a high-quality candidate pool becomes evident. Successful "process owners" from the private sector often lack interest in government employment because of mediocre salaries, frustration with bureaucracy, and general lack of opportunity. Although hiring and promoting from within can result in good people taking these key administrative positions, internal candidates do not always possess the new ideas and approaches that the private sector promotes. Thus the value of institutional memory and process knowledge is occasionally offset by the old government axiom of "but we've always done it that way" when trying to get something done (Kost 1996).

THE LEGAL ENVIRONMENT OF PUBLIC SECTOR SELECTION: FROM *GRIGGS* TO *ADARAND*

The state of Michigan's new approach to executive recruitment must be seen in context. Despite the suspicions of some, the human resources management world does not seek to make the recruitment and selection process as obtuse and complex as possible. Much of the direction human resources has taken was set by the American court system beginning in the early 1970s in its efforts to eliminate employment discrimination. The courts' involvement began with the unanimous U.S. Supreme Court decision in *Griggs* v. *Duke Power Company* (1971). *Griggs* was followed by various statutory laws and presidential executive orders, making discriminatory hiring practices a major target for elimination, but by the 1980s and President Reagan's appointment of several conservative judges, a rather different set of outcomes and decisions involving employment discrimination resulted in a change of course. Through several decisions in 1989, a badly divided Supreme Court ruled that while the goal of barring employment discrimination was still valid, the means to reach the goal were subject to dispute.

It should be pointed out before beginning this review of the legal context of employment selection that the cases in question are, in reality, the product of different Supreme Court environments. The landmark case that started everything—*Griggs* v. *Duke Power*—involved the personnel practices of the Duke Power Company's power-generating facility at Draper, North Carolina, known as the Dan River steam station. In 1964, the Dan River station employed 95 workers and was organized into five departments. All of the lowest-paying jobs were in its labor department, where the highest-paying job paid less than the lowest-paying job in the other four departments. Promotions within each department were generally based on seniority. The station employed 14 African Americans by 1964, all of whom worked in the labor department.

In 1955, the company began to require a high school education for initial placement in all departments except labor. This policy effectively prohibited African Americans from working in any department but labor. Then, on July 2, 1965 (coincidentally, the effective date of the Civil Rights Act of 1964), the company added an additional requirement for new employees. In order to qualify for placement in any department but labor, it was necessary to pass two aptitude tests. Later that year, the company eased up on its policy of requiring high school diplomas for transfers from the labor department to any of the other departments; it was now willing to allow incumbent employees to qualify for transfer by simply taking the two aptitude tests.

The tests used by the Dan River steam station were the Wonderlic personnel test, designed to measure general intelligence, and the Bennett mechanical comprehension test. These tests did not and were not intended to measure the ability to perform successfully in any particular type of job. Not surprisingly, the tests were actually more restrictive than the previous requirement for a high school diploma because the requisite scores used by the company approximated the national median for high school graduates. In other words, on a national basis only about half of all high school graduates would have been able to gain the requisite scores.

In early 1966, the "racial barrier" at the Dan River station was broken. An African-American employee, a high school graduate who had worked for Duke Power since 1953 in the labor department, was promoted. His promotion came five months after charges had been filed with the Equal Employment Opportunity Commission (EEOC) against the company. The next year, 13 of the African-American employees at Dan River steam station, all of whom had been denied promotion because they scored low on the aptitude tests, filed a class-action suit against their employer, the Duke Power Company. They charged that the company's requirements of a high school education and passing scores on intelligence tests for selection or promotion within the company were discriminatory and violated Title VII of the Civil Rights Act of 1964. While Title VII forbids discriminatory employment practices, it does allow the use of professionally developed ability and aptitude tests for employment practices, provided there is no intent to discriminate. The *Griggs* case finally made its way to the U.S. Supreme Court only after a district court and a court of appeals rejected the contentions of the African-American employees at Dan River.

A unanimous Supreme Court in 1971 reversed the lower court decisions and ruled in favor of the African-American employees. The Court ruled that Title VII of the Civil Rights Act of 1964 "proscribes not only overt discrimination but also practices that are fair in form, but discriminatory in operation," thus if employment practices that are operating to exclude African Americans or other protected-class persons "cannot be shown to be related to job performance, the practice is prohibited." The Court dealt a blow to restrictive credentialism when

What Exactly Is Adverse Impact?

The *Uniform Guidelines* state that evidence of adverse impact exists when "a selection rate for any race, sex or ethnic group . . . is less than four-fifths (4/5ths) or eighty percent (80%) of the selection rate for the group with the highest selection rate."

The *Guidelines* provide the following example:

"A comparison of the black selection rate (30%) with the white selection rate (60%) shows that the black rate is 30/60, or one-half (50%) of the white rate. Since the one-half (50%) is less than 4/5ths (80%) adverse impact is usually indicated."

Source: "Questions and Answers to Clarify and Provide a Common Interpretation of the Uniform Guidelines on Employee Selection Procedure," *Federal Register*, vol. 44, no. 43 (March 2, 1979), p. 11998.

it stated that while diplomas and tests are useful, "Congress has mandated the common-sense proposition that they are not to become masters of reality." In essence, the Court found that the law requires that tests used for employment purposes "must measure the person for the job and not the person in the abstract."

The *Griggs* decision originally applied only to the private sector, but since passage of the Equal Employment Opportunity Act in 1972, which extended the provisions of Title VII of the Civil Rights Act to cover public employees, the *Griggs* decision opened the doors to a new era in public employee testing and selection. What was at stake, as most organizations were to find, was not the actual practice, selection policy, or testing device in use, but the applied *results*, or the ways in which policies or practices brought about discriminatory *impact* on various special groups (gender, age, ethnicity, and race being the most important categories for which adverse impact must be avoided). So, as the *Griggs* Court said, "good intent or absence of discriminatory intent does not redeem employment procedures or testing mechanisms that operate as 'built-in headwinds' for minority groups and are unrelated to measuring job capability. . . . Congress directed the thrust of the [Civil Rights] Act to the *consequences* of employment practices, not simply the motivation."

Fast forward 15 years to 1989, when a very different Supreme Court tackled a second landmark case, *Wards Cove* v. *Atonio*. The case facts are as follows. Wards Cove Packing Company operated several salmon canneries in Alaska, essentially using two types of employees. There were unskilled jobs on the can-

---

In Search of the "Best Qualified" Job Candidate

The U.S. Supreme Court, in its 1987 *Johnson* v. *Transportation Agency* (107 S.Ct. 1442, 1987 at p. 1457) ruling said that there may *never* be a best qualified job applicant. Quoting from a brief submitted by the American Society for Personnel Administration, the Court said that "[i]t is a standard tenet of personnel administration that there is rarely a single, 'best qualified' person for a job . . . final determinations as to which candidate is 'best qualified' are at best subjective."

---

nery lines that were held predominantly by nonwhites, while the noncannery jobs (skilled positions such as boat operators, accountants, and medical personnel) were held predominantly by whites. Almost all the cannery jobs paid wages below the noncannery jobs. Furthermore, there was almost complete separation between the two groups of employees in that nonwhite and whites lived in separate dormitories and ate in separate dining facilities. In their dissenting opinions in this case, Justices Stevens and Blackmun went as far as to remark that "the salmon industry, as described by this record takes us back to a kind of overt and institutionalized discrimination we have not dealt with in years: a total residential and work environment, organized on principles of racial stratification and segregation, which resembles a plantation economy."

Justice White delivered the majority opinion for this 5–4 decision by refuting the interpretation provided in *Griggs* that forbade employment practices that result in "disparate impact" (i.e., that produce discriminatory results even if the practices themselves are neutral). The majority ruling rejected the standard of comparison established by *Griggs* in which a prima facie disparate-impact case could be established by comparing simply the percentage of minorities in each job category. In its place was a new standard, which compared the "qualified job force" in the labor market to the racial makeup of the jobs in question. The Court majority said: "If the absence of minorities holding such skilled positions is due to a dearth of qualified nonwhite applicants (for reasons that are not petitioners' fault), petitioners' selection methods or employment practices cannot be said to have had a 'disparate impact' on nonwhites."

The Court went the extra step to make clear its new position on where the burden of proof was regarding disparate impact. It stated that "any employer having a racially unbalanced segment of its work force could be hauled into court, and made to undertake the expensive and time-consuming task of defending the business necessity of its selection methods." *Wards Cove* effectively overturned the landmark *Griggs* ruling by shifting the burden of proof to the plaintiffs, requiring them to demonstrate that specific employment practices of the company have *caused* the statistical disparity between workforce groups and jobs. The *New York Times* commented that this places ''insurmountable obstacles in the path of workers seeking to bring a common type of employment discrimination lawsuit under the Civil Rights Act of 1964.'' Moreover, it ''could prove so onerous to plaintiffs that employers might feel free to abandon affirmative action plans.''

Of course there was vigorous dissent bordering on disbelief on the part of the four dissenting justices. They stated that the majority ruling in *Wards Cove* reargues the intentions of *Griggs*, the Title VII precedents, and even the acceptance within society of the *Griggs* decision as a fundamental ruling. The dissenting justices ended with a cynical note: ''One wonders whether the majority still believes that race discrimination—or more accurately, race discrimination against nonwhites—is a problem in our society, or even remembers that it ever was.''

Wards Cove was not destined to have a long-term impact. Along with several other related conservative Court actions, it generated a backlash and spurred legislative reaction in the form of a new 1990 civil rights act. The 1990 bill was vetoed by President Bush on the grounds that it was a ''quota bill'' that he could not support even though his personal record in support of civil rights was excellent. Although the Senate failed to override the veto by one vote, business leaders joined with moderate congressional representatives under the leadership of Senator Danforth of Missouri to reformulate the act and pass the Civil Rights Act of 1991. (See Chapter 9.)

Although the Civil Rights Act of 1991 made *Wards Cove* obsolete, the stage was now set for new court rulings, which came not in the form of employment selection or hiring rulings, but rather in two cases regarding business set-asides. The Supreme Court had ruled in 1989 in *City of Richmond* v. *J. A. Croson Co.* that any state affirmative action using racial or ethnic criteria as a basis for decision making would be subject to ''strict scrutiny.'' (Again see Chapter 9 for a more in-depth discussion.) Croson had sued the city of Richmond for requiring prime contractors who were awarded contracts with the city to subcontract at least 30% of the dollar value of the total contract into subcontracts to minority business enterprises. Suffice it say here, the Court's strict scrutiny standard meant if a government program wanted to take race into consideration, it had to be able to show a ''compelling government interest'' and that the program action was ''narrowly tailored.'' The acting assistant attorney general for the civil rights division remarked in an address in 1997 that ''The one thing that is clear is that the mere fact that African Americans, women, or any group have been discriminated against by society as a whole is *not* an acceptable basis for race based affirmative action by a federal agency. In other words, remedying societal discrimination is not considered a compelling government interest. What is generally accepted as a compelling interest is remedying the lingering effects of the government's own discrimination or the effects discrimination by others has had on government's own activities.''

In Croson, however, the Court had ruled that Congress and therefore the federal government might not be held to the strict scrutiny of the state and local governments. That stand was dropped however, in a 5–4 decision in 1995 in *Adarand Constructors Inc.* v. *Pena.* The facts were simply that Adarand, a nonminority firm had submitted the lowest bid of a subcontract for the Department of Transportation (DOT). The prime contract, responding to a financial incentive from the DOT to aid minority business enterprises, awarded the subcontract to a minority firm. Adarand sued that DOT's program, which required that 10% of all contracts be set aside for "small business concerns owned and controlled by socially and economically disadvantaged individuals."

Justice O'Connor wrote the 5–4 majority decision, which said unequivocally that strict scrutiny would now apply to all federal programs. It also explicitly stated that an earlier ruling in Metro Broadcasting that allowed a more lenient standard for federal affirmative action measures was overruled. Why would Adarand, a case about set-aside programs, apply to government hiring programs? The answer is simply that although a federal contracting program was the spark, the Court's decision on the strict scrutiny standard would apply, as the acting assistant attorney general noted in 1997, to all "race-based decisionmaking in all areas of federal activity, including employment. That reaches not only official government or agency employment policies or procedures but also individual employment decisions.''

A final example—that of *Dallas* v. *Dallas Fire Fighters Association* (1998)—shows where the Court stands on matters of personnel policy. In 1988, the Dallas City Council established a five-year plan that promoted minorities and women ahead of white males who had scored higher on promotion tests for advancement. In 1988, women and minorities held less than 15% of one key occupational group, driver-engineers, and less than 3% of all fire lieutenant positions. The affirmative action plan developed by the city was in response to a 1976 consent order signed by the city admitting past discrimination. By 1992, the city council's plan had raised minority and women rates to 23% and 18% in the two key posts, so the council approved a five-year extension of the program. This time, the Dallas firefighters association and other individual firefighters filed suit to stop the program. The lower courts all ruled against the city on the grounds that there was little evidence of past discrimination and that the city had failed to demonstrate a "compelling interest." On appeal to the U.S. Supreme Court in March 1999, only Justices Breyer and Ginsburg voted to review the case. Since the votes of at least four justices are required to even grant a review, the Supreme Court thus let stand the lower court decision and struck down the Dallas promotional program as discriminatory against white males.

THE DEVELOPMENT (AND DECLINE) OF THE
UNIFORM GUIDELINES

The first impact of the Court rulings in job discrimination cases was the establishment of a legal framework that regulated selection and hiring practices. Following the *Griggs* decision, the courts provided more specific guidance on testing practices. In 1973, in *U.S.* v. *Georgia Power Company*, the Fifth Circuit Court of Appeals reaffirmed job-relatedness as the critical requirement. In this case, the Georgia Power Company had used a separate validation process for its testing instruments that did not correspond with how the tests were being used for making employment and promotions decisions. The court ruled that job-relatedness in this case can only be construed as part of the selection decision-making process.

Then in 1975 the Supreme Court provided more definitive instructions on what job-relatedness entailed. In *Albemarle Paper Company* v. *Moody*, the Court struck down a rather late-constructed job-testing and validation procedure because it failed to demonstrate job relevance. The company in this case had conducted a job analysis based on only a few select jobs and concentrated on the job requirements for employees at the highest levels in those jobs. Basically, tests were developed that were keyed to higher-level, job-experienced whites, but were used to make hiring decisions for inexperienced minorities for lower-level jobs. In rejecting this practice, the Court ruled that it was essential for valid testing that a job analysis study relate entry-level applicants to higher positions and that criteria measurement be established to determine job-specific abilities to the positions in question. The message to all employers using examinations was rather clear: a well-planned and rigorously constructed validation study would be required to ''ensure'' any examination from legal challenges.

These early 1970s legal decisions about testing and selection helped lead to the development of the *Uniform Guidelines on Employee Selection Procedures* issued jointly by the EEOC, the former U.S. Civil Service Commission, and the Departments of Labor and Justice. (See Figure 6.1.) They were the result of nearly 15 years of arguments among federal agencies and scores of individually issued procedures that often created more chaos than clarity. Finally, in 1978, the guidelines were formally issued, completing a process that established a uniform government employment policy.

The *Uniform Guidelines* were intended to be the central set of rules for selection procedures applying to both the public and private sectors. Of course, most federal government agencies are covered, as are any state and local government agencies that employ more than 15 people or receive federal revenue assistance. The same concept applied to private sector employers; if they had 15 or more employees hired for 20 weeks in the year or received any form of government contract or subcontract, they also had to abide by the *Uniform Guidelines*.

Comprehensive Table of Contents

GENERAL PRINCIPLES

1607.1. Statement of Purpose
  A. Need for Uniformity — Issuing Agencies
  B. Purpose of Guidelines
  C. Relation to Prior Guidelines
1607.2. Scope
  A. Application of Guidelines
  B. Employment Decisions
  C. Selection Procedures
  D. Limitations
  E. Indian Preference Not Affected
1607.3. Discrimination Defined: Relationship Between Use of Selection Procedures and Discrimination
  A. Procedure Having Adverse Impact Constitutes Discrimination Unless Justified
  B. Consideration of Suitable Alternative Selection Procedures
1607.4. Information on Impact
  A. Records Concerning Impact
  B. Applicable Race, Sex and Ethnic Groups For Record Keeping
  C. Evaluation of Selection Rates. The "Bottom Line"
  D. Adverse Impact And The "Four-Fifths Rule"
  E. Consideration of User's Equal Employment Opportunity Posture
1607.5. General Standards for Validity Studies
  A. Acceptable types of Validity Studies
  B. Criterion-Related, Content, and Construct Validity
  C. Guidelines Are Consistent with Professional Standards
  D. Need For Documentation of Validity
  E. Accuracy and Standardization
  F. Caution Against Selection on Basis of Knowledges, Skills or Abilities Learned in Brief Orientation Period
  G. Method of Use of Selection Procedures

  H. Cutoff Scores
  I. Use of Selection Procedures for Higher Level Jobs
  J. Interim Use of Selection Procedures
  K. Review of Validity Studies for Currency
1607.6. Use of Selection Procedures Which Have Not Been Validated
  A. Use of Alternate Selection Procedures to Eliminate Adverse Impact
  B. Where Validity Studies Cannot or Need Not Be Performed
    (1) Where Informal or Unscored Procedures Are Used
    (2) Where Formal And Scored Procedures Are Used
1607.7. Use of Other Validity Studies
  A. Validity Studies not Conducted by the User
  B. Use of Criterion-Related Validity Evidence from Other Sources
    (1) Validity Evidence
    (2) Job Similarity
    (3) Fairness Evidence
  C. Validity Evidence from Multi-Unit Study
  D. Other Significant Variables
1607.8. Cooperative Studies
  A. Encouragment of Cooperative Studies
  B. Standards for Use of Cooperative Studies
1607.9 No Assumption of Validity
  A. Unacceptable Substitutes for Evidence of Validity
  B. Encouragement of Professional Supervision
1607.10. Employment Agencies and Employment Services
  A. Where Selection Procedures Are Devised by Agency
  B. Where Selection Procedures Are Devised Elsewhere
1607.11. Disparate Treatment
1607.12. Retesting of Applicants

(continued)

FIGURE 6.1 Uniform guidelines (table of contents) on employee selection procedures.

1607.13. Affirmative Action
   A. Affirmative Action Obligations
   B. Encouragement of Voluntary
      Affirmative Action Programs

TECHNICAL STANDARDS

1607.14. Technical Standards for Validity
    Studies
   A. Validity Studies Should be
      Based on Review of Informa-
      tion about the Job
   B. Technical Standards for Cri-
      terion-Related Validity Studies
     (1) Technical Feasibility
     (2) Analysis of the Job
     (3) Criterion Measures
     (4) Representativeness of the
        Sample
     (5) Statistical Relationships
     (6) Operational use of Selec-
        tion Procedures
     (7) Over-Statement of Validity
        Findings
     (8) Fairness
       (a) Unfairness Defined
       (b) Investigation of Fairness
       (c) General Considerations
          in Fairness Investi-
          gations
       (d) When Unfairness Is
          Shown
       (e) Technical Feasibility of
          Fairness Studies
       (f) Continued Use of
          Selection Procedures
          When Fairness Studies
          not Feasible
   C. Technical Standards for
      Content Validity Studies
     (1) Appropriateness of
        Content Validity Studies
     (2) Job Analysis for Content
        Validity
     (3) Development of Selection
        Procedure
     (4) Standards For Demon-
        strating Content Validity
     (5) Reliability
     (6) Prior Training or
        Experience
     (7) Training Success
     (8) Operational use

     (9) Ranking Based on Content
        Validity Studies
   D. Technical Standards For
      Construct Validity Studies
     (1) Appropriateness of
        Construct Validity Studies
     (2) Job Analysis For
        Construct Validity Studies
     (3) Relationship to the Job
     (4) Use of Construct Validity
        Study Without New
        Criterion-Related Evidence
       (a) Standards for Use
       (b) Determination of Com-
          mon Work Behaviors

DOCUMENTATION OF IMPACT AND
VALIDITY EVIDENCE

1607.15. Documentation of Impact and
    Validity Evidence
   A. Required Information
     (1) Simplified Recordkeeping
        for Users With Less Than
        100 Employees
     (2) Information on Impact
       (a) Collection of Informa-
          tion on Impact
       (b) When Adverse Impact
          Has Been Eliminated in
          The Total Selection
          Process
       (c) When Data Insufficient
          to Determine Impact
     (3) Documentation of Validity
        Evidence
       (a) Type of Evidence
       (b) Form of Report
       (c) Completeness
   B. Criterion-Related Validity
      Studies
     (1) User(s), Location(s), and
        Date(s) of Study
     (2) Problem and Setting
     (3) Job Analysis or Review of
        Job Information
     (4) Job Titles and Codes
     (5) Criterion Measures
     (6) Sample Description
     (7) Description of Selection
        Procedure
     (8) Techniques and Results
     (9) Alternative Procedures

FIGURE 6.1   *(continued)*

Investigated
(10) Uses and Applications
(11) Source Data
(12) Contact Person
(13) Accuracy and
     Completeness
C. Content Validity Studies
   (1) User(s), Location(s), and
       Date(s) of Study
   (2) Problem and Setting
   (3) Job Analysis—Content of
       the Job
   (4) Selection Procedure and its
       Content
   (5) Relationship Between
       Selection Procedure and
       the Job
   (6) Alternative Procedures
       Investigated
   (7) Uses and Applications
   (8) Contact Person
   (9) Accuracy and Completeness
D. Construct Validity Studies
   (1) User(s), Location(s), and
       Date(s) of Study
   (2) Problem and Setting
   (3) Construct Definition
   (4) Job Analysis
   (5) Job Titles and Codes
   (6) Selection Procedure
   (7) Relationship to Job
       Performance
   (8) Alternative Procedures
       Investigated

(9) Uses and Applications
(10) Accuracy and Completeness
(11) Source Data
(12) Contact Person
E. Evidence of Validity from
   Other Studies
   (1) Evidence from Criterion-
       Related Validity Studies
       (a) Job Information
       (b) Relevance of Criteria
       (c) Other Variables
       (d) Use of the Selection
           Procedure
       (e) Bibliography
   (2) Evidence from Content
       Validity Studies
   (3) Evidence from Construct
       Validity Studies
F. Evidence of Validity from
   Cooperative Studies
G. Selection for Higher Level Jobs
H. Interim Use of Selection
   Procedures

DEFINITIONS

1607.16. Definitions

APPENDIX

1607.17. Policy Statement on Affirmative
         Action (see Section 13B)
1607.18. Citations

Source: *Federal Register*, vol. 43, no. 166 (Friday, August 25, 1978).

FIGURE 6.1 *(continued)*

What the *Uniform Guidelines* cover is equally pervasive. Simply put, all procedures used in making "employment decisions" are covered. This would include, for example, application forms, minimum application requirements, any performance test, reviews of past training and experience, all written tests, all oral interviews or tests, and even performance reviews of someone hired on a trial or probationary basis. It is also important to add, as the courts have made abundantly clear, that employment decisions include more than the recruiting and hiring process. An employment decision includes retention, promotion, separation or firing, performance review, and training decisions. In effect, whenever one employee is chosen over another, this constitutes a "selection decision."

The *Uniform Guidelines* detail minimum standards for validation, explain different forms of validity, and document evidential requirements for demonstrating validity. Figure 6.1 is provided to give an indication of the scope of the guidelines. At the heart of the guidelines is the concept of "adverse impact." (This is the disparate impact controversy discussed in the review of Supreme Court rulings in this chapter.) This concept refers to the establishment of an "80%" or "4/5" rule, which is used to determine minimum evidence of "discrimination." The 80% rule stipulates that if the selection rate for any group is less than 80% of that for other groups, this constitutes evidence of adverse impact in the selection device. This does not mean that the selection device cannot be used, but it was to be carefully *validated* if the 80% rule is violated.

Essentially a "burden of proof" change was incorporated into the legal process surrounding selections, thus under the "old rulings" (i.e., beginning with *Griggs*), if there was adverse impact, the burden of proof shifted to the organization to defend and show that there are valid reasons for the result and that no intent to discriminate was involved. Under the later rulings (i.e., *Wards Cove*), adverse impact was not enough to reverse the burden of proof. The individual or "unselected one" had to demonstrate either the *intent* to discriminate or some causality between each employment practice and statistical job disparities. In the post-*Adarand* world, adverse impact is still valid, but it must be very carefully constructed. To withstand "strict scrutiny" and a compelling interest, adverse impact could still be demonstrated, but the comparison would have to be a specific racial percentage within an occupational group to the racial population of the occupational group in the general population. In some cases, the comparison might have to be even more narrowly drawn to a racial comparison of people who are qualified for the job. For example, it is no longer sufficient to compare the racial population of engineers in an agency to the racial characteristics of the general population and make the assertion that adverse impact exists because the group is underrepresented.

It is important to point out that prior to the 1990s it was only in cases arising under the Constitution that intent rather than results determined the existence of discrimination. This was made clear in the Court's landmark 1976 *Washington v. Davis* decision. In this case, an entry-level police officer exam administered by the District of Columbia's police department disproportionately screened out African-American applicants (four times as many African Americans failed the exam as whites). The African Americans filed suit, arguing that the police department's written exam was racially discriminatory and violated the Due Process Clause of the Fifth Amendment to the Constitution. Because the case was filed under the Fifth Amendment as opposed to Title VII, the adverse impact standard was not applied. The *Washington* Court said that this standard "is not the constitutional rule." The Court said: "Disproportionate impact is not irrelevant, but it is not the sole touchstone of an invidious racial discrimination forbidden by the Constitution. Standing alone, it does not trigger the rule." The Court instead relied on whether or not the police department *intended* to discriminate against the African-American job candidates. The Court found no intent to discriminate, therefore ruling in favor of the police department.

In 1978, the U.S. Supreme Court decided another precedent-setting case in *U.S. v. South Carolina.* In this case, a lower court ruling was upheld concerning the use of a test designed by a national testing corporation for selection decisions involving schoolteachers. Even though there was adverse impact, the Court ruled that there was no intention to discriminate and that proper validation procedures had been followed. (This case was brought under the Fourteenth Amendment, Title VII, and the Civil Rights Acts of 1866 and 1871.) While the legal verdict is still out in the selection and employment area, the technical vocabulary and methodological expertise required to understand the key issues involved is a permanent fixture, and more guidance is on the way. In 1982, the General Accounting Office, as well as such professional associations as the International Personnel Management Association, began urging the EEOC to undertake a comprehensive review of the *Uniform Guidelines* and make revisions. The EEOC's initial efforts were quietly halted after very critical congressional hearings on the guidelines were held in 1985.

Since the mid-1980s, the guidelines have been in what Chris Daniels calls a "state of polarized gridlock." Despite the need for revision they are trapped on the one hand between "civil rights advocates who identify the guidelines with effective enforcement of Title VII of the 1964 Civil Rights Act," and "Conservatives, on the other, who are generally critical of government regulation of economic life." Politics notwithstanding, Daniels concludes that the guidelines have been overtaken by considerable advancement in industrial and organizational psychology in selection and testing theory.

For starters, there has been a methodological revolution in the field of testing since the 1970s. In an assessment of employment testing in 1984, Frank Schmidt and John Hunter note that major improvements in methodology have resolved two major difficulties—first that "professionally developed cognitive ability tests are valid predictors of performance on the job and in training for all jobs," and second that "cognitive ability tests are equally valid for minority and majority applicants and are fair to minority applicants in that they do not underestimate the expected job performance of minority groups." These methodology advances led to revised validation guidelines that were released by the Society for Industrial and Organizational Psychology in 1987 and that are significantly different from the uniform guidelines. Daniels compares a key concept—"test fairness"—and contrasts the 1978 guidelines definition with the 1987 revised Society for Industrial and Organizational Psychology (SIOP; 1987: 18) guidelines.

> The 1978 Guidelines were based on the premise that tests which successfully predicted job performance for white males would not necessarily predict effectively performance by minorities and women. So, the

Guidelines required employers to conduct special studies of "test fair-ness," determining validity for demographic groups within applicant pools (U.S. EEOC, 1978, Section 14, B8a). In contrast to the Guidelines, SIOP's 1987 Principles view this concept, called "differential predic-tion" very critically.

        Fairness is a social rather than a psychometric concept. . . . Fair-ness or lack of fairness is not a property of the selection procedure, but rather a joint function of the procedure, the job, the population, and how the scores derived from it are used . . . There is little evidence to suggest that there is differential prediction for the sexes, and the literature indi-cates that differential prediction on the basis of cognitive tests is not supported for the major ethnic groups . . . There is no compelling re-search literature or theory to suggest that cognitive tests should be used differently for different groups.

Human resources management can only hope that sometime soon in this new century there will be revised uniform guidelines and clarity on the legal foundation of employment selection. In addition to those nonforthcoming uni-form guidelines, federal personnel offices along with the Office of Personnel Management (OPM) are still waiting for the Department of Justice to issue some form of formal guidance on federal personnel policies in light of the *Adarand* decision.

THE IMPORTANCE OF PUBLIC EMPLOYMENT

Perhaps the biggest reason that employment practices—recruitment, selection, and placement—have emerged as such a highly controversial area of personnel management is that the stakes are so high. Like government employment, public sector employment was at one time relatively small, but by the late 1980s, over 17 million persons (nearly 3 million federal, about 4 million state government, and over 10 million local government) worked for the government, accounting for almost 15% of the total workforce. (See Figure 6.3 for the percentage of change in state and local government employment from 1986 to 1996.) By 2000, despite some marked declines in federal employment numbers, the numbers stood at 4.6 million state employees and 12.8 million local government employees, making almost 20 million public sector employees. Add in contractors and non-profits working for government and the numbers shoot even higher.

    In 1996 *Governing* magazine pitched the size and importance of public sector employers by introducing their own version of the *Fortune* 500, or what they called America's billion-dollar governments. (See Table 6.1.) That amounted to 98 governmental entities that generated more than $1 billion in an-nual general revenue. The list is replicated in Table 6.1 to provide a sense of

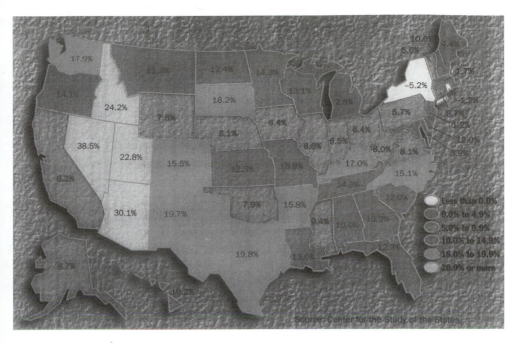

Figure 6.2 Hiring in the 1990s—more ups than downs.

Table 6.1 America's Billion-Dollar Governments

	Billions	Employees
1. California	89.370	343,781
2. New York	76.055	267,359
3. New York City	39.593	380,851
4. Texas	38.044	247,494
5. Pennsylvania	30.561	144,945
6. Florida	29.483	167,056
7. Ohio	27.051	141,286
8. Illinois	26.688	131,878
9. Michigan	25.982	135,864
10. New Jersey	24.028	110,176
11. Massachusetts	20.345	80,524
12. North Carolina	17.959	110,640
13. Washington	15.771	96,414
14. Georgia	15.529	118,527
15. Virginia	14.816	118,071
16. Indiana	14.678	97,843
17. Wisconsin	14.466	69,577
18. Minnesota	14.212	67,059

TABLE 6.1 Continued

	Billions	Employees
19. Maryland	12.870	83,871
20. Los Angeles Co.	12.101	82,941
21. Louisiana	11.846	90,417
22. Connecticut	11.336	59,991
23. Missouri	11.273	78,829
24. Tennessee	10.939	77,223
25. Kentucky	10.098	71,725
26. Alabama	10.014	82,886
27. Arizona	9.706	56,683
28. South Carolina	9.020	77,885
29. Oregon	8.511	47,160
30. Colorado	8.039	54,542
31. Iowa	7.619	51,018
32. Oklahoma	7.467	68,207
33. Mississippi	6.607	47,746
34. Kansas	6.462	47,746
35. Arkansas	5.982	46,655
36. New Mexico	5.511	42,862
37. West Virginia	5.332	33,412
38. Alaska	5.279	21,829
39. Hawaii	5.056	51,787
40. Utah	4.808	42,031
41. Washington, D.C.	4.731	43,142
42. Los Angeles	4.077	46,880
43. Nebraska	4.026	29,158
44. L.A. school dist.	3.706	58,307
45. Dade County	3.601	35,499
46. Maine	3.534	21,285
47. Nevada	3.460	19,059
48. Chicago	3.436	39,630
49. Rhode Island	3.177	19,834
50. Philadelphia	3.146	29,048
51. San Francisco	2.962	23,875
52. Idaho	2.837	20,555
53. Delaware	2.823	20,425
54. New Hampshire	2.649	16,902
55. Chicago schools	2.616	46,258
56. Montana	2.518	17,343
57. Orange Co., CA	2.370	15,544
58. San Diego County	2.282	17,092
59. NY/NJ Port Authority	2.060	9,455
60. Dade Co. schools	2.043	30,476
61. Nassau Co., NY	2.027	16,297
62. North Dakota	2.009	15,874

TABLE 6.1 Continued

	Billions	Employees
63. Wyoming	2.004	10,874
64. Montgomery Co.	1.935	25,533
65. Fairfax Co., VA	1.930	29,679
66. Baltimore	1.854	27,830
67. Santa Clara Co.	1.809	16,269
68. Cook Co., IL	1.807	24,985
69. Boston	1.804	20,658
70. LA Metro Transit	1.791	8,420
71. Vermont	1.781	12,686
72. South Dakota	1.741	13,895
73. San Bernardino Co.	1.692	13,663
74. Detroit	1.623	18,515
75. Sacramento Co.	1.565	13,307
76. Prince Georges Co.	1.528	22,249
77. Harris Co., TX	1.517	18,539
78. Suffolk Co., NY	1.516	11,635
79. Riverside Co., CA	1.515	11,947
80. Westchester Co.	1.507	10,680
81. Houston	1.486	22,015
82. Alameda Co., CA	1.403	10,092
83. Baltimore Co.	1.374	20,495
84. Philadelphia schools	1.371	30,308
85. Wash., D.C. Metro	1.316	8,313
86. Maricopa Co., AZ	1.255	15,631
87. Denver	1.231	12,452
88. Clark Co., NV	1.224	9,900
89. Erie Co., NY	1.220	9,542
90. Broward Co. schools	1.217	19,723
91. San Diego	1.209	10,140
92. Detroit school dist.	1.150	17,027
93. Dallas	1.144	13,607
94. Hillsborough Co., FL	1.129	12,204
95. Cuyahoga Co., OH	1.109	15,807
96. Hennepin Co., MN	1.109	10,336
97. Phoenix	1.106	10,932
98. Houston School Dist.	1.089	23,199
99. Nashville	1.083	16,594
100. Wayne Co., Mich.	1.066	5,682

* Also included in Governing's Billion Dollar government "club" but not listed here are Shelby County, TN, the City of Indianapolis, Contra Costa County, CA, Memphis, Broward County in Texas, Honolulu, Mechlenburg County, NC, and Monroe County, NY. For 108 total. And these are 1997 numbers—by now there are surely another 20–25 school districts, cities and counties.

Industry	Thousands of jobs			Change		Percent distribution			Average annual rate of change	
	1986	1996	2006	1986–96	1996–2006	1986	1996	2006	1986–96	1996–2006
Total [1]	111,374	132,352	150,927	20,978	18,575	100.0	100.0	100.0	1.7	1.3
Nonfarm wage and salary [2]	98,727	118,731	136,318	20,004	17,587	88.6	89.7	90.3	1.9	1.4
Goods producing	24,538	24,431	24,451	−107	20	22.0	18.5	16.2	.0	.0
Mining	778	574	443	−204	−131	.7	.4	.3	−3.0	−2.5
Construction	4,810	5,400	5,900	590	500	4.3	4.1	3.9	1.2	.9
Manufacturing	18,951	18,457	18,108	−493	−350	17.0	13.9	12.0	−.3	−.2
Durable	11,200	10,766	10,514	−433	−252	10.1	8.1	7.0	−.4	−.2
Nondurable	7,751	7,691	7,593	−60	98	7.0	5.8	5.0	−.1	−.1
Service producing	74,189	94,300	111,867	20,111	17,567	66.6	71.2	74.1	2.4	1.7
Transportation, communications, utilities	5,247	6,260	7,111	1,014	851	4.7	4.7	4.7	1.8	1.3
Wholesale trade	5,751	6,483	7,228	732	745	5.2	4.9	4.8	1.2	1.1
Retail trade	17,878	21,625	23,875	3,747	2,250	16.1	16.3	15.8	1.9	1.0
Finance, insurance, and real estate	6,275	6,899	7,651	625	752	5.6	5.2	5.1	1.0	1.0
Services [2]	22,346	33,586	44,852	11,240	11,266	20.1	25.4	29.7	4.2	2.9
Federal Government	2,899	2,757	2,670	−142	−87	2.6	2.1	1.8	.5	.3
State and local government	13,794	16,690	18,480	2,896	1,790	12.4	12.6	12.2	1.9	1.0
Agriculture [3]	3,327	3,642	3,618	314	−24	3.0	2.8	2.4	.9	−.1
Private household wage and salary	1,235	928	775	−307	−153	1.1	.7	.5	−2.8	−1.8
Nonagricultural self-employed and unpaid family workers [4]	8,085	9,051	10,216	966	1,165	7.3	6.8	6.8	1.1	1.2

[1] Employment data for wage and salary workers are from the BLS Current Employment Statistics (payroll) survey, which counts jobs, whereas self-employed, unpaid family worker, agricultural, and private household data are from the Current Population Survey (household survey), which counts workers.

[2] Excludes SIC 074,5,8 (agricultural services) and 99 (nonclassifiable

establishments), and is therefore not directly comparable with data published in *Employment and Earnings*.

[3] Excludes government wage and salary workers, and includes private sector SIC 08, 09 (forestry and fisheries).

[4] Excludes SIC 08, 09 (forestry and fisheries).

Occupational group	Employment						Change			
	Number			Percent distribution			Number		Percent	
	1986	1996	2006	1986	1996	2006	1986–96	1996–2006	1986–96	1996–2006
Total, all occupations	111,375	132,353	150,927	100.0	100.0	100.0	20,978	18,574	18.8	14.0
Executive, administrative, and managerial	10,568	13,542	15,866	9.5	10.2	10.5	2,974	2,324	28.1	17.2
Professional specialty	13,589	18,173	22,998	12.2	13.7	15.2	4,584	4,826	33.7	26.6
Technicians and related support	3,724	4,618	5,558	3.3	3.5	3.7	894	940	24.0	20.4
Marketing and sales	11,496	14,633	16,897	10.3	11.1	11.2	3,137	2,264	27.3	15.5
Administrative support, including clerical	20,871	24,019	25,825	18.7	18.1	17.1	3,147	1,806	15.1	7.5
Service	17,427	21,294	25,147	15.6	16.1	16.7	3,867	3,853	22.2	18.1
Agriculture, forestry, fishing, and related occupations	3,661	3,785	3,823	3.3	2.9	2.5	124	37	3.4	1.0
Precision production, craft, and repair	13,832	14,446	15,448	12.4	10.9	10.2	614	1,002	4.4	6.9
Operators, fabricators, and laborers	16,206	17,843	19,365	14.6	13.5	12.8	1,637	1,522	10.1	8.5

(Numbers in thousands of jobs)

FIGURE 6.3 Projected employment data. (From *Monthly Labor Review*, Nov. 1997.)

what kinds of governments are in the billion-dollar category and in keeping with this chapter's theme of how many full-time employees they have.

Does size really matter? Of course it does. Governments at all levels must make intelligent and legal decisions about their workforces, whether they are in the billion-dollar "club" or a much smaller entity. As will be discussed, obtaining the talent needed to operate effectively can no longer be taken for granted. There must be a well-planned approach that proves to the potential workforce candidate that the organization knows what it's doing.

PERSONAL RANK VERSUS POSITION RANK

Before tackling the essentials of the public sector employment process, one final distinction should be made about the core concept of career in a civil service system. There are essentially two kinds of jobs for which governments recruit: those that offer personal rank and those that only offer position rank. Rank-in-person systems, such as the foreign service and the military, are oriented toward bottom-entry career ladder patterns, whereby individuals normally progress from the lowest to higher ranks. These systems usually have an "up or out" feature whereby a member who is not promotable to the next higher grade after a set period of time is either dismissed or forced to retire. Employment decisions are therefore related to overall career potential and the capability to perform a wide range of responsibilities. Rank-in-position systems, based primarily on the classification and level of the position held by the employee, are far more common. Here it is the set of work responsibilities ascribed to the position that carries authority. By virtue of having qualified for the position, individuals being selected for the position or holding the position take its authority as their own only during tenure in that particular position.

These two systems, rank-in-person and rank-in-position, have employment processes that differ markedly in the following respects:

Concerning recruitment—The rank-in-person system seeks relatively inexperienced high-potential young people to start a career at the entry level, while the rank-in-position system seeks individuals who can perform a specific position's duties.

Concerning selection—The rank-in-person system selects individuals on the basis of their long-range potential and aptitude to perform at various levels through the course of a career, while the rank-in-position system selects individuals on the basis of their ability to perform a specific set of duties for one position or for positions in a certain job family.

Concerning placement—The rank-in-person system has flexible assignments that periodically change. Training is often included as part of an assignment change in order to provide newly needed skills. Individuals

must keep themselves available for any geographic or functional assignment. In contrast, with the rank-in-position system new assignments are
tied to promotions and to the meeting of specific standards. Individuals
must usually initiate and consent to placement changes.

While these two systems are nearly separate as analytical constructs, in
reality both systems tend to pay attention to both aspects—the person and the
position. The intermingling of these systems, their standing side by side in many
organizations with some means of access into each other (what is termed conversion), has further ensured this common perspective, yet the orientations of rank-
in-person and rank-in-position systems are quite different in terms of who is to be
employed and for how long. As such, employment practices will be appropriately
oriented.

ESSENTIALS OF THE EMPLOYMENT PROCESS

The process of employment has three basic components: recruitment, selection,
and placement. Once an organization has ascertained a specific staffing need and
a corresponding funding source for a new human resource, it will initiate an
employment process. The first step is some form of recruitment—the process of
advertising staffing needs and encouraging candidates to apply from both inside
and outside the organization. *Recruitment* is designed to provide the organization
with an adequate number of viable candidates from which to make its selection
decision. *Selection* is the process of reviewing the job candidates and deciding
who will be offered the position. *Examinations* in their many varieties are still
the dominant selection tool. Selection will tend to automatically order the last step
in the process, *placement*—the assignment of the new employee to the position so
that work can begin.

The main objective of recruitment can be said to be the generation of an
adequate number of qualified applicants from which a good selection decision
can be made. An applicant is any individual who submits a completed application
form for consideration. Indeed, it is often said that the first phase of the examining
process consists of filling out the application blank. If applicants do not provide
the necessary information documenting their minimum qualifications, they are
not given any further consideration; that is, they are not permitted to take the
formal examination. It is not uncommon for applicants who qualify in every
respect for a position to be refused consideration, however. Many positions above
the entry level are open only to individuals already employed with the jurisdiction. No matter how qualified outsiders may not be admitted to such promotional
examinations. Sometimes union agreements make the recruiting base even more
restrictive. When promotional examinations are held on a departmental basis, a
department may have no choice but to accept all of the low scorers in its own

department before it may consider higher-scoring individuals from other departments.

The heart of the selection process is the examination, however. While there are a variety of examination formats, their common objective is to determine whether or not an individual has a specified skill or ability. The idea of using tests to select individuals for "positions in the public trust" is a very old one dating back to ancient China, which initiated the use of examinations for employee selection. The Pendleton Act of 1883, which put the federal government on the road to widespread merit system coverage, foreshadowed the character of the examination process when it mandated "open competitive examinations" that "shall be practical in their character, and so far as may be possible shall relate to those matters which will fairly test the relative capacity and fitness of the persons examined." As the British Civil Service was the greatest single example and influence upon the American reform movement, there was considerable concern that a merit system based upon the British system of a competitive academic examinations would be automatically biased in favor of college graduates. As higher education was essentially an upper-class prerogative in the America of the last century, this was reminiscent of the aristocratic civil service that the Jacksonian movement found so objectionable only 50 years earlier. Mandating that all examinations be "practical in their character" presumably neutralized any advantage that a college graduate might have. (The first entrance examination designed specifically for liberal arts graduates would not be offered by the U.S. Civil Service Commission until 1934.)

Over the years, the primacy of examination practicality was often breached. As discussed earlier, that primacy was loudly reaffirmed by the U.S. Supreme Court's 1971 *Griggs* v. *Duke Power Company* decision. The intent of the original civil service reform of the 1880s, that the more privileged elements of society not have an elitist advantage over the less privileged in seeking public employment, was in essence supported by the U.S. Supreme Court in 1971, albeit in the context of a private sector case. Although the later Court rulings have modified the disparate impact theory, the doctrine of job-relatedness remains. Job-relatedness remains the paramount consideration in choosing a selection device. The legality of any test now hinges on its ability to predict success on the job, casting everything else under intense scrutiny.

Even jobs in police and fire departments, which for years maintained certain physical requirements, have had to be reviewed in the light of real job-relatedness. Many women and disabled individuals were formerly excluded from jobs requiring high levels of physical capabilities. Police and fire departments have to conduct detailed job analyses to determine what the "real" requirements are in terms of strength, height, weight, or physical endurance. Taking such steps may not resolve the problem of getting more women into protective services, however. The *New York Times* reported in March 2000 on the trials and tribulations of the

Early Recruiting Effort of the U.S. Civil Service Commission

THE EDITOR   May 22, 1891
American Architect
Boston, Massachusetts

SIR:

The Commission tenders the inclosed notice of examination for draftsman for publication, but has no means of paying for its publication, and neither such tender nor this letter must be regarded as in any sense creating a liability on the part of any one to pay for inserting the notice. It is simply hoped that you will regard it as an act of justice to those who wish to be examined for the public service to give them, as far as practicable, the information needed for that purpose, and that you will think the notice of so much interest for your readers and the public generally that you will be willing to publish it as information.

Thanking you for past favors,

Very respectfully,

THEODORE ROOSEVELT
Acting President

Source: *Letters of Theodore Roosevelt, Civil Service Commissioner, 1889–1895.* Washington, D.C.: U.S. Civil Service Commission, 1958, p. 16.

New York City Fire Department in this regard. The trials, almost literally, come from having an 11,000-member department with only 36 women employees, which has invited legal challenges. Getting into the numbers, as the *Times* reports, shows the tribulations of recruitment and examination. In terms of examination, there is both a written and a physical portion of the exam. In 1999, 850 women registered to take the written exam. About 450 women actually took the exam, with 354 passing the written test. Then about 125 of the women who passed the test actually took the physical test, with only 11 passing. On the physical exam, a perfect score of 100 is generally required in order to get hired. Nearly 600 of the more than 1000 men who passed the physical exam got a perfect score.

From a recruitment perspective, the fire department can probably do more, since only about 450 or 2.5% of the more than 17,000 candidates who took the written test in 1999 are women. When the final outcome of the selection process

Advertisement for a Programming Position, San Francisco Bay Area Newspapers, 1999

Do You Have What It Takes?

Programming Position (with Apologies to Dr. Seuss)

That special geek
That special geek
We want to find that special geek.

Do you like
To bang out code?
Do you run
Protected mode?

Do you Java
All day long?
Do you C++
In song?

Do you love
Your power Mac
Or prefer
A linux hack?

If you're cut
Do you bleed bits
Do you live
On caffeine hits?

Is your DCOM
Without equal?
Sleeping
Do you mumble SQL

Would you script
In Perl or Bourne
Can you shell
In C or Korn?

If you want to fax us, do
415 _____

Would you, could you
ASP?
Would you, could you
Just for me?

Do you like bureaucracy?
Say I don't, I don't, you see
Do you savor meetings long?
Say No, no you're wrong!

Would you like them
Here or there
Say I hate them
Everywhere

Come work a week
That's forty hours
Come use the Gym
The sauna, the showers

Come on trips
That build our team
Belize or skiing
What's your dream?

Come to _____
Come here now
Listen up
We'll tell you how
Resume and cover letter
References, three or better

Jobs@ _____ .com
(Please don't send a letter bomb)

History Validating the New York City Civil Service Exam for Firefighter

A 1982 court-imposed effort to hire women into the New York City Fire Department involved the validation of a physical agility exam. In *Berkman* v. *City of New York*, the exam was found by a federal district court judge to have an adverse impact on women. To validate the test, the city established standards based on the performance of incumbent male firefighters (i.e., the city used a concurrent validity strategy). Although a number of women passed the exam, many failed, particularly the second time it was administered. . . . The test was once again challenged under Title VII because of its adverse impact on women, but it was upheld on appeal in 1987 on the grounds that it was valid. . . . In effect, the "valid" test did not facilitate a determination of necessary physical strength or predict qualifications for the job. Rather, it simply showed that some women can perform equally as well as incumbent men.

Source: Riccucci, Norma M. "Merit, Equity and Test Validity: A New Look at an Old Problem," *Administration and Society* (May 1991).

is 11 passing scores out of 850 applicants, that makes recruitment very difficult, however. The fire department has already changed its physical exam since a 1982 court ruling that the old exam was not job-related. The new physical exam has eight different events that match well with what firefighters have to do (e.g., raise a 20-foot ladder, "feed" or pass 50 feet of fire hose in less than 19 seconds), but still are very difficult physically for the average woman. New York is trying to reach out to the military and to sports leagues to recruit more athletic women. They also have initiated a training program for women candidates with exercise professionals. In fact, nine of the 10 who passed the 1999 physical exam with perfect scores were in this four-month program. New York will keep searching and trying to build its recruitment efforts against very difficult odds in its examination process.

EXAMINATIONS AND VALIDATION

Job relatedness, validity, prediction, criterion measurement—what do these mean? More important, what requirements do they establish for personnel managers who wish to develop and use examinations? One must begin with the purpose of an examination. Exams are devices or instruments designed to measure individual differences. In some cases, the measurement problem can appear to be quite simple. Take for example a written examination to obtain a driver's license. The measurement accomplished through the exam is that those who achieve a prespecified minimum score (usually 70%) receive licenses; those who fail get to take the test again. The more basic question involves what's being measured, or what the criteria are. In this case, questions about state traffic laws, driving safety practices, and traffic signs are used as the criteria for measurement. The assumption behind the driver's test is that a passing score represents an adequate measurement of who will be a relatively safe driver. The criteria are thus, as Wayne Cascio defines them, "operational statements of goals or desired outcomes." While there are many problems with licensing drivers from an examination-selection perspective that could be discussed, it must be recognized that the problems of individual measurement for personnel selection decisions are of much greater magnitude and infinitely more complex.

The use of examinations in employment selection faces two critical problems of measurement: reliability and validity. Reliability concerns stability and consistency: Does the test measure accurately over time? Validity speaks to *relevance* and inherent accuracy: Does the test measure what it is designed to measure? Organizations have not been very concerned with reliability, in part because exams are changed so frequently and in part because of the primacy of validity and job relevance. The key dimension to validity, as previously mentioned, has been job-relatedness, which means essentially that the criteria being measured in the test are relevant and significant factors in the jobs for which selection decisions are to be made.

There are two kinds of examinations: assembled and unassembled. The latter are typically used for professional and managerial positions. They mainly consist of an extensive review and evaluation of a candidate's background. Many professional job candidates have already demonstrated their proficiency. Physicians need a state license to practice medicine; lawyers cannot practice law until they pass a state bar examination. It is obviously wasteful for a jurisdiction to seek to duplicate professional examinations. Sometimes it is even forbidden to do so. For example, Congress has mandated that OPM not offer written examinations for legal positions.

Assembled examinations are far more common, being any means by which individuals are tested to see if they have the ability to perform the prescribed responsibilities of a particular work assignment or position. There are three basic varieties of assembled examinations: written, oral, and performance. Written examinations, which are the least expensive to administer to large candidate populations, are the most common. Performance examinations are essential when specific skills must be demonstrated (e.g., typing, pipefitting, or truck driving). Oral examinations are appropriate when interpersonal skills are needed for a position and/or when the position is at such a level of sophistication that it is not cost-

Winston Churchill on Examinations

I had scarcely passed my twelfth birthday when I entered the inhospitable regions of examinations, through which for the next seven years I was destined to journey. These examinations were a great trial to me. The subjects which were dearest to the examiners were almost invariably those I fancied least. I would have liked to have been examined in history, poetry and writing essays. The examiners, on the other hands, were partial to Latin and mathematics. And their will prevailed. Moreover, the questions which they asked on both these subjects were almost invariable those to which I was unable to suggest a satisfactory answer. I should have liked to be asked to say what I knew. They always tried to ask what I did not know. When I would have willingly displayed my knowledge, they sought to expose my ignorance. This sort of treatment had only one result: I did not do well in examinations.

This was especially true of my Entrance Examination to Harrow. The Headmaster, Dr. Welldon, however, took a broadminded view of my Latin prose: he showed discernment in judging my general ability. This was the more remarkable, because I was found unable to answer a single question in the Latin paper. I wrote my name at the top of the page. I wrote down the number of question 'I'. After much reflection I put a bracket around it thus '(I)'. But thereafter I could not think of anything connected with it that was either relevant or true. Incidentally there arrived from nowhere in particular a blot and several smudges. I gazed for two whole hours at this sad spectacle: and then merciful ushers collected my piece of foolscap with all the others and carried it up to the Headmaster's table. It was from these slender indications of scholarship that Dr. Welldon drew the conclusion that I was worthy to pass into Harrow. It is very much to his credit. It showed that he was a man capable of looking beneath the surface of things: a man not dependent upon paper manifestations. I have always had the greatest regard for him.

Source: Churchill, Winston S. *A Roving Commission: My Early Life*. New York: Scribner's, 1931, pp. 15–16.

effective to create a special written examination for it. Sometimes examinations are given in two parts (oral or performance sections may only be given to candidates who have previously passed a written portion). In such cases, the scoring process is weighted; for example, 70% of the total examination may be for the written portion and 30% for the oral. Examinations used to be expensive to develop and monitor, thus only very large or very ''rich'' jurisdictions such as the federal government and the more highly populous cities and states could afford the staffs of psychologists, the consulting expenses, and other sources of testing expertise that were necessary to develop and maintain a comprehensive testing system. Over time, however, it became economical to grant contracts to private testing firms to acquire on-the-shelf examinations, or modify or develop examinations, analyze results, and even evaluate the testing system's effectiveness. Contractors even stand by their work, or at least their lawyers will stand by your agency's legal team in the event of a court challenge.

The utility, economy, and equity of selecting individuals for public service by using objective examinations is obvious, yet the examining process itself poses many problems. The complexity of successful job performance involves a great many variables—quality of supervision, adequacy of training and orientation, motivation, working conditions, peer relationships, and interpersonal environments, among others—any of which may surpass in importance the cognitive skills that are evaluated on written tests. Added to the problem of predicting job performance are categories of potential bias in testing itself—namely, test fairness.

Test content has been the subject of the most intense scrutiny in the area of fairness. For example, efforts to counter cultural bias have led to the inclusion in reading tests of passages by minority authors or about various racial groups, but most subsequent work by psychologists has led to the conclusion that test content (except in cases in which specialized historical and cultural background knowledge is being examined) does not make a sizable difference. As discussed earlier, Schmidt and Hunter have noted that a large part of the problem was methodological in that minority sample sizes were much smaller than majority sample sizes in creating a theory of test unfairness. The revisionist case, as Hunter and Schmidt argue, is that it is not testing that causes "adverse impact" against minorities. They conclude that "The cumulative research on test fairness shows that the average ability and cognitive skill differences between groups are directly reflected in job performance and thus are real. They are not created by the tests. We do not know what all the causes of these differences are, how long they will persist, or how to eliminate them."

Finally, there is a process for validation. Just as there are different kinds of tests, there are different methods of assessing how well a test measures what it purports to measure. The process of compiling data to evaluate tests is referred to as validation. The more common kinds of test validity are *content, criterion*, and *construct*. Additionally, the term *face validity* must be distinguished and examined for its own separate importance. At the outset it is important to note that the concepts of validity mentioned above are related to each other, although they can be examined as separate factors. In fact, educational psychologists generally insist that a complete review of any examination must necessarily examine all three types of validity.

Content validity means that the questions on the examination are directly related to the duties and responsibilities (i.e., the content) of the position, but how does a test become content-valid? Before the examination is assembled, the personnel or test technician must discover the abilities required for the job title for which the test is being developed. There are different ways to get this information: (1) from the knowledge, skills, and abilities section of the job description or class specification; (2) by interviewing managers who supervise individuals who are presently in the positions for which the test is being written; or (3) via a job analysis. A job analysis is akin to a position classification field audit in that the technician goes into the organization in order to talk with and observe individuals presently in the job. From these data the technician can identify the *elements* of a position for which test questions must be written. In short, a testing device has content validity if it is developed to measure the specific requirements for a job (i.e., several related positions). It is generally conceded that if the area of knowledge to be examined is well defined with considerable consensus about field boundaries and emphasis, content validity is an important aspect of validation. As might be expected, however, agreement about the application of content validation parallels that of commonly accepted well-defined fields of knowledge and well-defined jobs. Let us suppose as an example that a social case worker position required fluency in Spanish. A content-valid examination for Spanish proficiency would be one that tested for specific vocabulary, speaking, and writing skills needed in that position.

Criterion-related validity involves another set of questions. Essentially we attempt to compare the test with certain external variables that are assumed to be characteristic of the behavior in question. This sounds more complicated but it really entails making an indirect prediction about future success. Suppose, using our case worker example, we wanted to select case workers who could learn Spanish over a two- to three-year period. We might use a language aptitude test that measured an individual's ability to learn languages. In actuality, this type of exam makes a prediction about the individual's likely success in foreign language acquisition by measuring memorization, speaking facility, and mental organization skills that are predictors of success in learning languages.

There are two strategies for demonstrating criterion-related validity—concurrent validity and predictive validity. Concurrent validity may involve giving a prospective examination to individuals already performing successfully on the job. Each of the incumbents could be independently rated by their supervisors on their actual job performance, then the test scores and the ratings are correlated. If the better workers also obtain the better test scores, then the examination can be said to have concurrent validity.

Predictive validity could seek a similar correlation but would involve a time interval. An examination might be given to all applicants, and at a later date their test scores could be correlated with performance to see how accurate the original scores were in predicting success.

Both of these approaches to criterion validity have drawbacks. Concurrent validity has two particular problems. First, if previous employment decisions reflected discriminatory practices, validation results might be distorted by examining a group of ''wrong employees.'' The difficulty relates to the time factor of experience. It may be that the variable being tested will be validated in experienced employees. Some capabilities can only be acquired via experience, however, therefore such experience-based capabilities should not be a critical factor for entry. Concurrent validity is more an aid in the diagnosis of existing conditions than a predictor of future performance.

In contrast, predictive validity in contrast, may provide accurate distinctions about future performance, but unfortunately most organizations cannot afford it—either in terms of organizational disruption or expense. It is rather unrealistic to expect any jurisdiction to establish an examinations program, hire a full range of scorers, place them, and wait a year or more to evaluate how well the test scores predicted success, and yet some jurisdictions are doing just that in response to or in anticipation of court pressures.

Construct validity involves examining the personal traits being measured by a test, such as honesty, enthusiasm, or reliability. This is an important step in compiling a valid examination process, but it necessitates a lengthy and rather theoretical evaluation. While it is important to understand what the test is measuring, the emphasis to date has been on content and criterion validity, which are more direct measurements of how test results are being used.

A fourth type of validity—*face validity*—is not a true measurement of validity at all. It is simply an indication that on the face of it, the test is relevant; that is, it seems to measure what it purports to measure to the perception of the test taker. Face validity is really a measure of the appropriateness, overall acceptance, or legitimacy of the test. Perhaps the most important thing about face validity is its power. Although not a true statistical measure of an examination, it can make an invalid test appear valid or, conversely, can cause test takers to have considerable anxiety and disbelief about a valid test.

These approaches to validation speak to the heart of the selection process. Psychological and statistical measurement problems abound, but jurisdictions have reduced their questions to one: Will it hold up in court? While examinations were once simply a technical and administrative problem of the personnel department, as was made clear at the beginning of this chapter, they are now of equal concern to a jurisdiction's legal office.

A FEDERAL CASE HISTORY FROM PACE TO ACWA TO OTHER

Throughout the 1960s and 1970s, examinations were the mainstay of the public service employment process. Of the nearly 2 million persons who applied for federal employment annually, between 50 and 60% of them took written examinations, and although about 60% of all candidates taking written examinations passed them, the likelihood of obtaining a job was considerably less. The case of the federal government's former PACE exam (Professional and Administrative Career Examination) illustrated the problem. Between 200,000 to 300,000 applicants competed annually for fewer than 15,000 PACE jobs. About 40% of those applicants were in the Washington, D.C., metropolitan area, where some 2,000 PACE jobs were available. To be considered for a PACE job in Washington meant scoring among the top 3% of all test takers.

Despite the almost impossible odds for the individual, from an organizational perspective, one can see the attractiveness of offering a nationwide, written, highly competitive (but open to all) examination, especially when the goal was to hire candidates for entry-level jobs representing a broad range of professional and administrative careers. The federal government had used such a testing concept since 1948, beginning with the junior management assistant exam and then moving to the FSEE (Federal Service Entrance Examination) in 1955. Such exams were geared primarily toward college graduates or college seniors looking for work in the government. Of course, as long as the exam was testing applicants at a 20-to-1 ratio of applicants for jobs, it stood a reasonable chance of selecting top candidates. In 1974, the FSEE was replaced with PACE, which covered 118 occupations and brought entrants into the civil service at grades GS-5 or GS-7. Obviously there were exceptions, and college graduates with distinguished academic records could obtain exemptions from taking the PACE for certain occupational series, but the exam was the centerpiece for federal entry-level hiring.

The deathblow to the PACE examination came in 1980 as a result of a consent decree signed by the OPM in an out-of-court settlement over a suit alleging discrimination. The suit, *Luevano* v. *Campbell* (later *Luevano* v. *Devine*), claimed that PACE had not been validated correctly and that it resulted in an adverse impact against African Americans and Latinos. The case facts were these. In January 1979, a group of minority candidates who had failed to achieve passing scores on the PACE charged that the PACE discriminated unfairly against minorities. They cited differences in the pass rates for whites (approximately 42%), blacks (approximately 5%), and Hispanics (approximately 13%), contending that the differences were caused by test bias. Rather than go to trial, a consent decree was negotiated by the plaintiffs and the Department of Justice on January 9, 1981, which included abolishing PACE.

While the OPM denied the allegations stated above, it agreed to phase out PACE over a four-year period in favor of a more specific occupational testing procedure. In fact, in 1982, OPM changed its decision and abolished the PACE examination immediately. To handle entry-level hiring, it established a highly decentralized "schedule B" appointment authority for use until a new exam could be developed. Schedule B appointment authority had a long history (since 1910), but had been primarily used by agencies to make "co-op" appointments

Culturally Fair Tests

During the first few years of the controversy concerning test bias against minority-group members, many individuals felt that an answer to this problem was to develop a test or set of tests that were "culture fair," thus limiting the effects of disadvantaged backgrounds. A basic assumption behind this approach was that differences between minority- and majority-group members on traditional pencil-and-paper verbal tests were due to factors associated with the tests themselves.

One factor often suggested is that test items are culturally "loaded" or familiar only to those individuals who share white middle-class experiences. For example, the content of many intelligence tests may not be familiar to the culturally deprived. An item that has the word "umbrella" in one of the questions might be "unfair" because some people in our society may not know what it is. A 100-item test developed by Williams (1975) provides a dramatic example of this "effect" operating in reverse. The test is called the Black Intelligence Test of Cultural Homogeneity (BITCH) and is intended to be a "cultural-specific" test that taps the cultural experiences of blacks in this country. (Another such test is the Scales Inner City Intelligence Test [Scales, 1973]). When the BITCH is administered to both white and black subjects, there is virtually no overlap between the two distributions—the blacks score considerably higher. However, just because race correlates highly with test scores does not necessarily mean race has anything to do with performance on this test. That is, a middle-class black person raised in suburbia may perform just as poorly on the BITCH as a middle-class white person.

Source: Arvey, Richard D. and Robert H. Faley. *Fairness in Selecting Employees*, 2nd ed. Reading, Mass.: Addison–Wesley, 1988, p. 192.

in which students from universities or other schools were brought in under noncompetitive status; later (after successful completion of their degree program and institutional training program) they would be converted to career conditional status. Agencies now became the focal point of the entry-level hiring practices. By 1985, OPM had developed several new examinations to cover more than half of the old PACE positions.

In their comprehensive assessment of the schedule B system in a 1988 *Public Administration Review* article, "Retaining Quality Federal Employees: Life After PACE," Ban and Ingraham reported, "The good news," they report, "is that agencies are 'satisfied' with the Schedule B and new examinations processes, and that minority hiring has increased (about double the rate under PACE). The bad news is that the effect on the quality of the public service is difficult to determine and that the very few studies that have been done seem to indicate that internal hires are not as good as general exam hires.'' Ban and Ingraham, however, questioned a more serious concern: the compatibility of a decentralized, more narrowly specific job-focused hiring process with the longer-range, more career-oriented needs of a quality workforce premised on an effective merit system. Addressing just such needs, the OPM announced the opening on May 1, 1990, of a replacement examination process, called Administrative Careers with America (ACWA).

The OPM's new examination system was premised on what it calls a ''whole person approach.'' To measure the whole person, the process has both job-specific skills tests, using traditionally recognized verbal and quantitative testing elements, and an individual achievement record (IAR), which analyzes the prospective employee's experiences and accomplishments in academic and other work experiences. The IAR in effect supplements the skills tests through a multiple choice questionnaire that examines other job-relevant performance factors.

To create ACWA, 96 different occupational series were grouped into six categories according to specific job-related knowledge, skills, and abilities (KSAs). A seventh category with job-specific requirements that has no testing component was also created. Overall, this establishes the following:

Group 1: health, safety, and environmental occupations
Group 2: writing and public information occupations
Group 3: business, finance, and management occupations
Group 4: personnel, administrative, and computer occupations
Group 5: benefits, tax, and legal occupations
Group 6: law enforcement and investigative occupations
Group 7: positions with positive education requirements (e.g., a specific
    degree to qualify, such as economics or psychology)

The actual examination process of the six groups requiring exams involves a written test keyed to occupational context (i.e., typical questions and materials that one might encounter in a specific job situation). Logic-based testing is also a critical dimension of the testing process. In this case the verbal-based reasoning tests use the principles of logic, whereby the correct response to a question posed is a logical conclusion to a series of statements that are connected or related to each other. The use of logic-based testing is designed to avoid ambiguity and other forms of cultural wording bias. The total examination process weighs the test and the IAR equally in calculating a rating for each occupational group. As with past practices, an academically high achievement exemption is provided for

---

Leo Rosten's Maxim

When you get farther along, remember Leo Rosten's maxim: "First-rate people hire first-rate people; second-rate people hire third-rate people." Hire the best you can. Whenever I hired anybody, I'd ask myself: "How would I like to work for him—or her—someday?" The nod will go to the one I'd rather work for. This question is a real sleeper. It gets to such issues as: Are you protecting yourself against potential threats, or are you trying to get the best people you can? It also gets to the root of leadership. Once you've hired those assistants, if you're a true leader, you *will* be working for them—to help them become the best they can be.

Townsend, Robert. *Up the Organization*. Greenwich, Conn.: Fawcett, 1970, pp. 213–214.

---

college graduates with a 3.5 average or those graduating in the top 10% of their class.

Ironically, ACWA has essentially erased the painful memories of the federal government's experience with career entry-level testing. It signaled a return to a single examination process designed to make recruitment efforts easier and open the federal examination process to more potential college applicants. The new designs in the selection procedure were intended to maintain job-relatedness and avoid future legal problems, while at the same time improving affirmative action efforts. Initial studies showed the ACWA pass rates for minorities at more than seven times the old 4% pass rate of the PACE examination. The OPM also hoped to speed up the hiring process with a variety of automated options, including computer-based delivery of examinations that might allow immediate testing at actual agencies.

Despite the impressive test validity credentials of the new ACWA, however, formidable challenges remained. Initially there was a considerable education and awareness process in getting the word out to universities and colleges about the new exam. For the first offering in May 1990, the number of test takers was considerably below (less than 20%) the average number of test takers for the PACE in its heyday. Some contended that this was attributable in part to the lower prestige of federal public service; but more likely the largest factor was the rather daunting task of simply informing prospective applicants about the exam and the new process. A more telling problem was revealed in an article in the December 17, 1990, edition of the *Federal Times* entitled "Budget Crises Snarls Recruitment." It reported that of the 55,000 applicants who passed the

TABLE 6.2   Where Do Federal Hires Come From?

Entry method	Number of hires from entry source
OPM certificates (ACWA)	1,047
Outstanding scholar	6,388
Noncompetitive appointments/direct hire	22,310
OPM certificates (non-ACWA)	7,512
Agency certificates (delegated examinations)	6,482
Internal selections (merit promotion)	31,601
Cooperative education (Coop/SECP program)	3,665
Presidential management intern program	553
Total hires (analyzed)	79,918

Source: NAPA 1999.

May exam, only 127 had been placed in federal jobs as of that month, concluding that the best testing process in the world wasn't going to work if agencies couldn't hire those who passed the exams.

Something else was happening to federal government hiring, however. The reinvention/downsizing efforts of the Clinton administration were starting to affect overall hiring numbers, and federal attrition rates continued to stay flat (well under national averages). More important, agencies that had been forced to use alternative means for hiring in the 1980s kept control of their hiring processes. A fascinating study done by the National Academy of Public Administration (NAPA) with the help of the MSPB looked at the nearly 80,000 entry-level hires for the federal government from fiscal year 1991 to fiscal year 1993. Its purpose was to show how federal recruitment and hiring could be improved, which will be discussed shortly. As Table 6.2 demonstrates from the report, however, ACWA accounted for less than 2% of all hires.

NAPA concluded in its November 1999 report that agencies weren't using ACWA, that the quality of entry-level hires was higher through other sources than ACWA, and that OPM's process for filling positions via ACWA was too complex and administratively burdensome. Perhaps the final lesson in the federal experience for the 1990s was that even a legally sound, validatable examination process may fail if other parts of the public employment process are flawed.

HUMAN CAPITAL IN GOVERNMENT: THE NEXT FRONTIER

The NAPA study's examination of eight different hiring methods used by the federal government concludes that a new emphasis is needed on timeliness.

How New Hires First Learned About Their Job

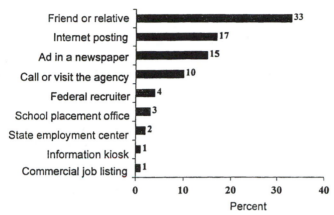

Source: Competing for Federal Jobs: Job Search Experiences of New Hires, p. 7.
Note: "Other" category totaled 14 percent.

Competing for Federal jobs
(The Applicants' Viewpoint)

- Internet advertising -- good but not sufficient
- Applying for jobs relatively easy
- Hiring process still seen as too long
- Feedback on application status hard to get
- Need faster process -- but still a good process
- Treat applicants as "customers"
- Pay attention to appearances

Source: Competing for Federal Jobs: Job Search Experiences of New Hires

FIGURE 6.4 Competing for federal jobs; job search experiences of new hires.

It supports what seems rather obvious in today's Internet economy with very low levels of unemployment—that good employees won't wait. In its 1999 report *Competing for Federal Jobs*, the MSPB issued its own warning. (See Figure 6.4.) The MSPB examined hiring from the applicant's perspective and concluded that considerable improvement is warranted. They asked respondents what a reasonable time was for a hiring decision to be made. The results are as follows:

Time from application to job offer	Percentage agreeing time period is "reasonable"
1–2 months	77%
3–4 months	52%
5–6 months	43%
More than 6 months	29%

The MSPB's report also concluded that while the entire federal job application process was easy enough, feedback on applications was difficult to get, applicants weren't really being treated like "customers," and of course the entire process took much too long. In normal times, those findings might not seem very important. One might even argue that government employment in the public service is about things other than treating every job applicant as though he or she were a customer and providing feedback on every application. One might even scoff at one of MSPB's minor findings that applicants felt they were often being asked to provide too much information in order to apply for a position.

Key Human Capital Principles From Nine Private Sector Organizations

Each of the nine private sector organizations in our review implemented human capital strategies and practices that were designed to directly support the achievement of their specific missions, strategic goals, and core values.[a] Although human capital management alone cannot ensure high performance, proper attention to human capital is a fundamental building block for achieving an organization's mission and goals. On the basis of the information they provided, we identified 10 underlying and interrelated principles of human capital management that are common to the nine organizations:

1. *Treat human capital management as being fundamental to strategic business management.* Integrate human capital considerations when identifying the mission, strategic goals, and core values of the organization as well as when designing and implementing operational policies and practices.
2. *Integrate human capital functional staff into management teams.* Include human capital leaders as full members of the top management team rather than isolating them to provide after-the-fact support. Expand the strategic role of human capital staff beyond that of providing traditional personnel administration services.

3. *Leverage the internal human capital function with external expertise.* Supplement internal human capital staff's knowledge and skills by seeking outside expertise from consultants, professional associations, and other organizations, as needed.

4. *Hire, develop, and sustain leaders according to leadership characteristics identified as essential to achieving specific missions and goals.* Identify the leadership traits needed to achieve high performance of mission and goals, and build and sustain the organization's pool of leaders through recruiting, hiring, development, retention, and succession policies and practices targeted at producing leaders with the identified characteristics.

5. *Communicate a shared vision that all employees, working as one team, can strive to accomplish.* Promote a common understanding of the mission, strategic goals, and core values that all employees are directed to work as a team to achieve. Create a line-of-sight between individual contributions and the organization's performance and results.

6. *Hire, develop, and retain employees according to competencies.* Identify the competencies—knowledge, skills, abilities, and behaviors—needed to achieve high performance of mission and goals, and build and sustain the organization's talent pool through recruiting, hiring, development, and retention policies and practices targeted at building and sustaining those competencies.

7. *Use performance management systems, including pay and other meaningful incentives, to link performance to results.* Provide incentives and hold employees accountable for contributing to the achievement of mission and goals. Reward those employees who meet or exceed clearly defined and transparent standards of high performance.

8. *Support and reward teams to achieve high performance.* Foster a culture in which individuals interact and support and learn from each other as a means of contributing to the high performance of their peers, units, and the organization as a whole. Bring together the right people with the right competencies to achieve high performance as a result, rather than in spite, of the organizational structure.

9. *Integrate employee input into the design and implementation of human capital policies and practices.* Incorporate the first-hand knowledge and insights of employees and employee groups to develop responsive human capital policies and practices. Empower employees by making them stakeholders in the development of solutions and new methods of promoting and achieving high performance of organizational missions and goals.

10. *Measure the effectiveness of human capital policies and practices.* Evaluate and make fact-based decisions on whether human capital policies and practices support high performance of mission and goals. Identify the performance return on human capital investments.

[a] *Human Capital: Key Principles From Nine Private Sector Organizations.* GAO/GGD-00-28, Jan. 31, 2000.

Those were other times, however. Now the public sector at all levels is in what some call a ''war for talent.'' Along with the escalating challenges of competing in the Internet economy, there is an increasing worry that the federal government will be unable to attract new employees in an economy with record levels of low unemployment. Recently, Comptroller General David Walker and OPM director Janis LaChance testified before Senator Voinivich about their concerns in this area. The comptroller general has made human capital a core theme since his confirmation in 1998, and OPM proposed new legislation in 2000 to obtain new flexibilities and discretionary authorities for agencies on the three R's—recruitment, retention, and relocation. Clearly there is consensus about the importance of human capital, but agreement on the ''how''—or how government will improve its recruitment, examination, and selection processes will be more difficult.

BIBLIOGRAPHY

''America at Work: The 1990's Labor Market,'' *Brookings Review*, (fall 1999), pp. 4–43. Washington, D.C.

American Psychological Association. *Standards for Education & Psychological Tests*. Washington, D.C.: APA, 1966.

Arvey, Richard, D. and Farley, R. *Fairness in Selecting Employees*. 2nd ed. Reading, Mass.: Addison-Wesley Longman, 1988.

Ash, Ronald A. ''Job Elements for Task Clusters: Arguments for Using Multi-Methodological Approaches to Job Analysis and a Demonstration of their Utility,'' *Public Personnel Management*, vol. 11 (spring 1982).

Ban, Carolyn and Patricia W. Ingraham. ''Retaining Quality Federal Employees: Life After PACE,'' *Public Administration Review* (May–June 1988).

Berwitz, Clement Jr. *The Job Analysis Approach to Affirmative Action*. New York: Wiley, 1975.

Blumrosen, Alfred W. ''Strangers in Paradise: *Griggs* v. *Duke Power Co.*, and the Concept of Employment Discrimination,'' *Michigan Law Review*, vol. 71 (November 1972).

Byham, W. C. and M. D. Spitzer. *The Law and Personnel Testing*. New York: American Management Association, 1971.

Campbell, Joel T. ''Tests Are Valid for Minority Groups Too,'' *Public Personnel Management*, vol. 2 (January–February 1973).

Campion, Michael A. ''Personnel Selection for Physically Demanding Jobs: Review and Recommendations,'' *Personnel Psychology*, vol. 36, no. 3 (autumn 1983).

Cronback, Lee J. *Essentials of Psychological Testing*. New York: Harper & Row, 1970.

Crum, John. ''Building a Quality Workforce,'' *Bureaucrat*, no. 2 (1990), pp. 30–34.

Daniels, Christopher. ''Reconciling Science and Politics: Do the Uniform Guidelines Still Help Managers?'' *Review of Public Personnel Administration* (2000).

Donovan, J. J., ed. *Recruitment and Selection in the Public Service*. Chicago: International Personnel Management Association, 1968.

Elliot, Robert H. "Selection of Personnel," in Jack Rabin et al. (eds.), *Handbook on Public Personnel Administration and Labor Relations*. New York: Marcel Dekker, 1983.

Equal Opportunity Opportunity Commission. *Uniform Guidelines on Employee Selection Procedures*. CFR 1997 vol. 29, sec 1607, (originally published in 1978).

Flynn, Kevin. "Most Women Applicants Fail Physical Test for Fire Department," *New York Times* (February 3, 2000) p. A25.

Gandy, Jay A. et al. "Development and Initial Validation of the Individual Achievement Record (IAR) Study." Washington, D.C.: U.S. Office of Personnel Management (November 1989).

Gatewood, R. D. and H. Field. *Human Resource Selection*. Fort Worth, Tex.: Harcourt Brace, 1994.

Ghiselli, Edwin E. "The Validity of Aptitude Tests in Personnel Selection," *Personnel Psychology* (1973).

Greenhouse, Linda. "The Court's Shift to Right," *New York Times* (June 7, 1989), pp. A1/A22.

Gullett, C. Ray. "The Civil Rights Act of 1991: Did It Really Overturn *Wards Cove*? *Labor Law Review* (July 1992), pp. 462–465.

Hayes, Stephen W. "Staffing the Bureaucracy: Employee Recruitment and Selection" in Stephen Condrey (ed.), *Handbook of Human Resource Management in Government*. San Francisco: Jossey-Bass, 1998, pp. 298–321.

Holmen, Milton G. and Richard F. Docter. *Educational and Psychological Testing*. New York: Russell Sage Foundation, 1972.

Howell, William C. and Robert L. Dipboye. *Essentials of Industrial and Organizational Psychology*, rev. ed. Homewood, Ill.: Dorsey Press, 1982.

Hunter, J. E. and R. F. Hunter. "Validity and Utility of Alternate Predictors of Job Performance," *Psychological Bulletin*, vol. 96 (1984), pp. 72–98.

Isaac, Stephen with William B. Michael. *Handbook in Research and Evaluation*. San Diego: Robert R. Knapp, 1981.

Kost, John M. *New Approaches to Public Management: The Case of Michigan*. Washington, D.C.: Brookings Institution Center for Public Management, July 1996.

Lawsche, C. H. "A Quantitative Approach to Content Validity," *Personnel Psychology*, vol. 28 (1975).

Ledvinka, James and Vida G. Scarpello. *Federal Regulation of Personnel and Human Resources Management*. Boston: PWS-Kent Publishing, 1991.

National Academy of Public Administration (NAPA). "Entry-Level Hiring and Development for the 21st Century: Professional and Administrative Positions." Washington, D.C., November 1999.

McClung, Glenn. " 'Qualified' vs. 'Most Qualified': A Review of Competitive Merit Selection," *Public Personnel Management*, vol. 2 (September–October 1973).

Nelson, Jodi B. "The Boundaryless Organization: Implications for Job Analysis, Recruitment, and Selection," *Human Resources Planning*, vol. 20, no. 4 (1997).

Pearlman, Kenneth. "Job Families: A Review and Discussion of Their Implications for Personnel Selection," *Psychological Bulletin*, vol. 80, no. 1 (January 1980).

Pinzler, Isabelle K. "The Future of Equal Opportunity Policy in the Public Sector," address to Brookings Institution, May 14, 1997.

Primof, Eanest S. *How to Prepare and Conduct Job-Element Examinations*. Washington, D.C.: U.S. Government Printing Office, 1973.

Riccucci, Norma M. "Merit, Equity and Test Validity: A New Look at an Old Problem," *Administration and Society* (May 1991).

Robertson, David E. "Update on Testing and Equal Opportunity," *Personnel Journal* (March 1977).

Rosenbloom, David H. and C. Obuchowski. "Public Personnel Examinations and the Constitution: Emergent Trends," *Public Administration Review*, vol. 37 (January–February 1977).

Rouleau, Eugene and Burton F. Krain. "Using Job Analysis to Design Selection Procedures," *Public Personnel Management*, vol. 4 (September–October 1975).

Scales, R. Jr. *Scales Inner City Intelligence Test*. Wilmington, N.C.: Scales, 1973.

Schlei, Barbara and Paul Grossman. *Employment Discrimination Law*, 2nd ed. Washington, D.C.: Bureau of National Affairs, 1983.

Schmidt, Frank L. and John E. Hunter. "Employment Testing: Old Theories and New Research Findings," *American Psychologist*, vol. 36, no. 10 (October 1981), pp. 1128–1137.

Society for Industrial and Organizational Psychology. *Principles for the Validation and Use of Personnel Selection Procedures*, 3rd ed. College Park, MD: 1987.

Sylvia, Ronald D. *Critical Issues in Public Personnel Policy*. Pacific Grove, CA: Brooks-Cole, 1989.

Taylor, Vernon T. *Test Validity in Public Personnel Selection*. Chicago: International Personnel Management Association, 1971.

Tenopyr, Mary L. "Content-Construct Confusion," *Personnel Psychology*, vol. 30 (1977).

Thomas, John C. and W. Donald Heisal. "The Modernization of Recruitment and Selection in Local Governments," in Steven Hays and Richard Kearney (eds.), *Public Personnel Administration: Problems and Prospects*. Englewood Cliffs, NJ: Prentice-Hall, 1983.

Thompson, Duane E. and Toni A. Thompson. "Court Standards for Job Analysis in Test Validation," *Personnel Psychology*, vol. 35, no. 4 (winter 1982).

Trattner, M. H. *The Validity of Aptitude and Ability Tests Used to Select Professional Personnel*. Report for U.S. Office of Personnel Management, 1988. Washington, D.C.

U.S. General Accounting Office. *Federal Recruitment and Hiring*. Washington, D.C.: August 1990.

U.S. General Accounting Office. *Federal Hiring. Practices*. Washington, D.C.: May 1992.

U.S. Merit Systems Protection Board. *Competing for Federal Jobs: Job Search Experiences of New Hires*. Washington, D.C.: February 2000.

———. *In Search of Merit: Hiring Entry-Level Federal Employees*. Washington, D.C.: September 1987.

———. *Restoring Merit to Federal Hiring: Why Two Special Hiring Programs Should Be Ended*. Washington, D.C.: January, 2000.

Walker, David M. "Human Capital: Managing Human Capital in the 21st Century," testimony of the Comptroller General, U.S. General Accounting Office before U.S. Senate Subcommittee, Committee on Governmental Affairs, U.S. Senate, March 9, 2000.

Werbel, James. "A Review of Research Regarding Criteria Used to Select Job Applicants," in J. Rabin, T. Vocino, W. B. Hildreth, and G. J. Miller (eds.), *Handbook of Public Personnel Administration*. New York: Marcel Dekker, 1995, pp. 267–284.

"The Wild New Workforce: What It Takes to Hire and Keep the Modern Worker," *Business Week* (December 6, 1999), pp. 38–46.

Williams, R. L. *Black Intelligence Test of Cultural Homogeneity*, 1975 (available from Williams & Associates, 6374 Delmar Boulevard, St. Louis, Missouri 63130).

Zeidner, Rita L. "Budget Crises Snarls Recruitment," *Federal Times* (December 17, 1990).

CASES

Adarand Constructors Inc. v. *Pena*, 63 U.DS. L W 4523 (June 12, 1995).

Albemarle Paper Co. v. *Moody*, 422 U.S. 405 (1975).

City of Richmond v. *J.A. Croson*, 488 U.S. 469 (1989).

Dallas Firefighters Association. v. *The City of Dallas*, 98–966 (1998).

Griggs v. *Duke Power Co.*, 401 U.S. 424 (1971).

Metro Broadcasting, Inc. v. *FCC* 497 U.S. 547 (1990).

U.S. v. *South Carolina*, 434 U.S. 1026 (1978); *sub nom. National Educ. Ass'n.* v. *South Carolina.*

Wards Cove Packing Co. v. *Atonio*, 57 *Law Week* 4583 (June 6, 1989).

Washington v. *Davis*, 426 U.S. 229 (1976).

7

Performance Appraisal

**PROLOGUE: 360-DEGREE APPRAISAL: RISING STAR OR
WRECK ON THE PERFORMANCE APPRAISAL HIGHWAY?**

A number of government agencies have been experimenting with a new concept
in performance appraisal entitled 360-degree assessment. One such experiment
has been conducted by the Corpus Christi army depot (CCAD) in Corpus Christi,
Texas. With over 2700 employees, the depot is the U.S. Army's primary facility
for overhauling and repairing helicopters for the army as well as for other services. It is a highly regarded organization that has been cited as a benchmark for
excellence in management and for "best practices" in industry. The Corpus
Christi army depot has been in existence since 1961, first as a depot maintenance
center and by the late 1960s as primarily a helicopter repair center.

It has also been in the business of pursuing management innovation, having
conducted pilot projects with work teams, quality management, and activity-
based costing, among other things. In that sense, 360-degree assessment was a
natural outgrowth of how the depot was doing business, pursuing results-oriented
management using teams and close collaboration with contractors and suppliers.

In keeping with this philosophy, a pilot project using a 360-degree assessment was launched in 1997 in the corporate performance office. The following
is the depot's write-up of its model.

This method of feedback to an individual (by peers, customers, and supervisors) is designed to provide more accurate feedback about an individual's performance. Implementation of 360-degree assessment is intended to provide the organization with a measurement tool that identifies individual, team, and organizational strengths and weaknesses, as well as areas for development. Prior to implementing this program in the CPO, performance feedback came from two possible sources. The first source was the traditional supervisor/subordinate performance appraisal, and the second source was a limited feedback form provided by the individual's customers. The limited feedback form involved ten questions in areas of general competencies; however, a subsequent action plan was not developed as a result of this feedback.

With the 360 degree assessment program, six people (four peers selected by the rated individual, the supervisor, and a self assessment by the individual) assess the individual in the six general areas of Mission/Vision/Value, Team Work, Managing Resources, Professional/Technical Knowledge, Business Skills, and Customer Service. There are 45 measurable elements in these six areas as well as narrative comments. Each element is measured on a scale of one to ten. Confidential feedback is received only by the individual on which he or she can analyze strengths and weaknesses. The individual uses this feedback as the basis to develop a personal action plan. The personal action plan can be used at the individual's option as a point of discussion to develop performance factors for official evaluation.

The depot viewed the 360-degree assessment as an excellent tool to pursue its larger goal of becoming a high-performance organization. When the results of the first round of 360-degree assessments was tabulated, the area of greatest strength was customer service, while "managing resources" was identified as the weakest area. Of course the individual's appraisal was kept confidential, but the depot was very optimistic about the overall process.

It should be said, however, that this 360-degree appraisal process was only mildly revolutionary. It wasn't being tied to compensation or adverse actions, nor was it actually part of the official evaluation file. An individual could use the information for self-improvement planning, but the supervisor knew only of the rating of the individual, and of course the overall ratings of the corporate performance office. Finally, customer information, which was a general component of the organizational evaluation process, was still not specifically linked to any individual. [Technically, this would make the 360-degree assessment used by the depot a 270-degree process (self, peers, and supervisor).] The depot announced in 1998 that it hoped to implement the 360-degree assessment program in other parts of the facility.

Such plans were never realized, however; 360-degree assessment was abandoned. The stated reason was the reorganization of the depot and the elimination of the corporate performance office. The depot, like many installations and units within the Defense Department, is under tremendous pressure to reduce costs and deliver more results and therefore guards its bottom line carefully. It's quite rational to conclude that the 360-degree performance appraisal lacked a real connection to "managing results." Faced with finding ways to enhance resource maximization, it would be difficult to make the business case even for an interesting new approach (that basically tripled the amount of time being allocated) to an old process generally questioned as to its validity and value. That would be one assessment, but in the spirit of 360-degree assessment, the Corpus Christi army deport was asked to respond to this prologue and provided the following appraisal of our appraisal (which we gratefully quote in full in the box that follows).

THE PROBLEM OF PERFORMANCE APPRAISAL

Historically, few problems have been as vexing to personnel administrators as that of performance appraisal. Certainly it has been the most maligned area of personnel and in many cases seems to be tolerated only because no one can think of any realistic alternatives. At stake is a process that should control the development and growth of the organization itself. Performance appraisal can be restated as a series of questions.

What qualities are we now recognizing, rewarding, and developing in employees?

What messages are we conveying to individuals about their behavior, skills, and attitude?

What ideal qualities do we wish to see developed and enhanced in our employees for the accomplishment of our objectives in the future? (See Figure 7.1.)

The development process, however, is rarely considered in a long-range perspective. The functions that performance appraisal seeks to support are much more short range, relating to positions being held now or, at best, to the next promotion. Even career systems with their "tenure" reviews generally have very static views of the qualities built into their minimal standards for career status. This static focus of performance appraisal is well reflected in the major functions it is designed to serve, such as the following:

1. To change or modify dysfunctional work behavior
2. To communicate to employees managerial perceptions of the quality of their work

CCAD Responds

To the Authors of *Personnel Management in Government*

The 360-degree feedback pilot at the depot was done in one work center—the Corporate Performance Office. These employees were allowed to select 4 peers which could be other individuals in the work center, others in the CCAD organization (internal customers), or outside customers, vendors or other agencies (external customers). Many of the employees did in fact include customers as part of their raters.

The data collected from the 360-degree feedback process in this pilot was provided to the individual, was consolidated by various teams within the corporate performance office and was consolidated as a group—the entire work center. Confidential ratings were given back to the individual to analyze strengths and weaknesses within each of the six core competencies. This analysis by the individual was used as the basis for developing a personal action plan. The personal action plan was then discussed between the individual and the supervisor and was subsequently used to develop the performance factors used in the next official performance appraisal.

The Depot's plan was to eventually use the 360-degree feedback mechanism as a measurement tool in recontracting the new responsibilities to individual positions. The pilot was an opportunity for the Depot to learn and understand the 360-degree process. One of our lessons learned was that the 360-degree feedback process is an excellent tool that was positively received, and the pilot provided very useful information to the individual and to the supervisor about his (or her) work center.

We also learned that it is critical to the success of 360-degree feedback to implement it at the right time in your strategic planning process. We realized that we needed to cascade our strategic plan to business unit operational plans, and from there individual performance standards based on our overall Depot strategy. We learned a lot from the pilot, but we found that we were not ready, in our 5-year strategic process, to implement the 360-degree feedback process. It would have been premature to implement 360-degree feedback without having adjusted individual performance plans in place.

In regard to your paragraph that began "It should be said however that this 360-degree appraisal process was only mildly revolutionary," it should be rewritten to reflect the accuracy of CCAD's 360-degree feedback program. First, CCAD completed only the pilot phase of the 360-degree feedback program and evaluated only one work center. The Best Manufacturing Practices article on CCAD identifies it to be used for individual performance and feedback not as part of the appraisal: "the 360-degree assessment on individual performance" and "feedback in pursuing a Higher Performing

Organization.'' Our long term goal was to phase in 360-degree feedback in stages, to review the results, and based upon the results to consider incorporating 360-degree feedback into the official appraisal process that would be tied to compensation and adverse actions. However, it was clear after the pilot, that other phases of our strategic plans must be completed first to enable 360-degree feedback to be successful.

Secondly, although in the pilot, we did not calculate a specific ''customer ratee'' field, customers were included as part of the peer group, and verbatim comments were provided to the individual which included those from customers, therefore we considered it to be a 360-degree survey and not a 270-degree survey. The survey included six of our most critical core competencies, one of which was ''Customer Service.'' The next planned phase of the 360-degree feedback program included expansion of the survey to include a specific customer ratee field, and reports with data from our customers.

Thirdly, CCAD has no data to support the implication that the time factor was increased by one-third. The time factor was not compared or weighed against the tools validity or value at CCAD.

In conclusion, CCAD found that 360-degree feedback is an excellent tool. It provides valuable statistical data to the individual and the superior that can be used to improve the organization. The appraisal system itself is improved by using 360-degree feedback whether directly tied to the appraisal system or not.

3. To assess skill deficiencies in employees and to recommend appropriate compensation levels
4. To assess whether or not the present duties of an employee's position have an appropriate compensation level
5. To provide a documented record for disciplinary and separation actions

In theory, performance appraisal is well suited to supporting these functions, but in reality most performance evaluation systems have not been very successful. Why? The main reason may be because supervisors have a great deal of difficulty writing useful and objective performance reports. They submit appraisals that tend to be very subjective, impressionistic, and noncomparable to the reports of other raters. Strong-minded supervisors with very high standards will do their better employees an injustice when compared with raters who have low standards or are less professional. The result is a vast quantity of inflated reports filled with superlatives; in effect, any review of performance appraisals boils down to a consideration of who wrote the report, what other reports have

Human Resources Management Factors (Individual)	Traditional Personnel Management Factors (Organization)
1. *Equity*—Does appraisal measure accurately, without bias, skills/potential of employees.	1. *Linkage to Compensation/Productivity*—documents productivity objectives to lead to some form of reward.
2. *Development*—Does appraisal help individuals grow: vertically; (i.e. role/responsibility/horizontally (i.e. master various skills, work content).	2. *Career Selection*—Organization identifies best, selects out worst.
3. *Individuation/Security*—Does appraisal help to maintain individuals in their jobs and their careers.	3. *Training Needs Assessment*—Identify performance gaps.
4. *Participation*—How do individuals participate in the appraisal process.	4. *Improving Supervisory-Subordinate Communication.*
5. *Integration/Support of other HRM* functions.	5. *Documentation of Work Agreements*—Used to provide form of accountability for areas of high task ambiguity and employee independence.

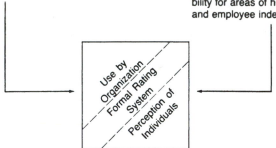

FIGURE 7.1   The objectives of performance appraisal viewed from two perspectives.

they prepared, and what they didn't say that they should have. More often than not, reports submitted about employees will reflect primarily the strengths and weaknesses of the rater. (The impact of this factor substantially limits the validity and use of any individual performance appraisal.) To complicate matters even further, supervisors are often not sure "what" is really being rated—their subordinates' work performance or their own writing ability.

Another difficulty with the concept of performance appraisal is that some of the functions it is designed to serve conflict with each other. For example, appraisal of performance (what has been done on the job) and potential (the capacity to do other jobs) may be in contrast to one another in that the qualities desirable for performance in one job aren't necessarily those needed in a higher-level job. The individual who works well independently in one particular job may be a total loss in another job that requires considerable social interaction.

Perhaps the best assessment of the general utility of performance appraisal systems has been provided by Harry Levinson, a leading writer on organizational psychology, who wrote in a classic *Harvard Business Review* article that despite its significance for effective management and the great deal of effort expended in developing such systems, the results have been fairly dismal. Levinson asserts that "there are few effective established mechanisms to cope with either the sense of inadequacy managers have about appraising subordinates, or the paralysis and procrastination that result from guilt about playing God." To those who might argue that these problems are deficiencies of individual managers and not of the managerial system, Levinson holds that "even if that were altogether true, managers are part of the system. Performance appraisal needs to be viewed not as a technique but as a process involving both people and data, and as such the whole process is inadequate."

Probably one of the most damning indictments of performance appraisal systems can be found in comparing the viewpoints of employees themselves over time. In OPM's (the Office of Personnel Management) 1979 *Federal Employee Attitudes* survey, only about half of the 14,000 employees who participated in the survey felt their performance appraisals were accurate and fair; over half thought their superiors gave the same rating regardless of performance. In a model of understatement, the 1979 report summary observed that "the current usefulness of performance feedback is questionable at best." The report found that "almost half of the employees said their performance ratings are not useful in assessing their strengths and weakness, improving their performance or determining their contribution to the organization. Even more say that feedback is not helpful either in planning for or receiving needed training."

A decade later, the MSPB stated in its 1989 report, *Working for America* (involving over 16,000 federal-worker respondents), that two-thirds of all employees felt their ratings were accurate but that over 60% received ratings of above fully satisfactory. This perception that the large majority of the workforce is above fully satisfactory is shared by both supervisors and employees, as noted in a 1999 report by MSPB. (See Table 7.1.)

Even when rating inflation largely dominates, however, there still remains a significant portion of employees who disagree with their ratings. In the 1989 survey, over 60% of the survey respondents reported that they had little or no involvement in the determination of their performance standards. The survey ratings don't differ much from OPM's central personnel data files on the distribution of performance ratings. The MSPB concluded: "What is to be made of a performance rating system in which two-thirds of all employees are rated 'above the norm' on their performance? What, indeed, when most of the remaining one-third are rated as meeting the 'fully successful' norm and many of them disagree with the accuracy of their ratings? What do these employee responses say about the system? Or about the perception of a 'fully successful' rating?"

TABLE 7.1 MSPB Survey Supervisory vs. Employee Ratings of Performance

	Supervisors Rating Employees			Employees Rating Employees		
	(1989)	(1992)	(1996)	(1989)	(1992)	(1996)
Outstanding	9	14	20	9	11	16
Above average	52	51	58	43	44	50
Average	33	28	19	37	34	27
Below average	4	5	2	7	6	4
Poor	1	1	1	2	3	2
Unable to judge	1	1	1	2	2	2

Source: MSPB. *Federal Supervisors and Poor Performers.* July 1999.

In its 1996 merit principles survey the MSPB gave up asking employees (*The Changing Federal Workplace*) whether or not they felt their performance appraisals were accurate. Instead it asked federal workers if they felt they had been treated unfairly. On the positive side, performance ratings were ranked the highest in terms of "fairness" (see box), although there were differences between minorities and nonminorities. On the negative side, performance ratings were most closely equated with disciplinary actions. Federal workers feel much more strongly that they have *not* been treated fairly on promotions and awards, which of course are supposed to be directly linked to performance ratings.

Can the same discouraging note be sounded for state and local government efforts? The credibility of performance appraisal programs at the state and local level is up considerably, but is still behind that of the federal government or of private industry. Of course private industry has traditionally found that unless the evaluations are kept confidential, they too end up overinflated and of little use.

THE TRADITIONAL APPROACH TO PERFORMANCE APPRAISAL

The standard method of performance appraisal is a written performance evaluation report prepared by the supervisor for a specific time period of an employee's performance. Many jurisdictions require annual evaluations and tie time-in-grade salary increases to satisfactory performance. Written evaluations generally include one or more of the following:

1. A delineation of specific duties and responsibilities
2. Specification of objectives or results to be produced for the time period (as previously agreed upon)
3. Rating scales to evaluate specific performance factors
4. A narrative about specific work accomplishments
5. A rating and/or narrative about the employee's potential for advancement
6. An overall scoring of the employee's performance

Most written evaluations begin with some form of descriptive listing of the work being accomplished. This provides a frame of reference for reviewing the report and can often be used for classification purposes. A more elaborate aspect of this type of work specification is to spell out performance objectives or indicate work products that will be produced over a certain period. In addition, this type of performance-by-objectives narrative normally includes a section to indicate any special circumstances or environmental constraints that may arise during the rating period. While this approach seems well designed to clarify working objectives, the written objectives tend to be either too vague or simply unmeasurable. There is no way to evaluate the apparent difficulty or the qualitative aspect of meeting the objective, much less to make valid comparisons against other reports. Too many unanswered questions remain: Were they appropriate for the individual? Were they actually under the individual's control? What do the objectives indicate about the "how" of performance as opposed to the "what?"

Rating scales represent a "multichoice" dimension of the performance report. The degree to which closed-ended scales or forced choices are used will increase the degree of capability to compare reports. Scales can be of several varieties, the most common being continuous (or integer) scales and discontinuous (discrete-unit) scales. The latter, a discrete-unit scale, forces the rater to choose one out of the four or five responses that is most descriptive, as seen in the following example:

Written communication
_____ Does not get ideas across clearly on paper.
_____ Can do simple drafting. Writing often lacks clarity, brevity, or effectiveness. Composition usually requires extensive editorial revision.
_____ Writing is understandable, to the point, and acceptably organized. Composition usually requires little editing.
_____ Writes clearly and effectively. Composition and style are admirably suited to the objective. Product rarely requires editing.
_____ Composition has all qualities of excellence: clarity, precision, conciseness, good organization, persuasiveness, and style. Only occasional minor editing is ever required.

A continuous scale provides more latitude for choice in that the rater scores the quality on a scale of, for example, 1 to 10 and is provided with descriptions of certain interval points on the scale, as the following example shows:

Dependability
0   Fails to follow instructions, unable to meet commitments or complete work on time.
1
2
3   Needs undue amount of supervision to comply with instructions or to meet deadlines and commitments.
4
5   Conscientious and steady worker. Fulfills commitments, meets deadlines, and produces useful work with normal supervision.
6
7   Conscientious and reliable worker. Completes each task, meets deadlines and commitments with a minimum of supervision.
8

9
10 Invariably meets the most difficult deadlines and commitments. Follows through even without special supervision.

The narrative portions of a written evaluation report can be undirected and designed to allow the rater maximum discretion, or they can be directed so that the rater must describe preselected qualities, providing examples and a general assessment of the quality involved. Narrative exercises can also be designed to address areas for improvement or weaknesses in an effort to combat inflated performance reports. Unfortunately, this tends to encourage supervisors to search for and relate weaknesses that are not really weaknesses or are so general as to be applicable to everyone.

Since written evaluations can be constructed in various ways, there is a tendency to constantly experiment and change the format of the performance evaluation report. In actuality, this represents an attempt by personnel managers to continually change the evaluation "system" so as to beat down "inflated reports." Making constant revisions in the reporting format may achieve the objective of keeping the system one step ahead, but at the cost of making historical comparisons of performance reports virtually impossible and creating uncertainty among supervisors as to what the "current" instructions are for completing the reports.

The inadequacies of written evaluation reports have led to the use of other methods of performance appraisal that essentially reflect different modes of the standard written evaluation technique. Many of these new methods have focused on changing who actually writes the performance report. Four such methods are the following:

1. *Self-appraisals*—Where individuals write some form of narrative or submit some work product to document their work performance.
2. *Peer ratings*—Where each individual rates every other employee in the division or office at a parallel level in the organization.
3. *Subordinate ratings*—Where the subordinates rate the performance of a supervisor.
4. *Group or external ratings*—Where an independent rater, usually a counselor or other qualified expert, will rate performance based on selected interviews or on-the-job visits. Assessment centers would be an example.

By changing the rater, an entirely different perspective can be obtained. The use of new performance appraisal methods seems to primarily represent a general dissatisfaction with traditional written reports, however. Most studies have found no significant relationships between size or type of organization and the type of performance appraisal system in existence. If there is no trend toward

one particular system, it is also difficult to say whether these new modes of evaluation represent advances in evaluation methodologies. They do indicate, however,
a trend toward more collaborative systems—like the 360-degree assessment
model discussed in the prologue.

Back in 1989, the MSPB study *Working for America* addressed some possible changes. It asked about the possibility of converting performance ratings to
a pass–fail approach, and 60% disagreed. The idea of limiting the number of
high performance ratings was suggested, and 50% percent disagreed. Figure 7.2
shows the responses to the survey question regarding other involvement in the
rating process. Fifty-six percent rejected the idea of involving co-workers or
peers, 27% rejected second-level supervisors, and 7% even rejected individual
involvement. (Given this lack of support, the use of 360-degree performance
appraisal experiments seems all the more remarkable.) Alas, performance appraisal seems destined to be subject to both universal complaint and universal
rejection of any ideas for change. This is not to imply that appraisal hasn't
changed at all; indeed, it has gone through a profound metamorphosis over the
past two decades.

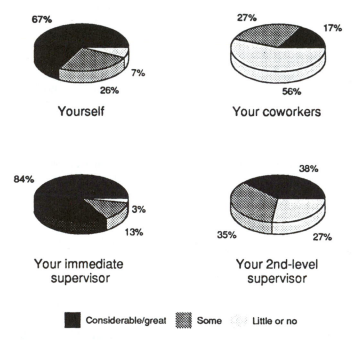

FIGURE 7.2   Who should be allowed to provide input into performance ratings?

CHANGING THE SYSTEM: THE BEHAVIORAL FOCUS

Beginning in the 1970s, a new focus emerged from the failures of the past. While it would be unfair to attribute it to any one specific source, the works of John Campbell, Larry Cummings, and Donald Schwab have been particularly significant in signaling this change. In brief, the argument has been to shift performance measurement to observable work *behaviors* as opposed to measures of organization effectiveness. The point is that effectiveness generally involves additional factors that are beyond the control of the individual. The emphasis, it was argued, should be to construct behaviorally based rating scales or behaviorally anchored rating scales (BARS). Statistical results showed considerably less distortion, bias, and variance when this technique was used.

The new thrust in performance appraisal was to write performance standards that were behaviorally based. What was added to the methodology is the job analysis technique that is used to determine which job behaviors are most important and thus should be measured. Job analysis would involve an extensive review of positions to determine what the job elements were. A job element is defined as a distinguishable, goal-oriented unit of work required by the position. Once the job elements are listed, some form of ranking process would be used to identify which elements were critical (i.e., defined in performance terms as an area in which below-minimum performance would be a basis for removal or demotion). Finally, performance standards would be established for those critical job elements and incorporated into a performance evaluation reporting format.

This concept was described in a 1978 OPM document, *A Guide for Improving Performance Appraisal.*

"Since job duties and performance standards are interrelated, it is common practice to develop them at the same time. Any standard needs to be consistent with the grade level of the position and reflect duties and responsibilities contained in the position description. There are several methods for analyzing jobs to develop job duties and performance standards. Whichever method is used should take into account both the quantitative and qualitative aspects of performance as well as timing and level of achievement. Quantitative measures include such things as number of forms processed, amount of time used, number of errors, number of pages typed, etc. Qualitative measures include accuracy, quality of work, ability to coordinate, analyze, evaluate, etc.

Almost all jobs involve both aspects of performance, but in varying proportions depending on the nature of the job. A production job on an assembly line may depend as much on quantity as on quality of production whereas a research job may emphasize the quality of results with quantity being a minor consideration. Most work situations vary between these examples. It is easier, of course, to measure performance against standards which can be stated and measured in quantitative terms. However, a complete set of performance standards for a job probably will contain some objectives which cannot be quantitatively measured.

Supervisory and managerial positions have an added component because of the nature of the positions. Some duties and responsibilities reflect individual performance. Examples are fulfilling equal employment opportunity responsibilities, recommending or making personnel decisions in accordance with merit principles, appraising subordinates fairly and accurately in accordance with previously established standards, and developing subordinates. Other duties and responsibilities of supervisors and managers reflect the performance of the organization for which the individual is responsible—i.e., the degree to which the organizational objectives are met.

This focus places special emphasis on performance standards and how they should be developed. A detailed discussion of these approaches and the advantages and limitations of each follows.

1. Position description method
   a. *Description and uses*—The position description, in addition to containing the classification series and grade, should also serve as a written record of what the employee is expected to do. It includes information such as job duties, responsibilities, work products, and level of supervision received. It is typical for the position description to be written by a manager or supervisor and revised as needed when the duties of the job change. Refinements in the process are made by classification specialists and others who base their results on observations of employees and analysis of the job. The resulting position description is more objective and accurate than the one developed by the supervisor alone.
   b. *Advantages and limitations*—The economy, speed, convenience, and job knowledge of a single person who knows the job thoroughly (i.e., the supervisor) are advantages of using the position description method. Shortcomings include the single point of view on which the standard is based and the supervisor's frequent lack of training in carrying out job analysis and preparing position descriptions. One of the major problems in writing job descriptions and performance standards is in incorporating the qualitative aspects of the job because they are so difficult to assess objectively.
2. Expert individual or group approach to job analysis
   a. *Description and uses*—Many organizations use either a job analysis expert or a team composed of specialists in fields such as position classifi-

cation, job analysis, and personnel management to improve the process of collecting data and making judgments about all of the pertinent information relating to the nature of a specific job.

As a first step, the individual specialist or the team collects such background information as organization charts, classification specifications, training manuals, and pertinent regulations. Second, a sample is selected of positions that are representative of the job, keeping in mind such factors as location, size of the organization, and amount of public contact. The next step involves gathering job data. This may be done by using one or more of the following methods: interviews, questionnaires, work plans, and job diaries or time sheets (records of job duties over a period of time). Information that is collected from different sources and obtained by more than one method of collection is more reliable than data collected from one source. At the same time that data on job duties are being obtained, information can be collected to use in developing standards to measure performance of those job duties. The final steps involve analyzing the information, knowledge, skills, abilities, and other characteristics needed for the job.

Another type of expert group approach to job analysis is called the *job element method*. It is based on quantifying the opinions of job experts who, as supervisors or as expert workers, know the requirements of the job. They work under the direction of a person who is familiar with the job element method of analysis. An interesting sidelight of this technique is a self-report checklist by which employees may describe their own qualifications in terms of the pertinent job elements. The checklist may be useful in making selections and in identifying possible causes of poor performance.

b. *Advantages and limitations*—The various methods that make use of one or more job analysis experts may be expected to yield more complete, accurate, and precise job information, which in turn leads to clearer, more useful performance standards. The job element method has the advantage of yielding job-related data that are useful for several purposes, such as developing rating checklists and constructing examinations. There is also an optional procedure for selecting job elements that are important in developing training programs. Although the job element method has been used primarily for examining blue-collar occupations, it is now being expanded to include a variety of white-collar occupations in the federal government.

3. Participative methods

a. *Description and uses*—Although the above-mentioned methods provide for obtaining job information from employees, none of them involves employees to the extent that the participative method does. Active participation is an important characteristic of techniques such as management by objectives (MBO) and the related but more limited work planning and review (WPR) systems. These systems are not, however, job analysis methods for developing performance standards for most jobs. For those higher-level jobs characterized by few measurable work products and great involvement in planning and decision making, performance standards and goals may be determined not by job analysis but by agreement between employee and supervisor using MBO and WPR methods. For most jobs, however, it is a good idea to have initial performance standards determined by job analysis, even if some of the standards may be later modified by agreement between supervisor and employee. In the participative methods, employees and their supervisors are involved in planning work, setting goals and objectives to be met, and periodically reviewing and revising work plans. Goals and objectives that meet at least minimum standards are documented in quantitative terms if possible (i.e., a specified kind and amount of work will be done within a certain time limit). Employees can thus readily assess their progress before any formal appraisal takes place. Some participative plans have provisions for employees to actively contribute to the appraisal process by carrying out self-ratings.

Management by objectives uses a participative approach as part of a broad plan to integrate organizational and personal goals at all organizational levels. Usually, this approach calls for all employees to participate in varying degrees in setting organizational objectives as well as planning their work, appraising their performance, and planning their career development. Target dates are set, and at predetermined times, the results are measured against the projected goals. To be successful, MBO programs require of management: careful planning, active participation, follow-up, and a regular review procedure.

The WPR method, which is narrower in scope than MBO, emphasizes the periodic review of work plans by employee and supervisor to acknowledge goals reached, identify problems and hindrances, exchange ideas and information about solutions, determine areas of specific need such as training, and review and update the goals and objectives in the work plan.

b. *Advantages and limitations*—The participative approach, by being oriented to the amount and quality of work accomplished, makes it possible to appraise performance more in terms of specific work goals rather than of ambiguous personal qualities, thus an advantage of this method is that its emphasis is on evaluating the characteristics of the work being done, not the characteristics of the employee doing the work. Employee involvement in work planning, performance standards, and appraisals promotes fairer, more objective performance appraisal and results in improved work performance and motivation. The MBO approach appears to be more successful when applied to managerial, executive, and professional jobs than to other kinds of positions. There are some organizations, however, using variations of the participative approach in work planning and review with employees in other occupational fields at several organizational levels.

THE HISTORY OF MERIT PAY

Few things seem more basic to a personnel system than the requirement to appraise individual performance regularly and ensure that the organization uses this information in making training, compensation, and advancement decisions. The federal government initially addressed the appraisal process with the enactment of the Performance Rating Act of 1950. This act provided guidelines for appraisal goals and processes and included rules for removing those individuals with unsatisfactory performance ratings. Prior to 1950, the federal government relied on the uniform efficiency rating system, which required employees to be rated on their quality of performance, productivity, and qualifications. Employees would be graded at one of five rating levels under each category and then receive a summary rating.

Dissatisfaction with performance appraisal ran rampant over the 1960s and 1970s, however, and when the Civil Service Reform Act (CSRA) was passed in 1978, a major target for change was the performance appraisal process. The CSRA established a merit pay system to cover supervisors and managers from GS-13 to GS-15, and also required that compensation decisions be linked with employee appraisals. In essence, performance appraisals were to serve as the primary basis for annual salary changes.

This merit pay system rapidly drew fire from all sides, however. Severely hampered by limited funding levels (it was tied to general schedule funding), the initial procedures were extremely cumbersome and ineffective. In 1985, merit pay was replaced with a new pay-for-performance system called PMRS (performance management and recognition system). Interestingly, Congress ''sunseted'' PMRS with a five-year lifeline, requiring legislation to revive it after September 1989. The details were as follows:

> Performance appraisals were to have five rating levels ranging from 1 (unacceptable) to 3 (fully successful) to 5 (two levels above fully successful).
> Employees rated 3 or above would get the full general annual pay increase with some kind of merit increase based on their overall rating and where they stood in terms of pay.

Fundamental Flaws in Employee Performance Appraisal

Consider the pyramiding required for performance appraisal to be objective. Most contemporary organizations are not assembly lines with clear inputs and material outputs. The majority of occupations are office based and deal with intangible information exchanges. Especially in the public sector we serve diverse clientele, respond to requests, and communicate. Our days are varied; they vary by season, budget cycle, and externally generated deadlines. All these activities are somewhat artificially gathered under the umbrella and named such and such unit, agency, or department. Such organizations are vastly complex macro organizations made up of already extremely complex subgroups in turn made up of multifaceted individuals. Out of this "primordial stew" we first evaluate jobs by breaking them down to minute components, attempting thereby to distill the essential tasks by removing their human incumbents from consideration. We then articulate a position classification system that arrays clusters of tasks according to various criteria by which their comparative worth can be assessed . . . We must then take *each* task or cluster of tasks and figure out precisely what level of performance, or which performance targets, may be termed "unsatisfactory," "needs improvement," "satisfactory," "fully satisfactory," and "outstanding." Once all this has been done we then ask a supervisor semiannually or annually to take the results of this fantastic series of abstract calculations, now reduced to a form, and use it to gauge the complex, interdependent, variegated activities of individual job incumbents. The end result of this process is to be objective data of sufficient validity to compare and reward or punish employees from across the entire organization.

If, for public relations purposes, or to save face, the political powers that be feel the need to maintain some sort of performance appraisal system, let them have the shadow of one. They will, over time, probably become that anyway as organizations adjust to the human reality that full-blown, objective, performance audits simply cannot be done . . . that seems to be the direction that the federal government was heading as it switched from the extremely punitive Merit Pay System . . . to the more lenient and flexible Performance Management and Recognition System in 1984. . . . A less complicated approach that I recommend in order to establish a defensible legal base for the occasionally needed adverse personnel action—firing or demoting, for example—is a simple form outlining position duties with only two rating categories: "unsatisfactory" and "fully satisfactory." . . . "Courts do not reject the subjective approach." You just have to be consistent in your subjectivity.

Whatever the strategy, we should work to abolish or mitigate formal performance appraisal as we know it.

Source: Fox, Charles J. "Employee Performance Appraisal: The Keystone Made of Clay," in Carolyn, Ban and Norma M. Riccucci (eds.), *Public Personnel Management: Current Concerns, Future Challenges*. White Plains, N.Y.: Longman Press, 1991, pp. 63, 68.

Level 5 awards range from a minimum of 2% to a maximum award of 10% of their pay. Provisions existed to give exceptions up to 20%.

Level 4 employees were intended to obtain some kind of award, and level 3 employees were eligible for a similar type of award. Those below level 3 were penalized. Level 2 employees were to get only 50% of the general pay raise and level 1 employees received no increase at all.

All the funding for these performance awards was to come from a performance award budget of 1.5% of the total salary budget for all PMRS employees. Again the system was to apply to all supervisors and managers from GS-13 to GS-15, but even the revised PMRS, which most federal personnel offices felt was an improvement over the original merit pay plan, ran into trouble.

To begin with, there simply wasn't enough money in the budget to reward all the high performers. Consider MSPB's findings in its 1987 report, *Performance Management and Recognition System*, that over two-thirds of all employees covered under PMRS had bonus-eligible ratings of 4 or 5 in the first year of the new plan! Agencies varied considerably in their ratings, which further discredited the system. Managers at the Departments of Justice and State were rated the highest (48% and 59%, respectively, had ratings of 5), while managers at the Departments of Labor and Treasury had tougher ratings (8% and 7%, respectively, had ratings of 5). Could this mean that one set of agencies had much better managers than another or is it that one set of performance raters took the rating process more seriously? Even OPM was not immune from rate inflation. Of its eligible managers, 10% had ratings of 5, but 40% had ratings of 4.

The MSBP concluded in a 1988 report, *Toward Effective Performance in the Federal Government*, that "There were many complaints that the procedures were so complex that employees could not understand how their increases were derived. Employees also were concerned about the fairness of the Performance Appraisal System which was the basis for the merit pay and cash award determinations."

Faced with inflated ratings, agencies either enforced informal quotas (limiting the number of high ratings) or developed subtle rotation polices, whereby one group of managers would get the high ratings one year and a second set would get the high ratings the next. The system's credibility was ripped apart by the resulting chaos. In MSPB's merit systems principles survey, as reported in *Performance Management and Recognition System*, nearly 70% of all top supervisors and managers responding agreed that there was an arbitrary limit on the number of high performance ratings. An even more critical question drew this mixed response. Forty-five percent agreed with the statement that if they performed better on the job they would likely be paid more, while nearly 39% disagreed.

Do Federal Government Employees See a Link Between Pay and Performance?

Here is how federal government employees* responded to the following question: "If you perform better in your present job, how likely is it that you will receive more pay?"

Pay category of respondent	Percentage responding very likely or somewhat likely
Prevailing rate	33
General schedule	30
Performance management and recognition system (GM)	45
Senior Executive Service	39

* Based on a sample of 21,620 employees.

Source: U.S. Merit Systems Protection Board. *Federal Personnel Policies and Practices*. Washington, D.C.: USMSPB, 1987, p. 7.

Despite problems with employee perceptions and inflated ratings, however, concern about PMRS was overshadowed by the increasing pay gap. As the sunset date approached, Congress moved to extend PMRS for an additional two years, or until March 1991. In the interim, OPM commissioned a major study by the National Academy of Sciences for completion in early 1991 and established a pay-for-performance management committee to make recommendations for action by November 1991. The latter committee was charged with reviewing pay raises in general and with evaluating all the studies to date on pay-for-performance problems experienced by the federal government.

The 1991 report of National Academy of Sciences, *Pay for Performance*, examined both pillars of the merit pay system–performance appraisal and performance-based pay systems. Overall, this very comprehensive but cautious report supported the objectives of merit pay, but felt that the costs of implementation outweighed the benefits. Their conclusions on appraisal and performance-based pay follow:

On appraisal: "The search for a high degree of precision in measurement does not appear to be economically viable in most applied settings; many believe that there is little to be gained from such a level of precision. The committee further concludes, that for most personnel management decisions, including annual pay decisions, the goal of a performance appraisal system should be to support and encourage informed managerial judgement, and not to aspire to the degree of standardization, precision, and empirical support that would be required of, for example, selection tests.''

On merit pay: ''On the basis of analogy from the research and theory on variable pay plans, the committee concludes that merit pay can have positive effects on individual job performance, These effects may be attenuated by the facts that, in many merit plans, increases are not always clearly linked to employee performance, agreement on the evaluation of performance does not always exist, and increases are not always viewed as meaningful.''

The National Academy's report concluded pessimistically

Our entire review has stressed the importance of viewing performance appraisal and merit pay as embedded within the broader pay, personnel, management and organizational contexts. The latter changes suggested by an analysis of the context can be costly, but we suggest that making programmatic changes to the Performance Management and Recognition System [PMRS] in isolation is unlikely to enhance employee acceptance of the system or improve individual and organizational effectiveness in the long run, may prove no less costly.

Faced with this pessimistic forecast, OPM then presided over the termination of PMRS. Employees were phased back into the regular pay step system. By 1995, OPM had essentially turned pay for performance over to the individual agencies. Agencies were allowed to design their own merit pay programs and simplify their performance appraisal systems although awards had to meet standards established in the CFR by OPM. Pay for performance was basically decentralized. (See Figures 7.3 and 7.4 for a summary of performance ratings by pay plan and grade from 1991 to 1996.)

Reactions by federal managers have been muted. Being given control of their own merit pay destiny has not meant that the system works any better. Agencies have always been in a quandary over what to do about merit pay and bonuses—at least under the old rules, they had someone else to blame for the problems. Now, as a 1994 MSPB survey showed (see Table 7.2), there was no strong consensus on how to fix merit pay or performance appraisal.

Fiscal Year (FY)	Unacceptable	Minimally Successful	Fully Successful	Exceeds Fully Successful	Outstanding	Average Rating	Number of Ratings Reported
General Schedule 13-15 (Supervisors and Management Officials) [1]							
FY 1991	0.06	0.14	17.85	47.25	34.70	4.16	148,983
FY 1992	0.06	0.14	16.62	46.41	36.77	4.20	149,810
FY 1993	0.07	0.14	13.98	44.69	41.12	4.27	151,728
FY 1994	0.04	0.13	12.11	41.92	45.79	4.33	147,041
FY 1995	0.03	0.15	9.47	37.52	52.83	4.43	132,444
FY 1996	0.00	0.10	11.20	32.70	56.00	4.45	129,859
General Schedule 13-15 (Other)							
FY 1991	0.09	0.21	22.71	45.27	31.72	4.08	85,973
FY 1992	0.04	0.13	22.66	45.26	31.91	4.09	91,484
FY 1993	0.06	0.14	20.61	45.71	33.48	4.12	103,342
FY 1994	0.05	0.19	17.87	40.22	41.66	4.23	120,917
FY 1995	0.04	0.17	15.33	38.57	45.88	4.30	135,736
FY 1996	0.00	0.10	16.40	34.70	48.60	4.32	163,838
General Schedule 1-12							
FY 1991	0.12	0.37	31.16	41.17	27.19	3.95	1,126,784
FY 1992	0.13	0.36	29.55	41.32	28.64	3.98	1,174,895
FY 1993	0.13	0.34	26.52	41.96	31.05	4.03	1,145,962
FY 1994	0.14	0.31	24.20	41.63	33.72	4.08	1,096,553
FY 1995	0.16	0.42	22.78	39.87	36.77	4.13	1,053,375
FY 1996	0.10	0.30	22.30	38.10	39.20	4.16	1,026,496
Federal Wage System							
FY 1991	0.05	0.26	33.71	43.78	22.20	3.88	310,381
FY 1992	0.04	0.23	30.46	44.66	24.61	3.94	308,661
FY 1993	0.05	0.19	26.13	45.11	28.53	4.02	283,381
FY 1994	0.03	0.15	23.92	44.61	31.29	4.07	263,182
FY 1995	0.03	0.26	21.57	41.99	36.16	4.14	243,334
FY 1996	0.00	0.30	21.00	39.70	39.00	4.17	235,667

[1] Prior to FY 1994, these employees were covered by the Performance Management and Recognition System (PMRS), which terminated November 1, 1993.

NOTE: Percentages may not add to 100 due to rounding.

FY 91-95 Source: Performance Management Information System (PERMIS) Data File, Office of Compensation Policy.

FY 96 Source: Central Personnel Data File (CPDF), Office of Workforce Information

***Until September 1995, most agencies operated performance appraisal programs that used five summary performance rating levels. 1995 regulatory changes allowed the use of differing numbers of levels. OPM is currently developing new methods of reporting performance data that will accommodate these patterns.*

FIGURE 7.3 Percentage distributions of performance ratings (fiscal years 1991–1996).

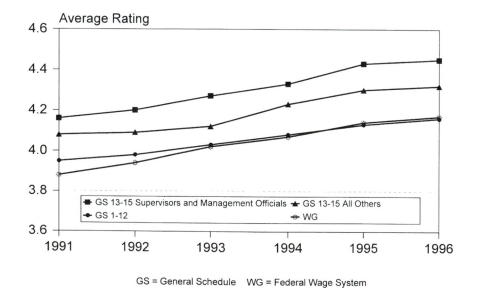

GS = General Schedule   WG = Federal Wage System

FIGURE 7.4 Performance ratings by pay plan and grade (1991–1996).

TABLE 7.2 1994 MSPB Survey of Federal Managers and Supervisors

What should be done to performance management systems	Yes	No	DK
Reduce ratings to two levels (pass–fail)	66%	27%	6%
Not use performance ratings as basis for cash awards	55%	37%	8%
Drop requirements for performance standards	42%	50%	9%
Eliminate requirement for performance-improvement plan	37%	43%	21%
Not use performance ratings as a basis for promotion	37%	54%	9%
Reduce advance notice from 30 to 15 days	35%	40%	26%
Not use performance ratings in reduction in force	35%	38%	16%

DK = Don't know.

SOME STATE GOVERNMENT PERSPECTIVES ON MERIT PAY

The question might be asked if the federal government's great step backwards on merit pay (see Table 7.3) has influenced thinking among other governments. Ed Kellough and Sally Selden addressed exactly that question in a 1994 survey of state personnel managers. Their survey covered numerous questions about motivation and the effectiveness of merit pay systems in state governments, but a more basic finding was that states had not retreated from merit pay. Fifty-two percent of their survey respondents indicated that they were using individualized pay-for-performance bonuses and 11% were using group-based bonuses. While there was a mix of approaches, over 48% of the survey respondents indicated that merit pay was the sole system used. Kellough and Selden conclude that despite all the perceived problems with merit pay, it remains the dominant form of performance management and is even more widespread than it was in the 1980s.

In 1998 the Government Performance Project at Syracuse University conducted a major survey of state governments in terms of performance evaluation and reward systems, among other personnel functions. This survey confirms that a majority of states are still using pay-for-performance systems, despite the difficulties, but survey results from the project (see Table 7.4) show that another trend is discernible—the emergence of nonmonetary rewards.

Fittingly, this lends strong support to an analysis by another leading expert, Gerald Gabris, that merit pay is unlikely to become extinct. He concludes that there are four key strategies for making merit pay work.

1. ''Move away from using financial or monetary incentives as the primary or sole incentive.''

TABLE 7.3 Chronology of Employee Performance Management
in the Federal Government

Year	Actions
1883	Pendleton Act, or Civil Service Act Attempted to provide a merit system to end favoritism. Required promotions by merit competition, but no centralized appraisal system was established.
1912	First law on appraisal An appropriations act directed the U.S. Civil Service Commission (now the U.S. Office of Personnel Management) to establish a uniform efficiency rating system for all agencies.
1923	Classification Act of 1923 Resulted in establishment of a "graphic rating scale" in 1924, which was used until 1935. Was effective but unpopular. Supervisor marked along a scale for each "service rendered."
1935	Uniform efficiency rating system The Civil Service Commission established the uniform efficiency rating system by regulation, which was used until 1950. Factors were grouped under the headings Quality of Performance, Productiveness, and Qualifications. There were five rating levels for each of the three categories, and also five summary rating levels.
1940	Ramspeck Act Directed establishment of independent boards of review to decide rating appeals in each agency. Boards included the Civil Service Commission and employee representatives.
1950	Performance Rating Act Purpose was to identify the best and weakest employees and to improve supervisor–employee relations. Required the establishment of appraisal systems within all agencies with prior approval by the Civil Service Commission. Established three adjective summary rating levels: outstanding, satisfactory, and unsatisfactory. Employees could still appeal ratings, but now through a statutory board of three members, one from an agency, one selected by employees, and the chairman of the Civil Service Commission.
1954	Incentive Awards Act Authorized honorary recognition and cash payments for superior accomplishment, suggestions, inventions, special acts or services, or other personal efforts.
1958	Government Employees' Training Act Provided for training to improve performance and to prepare for future advancement.

TABLE 7.3 Continued

Year	Actions
1962	Salary Reform Act

1962 Salary Reform Act
  Required an "acceptable level of competence" determination for granting general schedule within-grade increases.
  Provided for the denial of the within-grade increase when performance is below the acceptable level.
  Authorized an additional step increase for "high-quality performance."

1978 Civil Service Reform Act
  Agencies required to develop appraisal systems for all federal employees
  Office of Personnel Management approval of appraisal systems required.
  Appraisals must be based on job-related performance standards.
  Agencies must encourage employee participation in establishing performance standards.
  Appeal of appraisals outside an agency was eliminated.
  Results of the appraisal must be used as a basis for training, rewarding, reassigning, promoting, reducing in grade, retaining, and removing employees.
  Employees can be removed for unacceptable performance on one or more critical elements, but only after being provided an opportunity to demonstrate acceptable performance. The standard of proof was reduced from preponderance of the evidence to substantial evidence.
  Reductions in grade and removals are appealable to the Merit Systems Protection Board.
  Established a separate performance appraisal system for Senior Executive Service employees.
  One or more fully successful rating levels, a minimally satisfactory level, and an unsatisfactory level required.
  Agency performance review boards to make recommendations to appointing officials on final ratings required.
Established performance-related pay authorities.
  Provided for performance awards for career executives; at least a fully successful rating required, and recommendation of the performance review board.
  Provided for Senior Executive Service meritorious (career) executive awards ($10,000 for sustained accomplishment over a period of years; limited to 5% of executives) and distinguished (career) executives awards ($20,000 for sustained extraordinary accomplishment, limited to 1% of executives).

TABLE 7.3 Continued

Year	Actions
	Merit pay established for supervisors and management officials in grades GS-13 to GS-15 with funding for merit increases limited to what would have been paid as within-grade increases, quality step increases, and half of comparability adjustment. (Employees were guaranteed half of comparability adjustments only.)
1984	Civil Service Retirement Spouse Equity Act
	Established a 5% minimum performance award for Senior Executive Service employees.
	Merit pay system abolished and performance management and recognition system (PMRS) established.
	PMRS employees rated fully successful or higher guaranteed full comparability increases, with minimally successful getting half, and unacceptable getting none.
	PMRS employees guaranteed merit increases of specific amount based on their performance ratings and position in pay range for their grade level.
	Performance awards program for PMRS employees established, with a minimum funding level from .75% to 1.15% of estimated aggregate salaries over five years and a minimum performance award of 2% of employee's salary required for an outstanding rating. Maximum award funding was set at 1.5% of estimated aggregate salaries.
	Performance appraisal revisions in PMRS include five summary rating levels required, no forced distributions of ratings allowed, and joint participation in setting standards required.
1985	Final performance management and recognition system appraisal and pay regulations issued
	Implemented legal provisions regarding general increases, merit increases, and performance awards.
	Established procedures for determining merit increases and performance awards for "unrateable" employees.
	Described pay-setting procedures when employees move between pay systems.
	Established minimum appraisal periods and procedures for rating employees who are detailed to other positions.
	Required higher-level approval of ratings and performance-based personnel actions.
1986	Final performance management system regulations issued
	Appraisal regulations for general schedule and prevailing rate employees and for SES employees issued, which paralleled performance management and recognition system appraisal regulations of 1985.
	Regulatory pay-for-performance system established

TABLE 7.3 Continued

Year	Actions
	Fully successful rating required for within-grade increases.
	Outstanding rating required for quality step increases.
	Fully successful rating required for career-ladder promotions.
	Performance award program required for general schedule and prevailing rate employees.
1989	Legislation extends PMRS
	Revised merit increase amount for fully successful employees in the middle third of the pay range from one-third to one-half of a merit increase, to parallel step increases in the general schedule.
	Set minimum performance awards funding at 1.15% of estimated aggregate salaries for duration of the extension.
	Allowed for the reassignment, removal, or reduction in grade of PMRS employees who did not attain a fully successful level of performance after being given an opportunity to do so.
	Revised Senior Executive Service appraisal regulations
	Permitted three to five summary rating levels. Must include an unsatisfactory, minimally satisfactory, and fully successful level.
	Deleted requirement for rating period to end between June 30 and September 30.
1991	Legislation again extends the PMRS
	Allowed using a written statement of work objectives to establish performance requirements.
	Removed requirement for mandatory performance award for employees rated outstanding and the accompanying 2% minimum award.
	Federal Employees Pay Comparability Act
	Provided specific legislative authority for payment of rating-based cash awards to general schedule employees like those authorized under the PMRS.
	Provided authority to grant time off as an incentive award.
1992	Revised regulations on summary rating levels for general schedule and prevailing rate appraisal systems
	Allowed summary ratings at 3, 4, or 5 levels but required agencies to include unacceptable, fully successful, and outstanding levels.
1993	PMRS terminated
	Provided for orderly termination of the PMRS and payout of merit increases and performance awards based on October 1993 ratings.
	Provided for phased conversion of employees not on a step rate back to step rats based on specified personnel changes.
	Retained authority to pay employees at nonstep rates until changes occur to place all employees on a step rate.

TABLE 7.3   Continued

Year	Actions
1995	Performance management regulations revised
	Further decentralized the performance management program to allow agencies to develop programs to meet their individual needs and cultures.
	Established eight permissible summary rating patterns allowing from two to five levels for summary ratings.
	Combined all award authorities in one part of the regulations, 5 CFR 451.
	Streamlined the appraisal system approval process.
1997	Revised regulations on reduction in force and performance management
	Allowed flexible crediting between 12 and 20 additional years of service retention credit for ratings of record given under different summary level patterns.
	Retained traditional 12–16–20-year crediting when all ratings of record being credited were given under a single summary level pattern.
	Revised credit averaging to use actual ratings of record given without "filling in the blanks" with presumed fully successful.
	Removed use of presumed fully successful ratings and replaced them with credit based on the modal rating when employee had no ratings of record.
	Provided for immediate or delayed implementation at agency discretion to allow for education, partnership, and automated system revision efforts.
1998	Revised regulations on ratings of record
	Codified long-standing Office of Personnel Management policy regarding ratings of record.
	Described when a rating of record is considered final.
	Prohibited retroactive, carryover, and assumed ratings of record.
	Provided limited circumstances under which an agency can change a rating of record.

2. ''Cannot be implemented as an isolated, separate reform detached from the larger bureaucratic system.''
3. ''Should not target individuals as sole recipients; need to reward intact work teams and groups.''
4. ''Should reflect a balance among concerns for individuals, internal, and external equity.''

TABLE 7.4 Survey of State Government Performance Evaluation
and Reward Systems

	Not used (%)	Some use (%)	Major use (%)
Monetary			
Individual performance	40.8	44.8	14.3
Group performance	65.2	32.6	2.0
Nonmonetary			
Job flexibility	34.7	51	14.3
Time flexibility	22.4	38.7	38.8

Certainly state and local trends are moving toward nonfinancial and group awards, and other reforms, such as skill-based pay and results-based bonus concepts, are likely to garner more attention in the next decade. Perhaps the best conclusion is simply to note that merit pay's resiliency has less to do with its own inherent value and more to do with the lack of viable alternatives. As performance appraisal systems become more and more separated from compensation decisions, there may yet be the kind of comprehensive reform envisioned by the 1991 National Academy of Science report but never enacted.

OTHER ALTERNATIVES: ASSESSMENT CENTERS AND ASSESSMENTS OF MULTISOURCE APPRAISALS

For those who have advocated truly radical changes in the idea of individual performance appraisal, there have been two alternatives. The first alternative is to develop an external methodology for discovering what qualities were essential for successful performance in the organization. This concept involves establishing an assessment center for identifying individuals with future executive potential.

Actually, the term assessment center never implies a particular place; rather, it is a method—a comprehensive standardized measurement process that requires that the employees being evaluated participate in simulated real-life situations. Multiple evaluation techniques are used that include a range of approaches to simulating work situations: group discussions, in-basket exercises, simulation of interviews with subordinates, oral presentations, and written communication exercises. The assessment center is designed to evaluate candidates in a number of stressful situations over a period of several days for behaviors and abilities that are crucial for successful performance. How does an organization know which behaviors and abilities to test for? This information is provided by a job analysis of potential future positions. If first-line supervisors are being evaluated for middle-management potential, then the assessment center's exercise should test for the traits via a job analysis so that assessment center exercises could be selected or invented to test for those qualities.

The assessment center concept is far from new. Assessment center techniques were used by the German army for selecting officers in World War I. The American Office of Strategic Services (OSS) used them for selecting secret agents in World War II. The assessment center concept did not reach American industry until the mid-1950s, however, when AT&T pioneered such a program. The practice spread during the 1960s, but it wasn't until 1969 that a government agency, the Internal Revenue Service, used assessment center methodology on a large scale. Today such techniques have been used by government agencies at all jurisdictional levels, including the state of Illinois, the city of Philadelphia, and a host of federal agencies.

The assessors used in an assessment center are usually employees in the organization who are several levels higher than the candidates and have been specially trained in assessment center evaluation methods. The assessors function as a team—usually one assessor for each of two candidates—and they rotate so they can observe different candidates in each exercise. After the candidates have completed their exercises, the team of assessors confers and produces a report or assessment for each candidate.

Assessments are frequently used as justifications for both advancement and career development opportunities. It is not uncommon for an employee's assessment to recommend a particular course of training that could compensate for a noticed deficiency. To assure the validity of an assessment process and to meet equity requirements, assessment center exercises must demonstrably test for qualities that can be shown to be necessary to the job level in question. Position requirements, which must be determined through a prior job analysis, are reviewed, and those that can be assessed adequately by the employee's current job performance should be deleted since the appropriate evaluation mechanism for "current" performance is the regular performance appraisal.

While the assessment center methodologies are still so new as to be aptly termed experimental, they have proven to be substantially more reliable predictors of future performance than traditional written examinations or panel interviews. While assessment centers may have resolved one set of problems, however, they also generate their own unique problems. Most organizations base their decisions on who will be assessed on some form of supervisor's recommendation or individual voluntary basis, so as the assessment center concept is more widely adopted, one question arises as to who determines who goes through the assessment center or who will be the gatekeeper. Unless the organization can afford to process its entire management cadre through assessment centers, those individ-

Typical Assessment Center Exercises

Assigned role group discussion. In this leaderless group discussion, participants, acting as a city council of a hypothetical city, must allocate a one-million dollar federal grant in the time allotted or make other judgments on the varying proposals offered. Each participant is assigned a point of view to sell to the other team members and is provided with a choice of projects to back and the opportunity to bargain and trade off products for support.

Nonassigned role group discussion. This exercise is a cooperative, leaderless group discussion in which four short case studies dealing with problems faced by executives working in state government agencies are presented to a group of six participants. The participants act as consultants who must make group recommendations on each of the problems. Assessors observe the participant's role in the group and the handling of the content of the discussion.

In-basket exercise. Problems that challenge middle- and upper-level executives in state governments are simulated in the in-basket exercise. These include relationships with departmental superiors, subordinates and peers, representatives of other departments, representatives of executive and legislative branches, the public, and the news media. Taking over a new job, the participant must deal with memos, letters, policies, bills, etc., found in the in-basket. After the in-basket has been completed, the participant is interviewed by an assessor concerning his/her handling of the various in-basket items.

Speech and writing exercises. Each participant is given a written, narrative description of a policy, event, situation, etc. and three specific situational problems related to the narrative, each requiring a written response. The participant is also required to make a formal oral presentation, based upon the background narrative description, before a simulated news conference attended by the Capitol Press Corps and interested government officials and citizens (assessors).

Analysis problem. The analysis problem is an individual exercise. The participant is given a considerable amount of data regarding a state agency's field operations, which he/she must analyze and about which he/she must make a number of management recommendations. The exercise is designed to elicit behaviors related to various dimensions of managerial effectiveness. The primary area of behavior evaluated in this exercise is the ability to sift through data and find pertinent information to reach a logical and practical conclusion.

Paper and pencil tests. Three different commercially available objectively scoreable tests are included in the assessment: a reading test used for self-development purposes, a reasoning-ability test, and a personality test. The latter two are being used experimentally at present, and as with the reading test, are not made available during assessor discussions.

Source: Byham, William C. and Carl Wettengal. ''Assessment Centers for Supervisors and Managers,'' *Public Personnel Management*, vol. 3 (September–October 1974), p. 241. Reprinted by permission of the International Personnel Management Association, 1850 K Street, N.W., Suite 870, Washington, D.C. 20006.

uals not selected for attendance might justifiably conclude they have been negatively evaluated because the organization did not judge them to be worthy of
formal evaluation. The decision (or nondecision) not to send an individual to an
assessment center while peers are being sent could even have considerable legal
ramifications. Since management development funds always seem to be a scarce
resource, any jurisdiction implementing an assessment center program must also
be concerned with designing an equitable nomination process.

Another potential problem with assessment centers is that they may be too
efficient in replicating existing management values. A possible danger in any
assessment center program is that the assessors will seek to reproduce themselves
by scoring high those individuals who tend to reflect their personalities, leadership styles, and lengths of hair; or that the exercises used will self-select the past.
The last thing any management development program should do is produce a
management corps with the same values and attitudes as the previous managerial
generation. The best way of guarding against this potential nightmare is to use
the organization's best and most active line managers as assessors. It should go
without saying that any manager the organization is willing to spare to use as a
"full-time assessor" should not be allowed to assess anyone. This especially
includes the personnel operatives. Personnel's job is to facilitate a decisional task
that belongs to line management. Another possibly dysfunctional aspect of an
assessment center program is the "crown prince" phenomenon. Some individuals who do exceedingly well at the assessment center may feel that their future
is so assured that their on-the-job performance slackens. No organization should
rely entirely on assessment center reports. Such scores comprise only one of a
variety of factors that should be considered when it is time to make decisions
on management development and advancement. The above-mentioned caveats
notwithstanding, assessment centers have already proven to be of such value that
personnelists should not only be aware of their procedures, but they should also
be prepared to install centers in their own organizations.

The other alternative to individual performance appraisal is the multisource
appraisal process discussed in the prologue debate; that is, the 360-degree performance appraisal. What makes this most attractive to organizations is the lessening
of reliance on the supervisor–subordinate relationship. By providing multiple
perspectives on an individual's strengths and weaknesses, it is felt that the process
will be more objective and more comprehensive by covering the wider range of
relationships as opposed to the simple hierarchical relationship.

While it is early (in performance management time), there have been a few
evaluation reports on the 360-degree appraisal systems. Linda deLeon and Ann
Ewan conducted a study of a mid-1990s field experiment with a large federal
agency at the regional level. The field office included 450 employees who were
given a pretest and a posttest survey on the application of a multisource performance appraisal system. In terms of the system, employees were actually given

training in doing both ratings (they would, of course, be rating peers) and understanding ratings. In this case, the 360-degree system was really more of a 270-degree system, since only appraisals by the individual, supervisors, and peers were included. To complete a 360-degree appraisal would technically require some appraisal by customers or cooperators, to get an truly external service perspective.

DeLeon and Ewan's evaluation of the survey, along with interviews, underscored the difficulties in using one pre- and one posttest survey to validate a new system's effectiveness. They respectfully note that a pretest survey tends to overestimate the amount of dissatisfaction with the old system and that the posttest survey will have difficulties controlling for the Hawthorne effect (i.e., overestimating the positive impact of the new system simply because it is an experiment). Nonetheless, their study showed significant improvement in the perception by employees of the fairness of the appraisals and their effectiveness. A byproduct was the improvement in promoting teamwork and work group cooperation. Also of interest was the result that "protected classes" (e.g., women, minorities, and older and younger employees) rated the multisource appraisal system as fair and effective to a greater degree than the employee average.

With this favorable result, it would be of great interest to see how the system would have been affected by tying pay increases to individual or group performance. That was not part of the experiment and indeed, from the few other federal examples that have been reported on (i.e., FAA, Office of Veterans Affairs, and some defense installations), even for groups, merit pay is not tied directly to 360-degree appraisal. What this early 1997 study does demonstrate is that multisource appraisal, in a team-based organizational work environment with appropriate training, can improve the state of performance appraisal.

Another study of 360-degree appraisal was conducted in a large midwestern city using two city departments. Lynn Harland and Deborah Sander have reported on Omaha's experience. Like the federal regional agency experiment, pre- and post-test surveys were administered to employees, and the system did not include customers, just peers, the supervisor, and self-ratings. Harland and Sander's analysis shows positive but more limited results. Two variables showed significant positive impact of the 360 appraisal experiment: the level of conformity among workers over co-workers rating their performance and a significant improvement in the need for feedback about job performance. The latter variable effectively means that individuals saw less need for additional feedback on their work because of the value of the 360 process. There were no significant differences on several other key factors, however—most notably the fairness of the appraisal system or the degree to which employees' felt that they had a more accurate view of their performance on the job. Finally, there was no improvement in the employees' perception of their comfort level of rating other employees. If the Omaha study results were to be replicated in other studies of 360-degree appraisal, it might be rather ironic. Employees essentially are finding out first hand just how difficult it is to write a performance appraisal.

BIBLIOGRAPHY

Adelsberg, Henri van. "Relating Performance Evaluation to Compensation of Public Employees," *Public Personnel Management*, vol. 7 (March–April 1978).

Bann, Charles and Jerald Johnson. "Federal Employee Attitudes Toward Reform: Performance Evaluation and Merit Pay," in Patricia W. Ingraham and Carolyn Ban (eds.), *Legislating Bureaucratic Change: The Civil Service Reform Act of 1978*. Albany, N.Y.: SUNY–Albany Press, 1984.

Borman, W. D. and Marvin Dunnette. "Behavior-Based Versus Trait-Oriented Performance Ratings: An Empirical Study," *Journal of Psychology*, vol. 60 (1975).

Bowman, James T. "At Last, An Alternative to Performance Appraisal: Total Quality," *Public Administration Review*, vol. 54, no. 2 (1994), pp. 129–136.

Brumback, Gary B. "Toward a New Theory and System of Performance Evaluation: A Standardized, MBO-Oriented Approach," *Public Personnel Management*, vol. 7 (July–August 1978).

Byham, William C. and Carl Wettengel. "Assessment Centers for Supervisors and Managers," *Public Personnel Management*, vol. 3 (September–October 1974).

Campbell, John P. et al. "The Development and Evaluation of Behaviorally Based Rating Scales," *Journal of Applied Psychology*, vol. 57 (1973).

Cascio, Wayne F. "Scientific, Legal and Operational Imperatives of Workable Performance Appraisal Systems," *Public Personnel Management*, vol. 11 (1982), pp. 367–375.

Clement, Ronald W. and Eileen K. Aranda. "Performance Appraisal in the Public Sector: Truth or Consequences," *Review of Public Personnel Administration* (fall 1984).

Daley, Dennis M. *Performance Appraisal in the Public Sector: Techniques and Applications*. Westport, Conn.: Quorum Books, 1992.

Daley, Dennis M. "Designing Effective Performance Appraisal Systems," in Stephen E. Condrey (ed.), *Handbook of Human Resource Management in Government*. Jossey-Bass, 1998, pp. 368–386.

Daley, Dennis M. "Public Sector Supervisory Performance Appraisal: Core Functions, Effectiveness Characteristics, and the Identification of Superstar Supervisors," *Review of Public Personnel Administration*, vol. 19, no. 4 (fall 1999), pp. 65–75.

DeLeon, Linda and Ann J. Evans. "Multi-Source Performance Appraisals," *Review of Public Personnel Administration*, vol. 17, no. 1 (winter 1997), pp. 22–36.

Feild, Hubert S. and William H. Holley. "The Relationship of Performance Appraisal System Characteristics to Verdicts in Selected Employment Discrimination Cases," *Academy of Management Journal*, vol. 25 (1982).

Fox, Charles J. "Employee Performance Appraisal: The Keystone Made of Clay," in Carolyn Ban and Norma M. Riccucci (eds.), *Public Personnel Management: Current Concerns, Future Challenges*. White Plains, N.Y.: Longman Press, 1991.

Gabris, Gerald T. "Merit Pay Mania: Transforming Polarized Support and Opposition into a Working Consensus," in Stephen E. Condrey (ed.), *Handbook of Human*

Resource Management in Government. San Francisco: Jossey-Bass, 1998, pp. 627–657.

Gabris, Gerald T. and Kenneth Mitchell. "Merit Based on Performance Appraisal and Productivity: Do Employees Perceive the Connection?" *Public Productivity Review,* vol. 9 (1985), pp. 311–327.

Halachmi, Arie and Marc Holzer. "Merit Pay, Performance Targeting, and Productivity," *Review of Public Personnel Administration,* vol. 7, no. 2 (1987), pp. 80–91.

Harland, Lynn K. and Deborah K. Sanders. "Evaluating the Impact of a 360 Degree Feedback Performance Appraisal System: A Field Experiment," study for city of Omaha, Nebraska, Personnel Department, 1999.

Hughs, Garry L. and Erich P. Prien. "An Evaluation of Alternate Scoring Methods for the Mixed Standard Scale," *Personnel Psychology,* vol. 39 (1986), pp. 839–848.

Kellough, Edward J. and Sally Coleman Selden. "Pay for Performance in State Government," *Review of Public Personnel Administration,* vol. 17, no. 1 (1997), pp. 5–21.

Kellough, Edward J. and Henry Lu. "The Paradox of Merit Pay in the Public Sector," *Review of Public Personnel Administration,* vol. 13, no. 2. (1993), pp. 45–64.

Kleiman, Lawrence S. and Richard L. Durham. "Performance Appraisal, Promotion and the Courts: A Critical Review," *Personnel Psychology,* vol. 34 (1981).

Landy, Frank J. et al. "Behaviorally Anchored Scales for Rating the Performance of Police Officers," *Journal of Applied Psychology* (December 1976).

Latham, Gary P. and K. N. Wexley. "Behavioral Observation Scales for Performance Appraisal Purposes," *Personnel Psychology,* vol. 30 (1977).

Levinson, H. "Appraisal of What Performance?" *Harvard Business Review,* vol. 54 (July–August 1976).

Levinson, Priscilla. *A Guide for Improving Performance Appraisal: A Handbook.* Washington, D.C.: U.S. Office of Personnel Management, 1979.

Lovrich, Nicholas P. Jr., Paul L. Shaffer, Ronald H. Hopkins, and Donald A. Yale. "Do Public Servants Welcome or Fear Merit Evaluation of Their Performance?" *Public Administration Review,* vol. 44 (1980), pp. 214–222.

McEvoy, Glenn M. "Predicting Managerial Performance: A Seven Year Assessment Center Validation Study," *Proceedings of the Academy of Management,* vol. 48 (1988), pp. 277–281.

McGregor, Douglas. "An Uneasy Look at Performance Appraisal," *Harvard Business Review* (May-June 1957; reprinted May–June 1975).

McNish, Linda C. "A Critical Review of Performance Appraisal at the Federal Level: The Experience of the PHS," *Review of Public Personnel Administration,* vol. 7, no. 1 (1986), pp. 42–56.

Marcoulides, George A. and R. Bryant Mills. "Employee Performance Appraisal: A New Technique," *Review of Public Personnel Administration,* vol. 8, no. 3 (1988), pp. 105–115.

Nachmias, David and Paul J. Moderacki. "Patterns of Support for Merit Pay and EEO Performance: The Inherent Difficulties of Implementing Innovation," *Policy Studies Journal,* vol. 11 (1982), pp. 318–327.

Nalbandian, John. "Performance Appraisal: If Only People Weren't Involved," *Public Administration Review* (May–June 1981).

National Research Council. Pay for Performance. Washington National Academy Press, 1991.

Newton, Tim and Patricia Findley. "Playing God: The Performance of Appraisal," in *Strategic Human Resource Management (The Open University)*. London: Sage, 1998, pp. 128–143.

Nigro, Lloyd G. "Attitudes of Federal Employees Toward Performance Appraisal and Merit Pay: Implications for CSRA Implementation," *Public Administration Review*, vol. 41 (1981), pp. 84–86.

Pearce, Jane L. and James L. Perry. "Federal Merit Pay: A Longitudinal Analysis," *Public Administration Review*, vol. 43 (1983), pp. 315–325.

Perry, James L. "Merit Pay in the Public Sector: The Case for a Failure of Theory," *Review of Public Personnel Administration*, vol. 7, no. 1 (1986), pp. 57–69.

Perry, James L. "Linking Pay to Performance: The Controversy Continues," in Carolyn Ban and Norma M. Riccucci (eds.), *Public Personnel Management: Current Concerns, Future Challenges*. White Plains, N.Y.: Longman Press, 1991.

Schay, Brigitte W. "Effects of Performance-Contingent Pay on Employee Attitudes," *Public Personnel Management*, vol. 17 (1988), pp. 237–250.

Schinagl, Mary S. *History of Efficiency Ratings in the Federal Government*. New York: Bookman Associates, 1966.

Selden, Sally Coleman. "Human Resources Practices in State Government: Findings from a National Survey, Government Performance Project, Maxwell School, Syracuse, New York, Syracuse University, 1999.

Sherwood, Frank and Barton Wechsler. "The 'Hadacol' of the Eighties: Paying Senior Public Managers for Performance," *Review of Public Personnel Administration*, vol. 7, no. 1 (1986), pp. 27–41.

U.S. General Accounting Office. *Performance Management: How Well Is the Government Dealing with Poor Performance?* Washington, D.C.: USGAO, 1990.

U.S. Merit Systems Protection Board. *Federal Personnel Policies and Practices—Perspectives from the Workplace*. Washington, D.C.: USMSPB, 1987.

U.S. Merit Systems Protection Board. *The Changing Federal Workplace*. Washington, D.C.: USMSPB, 1998.

U.S. Merit Systems Protection Board. *Performance Management and Recognition System: Linking Pay to Performance*. Washington, D.C.: USMSPB, 1987.

U.S. Merit Systems Protection Board. *Working for America: A Federal Employee Survey*. Washington, D.C.: USMSPB, 1990.

U.S. Merit Systems Protection Board. *Federal Supervisors and Poor Performance*. Washington, D.C.: USMSPB, July 1999.

8

Training and Development

**PROLOGUE: THE FUTURE OF TRAINING IN THE NEW ERA
OF KNOWLEDGE MANAGEMENT**

Perhaps the most interesting management movement of the last century has been the effort to lead organizations to re-examine both what investments are being made in human assets and how organizations can promote knowledge sharing within their own workforces. Organizations faced with being both more productive and more innovative in order to compete are realizing that there's a huge problem capturing their collective expertise. Some have called this the "you don't know what you know" problem.

The movement, in terms of names, goes under the label "knowledge management" (KM, or "intellectual capital," if you like a more financial management edge), but behind these innocuous terms there's a major organizational initiative that is verging on becoming a revolution or at least the next big management fad. The consulting leaders in this arena see tremendous growth. According to *Information Week*, the Gartner Group reported $1.5 billion in consulting fees for knowledge management services, using the period for 1996 to 1997 as its baseline, and predicts it will reach $5 billion by 2001. Major corporations have set up corporate knowledge programs and designated CKOs or CLOs (i.e., chief knowledge officers or chief learning officers). By the close of the 1990s, a handful of federal agencies—National Security Agency (NSA), National Institutes of Health (NIH), and Social Security Administration (SSA), among others—had also created CKO positions or something akin to a chief knowledge strategist.

What's happening here? More appropriately, one might want to ask the following key questions:

How important is knowledge work to organizations?
What is KM and what significant difference does it make?
What's the relationship between investments in employee development and KM?

In its 1997 report on KM, the Delphi Group, a Boston-based research consulting firm in this area offers a start at some answers. Its surveys show that most organizations (60% of 700 corporations surveyed) recognize that the majority of their workforces consists of "knowledge workers." Of course, public sector agencies have always known that the vast majority of their workforce are knowledge workers, but that doesn't necessarily mean that a new management concept has to be developed. On the issue of what organizations are doing about KM, Delphi reports the following breakdown of responses:

Latest management fad, 3%
New spin on old technologies, 12%
Valuable way to organize and use organizational information, 53%
Major new strategic imperative for staying competitive, 32%

On the one hand these numbers are encouraging; only 15% are skeptical about intent (it's a fad) and original value (it's recycled). On the other hand, there is a very large gap between "valuable way to organize" and "major new strategic imperative."

Knowledge management is mostly about innovation, but not the old idea of innovation as individual invention. Knowledge management accepts that there will always be great inventors or individuals with great original ideas—but innovation is seen differently today. Primarily this is because of the overwhelming amount of information available and quickly accessible via the Internet, the dramatic pace of change in technology change, and the necessity of engaging different participants (contractors, customers, co-workers, even competitors) in the discovery, creation, application, and growth aspects of new solutions. Also, technology change makes possible much greater and faster exchange of ideas and raises expectations about responsiveness, so a core principle of KM is connection and collaboration—across all parts of the organization. Conversely, KM reminds professionals that one of the greatest barriers to connecting people in organizations is vertical structure and hierarchy.

What elevates it as a concept is that it's much more than a compilation or assembly of data and information or a new technology for exchanging E-mail or messages. Knowledge management emphasizes "tacit knowledge," or what

Thomas Davenport has termed the outcome of "minds at work." Putting it all together means that organizations must create specific strategies and processes to link workers and share information and experiences on old and new problems. One corporate KM leader calls its process for KM "shared learning," which is defined as the capability to "capture, store, transfer, and use our knowledge, learning, and effective practices across the corporation to accelerate improvement." The only quibble one might have with this shared learning definition is the omission of "and to promote new innovations."

How does an organization practice KM? Most consultants and advocates would argue that some kind of CKO or CLO is required. There must also be dedicated resources for educational investments, technology support and new systems for collaboration and the exchange of ideas, more accessible archives for obtaining and storing information, directories and listings of individuals' expertise and interests to create new networks or what some call "communities of practice," and such forums as "knowledge fairs" to provide employees with opportunities to share ideas and discuss problems and projects. Finally, organizations must create measurements that show both the economic value they are creating with KM investments and levels of innovation.

While the above list may sound formidable, the big problem with moving to KM, consultants state, is cultural. In theory, the majority of the public sector workforce is made up of knowledge workers, and the need to communicate and share information and knowledge is widely accepted. Too many professionals equate their knowledge and the information to which they have access as "power," however; sharing without getting something in return is seen as politically naive. In addition, there are all those functional hierarchical boundaries that are also major barriers. Indeed, the organization must carefully examine how its culture promotes—or in most cases—impedes knowledge sharing. Delphi's 1997 survey confirmed that the majority of the industry firms surveyed identified culture as the largest obstacle to KM.

That will be no surprise to anyone in the public sector, which is still struggling with how to make teams work and how to share information both within and across agencies, but public sector professionals will find much to like about KM. Most significant is how it addresses the third and final question of the relationship to employee development. Knowledge management creates a much larger framework in which to put training and employee development programs. In the early days of the Clinton administration, the promise was made and repeated often that in exchange for cuts in the workforce and restructuring, training programs for the workforce would be fixed at a minimum percentage of personnel salary cost—at least 4%. After all, more work would be demanded from fewer workers, so a greater investment in that workforce's knowledge, skills, and competencies would be essential. Public sector training investments are not even calculated or reported on in most governments and are generally thought to significantly lag behind the private sector, which uses 6% and sometimes 8 to 10% as its budget baseline. As any KM theorist would note, the mere fact that you don't know what your investment is in your human capital says it all.

THE EVOLUTION OF TRAINING AND DEVELOPMENT

Traditionally, of all the major functions of personnel, training and development has been the most neglected. Part of this was due in to where training came in the personnel functional hierarchy. Organizations would be first concerned identifying staffing requirements, then making decisions about where employees work in fulfilling those requirements, followed by evaluation and advancement, recruitment, and hiring new employees to replace those who leave. Only after all of these priorities are attended to would an organization begin providing for some form of training and development in an effort to improve the capabilities of its employees. Given the scarce resources environment that many public organizations confront, there was little doubt as to which personnel area would be the first to be sacrificed in a budget crunch. Recessions in the 1980s and then the early 1990s were textbook examples of how state and local organizations drastically cut training in order to meet emergency budget cutback targets. Many jurisdictions met budget shortages via meat-axe approaches (e.g., they cut certain categories of line-item expenditures reputed to be "luxuries," such as travel, overtime, and especially training program costs). Consequently, training was hard-pressed to maintain any continuity, much less identity.

There is more to this problem than simple neglect or fiscal scarcity, however. Employee training and development efforts are sometimes viewed as problematical since such efforts entail the expenditure of public funds to develop human resources over which the organization has no real control. Although some organizations, such as the military, have linked many of their training programs to contractual arrangements whereby individuals promise to stay in the organization for certain periods of time (or provide reimbursement for the training received), most public organizations, unfortunately, have viewed training expenditures as a less-than-certain investment. Perhaps that is what is so encouraging about the KM movement—that it restates the fiscal proposition that if an organization is to be competitive it must make certain of its investments in its workforce.

If organizations can get by the fiscal dilemma, there are other conceptual problems inherent in training. Just as employees as individuals differ, they naturally have different training needs. Should training programs be shaped to fit the individual needs of the employee or the overall needs of the organization? An agency may develop one set of training assumptions tailored to meet what it considers to be its short- and long-range needs (in that order). At the same time, depending upon his or her previous background and aptitudes, an individual employee will have an independent set of training assumptions oriented toward different long- and short-range needs (in this order). There is a continuous degree of conflict between the assumed training needs of the organization and the assumed training needs of the individual. The task of any manager—indeed, an essential function—is to ensure equity for both sides, to the organization as well as to the individual. This question of equity is further complicated by the fact that many public employees (and their unions) have taken the view that training opportunities are basically another fringe benefit and should be part of the employee's compensation package.

Despite all these obstacles, however, public sector organizations have increasingly placed more emphasis on training and development. Surface acceptance has progressed to increasing commitment to training and development programs by many private and public sector organizations. First there was the establishment of larger and more sophisticated training programs, greater numbers of staff being hired as training specialists, and increasing support for external educational and tuition assistance programs. Second, training itself became somewhat of a growth industry—universities, contractors, consulting firms, technology vendors, conference management, and others began to offer a wide array of training courses—some supplementing, others in direct competition to what agencies were providing themselves. These "providers" would advertise and market their programs directly to employees at all levels to generate interest and stimulate demand for training.

Supervisors were also more supportive of training programs (within reason, of course), and expected to receive a fair share of training opportunities to develop and reward their employees. Employees perceived of training as a job right and expected to have both formal training during work time and informal training on the job. Perhaps James O'Toole, a leading quality of work life theorist, has said it best: "Most workers have an innate desire to grow . . . Apparently being able to satisfy the desire to grow and to learn on the job enhances worker self-esteem, satisfaction, loyalty, motivation, and *occasionally*, productivity."

As training evolved into sustainable and significant personnel management functions, it also became more decentralized. In the 1970s and 1980s, many training offices were established outside the usual personnel organization, frequently under the separate title of human resources or employee development. This raised the question as to where training belonged in the personnel management world, but by the mid-1990s, even within training organizations, decentralization had its impact. More organizational units and functions began taking care of their own training planning and took control of their training budgets, and at the higher level—executive development—some agencies have established their own "corporate university" or "corporate management development program." Essentially, as training has become more decentralized, executive development has

TABLE 8.1   Plans to Increase or Decrease Organizational Training
Budget (1997–1999)

Industry sector	Greater (%)	Same (%)	Less (%)
Manufacturing	37	60	3
Transportation/communications/utilities	35	58	6
Wholesale/retail trade	40	59	1
Finance/insurance/banking	41	48	11
Business services	52	46	2
Health services	28	63	9
Educational services	27	70	2
Public administration	27	60	13
All industries	35	60	5

Source: *The Public Manager* (summer 1999).

emerged as a separate enterprise within employee development. Naturally there
are numerous hybrid models, but training and development have clearly reached
a new plateau in terms of importance and value.

This does not mean, however, that training investments in the public sector
are keeping pace. As an industrywide survey taken in the late 1990s reveals about
plans for training budgets, the public sector is still "trailing edge" compared to
the private sector (see Table 8.1), but at least 85% of the agencies surveyed were
planning on maintaining or increasing funding levels.

TRAINING AND PERSONNEL RELATIONSHIPS

If there is such a thing as a traditional approach to personnel management, it
clearly includes training. Training is part of the process of development that advances and maintains individuals within an organization. While the words training and development have often been used interchangeably, there is a highly
significant line of demarcation between the two. Training is a tool; it is instruction
in a myriad of forms and settings, in which both technical and conceptual knowledge and skills are imparted to employees, both nonmanagers and managers.
Development is a process of advancing or progressing within an organization
while acquiring skills and experience. Development incorporated all training and
previous job assignments and organizational experiences into a total capability
package.

Viewed in this light, training is a primary tool or method of facilitating
development. It will necessarily vary, depending upon the stage of development
and the aspect of work involved. What kinds of training programs will be offered
and what emphasis will be placed on employee development are usually based

on several key criteria: (1) that training be job- or career-related; (2) that it be relevant to enhancing advancement potential; (3) that it be useful in improving organizational effectiveness; and (4) that it be of sufficient relevance and interest to employees. In the public sector, decisions about training programs are more often focused on the first criterion mentioned—job- or career-relatedness. In fact, this criterion is generally used as a guideline by most personnel units to approve or deny requests by employees for training.

How do the objectives of training and development fit into the objectives of personnel management? This can only be answered in organizational terms. First, what are the functions of personnel? What is personnel designed to do? As already mentioned, the most realistic answer is to ensure organization continuity or organizational survival. What personnel is most concerned with is making sure that organizations, through the people who make them up, have "human continuity."

Unfortunately, personnel all too often uses its responsibility in this area much too narrowly. Personnel generally sees its function as making sure that the organization can at any point bring to bear on any type of problem the right kinds of people to provide the right kinds of solutions. Personnel purports to develop those people, place them in the organization in the right positions, and ensure that for those people who are leaving the organization there are adequate replacements. Training, then, has its place in this organizational human resources cycle—staffing, placement, advancement, training and development, replacement, and informational support.

What seems conceptually logical falls far short in practice, however. Personnel management has often so specialized its functions that its focus has become concerned largely with the impacts of its own services. Personnel often doesn't compare in any systematic fashion *how* or even *if* it should face an organizational resource problem; for example, by new hiring, reassignment or transfer, training, *or* job redesign or some combination of these options. Rather, it prefers to solve recruitment, assignment, training, and work organizational problems as they are handed down to personnel management specialists and different personnel management divisions. Personnel all too often and by its own choice prefers to facilitate the implementation of organizational solutions rather than actively help shape the decision in the problem-solving phase.

As a result, trainers have become increasingly concerned about what they view as personnel's self-prescribed isolationism. In many cases this has moved training toward secession. Trainers seek autonomy in part to establish the creditability of their trade and in part to avoid the regulatory image that personnel so often conjures up. In a sense, trainers want to disassociate themselves from "those people who are always saying no because of this regulation or that"; they want to establish their own image. Further impacting this movement toward autonomy has been the drive to contract out training, or what is commonly re-

Training for Results

Training is inevitable. Like old age, it attacks each of us whether we like it or not. At birth, or before, we begin training to operate within our environments. When the training is satisfactory, we speak of adjustment or adaptation to life. When the training is unsatisfactory, the result is failure, neurosis, or perhaps psychosis. This generalization provides a fairly valid basis for further discussion of training or development, since any action taken to train an individual must be considered in the light of his or her prior experience and behavior which must be developed in the current environment.

But if training is inevitable, why all the fuss about training program development, development planning, need identification, etc., in an organization? It would seem that since "Experience is the best teacher," training in an organization is also inevitable. All that is really needed is a hire and a job; in time the hire will be trained.

An intelligent management looks at this inevitable process and asks some questions. Is experience actually the best teacher? What is the cost of training a qualified person? How do we know when the person has been trained? How long do we mean when we say, "In time, the hire will be trained?" Most important, management asks, "How do we know that the person has been trained to meet the goals we have set?"

These questions and the implications they raise require that training or personnel development be clearly defined in terms of management's goals, the fulfillment of which is the organization's first concern. From this viewpoint, training must be evaluated in terms of its contribution to these goals. The first question is not how, or even who but rather why. If experience is the "trainer" who can best help the organization meet its goals, then experience will be chosen to run the training function.

Source: Warren, Malcolm W. *Training for Results*. Reading, Mass.: Addison-Wesley, 1979, p. 1. © 1979 Addison-Wesley Publishing Company, Inc. Reprinted with permission.

ferred to as "outsourcing." Much of the movement toward outsourcing has been caused by public sector organizations requiring that training pay for its own costs by charging organizational unit fees for each employee who attends a training course. From a management perspective, this has a number of implications. First, it forces training programs to adopt a value-added mentality. Since the organization is paying fees to cover training costs, then the organization will want to ensure that it's getting its money's worth. Second, the fees charged invite a comparison to the competition (in short, other training sources). This is particularly the case with technology or computer training or other highly specialized training courses. Organizations can "shop around" and compare what it would cost to send their employees to a computer software supplier, university, or other training supplier that offers its own training courses taught by its experts.

It is little wonder, then, that by the 1980s contracting out training was applied to more and different types of programs. Montgomery County, Maryland (a suburban county on the north border of Washington, D.C.) provides a good case study of why a prosperous county would contract out its basic management development program. Dennis Misler, the county's training director at the time, explained in an article that the county's six-person training staff was only able to offer four sections each year to approximately 100 of the 1,300 supervisors in the county. Simple math dictated that at that rate the county would have needed over 13 years to reach existing supervisors, not to mention any new supervisors hired or promoted. The county was facing a severe budget crisis and opted to reduce its training staff by two-thirds. Half the savings were returned to fund outside contracts for contracted training courses. Eight contractors were selected after a carefully developed request for proposal (RFP) was submitted and responded to with 159 different new course proposals in a highly competitive local area. The county was able to revamp its management program and offer at least some courses in the program to over 1,200 supervisors the first year. By the mid-1980s, four of the original contractors remained with the city, and supervisory participation remained quite high. From Misler's standpoint, this was a major success. In his words, "It has been a happy marriage. Ironically, as the training unit got smaller, it became able to do more . . . Contracting out and the circumstances that brought it about in Montgomery County at first seemed like the death knell for training. It has in fact turned out to be an injection of invigorating new life."

The above case illustrates some of the sought-after advantages from a resources perspective for outsourcing, but there are major implications. Somewhere in the organization (the training staff?) must reside the expertise to plan and prioritize training needs and then evaluate and assess outcomes. Freedom from the direct instructional responsibility does not mean that training staffs are nothing more than contract management specialists. Training must continue the major effort it embarked upon since the 1980s to professionalize itself. This process begins with training staff members who are being urged to move through their own professional development process. The American Society for Training and Development (ASTD), which has long played a key role in both developing the training and development profession and professionalizing training, issued numerous statements in the mid-1980s on what this must include. The ASTD's required activity categories include the following:

1. Analyzing needs and evaluating results
2. Designing and developing training programs and materials

3. Delivering training and development programs and services
4. Advising and counseling
5. Managing training activities
6. Maintaining organization relationships
7. Doing research to advance the training field
8. Developing professional skills and expertise
9. Developing basic skills and knowledge

The impact of ''professionalization'' on training's separate identity remains to be seen. Certainly such an effort takes training far beyond presenting orientation programs, explaining affirmative action policies, and providing 40 hours of supervisory management training for new supervisors, and it means more than simply negotiating contractors' proposals and doing contract oversight. Above all, trainers must be concerned about human development objectives and then focus on upgrading the activities and techniques to be used. These objectives can be condensed into the following three critical functions:

To plan what people need to know, both now and in the future
To stress the ability to communicate and apply—to ensure that what needs to be known is actually learned and used
To be *seriously* involved with the whole process of human development in helping people learn more about themselves

To do the above requires accomplished expertise in the designing methods of training, planning training, and training evaluation regardless of whether training is being provided internally or externally.

METHODS OF TRAINING: THE DESIGN ISSUE

The primary variables that organizations consider when implementing their training objectives are format (i.e., in what way and by whom training should be presented) and time (i.e., how often and how long training sessions should last). It is generally assumed that training programs with longer time intervals between the program segments will have more impact than those with segments that are bunched together. This is especially true for supervisory training, in which some form of behavior modification is the ultimate objective. While there is a great variety of training formats, almost all would fall into one of the following general categories:

1. *Skills training or demonstration*—Training to teach specific craft or equipment skills, either in-house or through an outside contractor, in which the employee receives initial or refresher instruction about specific processes or skills.

2. *Coaching or on-the-job training*—Direct personal instruction, usually in the work setting, in which an "expert" oversees initial work efforts by a learner and provides corrective advice and continued monitoring of work output.

3. *Formal or informal lecture or classroom instruction*—A variety of classroom methods are available to organizations whereby they can assemble and instruct groups of employees or assist employees in obtaining instruction on their own at nearby academic institutions. Organizations can and often do provide tuition reimbursement for outside course work that can be shown to be job-related.

4. *Role playing or "sensitivity/T-group" training*—A group of techniques has evolved from this concept of assembling small groups of employees to directly and openly approach problems of human behavior and interpersonal relationships. Used as a major tool to developing more "sensitive" and aware managers or more emphatic or responsive employees, sensitivity training usually requires the services of a professional "facilitator" and relies heavily on the willingness of individuals to confront emotional and subjective aspects of their behavior openly. Many variations of role playing or sensitivity training are being incorporated into work behavior areas, such as workforce diversity, sexual harassment, or team-building.

5. *Job rotation programs*—This technique can be established on a number of levels and is designed to provide employees with varying work tasks and assignments in order to increase employee experience. Some offices have developed limited versions of this concept (usually called cross-functional training), in which each job and thus the entire work of the office is learned by each employee. More formal systems also exist in which new employees are rotated through different offices to facilitate organizational familiarity or develop more general work skills. As teams have gained in prominence in modern organizations, job rotation has become almost a continuous process for building new work skills and promoting collaboration and worker cooperation.

6. *Special conferences and seminars*—These are special meetings of employees to discuss and exchange ideas about process, problems, and techniques. The great advantage of this conference or "retreat" (some organizations have taken to calling such off-site learning sessions "advances") concept lies in assembling employees away from day-to-day operations to focus on a specific agenda that is usually change-oriented or evaluative in terms of assessing the need for future change.

7. *Modeling, simulation, and self-paced learning training*—A plethora of simulated real-life situations have been developed to provide individuals with various contrived experiences. Many "games" involve

extensive applications of role playing, which affords participants the opportunity to view, analyze, and practice behavior patterns and related outcomes. Some of the major advances in this area involve the use of computers and videos that rely on self-paced learning methods, whereby the individual reads, responds, and is evaluated at the end of each session. Technology and computer training is especially well-suited for this type of training method.

8. *Exchange and sabbatical programs*—The concept of getting the individual out of the organizational environment and into a totally different one for a substantial period of time—up to two years—represents the most advanced training concept. Exchange programs are worked out between different organizations to send their professionals to work in new positions, while sabbaticals involve sending an individual off to an academic or research program.

The determination of which training methods should be employed will depend on the subject matter, the instructional preferences of the employees involved, and the appropriateness of the method to the organizational environment. It could be said up until the 1990s that little systematic work had been accomplished that effectively monitored what kinds of methods work better with what kinds of subjects and what types of employees. This simply is no longer true. In his recent assessment of employee development trends in government, Montgomery Von Wart notes that training as a whole comprehends the importance of linking the basics of learning theory to instructional methods to results. Essentially there are training principles that recognize the importance of learning theories. For example, Von Wart identifies the following four different learning theories:

Behavioralism, which "stresses the idea that learning is behavioral change produced by the effect of external stimuli"

Social learning, which "stresses the importance of observation and social context"

Cognitive theory, which "emphasizes learner activity in putting together patterns in unique and meaningful ways"

Adult learning, which "reminds educators of the adult learner's active curiosity, motivation for self-improvement, preference for practical (as opposed to academic) problem solving and capacity for self-imposed learning management"

To Von Wart's categories, one might now add "virtual learning," a powerful new learning model advanced by Roger Shank and his colleagues at the Institute for Learning Sciences at Northwestern University. Virtual learning stresses learning by doing through computer simulations presented via multimedia technology that allows the learner to discover situations, to fail in training exercises, and to learn from failure. Shank's indictment of current "learning systems" used in training is scathing—"The way managers attempt to help their people acquire knowledge and skills has absolutely nothing to do with the way people learn. Trainers rely on lectures and tests, memorization and manuals. They train people just like schools teach students. Both rely on 'telling,' and no one remembers what's taught, and what's told doesn't translate into useable skills." As will be discussed at the end of the chapter, there may still be a future for classroom training (and even graduate programs at universities). The point is simply that the choice of instructional methodology must be based on learning theories, whether traditional or radical.

CAREER DEVELOPMENT AND THE EMPLOYEE

Training and development are also vital to the employee's perspective of what is termed career development. A career can be defined as the sequence of positions within job fields that an individual holds over time. Career planning and development is the ongoing process of evaluating an individual's strengths and weaknesses in order to determine a personal strategy by which to pursue individual growth. Unfortunately many individuals don't know what they want in the way of a "career" path, and their organizations frequently don't have any better idea about what their employees should be doing in this regard. (See Figure 8.1.) This is all the more complicated in the current professional work environment, in which many workers don't think of spending their career in one organization and are inclined to think of their career as a series of five to seven years within one sector. Couple this with the psychological impacts of downsizing in the 1990s and one could argue that the entire concept of career has been discredited, if not made unrealistic.

Still, generally speaking, there are four basic phases of career or professional development.

Entry phase—A break-in time period in which the new employee will achieve a journeyworker's level (i.e., adequate working level of operational competence)

Specialist/professional phase—A period in which the employee concentrates on performing a set of specific work assignments involving technical and work skills

Generalist/team leader phase—A period in which specific technical skills are less important and broader work group or supervisory coordination responsibilities are involved

Management/executive phase—A period in which the employee assumes responsibilities for administering and directing work operations, for managing the execution of programs, and for formulating plans for future organizational action

Type of Training

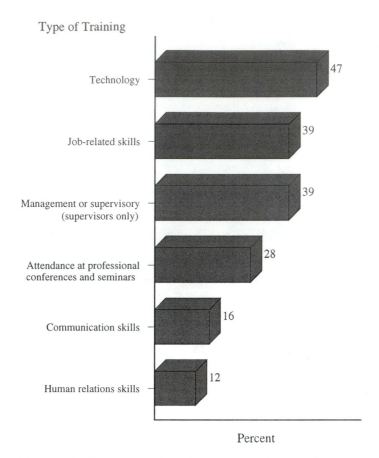

Percent

FIGURE 8.1   Percentage of employees saying they need various types of training. *Source*: MSPB Merit Principles Survey, 1992.

While employees may pursue a career path in any of the latter three phases, many employees are expected to and do chart their career paths through each of the four phases, culminating in a top managerial position. Training priorities obviously vary for each of the career path phases. Presumably new employees are hired with a modicum of skills so that they are capable of immediately performing work related to their assignment. The primary development need here is to acquaint new employees with the organizational structure in which they have been placed. Some form of orientation can generally accomplish this. As employees become full-fledged specialists, their development needs will require even more knowledge of organizational structure and increased technological

---

Leadership

The only real training for leadership is leadership: You do not learn it by being an assistant or a deputy, only by being a boss. The advice Peter O'Toole gave to Michael Caine was that if he wanted to be a leading actor he must only play leading parts: much better to play Hamlet in Denver than Laertes on Broadway. In the same way, the best way to learn how to lead a big organization is by leading smaller ones.

Source: Jay, Antony. *Management and Machiavelli: An Inquiry into the Politics of Corporate Life*. New York: Holt, Rinehart and Winston, 1967, p. 177.

---

skills. They must stay abreast of changes in the state of the art concerning their specialties. Generalists will be concerned both with technical advances and the direct oversight of the specialists. In a knowledge-based work environment, generalists are sometimes referred to as multibased specialists; that is, they have to have multiple specialties that enable them to make different contributions to projects, cross-functional work teams, or other special efforts. Development, of course, will necessarily involve interpersonal social skills to be effective in different cultures and different work settings.

Managers must be fully adept with those interpersonal skills relating to the communication, motivation, and leadership aspects of employee interactions. Traditionally the number of individuals who were developed along these last lines would depend upon the organization's hierarchical structure. Training and development have always been tailored to individuals at each level of development. This in itself is one definition of the objectives for a training and development program. As organizations become flatter, consist more and more of multiple teams or projects, or have numerous professionals linked through technology across the country (or the globe), the importance of collaboration or teamwork (i.e., excellent interpersonal workskills) thus becomes paramount. Public sector organizations are reaching the point where interpersonal skills are essential for every professional and critical for every manager. Perhaps the most comprehensive summary of how the career path of a public manager defines itself over time is the statement of core competencies for the federal senior executive service.

As organizations have changed shape over time, so have careers. For comparison purposes, take one of the first examples of a career development guide or model, developed by the U.S. Department of Labor in the late 1970s, which presents training objectives for the organization to provide and the employee to

Executive Core Qualifications for the Federal Senior Executive Service (SES)

The Executive Core Qualifications (ECQ's) define the competencies and characteristics needed to build a federal corporate culture that drives for results, serves customers, and builds successful teams and coalitions within and outside the organization. The Executive Core Qualifications are required for entry to the Senior Executive Service and are used by many departments and agencies in selection, performance management, and leadership development for management and executive positions.

ECQ 1: Leading Change

This core qualification encompasses the ability to develop and implement an organizational vision that integrates key national and program goals, priorities, values, and other factors. Inherent to this ECQ is the ability to balance change and continuity; to continually strive to improve customer service and program performance within the basic government framework; to create a work environment that encourages creative thinking; and to maintain focus, intensity and persistence, even under adversity.

Key Characteristics

1. Exercising leadership and motivating managers to incorporate vision, strategic planning, and elements of quality management into the full range of the organization's activities; encouraging creative thinking and innovation; influencing others toward a spirit of service; designing and implementing new or cutting-edge programs/processes.
2. Identifying and integrating key issues affecting the organization, including political, economic, social, technological, and administrative factors.
3. Understanding the roles and relationships of the components of the national policy making and implementation process, including the President, political appointees, Congress, the judiciary, state and local governments, and interest groups; formulating effective strategies to balance those interests consistent with the business of the organization.
4. Being open to change and new information; tolerating ambiguity; adapting behavior and work methods in response to new information, changing conditions, or unexpected obstacles; adjusting rapidly to new situations warranting attention and resolution.

5. Display a high level of initiative, effort and commitment to public service; being proactive and achievement-oriented; being self-motivated; pursuing self-development; seeking feedback from others and opportunities to master new knowledge.
6. Dealing effectively with pressure; maintaining focus and intensity and remaining persistent, even under adversity; recovering quickly from setbacks.

ECQ 2: Leading People

This core qualification involves the ability to design and implement strategies that maximize employee potential and foster high ethical standards in meeting the organization's vision, mission, and goals.

Key Characteristics

1. Providing leadership in setting the work force's expected performance levels commensurate with the organization's strategic objectives; inspiring, motivating, and guiding others toward goal accomplishment; empowering people by sharing power and authority.
2. Promoting quality through effective use of the organization's performance management system (e.g., establishing performance standards, appraising staff accomplishments using the developed standards, and taking action to reward, counsel, and remove employees, as appropriate).
3. Valuing cultural diversity and other differences; fostering an environment in which people who are culturally diverse can work together cooperatively and effectively in achieving organizational goals.
4. Assessing employees' unique developmental needs and providing developmental opportunities that maximize employees' capabilities and contribute to the achievement of organizational goals; developing leadership in others through coaching and mentoring.
5. Fostering commitment, team spirit, pride, trust, and group identity; taking steps to prevent situations that could result in unpleasant confrontations.
6. Resolving conflicts in a positive and constructive manner. This includes promoting labor/management partnerships and dealing effectively with employee relations issues, attending to morale and organizational climate issues, handling administrative, labor management, and EEO issues, and taking disciplinary actions when other means have not been successful.

ECQ 3: Results Driven

This core qualification stresses accountability and continuous improvement. It includes the ability to make timely and effective decisions and produce results through strategic planning and the implementation and evaluation of programs and policies.

Key Characteristics

1. Understanding and appropriately applying procedures, requirements, regulations, and policies related to specialized expertise; understanding linkage between administrative competencies and mission needs; keeping current on issues, practices, and procedures in technical areas.
2. Stressing results by formulating strategic program plans that assess policy/program feasibility and include realistic short- and long-term goals and objectives.
3. Exercising good judgment in structuring and organizing work and setting priorities; balancing the interests of clients and readily readjusting priorities to respond to customer demands.
4. Anticipating and identifying, diagnosing, and consulting on potential or actual problem areas relating to program implementation and goal achievement; selecting from alternative courses of corrective action; taking action from developed contingency plans.
5. Setting program standards; holding self and others accountable for achieving these standards; acting decisively to modify standards to promote customer service and/or the quality of programs and policies.
6. Identifying opportunities to develop and market new products and services within or outside of the organization; taking risks to pursue a recognized benefit or advantage.

ECQ 4: Business Acumen

This core qualification involves the ability to acquire and administer human, financial, material, and information resources in a manner that instills public trust and accomplishes the organization's mission, and the ability to use new technology to enhance decision making.

Key Characteristics

1. Assessing current and future staffing needs based on organizational goals and budget realities; applying merit principles to develop, select, and manage a diverse work force.

2. Overseeing the allocation of financial resources; identifying cost-effective approaches; establishing and assuring the use of internal controls for financial systems.

3. Managing the budgetary process, including preparing and justifying a budget and operating the budget under organizational and congressional procedures; understanding the marketing expertise necessary to ensure appropriate funding levels.

4. Overseeing procurement and contracting procedures and processes.

5. Integrating and coordinating logistical operations.

6. Ensuring the efficient and cost-effective development and utilization of management information systems and other technological resources that meet the organization's needs; understanding the impact of technological changes on the organization.

ECQ 5: Building Coalitions/Communications

This core qualification involves the ability to explain, advocate, and express facts and ideas in a convincing manner and to negotiate with individuals and groups internally and externally. It also involves the ability to develop an expansive professional network with other organizations and to identify the internal and external politics that impact the work of the organization.

Key Characteristics

1. Representing and speaking for the organizational unit and its work (e.g., presenting, explaining, selling, defining, and negotiating) to those within and outside the office (e.g., agency heads and other government executives, corporate executives, Office of Management and Budget officials, congressional members and staff, the media, and clientele and professional groups); making clear and convincing oral presentations to individuals and groups; listening effectively and clarifying information; facilitating an open exchange of ideas.

2. Establishing and maintaining working relationships with internal organizational units (e.g., other program areas and staff support functions); approaching each problem situation with a clear perception of organizational and political reality; using contacts to build and strengthen internal support bases; getting understanding and support from higher level management.

3. Developing and enhancing alliances with external groups (e.g., other agencies or firms, state and local governments, Congress, and clientele groups); engaging in cross-functional activities; finding common ground with a widening range of stakeholders.

4. Working in groups and teams; conducting briefings and other meetings; gaining cooperation from others to obtain information and accomplish goals; facilitating win–win situations.
5. Considering and responding appropriately to the needs, feelings, and capabilities of different people in different situations; being tactful and treating others with respect.
6. Seeing that reports, memoranda and other documents reflect the position and work of the organization in a clear, convincing, and organized manner.

Source: U.S. Office of Personnel Management (http://www.opm/gov/leader/ecq.htm).

achieve. The department created model career patterns for its various occupational fields. It then charted out the various phases of myriad careers by grade level, indicating the objectives for each phase, desirable assignments, and appropriate education and training activities. Employees wishing to advance would know what was specifically expected of them in one career period if they were to be advanced to the next. Of course, as with any such program, there was always the possibility that luck or politics will intervene in the normal process; but at the very least, the rules of the game—the way to the top—were clearly defined and highly visible.

In 2000, such career development models still exist in concept, but they take into consideration two additional elements—horizontal development and new skills requirements. Career models have been supplanted by what are called ''learning paths.'' Within a professional specialization, there are now other assignments, projects, details, and work units whereby an individual can consider moving ''horizontally'' to acquire new skills and stay on his or her employee development track.

Even more important, learning paths now define what new skills and knowledge, technology capabilities, and other competencies are needed for positions at different levels (actually, more plateaus). For a good example, look at the descriptions of the core competencies for federal senior executives in the box labeled ''Executive Core Qualifications for the Federal Senior Executive Service (SES).'' Also tied to this knowledge of what you need to know to do a job at a higher level (your next promotion) is the knowledge of what's changing in your own position, what you need to learn to keep current, and what's available for training (see figures 8.2 and 8.3). For years, trainers warned about professional obsolescence or the rate of change of knowledge and skills in a profession to no avail, but technology finally made organizations realize that job skills must be

"Our budget for training has..."

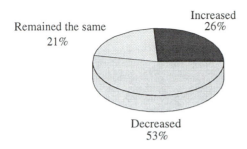

Remained the same
21%

Increased
26%

Decreased
53%

"Our budget for training is adequate."

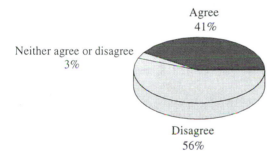

Agree
41%

Neither agree or disagree
3%

Disagree
56%

FIGURE 8.2 Views of survey respondents on two questions concerning training budgets. *Source*: MSPB telephone survey of HRD specialists, April 1994.

continually increased to keep pace with new demands on the organization and new developments. The question is no longer why invest in training and for whom; it is now how much and how often.

The questions of how much and how often lead directly to how organizations plan and evaluate their training investments. To integrate training effectively into career development requires two levels of planning. The first occurs on an individual level, during which employees schedule and evaluate what kinds of training they will need and when. The second level involves planning the total training program for the organization, or what is termed *training needs assessment*.

ON PLANNING TRAINING: THE STRATEGY ISSUE

"Failing to plan is planning to fail," or so the management adage goes. Few would argue that some form of planning effort for training is a vital first stage

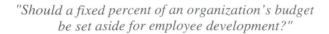

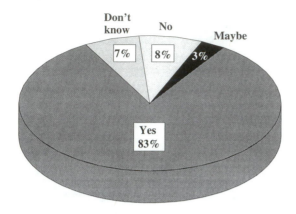

FIGURE 8.3 Views of survey respondents on a question concerning a fixed budget allocation for employee development. *Note*: Totals do not add to 100 because of rounding. *Source*: MSPB telephone survey of HRD specialists, April 1994.

in developing training programs. Planning is so significant in the training and development area that it falls under its own title: training needs assessment. If training is to be effective, it is argued, a careful diagnosis of what training is needed is essential. As a diagnostic tool, needs assessment will ensure that training is relevant to both the short-run performance deficiencies and long-run career development needs of employees by identifying training priorities. In the current environment of resource scarcity, the necessity of making such determinations seems almost absolute.

Of course, the planning of training goes beyond identifying in what subject areas training should be conducted. Needs assessment rightfully must consider the level of training needed for different kinds of employees, the best learning sequence for conducting the training, and the most effective methods and techniques of presenting the training. While more attention is being paid to these latter problems of level, sequence, and methods, the major difficulty facing most trainers is to ascertain what training employees need. (See Figure 8.4.)

A variety of techniques of needs assessment has been established; most training handbooks and numerous how-to-do-it training publications review some of the possible methods, such as interviews, discussion meetings, questionnaires, review of career plans, critical incident analysis, task or job analysis, and review of performance appraisal data. These techniques fall into the following six generally accepted categories:

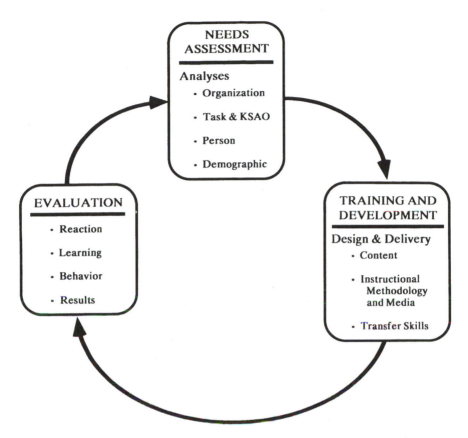

FIGURE 8.4 A systems approach to training and development. *Source*: Ban, Carolyn, Sue Faerman, and Norma M. Riccucci. "Productivity and the Personnel Process," in Marc Holzer (ed.), *Public Productivity Handbook*. New York: Marcel Dekker, 1991.

1. Survey of employees
2. Interviews of employees, supervisors, or work experts
3. Review of performance evaluation and assessment center data
4. Model career planning
5. Job analysis
6. Human resources information systems approaches

The first, employee surveys, involves written individual opinion questionnaires (in which individuals are asked to estimate their skill levels, corresponding training needs, and interests). A second approach involves extensive interviewing of a sample of individuals, supervisors, or work experts in specific occupational or job categories. The oral interview may be both direct (e.g., What kinds of training do you need?) or indirect (e.g., How would you go about doing this kind of task or handling this type of situation?). This format requires that the interviewer identify a training or skill need level that is related to job performance and level. A third approach involves a review of performance evaluation reports or assessment center data results whereby a group of supervisors or some other designated group reviews individual performance records, tests, inspection reports, career plans, and/or other data in order to assess what would be the most relevant training programs to offer various employees.

As discussed in the previous section, model career planning constitutes a fourth approach, whereby each functional or occupational work category is planned out against time and career grade objectives with approximate work assignment and training program objectives. Such model career paths are usually planned and modified by work groups of highly superior professionals in the various categories. The model career path functions quite similarly to a college bulletin, which lists courses and degree requirements. Both the individual and the supervisor retain the option to make choices and select only those developmental experiences that they deem appropriate.

The fifth approach is that of functional job analysis, whereby managerial positions are analyzed for functions, activities, and tasks performed. This level of detail affords a further basis for the determination of the corresponding knowledge, skills, and aptitudes needed to perform each task successfully. Functional job analysis involves extensive survey work and position analysis on a continuing basis.

The sixth and last approach, originally referred to as HRIS (human resources information system), involves the development of an extensive computerized position–person inventory data system that now incorporates learning paths. Initially, an HRIS would compare all position requirements against the current skill levels of employees and project training priorities. The HRIS conceptualized training as one of several planning alternatives for professional development, and compared training to position redesign, employment, and placement options. In 2000, what was once a massive database system is now off-the-shelf human resources management software that comes as one option for managing the personnel and training departments. Many of these systems incorporate annual surveys of employees, appraisals by supervisors, and assessments by unit managers and executives into the framework as well.

While there is a plethora of methods for conducting a training needs assessment, this does not mean that there still aren't issues over validation. There are still problems inherent in the definition of need. Most troublesome is time. What is the need for training for work being performed now and what will it be for work that is to be done three to five years from now? What if present work skills and most probable future work skills are in conflict? What should be the training program then? Technology training is a superb example of the problem here. A review of training catalogs in the 1980s and 1990s will show any number of courses from word processing to programming to Website design. Should anyone be given training in a skill that has become obsolete via advancing technology? Oddly, one might look back at the 1990s and wonder why so much training was invested in "team building" and "diversity training" and wonder why such basics were taught in the classroom.

When it comes to "training needs," we have to consider the opinions of superiors, subordinates, peers, and professional training specialists. All can be involved in the process of identifying training needs, and all are likely to have different opinions. Still, what individuals want to do is as important as any other factor in the needs assessment process. Training needs assessment strives to be what Roger Kaufman and Fenwick English have defined as "a humanizing process to help make sure that we are using our time and the learner's time in the most effective and efficient manner possible." No matter what theory of learning or method of training is involved, the motivation of the learners still counts.

ON ASSESSING TRAINING: THE EVALUATION ISSUE

Last but not least, the problem of evaluation stands at the core of the entire training and development knot. While many an annual report will boast of the employees who have been trained during the past year, such statistics must be viewed with great suspicion. It is a common mistake to assume that the number of individuals who have been subjected to a training experience is equal to the number of individuals who have acquired a new skill or expertise. The only way of even knowing what has been gained through training is to have developed evaluation criteria prior to all training experience. Without baseline points of performance, subsequent attempts to measure results will be futile. A further distinction must be made between measurement, which quantifies the results of training, and evaluation, which seeks to ascertain whether a training effort is worth its cost. A principal factor in the disincentive cycle of training is that public managers generally have neither measures of training effectiveness nor evaluations of training program utility.

Evaluations of training and development efforts are necessarily multifaceted. Do you measure the individual's subjective reaction to a training experience or do you seek an objective measure of what was learned? Another approach is to measure the change in job behavior—perhaps an increase in productivity— that might have occurred as a result of training, but if large elements of the organization have been recently taught new techniques, a more rational method of assessing utility would be to seek a measure of overall organizational effectiveness. Did it increase, decrease, or stay the same?

What Are the Implications of the Demographic Changes in the Workforce for Training and Development?

First, government agencies will need to begin to conduct more extensive needs assessments to determine the types of training and development experiences that are needed to meet both organizational and individual needs. Specifically, government agencies will need to conduct organizational analyses to determine the existing levels of support, both financial and philosophical, available to training and development efforts, and work to increase those levels of support, as necessary. Further, government agencies will need to conduct demographic analyses focusing on protected class people, including older workers, examine current training and development practices, determine the extent to which these practices meet the needs of these demographic groups, and develop new training and development programs, as appropriate.

Second, since the available pool of entry level workers will include increasing numbers of individuals who have had inadequate education and training opportunities, government agencies must be willing to provide more training in basic remedial skills. . . . Given the decreased number of entry-level employees, government agencies must be more willing to establish integrated recruitment and training programs that are based on potential and aptitude for necessary knowledge, skills and abilities (KSAs) rather than current possession. For example . . . New York State has adopted a grow-your-own approach to meeting work force needs that includes pre-employment training and job preparation for underskilled applicants, school-to-work bridge programs for non-college bound students, and traineeship, internship, apprenticeship and transition programs.

Third, government agencies need to examine their current organizational climates and provide necessary training to the people already in the organization in order to make the organizational culture more receptive to people from all cultures, to women and to older workers. . . . Affirmative action programs have been designed to recruit underrepresented people to the workplace. They have not, however, focused on creating supportive work environments. As the demographic changes bring new people into the workplace, it is the responsibility of the organization to provide work environments that are free from discrimination and that value diversity.

Source: Ban, Carolyn, Sue Faerman, and Norma M. Riccucci. "Productivity and the Personnel Process," in Marc Holzer (ed.), *Public Productivity Handbook*. New York: Marcel Dekker, 1992.

If a training effort seeks to prepare employees for positions that lend themselves to engineered work standards, then corresponding evaluations will be relatively simple mathematical efforts. As work moves up the scale of task ambiguity however, corresponding training efforts and their evaluations become more difficult to design, conduct, and measure. Training can be said to be validated if quantifiable measures of its effectiveness can be produced, but while many of the individual training elements of a management development program may be amenable to validation, management development itself in almost all jurisdictions is undertaken as an ''act of faith.''

The act may be covered in social science rhetoric, but it is faith—not science—that causes public organizations to put resources into management development, because these programs have simply not been validated. There are two basic reasons for this—time and numbers. Remember, the federal government was not even authorized to spend any significant sums on training until passage of the Government Employees Training Act of 1958. Even today, while most state and local jurisdictions have training efforts, most do not have extensive training staffs. The movement toward outsourcing, especially as a result of budgetary shortfalls, generally reduces the number of training staff members who are available to plan and evaluate training programs. Of course, a public sector agency can contract out the evaluation of the training to an outside consultant, but that means contracting out the evaluation of contractors doing the training!

As the number of public managers who have had the opportunity to participate in a comprehensive management development program increases, there should be growing confidence in training evaluation. Even if there aren't large-scale studies that empirically demonstrate the utility of the components of such programs, further funding of them will continue to be matters of faith. Part of it is an act of faith—and it is a faith that most managers and personnelists subscribe to, but part of it is also a recognition that training and development are critical dimensions of human resources management, that the technical, technological, and managerial requirements of most public sector jobs are not static. In fact, the reverse is the case; job dimensions are so dynamic that ongoing evaluation of training to ensure that ''learners'' are satisfactorily mastering new skills and competencies and applying them effectively in their positions is critical.

Of course, that still leaves the difficulty of deciding upon what evaluation approach to use. It is much easier to determine whether or not employees found a specific training program interesting, well organized, and relevant than to survey individuals and units several months later to see if productive job behavior changes have occurred that can be attributed to a specific training program. Furthermore, most jurisdictions that are beginning the task of assembling or reassembling a major training effort see the thorny problems of evaluation as a second priority. Their rationale, which basically amounts to ''let's build a good program first and then we'll worry about evaluation,'' seems quite logical.

The fact is, however, that training evaluation has now been upgraded from simply a cost-benefit resource question to a new series of questions about validation. Reflecting a more scientific perspective, training programs in public organizations must stand on the same grounds as examinations and promotion decisions. This will mean, at a minimum, the development of performance-relevant training programs that must be capable of demonstrating improvement in appropriate skills.

As such, the training evaluation question, which essentially focuses on the more intangible aspects of improving employee morale and perceptions, must yield to more rigorous evaluation questions. Consequently, validity in the context of the evaluation of training can be conceptualized, as Irwin Goldstein has hypothesized, in the following four-stage hierarchy:

1. The validity of the training itself based upon demonstrated performance in the training environment
2. Performance validity based upon demonstrated performance on the job
3. Intraorganizational validity, which considers the question of the training program's generalizability to new groups of trainees in the same organization
4. Intraorganizational validity, which considers the training program's generalizability to trainees in different organizations

These stages of training validity necessarily incorporate increasingly difficult levels of measurement. Most public sector organizations have been hard-pressed to reach much beyond the first stage. Most simply choose to administer various forms of subjective questionnaires to trainees about their reactions. Some, like the military, use extensive pre- and posttesting procedures to determine what was learned.

How much of this newly learned knowledge is imparted on the job (performance validity) is only indirectly addressed? Postcourse questionnaires to supervisors and employees asking numerous subjective questions about job improvement are very general and of little utility in producing any real measurement. As for inter- and intraorganizational validity, a great deal must still be done before these dimensions are successfully integrated into training evaluation. Perhaps it is in this sense that the experience of many public sector organizations with outsourcing or contracting out of training programs provides a silver lining. Much more emphasis has been placed on evaluation and developing more comprehensive and sophisticated evaluation methods to demonstrate that the training con-

What Is Evaluation?

. . . evaluation is an information gathering process that should not be expected to reach decisions that declare a program totally good or poor. Instructional programs are never complete but instead are designed to be revised on the basis of information obtained from evaluations that examine relevant multiple criteria that are both free from contamination and reliable. One role of the previously described need assessment process is to suggest relevant criteria which can be utilized to measure the achievement of the multiple objectives of the training program. Evaluation must be treated as one part of a long term systematic approach to the *development* of effective programs. Unless such a systematic approach is developed, the feedback process that could result from effectively designed evaluations built around relevant multiple criteria has been more likely to conclude in emotional reactions rather than decisions to use the information to improve programs.

The better experimental procedures control more variables permitting a greater degree of confidence in specifying program effects. While the constraints of the training environment may make laboratory type evaluation impossible to achieve, an awareness of the important factors in experimental design makes it possible to conduct a useful evaluation. Certainly, the real world has many constraints and these affect the designs employed. Thus, a pure do-nothing control group is sometimes not useful in the examination of instructional programs. At least, this author would not be interested in being flown across the Atlantic Ocean in a 747 jet plane by a pilot who was randomly placed in the uninstructed control group. However, there are many instances where controls consisting of the old technique as compared to the institution of a new type of program are appropriate. It is time to begin comparing methodologies to the constraints of the environment. This process should be characterized by careful consideration of threats to validity, and the creative application of design methodology to the questions being investigated.

Source: Goldstein, Irwin L. ''The Pursuit of Internal and External Validity in the Evaluation of Training Programs,'' *Public Personnel Management*, vol. 8 (November–December, 1979), p. 419. Reprinted by permission of the International Personnel Management Association, 1850 K Street, N.W., Suite 870, Washington, D.C. 20006.

tractor is in compliance and that the programs contracted for are effective in meeting the organization's needs. (See Table 8.2.)

Perhaps the most accepted framework for evaluating training has come from the work of Donald Kirkpatrick, who has proposed four levels of training evaluation measurement, which are summarized as follows:

Level 1:	Reaction	Participant satisfaction with the training event
Level 2:	Learning	Learning assessment (did participants learn the subjects?)
Level 3:	Behavior	Skills application (Do participants apply learning on the job?)
Level 4:	Results	Organizational change or impact—ROI for organization

Kirkpatrick's evaluation framework is really about determining training value. Level 1—the most basic and usually conducted by a postcourse survey—is now viewed as simply insufficient for determining value. At the other extreme, level 4 results would seem to be the essence of what training evaluation is all about. Level 4 is very hard to accomplish, however, and many leading training experts at corporate universities have abandoned their efforts to measure this. Their viewpoint is more that training and development is a given and that in the coming KM world, training is an ongoing part of the work process and should be measured directly in terms of how it contributes to employee retention. It is the ultimate irony that if participants like the organization's training program and are highly satisfied, it will be seen as a plus in attracting and retaining human capital.

TABLE 8.2 Timing of Posttraining Performance Evaluation (1997 Survey)

At the completion of training	29%
1 to 3 months after training	13%
4 to 6 months after training	8%
7 or more months after training	3%
No assessment of employee performance after training	47%

Source: *Public Personnel Management* (summer 1997).

TRAINING AND DEVELOPMENT AND TECHNOLOGY: THE ISSUE OF CHOICE

How much will training and development change in the next decade? Indeed, it may not even be appropriate to think of a decade as the appropriate interval of measurement; it may be three years or five. Organizationally, training has now reached a crossroads. It's finally sunk into both the private and public sector that the real value of human resources is measured in the development of the workforce's intellectual capital. Investment in training and development is both fashionable and good business. As expected, high technology-based firms are leading the way, with strategies ranging from requiring 40 hours of training for every employee or giving every employee a $2500 annual training allowance to those companies that have constructed "learning paths" and "curriculum maps" that show employees and managers what learning (i.e., training interventions) is needed for each position and the position above.

Behind the new (or latest, depending upon how skeptical you are) training renaissance is a major shift in training economics, however. Once organizations redefine training as a required resource for everyone, cost considerations become crucial. More and more organizations are adding up the expense of putting employees in a classroom versus other platforms that use technology to deliver training to employees when they want it and where they want it. New technology platforms using internal computer networks or the Internet are creating new formats from site learning centers to "exchange parks" that provide 24-hour access to mentors around the world. Such major IT firms as Lotus, Oracle, and Hewlett Packard (HP) are rushing to release new software products and consulting services, from canned computer courses to highly interactive knowledge-sharing forums. Some universities are responding by creating an Internet strategy for the delivery of learning. An excellent example is Stanford's online educational course series, which for those interested in industry trends has an industry thought leaders seminar, which has a series of hour-long video lectures that can be downloaded and discussed over the Web.

Of course, no one dares (except for Roger Schank) to say the obvious — that classroom training is too expensive and outmoded to be of much value in the future. Criticism of the classroom, or what is technically termed reception-based learning, is growing. In an article in the January/February 1999 issue of the *Journal of Higher Education*, Paul Privateer of Arizona State holds academia accountable for perpetuating what he calls "18th century models of learning with 19th century notions of organizational management" that completely misunderstand the potential of new information technology applications for learning. He does not doubt academia's resilience in being able to use new technologies to reengineer the classroom and even other university processes, but to do so without reinventing the product (what students will learn) would be as his article's subtitle implies, a tragic case of the strategic path not taken.

Others are not ready to count the classroom (and by inference, universities) out. In their new book, *The Social Life of Information*, John Seely Brown and Paul Duguid discount the idea that teaching and training are simply a delivery system and that educational technology is a new form of "intellectual forklift"; rather, they argue, learning is about "enculturation"— about what someone wants to be. To learn effectively demands people be put in touch with others, not just in touch with information. Classroom experiences, whether the individual learner has direct contact with an expert (i.e., the instructor) or the opportunity to be in touch with peers in an intellectually stimulating environment, are still one of the most effective settings for this.

Clearly, however, of all the functions of human resources management, training is going to be the most dramatically impacted by technology. On January 12,1999, the White House released an executive memorandum updating Executive Order 11348 (Providing for the Further Training of Government Employees," establishing a President's Task Force on Federal Training Technology) to consist of the usual cabinet agencies along with NASA, Small Business Administration (SBA), SSA, and other agency representatives to be designated. Their task is to produce in 18 months a new policy document on how the federal government will use TBT (technology-based training). Also of interest (hidden in subpart 8b of section 2) is the charge to develop options and recommendations for "federal individual training accounts" for federal workers so that they can obtain relevant training (which is subject, of course, to their individual manager's approval). How radical would that be? Technology may yet finally push training in the public sector to a place above the budget threshing floor so that it is no longer the first optional expense cut in times of budget cutbacks and is seen as the single most important factor in recruitment, retention, and even morale.

BIBLIOGRAPHY

Baird, L. S. and Kathy L. Kram. "Career Dynamics: Matching the Supervisor/Subordinate Relationship," *Organizational Dynamics*, vol. 11, no. 4 (spring 1983).

Bellman, Geoffrey. "Doing More with Less," *Public Personnel Management*, vol. 15, no. 4 (winter 1986).

Brown, F. Gerald and Kenneth R. Wedel. *Assessing Training Needs*. Washington, D.C.: National Training Development Service Press, 1974.

Brown, John Seely and Paul Duguid. *The Social Life of Information*. Boston: Harvard Business School Press, 2000.

Byers, Kenneth T., ed. *Employee Training and Development in the Public Service*. Chicago: International Personnel Management Association, 1970.

Clement, Ronald W. "Testing the Hierarchy Theory of Training Evaluation," *Public Personnel Management*, vol. 11, no. 2 (summer 1982).

Cooke, Kathleen. "A Model for the Identification of Training Needs," *Public Personnel Management* (July–August 1979).

Cole, Robert E., ed. "Special Issue on Knowledge and the Firm," *California Management Review*, vol. 40, no. 3 (spring 1998).

Craig, Robert, ed. *Training and Development Handbook*. New York: McGraw-Hill, 1987.

Davenport, Thomas and Lawrence Prusak. *Working Knowledge*. Boston: Harvard Business School Press, 1998.

Edvinson, Leif and Michael S. Malone. *Intellectual Capital*. Harper Business, 1997.

Ferman, Louis A. et al., eds. *New Developments in Worker Training: A Legacy for the 1990s*. Madison, Wis.: Industrial Relations Research Association, 1990.

Fraser, Richard F., John W. Gore, and Chester C. Cotton. "A System for Determining Training Needs," *Personnel Journal* (December 1978).

Goldstein, I. L. *Training: Program Development and Evaluation*, 2nd ed. Monterey, Calif.: Brooks/Cole, 1986.

Goldstein, I. L. "Training: Methodological Considerations and Empirical Approaches," symposium for *Journal of Human Factors*, vol. 20, no. 2 (April 1978).

Gray, George R. et al. "Training Practices in State Government Agencies," *Public Personnel Management*, vol. 26, no. 2 (summer 1997), pp. 187–202.

Hamblin, A. C. *Evaluation and Control of Training*. New York: McGraw-Hill, 1974.

Hinch, Gerald K. and Clement D. Pangallo. "Federal Training in Tight Budget Years," *Public Personnel Management*, vol. 15, no. 4 (winter 1986).

Jones, Andrew N. *Combatting Managerial Obsolescence*. Oxford, England: Philip Allan, 1980.

Kaufman, Roger and Fenwick W. English. *Needs Assessment: Concept and Application*. Englewood Cliffs, NJ: Educational Technology Publishers, 1979.

Kirkpatrick, Donald L. *Evaluating Training Programs: The Four Levels*, 2nd ed. San Francisco: Berrett-Koehler, 1998.

Knowles, Malcolm S. *The Adult Learner: A Neglected Species*. Houston: Gulf Publishing, 1973.

Leonard-Barton, Dorothy. *Wellsprings of Knowledge*. Harvard Business School Press, 1995.

Mager, Robert F. *Developing Attitudes Toward Learning*. Palo Alto, Calif.: Fearon Publishing, 1968.

Mager, Robert F. *Preparing Instructional Objectives*. Palo Alto, Calif.: Fearon Publishing, 1962.

McCullough, Richard C., ed. "Training in Tough Times," *Public Personnel Management*, vol. 15, no. 4 (winter 1986, special issue).

Misler, Dennis I. "Management Development and More: Contracting Out Makes It Possible," *Public Personnel Management*, vol. 15, no. 4 (winter 1986).

Nadler, Leonard. *Developing Human Resources*, 2nd ed. Austin, Tex.: Learning Concepts, 1979.

Nonaka, Ikujiro and Hirotaka Takeuchi. *The Knowledge-Creating Company*. New York: Oxford University Press, 1995.

Odiorne, George S. *Training by Objectives: An Economic Approach to Management Training*. New York: Macmillan, 1970.

Passett, Barry A. *Leadership Development for Public Service*. Houston, Tex.: Gulf Publishing, 1971.

Pomerleau, Raymond. "The State of Management Development in the Federal Service," *Public Personnel Management*, vol. 3 (January–February 1974).

Ravet, Serge and Maureen Layte. *Technology-Based Training*. Houston: Gulf Publishing, 1997.

Sanchez, Ron and Aime Heene eds. *Strategic Learning and Knowledge Management*. New York; Wiley, 1997.

Schreiber, Deborah A. and Zane L. Berger, ed. *Distance Training*. San Francisco: Jossey-Bass, 1998.

Sims, Ronald, John G. Veres, and Susan Heninger. "Training for Competence," *Public Personnel Management*, vol. 18, no. 2 (spring 1989).

Sims, Ronald. "Evaluating Public Sector Training Programs," *Public Personnel Management*, vol. 22, no. 4 (winter 1993).

Public Personnel Management, vol. 18, no. 2 (spring 1989), pp. 591–615.

Stewart, Thomas. *Intellectual Capital*. New York: Currency Doubleday, 1997.

Sveiby, Karl. *The New Organizational Wealth*. San Francisco: Berrett Koehler, 1997.

Sylvia, Ronald D. and C. Kenneth Meyer. "An Organizational Perspective on Training and Development in the Public Sector," in Stephen Hays and Richard Kearney (eds.), *Public Personnel Administration*. Englewood Cliffs, NJ: Prentice-Hall, 1990.

Training Needs Assessment: A Study of Methods, Approaches, and Procedures Used by Government Agencies. Philadelphia: Regional Training Center, 1978.

Ulshcack, Francis L. *Human Resource Development: The Theory and Practice of Needs Assessment*. Reston, Va.: Reston, 1983.

Van Wort, Montgomery. "Organizational Investment in Employee Development." In Stephen E. Condrey (ed.), *Handbook of Human Resource Management in Government*. San Francisco: Jossey-Bass, 1998, pp. 276–297.

Werth, Jackie Baker. "Training for Reality: Making Training Come Alive," *Public Manager*, vol. 28, no. 3 (fall 1999), pp. 27–31.

Williams, Marcia L., Kenneth Paprock, and Barbara Covington. *Distance Learning: The Essential Guide*. Thousand Oaks, Calif.: Sage, 1999.

Yi, Hyong U. "Computer-Based Training/Distant Learning," *Public Manager*, vol. 28, no. 2, (summer, 1999), pp. 61–64.

9

Quality Management and Reengineering

PROLOGUE: TQM AND *THE INVISIBLE MAN*

Over a century ago the British novelist H. G. Wells wrote a series of novels that he described as "fantastic stories" and that which have become classics. One in particular tells the strange tale of Griffin, who while a young student of 22 abandons his studies to devote himself to finding a way to become invisible. *The Invisible Man* is perhaps better known today for the concept than the actual details of the story, in which the student Griffin becomes more depraved and violent once he has accomplished his objective of becoming invisible. This prologue is not really a story as much as an attempt at an analogy to describe a similarly strange fate of the federal quality movement in the 1990s. Rest assured, quality management did not become "depraved and violent," but essentially, after a decade of good intentions and much hard work, the federal sector quality movement became practically invisible.

As will be discussed in the next section, quality management came upon the management scene in the 1980s. A number of leading American corporations, such as Motorola, Xerox, Hewlett Packard, and Johnson & Johnson, began adapting the principles of quality management (then called TQM for total quality management). Governments at all levels became interested as well, enough so that by the late 1980s, the Department of Defense (DOD) and NASA, among others, were forging ahead with their own quality management initiatives. There was sufficient interest governmentwide so that a clearinghouse was created called the Federal Quality Institute (FQI) to serve as a source of information and shared experiences and to house a few government executives on loan for consulting and training assignments. The FQI served as clearinghouse, training shop, evaluation and awards headquarters, and consulting enterprise. The FQI also published numerous reports, studies, and handbooks to get agencies started in quality. FQI sponsored an annual federal quality conference, in which quality awards were given to federal agencies that had applied and been reviewed. At its most successful point over 2000 attendees would come to Washington in July to talk about quality and share quality knowledge.

How, then, did something so successful end up being dismantled in the mid-1990s by an administration whose leader—a former governor from Arkansas—was one of the earliest converts to TQM, which he instituted in his own state? The political problem however was where to put an entity such as FQI within the federal management structure. To be fair, this is a common problem within large corporations which also have struggled to ascertain where their quality management or ''infrastructure'' should be based—within training and education, planning, administration, contracting, or even the quality assurance function. The FQI had been placed within the Office of Personnel Management (OPM), which may not have been a great location to begin within. When the new director of OPM, Jim King, took over and unveiled his plan for a drastically smaller OPM to become one of the five reinvention ''model agencies,'' what little room that had existed before at the inn was no longer viable.

As a result, the enterprise of the FQI was broken up. The award process and the annual conference was retained by OPM but managed by its executive development group, now led by the Federal Executive Institute. Quality training was effectively outsourced to the General Services Administration (GSA), which had already certified a large number of private sector quality training suppliers and added them to the GSA supply schedule. The FQI let go its lease on the fabulous space it held at the old Pension building (home of the National Building Museum). Only the consulting arm remained, which renamed itself the Federal Quality Consulting Group and spent a year or so searching for a new organizational home before becoming part of the franchise fund at the U.S. Treasury Department.

More disappointing developments followed the tenth annual quality conference in 1996, which suffered financial losses. The OPM's training arm, which functions as a revolving fund arrangement and technically cannot operate on a deficit basis, had to discontinue its sponsorship for future national conferences. The conference was molded into another externally funded effort, but quality, once the raision d'être of the conference, would be relegated to page 5 in the conference program simply as an award ceremony. Perhaps the final blow came in early 2000 when the Federal Quality Consulting Group renamed itself—dropping quality to become simply the Federal Consulting Group. Using our analogy to H. G. Wells, quality had finally become invisible.

All of these events in this dismal tale notwithstanding, one might ask if quality management even needs to have its own annual conference or have an institute bearing the name quality to serve as its standard bearer. In short, can quality survive without infrastructure? This chapter reviews the advent of quality over the last century and examines current trends. It will address the issue of quality as change management and assess its relationship to reengineering, another management fad of the 1990s that failed rather dismally and yet has left its own mark on management jargon, if not management practice. To begin, however—to put the prologue in context—one has to understand quality's evolution in American industry.

QUALITY MANAGEMENT: BACK TO THE FUTURE

The roots of quality can be traced back to quality assurance methods in the rise of the American system of manufacturing. Quality assurance evolved from inspection methods pioneered in large part by the United States Ordinance Department well before the American Civil War. When Frederick Taylor developed the principles of scientific management, he basically promoted the role of inspection to a core management function. The evolution of that inspection role over the first half of the twentieth century led to statistical quality assurance, first pioneered by Bell Laboratories in the 1930s with the efforts of Walter Shewhart and others. By the 1950s Joseph Juran, Arnold Feigenbaum, and W. Edwards Deming (usually referred to as America's quality gurus) had developed the core concepts of quantifying the costs of quality, establishing total quality controls and reliability engineering, and perhaps most controversial of all, advocating the pursuit of zero defects as an absolute goal of manufacturing. Almost inexplicably, however, quality management never emerged out of the assurance function in the United States. Instead, it would be Japanese management that would become the prototype for quality management.

Today most management students can recite the story of how quality management was developed first in the United States, exported to Japan following the Second World War, and then had to be imported back to the United States two decades later. David Garvin, a professor at the Harvard Business School and one of the earliest critics of shoddy American production processes, has lamented in his history of quality that quality control techniques have been one of "America's most successful exports."

What prevented the quality movement from really taking off in American Industry? It was important, yes, but it was just another department

Japanese vs. American Management Quality Perspectives

The question remains—Why did quality become a "thought revolution in management" in Japan but remain a highly specialized mathematical function in the United States? Kaoru Ishikawa, Japan's great quality guru, addressed this issue in his classic assessment of quality history and simply noted that the difference was Japan's "lack of professionalism." Japanese companies rotated their managers through all the core departments, including quality control, before they could garner a senior assignment. Western companies preferred to train specialized professionals to administer their quality sections and perform this work. The result of Western specialization, Ishikawa argued, is a large corps of managers with limited vision and little understanding of the vital role of quality in strategy and management, and a few statistical QC specialists who don't know how to communicate with the rest of management.

or inspection function in this case within the organizational hierarchy. In Japan, the viewpoint was different — quality would be seen as the core structural approach to management. When America's quality experts (first Deming, then Juran and Feigenbaum) visited Japan and gave lectures to Japanese business and government officials in the mid 1950's, they found a highly receptive audience. The rest of this story is industrial history.

To continue the story, the Japanese developed their own innovative approach to quality, but it began with an understanding of American quality management techniques and concepts that were, frankly, simply underappreciated in the United States. The Japanese, some have argued, sought to produce the best products in the world so that the label "made in Japan," once synonymous with junk, would set the standard for quality. In the 1960s and 1970s, they achieved exactly that.

The 1980s: From Quality Circles to TQM

By the late 1970s American industrial firms began to take notice of the rapidly improving competitive position of Japanese manufacturing. In some cases, such as with Hewlett Packard or Xerox, there was an existing company partnership or business relationship between American and Japanese corporate entities. Firms such as these with direct access to Japanese quality methods would be early champions of the quality movement's importation back into the United States, but many American companies and some government agencies were looking for a quick turnaround approach that would replicate the Japanese quality success without having to alter any of basic structural elements of American management. What seemed most attractive was the Japanese use of voluntary work groups, which met regularly to discuss how to improve the quality levels of products and work processes—a concept called quality circles (QCs).

So began the first rather tenuous quality experiment, the formation of QCs, in which small groups of employees and supervisors —''volunteers''—would receive some training in basic statistical quality control techniques and then under the leadership of a trained facilitator meet regularly to analyze, solve, and recommend solutions on quality problems to top management. While these early efforts were hailed as revolutionary first-time efforts at participative management, they largely failed. Indeed, just as some government agencies were starting up their QCs in the early 1980s, the private sector was abandoning the whole effort en masse. Of course there were many ''small successes'' within QC. Federal organizations as diverse as the Norfolk Naval Shipyards, NASA's Lewis Space Center, the U.S. Customs Service, and numerous other DOD installations and agencies tried QCs and reported varying degrees of success in cost-saving suggestions and quality improvements in products and services. Any comparison to the Japanese model revealed vast inadequacies, however.

Model Japanese companies had 75% or more of their workforce in QCs. In fact, most workers in Japan participated in several QCs. Top management relentlessly pushed all of its cost, quality, and performance data down to the lowest levels of the organization for rigorous evaluation and action. Every worker and supervisor already had extensive training in quality measurement concepts, and there were high degrees of trust among employees and between management and employees. In Japan, QCs were contributing hundreds of ideas and suggestions for improvement by the workforce each month, and ideas were routinely shared across the entire organization. In addition, most Japanese unions were company unions that strongly supported the idea of different kinds of employees meeting and discussing work process changes.

Few of these conditions were prevalent in American corporations and government organizations. Even those experimenting with QCs with the best intentions simply faced too many political and social obstacles. After a few successes, most organizations were willing to declare victory, abandon the circles, and then wait for the next stage of development, an organizationally comprehensive approach to quality under the banner of TQM.

By the mid- to late 1980s, TQM was the rage. Billions were invested in training, consulting, and management education efforts in an all-out effort to close the quality gap between the United States and Japan and to remake the basic management precepts of American industry. In 1987, the Congress created a national quality award competition to be named in honor of Commerce Secretary Malcolm Baldrige, who had died as a result of a rodeo accident. The Baldrige Award has been a central element both in promoting American quality progress and providing a comprehensive framework for evaluating any organization's management effectiveness. This latter aspect is even more prominent, with major changes having been made in 1997 in the award criteria, placing new emphasis

Quality Awards: The Baldrige Award, the President's Award, The Deming Prize

Using the quality process as an evaluation mechanism to review an organization's progress. There are three major competitive assessment processes in which organizations can apply to be evaluated against quality award criteria.

The Malcolm Baldrige Award

Created by Congress in 1987 (named after the late secretary of commerce), which provides two awards for companies (three eligibility categories: manufacturing, service, and small businesses) according to weighted criteria in seven areas: (1) senior executive leadership, (2) information and analysis, (3) strategic quality planning, (4) human resource development and management, (5) management of process quality, (6) customer focus and satisfaction, and (7) quality and operational results.

President's Award for Quality

The American public sector equivalent of the Baldrige, first established in 1988, which uses eight criteria that closely follow Baldrige guidelines. The additional criterion comes from dividing human resources into two categories: (1) employee training and recognition and (2) employee empowerment and teamwork. Two awards can be given each year, but the process also recognizes excellence in quality management by designating "prototype" or models. The process was formerly administered by the U.S. Federal Quality Institute.

The Deming Prize

The Japanese national quality award, which is awarded to Japanese and overseas companies for superior quality management practices. The award is named after W. Edwards Deming, but criteria for the award are developed by the Union of Japanese Scientists and Engineers.

on business results, markets, and strategic planning. It should be noted that several states followed suit and have created their own annual quality award competitions premised on the Baldrige criteria and award process.

THE ADVENT OF TQM

What exactly is TQM and how does it compare to the more generic terms, such as continuous improvement or quality management, that one encounters? Indeed, some make the case that TQM as a label was such an albatross that most organizations came up with their own terms—total quality leadership (TQL), total quality organization (TQO), or TQ.

As most management tools are, TQM was a consulting term. Quality itself was seen as some basic measure of ''goodness,'' or if you will, some measure of the organizational costs incurred because of defects (that's cost of quality!). Continuous improvement was the larger systematic effort that any organization through its work groups or teams (often called quality improvement teams) would undertake to refine its work processes and improve the quality levels of the resulting products or services. This concept of quality as continuous improvement is still too narrow, however; quality was to be integrated into an overall organizational approach that focuses management planning and workforce involvement on improving current and future quality levels to meet customer requirements. That's more a management system or what would be called TQM. The basic elements or what some call cornerstones of TQM, then, are customer focus, process measurement, contractor collaboration, and total workforce participation.

Total Quality Management was not viewed as a short-term accomplishment for any organization. Anyone who has ever worked in quality management would argue vehemently that it takes years for quality to evolve into a mature management system. Indeed, TQM was often described as a journey, not a destination. That instantly became one of the first major obstacles in applying TQM to the public sector—getting the needed long-term support from the usually short-term-focused politically appointed top leaders in government agencies who were most interested in results they could see (and take credit for) in their two-to-three-year average length of stay in office.

The full adoption of TQM in the public sector would be more difficult for many reasons. For starters, there was a counterargument that TQM was mostly applicable for manufacturing organizations. Critics were quick to point out that Japan, the basic model, did not use TQM within its government services. Second, there were numerous issues regarding customer focus. Major questions were raised regarding what government's perspective should be regarding the direct and indirect consumers of government products and services. Were they customers, clients, or citizens? How do customers relate vis-á-vis taxpayers? What were

The Cornerstones of Quality Management

Process Metrics: Linking to Business Results

Internal statistical process control and other quantitative process improvement methods that are used by the organization to evaluate work process quality, output variation, and service quality improvement. Quality has always involved different kinds of process measurement activities under the rubric of statistical process control. The seven tools of quality, as they often called, are basic, but other measurement components include baselining and benchmarking, whereby the organization creates a series of larger assessments of cost, rework, production or service cycle time, productivity, and perceived quality as performance indices, and compares these statistics over time (baselining) or to other organizations (benchmarking). Either method provides a gauge of what kind of progress is being achieved over time and anchors quality firmly in business results.

Customer Feedback: Focusing on Consumer Expectations

External measurements that quantify customer feedback and perceptions on satisfaction with service and product quality and market expectations. Customer focus is another area that has undergone tremendous development. Agencies began with tracking customer complaints and problem calls, but soon realized they must develop more sophisticated methods of tracking current customer satisfaction. Service follow-up surveys, phone interviews, and focus groups with current and potential customers in the marketplace all became staples of customer feedback. Surveys have become a mainstay for customer feedback; they can measure everything from customer complaint levels to expectations, satisfaction, loyalty, and image issues.

Participate Management: Changing Through Teams

Work Group participation efforts that involve the organizational workforce in new ways to improve, experiment with, and ultimately redesign production, service, and other organizational work processes. Understandably, there is little consensus on what the proper term is to describe the collective engagement of the supervisors and workers in redesigning work processes and work team structures. Some call it empowerment, others involvement or collaboration or even leadership. Whatever the name, it retains a significant effect on all aspects of the quality-improvement process since it holds the key to whether the organizational culture can be remolded to emphasize better teamwork, more cooperation, less control-focused supervision, more cross-functional and overlapping work roles and responsibilities. Examples of quality teams include corrective action teams, chartered teams, work process teams, and cross functional work teams.

Contractor Cooperation: Creating Supplier Partnerships

Initiatives that include vendors and suppliers involved in the production or service process through certification or preferred partnerships designed to ensure quality with minimum inspection. The participation or collaboration dimension that affects suppliers and contractors is no less dramatic. It requires organizations to work with fewer but preferred vendors and suppliers, to discontinue lowest bid procedures, and to work out standards, certification, and new partnership arrangements. The goal is to include all the "players" in an expanded conceptualization of a total production or service process focused on ultimate customers rather than an organizational process that emphasizes functional specialization and internal controls.

---

the major stakeholders (e.g., Congress or interest groups)? Debates ensued over who government was serving and how "competing customers" resulted in different costs of quality.

Still, despite a great deal of skepticism and all these serious questions, TQM began to make considerable inroads into government in the late 1980s. As mentioned, the Reagan administration charted the FQI and a parallel quality award process—the President's Quality Award—using a modified version of the Baldrige Award criteria. Certainly influenced by the less than enthusiastic agency response to President Reagan's ill-fated productivity improvement initiative of 1986, whereby the administration mandated a 20% increase in government agency productivity (to be matched by a commensurate reduction in staffing), there was not to be an executive directive requiring the adoption of TQM. Quality would be accomplished by example and promoted at the grassroots level.

Fortunately, the DOD saw TQM in much the same light as its prime contractors—as a valuable management philosophy and set of quantitative tools and techniques for widespread dissemination. The DOD committed the resources and internal expertise in the late 1980s to provide management directives and guidance, self-assessment processes, and training materials and handbooks to start up TQM in any part or place of the DOD empire. NASA did much the same, focusing on creating a high-profile management commitment to TQM that also encouraged subcontractors and suppliers to be TQM-"certified." Other domestic agencies, including the likes of the Veterans Administration and the IRS launched major quality initiatives, often with some semblance of real cooperation between management and their unions.

What Is Quality/What Is TQM?

Quality

There are probably as many definitions of quality as there are quality consultants or quality book authors. Early definitions focused on the concept of "conformance to requirements," which intended in part to broaden quality to include users' or customers' requirements. Current definitions emphasize "excellence" and use quality as a relative or ideal measurement to make comparisons against others. If there was to be only one definition allowed, perhaps that provided by the American Society for Quality Control would be the best: "Quality is the totality of features and characteristics of a product or service that bear on its ability to satisfy stated or implied needs."

TQM (to Include TQS, as in Service), TQL (as in Leadership), TQO (as in Organization), TQE (as in Excellence), and the like

Total quality management (TQM) is the term generally used to describe the range of organizational strategies focused on quality improvement spawned in the 1980s. The first use of the term total appears in the 1950s with the works of Fiegenbaum, Deming, and Juran, who applied statistical quality control theories to management labeling it total quality control. Total quality management appears in the 1980s with the expansion of these ideas to encompass workforce participation, customer satisfaction feedback, and supplier collaboration. Organizations have altered the title of their quality management effort to fit a particular emphasis or in some cases to signal their intention to adapt TQM to their needs rather than adopt the philosophy wholesale. As with quality, if there was to be only one definition allowed, the nod might go to the Defense Department's: "TQM is both a philosophy and a set of guiding principles that represent the foundation of a continuously improving organization. TQM is the application of quantitative methods and human resources to improve materials and services supplied to an organization, all the processes within an organization, and the degree to which the needs of the customer are met, now and in the future. TQM integrates fundamental management techniques, existing improvement efforts, and technical tools under a disciplined approach focused on continuous improvement."

THE 1990s: THE "DEMISE" OF TQM AND THE BPR CHALLENGE

By 1990, however, economic conditions in the United States were playing havoc with the TQM movement. Facing severe competitive pressures and a recession, American manufacturing had begun a massive downsizing effort. Plant closings and widespread layoffs had already taken much of the luster off TQM, which had promised manufacturing workers job security in exchange for being trained in quality techniques and participating in quality improvement teams.

The business pages of major newspapers ridiculed each major layoff or corporate failure by a TQM champion, including the bankruptcy of one Baldrige Award-winning firm whose top management team confessed that they had spent too much time the following year on the banquet tour lauding their own success as a Baldrige winner. The *Washington Post* ran an infamous front page article entitled "Totaled Quality Management" in its Sunday business section, complete with a cartoon showing how consultants were the primary beneficiaries of TQM. Editorials were written contemplating the lessons learned from the demise of yet another management fad. Robert Cole, a professor at the University of California at Berkeley, examined this premature demise of TQM in his book *The Death and Life of the American Quality Movement*. It was a logical reaction (and misunderstanding) against TQM for what it was not—mainly a quick fix. Cole argued that while TQM was fading, the quality movement was proving to be "remarkably durable, sinking deep roots in many companies."

Clearly, TQM—both the consulting program and label—was being jettisoned in favor of a more patient, fundamental approach called simply quality management. Quality management, or as some have called it, TQM without the bells, whistles, slogans, posters, consultants, and qualiticrats," sought to provide a foundation for management and workforce efforts to improve work processes and service quality. This reformed version of quality would also discard many of the fatal flaws of TQM that Cole had clearly identified: "the bellowing of top management about quality, without any follow-through, wholesale training of employees without immediate action, unrealistically high expectations for quick results, the bureaucratization of quality efforts, etc." Finally, this version of quality management would by definition be internally driven—not by consultants and vendors, but by managers, employees, and even unions who recognized that employee participation was inextricably linked to quality goals and objectives.

Quality management in the public sector also got some help from some unexpected quarters in the early 1990s. There was a major effort in the American service industry to embrace the principles of quality management, but in this sector there was no Japanese model to drive it. Telecommunications, banking, insurance, and yes, even health care organizations began to develop their own versions of quality with a distinct service focus. These industries all had major counterparts in the public sector at the federal, state, and local levels, and they strongly encouraged both benchmarking and the sharing of best practices with government executives. Many of these service industry corporations helped fund studies on quality practices among state and local governments and set up advisory committees to help launch governmentwide efforts.

The General Accounting Office (GAO) also contributed with two important studies on the quality movement, confirming the soundness of quality as a long-term management approach. Charles Bowsher, the comptroller general at that time, was impressed enough with GAO's findings that he launched a multiyear effort at GAO to make quality management an integral part of GAO's management approach. In 1992, GAO conducted a major study of quality management in the federal government, finding that quality had been introduced into the majority of federal agencies (over 77% of agencies responding) but that direct participation of the workforce lagged far behind. (Seventeen percent of the workforce was directly involved in quality activities.) Quality efforts were spreading everywhere, but the penetration was at best skin deep.

Then in 1993, the newly elected Bill Clinton came into the presidency with an enviable quality management background. As governor of Arkansas, he was the first politically elected leader at the state level to launch a major TQM initiative. Most Arkansas agencies had quality improvement teams led by a statewide quality council that oversaw quality and provided training support and resources. Total Quality Management advocates salivated at the prospects of a newly led presidential effort in quality in the federal government.

In retrospect, TQM advocates would be disappointed but perhaps were fortunate that they didn't get what they wished for. Clinton's priorities were in public policy arenas—the TQM governor of Arkansas focused primarily on a major budget package that would move the country toward deficit reduction and of course the now infamous health care reform debate (which would have to be paid for by that same budget deficit package). Major management change was delegated to the vice-president and his internal executive review, to be called the National Performance Review (NPR), which saw quality as part of the strategy but had a much more encompassing vision for change.

The NPR did not have to wrestle with the issue of whether or not to make TQM its primary management strategy. Its blueprint was the best-selling book by Osborne and Gaebler *Reinventing Government,* which had a substantial role for TQM among its various prescriptions for a new form of entrepreneurial government—mainly, creating customer-focused government. When the September 1993 report of the NPR was issued, TQM was not a primary reference point, but Chapter 2 "Putting Customers First," was quality management 101 from top to bottom. Executive order 12862, issued after the report, put all of these expectations into agency requirements. All federal agencies dealing with the public were

Quality Performance Measurement: Benchmarking vs. Baselining

Most organizations equate performance with results. Since quality management stresses the long run and insists that "continuous improvement" should be based on improving the quality of processes and products, there is resistance to traditional performance measurement based on achievement of certain objectives or results within a specific time frame. Quality measurement theorists further argue that performance measurement based on any one set of measures can lead to significant problems. One set of results can be obtained by neglecting other areas or substituting resources or attention. Goals can also be achieved by exhorting workers to work harder toward that particular goal rather than correct the process or make needed changes.

So, in quality management terms, performance should be defined in systemwide or global terms, to include customers, employees, organizational, and community and external environmental terms. Quality management does include two types of performance measurements that focus on whole processes and quality concerns: baselining and benchmarking.

Baselining entails taking a comprehensive set of measurements of organizational work and service processes and establishing a starting evaluation mark. As work and service process changes are made, the organization conducts periodic reassessments of its initial performance measurement set and notes levels of changes from the initial baseline. These measures should include a representative set of indices (internal employee ratings, external customer ratings, process quality, cost, rework levels, etc.).

Because baselining is a "relative" measurement concept (i.e., the organization is measuring progress using itself as a standard), there has been considerable attention given to another form of improvement strategy through performance measurement—*benchmarking*. Benchmarking was made famous by Xerox corporation in the early 1980s as an attempt to compare an organization's production and service processes and output quality levels against a special set of competitors who are by reputation viewed as the "best in the business." Benchmarking can take one of the following three formats:

Internal process, whereby comparisons are made among different subunits and locations within the same organizations

External competitive, whereby comparisons are made to comparable organizations or competitors who are in the same basic industry or have similar customers

Functional processes, whereby comparisons are made to organizations with reputations for specific processes or services, with just that specific process or service being compared.

> Of course benchmarking requires considerable cooperation among participating organizations and units and extensive sharing of information. While there are now several works appearing on benchmarking (and consulting companies offering benchmarking services), the initial text was by Robert Camp (a Xerox engineer) in 1989—*Benchmarking: The Search for Industry Best Practices That Lead to Superior Performance.*

required to identify their customers, set quality standards for service, survey their customers, and act to make government services "equal to the best in business."

This was a major victory for quality management in everything but name. Unfortunately, customer service improvement would still have to compete with the more than 200 other recommendations of the NPR, but at least it was a prime directive. Later, as the NPR got bogged down in controversies with first the Democratic Congress and then its Republican successor over fast-track legislation for NPR budget, procurement, and civil service reforms, and mired in a larger controversy over having the reduction of more than 250,000 positions as its primary goal, the distance between NPR and TQM proved a useful buffer.

It should said, however, that the NPR never lost sight of customer service improvement. In the last days of 1999, NPR, renamed the National Partnership for Reinventing Government (NPRG) finally accomplished one of its most cherished objectives; it generated comparisons on customer satisfaction between the federal government and the private sector using a third part benchmark, the American Customer Satisfaction Index. (See Figure 9.1.)

Quality management might have been rearranged to meet agency needs in the mid-1990s, but another management revolution emerged that grabbed most of the headlines. The business process reengineering (or BPR) movement was launched by a 1990 article by Michael Hammer in the *Harvard Business Review* entitled "Reengineer Work: Don't Automate—Obliterate" followed by a best-selling book in 1992, *Reengineering the Corporation,* coauthored with James Champy. The reengineering premise was simple enough: Continuous improvement quality style was insufficient and too slow; organizations could and should discard current cumbersome and redundant work processes and radically redesign them!

The immediate result of most of this was a reengineering frenzy that matched another wave of corporate downsizing, this time hitting much of the service sector. Over on the sidelines, quality consultants squared off against reengineering consultants in a war of consulting jargon. About the only real clear-cut winner was Scott Adams, the cartoonist who created Dilbert, who now had

The National Quality Research Center annually surveys customers of 175 companies and 30 government agencies, but each quarter only a selected group is updated. Here are the index scores, out of a possible 100, for government agencies that provide consumer and business services.

Group/Manufacturer	1999 Score
AGENCY/DEPARTMENT	
Overall Federal Government Score	**68.6**
FAMILY SERVICES	**80**
Administration for Families & Children, HHS	87
Food and Nutrition Service, Agriculture	83
Department of Housing & Urban Develop.	69
CLAIMS, BENEFITS, PAYMENTS	**77**
Social Security Administration	82
Veterans Health Administration, VA	79
Office of Personnel Management	75
Health Care Financing Administration, HHS	71
Veterans Benefits Administration, VA	61
PUBLIC INFORMATION	**75**
Education Publications, Education	80
National Aeronautics & Space Admin.	80
General Services Administration	77
Bureau of the Census, Commerce	70
Environmental Protection Agency	69
RECREATIONAL SERVICES	**72**
National Park Service, Interior	73
National Forest Service, Agriculture	70

Group/Manufacturer	1999 Score
RECREATIONAL SERVICES (cont.)	
Bureau of Land Management, Interior	64
PATENTS, GRANTS & ASSIST.	**71**
U.S. Mint, Treasury	86
Federal Emergency Management Agency	73
Student Financial Assistance, Education	63
National Science Foundation	57
Patent & Trademark Office, Commerce	57
TRAVEL SERVICES	**68**
Consular Affairs, State	73
Immigration & Naturalization Svce, Justice	69
Customs Service, Treasury	66
FOOD SAFETY	**63**
Food & Drug Administration, HHS	66
Food Safety & Inspection Svce, Agriculture	62
INTERNAL REVENUE SERVICE	**57**
IRS (electronic filers)	74
IRS (traditional filers)	51
REGULATORY SERVICES	**55**
Federal Aviation Admin., Transportation	58
Occupational Safety & Health Admin., Labor	51

Source: The American Customer Satisfaction Index is produced through a partnership of the University of Michigan Business School, American Society for Quality, and Arthur Andersen.

FIGURE 9.1 American customer satisfaction index: the government. Source: National Partnership for Reinventing Government.

enough material for a decade of new cartoons lampooning American management techniques.

In almost record time for a management fad, the BPR movement fizzled. The first major studies of BPR results showed 50 to 70% failure rates. Blame for corporate downsizing was fairly or unfairly pinned on BPR. Now the same type of headline that taunted TQM was recycled for BPR, proclaiming it as passé. Its gurus—Michael Hammer, James Champy, and Thomas Davenport—were on the defensive, explaining how BPR was misused, what went wrong, why organizations were incapable of implementing the radical redesigns and achieving the promised gains. They admitted that the problems of implementing radical new designs and the critical issues of preparing the workforce to embrace the levels of change inherent in BPR were greatly underestimated.

This unexpectedly quick failure of BPR returned some semblance of sanity, if not reason, to American change management. For one thing, the feud (if it can be called that) between the quality and BPR consultants presented organizations with a choice. Organizations could now see quality or continuous improvement as one component of how an organization manages what it does and see reengineering or radical redesign as another. Some understanding of both quality and especially BPR as change management strategies is in order.

UNDERSTANDING REENGINEERING (AND QUALITY) AS CHANGE MANAGEMENT

Few organizational change methodologies have hit the public sector with more power and potential impact than the reengineering movement of the 1990s. If ever there was a methodology that seemed a perfect fit for government organizations whose overextended and overregulated work flow processes and overrigid and overly bureaucratic organizational structures needed fundamental redesign, BPR was the match. Business Process Reengineering promised organizations radical improvements in quality, cycle time, and cost reduction if it was used correctly and uncompromisingly—mainly ensuring unwavering top management support to lead fast-track change efforts.

In government, where one normally thinks of the speed of change in terms of analogies to glaciers, BPR was greeted with great skepticism. For once, however, career bureaucrats and midlevel managers found genuine and enthusiastic support if not total commitment from top executives and the organizational leadership for reengineering. Executives were attracted to a change approach with objectives measured in quarters and months and one that promised complete redesigns, not just restructuring and tweaking existing systems. Executives seeking to make their marks in the short two- to three-year time frames of their average tenure saw great promise in a methodology that wanted dynamic breakthrough innovation as opposed to slow, incremental improvements in operating efficiency. For those executives with previous private sector experience or a consulting background, it offered an opportunity to shake up conventional organizational thinking and get their agencies to think about doing things differently or doing different things.

Of course, enthusiasm and strong support are not the same things as commitment and direct involvement; nor are they a guarantee for success, even in the private sector, which has more flexibility and arguably a more paranoiac appetite for change. This is part of the perspective that is shared by the emerging thinking about strategy. In a *Harvard Business Review* article in November 1996, Michael Porter stated flatly that doing things better, cheaper, and faster is insufficient. Today's competition is so intense, he argues, because of the "rapid diffusion (and knowledge through benchmarking and outsourcing) of best practices." In his words, "As rivals imitate one another's improvements in quality, cycle time, supplier partnerships, strategies converge and competition becomes a series of races down identical paths that no one can win."

Gary Hamel, another leading thinker on strategy, is even more pessimistic about how organizations change. In his 1998 article in the *Harvard Business Review* he challenged current thinking about strategic planning, stating that organizations are now reaching a diminishing rate of return vis-á-vis improvement. He sees a new "strategic convergence" in industry and (sooner than you think) in government where everyone learns and compares the same strategies. Even BPR along with benchmarking will be preferred approaches for those wanting to catch up—but they will not be capable of putting you in the lead.

Somehow this may sound far too draconian for government, but the pressures to provide services in government that are viewed as competitive and convenient (the FedEx effect on our expectations, as it is sometimes called) and the increasing ease of comparison of performance among public, private, and within may be leading governments to start thinking beyond quality and BPR to thinking about innovation and new forms of technology.

Even now there are new pressures that are spurring government agencies to think about making major changes in their modes of operations. Just as TQM became quality management, BPR may yet become simple reengineering (as in the verb) and be destined for more important things. Some recent events illustrate.

The GAO released the *Business Process Reengineering Assessment Guide* (April 1997) to assist federal agencies in applying this "private sector technique to help organizations fundamentally rethink how they do their work in order to dramatically improve customer service, cut operational costs, and become world-class competitors." The GAO has recognized the application and potential impact of BPR as a change strategy and expects agencies to use appropriate methodologies and planning approaches to do BPR well, should they choose to.

The Information Technology Management Reform Act (1996) explicitly requires all federal agencies in the stages of procuring any new information system to reengineer their work processes prior to selecting and installing any technology investment. The GAO has been reinforcing that message with its work on strategic information management. Agencies are being given a firm reminder that this is not just a smart step but a requirement. Former OMB director Raines's memorandum of October 25, 1996, to all federal agencies on Funding Information Systems Investments (known as Raines Rules) further reinforced this requirement.

The Quadrennial Defense Review (QDR) for the DOD takes very specific aim at a number of administrative, procurement, and management support processes and prescribes reengineering of those processes to improve service levels and make substantial cost reductions. While the QDR is not mandatory for domestic agencies, this pursuit of higher-level reengineering initiatives may set a standard for comparison that all federal departments will have to recognize. It also directly points to the need to integrate by redesign administrative systems as opposed to letting them function as separate business functional units.

The report released jointly by the NPR and the Government Information Technology Service Board in 1997 entitled *Access America: Reengineering Through Information Technology* recognizes the critical relationship between reengineering and technology. In then vice president Gore's introduction to the report the point is made that "The idea of reengineering through technology is critical. We don't want to automate the old worn processes of government. IT was and is the great enabler for reinventions It allows us to rethink, in fundamental ways, how people work and how we serve customers."

The above illustrations all envision using reengineering as a means to doing things differently and even thinking about providing very different kinds of services and products for the public. Unfortunately, all of this new emphasis on doing more reengineering may not make it any more successful than BPR's original dismal track record in the 1990s. The experiences of numerous leading-edge federal organizations with BPR indicates that even the best designs and the most expensive consulting advice is no guarantee of success when it comes to getting stakeholder and customer approval or supervisory, union, and workforce acceptance for implementation. Thinking of reengineering in more micro terms, however (again as a verb, if you will), has certain advantages that are likely to transform the way reengineering is used, as it ultimately impacts on what BPR becomes in the future.

Much of the thinking behind both quality and reengineering is cross-functional; that is, breaking down functional and business unit boundaries and redesigning work flows and service delivery systems in terms of what's value added to the customer and the market. What quality and reengineering shared was the same horizontal perspective of enhancing performance across the organization's line of sight from the customer through the organization back to suppliers and contractors. Both approaches were concerned with all of the problems, delays, excessive handoffs, inspections, rerouting, and managerial interventions and holdups (not to mention all of the administrative barriers) built by design into the old bureaucratic work processes. Quality has traditionally been far more interested in streamlining, running parts of the process in parallel, and reducing steps and handoffs accomplished by flowcharting and conducting a value-added analysis of the current system, however. More radical BPR theorists saw much of this as "picking the low-hanging fruit" and moved to make reengineering focus on a complete redesign that redrew organizational boundaries, lines of communication, and employee position responsibilities.

Quality and BPR also share certain disdains (albeit for different reasons). Both abhor simply applying new technology to solve old problems. Quality as continuous improvement saw these types of efforts as "paving cowpaths." Business Process Reengineering viewed IT applications as "installing new plumbing and electricity when the bulldozer was outside the door." Both despised the restructuring and downsizing efforts that were the rage in the 1990s recession, when portraits of CEOs graced the cover of *Newsweek* as "corporate killers." Restructuring was irrelevant because it focused on those vertical aspects of organization. Any creative effort expended on new structural visions of the organizational hierarchy was a waste of time in the view of quality and reengineering until the real work processes of the organization had been realigned. Finally, both quality and reengineering saw downsizing as nonsensical and irrational. While organizations raced to cut their headcount to please investors and Wall Street analysts, quality and reengineering saw these approaches as synonymous to cutting off one's head. Downsizing, they reasoned, as pointed out by Kim Cameron of the University of Michigan and the leading expert on this phenomenon, leads only to more downsizing because such strategies don't work, while at the same time demoralizing the very workforce that would be expected to change the culture and innovate the new process designs being created within quality and BPR.

Information technology reengineering is now clearly emerging as a major new variation. It's more difficult to make distinctions here about what's technology-driven and what's process reengineering-driven. A good example is the Social Security Administration (SSA). By now, everyone has heard of SSA's extraordinary success with its 800 phone service, which is cited as an example of how government can reach world-class customer service standards. In the words of the 1996 NPR report, "In just 18 months, Social Security almost doubled its telephone answering capacity without adding new hires. The agency did this, first, by working with AT&T to design a new network that provided the capacity and automated features found in the best toll-free business services.

But is this reengineering? Indeed, questions were raised in a June 1987 GAO audit of where the 800 service number technology will take SSA. Already 200 to 300 employees have been diverted from other tasks to handle phone calls now and the number must increase if other services are added to the 800 number list. Does the public expect to handle all of its SSA business over the phone? Is this desirable? In terms of comparison, when insurance companies put in their telephone service centers and reengineered their service processes, they found that many customers were concerned about losing track of their "agent," and that convenience provided a real trade-off against continuity. Then again, as more and more corporations put automated voice menus on their phone lines and train customers to push numbers or answer questions via automated command, SSA may yet be vindicated for having provided the best technical customer access and most accurate service.

It should be said that no criticism is implied here of what everyone, even the GAO, agrees was and still is a true government customer success story. Yet reengineering through IT provides a range of new services and access points that need to be viewed in the context of strategic thinking. Taking advantage of new technology is important for competitive purposes, but it may also fall somewhat short of the larger thinking that was envisioned in BPR. Consider another example. When it considered reengineering its core service process, the IRS thought long and hard about how to handle the 120 million phone calls it receives each year. Its final conclusion was that developing a system to handle that volume level would be going in the wrong direction—better to improve tax forms, simplify instructions, and find ways to reduce the number of calls rather than try to handle them more quickly.

Another hybrid on the reengineering change management continuum involves common process management. It involves integrating systems and communications among merging organizations. After undergoing major mergers many corporations are undergoing this type of process, which is required when different organizations merge or bind together in an alliance or partnership to work together. Their systems are not usually compatible and it is important to leverage best practice from within, to choose or create a common process, and to get everyone in on that process, hence the term common process management.

This is not yet a major hybrid for the public sector. Government doesn't have many mergers and acquisitions yet, but it may be coming. Furthermore, government is used to making its contractors and suppliers adopt government systems or crosswalk to their processes. This too will change. As technology affords more advantages and choices, the value of common platforms and linked Internet systems and networks will ultimately drive organizations to integrating systems. The full advantages of electronic commerce will not be realized without significant reengineering of the financial, procurement, and logistical information support systems within the federal agencies themselves.

The problems or lessons learned from poor quality and reengineering planning and methodology misuse pale in comparison with the issues of conversion and implementation, however. If the private sector has failed to use quality or BPR to its fullest extent, there are countless federal agencies who failed to see the implementation requirements in terms of workforce, customer, systems, and programmatic change. Despite countless reminders about the need to get ready for changes resulting from quality and BPR, agencies always underestimated what had to be done and when.

Part of this is thinking of improving and especially reengineering an organization's work processes as something mechanical or procedural as opposed to viewing it for the real thing that it is—changing the culture. One top executive, who directed a major reengineering project at the U.S. Customs Service, commented that it underestimated by tenfold how much work and how much communication would be required to get the workforce to change even when it basically knew the workforce (supported by the union) wanted to change. It is even more difficult, as Social Security has discovered in its major reengineering effort of its disability insurance process, when many of the stakeholders who are involved in the process are outside the agency (e.g., working in state governments). There are lessons to be learned through every stage of the implementation process. It begins with agencies building in delays between the redesign phase and decision approval. Indeed, there are numerous examples of excellent quality change and BPR efforts being completed, but because plans for implementation hadn't been started, other forces within the agency simply backtracked and savaged the redesign plan. They quite correctly interpreted top management's indecision to move forward as permission to move backwards.

Implementation problems abound because few of the supporting management systems are on board far enough in advance to "enable" the new designs. Teams can't be formed because human resources management hasn't figured out how to place and evaluate team members for teamwork. Information technology hasn't been aligned to fit cross-functional teams because the organization allocates budgets and procures its resources through functions. Finally, the workforce has not been prepared with training and learning new work skills. Instead, huge amounts of time are consumed reassuring the workforce about how the redesigned process will affect the workers' job responsibilities, who they report to, and who will fill out their performance appraisals to get them to buy into a change to a work process that they always found frustrating and hopeless. (See the appendix for a summary discussion of these and related issues.)

The lesson learned, of course, is to do concurrent implementation. That remains the final irony for quality management or BPR in the federal government. If there is one underlying premise of both quality and reengineering, it is that all work processes can be redesigned to work in parallel; that with appropriate technology, communications, and management support; work does not have to be done in a serial fashion. The same premise must drive quality or reengineering or any form of change in its application to the federal government. It must lay the foundation for phasing change and redesign, conversion, and implementation stages, and for making human innovation at work a never-ending part of the quality or reengineering processes.

QUALITY ON THE EDGE

As it happens, there is today a resurgence of interest in quality management in the American corporate sector. Quality is making headlines as several leading industries are promoting the value of training their management and professional cadre as "six sigma black belts or internal quality consultants (a sort of blend of quality and reengineering). One of Ford's automobile plants in Atlanta has overtaken the Japanese for the most productive and highest quality-level manufacturer in the world, and among the quality champions such as DOD or states such as Ohio, Florida, and Pennsylvania, quality programs are still highly valued (even if the infrastructure is still invisible).

Quality management now faces its own crises of relevance. In short, in this era of "results act, downsizing, and contracting out," how much value or return on investment can quality add? Tina Sung, the last director of the Federal Quality Consulting Group (before it changed its name), described the current environment this way: "The goals of quality haven't changed, but the organizational map has. Quality management in the future is about results, change and innovation, and most of all creating and sharing knowledge in the workplace."

Sung's vision of quality and its role in public management raises the level of effort and focus considerably. In fact, the question becomes Can continuous improvement become a goal for every employee? An interesting example of how this new expectation would work is the highly touted 1997 winner of the Baldrige Award, Dana Corporation's financial services group, which has a policy that requires every employee to submit two suggestions or ideas a month for improvements and change. The role of midlevel management at Dana is then to ensure that the majority of these employee ideas are implemented. Now that's continuous improvement and real empowerment.

Obviously, there has to be a very real level of trust and real communication among employees to make quality ideas work. This can only happen in an environment that is supportive and truly values people's ideas. If all you see is a bureaucratic nightmare for processing and reviewing suggestions, it won't work, but this does point out the larger issue, especially in government, of how quality management fits within the leadership and management framework. Part of the problem of adapting quality to government is culture and part of it is politics.

So what is the return on investment for management time? What is the economic value of a two-hour meeting of a top management team that focuses on continuous improvement ideas or the next stage of quality development compared to current budget issues, GPRA critical performance issues, strategic policy changes, or even workforce compensation and retention policies? What do you think most government executives prefer to discuss?

It depends, of course, but the prospects for quality aren't bright. Even having a quality coordinator sitting with the top management team isn't going to

Six Sigma Black Belts

Since the mid-1990s, a number of key corporations in the United States have been refocusing their quality management programs internally. Whether tied of paying expensive management consultants or finally having enough trained quality experts on their own staffs, there has been a movement toward creating a new quality culture using the "six sigma black belt" process.

Six sigma was the nearly zero-defects rate pioneered by Motorola a decade ago, which set a failure rate of 3.4 defects per million as the quality goal. That rather astronomical defect rate would translate into such standards as one wrong drug prescription in 25 years or one short or long landing at all the airports in the United States every 10 years.

But six sigma is more than just a numerical objective; it was designed to be the outcome of a process, and that is what is driving Motorola, General Electric (GE), IBM, Raytheon, Citibank, Allied Signal, and Kodak, among others. The concept is basically to convert all of their training investments in TQM by creating a group of internal quality consultants ("black belts") and turning them loose on redesigning work processes and product or service lines.

Motorola puts the work of six sigma belts into six core steps.

1. Identify the work performed (product or service provided)
2. Identify the customer who receives the product or service
3. Identify your work needs (and specify any suppliers)
4. Map the process
5. Mistake-proof the process and eliminate delays
6. Establish quality, cycle time, and improvement goals

The internal consultants are basically process improvement specialists, but their training prepares them for more than simply analyzing process flows and setting up metrics. They acquire additional skills in leadership development and application consulting. Motorola, one of the leaders in this field, emphasizes another dimension—what it calls change acceleration. It is not enough to be agile and flexible—organizations today have to be able to implement change rapidly and broadly, to be able to take project successes or any process innovation in any part of the organization and replicate it in weeks or months.

While Motorola has the longest association with the six sigma process, it is GE that has caused the biggest stir about six sigma black belts. Reportedly it had already trained 4,000 employees as black belts by 1997 and is on target to reach 10,000 for 2000. It measures its return on investment seriously, expecting each black belt project to produce $500,000 to $1,000,000 in annual savings. Jack Welch, arguably the most dynamic corporate leader in the United States in the 1990s made the importance of six sigma crystal clear. He set up senior leadership programs on the six sigma processes and made it clear how quality drives success at GE. As for his workforce, Website sources repute that he has said, "You haven't much future at GE unless you're selected to become a black belt."

What does that six sigma black belt translate to in terms of training? While it's not a master of business administration or master of public administration program, it is extensive. Motorola University (the training and educational consulting arm of Motorola) provides a good overview of what is involved. Motorola's program has four six sigma foundation courses, six black belt courses, and three leadership/personal skills development courses. Along with this training are focused project efforts wherein skills are applied in a real problem-solving environment. Motorola's effort does everything concurrently, but clearly this goes beyond a two-to-four-week government training or university executive course. Black belt programs will vary, but most involve an extensive application process, a half year of concurrent training and project work followed by more project work.

Changing Quality Tactics: Disappearing Quality Teams?

Assuming that the six sigma black belt movement continues to generate interest, what are likely to be the biggest effects? Surely the greatest will be on the future of quality improvement teams. A major attraction of TQM has been its emphasis on employee participation, generally accomplished by setting up employee problem-solving teams or self-directed work groups that are trained in quality tactics and expected to be the driving force behind continuous improvement. Many of quality's strongest advocates assumed that when quality teams were omnipresent in the organization, quality would finally win out.

Six sigma black belt may radically alter that prospect. For one thing, an organization may transfer its training investments from teams to internal consultants. More important, the core assumption of quality has always been that those closest to the work (i.e., the work team were the experts on quality. The roving consultant (i.e., the six sigma black belt may signal the arrival of a new problem-solving approach, fashioned more on process-reengineering methodology and external expertise. Clearly the relationship between work groups and this new kind of internal consultant—the six sigma black belt—may be just as complicated and fraught with potential difficulty as early quality efforts were with external consultants and the old TQM hierarchy.

Source: Adapted from: "Bruce Lee—As Quality Management Consultant," *Public Manager* (winter 1999–2000).

guarantee that top management will want to allocate much time to quality (unless there is a crisis involving work safety or customer service problems). Top management does want quality to work, but it wants to see it ingrained into workforce behaviors and attitudes. Some managers even talk about quality as a form of DNA.

Quality can have a major impact, but it has to be focused on all those "performance" things Tina Sung mentioned—results, change, innovation, and new knowledge—so the changing map confronting quality begins with the Government Performance Results Act (GPRA) or the metric connection. Quality has always had two strong sets of evaluation tools. One entails quality metrics that measure work processes and customer satisfaction levels; the other is the integrated set of self-evaluation organizational assessment measures developed from the Baldrige Award process as the President's Quality Award.

When federal agencies put together their indicators to measure outcomes or results, they will not, by and large, be looking at quality metrics, but quality metrics that are normally focused first on product and service reliability and work process efficiencies can be easily augmented to assess results. Many already do. The link to customer service outcomes is even more direct. Numerous measurement techniques that are now standard for agencies grappling with executive order 12862 all come from quality measurement—satisfaction, responsiveness, cost, and even corporate image. From a quality perspective, any agency that is including customer service outcomes in its GPRA measurement set is probably using service quality metrics to begin with.

As for the link to organizational self-assessment—conceptually this is usually done. Two years ago, the Baldrige criteria were revised to make strategic planning and leadership along with results major new categories for organizational evaluations. The quality organizational assessment process tracks very nicely with the objectives of the GPRA. For organizations already moving to the next wave of organizational measurement in this arena, such as using balanced scorecards (such as units within the FAA and the Veterans Administration), there are models to integrate Baldrige with the balanced scorecard approach.

Still, there's more to quality than simply supporting GPRA objectives. The major issue confronting quality is how to leverage change and alter bureaucratic culture. Ted Poister, a professor at Georgia State University and long-time observer of the quality scene in government, puts the issue this way: "The quality management movement has crested through the public sector over the past decade and managers who don't at least pay lip service to the principles of employee involvement, quality, and customer service are considered to be 'Jurassic.' In practice, however, while a few public agencies have developed a quality and customer focused culture that permeates all aspects of decision making and operations, the majority are still back in the dark ages on this score."

What's a Balanced Scorecard? What Does it Measure?

The balanced scorecard (BSC) first gained notice through the work of Harvard professor Robert Kaplan and consusltant David Norton. In their original *Harvard Business Review* article in 1992, followed by other articles and a book, they explained the concept and helped develop the application.

Simply put, a BSC provides performance measurements that expand on traditionald financial measures. In Kaplan and Norton's original description, they added three measurement areas or perspectives: from customers, internal processes, and an employee category entitled learning and growth. The idea was for the organization to surround its core business vision with financial, customer, process quality, and employee measures. For each of the four dimensions of the scorecard the organization would specify objectives, indicators, and targets, and would describe specific initiatives or activities that matched the targets.

A number of organizations have developed or are doing BSC, primarily because they want to align their strategic objectives with the more important "drivers" or "enablers" that bring about performance improvement. In government, balanced score users include a number of Department of Defense applications, several U.S. cities like Charlotte, NC, and a few state agencies like Arizona's Game and Fish Department and Minnesota's Department of Revenue. One very accessible example is the Federal Aviation Administration's logistics center in Oklahoma City, which, in addition to being a leader in applying BSC, has a reputation for being very generous in supplying information and examples of how to create and use the BSC.

In explaining what BSC is, it's important to stress its flexibility. An organization can add or sutract any number of perspectives. Some major corporations using BSC have added a fifth perspective on "core values" in which they put submeasures and goals for diversity, safety, employee development, and environment. Other corporate leaders that are heavily into quality management have modified their BSC perspectives to complement the Baldrige criteria for organizational assessment.

Why adopt a BSC? After all, most public agencies, especially federal, have their hands filled (or tied) with meeting the requirements levied by performance results budgeting or simply compiling with legislative mandates such as the Government Performance Results Act. The BSC notes that even the best outcome measurements of policy goals and program outcomes can't tell you waht causes good or poor performance. The logic of BSC is that good management can align people, processes, and customer (and contractor) activities as "drivers" of final performance and understand why they are succeeding or failing.

How does an organization go about creating another set of measures when the task of measuring financial or results measures is so consuming? BSC advocates will point out that many of the customer, employee, and internal process measures to be created are already entered into results measures in one form or another. Separating these measures and tracking initiatives in each area may seem onerous, but they are all related and essential to understanding what works and what doesn't.

Who takes responsibility for creating a scorecard, tracking the metrics, and most important, taking action? It begins with the management team. It selects the goals and sets the targets. The management team also devotes time (at least quarterly) to discuss progress and problems, but the organizational units must act, meaning that midlevel managers and employee work teams must understand the BSC metrics and take initiative for change when needed.

When does an organization create a BSC in light of other organizational priorities (i.e., long-term strategic planning, GPRA requirements, budget cycles, and other evaluations and assessments)? A BSC should complement all of these parts of the management cycle. If there's a weakness with BSC, it's that it's heavily internal environment-focused. The more dynamic and turbulent the external environment, the more difficulty for BSC to keep pace, but that's a weakness attributable to most strategic planning systems. BSC is very compatible with the quality management framework.

Source: Adapted from ''The Balance Scorecard—Moving Above the Bottom Line,'' *Public Manager* (Fall 1999).

THE GULF BETWEEN THE QUALITY HAVES AND HAVE NOTS

What puts quality on the edge is the growing gap between those who have assimilated quality in some meaningful way into their culture and those who still see quality as a management fad. No amount of persuasion from corporate leaders at GE, HP, Xerox, or Motorola, who have made quality an essential and integral part of their culture, seems to make a dent in lessening this gulf. There are in the federal government numerous quality haves, beginning with the DOD installations and NASA space centers that have picked up the vast majority of the President's Quality Awards and Special Awards over the past five years.

Some would argue that because of their contracting ties to private industry DOD and NASA have always had a natural advantage in the quality field, but it's hard to argue with success—and success in these cases begins with creating management frameworks and evaluation systems that integrate quality into the management and work team fabric. Likewise, the haves have not seen quality as a form of floor or foundation for performance. They have consciously raised the bar, whether it's in the pursuit of ISO 9000 and now 14000 standards (the European quality process and environmental standards for quality certification) or competing for state government quality awards or holding their own contractor quality conferences and competitions. Of course the drive to compete for awards and recognition can have its negative side. One commander from a recent federal quality award-winning unit candidly remarked that he didn't care what you called their quality process, as long as it provided recognition for his employees. In that regard, he viewed his quality coordinator as essentially his public relations unit.

The have nots who still regard TQM as a failed management fad and have a long memory see little redeeming value in the current successor—quality management—any more than "it's common sense management." More specifically, they see almost no reason for creating any form of quality infrastructure to jumpstart the quality process, much less create training and education programs about quality. They may accept the fact that their organizations have customers and/or may need to form work teams to fix internal problems, but say the c word for customer or the e word for empowerment, and one should be prepared for an argument about why neither concept works.

In terms of the growing gulf between these haves and have nots, the problem is not just visionary versus Jurassic leaders. There are just as many, if not more, Jurassic employees too; organizational culture is the difference. We know that a positive organizational culture supports quality, fosters work teams and cooperation, and enhances work satisfaction. We also know that a more negative and skeptical culture belittles quality, mocks teaming and empowerment, and reinvents the command and control model it supposedly has outgrown. What we don't know is how to change one for the other. Chris Argyris's 1997 article in the *Harvard Business Review,* entitled "Empowerment: The Emperor's New Clothes," comes at this problem of cultural change in a different way. First he argues that most managers like empowerment in theory but trust command and control in practice. Likewise he notes that many employees are "ambivalent about empowerment—it is great as long as they are not held personally accountable." Argyris sees no real transformation of workforce values and culture and blames change professionals as much as anyone for our lack of progress. Among those change professionals, he takes care to include quality and reengineering consultants.

Where is quality likely to go in the next decade in government agencies as they prepare for the new demands of E-government? In the now-emerging age of the horizontal or networked organization, quality will clearly have to convey its message and work its process with minimal infrastructure and even less consulting support. That is the part of quality that is on the edge; organizations facing more downsizing and contracting dilemmas are going to be cautious about any employee decisions. They don't want to get into the paradox that many corporations faced in the late 1980s when they made major training investments in quality basics and then conducted layoffs and outsourced parts of their organization.

Quality management and reengineering must strive to become more synonymous with innovation, however. Much of that will happen through the formation of work teams and cross-functional teams within the work setting. These teams will be different from the problem-solving work groups seen before in organizational environments. For starters, the organization will support these teams by providing them with their own support technology and even reclassifying positions and wage structures to make team work significant. More important, teams will be seen as permanent entities expected to continually assess their own work processes rather than serve as an ad hoc group trying to fix a bunch of organizational problems. The new teams will truly be based on quality culture aspects and may make a reality out of the illusion that Chris Argyris largely sees in empowerment today.

Unions are likely to be more supportive of this type of quality team effort than what has been seen in the past. They should see process teams with rotating team leaders and cooperation-focused work rules as more appropriate to the ideas of partnership. Some have argued that the federal unions were not really serious about the federal quality effort in the beginning, but that was a different time under different rules. The labor–management partnership framework under executive order 12863 of 1993 provides a more level playing field for labor to join management in the pursuit of organizational change and performance improvement. That's the true goal and the unions intend to play and contribute.

In one sense we're likely to see quality move from a position of leadership to followership. That's not meant as a negative. In today's environment, making things happen is the easy part; making things work is what's hard. Quality will be about that kind of implementation. It will still include pareto charts, team brainstorming sessions, customer feedback and focus groups, and even awards and occasional banners and celebrations. More and more, however, it will be about changing the culture, sustaining innovation, planning and accomplishing the next level of breakthroughs, and developing and sharing work knowledge.

APPENDIX

Can Your Personnel Management Policies and Quality Management Premises Coexist?

High on the list of implementation problems is the interface of quality management concepts with organizational or workforce ''culture.'' Since personnel often best represents (or at least codifies) culture through current human resources policies, organizations using quality as a central management philosophy must find ways to realign performance appraisal, compensation, training and development, and labor relations policies. Human resource management issues in the form of personnel policy, labor relations, and training and development are the major forces for making quality happen and making it work within an organization.

Quality and Personnel Policy Issues

While much has been made of the problems associated with getting management and employees to come together as partners to make quality a reality in the public sector, an even larger problem involves a series of issues revolving around the incongruence of quality principles and public personnel requirements. In a 1992 article in *Organizational Dynamics*, two leading advocates of quality applications, Bowen and Lawler, posed a challenge in direct and blunt terms, arguing that personnel offices should be leading organizational quality efforts, not confronting or hindering them. To do this, they contended, required two fronts of action.

First, all human resource management policies and procedures should be reconfigured to align with quality organizational effectiveness concepts. The following five key themes would be involved:

A focus on the organization rather than the job
Support for group performance rather than individual performance
Egalitarianism rather than hierarchy
change rather than stability
Participation rather than command and control

The second front was to apply quality within personnel itself as an organizing customer service principle and thus break down the excessive specialization and narrow functional units within human resource departments in most organizations. They argued that a better way would be to reconstruct personnel into service teams consisting of cross-functional work units that would provide unified answers and one-call access for answers and assistance from managers seeking help in putting together their executive teams or for employees seeking information about leave status or benefits.

Other theorists have tackled the different functional areas of personnel management itself and questioned how compatible existing policies and operating concepts are with quality precepts.

Quality and Performance Appraisal The opening salvo in this debate has been over the role of performance appraisal. The conflict is fairly direct; most public sector organizations have personnel rules requiring individual performance appraisal, while most quality theorists see individual performance appraisal as unacceptable. The conflict was nicely summed up in a letter to *Business Week* in 1991 by the country's generally acknowledged leading quality management consultant, W. Edwards Deming, who wrote: "It will be necessary to end practices such as ranking people, divisions, regions (i.e. performance appraisal), the merit system, pay-for-performance, quotas, and management by objectives (as practiced)."

Why are quality and performance appraisal so incompatible? The main problems are focus and context. In short, quality assumes that the major problems faced by most organizations are the lack of a quality focus caused by the work system and production process. Quality is achieved when workers cooperate with each other, not compete; and rely on customer feedback as the best measurement of whether the system is working effectively. Individual performance appraisal negates these points. Individuals are held accountable and evaluated against performance standards for a work system that is assumed to be optimal. Also, appraisals are focused on individual, not group actions, which breeds individual competition, not group cooperation.

Quality advocates prefer getting rid of individual performance appraisals altogether. What would this involve? First, there are existing legal requirements and labor relations bargaining hurdles that would have to be faced. Second, public sector organizations would have to find substitutes for more specific uses of performance appraisal; such as career retention decisions on new employees or adverse actions against poor performers or probationary employees.

Is there a quality alternative to performance appraisal? Unfortunately, no one seems to know. The one major federal sector experiment with quality, OPM's demonstration Pacer Share at McClellan Air Force Base, eliminated performance appraisal. Reorganization and downsizing have changed the scope and direction of the quality effort and the performance appraisal experiment, however. Even the private sector experience here is at odds with quality theory. An OPM survey in 1990 of private sector organizations that use quality as their central management philosophy found that very few of them actually discontinued their performance appraisal processes.

Still, the incompatibility between traditional human resources appraisal policies and quality management philosophy is very real. Public sector organizations need to recognize that adoption of quality means acceptance of a very different set of human resource management principles. As Dennis Daley has observed, "On the one hand, performance appraisal systems are intricate, complicated, and troublesome but necessary; on the other, they are inconvenient, subversive, and troublesome, but unnecessary. How can performance appraisal navigate between this Scylla and that Charybdis?"

Over time, quality advocates hope that perhaps performance appraisal will become primarily a "development appraisal" that supports training and career education goals. Another option is a model whereby employees and supervisors

are asked to complete annual organizational quality and performance evaluations—not assessments of individual efforts, but of the work processes, system
logistics, planning and communications, training and development needs, and
levels of teamwork within the organization. Such extensive "performance review" information would help focus joint participative management efforts on
"continuous improvement" rather than assessing how well an individual con-
forms to a specific set of work duties. It could examine how well the work unit
performs these same work processes through teams on change and innovation.
Individual appraisal in this model is done through some form of annual training
assessment and job assignment planning process.

Of course this would mean a true change in management perspective, as
James Bowman advocated in an article in *Public Administration Review*. Bowman admonishes public sector organizations.

> It is increasingly obvious that the only sustainable advantage an organi-
> zation has is its people. Traditional management attempts to improve
> performance by controlling employees; it confuses fear with discipline.
> Quality ensures that planning, organizing, staffing and directing take
> place by promoting teamwork, coaching, listening, and leading: pro-
> cesses are measured instead of people, and performance measurements
> are integrated into daily activates to meet real needs. Everyone is ex-
> pected to assume responsibility for problem solving to ensure quality
> and productivity.

Quality and Compensation Issues

Closely linked to appraisal, of course, are compensation questions that need to
be seriously addressed. One good indication of how critical both appraisal and
compensation issues are for quality organizations is the change in organizational
recognition processes. Most quality organizations have not been able to effectuate
any true gainsharing or equal-based proportionate financial reward system for
work groups. Instead there is a progression from "quality champions" or "quality employee of the month" (which most quality organizations now see as dysfunctional) to work team nonfinancial awards and attendant publicity.

Examples of such nonmonetary techniques are certificates of appreciation,
employee recognition days and ceremonies, newsletters and publicity, and even
lotteries with nominal gifts. Individual recognition is basically seen as an extension of team recognition that publicizes the value of team member suggestions,
innovative ideas, and exemplary service stories for customers. Because the majority of organizations involved in quality have yet to reach high levels of their total
workforce participating in some form of quality-oriented team effort, one can
only wonder how long it will take for the quality team award process to become

as dysfunctional as its predecessors, the paid suggestion award system and quality employee monthly recognition program.

Certainly the compensation issue is much bigger than simply recognizing individuals as a means to promote workforce cooperation. The bigger issue is employee empowerment. As long as quality teams are ad hoc and constitute a fraction of the total workforce efforts, most organizations can be creative (and somewhat successful) in providing nonmonetary recognition, but real change occurs when monetary award strategies are used.

Gainsharing is probably the ideal approach for compensating for quality. In gainsharing, a group of employees or teams receives an equal percentage of savings determined to have been produced by productivity and service-level improvement. It is important to have all employees benefit in the same way and to ensure that the system provides no payout if the organization is not successful. To provide some degree of compensation for individual achievement, knowledge-based pay systems can be created whereby education and work skills achievements are rewarded separately. The problem remains that gainsharing systems conflict with personnel policies that legally require pay to be determined by having individuals meet individual, position-determined performance requirements. While most studies point out that public sector pay-for-performance systems are dysfunctional and ineffective, it is hard to find support for alternatives.

There have been some interesting efforts to reconcile quality with current compensation policies. In the early 1990s, the U.S. Naval Aviation Supply Office created a model for team-based monetary awards. A pool of money is set aside (in this case approximately $200 per employee), and if the organization meets its overall performance goals, then all employees who have received at least a "fully satisfactory" rating get the same $200 bonus. Of course, top performers receive the same as everyone else, and because the award is split among everyone basically equally, the award is much less than if it were limited to a small number of high achievers.

To make the system work, the Naval Aviation Supply Office decoupled the performance rating from monetary awards. Much of the performance appraisal was based on team ratings of a common work plan. Here the problems of separating individual appraisals from team-based appraisals are more manifest. The Naval Aviation Supply Office candidly admits "It is difficult to design a system that is compatible with TQL (Total Quality Leadership) within existing Federal regulations"

Quality and Training and Development Issues

The relationship between quality and training has changed considerably over the past decade. In the initial stages of quality development, making investment decisions about quality training was easy to justify. The problem was making sure that the money was well spent. In response to a new management marketing area, there was a flood of training programs on quality, especially from outside vendors. Almost every consulting organization, university, and management association had a training program on quality to offer—for a price.

Variations on this theme included the following:

> Train every employee in the organization in quality improvement processes (QIP), whereby every individual was given (or inoculated with) a 1- to 2-day quality orientation or "awareness course" to present the organization's quality improvement process.
>
> Train every supervisor to be a quality on-the-job trainer. (All supervisors receive a week-long course in quality metrics and their application so that they "would manage by fact and data.")
>
> Educate top managers in quality principles and philosophy. (Send all managers to a "quality institute," a "quality college," "seminars with the gurus," or some other form of vendor seminars to learn quality and think through how they could apply it to their units. (Since usually the most receptive managers would go first, this would generate pressure over time to have everyone attend.)

Over time organizations put their quality-training efforts in a linear progressive relationship. All employees got some form of general quality orientation, supervisors got tools and measurement techniques, and managers received strategic thinking and analysis in quality, with maybe some participative management material to get them thinking in terms of teamwork and empowerment.

None of this was wrong. In fact, it was exactly what the quality gurus had prescribed: Use training to institute quality on the job. Most organizations contracted for their quality training anyway, although the more serious the organization was about quality, the more likely it was to (1) create its own "quality institute," (2) establish a quality training curriculum, and (3) create an internal training capability in quality.

Problems began to emerge, however, because training and quality usually weren't integrated. Most organizations created some form of quality infrastructure—a quality board, council, coordinator, or office—and that body of "qualiticrats" oversaw training in quality as one of its big functions. If the quality office hired consultants, they often fashioned a quality-training curriculum for the organization. The training office continued on as before, waiting for the quality office to complete the quality introductory process before taking over quality training as a maintenance function or a new employee orientation function.

The failure of this model of training for quality was inevitable. The choice of words is important here; failure is something one learns from, adapts to, and moves forward from. Failure is not decline or fall or demise. Orthodox quality was too long-term and too slow. Its use of training emphasized too much program and not enough process. Too much of quality pushed "doing things right" as opposed to asking whether the organization was "doing the right things."

Ironically, training figured prominently in the first wave of failure and adverse publicity involving quality. The most telling story was not the failure of some Baldrige Award winners (the national quality competition) or Florida Power and Light (winner of Japan's international quality prize). In these cases, several companies that competed for and won national and international awards for their quality and management efforts failed in or cut back their quality programs, contributing to the some of the skepticism about quality; rather, it was such cases as aerospace companies such as Mcdonnell Douglas going into a massive downsizing that resulted in laying off large numbers of their workforce, many of whom had been trained extensively in quality tools and methods. This story crystallized fears that training in quality (with its bottom-up, continuous improvement, process measurement emphasis) could not ensure that the organization was on the right course or prevent the loss of a considerable training investment if the organization had to radically change.

By the mid-1990s, the watchword had become balancing "improvement versus innovation." The question now was how training should respond to the demands of innovation (and learn from the mistakes made in the earlier 1980s quality partnership). Training's initial response was to become more multidimensional. Quality management now ranges from continuous improvement to radical innovation. Training must be more multifaceted. In the continuous improvement domain, it must balance awareness with methodological skills. The concept involves more "facilitation." In the innovation domain, it must play more of an "enabler role," whereby the driving concept is "consultation" or "mentoring."

Training now ranges from training and development for individuals to training for work groups. It seeks to support the organization by pursuing very different strategies. First, quality training has redefined its role in working with all sorts of work teams, from problem-solving teams such as QITs (quality improvement teams) to SAWTs (semiautonomous work teams) to PRTs (process redesign teams) and CFTs (cross-functional teams). This involves teaching a full range of core team skills (e.g., team dynamics and facilitation) and core quality and reengineering methodology skills (e.g., process measurement, customer value assessment, and modeling). Second, quality training is increasingly more focused on groups. Quality training is given to work teams and groups rather than individuals from all over the organization. Quality training has in effect become just-in-time, and just-in-need. The objective is to provide training as appropriate to employees, whether in quality problem-solving work groups or reengineering teams, just before they start their problem-solving efforts, redesign work, or even assume new work team responsibilities.

Like the central personnel policy function, training is being forced to reexamine its own role in the organization. The problem is both systematic (the way work groups perpetuate individual work preferences) and structural (the way organizations are aligned in tight functional disciplines), but training is increasingly being asked to pursue a multifaceted approach capable of supporting either broad-based incremental change efforts inherent in quality management or more selective and radically focused reengineering efforts in the organization.

The challenge to training is the same one being given to budget, procurement, information technology, and even human resource management offices. If the goal is to use quality and innovation as a framework to achieve ''government that works better and costs less,'' then surely the framework must be applied to training itself. Perhaps that is what is truly significant about this still-emerging quality revolution in public sector management. The lessons being learned in public sector training and development are significant. As training strives to install quality as a process management methodology within itself and concurrently support customer-focused organizational processes, it will be an excellent gauge as to how much progress the public sector is making on the path toward quality management or making quality an integral dimension of its approach to management and performance.

Quality and Labor Relations Issues

Finally, quality management calls for very high levels of workforce participation or what is generally called empowerment. Workers are expected (and trained) to join together in any number of variations of quality teams to analyze quality problems (improvement teams) or to devise new solutions (PRTs).

Most of these teams operate outside the classic formal hierarchical and representation structures that have evolved over the last century, with managers and supervisors managing work being performed and union stewards managing workers' behavior. The questions raised are not trivial. Some theorists have examined employee involvement in this new environment and foreseen several possible outcomes, ranging from false cooperation at one extreme to managerialism (essentially participation without unions) at the other. Given quality management's reliance on the workforce, the dangers of moving to either extreme are considerable and potentially disastrous.

One might wonder why these tensions did not come up in either of the quality movement's predecessors; the quality of work life (QWL) movement in the 1970s and quality circles (QCs) in the early 1980s. Two reasons may be offered. First, neither QWL nor QCs represented such sharply focused levels of participation. The QWL movement was very broad, usually involving elected representation, while QCs were very narrow, in part because they were almost always voluntary. Second, the seriousness of the need for change was much more muted. Up to the 1980s, there were problems in the American industrial public sector, but no real sense that the wolf was at the door. Today, economic climates are radically different and as some analysis has shown, when organizational survival is at stake, management and unions have learned very quickly how to employ radical forms of quality teaming as a measure for change.

By habit, both unions and management still know how to fight in the courts. A 1993 ruling by the National Labor Relations Board (NLRB) that a major corporation (Du Pont) had to eliminate seven management employee committees created as employee participation efforts to improve safety, fitness, and work conditions brings into question where unions stand on workforce empowerment through quality management. The NLRB ruling is limited, and NLRB officials were quick to point out that the ruling does not preclude "many of the types of participation programs now in place," such as productivity teams, quality circles.

Left unanswered is exactly what is covered, however. What types of employee participation committees do pass muster, within what scope of activity, and under what procedural guidelines? Unfortunately the path of labor–management cooperation continues to get rockier. On the one side is management pressing for employee involvement as a key to improve work quality and performance. On the other side are unions greatly concerned about avoiding co-optation and protecting workers' rights, and suspicious of participation as just another form of managerialism. Suspicions are further raised when participative management efforts are the first things called for when organizations face downsizing or severe budget and cost constraints.

To be fair, there are some excellent success stories in the private and public sectors involving quality and employee participation efforts. Little wonder that the Clinton administration has been so enthusiastic about them as role models for change. Again, the research suggests that when organizational situations are truly seen as "crises of survival," management and unions are quite capable of creating and supporting effective quality-oriented participate management efforts. Alas, the same research notes that in regulated or stable industries there is less interest, less support, and less success.

While current government budget situations at the federal and state levels are of crisis proportions, few believe survival is a problem. Most state governments and now the federal government continually opt for some mix of workforce size reductions, pay and benefit constraints, and revenue enhancements to cope with hard fiscal times. Despite their obvious potential, the fact that quality management and employee participation efforts are not focal points for major reform or restructuring speaks volumes to their real significance.

So where does that leave labor–management cooperation in the current quality environment? Of course there is always interest in labor–management cooperation, but real reform is another matter. The public sector is still regarded as a stable industry, and it is questionable how many unions or managers will perceive that their organizational survival is in question. Perhaps the larger question will be how quality management and labor–management cooperation will be affected in the oncoming wave of pressures to restructure, downsize, and reinvent government, as with the federal level or the next stages of competitive government at the state and local level.

Postscript

In summary, despite the skepticism of many, quality management has become a major element in public sector management. The core dimensions of quality management—internal process measurements, external customer focus, employee participation, and contractor involvement—are all highly compatible with public management premises and goals, and in some cases have been made formal policy goals such as customer service improvement.

Above all, however, quality management is a framework for organizational change that emphasizes work groups and processes with a customer focus over individuals and organizations focused on functional specializations. Within a quality framework, there are key conflicts with traditional human resource management functions. As quality management becomes more and more accepted as the public sector management standard, pressure can only mount for traditional personnel functions such as appraisal, compensation, training and especially labor–management relations to adapt and change to new organizational realities.

BIBLIOGRAPHY

Bowen, D. E. and E. E. Lawler. "Total Quality-Oriented Human Resources Management," *Organizational Dynamics,* vol 20, no. 4 (Fall 1992) pp. 29–41.

Bowman, James. "At Last, an Alternative to Performance Appraisal: Total Quality Management," *Public Administration Review,* vol. 54, no. 2 (March–April 1994) pp. 129–138.

Carr, David K. and Ian D. Littman. *Excellence in Government: Total Quality Management in the 1990's,* 2nd ed. Washington, D.C.: Coopers & Lybrand, 1993.

Champy, James. *Reengineering Management.* New York: Harper Business, 1995.

Cohen, Steven and Ronald Brand. *Total Quality Management in Government.* San Francisco: Jossey Bass, 1993.

Cole, R. E. "Introduction: Symposium on Quality Management," *California Management Review,* vol. 35 (spring 1993) pp. 7–11.

Cole, Robert E. *The Death and Life of the American Quality Movement.* New York: Oxford University Press, 1995.

Daley D. M. "Pay for Performance, Performance Appraisal, and Total Quality Management," *Public Productivity & Management Review,* vol. XVI (fall 1992) pp. 39–52.

Davenport, T. "Need Radical Innovation and Continuous Improvement: Integrate Process Reengineering and TQM," *Planning Review* (May–June 1993) pp. 18–23.

Davenport, Thomas. *Process Innovation: Reengineering Work Through Information Technology.* Harvard Business School Press, 1993.

Deming, W. E. *Out of the Crises.* Cambridge, MA: MIT-CAES Press, 1982.

Deming, W. E. "Letter to the editor," *Business Week* (April 15, 1991).

Devaney, D. *New York Times* (June 8, 1993), p. 14.

Farson, Richard. *Management of the Absurd: Paradoxes in Leadership.* New York: Simon & Schuster, 1996.

Federal Register, vol. 58 (September 16, 1993), p. 48583.

Federal Register, vol. 58 (October 6, 1993), p. 52201.

Garvin, David. *Managing Quality.* New York: Free Press, 1988, p. 4.

Hamel, Gary and C. K. Prahalad. *Competing for the Future.* Boston: Harvard Business School Press, 1994.

Hammer, Michael. *Beyond Reengineering.* Harper Business, 1996.

Hammer, Michael and Steven Stanyon. *The Reengineering Revolution.* New York: Harper Business, 1995.

Heckscher, C. C. *The New Unionism.* New York: Basic Books, 1988.

Hyde, A. C. "The Implementation of Quality Management: A Concept Assessment Report." Washington, D.C.: Center for Public Policy Education, the Brookings Institution, 1996.

Hyde, A. C. "A Primer for Business Process Reengineering," *Public Manager* (summer 1994).

Ishikawa, Kaoru. *What Is Total Quality Control? The Japanese Way.* Englewood Cliffs, N.J.: Prentice Hall, 1985, pp. 23–44.

Koehler, Jerry W. and Joseph M. Pankowski. *Quality Government.* Del Ray Beach, FL: St. Lucie Press, 1996.

Johnson, E. K. "Total Quality Management and Performance Appraisal: To Be or Not to Be." Washington, D.C.: U.S. Office of Personnel Management, 1990.

Levine. M. J. "Labor and Management Response to Total Quality Management," *Labor Law Journal* (February 1992) pp. 107–116.

Linden, Russell. *Seamless Government: A Practical Guide to Reengineering in the Public Sector.* San Francisco: Jossey Bass, 1994.

Milakovich, Michael. *Total Quality Service.* Del Ray Beach, FL: St. Lucie Press, 1996.

National Governor's Association. "Total Quality Management Initiatives in State Governments." Washington, D.C.: 1992.

National Performance Review. *From Red Tape to Results: Creating a Government That Works Better and Costs Less.* Washington, D.C.: U.S. Government Printing Office, 1993.

"The Costs of Quality: Business Sours on Total Quality Management," *Newsweek* (September 7, 1992).

Swiss. J. E. "Adapting Total Quality Management (TQM) to Government," *Public Administration Review,* vol. 52, no. 4 (1992).

Taylor, Frederick. *Shop Management.* New York: Harper & Brothers, 1919, p. 3.

U.S. General Accounting Office. (1992) "Quality Management: Survey of Federal Organizations." Report number GGD-93–9BR. Washington, D.C: 1992, p. 43.

U.S. Department of the Navy. "Recognizing, Awarding, and Appraising People in a Total Quality Leadership Organization." TQLO publication no. 92–04. Washington, D.C., 1992.

West, J., E. Berman, and M. Milakovich. "Implementing TQM in Local Government: The Leadership Challenge," *Public Productivity and Management Review* (1994).

10

Equal Employment Opportunity and Affirmative Action

PROLOGUE: FROM *BAKKE* TO *HOPWOOD*

In the early 1970s, Allan Bakke unsuccessfully sought admission to the medical school at the University of California at Davis. The medical school maintained a separate admission program for students of color, and reserved at least 16 seats for them. The program was developed in 1973 in order to increase the representation of African Americans, Mexican Americans, and American Indians, who were conspicuously absent from the entering classes ever since the medical school opened in 1968. Bakke, a white applicant who could not demonstrate that he would have been admitted to the school under the regular admissions program, sued on the grounds that his exclusion from competition for the 16 reserved admissions slots constituted a violation of the Fourteenth Amendment to the U.S. Constitution, the California Constitution, and Title VI of the Civil Rights Act of 1964. He claimed that he was a victim of "reverse discrimination."

A very divided U.S. Supreme Court struck down the affirmative action program developed by the medical school on the grounds that it was too obtrusive in reserving 16 slots exclusively for racial minorities. Allan Bakke was ultimately admitted to the medical school. A majority of the justices also upheld the constitutionality of a flexible admissions program, however, whereby under certain circumstances race could serve as one factor in admissions decisions. In effect, the 1978 *Bakke* decision upheld for the first time the principle of affirmative action.

Chapter 10

This paved the way for a number of other rulings whereby the legality of affirmative action would be upheld by the U.S. Supreme Court.

Fast forward to the 1990s.

In 1992, Cheryl Hopwood and three other white students were denied admission to the University of Texas School of Law, one of the nation's leading law schools. After decades of segregationist policies, the state's institutions of higher education were under pressure from the federal government to increase the representation of African Americans and Mexican Americans. The law school had a target of admitting a class that was 10% Mexican American and 5% African American. Hopwood and the other three applicants sued under the Equal Protection Clause of the Fourteenth Amendment as well as under civil rights laws. Their central claim was that they had been subjected to unconstitutional racial discrimination.

In *Hopwood* v. *State of Texas* (5th Cir. 1996), the U.S. Court of Appeals for the Fifth Circuit struck down the constitutionality of the law school's affirmative action program. In reversing the district court's decision, the appeals court issued a ruling that did not necessarily evaluate the actual admissions program of the law school, but rather ruled more broadly on the constitutionality of using race as a criterion in admissions decisions.

In effect, the ruling called into question the continued validity of the high court's 1978 *Bakke* ruling. The appeals court in *Hopwood* began by applying the first prong of the strict scrutiny test to the law school's use of race in admissions decisions. More specifically, the court asked:

1. Whether or not relying on race for the nonremedial goal of having a diverse student body could serve as a compelling governmental interest
2. Whether or not the use of racial classifications could be justified as a remedy for the present effects of past discrimination by not only the law school, but by the Texas educational system as a whole

What Is Strict Scrutiny?

In determining the constitutionality of an affirmative action program, courts will apply the strict scrutiny test. It is a two-pronged test that asks: (1) whether or not there is a compelling governmental interest for the program (e.g., to redress past discrimination), and (2) whether or not the program is sufficiently narrowly tailored to meet its specified goals (e.g., whether there are alternative programs that could be employed that do not classify people by, for instance, race).

In addressing the first point, the appeals court ruled that diversity in and of itself cannot serve as a compelling state interest in higher education. Interestingly, the court invoked the *Bakke* decision to support its ruling here. The *Hopwood* court reasoned that only one member of the high court—Justice Powell—had found that diversity could serve as a compelling governmental interest in *Bakke*. The Court of Appeals for the Fifth Circuit flatly rejected this aspect of the *Bakke*, opining that "Justice Powell's argument in *Bakke* garnered only his own vote and has never represented the view of a majority of the Court in *Bakke* or any other case . . . Justice Powell's view in *Bakke* is not binding precedent on this issue."

The appeals court concluded that "the use of race to achieve a diverse student body, whether as a proxy for permissible characteristics, simply cannot be a state interest compelling enough to meet the steep standard of strict scrutiny."

The appeals court next assessed the second point and determined that it was unconstitutional for the law school to employ racial classifications to remedy the present effects of past discrimination by the entire Texas school system. The appeals court rejected the lower court's argument that past, pervasive discrimination by the Texas primary and secondary educational systems against African Americans and Mexican Americans impeded their ability to compete fairly on the tests and other tools used in admissions decisions to the law school. The appeals court concluded that "the use of racial remedies must be carefully limited, and a remedy reaching all education within a state addresses a putative injury that is vague and amorphous. It has 'no logical stopping point.'"

It is interesting to note that even if the case turned on whether the use of race could be justified as a remedy for the effects of discrimination *solely* by the law school, the appeals court would have struck down the constitutionality of the program, because it took the further step of saying that the law school no longer discriminated against African Americans. It said that "While the school once did practice de jure discrimination in denying admission to blacks, the Court . . . struck down the law school's program (in a 1950 decision). Any other discrimination by the law school ended in the 1960's . . . when the school . . . implemented its first program designed to recruit minorities."

In short, the *Hopwood* appellate court ruled that the law school's affirmative action program could not meet the first prong of the strict scrutiny test. As such, the court went on to say, it need not apply the second prong of the test, which examines whether or not the program was sufficiently narrowly tailored to meet its goals.

For now, the *Hopwood* ruling governs at least the three states that make up the Fifth Circuit—Texas, Louisiana, and Mississippi—because in July of 1996 the U.S. Supreme Court said it would not hear the appeal by the state of Texas from the Fifth Circuit's ruling. Importantly, because the *Hopwood* decision addresses the *constitutionality* of an affirmative action program, it sets a precedent not only for admissions programs of educational institutions but also for public employment decisions. The challenge, then, is whether or not government employers in these jurisdictions will seek to ensure that their affirmative action programs meet the strict scrutiny test, thereby enabling the programs or policies to pass constitutional muster if challenged.

The controversy over affirmative action will continue into the twenty-first century. It remains one of the most hotly debated and contested personnel issues of the latter part of the twentieth century. It is an issue that every American has an opinion on, and one that employers, policy makers, and the courts have been challenged by since its inception. Grass roots efforts across the country have sought to dismantle or abolish affirmative action altogether. In California, for example, voters in the November 1996 election supported Proposition 209, a measure that outlaws the use of affirmative action programs based on race, color, gender, ethnicity, or national origin in public hiring, contracting, and college admissions. Overall, the legal status of affirmative action has been so mercurial that most are left to wonder what the future holds for affirmative action as an employment tool or social policy.

THE DIFFERENCE BETWEEN EQUAL EMPLOYMENT OPPORTUNITY AND AFFIRMATIVE ACTION

Equal employment opportunity (EEO) is largely viewed as a means to prevent discrimination in the workplace. Title VII of the Civil Rights Act of 1964 as amended, for example, is intended to prevent discrimination on the basis of race, color, religion, gender, and national origin in public and private sector workforces. Affirmative action, on the other hand, which emerged in response to pervasive employment discrimination, refers to proactive efforts to diversify the workplace in terms of race, ethnicity, gender, and even physical abilities. Its emphasis on proaction has been the cause for the controversy and public debate over its use as an employment tool or social policy. (See Table 10.1.)

ABUSES OF THE PAST

In the past three decades EEO has become a major concern of public personnel administration in the United States. There is now a myriad of statutes, executive orders, judicial decisions, and administrative regulations intended to further EEO at all levels of government. Equal Employment Opportunity means different things to different people, however, and how it should be defined and implemented touches directly upon one of the most persistent political questions facing America today. Here can be seen the full politicality and widespread ramifications of personnel practices in the public sector. It is impossible to understand recent developments in the EEO realm, especially reliance on affirmative action, without

TABLE 10.1   Chronology of Legal Actions Affecting Affirmative Action

1978   *Regents of the University of California* v. *Bakke*. U.S. Supreme Court
       upholds the principle of affirmative action, but strikes down its
       operation by the University at California under the Fourteenth
       Amendment and Title VI of the Civil Rights Act of 1964.

1979   *United Steelworkers of America* v. *Weber*. U.S. Supreme Court upholds
       legality of voluntarily developed affirmative action plan under Title VIII
       of Civil Rights Act of 1964.

1980   *Fullivove* v. *Klutznick*. U.S. Supreme Court upholds constitutionality
       (under Fifth and Fourteenth Amendments) of federal set-aside
       programs enacted by the U.S. Congress.

1984   *Firefighters Local Union and Memphis Fire Department* v. *Stotts*. U.S.
       Supreme Court upholds, under Title VII of the Civil Rights Act, as
       amended, the use of a seniority system in layoff decisions, despite its
       negative impact on affirmative action.

1986   *Wygant* v. *Jackson Bd. of Ed*. U.S. Supreme Court strikes down, under
       the Fourteenth Amendment to the Constitution, the use of affirmative
       action in layoff decisions.

1986   *Sheet Metal Workers' International Association* v. *EEOC*. U.S. Supreme
       Court upholds, under Title VII and Fifth Amendment to the
       Constitution, a court-ordered affirmative action program to remedy
       past discrimination by a union and apprenticeship committee against
       people of color.

1987   *Johnson* v. *Transportation Agency, Santa Clara County*. U.S. Supreme
       Court upholds, under Title VII, voluntarily developed affirmative action
       program intended to correct gender and racial imbalances in
       traditionally segregated job categories.

1987   *U.S.* v. *Paradise*. U.S. Supreme Court upholds, under the Fourteenth
       Amendment to the Constitution, a court-ordered affirmative action plan
       aimed at remedying discrimination against African Americans in hiring
       and promotion decisions in Alabama Public Safety Department.

1989   *City of Richmond* v. *Croson*. U.S. Supreme Court strikes down the
       constitutionality, under the Fourteenth Amendment, of a local
       government's set-aside program because it could not satisfy the
       criteria of the strict scrutiny test.

1989   *Martin* v. *Wilks*. U.S. Supreme Court allowed white firefighters to
       challenge, under Title VII, a consent decree to which they were not a
       party years after it had been approved by a lower court.

1990   *Metro Broadcasting* v. *F.C.C*. U.S. Supreme Court upholds the
       constitutionality (under the Fifth Amendment) of FCC's set-aside
       policy, which bears the imprimatur of longstanding congressional
       support.

1990   Civil Rights Acts vetoed by President Bush. Congress fails to override
       veto.

TABLE **10.1**   Continued

1991	Civil Rights Act passed. Restores affirmative action to its pre-1989 legal status.
1995	*Adarand* v. *Pena.* U.S. Supreme Court rules that the Equal Protection Clause of the Fifth Amendment requires that racial classifications used in federal set-aside programs must undergo strict scrutiny analysis.
1995	*In re Birmingham Reverse Discrimination Employment Litigation (BRDEL).* U.S. Supreme Court let stand, without comment, a decision by the U.S. Court of Appeals for the Eleventh Circuit, which invalidated a promotion plan aimed at promoting African American firefighters to the position of lieutenant.
1995	*Claus* v. *Duquesne Light Company.* U.S. Supreme Court let stand without comment a decision by the Third Circuit Court of Appeals, which awarded a white engineer for a utility company $425,000 in damages because, according to the court, he was "passed over" in favor of an African American for promotion to a managerial job.
1996	President Clinton suspends, for a minimum of three years, all federal set-aside programs.
1997	*Taxman* v. *Piscataway Township Board of Education* is dropped from the U.S. Supreme Court's calendar, because parties settled. Thus remains the 1996 opinion of U.S. Court of Appeals for the Third Circuit: the goal of achieving or maintaining diversity cannot be a justification for a race-based employment decision.

Note: Actions around EEO or employment discrimination (e.g., the U.S. Supreme Court's *Griggs* v. *Duke Power Co.* ruling) are not addressed here.

at least a cursory understanding of the discriminatory practices of the past. Although other groups have been subjected to unequal treatment, discrimination against African Americans and women is illustrative and perhaps has been the most prevalent.

Even as the American revolutionaries were fighting the British for the right to establish a new political order, it was reasonably clear that whatever improvements the struggle for independence might bring to whites in the new world, African Americans were not very likely to receive a substantial share of the prospective benefits. Symbolically, this was demonstrated at the outset by General Washington, who, although in need of increased human resources power, was unwilling to use African-American troops. The issue of slavery aside, the first formal application of such an outlook toward free African Americans came in 1810, when Congress enacted a law providing that "no other than a free white person shall be employed in conveying the mail." At least some of its proponents, including Postmaster General Gideon Granger, wanted to prevent African Americans from doing anything that "tends to increase their knowledge of natural rights, of men and things, or that affords them an opportunity of associating, acquiring and communicating sentiments, and of establishing a chain or line of intelligence.'' The law was subsequently modified, but remained on the books until it was repealed in 1865.

Although this provision applied only to postal employees, it is believed that there were no African Americans in the federal bureaucracy until 1867. After that date, African Americans made slow but generally steady numerical inroads. It appears that by 1928 they had achieved a proportion in the federal service roughly equal to their proportion in the nation as a whole. These gains came about both through politics and through the merit system. Politically, after the end of the Reconstruction period, the Republicans began to make a number of African-American civil service appointments as a form of compensation to the group as a whole. Eventually a tradition was established of appointing African Americans to some minor posts in the District of Columbia and to diplomatic posts in black nations such as Liberia and Haiti. Once white Southerners were able to disenfranchise African Americans through terror, poll taxes, and other devices, however, the Republicans began to lose interest in their lot and became reluctant to make additional African-American appointments.

During the latter part of the nineteenth century, as African-American gains under Reconstruction were wiped out, it appeared that the merit system might offer a lasting means of facilitating their appointment to the federal service. In 1883, when the merit system was enacted into law, there were 620 African Americans in the bureaucracy in Washington. By 1892 this number had increased to 2,393. In its *Eighth Annual Report*, the Civil Service Commission wrote: ''Another excellent feature of the examinations in the Southern States has been the elimination not only of the questions of politics and religion but of the question of race.'' It maintained that ''it is impossible to overestimate the boon to these colored [sic] men and women of being given the chance to enter the Government service on their own merits in fair competition with white and colored [sic] alike.'' Maintaining entry is sometimes more difficult than gaining entry, however. The civil service laws did little to prevent discrimination in dismissals and other aspects of personnel administration. Thus in 1894 civil service commissioner Theodore Roosevelt observed that over the three or four preceding years, the War Department dismissed about two-thirds of the African Americans placed through examination. Such practices were exacerbated by the Taft and Wilson administrations. Taft believed that African Americans should not hold federal posts where whites complained of their presence. Moreover, he began segregationist practices in the federal service by segregating census takers in Washington, restricting whites to whites and African Americans to African Americans.

The Wilson administration had an even greater impact on inequality. Although often considered one of the more liberal and enlightened presidents, Wilson, put simply, engaged in racist personnel policies. After openly appealing to the African-American vote, which was largely Republican at the time, and winning more of it than had any other Democratic candidate for the presidency, he created widespread segregation within federal agencies and sanctioned the dismissal of large numbers of African Americans. In the following years, segregationist practices were continued and gained the sanction of the Civil Service Commission (CSC). In the words of one of its officials, the commission was in the practice of "not certifying Negroes [sic] to bureaus where they would be turned down or made unhappy." It wasn't until the New Deal that the treatment of African Americans in the federal service began to undergo significant change.

While the employment of women in the government service in America actually predates the formation of the Union, women have generally not been treated as equals in the federal service. The relevant history of women and federal personnel administration began in 1861, when the Treasury Department first began the then scandalous practice of hiring female clerks. Similar to the experience of African Americans, discrimination against women was once formally sanctioned both by law and by official directive. The most important formal basis of inequality on the grounds of gender was derived from an 1870 statute, which ironically had been intended to give women greater equality: "Women may, in the discretion of the head of any department, be appointed to any of the clerkships therein authorized by law, upon the same requisites and conditions, and with the same compensations as are prescribed for men." The law was interpreted to allow appointing officers to exclude women for reasons unrelated to their capacity or the efficiency of the service, and until 1919 women were excluded from about 60% of the positions covered by examinations. Until the ratification of the Nineteenth Amendment in 1920 (guaranteeing women the right to vote), many women also found it difficult to compete for patronage positions. Unequal compensation had originally been provided for by law, and despite the 1870 statute it continued in some agencies until 1923, when the Classification Act established the requirement of equal pay for equal work, regardless of gender. It wasn't until 1937, however, that marital status became an illegal basis for discriminatory treatment.

Legal barriers and prejudice aside, women faced a number of substantial problems in gaining and retaining federal employment. First, as Cindy Sondik Aron points out in her book, *Ladies and Gentlemen of the Civil Service*, social norms frowned so much on middle-class women working outside the home that those "who chose to become federal employees might well have felt they were jeopardizing not only their class status, but their gender identity as well." Second, female federal employees faced sexual harassment. As early as 1864, a congressional committee began to investigate charges that supervisors were seeking sex from their female subordinates. Popular writers belabored the theme that a federal clerkship would often be won at the cost of a woman's virtue. The Treasury in particular gained notoriety for sexual improprieties, although it is impossible to say how widespread they were. Finally, as Aron notes, "government offices were clearly men's turf," for they spit, smoked, cursed, and sometimes showed up

---

What Are Veterans Preferences?

Veterans preference refers to a type of affirmative action for veterans. Most states and the federal service provide a five-point advantage to qualified veterans and a ten-point advantage to disabled veterans. In other words, a score of 90 on a civil service exam that is earned by a veteran eligible for a five-point preference will be raised to 95, giving him or her a higher ranking than those who earned less than 95 points on the list. In some places, absolute preference is afforded to veterans.

Veterans preference statutes have come under attack on the grounds that such preferences adversely affect women, who are less likely to be veterans. This issue was settled by the U.S. Supreme Court in its 1979 decision in *Personnel Administrator* v. *Feeney*, however. The Court ruled that veterans preference statutes provide legitimate rewards by government for military service and do not violate the Equal Protection Clause.

---

drunk—all of which the women workers were likely to find offensive at that time.

No doubt most of the women who joined the federal service in the latter half of the nineteenth century were "reluctant pioneers," as Aron puts it, yet the number of female employees in the executive departments in Washington, D.C. increased from none in 1859 to 6,882 by 1903. By 1930, about half of all federal clerical workers were women. Eventually, that proportion would rise to over 80%, creating new problems such as sex-segregated jobs and concerns over pay equity for women.

Despite the unique problems facing women, historically their experience in the federal service paralleled that of African Americans in many respects. For instance, until recent decades, both were confined almost entirely to the lower grades. Both groups also found it somewhat easier to obtain positions in factory-type operations, such as in mint and printing operations. As was the case for African Americans, the CSC formally supported equality for women while at the same time accepting and even abetting discrimination against them. As will be seen shortly, it was not until the 1960s that genuine change in this area began to occur.

THE DEVELOPMENT OF EEO

Although there were a few earlier provisions affecting equal opportunity in federal personnel procedures, it was in 1941 that a serious EEO effort was begun.

In order to forestall a threatened mass protest march by African Americans on Washington, President Franklin Roosevelt issued Executive Order 8802, which called for the elimination of discrimination based upon race, color, religion, or national origin within defense production industries and the federal service. The newly created Fair Employment Practice Committee was charged with the implementation of the program. By almost all accounts, however, the committee was weak and even somewhat uninterested in combating discrimination in the federal service. It met its demise in 1946 through an amendment to an appropriations bill. Through an executive order in 1948, President Truman created the Fair Employment Practices Board within the CSC. The board advanced EEO concepts considerably. Its "corrective action program" enabled individuals who believed that they had been subjected to illegitimate discrimination to launch a complaint. Such actions had to be initiated in the agency involved, so the board only heard cases on appeal, which limited its effectiveness. The board's other responsibilities were both ill-defined and ineffective. It held conferences with fair employment officers and outside organizations, conducted periodic surveys and appraisals, and sought the adoption of new recruitment techniques and better efforts at integrating the federal workforce. In a way the board's activities were a precursor of contemporary practices, although it believed that its direct action options were strictly limited by the need for "color-blindness" and "merit." In judging the board, it should be remembered that it existed during the McCarthy era, when being sympathetic to racial equality was sometimes taken as evidence of communist leanings under the loyalty-security programs in existence at the time.

In 1955, the board was replaced by the President's Committee on Government Employment Policy. The new program reaffirmed the government's interest in nondiscrimination, but it went further in declaring that "it is the policy of the United States Government that equal opportunity be afforded all qualified persons, consistent with law, for employment in the Federal Government." This was interpreted to mean that the government was obligated to take whatever action it deemed reasonable to overcome societal inequities and to equalize opportunity itself, not just equalize the treatment of individuals. Under the new policy it was necessary to channel special efforts in recruitment, training, and other areas of personnel administration toward minority or protected-class groups that were thought to be proportionally underrepresented in the federal service as a result of societal inequalities. Accordingly, the program moved further in the direction of affirmative action and compensatory treatment. At the same time it maintained an interest in individual complaints and strengthened the system for their consideration.

By the time President Kennedy took office, the basic EEO concepts of today had been developed, if not carried to their logical ends or effectively implemented. It was not until the Kennedy administration that EEO became a central and major aspect of federal personnel administration, however. Between 1961

and 1965, the civil rights movement reached the pinnacle of its political importance, and racial equality became a dominant national issue. Indeed, it was a sign
of the times when Kennedy declared, "I have dedicated my administration to
the cause of equal opportunity in employment by the Government." Accordingly,
he issued yet another executive order, this time creating the President's Committee on Equal Employment Opportunity. The new committee gained prestige and
some measure of political clout by including the vice president as its chair. It
stressed affirmative action in the sense of making efforts to bring more African
Americans, Latinos, and other protected-class groups into the federal service.
These included recruitment drives at high schools and colleges heavily attended
by these persons. Agencies were encouraged to provide better training opportunities for them as well. The committee also began the practice of taking an annual
census of the employment of African Americans, Latinos, and other protected-
class groups in government. Although it de-emphasized the importance of complaints, believing that they were of only remedial importance, it nevertheless
took steps to strengthen the complaint system. Finally, and most important, the
committee developed a new sense of realism in recognizing that "full equality
of employment opportunity requires that we face up to the whole problem of
equality itself." Accordingly, it began thinking along compensatory lines.

The Kennedy program was carried forward by President Johnson until
1965, when another reorganization occurred and a longer-lived program was initiated. The change was a result of many factors. The Civil Rights Act of 1964
declared that "it shall be the policy of the United States to ensure equal employment opportunities for Federal employees." It also created the Equal Employment Opportunity Commission (EEOC) to combat discrimination in the private
sector, and consequently the coordination of all federal civil rights activities became increasingly complex and difficult. Funding for the president's committee
on EEO ran into difficulty in Congress, and it was decided to shift its responsibilities to the CSC, where the program remained until 1979.

The Civil Rights Act also required EEO for women by prohibiting discrimination on the basis of gender. Prior to its enactment, Kennedy had created the
Commission on the Status of Women and subsequently issued a memorandum
requiring that appointments and promotions be made without regard to gender
except under circumstances whereby the CSC found differentiated treatment jus-
tifiable. In 1969 the women's program was fully incorporated into the overall
EEO program for the first time.

The next major development in the evolution of the EEO program came
in 1969, when President Nixon issued an executive order requiring agency heads
to "establish and maintain an affirmative program of equal employment opportunity." The following year, Nixon changed the nature of EEO activities still further by creating a Spanish-speaking program within the overall EEO program.
Designed to bring more members of the Spanish-speaking population into the

**Why Gender Was Added to the Language of Title VII
of the Civil Rights Act of 1964**

Gender discrimination in employment was by no means a significant concern of the civil rights advocates of the early 1960s. Its prohibition only became part of the Civil Rights Act of 1964 because of Congressperson Howard ''Judge'' Smith. As the leader of the South's fight against civil rights, he added one small word—*sex*—to prohibitions against discrimination based on race, color, religion, and national origin. He felt confident this amendment would make the proposed law ridiculous and cause its defeat. Smith was an ''old style'' bigot; in his mind one thing more ridiculous than equal rights for blacks was equal rights for women.

The ''sex discrimination'' amendment was opposed by the Women's Bureau of the Department of Labor, by the American Association of University Women, and by most of the Congress's leading liberals. They saw it as nothing but a ploy to discourage passage of the new civil rights law. The major support for adopting the amendment came from the reactionary southern establishment of the day. Because President Lyndon Johnson insisted that the Senate make practically no changes in the law as passed by the House, there was no discussion of gender discrimination by the Senate. The momentum for a new civil rights law was so great that Smith's addition not only failed to scuttle the bill, but went largely unnoticed.

Source: Adapted from Rosenbloom, David H. and Jay M. Shafritz. *Essentials of Labor Relations*. Reston, Va.: Reston Publishing Co., 1985, pp. 63–64.

federal service, it was subsequently renamed the Hispanic Employment Program and became an integral part of the government's EEO efforts. It has been effective in turning attention to the special circumstances of the Hispanic or Latino segment of the population.

The Equal Employment Opportunity Act of 1972 solidified the CSC's authority in this area and placed the program on a solid statutory basis for the first time. It reaffirmed the traditional policy of nondiscrimination and empowered the commission to enforce its provisions ''through appropriate remedies, including reinstatement or hiring of employees with or without back pay . . . [and issuing] such rules, regulations, orders and instructions as it deems necessary and appropriate.'' It also made the commission responsible for the annual review and approval of agency EEO plans and for evaluating agency EEO activities. The act also brought state and local governments under the federal EEO umbrella for the first time. The EEOC, heretofore primarily concerned with the private sector, was given similar authority over the nonfederal public sector.

In 1991, Congress again amended civil rights law with passage of the Civil Rights Act. The act not only overturned several negative U.S. Supreme Court decisions issued in 1989 on EEO and affirmative action, but is also did the following:

> Created the Glass Ceiling Commission to study the artificial barriers to the advancement of women and persons of color in the workplace.
>
> Extended coverage of antidiscrimination laws (including the 1991 act, the 1964 Civil Rights Act, the Age Discrimination in Employment Act of 1967, the Rehabilitation Act of 1973, and the Americans with Disabilities Act of 1990) to political employees in the executive branch and the employees of the Senate.
>
> Allowed compensatory and punitive damages to be recovered by victims of intentional discrimination based on gender, religion, or disability. (Previously such damages were available only to racial and ethnic minorities.) Damages are capped—at $50,000 to $300,000, depending upon the size of the employer—for cases of gender, religious, and disability discrimination only. The provision does not apply to government employers.
>
> Extended protections of the act and the Americans with Disabilities Act to U.S. citizens employed by U.S. companies abroad.
>
> Prohibited "race norming" of employment tests (i.e., score adjustments, use of different cutoff scores, or other alterations to the results of employment tests, on the basis of race, color, religion, gender, or national origin (Civil Rights Act of 1991).

In 1979, as a part of the overall federal civil service reforms then taking place, the enforcement aspects of the federal EEO program were transferred to the EEOC, but while the EEOC gained responsibility for reviewing affirmative action plans and processing complaints of discrimination, the newly created Office of Personnel Management (OPM) contained the Office of Affirmative Employment Programs, which had responsibility for the Federal Women's Program, the Hispanic Employment Program, and programs for veterans, the disabled, and the "upward mobility" of members of these groups and protected-class groups in general. This change was opposed by some high-ranking OPM officials and several members of Congress on the grounds that it undesirably fragmented authority for federal personnel management. The EEOC was also criticized for its huge backlog of cases and its history of ineffectiveness. These views notwithstanding, the transfer was part of the political price of building a consensus in favor of

---

The Principal Provisions of Title V of Rehabilitation Act of 1973, as Amended

Section	Provision
501	Requires affirmative action in federal employment
502	Requires that federal buildings be accessible
503	Requires federal contractors to develop affirmative action plans
504	Prohibits discrimination by federal agencies as well as institutions receiving financial assistance
505(b)	Requires that attorney's fees be provided for the prevailing party in a Title V action

Source: Adapted from Schlei, Barbara and Paul Grossman. *Employment Discrimination Law*, 2nd ed. Washington, D.C.: Bureau of National Affairs, 1983, p. 246.

President Carter's reform package and it was generally supported by African Americans and other groups especially interested in federal EEO. Obviously, the CSC's failure to develop much support for its implementation of EEO proved costly to the development of unified and coherent public personnel management. Once again, then, public personnelists were clearly reminded of the politicality of their jobs.

The transfer of major EEO responsibilities to the EEOC quickly turned out to be of major consequence for federal personnel administration. The EEOC was instrumental in forcing the OPM to discontinue the Professional and Administrative Career Examination (PACE). The exam had an adverse impact on the employment of African Americans (as well as Latinos). Only 5% of the African Americans taking the exam passed it, and only 0.7% percent received a score high enough to even win consideration for hiring. By contrast, as of 1979, the passing rate of whites was 51% and 9% of them scored a 90 or higher, thereby making appointment likely. The exam was discarded in 1982 after the OPM failed to demonstrate satisfactorily that it was valid in the sense of one's score being predictive of the quality of job performance later on. The PACE was the single major examination for entrance into the main career track in the general schedule. Its demise gave individual agencies far greater responsibility for developing their own approaches to selection. Many federal agencies began to place greater reliance on unassembled examinations. Much more use was also made of Schedule B, which allows hiring based on noncompetitive examination (i.e., the applicant must pass an examination but is not ranked competitively with other applicants by score). A variety of other techniques was also used. These included relying on college grade point averages, recommendations, interviews, and highly specialized exams for specific positions.

Constance Horner, former director of OPM, claimed that personnelists faced a "nightmarish" situation in trying to screen some 300,000 to 500,000 yearly applicants for roughly 10,000 positions in the general schedule's main administrative career track, but getting rid of the PACE also enhanced EEO. By 1990, OPM was set to try to maximize both efficient personnel administration and equal opportunity. It had spent about $100,000 to develop each of six broad examinations that did not appear to have an adverse impact on African Americans, Latinos, and other protected-class groups, and would be highly predictive of on-the-job performance. This battery of tests, called Administrative Careers with America (ACWA), was abandoned by OPM in 1994, however. The emphasis on centralized examining of entry-level job applicants, which ACWA (and PACE before it) was designed to accomplish, was replaced with a focus on decentralized examination.

The civil service reform of 1978 not only gave the EEOC a major role in federal personnel practices, it also changed EEO policy substantially. The reform makes it federal policy to seek a "work force reflective of the Nation's diversity" by establishing that "recruitment should be from qualified individuals from appropriate sources in an endeavor to achieve a work force from all segments of society." Further, it requires that each executive agency's recruitment should be "designed to eliminate underrepresentation of minorities in the various categories of civil service employment within the Federal service." Underrepresentation in turn is defined as a situation in which members of a designated minority or protected-class group "within a category of civil service employment constitutes a lower percentage of the total number of employees within the employment category than the percentage that the minority constituted within the labor force of the United States." Any such underrepresentation is to be eliminated within the framework of merit, and programs to do so would presumably have to be narrowly tailored to avoid violating the legal rights of nonminorities. The statute leaves no doubt, however, that federal personnel policy now views obtaining a socially representative workforce as a major objective. In the early days of EEO programs, there was often a contest of merit *versus* representation; today, the goal is clearly merit *and* representation.

There are several lessons of contemporary relevance to be learned from the past. Foremost among these is the simple fact that the government had engaged in widespread discriminatory practices. African Americans, women, and members of other groups were not excluded on the basis of their qualifications but rather on the basis of their social characteristics. The merit system once created did not fully apply to them. In addition, the development of the federal EEO program indicated that while organizational change came frequently, substantive change has been elusive. Although the first-stage problem of equalizing the opportunity of protected-class persons to gain entrance to the federal service has been more or less resolved, these government employees still remain disproportionately concentrated in the lower grades of the bureaucracy. Whether or not equal opportunity has been created remains debatable. It is abundantly clear, however, that more than five decades of federal EEO have not resulted in anything approaching substantive equality. (See Table 10.2.)

Table 10.2 captures the current federal EEO situation well. Great progress has been made in assuring that members of protected-class groups have equal opportunity in the federal personnel system. There is no pronounced underrepresentation of them in the federal workforce as a whole. Members of these groups are still disproportionately concentrated in the lower levels of the federal service, however, and they are seriously underrepresented in the upper grades. Consequently, today the EEO emphasis is less on eliminating barriers to the employment of protected-class persons than on developing greater upward mobility for them within the federal service. Affirmative action plans also stress recruitment to the higher levels to do away with marked imbalances in the social composition of the workforce. Overall, public employment at the state and local governmental levels reflects similar patterns and concerns. Just as there is considerable variation among individual federal agencies and regions in their employment patterns, however, there is great variation among the states, counties, municipalities, towns, authorities, and school and other districts that form all but one of the nation's 83,000 governmental jurisdictions.

THE ORGANIZATION OF EEO

Although public sector EEO programs can be organized in a variety of ways, several pertinent organizational lessons have been learned from past experience. First, an agency administering EEO must have a credible record in its own dealings with protected-class persons. Agencies administering EEO must practice what they preach. In this regard, the old CSC was particularly defective. In the 1970s it was harshly criticized by the U.S. Commission on Civil Rights for adopting a role that "was characterized more by passivity than by 'leadership'; more by neutrality than by 'guidance.'" Undoubtedly the CSC's inadequate performance contributed strongly to support for the transfer of much of the EEO program to the EEOC.

Second, efforts to decentralize EEO and to integrate it into all facets of public personnel management have not worked well at the federal level. The CSC's organizational scheme dispersed authority and responsibility among bu-

TABLE 10.2 Percentage Representation of Men, Women, Whites, and People of Color in Grade Groupings in the Federal Government (1997)

	Men	Women	White	African American	Latino	Asian/Pacific Islander	Native American	Total
GS 1–4	28	72	54	30	7	5	4	75,548
GS 5–8	39	61	66	22	7	4	2	442,860
GS 9–12	57	43	75	14	6	4	2	566,587
GS 1–15	74	26	83	8	4	4	1	314,422
Executives	79	21	88	6	3	2	1	13,956

Source: EEOC, Annual Report on the Employment of Minorities, Women & People with Disabilities in the Federal Government for FY 1997.

reaus and officials that were often more sympathetic to traditional personnel practices than to EEO. Consequently, change was difficult and the discriminatory status quo was maintained to a substantial extent. Agencies had considerable responsibility for the development of their own EEO programs, including the authority to establish and implement affirmative action plans and to deal with many aspects of complaints of discrimination within broad guidelines set forth by the CSC. Authority and responsibility were also divided among headquarters and regional offices in such a fashion that the CSC's Office of Federal EEO, the main policy-making and oversight bureau, had little direct information concerning federal employment outside the Washington, D.C., metropolitan area. In essence, this meant that the affirmative action plans and agency activities covering over 90% of the federal workforce were outside its purview. Moreover, the EEO offices in the headquarters of other agencies sometimes suffered from a similar problem and knew little about what was going on within their own field installations.

If decentralization of EEO activities in an effort to integrate equal opportunity with public personnel management generally have not worked well, however, efforts to implement EEO through a centralized enforcement agency also present difficulties. Historically, in the federal service at least, this approach has not worked well. Agencies administering EEO outside the mainstream of personnel have been frustrated by the commitment of personnelists to "merit" even in the face of clear evidence that aspects of the merit system can be discriminatory. Moreover, public personnel administration is rather complicated and difficult for outsiders to comprehend, especially in its netherworld aspects. Even today the EEOC and the OPM are sometimes seriously at odds concerning policies that are relevant to EEO. Nevertheless, there is now some evidence from local governmental experience that EEO efforts will be more effective if responsibility for them is placed under the chief executive rather than in a personnel department or a civil service commission.

Another positive lesson was learned regarding the organization of efforts to further the employment of members of different groups covered by EEO. In 1970, a special Spanish-speaking program (subsequently renamed the Hispanic Employment Program) was initiated within the overall framework of federal EEO. It included Hispanic Employment Program coordinators who were to address the special needs of Latinos and to facilitate the application of EEO to them. Similarly, Federal Women's Program coordinators were to advise agency officials on the "special concerns" of women and were "required" to "have empathy with and understanding of the special problems and concerns of women in the employment situation." Organization along these lines is important because the employment patterns of African Americans, women, and other protected-class persons are sufficiently dissimilar to indicate that these persons should be treated separately rather than as a bloc.

THE MANAGERIAL ASPECTS OF AFFIRMATIVE ACTION

There are two key affirmative action functions that human resource managers or affirmative action officers are responsible for: reporting and planning. Title VII of the Civil Rights Act as amended requires public sector employers with 100 or more employees to compile and submit to the EEOC reports on the gender and racial composition of their workforces on an annual basis. The purpose of these reporting requirements is to aid in EEOC's administration and enforcement of Title VII. In addition, once processed and summarized by the EEOC, the reports allow employers to make comparisons of the racial and gender makeup of their workforces with that of other jurisdictions across the country, and with their local labor markets.

The other critical affirmative action function performed by human resource managers or affirmative action officers is affirmative action planning. Let's take a closer look at what's involved in developing an affirmative action plan.

Developing a Plan

There is no definitive affirmative action plan, nor is there a "cookbook" approach to developing viable, effective plans. While there is a wide variety of types of affirmative action plans, there are nonetheless some common ingredients to well-developed plans, including the following:

1. Commitment of financial and human resources for administering the plan
2. Evaluation of current EEO/affirmative action efforts, and overall personnel policies and practices
3. A utilization analysis
4. Goals and timetables to achieve a representative workforce
5. Recruitment strategies to reach and attract job candidates from all sources
6. Training programs for employees and supervisors
7. A procedure for evaluating the organization's progress toward achieving its affirmative action goals

Perhaps one of the first steps in affirmative action planning is to ensure that the organization or government entity has invested an appropriate amount of resources to the overall effort. If serious about diversifying its workforce, a government employer must appropriate resources so that the *entire* plan can be implemented effectively.

In addition, organizations will often review and evaluate their current EEO and affirmative action efforts. This entails a host of activities, including examining current recruitment, hiring, promotion, retention, and transfer policies and practices, and their effects on all employees. Such a review may reveal inequities in the treatment or representativeness of protected classes throughout the organization.

Utilization analyses are also important to affirmative action planning. A utilization analysis compares the numbers and percentages of protected-class persons in the organization or government workplace with their percentages in the local or relevant labor market. Also involved is a review of the skills requirements for job vacancies, the skills utilization of protected classes (including disabled and older workers) within the organization, and the general availability of protected-class persons in the local labor market with the requisite skills. Organizations may also consider the availability of protected-class persons in the local geographic area who are promotable, and the training opportunities they will make available so that these persons are competitive for job advancement.

The development of goals and timetables has also been encouraged. Goals and timetables, which may be calculated in any number of ways, establish benchmarks and target dates for diversifying the workforce. Contrary to popular belief, goals are *not* quotas; quotas are generally set by courts after a finding of employment discrimination, and involve the imposition of sanctions if the quota is not met. If, for example, an organization does not fulfill a court-ordered quota, the court in theory can fine the organization. In practice, sanctions are rarely imposed because the courts tend to look favorably on an organization's good faith efforts toward fulfilling the established quota.

In contrast, goals are flexible benchmarks or indicators of an organization's desired level of protected-class employment. If not fulfilled within a given time period, the organization will reexamine its efforts and set more realistic goals. Needless to say, the organization does not impose sanctions on itself if the goals are not met.

Active recruitment efforts should also be outlined in the affirmative action plan. Outreach is critical for an organization's overall affirmative action efforts, and requires the development and maintenance of contacts with various groups and communities (e.g., women's groups, African Americans, Latinos, and groups representing citizens with disabilities). Contacts should also be maintained with schools, colleges, and universities that have large populations of women or students of color. It is also common to make job announcements with radio stations and other media outlets (e.g., newspapers) that appeal to people of color, women, and other protected-class groups.

Training and education programs for managers, supervisors, and rank-and-file employees should also be addressed in the affirmative action plan. Managers and supervisors should receive training on the overall EEO and affirmative action policies and programs of the organization, and employees should be offered training programs for skills acquisition, promotion opportunities, and career growth and development.

The Language of EEO

Adverse effect.   Differential rate of selection (for hire, promotion, etc.) that works to the disadvantage of an applicant subgroup, particularly subgroups classified by race, gender, and other characteristics on the basis of which discrimination is prohibited by law.

Adverse-inference rule.   An analytical tool used by the Equal Employment Opportunity Commission (EEOC) in its investigations. The EEOC holds that when relevant evidence is withheld by an organization when the EEOC feels that there is no valid reason for such a withholding, the EEOC may presume that the evidence in question is adverse to the organization being investigated. The EEOC compliance manual permits use of the adverse-inference rule only if "the requested evidence is relevant," the evidence was requested "with ample time to produce it and with notice that failure to produce it would result in an adverse inference," and the "respondent produced neither the evidence nor an acceptable explanation."

Adverse impact.   When a selection process for a particular job or group of jobs results in the selection of members of any racial, ethnic, or gender group at a lower rate than members of other groups, that process is said to have adverse impact. Federal EEO enforcement agencies generally regard a selection rate for any group that is less than four-fifths or 80% of the rate for other groups as constituting evidence of adverse impact.

Affected class.   According to the U.S. Department of Labor's Office of Federal Contract Compliance:

> persons who continue to suffer the present effects of past discrimina-
> tion. An employee or group of employees may be members of an af-
> fected class when, because of discrimination based on race, religion,
> sex, [sic] or national origin, such employees, for example, were as-
> signed initially to less desirable or lower paying jobs, were denied
> equal opportunity to advance to better paying or more desirable jobs,
> or were subject to layoff or displacement from their jobs.

Employees may continue to be members of an "affected class" even though they may have been transferred or advanced into more desirable positions if the effects of past discrimination have not been remedied. For example, if an employee who was hired into a lower paying job because of past discriminatory practices has been subsequently promoted, further relief may be required if the employee has not found his or her "rightful place."

Affirmative action.   When the term first gained currency in the 1960s, it meant the removal of "artificial barriers" to the employment of women and "minority" group members. Toward the end of that decade, however, the term got lost in a fog of semantics and came out meaning the provision of compensatory opportunities for hitherto disadvantaged groups. In a formal, *legal* sense, affirmative action now refers to specific efforts to recruit, hire, train, retain, and/or promote disadvantaged groups for the purpose of eliminating the present effects of past discrimination.

Bona fide occupational qualification (BFOQ or BOQ). *Bona fide* is a Latin term meaning "in good faith," honest, or genuine. A BFOQ, therefore, is a *necessary* occupational qualification. Title VII of the Civil Rights Act of 1964 allows employers to discriminate against applicants on the basis of religion, gender, or national origin, when being considered for certain jobs if they lack a BFOQ. However, what constitutes a BFOQ has been interpreted very narrowly by the EEOC and the federal courts. Legitimate uses for BFOQs include, for example, female sex for a position as an actress or male sex for professional baseball player. There are no legally recognized BFOQs with respect to race or color. Overall, a BFOQ is a job requirement that would be discriminatory and illegal were it not for its necessity for the performance of a particular job.

Bottom-line concept. In the context of equal employment opportunity, the bottom-line concept suggests that an employer whose total selection process has no adverse impact can be assured that EEO enforcement agencies will not examine the individual components of that process for evidence of adverse impact. However, not all EEO enforcement agencies subscribe to the concept.

Business necessity. The major legal defense for using an employment practice that effectively excludes protected-class persons. The leading court case, *Robinson* v. *Lorrilard Corp.*, 444 F.2d 791 (4th Cir. 1971); *cert. denied*, 404 U.S. 1006 (1971), holds that the test of the business necessity defense

> is whether there exists an overriding legitimate business purpose such that the practice is necessary to the safe and efficient operation of the business. Thus, the business purpose must be sufficiently compelling to override any racial impact; the challenged practice must effectively carry out the business purpose it is alleged to serve; and there must be available no acceptable alternative policies or practices which would better accomplish the business purpose advanced, or accomplish it equally well with a lesser differential racial impact.

Chilling effect. Employment practices, government regulations, court decisions, or legislation (or the threat of these) may create an inhibiting atmosphere or chilling effect that prevents the free exercise of individual employment rights. A "chilling" effect tends to keep protected-class persons from seeking employment and advancement in an organization even in the absence of formal bars. Other chilling effects may be positive or negative, depending upon the "chillee's" perspective. For example, even discussion of proposed regulations can "chill" employers or unions into compliance.

Consent decree. Approach to enforcing equal employment opportunity involving a negotiated settlement that allows an employer to not admit to any acts of discrimination yet agree to greater EEO efforts in the future. Consent decrees are usually negotiated with the Equal Employment Opportunity Commission or a federal court.

Discrimination. In the context of employment, the failure to treat equals equally. Whether deliberate or unintentional, any action that has the effect of limiting employment and advancement opportunities because of an individual's gender, race, color, age, national origin, religion, or physical disability is discrimination. Because of the EEO and civil rights legislation of recent years, individuals aggrieved by unlawful discrimination now have a variety of administrative and judicial remedies open to them.

Disparate effect. Tendency of an employment screening device or criteria to limit the appointment opportunities of protected-class persons at a greater rate than for white males.

Employment practice. In the context of equal employment opportunity, an employment practice is any screening device operating at any point in the employment cycle. If a discriminatory employment practice is not related to job performance, it will not be able to withstand a court challenge.

Equal Employment Opportunity (EEO). Concept fraught with political, cultural, and emotional overtones. Generally, it applies to a set of employment procedures and practices that effectively prevent any individual from being adversely excluded from employment opportunities on the basis of race, color, gender, religion, age, national origin, or other facts that cannot lawfully be used in employment efforts. While the ideal of EEO is an employment system that is devoid of both intentional and unintentional discrimination, achieving this ideal may be a political impossibility because of the problem of definition. One person's equal opportunity may be seen by another as tainted with institutional racism or sexism. Because of this problem of definition, only the courts have been able to say if, when, and where EEO exists.

Equal employment opportunity counselor. Specifically designated individual within an organization who provides an open and systematic channel through which employees may raise questions, discuss real and imagined grievances, and obtain information on their procedural rights. Counseling is the first stage in the discrimination complaint process. The counselor through interviews and inquiries attempts to informally resolve problems related to equal employment opportunity.

Equal employment opportunity officer. Official within an organization who is designated responsibility for monitoring EEO programs and assuring that both organizational and national EEO policies are being implemented.

Fair Employment Practice Commission (FEPC). Generic term for any state or local government agency responsible for administering/enforcing laws prohibiting employment discrimination because of race, color, gender, religion, national origin, or other factors.

Fair employment practice laws. All government requirements designed to prohibit discrimination in the various aspects of employment.

Gender differential, also RACE DIFFERENTIAL. Lower than ''regular'' wage rate paid by an employer to female and/or African-American and Latino employees. Such differentials were paid before the advent of current equal employment opportunity laws and are now illegal.

Gender discrimination. Any disparate or unfavorable treatment of an individual in an employment situation because of his or her gender. The Civil Rights Act of 1964 makes gender discrimination illegal except where a bona fide occupational qualification is involved.

Make whole. Legal remedy that provides for an injured party to be placed as near as may be possible, in the situation he or she would have occupied if the wrong had not been committed. The concept was first put forth by the U.S. Supreme Court in the 1867 case of *Wicker* v. *Hoppock*. In 1975, the Court held, in the case of *Albermarle Paper Company* v. *Moody* (422 U.S. 405), that Title VII of the Civil Rights Act of 1964 (as amended) intended a ''make whole'' remedy for unlawful discrimination.

Protected class. Any person covered by antidiscrimination legislation, including women, African Americans, Latinos, Asian/Pacific Islanders, Native Americans, persons over forty years of age, disabled persons, and Vietnam-era veterans.

Reading assistant. Reader for a visually impaired employee. Public Law 87-614 of 1962 authorized the employment of readers for visually impaired federal employees. These reading assistants serve without compensation from the government, but they can be paid by the visually impaired employees, nonprofit organizations, or state offices of vocational rehabilitation. They may also serve on a volunteer basis.

Reasonable accommodation. Once a disabled employee is hired, an employer is required to take reasonable steps to accommodate the individual's disability unless such steps would cause the employer undue hardship. Examples of ''reasonable accommodations'' include providing a reader for a visually impaired employee, an interpreter for a hearing-impaired person requiring telephone contacts, or adequate workspace for an employee confined to a wheelchair.

Religious discrimination. Any act that manifests unfavorable or inequitable treatment toward employees or prospective employees because of their religious convictions. Because of section 703(a)(1) of the Civil Rights Act of 1964, an individual's religious beliefs or practices cannot be given any consideration in making employment decisions. The argument that a religious practice may place an undue hardship upon an employer—for example, where such practices require special religious holidays and hence absence from work—has been upheld by the courts. However, because of the sensitive nature of discharging or refusing to hire an individual on religious grounds, the burden of proof to show that such a hardship exists is placed upon the employer.

Restrictive credentialism. General terms for any selection policy adversely affecting disadvantaged groups because they lack the formal qualifications for positions that, in the opinion of those adversely affected, do not truly need such formal qualifications.

Representative bureaucracy. Concept originated by J. Donald Kingsley, in *Representative Bureaucracy* (Yellow Springs, Ohio: Antioch Press, 1944), which asserts that all social groups have a right to participation in their governing institutions. In recent years, the concept has developed a normative overlay—that all social groups should occupy bureaucratic positions in direct proportion to their numbers in the general population.

Retroactive seniority. Seniority status that is retroactively awarded back to the date that a woman or other protected-class group member was proven to have been discriminatorily refused employment. The U.S. Supreme Court has interpreted the "make whole" provision of Title VII of the Civil Rights Act of 1964 to include the award of retroactive seniority to proven discriminatees; however, retroactive seniority cannot be awarded further back than 1964—the date of the act.

Rightful place. Judicial doctrine that an individual who has been discriminated against should be restored to the job—to his or her "rightful place"—as if there had been no discrimination and given appropriate seniority, merit increases, and promotions.

706 Agency. State and local fair employment practices agency named for Section 706(c) of Title VII of the Civil Rights of 1964, which requires aggrieved individuals to submit claims to state or local fair employment practices agencies before they are eligible to present their cases to the federal government's Equal Employment Opportunity Commission. State and local agencies that have the ability to provide the same protections provided by Title VII as would the EEOC are termed 706 agencies. The EEOC maintains a list of the 706 agencies that it formally recognizes.

Systemic discrimination. Use of employment practices (recruiting methods, selection tests, promotion policies, etc.) that have the unintended effect of excluding or limiting the employment prospects of protected-class persons. Because of court interpretations of Title VII of the Civil Rights Act of 1964, all such systemic discrimination, despite its "innocence," must be eliminated where it cannot be shown that such action would place an unreasonable burden on the employer or that such practices cannot be replaced by other practices which would not have such an adverse effect.

Source: Adapted from Shafritz, Jay M. *Dictionary of Personnel Management and Labor Relations*, 2nd ed. New York: Facts on File, 1985.

Finally, periodic reviews and evaluations of the affirmative action plan and its implementation will enable the organization to determine whether or not it is meeting its goals. Problems can thus be identified and rectified.

It is also worth noting that in developing and implementing a plan, employers will rely on EEOC's technical assistance, compliance manuals, and its *Guidelines on Affirmative Action*. These guidelines govern how the EEOC will handle complaints about actions taken in accordance with an affirmative action plan. The EEOC expressly issued these guidelines in conjunction with section 713 (b) (1) of Title VII, which protects from challenge an employer's omission or action taken ''in good faith, in conformity with, and in reliance on written opinions or interpretations of the [EEOC].'' Adhering to the EEOC's *Guidelines on Affirmative Action* thus protects employers who take ''reasonable actions'' under legitimate affirmative action plans.

There are many other components that may be included in affirmative action plans. As noted earlier, affirmative action plans are unique to each organization or government employer; effective plans depend upon each employer's attention to its own circumstances and the problems and opportunities it faces.

Monitoring the Plan

Affirmative action and EEO planning are ongoing processes that don't end once a plan has been completed and implemented. In particular, monitoring the plan involves constant attention to how the plan is being implemented and whether or not its goals are being met. Depending upon the circumstances, formal audits by administrative bodies may also take place. For example, the Department of Labor's Office of Federal Contract Compliance Programs (OFCCP) conducts periodic compliance audits of current federal government contractors as well as preaward audits of prospective contractors. The initiation of an audit does not depend upon the receipt of a complaint from an aggrieved individual; rather, the OFCCP routinely targets employers for review.

When targeted for review by the OFCCP, a copy of the employer's affirmative action plan is requested. The OFCCP reviews the plan and makes a determination as to its soundness. If the plan is sound, the audit is immediately terminated. If the plan is unsound, a ''desk audit'' is arranged. Here the OFCCP compliance officer or team is assigned to the case. The team will spend several days, sometimes weeks, randomly reviewing affirmative action files on hiring, promotions, and terminations within the *entire* organization, not just the program or unit receiving federal funding. The team will, for instance, (1) investigate the numbers of women and persons of color hired, promoted, and terminated within a designated time period; (2) ascertain whether or not any of the employer's personnel procedures have adverse impact; (3) conduct a compensation analysis to determine if there are pay inequities between women and men, or people of

Procedures for Processing Individual Complaints of Discrimination Based on Race, Color, Religion, Gender, National Origin, or Physical or Mental Disability

1. Employee contacts EEO COUNSELOR within 30 calendar days of alleged discriminatory action. COUNSELOR has 21 calendar days to attempt informal resolution.
   If final counseling interview is not completed in 21 days, COUNSELOR must on 21st day give written notice of right to file an individual complaint any time up to 15 calendar days after final interview.

2. If informal resolution fails, EMPLOYEE may file an individual formal complaint with DIRECTOR OF EEO, AGENCY HEAD, INSTALLATION HEAD, EEO OFFICER, or FEDERAL WOMEN'S PROGRAM MANAGER within 15 calendar days of final interview with COUNSELOR.

3. EEO OFFICER advises DIRECTOR OF EEO, who assigns INVESTIGATOR from jurisdiction or agency other than that in which the complaint arose.

4. Investigation conducted; COMPLAINANT given copy of investigative file. EEO OFFICER provides opportunity for informal adjustment.

5. If adjustment not made, EEO OFFICER notifies COMPLAINANT in writing (1) of proposed disposition, (2) of right to hearing and decision by AGENCY HEAD, and (3) of right to decision by AGENCY HEAD without a hearing.

6. If COMPLAINANT does not reply within 15 calendar days, EEO OFFICER may adopt proposed disposition as decision of the agency, providing he or she has been delegated this authority. Otherwise, complaint is forwarded to AGENCY HEAD (or his or her designee) for agency decision. Upon receipt of decision or any final decision, the EMPLOYEE may file a notice of appeal within 20 days to EEOC or may file a civil action in an appropriate U.S. District Court within 30 days.

7. If COMPLAINANT asks for hearing, agency requests EEOC to assign COMPLAINTS EXAMINER.

8. COMPLAINTS EXAMINER reviews file; remands complaint to agency if further investigation necessary; schedules and conducts hearing.

9. Hearings recorded and transcribed verbatim. COMPLAINTS EXAMINER makes findings, analysis, and recommends decision; forwards these and the complaint file to the AGENCY HEAD (or designee).

10. HEAD OF AGENCY (or designee) makes agency decision, based on file, giving COMPLAINANT a copy of COMPLAINTS EXAMINER'S report. Must give specific reasons for rejection or modification of COMPLAINTS EXAMINER'S recommended decision in detail.

11. COMPLAINANT has right to file a notice of appeal to EEOC's OFFICE OF REVIEW AND APPEALS within 20 calendar days of receipt of agency's notice of final decision.

Note:

1. COMPLAINANT has right to file civil action in an appropriate U.S. District Court:
   (a) Within 30 calendar days of his or her receipt of notice of final agency action on his or her complaint
   (b) After 180 calendar days from date of filing an individual complaint with agency if there has been no decision.
   (c) Within 30 calendar days of his or her receipt of notice of final action taken by EEOC on the complaint, or
   (d) After 180 calendar days from date of filing an appeal with EEOC if no EEOC decision.

Filing of a civil action does not end the processing of an individual complaint by the agency or EEOC.

2. The agency shall furnish EEOC monthly reports on all individual complaints pending within the agency. If an agency has not issued a decision or requested EEOC to supply a complaints examiner within 75 calendar days of the date a complaint was filed, EEOC may require special action or assume responsibility for the complaint.

Source: Supervisory and Communications Training Center, U.S. Office of Personnel Management. *Workshops on Sexual Harassment, Trainer's Manual*. Washington, D.C.; u.d., pp. 74–75.

color and whites; and (4) randomly select employees to be interviewed on the employer's EEO and affirmative action practices.

The purpose of the desk audit is to determine which areas, if any, warrant further investigation. For example, if a compensation analysis reveals pay inequities, a more comprehensive investigation into the pay policies and practices of the employer is launched. The employer is then given the opportunity to explain or justify the pay disparities. If the employer can provide a satisfactory explanation, the investigation is terminated. If it cannot, the OFCCP compliance team will offer recommendations as well as remedies as to how the employer can come into compliance with federal law.

The employer is required to provide periodic progress reports to the OFCCP indicating what steps it is taking to remedy the problem. For example, if the OFCCP found that the employer's recruitment efforts failed to yield female job candidates, the employer would need to illustrate that it is making a good faith effort to recruit women. If the employer fails to demonstrate a good faith effort toward remedying the problem, it may be sanctioned. As noted earlier, while the employer's federal funding can be suspended or terminated, this rarely happens, even when employers are not in compliance with OFCCP requirements.

While there is no definitive manner in which to prepare for OFCCP audits, it appears rather clear that employers can eschew sanctions—indeed a full-fledged audit—if they have well-developed affirmative action plans in place.

Affirmative action plans are also monitored by the courts, insofar as employment discrimination claims may arise from the plan. In addition, plans may be monitored by administrative bodies such as the EEOC. As noted earlier, the EEOC reviews and monitors EEO and affirmative action progress through the EEO reports submitted to it by public employers. Any commissioner of the EEOC may initiate an investigation under Title VII to address what is perceived to be a widespread pattern of employment discrimination. Such an investigation can lead to a finding of systematic discrimination, in which case the EEOC may seek to conciliate a settlement between the employer and the aggrieved person(s). If this fails, the attorney general, on behalf of the EEOC and the aggrieved public employee(s), may bring a civil action in federal court. The court may enjoin the employer from engaging in the unlawful employment practices, with or without back pay.

In sum, an important managerial function of affirmative action planning is monitoring the plan once it has been implemented. Not only is this sound management practice, but it can also prove cost-effective for the organization since the costs of challenges to affirmative action plans are staggering.

Sexual Harassment

In 1991, the nation's attention was centered on the confirmation hearings of Clarence Thomas to become a justice on the U.S. Supreme Court. University of Oklahoma law professor Anita Hill alleged that Thomas sexually harassed her while he was the director of the EEOC and she was a staff member there. After several days of grueling testimony, Thomas barely won confirmation—by a vote of 52 to 48—to the high court. Notwithstanding, the Hill–Thomas hearings brought new ferment to the insidious problem of sexual harassment in the workplace.

Not long after the Hill–Thomas debacle, the federal government was inundated by sexual harassment claims. The Tailhook scandal, in which dozens of female navy pilots were sexually assaulted at an annual convention of naval aviators, was the first in a succession of cases in which women were awarded millions of dollars in damages for successful sexual harassment claims. Paula Coughlin, a former navy helicopter pilot who was one such victim, was awarded $6.7 million by a jury in Las Vegas, Nevada.

Then in 1994 Paula Corbin Jones filed suit against President Clinton, alleging that he sexually harassed her while she was a state worker and he was governor of Arkansas. The national attention drawn to the sexual proclivities of the president ultimately led to "sleazegate" or the Monica Lewinsky "affair." Lewinsky was alleged to have had a consensual sexual relationship with President Clinton while she was a twenty-one-year-old intern at the White House. Although not a sexual harassment case, the putative affair galvanized the nation's attention around appropriate sexual or romantic behavior in the workplace. It was precedent-setting in that never before had a president's sex life come under such scrutiny, and Clinton's videotaped deposition on the matter was the first time a sitting president was interrogated as a defendant in a court case. The president's wife, Hillary Rodham Clinton, dismissed the Lewinsky charges as a "vast right-wing conspiracy" out to get her husband.

Sexual harassment is a serious EEO concern and a form of prohibited discrimination. It is considered discrimination because it bases job actions or work arrangements on gender, which is prohibited by the Civil Rights Act of 1994 as amended. There is no single standard definition of sexual harassment. It is usually thought of as "unwanted sexual attention," however. This definition is broad enough to encompass everything from coercion to touching to leering to offhand comments with sexual overtones. (See Table 10.3.)

TABLE 10.3 Reported Incidents of Sexual Harassment (*Percentage of Federal Survey Respondents Who Experienced the Indicated Behaviors During the Preceding 2 Years*)

	Men	Women
Sexual remarks, jokes, teasing	14	37
Sexual looks, gestures	9	29
Deliberate touching, cornering	8	24
Pressure for dates	4	13
Suggestive letters, calls, materials	4	10
Stalking	2	7
Pressure for sexual favors	2	7
Actual/attempted rape, assault	2	4

Source: U.S. Merit Systems Protection Board. "Sexual Harassment in the Federal Workplace," 1995.

What Is Sexual Harassment?

Sexual harassment* is any unwanted verbal or physical sexual advance or sexually explicit derogatory statements made by someone in the classroom or workplace, which are offensive or which cause the recipient discomfort or humiliation or which interfere with the recipient's education or job performance. It can include:

> Leering at a person's body
> Verbal harassment or abuse of a sexual nature
> Unnecessary touching, patting, pinching, or constant brushing against a person's body
> Subtle pressure for sexual favors
> Demanding sexual favors accompanied by implied or overt threats concerning one's grades, recommendations, job, performance evaluation, promotion, etc.
> Physical assault

Note: Although the majority of incidents involve a male supervisor, co-worker, or instructor harassing a woman, the law also covers women harassing men, women harassing women, and men harassing men.

*Definition from N.O.W. and the Working Women's Institute, as it appears in a pamphlet prepared by the Affirmative Action Office, the University at Albany, State University of New York.

Although its scope is inherently unknowable, there is considerable evidence that sexual harassment is very widespread. Several surveys have indicated that a large number of women believe they have been subjected to sexual harassment in the workplace at one time or another. A 1995 study conducted by the Merit Systems Protection Board (MSPB), *Sexual Harassment in the Federal Workplace*, found that sexual harassment is widespread: "In 1994, 44 percent of women and 19 percent of men responding to [the MSPB] survey reported that they had experienced some form of unwanted sexual attention during the preceding two years." The study also found that the primary source of sexual harassment in the government is co-workers and other employees rather than those in the supervisory chain. The MSPB further noted that "Sexual harassment cost the Federal Government an estimated $327 million during the two-year period April 1992 to April 1994." This amount includes the cost of sick leave, job turnover, and productivity losses resulting from sexual harassment. Tables 10.3 and 10.4 illustrate the problem of sexual harassment in the federal government.

TABLE 10.4 Who Are the Harassers? (*Percentage of Victims Sexually Harassed by Supervisors and Others*)

	1980		1987		1994	
Harasser	Men	Women	Men	Women	Men	Women
Coworker or other employee	76	65	77	69	79	77
Immediate and/or higher level supervisor	14	37	19	29	14	28
Subordinate	16	4	10	2	11	3
Other or unknown[a]	5	6	10	10	6	7

[a] For example, contractor personnel, anonymous person(s).
Note: Because some victims reported harassment from more than one source, these percentages cannot be added together to obtain aggregate percentages. *Source*: See Table 10.3.

Currently sexual harassment is illegal in the public and private sectors under a number of statutes. Most important for noncriminal sexual harassment is Title VII of the Civil Rights Act of 1964 as amended by the Equal Employment Opportunity Act of 1972. Under these statutes, the EEOC has authority to hear and resolve complaints of sexual harassment. Also, in its important 1980 "Guidelines on Discrimination Because of Sex," the EEOC took the position that sexual harassment is a form of gender discrimination.

In 1986, the U.S. Supreme Court issued a landmark ruling, making sexual harassment a prohibited form of gender discrimination. In *Meritor Savings Bank* v. *Vinson*, the Court ruled that "a violation of Title VII may be predicated on either of two types of sexual harassment: harassment that involves the conditioning of concrete employment benefits on sexual favors, and harassment that, while not affecting economic benefits, creates a hostile or offensive working environment." The first type of sexual harassment, known as quid pro quo sexual harassment, is where the plaintiff attempts to prove that he or she was denied job benefits, such as a pay increase or promotion, because sexual favors were not granted to the harasser.

The second type of sexual harassment involves the hostile environment standard; this is an important one because it suggests that a violation of Title VII on a sexual harassment claim is not dependent upon the victim's loss of promotion or employment. Ultimately, the Court's ruling encourages employers to develop policies and complaint procedures that will protect employees from unwanted, unwelcome sexual advances.

In 1993, the U.S. Supreme Court issued another ruling in *Harris* v. *Forklift Systems, Inc.*, which further refined the standards for determining harassing conditions. In a unanimous ruling, the *Harris* Court said that "Whether an environment is 'hostile' or 'abusive' can be determined only by looking at all the circumstances. These may include the frequency of the discriminatory conduct; its severity; whether it is physically threatening or humiliating, or a mere offensive utterance; and whether it unreasonably interferes with an employees' work performance." This decision held that psychological harm need not be demonstrated by a woman alleging hostile environment. Justice Sandra Day O'Connor, who wrote the opinion, stated that you don't need to have a nervous breakdown before Title VII will protect you from sexual harassment.

In 1998, the U.S. Supreme Court widened workplace sexual harassment claims, ruling that Title VII also protects employees from same-sex harassment. The unanimous decision in *Oncale* v. *Sundowner Offshore Services*, extended the law beyond male–female sexual harassment to cover people of the same sex. The Court ruled that it was the conduct itself and not the sex or motivation of

President Clinton Is Accused of Sexual Harassment

Paula Corbin Jones filed a lawsuit again President Clinton in 1994, alleging that he propositioned her and exposed himself to her in a Little Rock hotel room three years earlier. At the time, he was governor of Arkansas and she was a low-level state employee. Clinton denied any wrongdoing, and accused Jones of being an opportunist who went public with her story to make money and harm him politically.

Clinton sought to delay a court trial until he left office, but in May of 1997, the Supreme Court dismissed his appeal, claiming that it was unlikely that Jones's lawsuit would burden Clinton's time as president. (The following month, Clinton offered a $700,000 settlement payment to charity, but Jones said she also wanted an apology.)

In April 1998, U.S. District Court Judge Susan Webber Wright sided with the Clinton team motion for a "summary judgment" dismissing the case before it could come to trial. Even if Clinton did make a crude proposition, the judge wrote, it would not constitute sexual harassment. There was no proof that Jones was emotionally afflicted or punished in the workplace for rebuffing him. "There are no genuine issues for trial in this case," Wright concluded. Jones appealed, but the parties reached a settlement agreement before the appeal was heard. A year after settlement, the case was back in the news when Judge Wright held the president in contempt of court for deliberately making misleading statements and ordered him to pay legal fees to Jones's lawyers.

the people involved that determined whether sexual harassment amounted to discrimination because of sex. Sexual desire, whether heterosexual or homosexual, the Court said, is not a necessary element of such a case.

Also in 1998, the U.S. Supreme Court issued two other rulings that will greatly affect employer liability in sexual harassment suits. In *Faragher* v. *City of Boca Raton* and *Burlington Industries* v. *Ellerth*, the high court, in 7-to-2 votes (Justices Clarence Thomas and Antonin Scalia dissented from the majority) ruled that an employer is liable under Title VII for its supervisors' sexual harassment, even if it did not know about the misconduct. The Court further ruled that in some cases, an employer can defend itself by showing that it took reasonable steps to prevent harassment on the job.

COMPARABLE WORTH AND PAY EQUITY

Depending upon the source, women earn anywhere from 60 to 89 cents for every dollar earned by a male. (See Table 10.5.) This pay disparity is at the heart of the comparable worth or pay equity debate.

Comparable worth differs considerably from "equal pay for equal work." The latter, which is explicitly mandated by the Equal Pay Act of 1963 for public and private employers, is aimed more at pay *equality* between women and men performing similar or equal work. A female maintenance worker, for example, must be paid the same wages as a male maintenance worker, assuming that the content of the jobs is the same. Equal pay may be required even if the jobs are not identical, provided that they are similar in functions and required skills (*Schultz* v. *Wheaton Glass Co.*, 1970).

Comparable worth, on the other hand, is aimed at pay *equity*, seeking to pay women and men equal wages for different or dissimilar jobs of comparable value to an employer. It is much more abstract as well as political in nature than pay equality, given its emphasis on measuring the intrinsic worth of jobs. Pay

TABLE 10.5   The Jobs and Earnings of Women in Full-Time Jobs (1997)

	Women		Men	
	1990	1996	1990	1996
Total workers	31,414,000	39,023,000	45,489,000	51,895,000
Median weekly earnings	$346	$418	$481	$557

Source: Adapted from *U.S. Statistical Abstracts*, 1997 (online).

equity measures have been more popular in the public sector than in the private sector, perhaps because public sector jobs are not specifically linked to the "free labor market" ideology that has been a major deterrent to the implementation of pay equity in the private sector. It is also important to note that comparable worth is not explicitly mandated by any federal legislation.

Comparable worth proponents argue, quite correctly, that jobs traditionally associated with women have been systematically undervalued in the marketplace. The net result is a disparity in pay for women when compared with that for jobs largely held by males. This compensatory bias against women, it is argued, can be demonstrated and subsequently eliminated by assessing the economic value of disparate occupations through the use of objective standards of evaluation. For example, although secretarial and janitorial jobs are dissimilar in function, it is argued that pay equity can be achieved by assessing such factors as working conditions and the amount of training, responsibility, and effort required for each job—in effect, using the classification function to determine the true value of the work being performed.

Critics of comparable worth vigorously counter those arguments. They state that the wage differential between men and women is more the result of career choice and market forces than sex discrimination. They point out that any pay gap that develops is produced over time. For example, male and female college graduates start out at comparable salaries once out of school. Moreover, opponents contend that employers by definition will pay higher wages for some occupations than others in order to remain competitive and to attract the best qualified personnel. Their responsibility is to be sensitive to the forces of supply and demand. Finally, critics of comparable worth maintain that job evaluation systems are inherently subjective, therefore any comparison of dissimilar jobs is at best arbitrary.

The issues inherent in comparable worth are complex and reflect a great deal about American social, political, and economic forces. By the late 1980s, there were approximately 60 million women working in the American labor force, compared to 65 million males. This tremendous increase in female participation itself represents one of the most dramatic changes in labor economics over the last 25 years. Women are also remaining in the labor force. Traditionally, women would quit the labor force in high percentages for marriage and family responsibilities. Under this situation, it was argued that the marketplace would reward males for remaining. Of course, the counterargument runs that the lack of advancement opportunities and the wage gap provided negative incentives for women to stay.

This is no longer the case, however. Why then, if female participation (in terms of entering and leaving) is comparable to male rates, should there be a wage gap? This question stands at the heart of comparable worth.

What Is the Pregnancy Discrimination Act of 1978?

An amendment to Title VII of the Civil Rights Act of 1964, which holds that discrimination on the basis of pregnancy, childbirth, or related medical conditions constitutes unlawful sex discrimination. The amendment was enacted in response to the Supreme Court's ruling in *General Electric Co.* v. *Gilbert*, 429 U.S. 125 (1976) that an employer's exclusion of pregnancy-related disabilities from its comprehensive disability plan did not violate Title VII. The amendment asserts that

1. A written or unwritten employment policy or practice which excludes from employment opportunities applicants or employees because of pregnancy, childbirth or related medical conditions is in prima facie violation of Title VII.
2. Disabilities caused or contributed to by pregnancy, childbirth, or related medical conditions, for all job-related purposes, shall be treated the same as disabilities caused or contributed to by other medical conditions, under any health or disability insurance or sick leave plan available in connection with employment. Written or unwritten employment policies and practices involving matters such as the commencement and duration of leave, the availability of extensions, the accrual of seniority and other benefits and privileges, reinstatement, and payment under any health or disability insurance or sick leave plan, formal or informal, shall be applied to disability due to pregnancy, childbirth, or related medical conditions on the same terms and conditions as they are applied to other disabilities. Health insurance benefits for abortion, except where the life of the mother would be endangered if the fetus were carried to term or where medical complications have arisen from an abortion, are not required to be paid by an employer; nothing herein, however, precludes an employer from providing abortion benefits or otherwise affects bargaining agreements in regard to abortion.
3. Where the termination of an employee who is temporarily disabled is caused by an employment policy under which insufficient or no leave is available, such a termination violates the Act if it has a disparate impact on employees of one sex and not justified by business necessity.

Source: Shafritz, Jay M. *Dictionary of Personnel Management and Labor Relations*, 2nd ed. New York: Facts on File, 1985.

THE FEMALE–MALE PAY GAP: CAUSES AND CURES

A number of explanations for the wage gap between women and men as well as whites and people of color have been advanced in recent years. One explanation relates to occupational segregation. Women entering the labor force tend to go into certain occupations that society deems "appropriate" for them; that is, they are socialized into thinking about jobs and professions as being either "female" or "male." The argument (which is specious at best!) then runs that as women begin to "crowd" certain job categories, the salary rate for such jobs becomes low because there is an abundant supply of workers. Moreover, the conclusion is then reached by opponents of comparable worth that women desire or choose these low-paying jobs, and therefore the government should not interfere with women exercising their choice. A great deal of the female–male wage differential is attributed to patterns of occupational segregation. In effect, women and men are in different jobs to begin with and female-dominated jobs are the lesser-paying occupations.

Further compounding patterns of occupational segregation is the higher percentage of females in part-time jobs compared to full-time. The part-time/full-time dimension has interesting side effects that show how difficult it is to untangle the long-standing patterns of occupational segregation. Hospital nursing, for example, with its extensive shift work requirements, has major staffing demands. One solution would be to raise salaries dramatically to attract more people (including men) into the profession. Other solutions involve creating weekend shift packages or other innovative flexible part-time arrangements that attract female nurses. Hospitals that employ flexible time plans solve their staffing problems in the short term, but their wage and compensation structures are preserved, thereby perpetuating patterns of occupational segregation. Nursing remains a 95% female-dominated job.

Others have argued that the female–male earnings gap is due to "market forces." They argue that organizations should pay only what the prevailing wage rate is for librarians, secretaries, nurses, and so forth. If there is an ample supply of qualified applicants for the organization's needs, the salary rate should reflect this. Conversely, if the organization needs truck drivers, computer programmers, or sanitation workers, it must pay the market rate, which reflects, as the organization will argue, a scarcer supply of labor. One result is organizations paying truck drivers higher salaries than librarians or nurses, even though the educational qualifications and professional responsibilities of the latter may far exceed the former. Another by-product, which raises legal concerns, is the organization's creation of a major disparity in relative wages between female and male jobs, or what is called "gender-based wage discrimination."

What happens when the organization has a comprehensive classification and compensation system? Modern "class and comp" systems use job evaluation techniques to relate all jobs in the organization to each other. In public sector organizations, this affords a unique perspective. Nurses can be compared to truck drivers, librarians to sanitation workers, and so on. In short, since the job evaluation methods focus on the position requirements, they ignore the marketplace arguments of supply and demand. What does an organization do when it compares the position value of each of its occupations with the market-created realities of prevailing wages? When it follows the marketplace, it then builds in the discrimination in wages that the marketplace has created.

Welcome, then, to comparable worth. It is a world of many dilemmas for public sector organizations. The public sector has always led the battle against discrimination, but its leadership in comparable worth has been a true test. Public sector organizations are particularly vulnerable to the conflicting political and economic currents within comparable worth. For example, if governments pay higher salaries for women, what will the budgetary effects be? Will higher salaries mean a reduction in the number of new jobs in various occupational groups? Will higher salaries for female jobs create incentives or disincentives to break down occupational segregation? Is the breakup of "male jobs" and "female jobs" a public policy objective arising out of comparable worth? Incidentally, shouldn't any compensation correction policy entail some kind of reduction in male wages presently or over time? The solutions to these many problems are tied tightly to the political processes and strategies of implementation. The potential impacts are simply enormous.

The lessons of the marketplace are clear, however. A decade's progress has added one cent a year toward closing the gap. A penny for your thoughts!

LEGAL AND JUDICIAL DEVELOPMENTS

The chief legal devices employed by advocates of comparable worth to achieve pay equity have included the Equal Pay Act of 1963 and Title VII of the Civil Rights Act of 1964, as amended. The two acts are closely linked. As noted earlier, the Equal Pay Act generally prohibits gender-based pay inequality for "equal work," but it also provides for four "affirmative defenses," or exceptions. In other words, lower pay for one sex can be justified when such payments are based on:

1. A nondiscriminatory system
2. A merit system
3. A system that measures earnings by quantity or quality of production
4. A wage differential based on any additional factor other than gender

The other statute, Title VII, specifically prohibits all employers from discriminating in their business practices on the basis of gender. In an attempt to avoid a conflict between the two acts, Congress added the so-called Bennett amendment to Title VII in 1964. This amendment provides that an employer may "differentiate" the amount of employee's wages if such payments are based on the affirmative defenses of the Equal Pay Act.

The case law around comparable worth has not yet been clearly resolved. In 1981, the U.S. Supreme Court in *County of Washington, Oregon v. Gunther*, ruled that Title VII of the Civil Rights Act as amended could sustain comparable worth suits. This was a procedural ruling, however, not a ruling on the merits of pay equity. Four years later, the U.S. Court of Appeals for the Ninth Circuit in *American Federation of State, County and Municipal Employees (AFSCME) v. State of Washington* (1985) virtually killed comparable worth on substantive grounds. In an opinion written by Judge Anthony Kennedy (now on the U.S. Supreme Court, a Reagan appointee), the Ninth Circuit Court held that the state of Washington could not be in violation of Title VII if it based its wages on prevailing market rates, even if the outcome meant lower salaries for women. The Court, subscribing to the free-market theory, ruled that the state did not create the market disparity, and "neither law nor logic deems the free market system a suspect enterprise." In effect, the Ninth Circuit's ruling remains intact, and the question of the ability of state or federal courts to require comparable worth consistent with or in enforcement of Title VII of the Civil Rights Act as amended is unresolved.

ADDITIONAL EEO CONCERNS

Equal opportunity essentially requires that artificial barriers not be placed in the way of qualified individuals seeking public or private employment and that once on the job all employees be treated in a nondiscriminatory fashion.

Age Discrimination

In 1967, Congress enacted the Age Discrimination in Employment Act (ADEA), which made it illegal for private businesses to refuse to hire, discharge, or otherwise discriminate against an individual in compensation or privileges of employment between the ages of 40 and 65. The act was amended in 1974 to apply to federal, state, and local governments.

The ADEA was amended again in 1978 to raise to 70 the minimum mandatory retirement age for employees in private companies and state and local government. The 1978 amendment also banned forced retirement for federal employees at any age. Enforcement authority over the ADEA was originally vested in the Department of Labor but was transferred to the EEOC as part of the federal service reform of 1978.

The ADEA was once again amended in 1986 to remove the upper age limit of 70 for all employees (private and state and local government) except for (1) firefighters; (2) policy-making executives who held such a position for at least two years and whose pension and benefits amount to at least $40,000 per year; (3) law enforcement officers; and (4) tenured university professors. These exceptions for law enforcement officers and tenured professors expired on December 31,1993.

Employers who put conditions around age must be able to defend their actions under the bona fide occupational qualification (BFOQ) standard; that is, the courts have required employers to demonstrate that setting a certain age for a particular job is a necessary requirement for the job.

Disability Discrimination

Various laws prohibit discrimination on the basis of a disability. The Vocational Rehabilitation Act of 1973 as amended prohibits discrimination against disabled persons. Protections against employment discrimination as well as other forms of discrimination (e.g., access to public accommodations and services) were strengthened by Title I of the Americans with Disabilities Act (ADA) of 1990. The ADA covers employers, employment agencies, labor unions, and joint labor–management committees with 15 or more employees. The federal government, which is excluded from the ADA, continues to be covered by executive orders and the Rehabilitation Act.

Both the Rehabilitation Act and the ADA state that an individual can claim to be disabled if she or he

1. Has a physical or mental impairment that substantially limits one or more of the major life activities of the individual
2. Has a record of having such an impairment
3. Is regarded as having such an impairment

Physical impairments include: anatomical losses, cancer, deformities, HIV/AIDS, heart disease, impairments that affect speech, hearing, and sight, and mental impairments such as mental retardation and mental illness. Employers must be prepared to provide reasonable accommodations, special assistants, and modification of workplace equipment.

Discrimination Based on HIV/AIDS

Several lower court rulings (e.g., *Chalk* v. *U.S. District Court*, 1998) were incorporated into the language of the ADA to prohibit discrimination against persons who have acquired immunodeficiency syndrome (AIDS) or the retrovirus, human immunodeficiency virus (HIV), that causes AIDS.

Frequently Asked Questions Under the ADA

Q: May an employer inquire as to whether a prospective employee is disabled?

A: No. An employer may not make a pre-employment inquiry on an application form or in an interview as to whether, or to what extent, an individual is disabled. The employer may, however, ask a job applicant if she or he can perform particular job functions.

Q: Can an employer refuse to hire an applicant or fire a current employee who is illegally using drugs?

A: Yes. Individuals who currently engage in the illegal use of drugs are specifically excluded from the definition of a "qualified individual with a disability" protected by the ADA when an action is taken on the basis of their drug use.

Q: Does the ADA mandate affirmative action?

A: No. But it also *does not* preclude an employer from taking affirmative steps to hiring disabled persons.

First detected in the early 1970s in tropical Africa, HIV quickly spread throughout the world. By the mid-1990s, it was estimated that well over 1 million persons in the United States were infected with HIV and 20 to 50 million people throughout the rest of the world.

In the workplace, HIV/AIDS has resulted in such hysteria that people were afraid to drink from the same water fountains, use the same bathrooms, or touch the same doorknobs as persons suspected of having HIV or AIDS. Employers gradually responded with policies to protect persons with HIV/AIDS (e.g., around discrimination, privacy, and confidentiality), but despite enhanced knowledge about its causes, people continue to react negatively to co-workers or clients suspected of being infected. Despite the ADA, discrimination in the workplace and in social settings prevails, thereby challenging government to better protect persons with HIV/AIDS.

THE FUTURE OF EEO AND AFFIRMATIVE ACTION

As we move into the next millennium, it would appear that the system of law around affirmative action will continue to break down. We may no longer see affirmative action programs supported or mandated by the courts, or as we saw in California, by some state governments. Moreover, given popular sentiment, it is unlikely that the U.S. Congress or the White House can be relied upon to defend its use. Indeed, President Clinton, who has vowed not to end affirmative action, has ordered the first major revision of affirmative action programs since President Reagan in the 1980s. Although his slogan for affirmative action came to be "mend it, but don't end it," he has taken such actions as suspending all federal set-aside programs for at least three years. In addition, after many months of studying affirmative action, his long-awaited affirmative actions directive issued in 1995 to all federal departments and agencies merely called for additional studies.

In light of the recent as well as prospective changes to affirmative action, it appears that public personnelists and human resources managers will turn their attention toward workplace diversification endeavors, which represent the next stage in the evolutionary process of EEO. Private corporations have been silently supporting diversity amidst a backlash against affirmative action because they recognize the economic exigencies of doing so. Many government employers are also voluntarily developing and maintaining diversity programs, even in the wake of efforts to dismantle affirmative action programs because of the changing demographics of the populations they serve. Quite simply, if the labor pools from which public organizations are recruiting are increasingly diverse, government employers will as a corollary hire persons with diverse social and economic backgrounds, and as their workforces become more diverse, there will be a greater incentive to develop training programs to promote and maintain diversity in the workplace. Voluntary diversity efforts without some legal stimulus may be ad hoc, sporadic, and ephemeral, however.

BIBLIOGRAPHY

Ban, Carolyn and Norma M. Riccucci. *Public Personnel Management: Current Concerns, Future Challenges*, 2nd ed. New York: Longman, 1997.

The Bureau of National Affairs (BNA). *Pay Equity and Comparable Worth: A BNA Report*. Washington, D.C., 1985.

Cayer, N. Joseph. *Public Personnel Administration in the United States*, 3rd ed. New York: St. Martins Press, 1996.

Civil Rights Act of 1991: Text and Analysis. *Employment Guide*. Special Supplement, vol. 6, no. 23. Washington, D.C.: Bureau of National Affairs, November 11, 1991.

Crampton, Suzanne M., John W. Hodge, and Jitendra M. Mishra. "The Equal Pay Act: The First 30 Years," *Public Personnel Management*, vol. 26 (fall 1997), pp. 335–344.

Dresang, Dennis L. and Paul J. Stuiber. "Sexual Harassment: Challenges Are Personnel," in Carolyn Ban and Norma M. Riccucci (eds.), *Public Management: Current Concerns, Future Challenges*. White Plains, N.Y.: Longman Press, 1991.

Elliot, Robert H. "Human Resources Management's Role in the Future Aging of the Workforce," symposium, *Review of Public Personnel Administration*, vol. 15 (spring 1995).

Equal Employment Opportunity Commission. Title 29-Labor, Chapter XIV-Part 1604. "Guidelines on Discrimination Because of Sex Under Title VII of the Civil Rights Act of 1964, as Amended: Adoption of Interim Interpretive Guidelines." Washington, D.C.: April 1980.

Graham, Cole Blease, Jr. "Equal Employment Opportunity and Affirmative Action: Policies, Techniques, and Controversies," in Steven W. Hays and Richard C. Kearney (eds.), *Public Personnel Administration: Problems and Prospects*. Englewood Cliffs, N.J.: Prentice Hall, 1995, pp. 202–216.

Guy, Mary E. "Public Personnel and Gender," symposium, *Review of Public Personnel Administration*, vol. 16 (winter 1996).

Haigner, Lois. "Comparable Worth," in Jay M. Shafritz (ed.), *International Encyclopedia for Public Policy and Administration*, New York: Henry Holt, 1998.

Hale, Mary M. "Gender Equality in Organizations," *Review of Public Personnel Administration*, vol. 16 (winter 1996), pp. 7–18.

Johansen, Elaine. *Comparable Worth: The Myth and the Movement*. Boulder, Colo.: Westview Press, 1984.

Kellough, J. Edward. "The Supreme Court, Affirmative Action, and Public Management: Where Do We Stand Today?" *American Review of Public Administration*, vol. 21, no. 3 (1991), pp. 255–269.

Kellough, J. Edward. "Affirmative Action and Equal Employment Opportunity," symposium, *Review of Public Personnel Administration*, vol. 17 (fall 1997).

Kelly, Rita Mae and Jane Bayes, eds. *Comparable Worth, Pay Equity, and Public Policy*. Westport, Conn.: Greenwood Press, 1998.

Klingner, Donald E. "Work Force Diversity," in Jay M. Shafritz, (ed.), *International Encyclopedia for Public Policy and Administration*, New York: Henry Holt, 1998.

Klingner, Donald E. and John Nalbandian. *Public Personnel Management: Contexts and Strategies*, 4th ed. Englewood Cliffs, N.J.: Prentice-Hall, 1998.

Krilsov, Samuel and David H. Rosenbloom. *Representative Bureaucracy and the American Political System*. New York: Praeger, 1981.

Lewis, Gregory. "Women, Occupation and Federal Agencies: Occupational Mix and Interagency Differences in Sexual Inequality in Federal White-Collar Employment," *Public Administration Review*, vol. 54 (May–June 1994), pp. 271–276.

Lovrich, Nicholas P., Brent S. Steel, and David Hood. "Equity Versus Productivity: Affirmative Action and Municipal Police Services," *Public Productivity Review*, vol. 39 (fall 1986).

Mackinnon, Catherine A. *Sexual Harassment of Working Women*. New Haven, Conn.: Yale University Press, 1979.

Reese, Laura A. and Karen E. Lindenberg. "*Victimhood and the Implementation of Sexual Harassment Policy*," *Review of Public Personnel Administration*, vol. 17 (winter 1997), pp. 37–57.

Remick, Helen, ed. *Comparable Worth and Wage Discrimination*. Philadelphia: Temple University Press, 1984.

Riccucci, Norma M. "A Practical Guide to Affirmative Action," in Steve Condrey (ed.),

The Handbook of Human Resource Management in Government. San Francisco: Jossey-Bass, 1998, pp. 165–182.

Riccucci, Norma M. "Will Affirmative Action Survive into the 21st Century?" in Carolyn Ban and Norma M. Riccucci (eds.), *Public Personnel Management: Current Concerns-Futures Challenges,* 2nd ed. White Plains, N.Y.: Longman Press, 1997, pp. 57–72.

Rosenbloom, David H. "Diversity in Public Higher Education and Current Equal Protection Analysis," presented at SUNY-Oswego, March 19,1998.

Rosenbloom, David H. *Federal Equal Employment Opportunity.* New York: Praeger, 1977.

Selden, Sally Coleman. "Minorities in the Farmers Home Administration," *Review of Public Personnel Administration* (winter 1998), pp. 39–67.

Selden, Sally Coleman. *The Promise of Representative Bureaucracy.* Armonk, N.Y.: M.E. Sharpe, 1997.

Sexual Harassment in the Federal Workplace. Washington, D.C.: Merit Systems Protection Board (MSPB), 1995.

Slack, James D. "The Americans with Disabilities Act and the Workplace: Observations about Management's Responsibilities in AIDS-Related Situations," *Public Administration Review* (July–August, 1995).

Treiman, D. and H. Hartman, eds. *Women, Work, and Wages: Equal Pay for Equal Value.* Washington, D.C.: National Academy Press, 1981.

U.S. Commission of Civil Rights. *Comparable Worth: Issue for the 80's, A Constitution of the U.S. Commission on Civil Rights,* vol. 1, Papers; vol. 2, Proceedings, June 6–7, 1984.

CASES

AFSCME v. *Washington State,* 770 F. 2d 1401 (9th Cir. 1985).

Burlington Industries v. *Ellerth,* cite.

Chalk v. *U.S. District Court, Central District of California and Orange County Superintendent of Schools,* 840 F. 2d. 701 (9th Cir. 1988).

County of Washington v. *Gunther,* 452 U.S. 161 (1981).

Farragher v. *City of Boca Raton,* cite.

Fullilove v. *Klutznick,* 448 U.S. 488 (1980).

Griggs v. *Duke Power Company,* 401 U.S. 424 (1971).

Hopwood v. *State of Texas,* 861 F. Supp. 551 (W.D. Tex. 1994), rev'd and remanded in part, diss'd in part, 78 F. 3d. 932 95th Cir. 1996, cert. Denied, 1996 WL 227009 (1996).

Johnson v. *Transportation Agency of Santa Clara County,* 480 U.S. 624 (1987).

Lorance v. *AT&T,* 490 U.S. 900 (1989).

Martin v. *Wilks,* 490 U.S. 755 (1989).

Memphis v. *Stotts,* 104 S. Ct. 582 (1984).

Meritor Savings Bank v. *Vinson,* 477 U.S. 57 (1986).

Metro Broadcasting v. *F.C.C.,* 111 L. Ed. 2d 445 (June 27, 1990).

Patterson v. *McLean Credit Union*, 491 U.S. 164 (1989).
Price Waterhouse v. *Hopkins*, 490 U.S. 228 (1989).
Regents v. *Bakke*, 438 U.S. 265 (1978).
Richmond v. *Croson*, 488 U.S. 469 (1989).
State of Washington v. *AFSCME*, 770 F2d 1401 (1985).
United States v. *Paradise*, 480 U.S. 149 (1987).
Wards Cove Packing Co. v. *Antonio*, 490 U.S. 642 (1989).
Washington v. *Davis*, 426 U.S. 229 (1976).
Wirtz v. *Wheaton Glass Co.*, 421 F. 2d 259 (3rd Cir.) cert. denied, 398 U.S. 905 (1970).

11

Diversity in the Workforce

PROLOGUE: A SUCCESS STORY
IN SEATTLE, WASHINGTON

The city of Seattle has a long-standing commitment to diversity. Since the early 1980s, when Seattle was undergoing significant demographic shifts, the city attempted to create a workforce that would be representative of the city at large. In the early 1990s, just after Norman Rice, an African American, was elected mayor, diversity efforts began to surpass traditional affirmative action programs and were linked to cultural and institutional changes in the city. The city's diversity coordinator, Joanne Anton, explained that "diversity efforts would not only be long-term, sustainable ones but they would be part of the city's corporate culture; they would be integrated into the psyche of the city and its work force. Diversity efforts must be given priority status and actively reinforced by top-level officials to be successful and to be credible in the eyes of employees."

The success of Seattle's programs has largely been attributed to Mayor Rice's strong commitment to diversity as a cornerstone of his administration and his insistence that department heads actively support diversity initiatives. Seattle's diversity efforts are multifold. First, the city designed its own comprehensive two-day diversity training that is *mandatory* for all supervisory and management staff. Second, each city department is required to develop a diversity plan. The key here is to decentralize the operations as much as possible so that the specific

421

diversity efforts would not be mandated by the mayor's office. This gives departments more flexibility and control over diversity initiatives, and as such leads to
less resistance. In addition, department heads are accountable to the mayor for
ensuring that diversity exists throughout the department, and not simply at the
bottom of the organizational structure. The extent to which their stated diversity
goals are met is a factor in the performance evaluation of department heads.

Diversity training for all employees is significant. In Seattle, diversity is
not treated as warmed-over affirmative action, but is considered a business issue.
It is not a racial or gender issue with a business concern on the side, but a business
issue that deals with the inclusion of all people. In this sense the city has worked
hard to ensure employees value diversity and to clarify the distinctions between
EEO, affirmative action, and managing diversity. (See Table 11.1.) While ac-
centing the distinctions among the three concepts, however, the city also stresses
the importance of recognizing the common ground and connections they share.

The city of Seattle's diversity efforts go beyond recruitment, hiring, and
training, to include mentoring, promotion, and retention, and the city has been

TABLE 11.1 A Comparison of EEO, Affirmative Action, and Diversity

EEO	Affirmative action	Managing diversity
A business issue	A business issue	A business issue
Mandated by federal leg- islation and city policy	Mandated by executive order and city policy	Voluntary, proactive tool to benefit all em- ployees
Ensure EEO for all em- ployees and potential employees	Requires long-range planning, recruiting, goal setting, staff de- velopment	Recognizes and utilizes individual differences in working and learn- ing styles
Compliance with law	Voluntarily develop goals to comply with law	Not mandated by law; proactive
Necessitated by a past history of discrimi- nation	Necessitated by a past history of discrimi- nation	Organization views dif- ferences as an asset
Outcome: To provide a workplace free of dis- crimination and to guarantee the right of equal opportunity for all	*Outcome*: To remedy past practices of dis- crimination	*Outcome*: To contrib- ute to productivity and quality work; support workplace equity; im- prove customer ser- vice; contribute to or- ganizational success

Source: City of Seattle, 1995.

successful in all categories for a variety of reasons. Once hired, the city works to ensure that new hires receive the orientation and mentoring needed to perform well on the job and to ensure that they are part of a supportive work environment. The city holds department heads accountable for providing their employees with opportunities for upward mobility. Unions support the city's diversity initiatives. While there was some resistance initially, unions have been cooperative because they, too, recognize the realities of a changing workforce.

The city has not yet developed formal measures to evaluate the success of its diversity efforts because measurement presents a conundrum of sorts. As Seattle's diversity coordinator observed, "How do we measure the sense of worth and well-being that employees now feel as a result of the program? Some of the outcomes of our diversity programs are simply not quantifiable." With the implementation of a new human resource information system currently in development, the city hopes to identify means of meaningful measurement.

In the meantime, the city has looked for other creative ways to highlight the successes of its diversity programs. For example, in early 1994 an awards ceremony was established to honor employees for their distinctive accomplishments related to diversity. In one case, two police captains were nominated by a female lieutenant for creating a safe, hostile-free environment for women police officers and for creating opportunities for women to advance within the department. In another case, park employees responsible for cleaning parks were honored for their efforts to assist homeless families and individuals. The employees were successful in developing linkages with social service agencies to provide these persons and families with food and shelter.

Seattle's diversity efforts have received recognition because the city successfully parlayed the mayor's political leadership into multiple interventions in its human resource management processes. The city understood the value of a workforce representative of the community it serves, and developed a wide range of programs to ensure that department heads shared that awareness and were held accountable for making opportunities available for traditionally underrepresented groups.

THE CHALLENGE OF ENSURING EQUAL OPPORTUNITIES

The efforts of the city of Seattle demonstrate that whether or not an agency's policies and practices would meet the legal definition of discrimination, real equality of opportunity in employment is an objective that management must resolutely strive for. Employees who believe they are being discriminated against may not file a complaint, but their motivation to contribute their full potential to the organization may be lost, at a cost to the agency. Similarly, an organization may have formal or informal policies or programs that appear on their face to offer everyone the same opportunities but in fact work to the advantage or disad-

vantage of one group. Research has also documented the persistence of stereotypes, whereby assumptions are made about individuals based on their membership in a group. Such stereotypes can sometimes result in a negative evaluation
of the accomplishments or potential accomplishments of another person. This
chapter begins by describing the changes in the workforce necessitating attention
to the management of diversity and the subtle ways in which equal opportunity
is sometimes limited in organizations. It then discusses some strategies undertaken by organizations to provide a more inclusive environment for all segments
of the workforce.

Workforce 2020

In 1987, under a contract with the Department of Labor, the Hudson Institute
issued a report entitled *Workforce 2000*, which forecasted the key trends that
would shape the nature of the American workplace and workforce at the end of
the twentieth century. A year later, under contract with the Office of Personnel
Management (OPM), the Hudson Institute produced a similar report, *Civil Service
2000*, that described anticipated changes in the federal civil service over the same
time period. These reports served as a wake-up call to employers by documenting
the increasing diversity of the American workforce. Workplace policies that had
worked well when the workforce was largely young, white, and male, warned
the institute, may no longer be effective as women and people of color become
a larger share of the labor force and as the average age of employees rises. *Workforce 2000* was later criticized because it appeared to overstate the extent to which
white men would shrink as a percentage of the labor force. Nevertheless, the
reports induced a flurry of activity and the development of an industry of consultants, books, and videos designed to sensitize employers and employees as to the
different perspectives and needs of a more diverse workforce.

A decade later, the Hudson Institute published a sequel to *Workforce 2000*,
entitled *Workforce 2020*. Their latest study predicts an incremental but continued
diversification of the workforce. The percentage of women in the workforce already increased from 33% in 1950 to 60% in 1997. During the same 47-year
period, the proportion of men in the workforce dropped from 88% to 75%.
Whereas fewer than one-third of American jobs were held by women in 1950,
they soon will hold as large a share of jobs as men. Nearly two-thirds of married
women with children under six years of age are working today. These changes
have implications for work conditions and benefits offered by employers, but as
discussed in more detail later, they also have implications for such issues as how
promotion decisions are made. For example, an ability to travel extensively may
have been an impartial criteria when men could leave their children with stay-
at-home wives, but can limit opportunities for single parents or dual-career couples.

The institute also predicts a gradual increase in the racial and ethnic diversity of the workforce. By 2020, white non-Hispanics are projected to represent 68% of the workforce, down from 76% in 1995. While the proportion of jobs held by African Americans will remain steady at about 11%, the share of jobs help by Hispanics will grow from 9% in 1995 to 14% in 2020, and Asian non-Hispanics will increase their share from 4% to 6%.

As with women, many of the informal workplace norms that evolved at a time when the workforce in general and upper management positions in particular were dominated by white men may no longer be appropriate as the workforce becomes more diverse. This is a concern in any workplace, regardless of whether it is in the private or public sector. An employer that is not equipped to tap the full potential of its workforce will likely pay a price in terms of lower motivation, lost productivity, and undesirable turnover. There are reasons that *public* sector agencies should be even more interested in ensuring that the career development of women and people of color isn't hindered by any such barriers, however, and that has to do with the notion of a "representative bureaucracy."

The Importance of a Representative Bureaucracy

This term representative bureaucracy was coined by J. Donald Kingsley in his 1944 book about the British government. The term refers to the notion that since public sector agencies affect public policy they must be made responsive to democratic values. In Kingsley's view, the way to ensure that bureaucracy is responsive to the citizenry it serves is to make sure it "mirrors the dominant forces in society." Kingsley originally conceived of "representativeness" in terms of social class. By the 1960s the composition of this country's bureaucracy was being evaluated in terms of the extent to which women and people of color held civil service jobs. This transition occurred because of the salience of race in American politics at that time and the entrance of substantial numbers of women into the labor force.

In his 1967 book *The Negro in Federal Employment*, Samuel Krislov proposed additional purposes served by a diverse civil service beyond those suggested by Kingsley. Krislov suggested that a representative bureaucracy serves as a funnel for divergent points of view and is more likely to have diverse skills and talents, making it better able to deal with a wider variety of problems that emerge in the modern industrial society. In addition, agencies that are representative ensure that social responsibility is shared, leading to a greater acceptance of governmental policies. A representative bureaucracy brings members of the segments of the society holding civil service positions a broader social point of view, which is in turn transmitted back to the groups they represent. Moreover, Krislov suggested, governmental employment offers a coveted economic and social status. The extent to which that status is available to all provides an index of the concentration of power, while the lack of access serves as an affront to unincluded groups. The importance of representative bureaucracy lies not just in its function as a mirror of the community; rather, "bureaucracies by their very structure represent truths about the nature of the societies they administer and the values that dominate them."

The importance of a representative workforce was officially recognized by Congress in the Civil Service Reform Act of 1978. The act called for a civil service "representative of the nation's diversity," and established the Federal Equal Opportunity Recruitment Program (FEORP). The FEORP program, administered by the OPM, requires federal agencies to establish affirmative recruiting plans in order to correct the underrepresentation of women and people of color at all grades in all occupations. Agencies are required to submit annual reports on their progress toward meeting this goal to both OPM and the Equal Employment Opportunity Commission (EEOC).

The need for representative agencies has also long been recognized at the state and local levels. In its 1993 report the National Commission on the State

Diversity Within and Across Occupations

As employers strive to diversify all job levels in their organizations, governments must also work to diversify traditionally male occupations. Here's a look at a few of them at the state and local levels of government:

	Percentage women	
	1985	1995
Fire fighting	.9	6.3
Police	9.2	26.8
Corrections	15.4	33.7
Sanitation	2.4	13.6

Source: "State and Local Government Information, Summary Report for 1985 EEO-4 Survey." Washington, D.C.: Equal Employment Opportunity Commission (EEOC), 1985, and "Job Patterns for Minorities and Women in State and Local Government." Washington, D.C.: EEOC, 1995.

and Local Public Service (the Winter commission) stated that "There is a very legitimate question as to whether a government that does not reflect the demographic makeup of the governed can operate effectively over the long haul, or in the face of widespread hostility or resentment on the part of disenfranchised groups." The continuing salience of this concept was further confirmed by the bipartisan Federal Glass Ceiling Commission, which emphasized that since governments at all levels have an active role in ensuring equal opportunity throughout American society they should lead by example.

To assess whether a representative bureaucracy does indeed serve a valuable purpose, one must agree on what constitutes a representative bureaucracy. How does one know if a particular agency or government meets this criterion or not?

Measurement Issues

The issue of how a representative bureaucracy should be defined and measured has never been definitively resolved. Most analyses have relied on what Frederick Mosher called "passive representation," or in today's parlance, the extent to which the government "looks like America." In assessing passive representation, the proportion of jobs any group holds in an agency is compared to some benchmark.

In early discussions of the notion of representative bureaucracy, it was assumed that the appropriate benchmark was the American population. If African Americans make up 15% of the population, they should make up 15% of the workforce in any given agency. The agencies now responsible for monitoring the representativeness of federal agencies—the EEOC and OPM—use a more limited benchmark, requiring agencies to compare the percentage of women and people of color with their proportion in the civilian labor force. The civilian labor force includes all persons in the United States who are 16 years or over and not employed by the military. In looking at how OPM and the EEOC make these comparisons, however, it is clear that there is more than one way to compute the civilian labor force.

The OPM relies on the annual current population survey (CPS), administered by the Bureau of Labor Statistics, for identifying the proportion of women and each ethnic group in the civilian labor force. Since these computations are based on only a sample of the population, however, CPS does not provide separate counts for Asian/Pacific Islanders or Native Americans. (There are not enough members of these groups in the sample to do so.) The OPM hence extrapolates those proportions using decennial census data. (See Figure 11.1.) Similarly, because CPS is only a sample, it cannot be used to make occupation-specific comparisons; hence OPM and the EEOC use decennial census data for this pur-

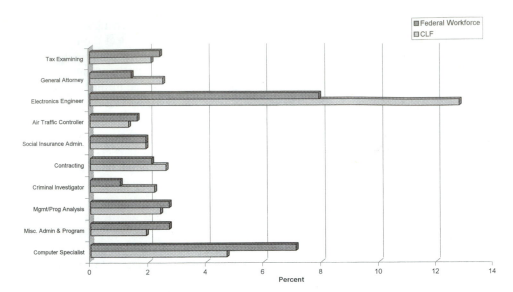

FIGURE 11.1   Asian/Pacific Islander representation in federal workforce and CLF in 10 most populous, professional and administrative positions. *Source*: OPM FY 1997 FEORP Report, p. 31.

pose. The problem with using census data is that 1999 data from federal agencies are compared with 1990 census data, even though the composition of the labor force has certainly changed in that nine-year period.

Moreover, OPM and EEOC use somewhat different numbers in computing representation in the federal workforce and civilian labor force. The EEOC includes the U.S. Postal Service and several other agencies that OPM does not. The OPM includes Puerto Rico in its computations, whereas the EEOC does not. As a result, the two agencies sometimes report slightly different percentages with respect to representation in the civilian labor force and in federal agencies. For example, for fiscal year 1997, OPM reported that Latinos made up 6.2% of the federal workforce and 11% of the civilian labor force. The EEOC reported that Latinos represented 6.4% of the federal workforce and 8% of the civilian labor force.

The EEOC and OPM routinely report the representation of women and people of color by grade level and within broad occupational categories (PAT-COB, or professional, administrative, technical, clerical, other, and blue collar.) In response to pressure to make sure that underrepresentation is determined based on comparing apples with apples, however, OPM recently began comparing representation within specific occupational categories. For example, suppose, using an aggregate measure, that African Americans make up 11% of the civilian labor force but only 5% of agency X's workforce. African Americans would be considered to be *underrepresented* in agency X. Suppose, however, that agency X primarily employs engineers, of which 20% are African American. If African Americans represent only 10% of engineers in the civilian labor force, they would be considered *overrepresented* in agency X, at least with respect to the engineering corps.

Because of such occurrences OPM's FEORP reports now include comparisons of people of color and women within specific occupations to their representation in those occupations in the civilian labor force. (See Table 11.2.) In addition, OPM now also reports representation within specific departments and agencies with the civilian labor force, based on agency-specific occupations. For example, the report shows that Native Americans hold 2.5% of agency-specific jobs in the Department of Agriculture, compared to .5% of those jobs in the civilian labor force. In order to make these comparisons, OPM must again rely on census data.

The need to use outdated census figures is only one problem with using the civilian labor force to determine representation. Other criticisms of the civilian labor force as a benchmark include the fact that the federal government generally does not hire people below the age of 18 or noncitizens, while 16- and 17-year-olds and noncitizens are included in the civilian labor force.

Even if agreement as to the appropriate benchmark could be secured, the U.S. General Accounting Office (GAO) and some scholars have criticized this method of comparing percentages as being too simplistic, and they have attempted to devise other measures. In a 1993 report, GAO advocated a "ratio-based approach" that compares the numbers of each EEO group to a benchmark such as white men, arguing that such a measure better states the extent to which each group makes progress relative to the others. Similarly, Nachmias and Rosen-

TABLE 11.2 Representation of Women and People of Color in the Population, Civilian, and Federal Workforces (1997)

	Representation (percent)			
	In U.S. population	In civilian labor force	In federal workforce	In senior federal jobs
Women	51.1	46.4	42.8	20.9
People of color	26.3	26.3	29.1	11.6

Note: The federal government defines "people of color" as African Americans, Asian and Pacific Islanders, Latinos, and Native Americans. *Source*: For U.S. population, Bureau of the Census; other percentages, OPM 1997.

bloom developed a measure of variation (MV) that compares the total number of observed differences within a group to the maximum number of possible differences; that is, it compares the total number of pairs of employees who are from different ethnic (or gender) groups to the total number of *possible* pairs of employees from different ethnic (or gender) groups. Nachmias and Rosenbloom favor this approach as one that facilitates comparison over time and among different nations. This measure continues to be used by scholars assessing the bureaucracy's representativeness, although not without evoking some questions and criticism.

Regardless of how representation is measured, it is generally agreed that women and people of color are well represented within the federal workforce in general, but not in the top grades within the federal workforce. (See Table 11.2.) Kenneth Meier was one of the first to take issue with many of his contemporaries who suggested that the American federal bureaucracy was representative by arguing that "Since most of the important decisions made by the civil service are concentrated at its higher levels, the unrepresentative nature of the elite of the civil service corps is cause for rejecting the notion that a representative bureaucracy exists in the United States." These analyses have raised some concern about the opportunities available to women and people of color, as research has shown that their lack of advancement cannot be entirely attributable to merit-based factors, such as education and experience.

Measurement issues aside, others criticize the utility of passive representation from a different angle of vision. In their view, the theory of representative bureaucracy is meaningless if passive representation does not result in what Mosher called "active" representation. Mosher argued that unless a civil servant can be shown to "press for the interests and desires of those whom he is presumed to represent" there is little point in even being concerned with whether or not the bureaucracy is representative in the passive sense.

There is some evidence that diversity does make a difference in the administration of public policy. Meier and Stewart have suggested that this is most likely to occur when administrators have some degree of discretion in how they implement their program, when the discretion can be employed in a way that could affect a minority community, and when those administrators are linked directly to their decisions. This is the situation in EEOC district offices, at which legal and investigative staffs have the discretion to pursue a case based on their own judgment as to whether or not any case brought to them by a complainant appears to have probable cause. John Hindera has found that the representation of African Americans and Hispanics in these positions is positively related to the number of charges filed on behalf of African-American and Hispanic complainants. Similarly, Meier found that the greater the representation of African-American teachers in schools, the less likely it is that African-American students will be subject to disciplinary action or tracked into noncollege preparatory classes. Selden showed that the percentage of favorable loan eligibility determinations by the USDA's Farmers Home Administration (FHA) for African Americans, Latinos, and Asian Americans are directly related to the number of African-American, Latino, and Asian-American supervisors, respectively, in FHA offices in a given county. There is some evidence that representativeness also matters to the clients of a service agency. Thielemann and Stewart found that African Americans, Latinos, and gays living with AIDS much preferred to receive services from members of their own group than from another group.

There is some evidence that the ethnic composition of a workforce does make a difference in government decision making. Other researchers have a contrary perspective, in part because there is no consensus as to how "active representation" should be measured. Rehfuss, for example, concluded that female and minority senior executives in the California civil service don't engage in active representation because they express a "management ideology" that is no different from that manifested by their white male counterparts. After reviewing many of these studies, Frank Thompson concluded "Both pessimists and optimists concerning linkage [between passive and active representation] can, then, find support for their conclusions in the existing theories and empirical findings of social science."

Determining whether or not a particular agency is indeed "representative" of the citizenry is not, then, a simple task. Moreover, given the myriad reasons that a representative bureaucracy is important, it is unclear whether proportional representation alone would satisfy the demands of women and people of color for equality of opportunity, power, and authority. Charles Levine wrote in 1974, "But knowing the number and percentage of employees from minority groups has increased and that more minority group employees are being promoted to higher grades tell us little about their work experiences and the extent to which racism and sexism persist in public manpower management systems." The ways in which race and sex may continue to pervade public sector agencies is the issue addressed in the next section of this chapter.

THE NATURE OF UNEQUAL TREATMENT
IN TODAY'S WORKPLACE

Governments have elaborate mechanisms in place for ensuring that all Americans have the same opportunities in employment, regardless of race, ethnicity, gender, and other such factors. Employees who believe they have been denied a job or job reward based on their race, ethnicity, or sex can file a complaint, which if not resolved to their satisfaction by their agencies can be pursued with the EEOC or the courts. In fiscal year 1994 alone, over 24,000 complaints were filed with the EEOC by federal employees. Very few of these cases result in findings of discrimination, largely because the EEOC attempts to settle cases before they reach this point. Another reason, however, is that the barriers to full equality in the workplace experienced by individuals are often so subtle that they do not demonstrate the manifest discrimination that the EEOC was set up to monitor or investigate.

The subtle ways in which women and people of color are often disadvantaged based on their race, ethnicity, and sex in organizations has been called "institutional discrimination," "treatment discrimination," or "second-generation discrimination." While specific definitions of these terms may differ, in general they all refer to the notion that factors other than merit or achievement, such as group membership, have an effect on the way opportunities, rewards, and punishments are distributed in organizations. Such factors continue to operate after formal structural barriers to inclusion have been eliminated. Thomas Pettigrew describes second-generation discrimination, for example, as racial discrimination that is "more indirect, subtle, procedural, and more ostensibly nonracial" than the blatant forms of discrimination that were attacked by the 1964 Civil Rights Act and 1965 Voting Rights Act. The next section is devoted to a discussion of these subtle barriers.

Subjective Discrimination

In a 1980 article Anne Hopkins argued that a focus solely on discrimination that could be said to exist by an outside observer—or "objective discrimination"—does not provide a complete understanding of the effects of a legacy of disparate treatment in organizations. Equally important is "subjective discrimination," or the perception by individuals or members of a group that their own situation is discriminatory. Such perceptions are important, she argued, because they adversely affect employee morale and productivity. Moreover, they can create a self-perpetuating cycle whereby women and people of color do not aspire to elite ranks because they perceive a lack of opportunity and engage in self-limiting behaviors.

A survey conducted by MSPB and discussed in a 1992 report suggests that a substantial portion of women in the federal government do experience subjective discrimination. (See Figure 11.2.) More than half (55%) of women expressed the belief that women must perform better than a man to be promoted, while nearly half (45%) reported that standards are higher for women than men. What is also noteworthy about Figure 11.2 is that men do not share these perceptions—fewer than 10% of male respondents expressed agreement with either of these statements.

Similarly, Figure 11.3 reports the results of a survey administered by MSPB and discussed in a 1996 report on minority employment in the government. Responses to this survey demonstrate that some members of minority groups in the federal government, particularly African Americans, believe their opportunities

In general, in my organization . . .

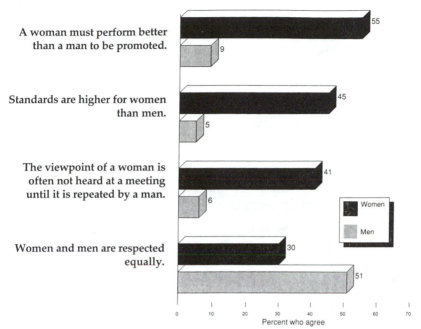

A woman must perform better than a man to be promoted. — 55 / 9

Standards are higher for women than men. — 45 / 5

The viewpoint of a woman is often not heard at a meeting until it is repeated by a man. — 41 / 6

Women and men are respected equally. — 30 / 51

Women / Men

Percent who agree

FIGURE 11.2 Perceptions of female and male survey respondents. *Source*: U.S. Merit Systems Protection Board, "A Question of Equity: Women and the Glass Ceiling in the Federal Government," 1992.

are not just limited, but also that they are subject to excessive discriminatory treatment. Specifically, more than half (55%) of African Americans reported that African Americans are subjected to "flagrant or obviously discriminatory practices" to a great or moderate extent. Again, non-African Americans do not share this perception; only 4% of white employees agreed with the statement.

Regardless of whether such perceptions are justified, the point here is that even the *perception* of such bias in the workplace places constraints on women and people of color. Those who perceive these disparities are likely to have lower job satisfaction and effectiveness. Moreover, they are less likely to put themselves in a position in which they believe they are expected to fail (e.g., by applying for promotions). No *objective* discrimination occurred, because the individual never applied for the job, but his or her ambitions and potential contributions to the organization have been thwarted. *Subjective discrimination*, while not falling into the category of prohibited discrimination, may thus be just as potent in limiting the aspirations and therefore the potential for career advancement of women

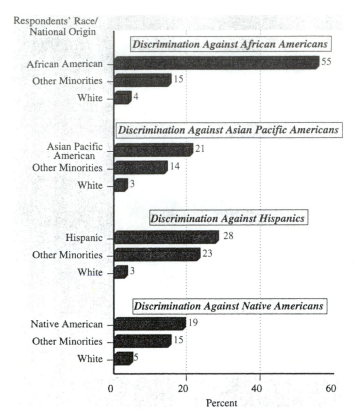

Respondents' Race/
National Origin

FIGURE 11.3 Extent to which employees believe minorities are subjected to "Flagrant or obviously discriminatory practices," by race/national origin. *Note*: Response percentages are for answers of "to a great extent" or "to a moderate extent." *Source*: MSPB survey of federal employees, January 1993, question 46.

and people of color. It is also important to note that such perceptions are often not shared by dominant groups in the workplace. Such a divergence may also have an adverse impact on collegiality and teamwork.

Stereotypes

Another factor that can be a powerful albeit subtle influence on how people of color and women are treated in the workplace is the propensity of people to stereotype. Stereotypes aren't necessarily false or damaging; they are a normal process by which people categorize information about the world around them. The problem is that in some cases assumptions are made about a group that are inaccurate or that simply don't apply to any one individual member of that group. The Federal Glass Ceiling Commission, for example, reported that Native Americans are often assumed to be irresponsible and lazy, while Asians tend to be stereotyped as passive, technically oriented, and ill-equipped for people-oriented work.

Jobs are also often stereotyped in that they are considered male or female, white or nonwhite, depending on which group has tended to predominate in the job. For example, although the image of what characterizes an effective manager is changing, the traditional notion is that a manager is strong, competitive, and assertive. Women, on the other hand, are assumed to be weak, passive, and uncompetitive. When the stereotype associated with an individual does not match that of the job, it is often assumed that the individual will fail in the job, both by him- or herself and others. In this way, stereotypes can be self-fulfilling.

This is not to say that white and/or male employees are not also subject to stereotypes. They are less likely to be adversely affected by them than people of color and women, however. Traditionally, white men have held a majority of professional and high-level jobs. Research has suggested that stereotyping is magnified when a particular group is in the minority. In these situations, members of minority groups are more visible, and hence their mistakes are as well. Moreover, since white men hold the majority of supervisory positions in organizations, they are more often in the role of evaluating others' prospects for employment and promotion rather than being evaluated themselves. In analyzing the results of a broad array of research in this area, Kraiger and Ford found that supervisors tend to rate employees from their own ethnic group higher than those from another group.

Stereotypes also tend to be self-reinforcing, in that people tend to disregard information that is counter to the stereotype and retain information that confirms it. A woman in a management position may thus find that her accomplishments are attributed to luck and her failures to her unsuitability for the job. In contrast, a male manager's achievements tend to confirm his skills, while his failings are minimized.

Stereotypes, then, can serve as a real impediment to equal opportunity in the workplace. Their effects may be subtle, but they are often powerful. Those who are subject to stereotypes are likely to avoid positions in which they will be highly visible and subject to particular scrutiny. As an example, 20% of respondents to a recent MSPB survey reported that they chose not to apply for a promotion or developmental assignment because they believed no one from their racial or ethnic group would be selected. Stereotypes, then, are no less potent than overt discrimination in denying individuals advancement opportunities and in denying organizations the opportunity to consider the full range of potential applicants.

Glass Ceilings

First used in a *Wall Street Journal* article in 1986, the term *glass ceiling* refers to elusive, almost invisible barriers that hinder people of color and women as they try to advance in organizations. The metaphor suggests that the underrepresentation of women and people of color in top-level positions cannot be entirely explained by a lack of qualifications, disinclination to hold such positions, or even overt discrimination; rather, the obstacles that impede them are nearly imperceptible.

Few would dispute that white men hold a disproportionate share of senior-level jobs in the public and private sectors. The Federal Glass Ceiling Commission noted in its 1995 report that 97% of senior-level managers in *Fortune* 1000 industrial and *Fortune* 500 service industries are white men. On a positive note, as shown in Table 11.2, in 1997 women held 21%, and people of color 12% of senior federal jobs. Some of this disparity can be explained by differences in qualifications, such as education and experience. In the federal government, for example, senior federal executives have on average about 22 years of federal service, and two-thirds of them have a degree beyond the bachelor's level. High-level federal employees are often expected to have relocated geographically in order to demonstrate a breadth of experience and commitment to one's career. Indeed, fewer people of color than whites hold college degrees, while women, who have only recently closed the educational gap with men, tend to have been in the workforce for shorter period of time and are less likely to have relocated.

In its study of the glass ceiling, however, MSPB found that even controlling for differences in education, experience, and geographic relocations, women have been promoted fewer times over the course of their federal careers than men. The MSPB also found that, with the exception of Asian-American men, minority men and women had not advanced as far as white men, even accounting for differences in education and experience.

The difference in advancement rates is no doubt influenced by two of the factors already discussed—subjective discrimination and stereotypes. In the case of the glass ceiling, it is likely that a particular set of stereotypes and expectations works to the disadvantage of people of color and women. In particular, expectations about the characteristics of an employee with promotion potential are based on a model that is out of date. That model is based on the assumption that those who will ascend to high levels are white men who demonstrate their commitment to the organization by, among other things, relocating geographically and working long hours. They were able to be mobile and flexible in the past because they had wives at home who did not pursue careers and could devote themselves to taking care of the family and household. That model also assumes, then, that women are more devoted to their families than their careers, placing them at a double disadvantage.

The first disadvantage women face is that those who have small children may not be able to put in the long hours expected of senior managers, at least as long as women continue to bear the primary responsibility for child rearing. A second disadvantage arises in that even if women *are* able to work late, it is often *assumed* that they cannot, and so women are often passed over for career-enhancing assignments and promotions. Even where organizations attempt to be ''family-friendly'' by offering flexible working hours, those who take advantage of such programs are often viewed as lacking the career commitment required for promotion. In a study of professionals in *Fortune* 500 companies, Wick and Company, a consulting firm, exploded the myth that the higher turnover rate among women as compared to men was attributable to women's desire to devote more time to their families; rather, women were leaving their companies to pursue opportunities in other corporations that offered more growth potential and respect for women as professionals.

In today's knowledge-based economy, promotion potential is not easily measured or judged, hence the hours devoted to the job each week become a visible, easily quantifiable surrogate for job commitment, and thus a reason to promote one individual over another one who is equally qualified. The quantity and quality of employees' work depends on a variety of factors, only one of which is the time they spend at the workplace. Hence, reliance on long hours as a criteria for judging employee performance means that high-quality employees, especially women, may be excluded from consideration.

Moreover, there is some evidence that such criteria also exclude women of childbearing age from consideration, as it is assumed it is only a matter of time before they become pregnant and choose to sacrifice their careers for their family. A participant in a focus group assembled by MSPB put it this way:

> There is this business that as a successful senior executive you come in at 7:00 and you stay longer and work harder than anybody else and you really don't start your rumination about really important things until 10: 00 or so at night. And the effect of this was that the only people who [they] wanted to discuss the job [vacancy with] were men of any age, single women and older women with no kids. I mean there were 2 or 3 names in the hat and they said I don't want to talk to her because she has children who are still home in these hours. Now they don't pose that thing about men on the list, many of whom also have children in that age group.

Some studies have found, in fact, that women with children are less likely to advance than single and childless women, even accounting for any leaves of absence they may have taken during their careers. In contrast, the presence of children has either no impact, or a positive effect, on men's likelihood to be promoted.

It is thus this particular set of expectations about what it takes to be a manager (demonstrated commitment to one's career by having relocated and worked long hours) that runs headlong into a particular set of stereotypes about women (more committed to their families than their careers and hence unable or unwilling to meet these expectations) that forms, at least in part, the glass ceiling. It will take conscious efforts on behalf of organizations to recognize and remove these kinds of subtle barriers.

Other Disparities

While the glass ceiling has received considerable attention, there are other subtle barriers that can arise in the workplace as well. Some of these have been described with similar "architectural" metaphors. For example, an article in the *Wall Street Journal* referred to the concentration of women and people of color in occupations that are not in the pipeline to management (e.g., support positions) as "glass walls." The Center for Women in Government dubbed the concentration of women and people of color in low-paying jobs "sticky floors." Beyond these issues, MSPB researchers discovered other inequities in their analysis of minority employment in the federal government.

The MSPB found, for example, that in professional and administrative positions, people of color receive on average lower performance ratings and cash awards than white employees. As noted before, research has suggested that this may result, at least in part, from the tendency of supervisors to rate employees of their own ethnic group more favorably than those of another group. While this research also suggests that people of color are likely to rate other people of the same ethnicity higher than nonminorities, it is nonminorities who hold the majority of supervisory positions. Low performance ratings in turn can adversely affect employees' likelihood to earn promotions or awards, as well as their status during a reduction in force (layoff). In fact, MSPB also found that in many federal occupations, white employees did receive more cash awards than minority employees.

Another employment area in which disparities among ethnic groups are found is the disciplinary process. In the federal government, African Americans and Native Americans are subject to disciplinary measures and discharged from their jobs at a significantly higher rate than white employees or Asian Pacific Americans (with Hispanics falling in between). A report produced by OPM in 1995 revealed that the disparity cannot be explained on the basis of grade level, education, kind of work, age, performance rating, seniority, or attendance record. Similar patterns with regard to disparate discipline rates have been found in a region of the U.S. Postal Service, in the Internal Revenue Service, and in the state of California's public workforce.

While the OPM report did not offer a definitive explanation for the disparity, it did offer some "reasonable explanations of possible causes of the disparity," such as that supervisors and managers may not always know how to communicate effectively and that African Americans and Native Americans may not receive timely feedback about their failure to meet management's expectations.

It is also possible that stereotypes and subjective discrimination play a role. Sometimes a cycle can be created whereby because of a stereotype a supervisor has lower expectations of an African-American employee and does not give him or her the kind of mentoring or access to networks that provides employees with greater opportunity to be successful on the job. The African-American employee may well perceive the difference in treatment, become unhappy, and as a result, his or her performance and/or conduct suffers.

The Power of Subtle Differences

In summary, there are many ways in which subtle barriers operate to the disadvantage of women and people of color in organizations. None of these disparities is great, but they are all interrelated. An employee who receives a lower performance rating than his or her peers or who is passed over for promotion may very well believe that the cause was discrimination. This is as true of white employees, many of whom believe people of color are treated more favorably than themselves, as it is of people of color, who believe the opposite. Even small disparities can thus increase the likelihood of subjective discrimination, which in turn can cause lower morale, job satisfaction, and productivity, and may prevent high-potential individuals from seeking promotion or even remaining with their organizations. It is for this reason that many organizations today, including the city of Seattle, realize that traditional EEO programs are not enough, and so are proactively seeking ways to foster greater inclusion.

STRATEGIES FOR GREATER INCLUSION

Identifying the ways in which racism and sexism have persisted in organizations is not a simple task, particularly when they take the subterranean forms described in this chapter. An even more difficult question is how to transform the organization into one in which women, people of color, and other nontraditional groups are truly on an equal footing with white men. Given the enormity of this task and the barriers to be surmounted, only a multifaceted approach will make a significant difference. This is because an effective strategy for fostering greater inclusion requires opening the minds of individuals who harbor assumptions and stereotypes they are often not even aware of and confronting an organizational culture grounded in an outmoded industrial model. This means that everything from work policies and human resource management practices to organizational norms and structures must re-examined in light of their potential exclusionary nature. While a wealth of literature exists today prescribing strategies for fostering greater inclusion (albeit mainly focused on the private sector), the remainder of this chapter will highlight some of the more promising ones.

Ensuring Effective Communication and Feedback

One of the most significant obstacles to ensuring that all employees are valued in an organization is a failure to ensure effective communication. Assumptions that are made about individuals based on their membership in a group (i.e., stereotypes) can reflect a lack of communication between the two parties involved. Substantive communication between the parties can go a long way to dispelling the notion that any particular individual fits the stereotype associated with him or her. Moreover, in many cases in which people allege discrimination (i.e., are experiencing subjective discrimination) it is because communication has broken down.

Imagine an African American who has unsuccessfully applied for a promotion he believes he is eminently qualified for and is not given feedback as to why he was not selected. If the selected individual were white, that African American may well assume that the selection decision reflected the supervisor's prejudice against African Americans. Similarly, it is not uncommon for a white employee, passed over for promotion by a person of color, to assume that "reverse discrimination" had occurred. Assuming there were no prejudice or discrimination, these charges would have occurred because these applicants were not given feedback as to why the successful candidate was selected rather than themselves. In response to a survey question posed by MSPB, only 8% of the respondents who reported that they had not been selected for a promotion indicated that they had asked for and had been given useful feedback as to why they were not selected.

Similarly, the disparity in rates of discipline and discharge discussed in this chapter are likely to result at least in part from ineffective communication between supervisors and their subordinates. Supervisors may think they are making their expectations clear, but the employee is not getting the message. The MSPB concluded in a study of the quality of first-line supervisors in the federal government that not all supervisors are willing or able to provide frank and frequent feedback to their subordinates about performance. This is partly a function of a climate that tends to pervade many federal agencies that provides more disincentives than incentives to supervisors when they consider confronting employees. This reluctance is often exacerbated when the two are from different ethnic groups. The supervisor may not feel comfortable with someone of a different ethnicity, and/or fears that negative feedback will cause the employee to file a discrimination lawsuit. In a survey administered to employees who had recently been subject to disciplinary actions and their supervisors, nearly 80% of supervisors reported that they had counseled their employees before taking the action, while less than 30% of those same employees reported receiving the counseling, indicating a breakdown in communication. The problem was worse when the two were of different ethnicities, however. White employees with white supervisors were much more likely than minority employees with white supervisors to report that they had received counseling before being disciplined.

Effective and timely feedback is as important to employees' development as it is to reducing the likelihood that their performance will become poor enough to warrant disciplinary action. It is clearly also important for creating an environment free of stereotypes, subjective discrimination, and other impediments to inclusion. Organizations must ensure that the ability to communicate effectively and impartially is an important component in the training of new supervisors.

Reorienting Personnel Policies and Processes

The system most public sector agencies continue to use today for managing employees was built on a set of assumptions about the nature of the workforce and a commitment to particular values that were important decades ago. It was assumed, for example, that the most efficient and fair way to treat employees was with maximum uniformity, a practice that made sense when the workforce was relatively homogeneous. It was taken for granted that open recruitment and the development of crediting plans would ensure that the most highly qualified candidate would apply for and be selected for a job. The benefits system was designed for a largely white male workforce with a wife and family at home. It was presumed that employee performance could be objectively evaluated and rewarded, and that these rewards would create an incentive for employees to do their best work.

Many organizations that are attempting today to create a more inclusive workplace are challenging these assumptions and reorienting their procedures for managing their human resources. In doing so, they are also altering the mix of values that either explicitly or implicitly underlie many personnel policies and procedures. The value of uniformity, for example, is less relevant today when organizations need to be flexible and adaptable to changing conditions. At the same time, traditional personnel policies do not typically emphasize inclusiveness as a value. The following are some examples of changes organizations are making to reflect the growing importance of that value.

Recruitment and Selection Practices

There are two ways in which recruitment and selection strategies can work for or against the creation of a diverse and inclusive environment. One way is in how the organization carries out its recruitment strategies, and the other is in how it establishes selection criteria.

In its 1991 report on the glass ceiling the U.S. Department of Labor noted that in many of the *Fortune* 1000 companies examined, recruitment practices inadvertently hampered the employment and advancement of people of color and women. This is because these companies tended to rely on word-of-mouth referrals from current employees for locating prospective candidates, and then promoted from within for their senior-level positions. This had the effect of bringing in new recruits that looked a lot like the current workforce, and hence perpetuated its homogeneity in both the lower and higher levels.

Recruitment practices in most public sector organizations generally do not fall into the same trap, as they are often required to announce job vacancies more broadly. However, an organization that is seeking to increase the diversity of its workforce often must make a conscious effort to ensure that nontraditional candidates are included in the applicant pool. This objective is often accomplished by targeting recruitment efforts in places in which there is a larger concentration of people of color (e.g., historically black colleges and universities). Agencies often establish partnerships with educational institutions to increase the exposure of the organization to a wider array of students. They can help ensure that nontraditional groups are interested in applying to their organizations by publicizing their own success in creating an inclusive environment.

This strategy mainly addresses the applicant pool for entry-level jobs, however. In many public sector agencies, people of color and women continue to hold a smaller share of midlevel or journey-level jobs. This means that when vacancies at senior levels are announced, which occurs less frequently, there will be considerably fewer women and employees of color at the right place in the pipeline to compete for those jobs. In that case, recruitment, which often only occurs in-house, may need to be expanded beyond the usual area of consideration in order to ensure that a sufficient number of women and people of color are included in the applicant pool.

The other issue that organizations must face is that there is no such thing as a perfectly objective system for assessing which applicant is ''best qualified'' for the job. Certainly merit systems within public sector agencies are designed to achieve as objective a process as possible, but no system can be installed that does not involve someone's judgment at some point.

Most public sector organizations, in an effort to be objective, will develop a crediting plan. This is done by attempting to determine in advance the qualifications needed for success on the job and the weight each particular qualification should be given. The crediting plan is then used to assign numerical scores to the candidates so that they can be ranked according to how well their qualifications match those required for the job. In designing crediting plans, however, organizations frequently rely on past behaviors, which are clearly an imperfect predictor of future success on the job, particularly when the new job is a different one than the candidate held previously. Moreover, the development of the crediting plan clearly requires subjective judgments about which skills or experiences are important in relation to the others.

For example, in hiring a team leader for a group of attorneys, is it more important for the candidate to have demonstrated leadership skills, teamwork, or success as a litigator? The decision is necessarily subjective. Moreover, a crediting plan often reflects the qualifications of incumbents in the job, giving an advantage to those who most closely resemble job incumbents, to the detriment of nontraditional candidates. This advantage is reinforced when the supervisor makes the final selection among the top qualified, as there is a natural tendency to select in our own image.

The other difficulty with this process for selecting employees is that it gives the illusion of a precise system that promises that the person most likely to succeed in the job is the one who attains the highest score. If for whatever reason (e.g., to achieve a diverse workforce) a person who received a score of 92 is selected rather than the one who achieved a score of 95, it is assumed that a less qualified applicant was chosen. This assumption is based on the belief that the score is a precise measure of a candidate's ability. A good illustration can be seen in the U.S. Supreme Court's decision in *Johnson* v. *Santa Clara County Transportation Agency* (1987). This case involved the promotion of a female applicant, Diane Joyce, to the position of road dispatcher in the county's transportation agency. Paul Johnson, another applicant for the position, filed suit, charging that he was denied the promotion based on his sex in violation of Title VII of the Civil Rights Act. One of the issues raised in the case was the difference in their scores from an oral interview. Diane Joyce earned a score of 73, while Paul Johnson earned a 75.

The U.S. Supreme Court ruled in favor of Joyce on the grounds that the county hired her pursuant to a voluntarily developed affirmative action plan aimed at correcting gender imbalances in traditionally segregated job categories. Indeed, one of the major goals of affirmative action programs is to neutralize the effect of recruitment and selection systems to hire those that most closely match job incumbents. Such a program, according to the Court majority, is legal under Title VII.

Sometimes the issue is more serious than just a small difference in the applicant scores. In some cases, applicants are given a written or oral exam that reflects cultural biases. The concern here is not whether an exam is translated into Spanish or an Asian language, but rather whether the job applicants have an equal opportunity to acquire the tools, skills, and education needed to perform well on the tests. One approach to addressing this problem is to tutor or coach all prospective candidates for a promotion on how to prepare for and take the test. Such methods have proven to be especially successful in preparing women and persons of color for entry-level police officer and firefighter exams.

Organizations that are committed to achieving a diverse and inclusive work environment recruit broadly for vacant positions and encourage nontraditional employees to apply by making their commitment to diversity clear. They also labor to accurately define the qualifications that are required for success on the job, and recognize that there is no perfect predictor of success or precise measure of qualifications. In some cases, coaching prospective candidates can help remedy any cultural or gender bias that the selection instruments may contain.

Performance Appraisals, Awards, and Development

Performance appraisals play a critical role in many organizations. They are intended to be used as a means for giving employees feedback as to how they can improve their performance on the job. They also often form the basis for important decisions regarding development, compensation, promotions, awards, discipline, and reductions in force. However, performance appraisals are no more likely to be precise and objective measures of employees' performance than crediting plans are of employees' qualifications.

That people of color in the federal government receive, on average, lower performance ratings than white employees has already been discussed, along with the reasons that may occur. In addition to the consequences a poor performance rating can have for an employee's status in the organization, it can cause low morale and increase subjective discrimination. Indeed, a poor rating can create a self-fulfilling prophesy, whereby the employee who received the low rating is convinced that the process is biased and unfair, and so puts even less effort into the job.

Performance appraisals frequently serve as the basis for granting employees pay increases and monetary awards, under the assumption that the potential for financial remuneration motivates employees to do their best work. This often means, however, that a de facto competition is set up among employees because there is not enough money in the budget to reward everyone. Those who don't win the award are often resentful, and a perception of racism or sexism may be reinforced. A lack of effective communication regarding how decisions were made will also exacerbate negative consequences.

Similarly, performance appraisals often serve as a starting point for the formulation of career development plans. Development programs are intended to provide employees with the skills necessary for full integration into the workforce and the knowledge, skills, and experiences they need to be competitive for future promotions. In her book *The New Leaders*, Ann Morrison suggests that in many organizations, even those in which women and people of color have successfully broken into management ranks, their affiliation and growth in the new position has been assumed rather than managed. In this situation, Morrison argues, development is the "Achilles' heal of many otherwise strong diversity efforts."

Development programs normally include several components, such as participation in classroom training on management skills, rotational assignments, opportunities to "act" for a supervisor who is out of the office for a period of time, and consultation with a mentor. Classroom training can impart necessary knowledge to participants, while mentors can provide guidance as to the more informal organizational requirements for success on the job. Both kinds of learning are critical to the success of nontraditional employees, as they are often excluded from the networks and relationships that traditional employees have benefited from.

In addition to providing important on-the-job training, rotational assignments and serving as an "acting" director furnish nontraditional employees with the opportunity to demonstrate their competence, thereby breaking down negative stereotypes. Selection into a formal management development program can also provide an employee with visibility and signal management's regard for his or her abilities. Table 11.3 shows the responses of men and women in mid- and senior-level federal jobs (GS-9 and above) to a series of questions about what they found helpful in their career advancement. Note that a much greater proportion of women than men found such activities as the opportunity to act in a position, completion of a formal development program, and developmental assignments to be very helpful in their career advancement.

Performance appraisals are also a means by which organizations communicate to their employees the behaviors they value. For example, organizations

TABLE 11.3 Employees' Views of Experiences That Helped Their Career Advancement

Experience	Percentage responding "helped a lot"	
	Women	Men
Opportunity to act in a position(s) prior to appointment	44	30
Completion of formal developmental program or managerial training	26	15
Developmental assignments	42	26
Having a senior person/mentor looking out for my interests	28	12
My performance or "track" record	79	67

Source: MSPB, *A Question of Equity*, 1992.

that are attempting to transition to team-based work structures should replace individual performance appraisals with assessments of team performance. To fail to do so would belie the organization's confidence in and commitment to teams. In this way, the performance appraisal system provides an opportunity to reinforce the organization's values, including its expectation that employees contribute to a diverse, inclusive work environment.

In short, performance appraisals serve a multitude of purposes, some of them contradictory. In response to this concern, some organizations are separating the purposes intended to be served by performance appraisals. Appraisals that are used to provide feedback and development for employees are separated from those that are used for rewards. To avoid the perception of "winners" and "losers" often engendered by monetary performance awards, some organizations recognize higher performers instead by granting them more autonomy, giving them special assignments, or increasing their visibility in the organization. Team awards are also becoming popular, with the recognition that cooperation and teamwork are valuable skills in today's environment.

Work Arrangements and Benefits

Most organizations today have recognized that the model of a husband working, with a wife at home taking care of the family and household, is no longer the predominant family arrangement. Increasingly employers are recognizing the conflict that can arise when a single parent or both parents have to cope with a full-time job and significant family responsibilities. A common response is to offer flexible work arrangements, including telecommuting, flexible schedules, job sharing, and benefits such as child care and elder care. Moreover, the Family Medical and Leave Act requires employers to make available twelve weeks of unpaid leave for personal medical problems or the birth or adoption of a child. This is an important step toward creating a work environment that is inclusive of members of nontraditional families, especially women.

To be fully inclusive, however, an organization has to go one step beyond providing these arrangements by *not* penalizing those who take advantage of them. The tendency for traditional managers to assume that women with children or even of childbearing age are less committed to their careers has already been discussed. Organizations need to make sure that such informal and non-job-related criteria do not limit women's opportunities for advancement. A 1995 article in the *Wall Street Journal* reported that some private sector companies have already recognized this issue and are developing ways to integrate work–family and career advancement initiatives. The Sara Lee Company, for example, visibly selected two mothers of small children for top-level jobs. Both women are trying to set an example by leaving the office in time for dinner with their families.

In short, organizations must re-examine their human resource management policies to ensure that they don't work to the disadvantage of nontraditional employees. They must ensure that recruitment and selection practices don't simply perpetuate the status quo. Performance appraisals should be used as a mechanism for satisfactory communication between supervisors and subordinates, and to reinforce the organization's commitment to diversity and inclusion. Employees who take advantage of flexible work arrangements should be assured that they will not be penalized when they pursue advancement. Reconstructing performance appraisals, awards systems, development programs, and recruitment and selection practices can go a long way toward providing an environment that is inclusive of nontraditional employees.

Data Collection and Training

The publication of *Workforce 2000* and *Civil Service 2000* in the late 1980s spawned the development of what Frederick Lynch calls a "diversity machine," which includes a host of consultants prepared to offer training in "diversity awareness." Attendance at such training sessions is increasingly becoming a requirement in public sector organizations. These training sessions generally focus on teaching employees (and especially supervisors) to be sensitive to differences among people from different cultural backgrounds and to see these differences in a positive light rather than as factors that limit employees' contributions to their organizations. The quality of such training varies greatly, sometimes causing a backlash of anger. One such training experience recently resulted in a lawsuit against the Federal Aviation Administration. (See box.)

Successful training programs generally include a number of components. A starting point for even designing a diversity training program (or any diversity-related interventions, for that matter) is the collection of data. In order to understand where an organization is having the greatest problems, the rates of hiring, promotion, awards, discipline, and other work actions should be examined for any disparities among groups within the workforce. In addition to suggesting where management's attention should be focused, these are important facts that can challenge assumptions made by employees. For example, a white employee may be convinced that "Latinos are getting all the promotions in this agency" when in fact Latinos are promoted at no greater a rate than any other group. An African American may assume that "the performance appraisal system is biased against us," when in fact African Americans have received a higher or equal proportion of outstanding performance ratings compared to others. Dispelling such myths and therefore reducing the potential for subjective discrimination, can be facilitated by incorporating accurate data about employment actions into diversity training sessions, and encouraging discussion about them.

Ann Morrison counsels that data collection should be more than "just the facts—perceptions count, too." As was discussed earlier, perceptions of discrimination or other unfair treatment can be just as damaging to employee morale

In September 1994 the *Washington Times* reported that the Federal Aviation Administration (FAA) agreed to settle complaints filed by a union representing air traffic controllers. According to the union, diversity training that FAA employees were required to attend left them traumatized and, in some cases, unable to work. The union asked that the 4,000 training participants be "deprogrammed" to undo the training's adverse affects, and that the employees who required medical treatment as a result of the training be reimbursed for their expenses. The lawyer representing a male FAA employee who filed a sexual harassment suit as a result of the sessions, called the training "a government-sponsored Tailhook." (Tailhook refers to an incident in 1991 in which female Navy officers were fondled and forced to pass through a gauntlet of male aviators during a convention in Las Vegas.) The FAA training, according to the *Washington Times* report, forced men to walk through a gauntlet of women who fondled their genitals and ridiculed their sexual prowess. Participants were also pressured into talking about intimate sexual experiences.

This is an example how training that may be intended to sensitize men to the treatment that women must sometimes endure can backfire. As one controller and former union vice president said, "This is horrendous. They took a very good idea—trying to help people get along—and they killed it."

and productivity as "objective" discrimination. Climate surveys, interviews, and focus groups are all means by which managers can identify the biggest areas of concern so that intervention strategies can be targeted effectively. These findings should also be a topic of discussion in diversity training sessions.

A good training program will also focus on breaking down stereotypes and educating managers about how they may be inadvertently contributing to mistreatment. These programs should also demonstrate the importance of open discussion and help to develop mechanisms whereby such discussion can continue after the training is ended.

One particular area in which training is often needed is with respect to how selection decisions are made in general and the use of affirmative action in particular. How affirmative action is used in practice is often greatly misunderstood, particularly by people from groups who are not underrepresented in their work unit and fear that affirmative action will impede their own career advancement. Such a misunderstanding can also lead to poor morale and distrust of the organization. Educating employees about actual hiring and promotion practices

The "Labeling Game"

A game called "labeling" has become a popular tool in diversity training for managers. It is intended to illustrate how such characteristics as race and gender can influence how a worker is treated. And, it shows how and why the way people are treated can perpetuate negative stereotypes. The game works like this:

"A piece of paper with a characteristic written on it is placed on a manager's forehead, but the manager can't see it. If the label ('CEO,' say,) causes others in the seminar to react with respect, the manager soon becomes confident and outgoing. If the words ('militant feminist,' say,) elicits negative responses, the manager often grows hostile and silent."

Source: Mabry Marcus. "Pin a Label on a Manager—and Watch What Happens," *Newsweek* (May 14, 1990), p. 43.

and the status of various groups at all levels of the organization can help to dispel employees' suspicions. Also important is education about the continuing nature of discrimination and more subtle forms of mistreatment. The MSPB found that a much greater percentage of the white federal employees who believed African Americans have not made much progress in career advancement in the government support the notion that underrepresentation should be considered in selection decisions than white employees who believe people of color have made at least some progress.

In summary, most experts agree that the education of the workforce at all levels is an important step in building a more inclusive work environment. Organizations should exercise caution when looking for diversity training to be made available to their employees, because poorly designed programs can cause more harm than benefit. Essential components of effective programs are discussion about how selection, promotion, and other such employment-related decisions are made, the status of various groups within the workplace, and how those groups perceive their own status. Also worthy of consideration are the nature of continuing mistreatment and the damage caused by stereotypes. These subjects are more difficult to address, and care must be taken that they are approached in a way that does not characterize victims and villains. Experts agree that training should be provided on an ongoing basis, and that it should be provided in conjunction with other interventions.

Leadership and Accountability

Organizational leadership plays a critical role in fostering an inclusive environment. Many management theorists go as far as to say that an organization cannot become inclusive without leadership that is both competent and committed to equality and trust. In his book *Race, Gender and Rhetoric*, John Fernandez warns that a lack of leadership skill can result in a belief among lower-level employees that management is not only incompetent but biased against them as well.

To demonstrate the priority given to diversity and inclusion, top management needs to becoming visibly involved in efforts to achieve these goals. Ann Morrison warns, however, that management should not dictate a strategy for fostering achievement, but rather commission and support a task force broadly representative of the workforce. The task force should be informed of the appropriate boundaries and the extent of resources available for the interventions it recommends.

Top managers also demonstrate their commitment to diversity by expending their own time and efforts on diversity-related activities. Such activities can include meeting with task forces and advocacy groups for underrepresented employees. Management also signals its commitment by setting specific diversity-related objectives to be met by subordinate managers, and constantly reminding them of the importance of achieving those objectives. Other actions include publicizing the organization's record on diversity by speaking to outside groups or getting the attention of the media.

Top management's commitment to diversity is not always accepted by agency staff, however. The *Washington Times* reported on a measure taken during Henry Cisneros's term as secretary of Housing and Urban Development (HUD). Agency managers were informed that "documented evidence" of performance in cultural diversity that distinctly shows actions or measurement achievements would be necessary for them to received highly successful or outstanding performance ratings. The newspaper quoted one HUD manager as saying, "good intentions run amok, which seems to be the theme of current HUD leadership." Similarly, the *Federal Times* reported that the defense undersecretary for personnel came under criticism for issuing a memorandum requiring special approval for the selection of white men without disabilities into high-level jobs (GS-15 and above) in the Office of Personnel and Readiness. Such criticism may be avoided if top management makes an effort to educate subordinate managers about the importance of diversity and inclusion and involve them in setting objectives and accountability measures.

Indeed, the HUD and DOD leadership were doing more than simply telegraphing their commitment to diversity. They were attempting to develop mechanisms for holding subordinate managers accountable for meeting diversity goals, another important component of leadership. The collection and analysis of employment-related and climate data should also augment management goal setting. Taylor Cox encourages organizations to set as their goal "zero correlation of sociocultural identity with opportunity, motivation, and achievement." Table 11.4 provides examples of potential interim objectives and strategies for achieving those objectives.

These are the kinds of measurable objectives for which top management should hold its staff responsible. In addition, training programs, recruitment efforts, and other interventions should be individually evaluated to determine their effectiveness in meeting these goals.

TABLE 11.4 Examples of Interim Organizational Objectives and Strategies for Achieving Them

Objective	Strategy
Reduce the proportion of employees resorting discrimination in the organization, as measured by the climate survey, by 50%	Provide diversity training to all employees Provide supervisors with training in effective communication and feedback Reinforce top management commitment to diversity
Increase the hiring rates of underrepresented groups so that they are equal to those of nonunderrepresented groups	Expand recruitment efforts to increase the number of members of underrepresented groups in the applicant pool Re-examine selection criteria to ensure they are free from bias and reflect only job-related qualification requirements
Increase promotion rates for underrepresented groups in top levels so that they are equal to the promotion rates for nonunderrepresented groups	Establish career development plans for all employees Ensure that members of underrepresented groups are given rotational assignments and other assignments that will increase their visibility and regard in the organization
Eliminate the disparity in performance among groups by improving the performance of lower-rated employees.	Provide training to employees receiving poorer evaluations Provide training to supervisors in effective communication and feedback

In demonstrating commitment to diversity, however, top management must also take steps to ensure that managers and employees understand that models of diversity are based on inclusion, not exclusion; that is, diversity programs do not seek to displace white males, but rather to prepare workers and managers to work in a heterogeneous environment, one in which everyone can compete equally for organizational resources. The desire is to avoid the same backlash against diversity programs that emerged out of the *Bakke* case in the late 1970s.

To frame the concern another way, efforts to diversify public and private sector workforces in the 1970s and 1980s were largely a result of legal pressures, which in turn engendered a good deal of resistance and enmity. Efforts to promote diversity in the workforce today are driven not so much by law as economics, which means that at least some employers will be less resistant. Nonetheless, workers and the general public may continue to resist and oppose diversity measures. As such, government employers in particular are challenged to frame the issue of diversity in a much more positive way so as to create an environment in which diversity is truly valued rather than begrudgingly pursued.

Change Organizational Structures and Work Processes

John Fernandez argues that the very nature of the hierarchical bureaucratic structure that characterizes most organizations today is one that defeats anything or anyone who is outside the established order. Fernandez agrees with many leading management theorists that bureaucratic organizations were effective in providing the efficiency, uniformity, and objectivity needed in this country as we moved through the industrial era. Bureaucracies have become an impediment, however, to the optimal functioning of organizations in today's environment of rapid change, a more demanding public, a more highly educated workforce, and technology that facilitates widespread information sharing, communication, and parallel work processing. The more effective organization in this new environment is likely to be one that is based on innovative thinking, which is best cultivated in a diverse workforce. It is also based on teamwork, which requires mutual respect and understanding. To succeed in this environment an organization must ensure it is tapping the knowledge and potential of its entire workforce. It must further ensure that all segments of the workforce trust each other and believe they are treated fairly by the organization. Employees must see the value of nontraditional employees and nontraditional thinking. In short, the kinds of mistreatment discussed in this chapter will have no place in the organization of tomorrow. If organizations (including those in the public sector) can face the reality that they need to evolve into a postbureaucratic form, they will necessarily take steps to eliminate overt and subtle forms of discrimination.

In particular, a growing number of private and public sector organizations are replacing their hierarchical structures with semiautonomous teams. They do so because teams provide the best means for capturing the diversity of perspectives and skills, and for acquiring the ability to respond flexibly and quickly as the organization is confronted by new challenges. In many cases ethnically diverse teams have been found to be more creative and innovative than homogenous ones. Taylor Cox has suggested that many organizations are shifting to team-based work structure as a means to reduce intergroup conflict. Properly structured teams can eliminate power imbalances systematically related to gender and/or race/ethnicity, which are the source of much intergroup conflict. In addition to providing the benefits of organizational flexibility and innovation, the development of cross-functional teams thus may in fact also serve the purpose of opening up new opportunities and gaining respect for women and people of color.

A massive overhaul of organizational processes and structures may seem like a radical approach to securing an inclusive workplace, and certainly every organization is not ready to undertake such an enterprise. However, as organizations find themselves having to respond to changing economic, fiscal, and political conditions, they should recognize that such a transformation of work systems and processes provides a target of opportunity for eliminating many of the underlying roots of mistreatment and bias. They should also be aware of the fact that failure to address these issues will likely prevent the organization from achieving the maximum benefit of the effort.

In summary, there is a wide array of interventions that an organization can undertake to improve the climate for its multicultural workforce. Experts agree that no single intervention is likely to be effective. Changing the culture that is deeply rooted in most organizations will require top management commitment. It will demand an interest in developing effective communication and feedback mechanisms, a willingness to re-examine personnel policies and practices, a commitment to investing in employee training and development, and the vehemence to develop and maintain accountability measures to track progress.

WHO IS RESPONSIBLE?

The previous section emphasized the measures that organizations can and should take to cultivate an inclusive, multicultural workplace. This does not mean that the responsibility lies solely with organizational management, however. There are issues that must be addressed by society as a whole, and steps that individuals can and should take to increase their own opportunities.

Peoples' attitudes and practices are generally developed long before they enter the workforce. Society as a whole needs to grapple with eliminating the effects of past discrimination and changing the socialization processes that steer women and people of color into a limited range of occupations and perpetuate harmful stereotypes. Society must also ensure that everyone has equal access to a high-quality education. According to *Workforce 2020* , the number of jobs in the least-skilled job classes will shrink over the next two decades, while high-skilled professions will grow rapidly. The report states that ''Upward mobility in the labor force depends, quite simply, on education. The single most important goal of workforce development must be to improve the quality of American public education substantially.'' *Workforce 2020* further points out that the future of people of color is at greater risk than whites because they are more likely to be inadequately educated. Disparities in educational opportunities result in lower graduation rates for people of color compared to whites, and ultimately fewer and poorer job opportunities for them.

Individuals also have a role to play in eliminating prejudice and advancing their own competitiveness. They should make the effort to gain the education and experience required for entry and advancement in professional jobs. They should be aware that stereotypes exist and that they can help to overcome them by taking advantage of opportunities to demonstrate their abilities. Such opportunities may include seeking rotational assignments or volunteering for difficult assignments or high-level task forces. Studies on the effect of sex stereotyping have found, for example, that women's potential is often more subject to exacting examination than their actual accomplishments. Margaret Heilman describes an experiment in which subjects were told that certain paintings were to be entered into a contest. The ones attributed to men were rated more favorably than the ones attributed to women. When the subjects were told the paintings had already won prizes in a contest, however, there was no difference in the evaluation of those attributed to women and those attributed to men. In other words, proving one's competence through developing a track record of successes can go a long way toward dispelling negative stereotypes.

EPILOGUE: "PROVING" DISCRIMINATION

A recent headline in the *San Francisco Chronicle* proclaimed that ''Ethnic Quotas Are Under Siege in San Francisco Schools.'' The article was referring to a challenge to the desegregation system under which the San Francisco Unified School District (SFUSD) now operates. The system, put in place in response to a 1983 lawsuit brought by the NAACP, requires that no ethnic group comprise more than 45% of any school's enrollment, and that at least four ethnic groups be represented at each school. The city receives substantial aid to pay for the desegregation effort, which it now stands to lose as a result of a lawsuit filed by Chinese-American families. The federal judge who will decide the case has warned SFUSD officials that they must justify the need for the system if they are to be permitted to keep it. Consequently, the article notes, the school superintendent is put "in the extraordinary position of stepping up efforts to prove that the district still discriminates."

The moral of this story is that our society is still a long way from recognizing that subtle barriers may continue to stand in the way of equal opportunity, even when overt discrimination has been eradicated. This chapter has discussed some of the barriers that confront women and people of color as they attempt to succeed and advance in organizational environments that were contrived in a time in which white men predominated. Most of these barriers do not rise to the level of discrimination specifically prohibited by the 1964 Civil Rights Act and enforced by the EEOC, yet their effects can be just as pernicious and require intention, attention, and time to overcome. There are many strategies that organizations have successfully employed to quell these barriers and create an inclusive work environment, but organizations that do engage in such efforts must keep in mind that an intense educational effort may be required to avoid challenges by those who don't see their need.

BIBLIOGRAPHY

Bridger, Chet. "Memo Worries White Men," *Federal Times* (September 26, 1994).

Center for Women in Government. "Women Face Barriers in Top Management," *Women in the Public Service* (winter 1991/1992).

City of Richmond v. *Croson*, 488 U.S. 469 (1989).

Civil Service 2000. Indianapolis: Hudson Institute (prepared for the U.S. Office of Personnel Management), June 1988.

Copeland, Lennie. "Learning to Manage a Multicultural Work Force," in Matzer (ed.), *Personnel Practices for the 1990s: A Local Government Guide*. Washington, D.C.: ICMA, 1988, pp. 56–63 (also appears in the May 1988 issue of *Training*).

———. "Valuing Diversity, Part 1: Making the Most of Cultural Differences at the Workplace," *Personnel* (June 1988), pp. 52–60.

———. "Valuing Diversity, Part 2: Pioneers and Champions of Change," *Personnel* (July 1988), pp. 44–49.

Cox, Taylor. *Cultural Diversity in Organizations: Theory, Research and Practice*. San Francisco: Berrett-Koehler, 1993.

Crampton, Suzanne M. and Jitendra M. Mishra. "Family and Medical Leave Legislation: Organizational Policies and Strategies," *Public Personnel Management*, vol. 24 (fall 1995), pp. 271–289.

Dothard v. *Rawlinson*, 433 U.S. 321 (1977).

"Ethnic Quotas Are Under Siege in San Francisco Schools," *San Francisco Chronicle* (December 1998), p. B-1.

Federal Glass Ceiling Commission. *Good for Business: Making Full Use of the Nation's Human Capital, the Environmental Scan*. Washington, D.C.: Federal Glass Ceiling Commission, March 1995.

———. *Good for Business: Making Full Use of the Nation's Human Capital, Recommen-*

dations of the Federal Glass Ceiling Commission. Washington, D.C.: Federal Glass Ceiling Commission, November 1995.

Fernandez, John P. *Race, Gender, and Rhetoric: The True State of Race and Gender Relations in Corporate America*. New York: McGraw-Hill, 1999.

Fullerton, Howard N. Jr. "New Labor Force Projections, Spanning 1988 to 2000," *Outlook 2000*, U.S. Department of Labor, April 1990, pp. 1–11.

Golembiewski, Robert T. *Managing Diversity in Organizations*. Tuscaloosa, Ala.: University of Alabama Press, 1995.

Gossett, Charles W. "Domestic Partnership Benefits," in Jay M. Shafritz (ed.), *International Encyclopedia of Public Policy and Administration*, Boulder, Colo.: Westview Press, pp. 706–707.

———. "Domestic Partnership Benefits: Public Sector Patterns," *Review of Public Personnel Administration*, vol. 14 (1994), pp. 64–84.

Hard Truths/Tough Choices: An Agenda for State and Local Government. National Commission on the State and Local Public Service, 1993.

Heilman, Madeline E. "Sex Bias in Work Settings: The Lack of a Fit Model," in L. L. Cummings and Barry M. Staw (eds.), *Research in Organizational Behavior*, vol. 5. Greenwich, Conn.: JAI Press, pp. 269–298.

Hindera, John J. "Representative Bureaucracy: Further Evidence of Active Representation in the EEOC District Offices," *Journal of Public Administration Research and Theory* (1993), pp. 415–429.

———. "Representative Bureaucracy: Imprimis Evidence of Active Representation in the EEOC District Offices," *Social Science Quarterly* (1993), pp. 95–108.

Hopkins, Anne. "Perceptions of Employment Discrimination in the Public Sector," *Public Administration Review* (March/April 1980), pp. 131–137.

Hopkins, Willie E., Karen Sterkel-Powell, and Shirley A. Hopkins. "Training Priorities for a Diverse Workforce," *Public Personnel Management*, vol. 23 (fall 1994), pp. 429–435.

Hostetler, Dennis and Joan E. Pynes. "Domestic Partnership Benefits: Dispelling the Myth," *Review of Public Personnel Administration*, vol. 15 (winter 1995), pp. 41–59.

Kim, Soonhee. "Toward Understanding Family Leave Policy in Public Organizations: Family Leave Use and Conceptual Framework for the Family Leave Implementation Process," *Public Productivity and Management Review*, (September 1998).

———. "Organizational Culture and New York State Employees' Work–Family Conflict: Gender Differences in Balancing Work and Family Responsibilities," *Review of Public Personnel Administration*.

Kingsley, J. Donald. *Representative bureaucracy: An Interpretation of the British Civil Service*. Yellow Springs, Ohio: Antioch Press, 1944.

Kraiger, Kurt and J. Kevin Ford. "A Meta-analysis of Ratee Race Effects in Performance Ratings," *Journal of Applied Psychology* (February 1975), pp 56–65.

Krislov, Samuel. *The Negro in Federal Employment*. Minneapolis: University of Minnesota Press, 1967.

———. *Representative Bureaucracy*. Englewood Cliffs, N.J.: Prentice-Hall, 1974.

Larson, Ruth. "FAA Men Charge 'Tailhook II,'" *Washington Times* (September 8, 1994).

Larson, Ruth. "FAA to Pay for Trauma of Groping Gauntlets," *Washington Times* (September 23, 1994).

Leonard, Arthur S. "Gay and Lesbian Rights Protections in the U.S." Washington, D.C.: National Gay and Lesbian Task Force, 1989.

Levine, Charles H. "Beyond the Sound and Fury of Targets," *Public Administration Review* (May/June 1974), pp. 240–241.

Loden, Marilyn and Judy B. Rosener. *Workforce America!* Homewood, Ill.: Business One Irwin, 1991.

Lopez, J. A. "Study Says Women Face Glass Walls as Well as Ceilings," *Wall Street Journal* (March 3, 1992), p. B1–2.

Lynch, Frederick R. *The Diversity Machine: The Drive to Change the "White Male Workplace."* New York: Free Press, 1997.

Meeting Public Demands: Federal Services in the Year 2000. Washington, D.C.: U.S. Treasury Department, 1988.

Meier, Kenneth J. "Representative Bureaucracy: An Empirical Analysis," *American Political Science Review* (June 1975).

———. "Teachers, Students, and Discrimination: The Policy Impact of Black Representation," *Journal of Politics* (February 1984), pp. 252–263.

Meier, Kenneth J. and Robert E. England. "Black Representation and Educational Policy: Are They Related?" *American Political Science Review* (June 1984), pp. 392–403.

Meier, Kenneth J. and Joseph Stewart. "The Impact of Representative Bureaucracies: Educational Systems and Public Policies," *American Review of Public Administration* (September 1992), pp. 157–151.

Morrison, Ann M. *The New Leaders: Guidelines on Leadership Diversity in America.* San Francisco: Jossey-Bass, 1992.

Mosher, Frederick C. *Democracy and the Public Service.* New York: Oxford University Press, 1968.

Nachmias, David and David H. Rosenbloom. "Measuring Bureaucratic Representation and Integration," *Public Administration Review* (November/December 1973), pp. 590–596.

Naff, Katherine C. "Through the Glass Ceiling: Prospects for the Advancement of Women in the Federal Government," *Public Administration Review* (November/December 1994), pp. 507–514.

———. "Subjective vs. Objective Discrimination in Government: Adding to the Picture of Barriers to the Advancement of Women," *Political Research Quarterly* (September 1995), pp. 535–557.

———. "Perceptions of Discrimination: Moving Beyond the Numbers of Representative Bureaucracy," *Policy Studies Journal* (Fall 1995), pp. 483–498.

National Organization for Women (NOW). *The Impact of Violence in the Lives of Working Women: Creating Solutions–Creating Change.* Washington, D.C.: National Organization for Women, 1996.

National Partnership for Women and Families. Website: www.nationalpartnership.org.

Nollen, Stanley D. "The Work–Family Dilemma: How HR Managers Can Help," *Personnel* (May 1989), pp. 25–30.

Offermann, Lynn R. and Marilyn K. Gowing. "Organizations of the Future," *American Psychologist*, no. 2. vol. 45 (1990), pp. 134–143.

Opportunity 2000: Creative Affirmative Action Strategies for a Changing Workforce. Indianapolis: Hudson Institute (prepared for the U.S. Department of Labor), September 1988.

Outlook 2000. U.S. Department of Labor, Bureau of Labor Statistics, April 1990.

Pachon, Henry P. "Hispanic Underrepresentation in the Federal Bureaucracy: The Missing Link in the Policy Process," in F. Chris Garcia (ed.), *Latinos and the Political System.* Notre Dame, Ind.: University of Notre Dame Press, 1988, pp. 306–313.

Pettigrew, Thomas F. "Racial Change and Social Policy," *American Academy of Political and Social Science* (January 1979), pp. 114–131.

Price, Joyce. "Cultural Diversity at HUD," *Washington Times (February 11, 1994).*

Reed, Christine M. and Willa M. Bruce. "Dual-Career Couples in the Public Sector," *Public Personnel Management,* vol. 22 (summer 1993), pp. 187–199.

Rehfuss, John A. "A Representative Bureaucracy? Women and Minority Executives in California Career Service," *Public Administration Review* (September/October 1986), pp. 454–460.

Riccucci, Norma M. "Affirmative Action in the Twenty-first Century: New Approaches and Developments," in Carolyn Ban and Norma Riccucci (eds.), *Public Personnel Management: Current Concerns—Future Challenges.* New York: Longman Press, 1991, pp. 89–99.

Riccucci, Norma M. "Merit, Equity and Test Validity: A New Look at an Old Problem," *Administration and Society* (May 1991).

Riccucci, Norma M. and Tamu Chambers. "Models of Excellence in Workplace Diversity," in Carolyn Ban and Norma Riccucci (eds.), *Public Personnel Management: Current Concerns, Future Challenges,* 2nd ed. New York: Longman Press, 1997, pp. 73–90.

Romzek, Barbara S. "Balancing Work and Nonwork Obligations," in Ban and Riccucci (eds.), *Public Personnel Management: Current Concerns—Future Challenges.* New York: Longman Press, 1991, pp. 237–239.

Rubaii-Barrett, Nadia and Ann C. Beck. "Minorities in the Majority: Implications for Managing Cultural Diversity," *Public Personnel Management,* vol. 22 (winter 1993), pp. 503–521.

Shellenbarger, Sue. "Some Firms Manage to Ease Family Duties and Aid Promotions," *Wall Street Journal* (December 13, 1995).

Selden, Sally Coleman. *The Promise of Representative Bureaucracy: Diversity and Responsiveness in a Government Agency.* Armonk, N.Y.: M. E. Sharp, 1997.

Thielemann, Gregory S. and Joseph Stewart. "A Demand-Side Perspective on the Importance of Representative Bureaucracy: AIDS, Ethnicity, Gender, and Sexual Orientation," *Public Administration Review* (March/April 1996), pp. 168–173.

Thompson, Frank J. "Minority Gains in Public Bureaucracies: Are Passive and Active Representation Linked?" *Administration and Society* (August 1976), pp. 201–248.

U.S. General Accounting Office. *Federal Workforce: Continuing Need for Federal Affirmative Employment.* Washington, D.C.: U.S. General Accounting Office. GAO/GGD-92-27BR, November 1991.

———. *The Changing Workforce: Comparison of Federal and Nonfederal Work Family Programs and Approaches.* Washington, D.C.: General Accounting Office, April 1992.

————. *Affirmative Employment: Assessing Progress of EEO Groups in Key Federal Jobs Can Be Improved*. Washington, D.C.: U.S. General Accounting Office, GAO/GGD-93-65, March 1993.

U.S. Department of Labor. *A Report on the Glass Ceiling Initiative*. Washington, D.C.: U.S. Department of Labor, 1991.

U.S. Merit Systems Protection Board. *A Question of Equity: Women and the Glass Ceiling in the Federal Government*. Washington, D.C.: U.S. Merit Systems Protection Board, October 1992.

————. *Evolving Workforce Demographics: Federal Agency Action and Reaction*. Washington, D.C.: U.S. Merit Systems Protection Board, November 1993.

————. *Fair and Equitable Treatment: A Progress Report on Minority Employment in the Federal Government*. Washington, D.C.: U.S. Merit Systems Protection Board, August 1996.

————. *Achieving a Representative Federal Workforce: Addressing the Barriers to Hispanic Participation*. Washington, D.C.: U.S. Merit Systems Protection Board, September 1997.

U.S. Office of Personnel Management. *Minority/Non-Minority Disparate Discharge Rates*. Washington, D.C.: U.S. Office of Personnel Management, April 1995.

————. *Annual Report to Congress: Federal Equal Opportunity Recruitment Program, October 1, 1996–September 30, 1997*. Washington, D.C.: U.S. Office of Personnel Management, 1997.

Wick and Company. "Don't Blame the Baby: Why Women Leave Corporations." Wilmington, Del.: Wick and Company, 1990.

Workforce 2020. Indianapolis: Hudson Institute, 1997.

Workforce 2000. Indianapolis: Hudson Institute, 1987.

12

Labor–Management Relations

PROLOGUE: THE BRAVE NEW WORLD OF LABOR–MANAGEMENT PARTNERSHIPS

As part of its reinvention efforts under the National Performance Review (NPR), President Clinton signed Executive Order 12871 on October 1, 1993, creating the National Partnership Council (NPC). The purpose of the NPC and partnerships in general is to improve overall relations between labor and management for the ultimate benefit of the taxpayers. The notion behind partnerships is that public employees and their unions work in the trenches, and so they know firsthand what is needed to get the job done effectively and efficiently. Any restructuring or reinventing of government thus cannot be management-driven but must necessarily involve workers and their unions. In announcing the national partnership concept, Vice President Al Gore proclaimed that ''We can only transform government if we transform the adversarial relationship that dominates federal union–management interaction into partnership for reinvention and change.''

The NPC comprises management representatives, a representative of the Public Employees' Department of the AFL-CIO, and the presidents of three major federal employee unions—the American Federation of Government Employees (AGFE), the National Treasury Employees Union (NTEU), and the National Federation of Federal Employees (NFEE). Its mandate was to ''propose the statutory changes needed to make the labor–management partnership a reality.'' A new era of labor relations was thus promised by the Clinton administration, with the NPC presumably having input in several of Clinton and Gore's plans to reinvent government, including reforming procurement procedures, reducing rigid personnel policies, and even cutting federal jobs. The number of partnership arrangements expanded quickly following the promulgation of the executive order. (See Figure 12.1.) By mid-1997, the Office of Personnel Management estimated that partnership agreements had extended to 35% of the bargaining units in the federal government and 70% of bargaining-unit employees.

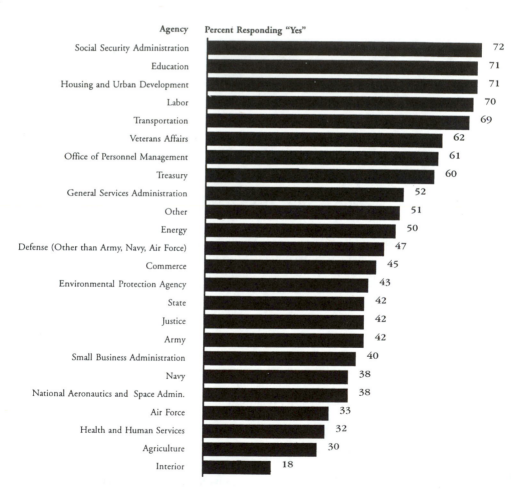

FIGURE 12.1 "Have management and the local federal employee unions established partnerships in your agency?"

One might well ask how this remarkable change of events came about after the very difficult decade of the 1980s, which began with President Reagan's breaking the air traffic controllers strike, and still harbored a climate of distrust, if not outright antagonism.

"AN UNAUTHORIZED HISTORY" OF THE ORIGINS OF FEDERAL LABOR–MANAGEMENT PARTNERSHIP

Back in the presidential campaign year of the 1992, then-candidate Clinton pledged that he would improve the operations of the federal government and as a result decrease the size of government by 100,000 positions. That rather minimal pledge may not have attracted much attention among voters or the media, but it was seriously regarded by the federal unions, which vigorously campaigned for the Democratic Party in 1992. When president-elect Clinton set up his transition teams very late in November of 1992, one of the documents circulated to all the transition teams was a list of campaign promises made by both Clinton and Gore. Transition teams were informed that their proposals and plans for the incoming cabinet appointees and their management teams should ensure that these campaign promises were kept. Indeed, in December 1992 the transition team preparing the agenda for the Office of Personnel Management (OPM) and civil service policy concluded that the 100,000 job cuts could easily be obtained through attrition rates and the remainder of the "peace dividend" that would reduce civil service levels in the Defense Department.

By March of 1993, however, the president's agenda had broadened. In launching the NPR and conducting an exhaustive six-month study of all the major cabinet agencies and governmental functions, the promised 100,000-position cut soon reached a promise of 12% over five years—what would amount to over 250,000 federal positions. The federal unions were deeply involved in the initial discussions about the size of the workforce reduction and their involvement in the reinvention efforts. Indeed, there are sources that indicate that the first draft of the executive order establishing the partnership came from one of the unions. The unions were prepared to back the downsizing of the federal workforce in exchange for two key promises—a policy objective on workforce restructuring that would increase the span of control from one to six or eight employees per supervisor to double that (one to 15), and the creation of the partnership concept, which would be a major expansion of the scope of bargaining.

When the official history of the NPR decade is written it will doubtlessly include a number of other factors that created the force for partnership. The early appointment of Robert Reich, who was a tireless advocate of labor–management cooperation, as the secretary of labor and the lengthy delay in picking the new director of OPM, which might have served as a counterviewpoint, created a powerful imbalance in favor of expanding bargaining for the unions. The timing was certainly right for change since the unions were tired of using the various legal devices (unfair labor practice charges, grievances, etc.) to stymie management actions. From 1987 to 1992, the number of unfair labor practice charges had increased nearly 50%, from about 5750 to 8750. From 1992 to 1995 after the partnership was launched, they would drop back to 6750. (See Figure 12.2.)

A "deal" was thus struck, and this "unofficial history" can turn to a rather intriguing source to show the final outlines of what would emerge from the NPR and why. The following excerpt, from a Federal Labor Relations Authority decision in a 1997 case between the Patent & Trademark Office and the Patent Office Professional Association, includes the following statement in member Donald S. Wasserman's dissent:

> The executive order embodied an attempt by the Administration to foster a major change in the way labor–management relations functioned within the federal government. Numerous contextual matters shed light on the meaning of the words of the order, and more specifically, explain the intention of the President's Order regarding expanded bargaining. The dialogue between the unions and the Administration is instructive as to the extent of the change contemplated by the Executive Order, as are the various interpretations of the Office of Personnel Management and agency officials. To ignore the context of the executive order while

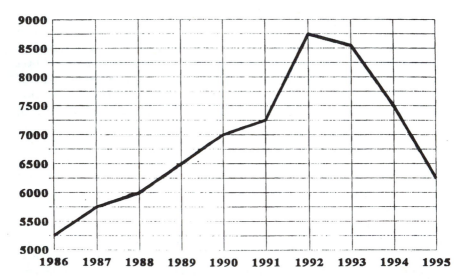

FIGURE 12.2   Unfair labor practice charges filed, FY 1986–FY 1995 (*Source*: Federal Labor Relations Authority).

looking only at its "precise words" is similar to looking only at the eye of the hurricane—the narrow focus leads to a misunderstanding of the calm existing within the surrounding swirl of activity. . . .

In determining whether the Order represents an election to bargain, I begin by looking at its opening terms, which are as follows: "The involvement of the Federal Government employees and their union representatives is essential to achieving the National Performance Review's Government reform objectives. Only by changing the nature of federal labor–management relations so that managers, employees, and employees' elected union representatives serve as partners will it be possible to design and implement comprehensive changes necessary to reform government" (Executive Order 12871 at 1).

The President thereafter involved his authority under the United States Constitution "to establish a new form of labor–management relations throughout the executive branch to promote the principles and recommendations adopted as a result of the National Performance Review [.]" Id. Thus the President's order regarding the scope of bargaining must be viewed in the context of his seeking to implement the goals of the National Performance Review (hereafter the NPR). Those goals include, inter alia, a 12% reduction in civilian personnel over five years. It is commonly understood that the federal unions struck an agreement with the administration to receive expanded bargaining rights in exchange for their cooperation in the National Performance Review. I take official notice of the various articles in the public domain: On September 29, 1993, three days prior to the execution of the Executive Order, the *Washington Post* reported that: "Federal agencies for the first time would be required to bargain with unions over items such as the number of workers assigned to tasks, their grade and pay levels and tours of duty under an executive order that the president is likely to issue this week. . . . Insiders believe [that] unions got most of what they wanted in return for soft-pedaling opposition to President Clinton's decision to eliminate 252,000 jobs or cancel January's 2.2 percent national pay raise."

On October 2, 1993, the day after the executive order was signed, the Austin American-Statesman reported that President Clinton sought legislation the previous day "to speed his cutback of the federal workforce by offering buyouts . . . and that the leaders of the three largest federal unions praised Clinton for 'broadening the scope of collective bargaining.'"

The federal unions "wanted a place at the negotiating table when agencies started reorganizing themselves" (*Government Executive*, March 1994). Vice President Gore wanted to "avoid the embarrassment'' of union opposition to his National Performance Review goals and the cost of union support was expanded bargaining and partnership.

We simply cannot ignore the quid pro quo aspect of the Executive Order and the obvious intent of the President in issuing the Order. He framed the entire document within the context of achieving cooperation in accomplishing his NPR goals and the tradeoff for acquiring union cooperation was his election to bargain over the permissive subjects listed in section 7106(b). [54 FLRA No 43, FLRA, U.S. Department of Commerce, Patent and Trademark (Respondent) Patent Office Professional Association (Charging Party/Union) June 19, 1998, pp. 33–35.]

THE DEVELOPMENT OF COLLECTIVE BARGAINING IN THE PUBLIC SECTOR

Collective bargaining is a fundamental feature of contemporary public personnel management. In many jurisdictions, such core aspects of personnel administration as position classification, pay, overtime, promotion procedures, and discipline are subject to labor–management negotiations. Collectively bargained agreements routinely limit managerial authority and flexibility. They deal with matters that were once considered part of a science or of management, such as position design. In some public organizations, there are very few working conditions that can be unilaterally changed by the employer.

This has not always been the case, however. Historically there was great opposition to collective bargaining in the public sector. It was considered antithetical to constitutional principles guaranteeing that public policy will be made by the voters or their representatives, and not by union leaders and their members. It was feared that unions would hold the public interest and welfare hostage in their demands for better treatment. Job actions, such as slowdowns, and strikes would cause chaos and anarchy—which sometimes did occur. (See the box on the Boston police strike of 1919 and the box on the postal strike of 1970.) This opposition was eventually overwhelmed by public employees' pressure for labor rights similar to those of private workers and politicians' quests for labor votes and peace in the workplace. The United States is still searching for an appropriate labor relations model for the public sector, however. The Clinton–Gore partnership initiative discussed in the prologue is based on the premise that ''old-style'' federal collective bargaining impedes productive, responsive, results-oriented public management.

The reasons why the United States has never developed a fully satisfactory public sector labor relations model are easily understood. In the 1960s and 1970s, when labor's demands for collective bargaining could no longer be pushed aside, the natural tendency was to fall back on private sector practices rather than to

The Boston Police Strike

On the afternoon of September 9, 1919, most of Boston's patrol officers turned in their badges and went on strike. Although there were many grievances, the major issue immediately involved was the right of the police to form a union and to affiliate with the American Federation of Labor (AFL). Should the police be allowed to form a union, engage in collective bargaining, strike? Would such activity be in the public interest? Would it pose a threat to the public order and democracy? Although the ensuing three-day strike did little to answer these questions, it shocked the nation's conscience and transformed a laconic, almost invisible state governor into a national hero.

The drive for unionization and collective bargaining had been spurred by the reprehensible conditions under which the patrol officers had to work. Their starting salary was $1,000, of which some $200 went for equipment and uniforms. Annual increases were $100, to a maximum salary of $1,600. In May 1919 the city had authorized the first pay raise in six years, $200 for all patrol officers. This increase was far outweighed by the skyrocketing cost of living, which had gone up 86% during the period. The patrol officers averaged an 87-hour work week and had to put up with outrageous working conditions. The patrol officers' wives constantly complained of the cockroaches which accompanied their husbands home and shared their clothing. Vermin-eaten helmets were also a source of displeasure. Although there was a civil service system, the police commissioner, a gubernatorial appointee, was not required to promote on the basis of promotion lists. Thus, a patrol officer could rank at the top of the eligible list and remain there, despite openings, until retirement. Personal acceptability to the commissioner was the key to success.

Once the strike began, politics came to the fore. Boston's mayor, a "good-government" Democrat, sought to work out a compromise despite his opposition to the union. The police commissioner, a gubernatorial appointee, was adamant in his desire to break the union. The Republican governor of Massachusetts, Calvin Coolidge, preferring inaction, did little until the strike's final day. The evidence suggests that all three sought some political advantage from the situation, and one, of course, won the whole show.

Despite the efforts of some police officers and volunteers to maintain order, Boston reverted to a Hobbesian state of nature. Criminals of all persuasions flocked to the city and joined Boston's home-grown hoodlums in sacking it. Van after van was filled with stolen bounty. When lawlessness and mob rule gained the upper hand, the mayor exercised authority, on the basis of two old state statutes, to wrest control of the police from the commissioner and to call upon men from the State Guard. He further requested not less than "three regiments of infantry fully equipped for field service" from the governor. Coolidge responded by sending the entire State Guard and by putting himself in control of these troops as well as the police department. By September 11, some 7,000 guards were patrolling Boston's streets, the strikers were summarily discharged, and order was more or less restored.

It was at this moment that Coolidge, whose luck was legendary, received the political break of his life. Samual Gompers, head of the AFL, unwittingly provided the opening that ultimately made Coolidge the thirtieth president of the United States. Gompers protested the police commissioner's refusal to allow the union to affiliate. As the nation watched, Coolidge responded with his famous assertion that "there is no right to strike against the public safety by anybody, anywhere, anytime." With those words, Coolidge, an unimpressive cold, and "sourish" man, captured the public's imagination. Amid civic disintegration and chaos appeared a commonsensical Yankee who knew what was right and what was wrong and was willing to take a forceful stand against elements that seemed threatening to the nation. The tidal wave of support for Coolidge among the press and public swept him into the vice-presidential slot on the 1920 Republican ticket. When Harding died in 1923, he became president.

The Boston police strike in 1919 was the nation's first genuine taste of a municipal labor problem. Although many years elapsed between the strike and the emergence of the present period of permanent crisis in public sector labor relations, the basic problems involved are essentially the same and remain without substantial resolution. In the past two and a half decades, governments have sought to come to grips with the public sector labor relations problem by creating a legal basis for collectively bargaining with public employees.

create something brand new. The problem is that the private sector model does not fit the public sector well, so it has to be adjusted. The adjustments in turn made public sector practices less coherent and systematic than those in the private sector. Expansive management rights clauses leave little to bargain over. Prohibitions on the right to strike made closure difficult and upset the fundamental principle of "bilateralism"; that is, contracts should be negotiated by management and unions, not determined by third parties such as arbitrators. As a result, public sector collective bargaining is still subject to a number of dysfunctions and frustrations, as the Clinton–Gore effort to find a new way suggests. Because it is very difficult to understand public sector labor relations systematically without appreciating how they evolved, the next section is devoted to this topic.

The Postal Strike

On March 17, 1970, members of the Manhattan–Bronx Branch 36 of the National Association of Letter Carriers (NALC) voted to strike the U.S. Postal Service. For the first time in the agency's 195-year history, it was neither "rain, sleet, nor gloom of night," but rather picket lines that stopped the U.S. mail.

At issue was the low wage scale for postal carriers. Starting pay was $6,100 per annum, "rising" to $8,442 over a 21-year period. In New York City alone, this left 7% of the carriers on welfare of one sort or another. The local union was seeking a new scale that would range from $8,500 to $11,700 and would provide cost-of-living increases. The union also wanted the maximum to be attainable after five years instead of 21 and sought a 20-year half-pay retirement option among other fringe benefits.

But the strike was not called simply for economic reasons; politics was involved as well. Specifically, a kind of three-cornered game of "chicken" had been developing, and the strike was used to break a deadlock. The Nixon administration, unhappy with the operating effectiveness and "organizational philosophy" of the post office, had sought to transform it from an ordinary department into a government corporation. Nixon made future pay raises dependent upon congressional and postal union support of his plan. A week prior to the outbreak of the strike, the House Post Office Committee, which is ordinarily heavily influenced by organized postal workers, approved a bill providing for a 5.4% pay increase for lower-grade employees. However, it failed to include the cost-of-living increases that were demanded by the postal unions. Feeling that no other recourse was available, the Manhattan–Bronx branch of the NALC opted to flex its muscle.

The strike was scheduled for 12:01 A.M. of March 18. By 1:00 A.M. police reported that picket lines had sprung up outside Manhattan's central postal facility. As the day progressed, the head of the Manhatten–Bronx Postal Union said he expected the 25,000 clerks, mail handlers, and other employees he represented to honor the picket lines. Then the strike spread across the East River to Brooklyn and Queens. Once the post office was shut down in New York, it was inevitable that tons of mail would begin to pile up not only there but in other post offices across the country.

Of course, there are laws against this sort of thing. Indeed, federal statutes provide for criminal sanctions against striking federal employees. However, despite these and court injunctions prohibiting the strike, the workers did not return to their jobs. Herman Sandbank, executive vice president of the NALC, in the style of many union leaders, told the government where to put its injunctions and what to do with its laws: "The men will defy any injunction. They'll stay out until hell freezes over."

Next, the strike spread across the Hudson River to New Jersey and northward to Connecticut. Eventually it went westward and southward, and soon postal facilities in many major cities throughout the nation were paralyzed. Union leaders seemed to lose control of the situation, and the strike took on a wildcat flavor. Ultimately, some 200,000 postal workers joined in.

Within a week, Nixon declared a national emergency and sent 27,500 National Guards to sort and deliver mail in New York City. However, to sweeten this coercive pill, the government for the first time in history agreed to allow wages, which hitherto had always been set through the legislative process, to be negotiated between union and government representatives. That ended the strike. Subsequently, the Postal Reorganization Act was passed, establishing the corporate framework sought by Nixon and providing for collective bargaining with postal employees in the future.

MODIFICATIONS FOR THE PUBLIC SECTOR

For most of the period during which the private sector model was evolving, there was nearly universal agreement that collective bargaining was inappropriate for the public sector. For the most part, until the 1960s and 1970s governments and their component units simply refused to engage in collective bargaining with their employees. Those that did recognize unions or employee associations sometimes sought to engage in a ''meet and confer'' approach, which allows employees to voice requests but does not provide a format for actual collective bargaining, yet labor's drive for full collective bargaining rights in the public sector rendered the earlier approaches politically and organizationally untenable. Public employees were a rapidly growing segment of the economy. They had the constitutional right to organize; once they did so, they wanted to assert their power through collective bargaining—and they were able to lobby and employ concerted action, such as picketing and strikes, in order to achieve this objective. The traditional opposition to public sector collective bargaining was overwhelmed by events. Nevertheless, doubts about the appropriateness of collective bargaining in the public sector were expressed in a number of ways that violated the premises of the private sector model.

1. Public sector collective bargaining regulations do not treat the parties as coequal. The government—that is, one of the parties—*establishes the process*, the rights of the other party, and the scope of bargaining (i.e., what can and cannot be legally bargained over). Management rights—that is, the government's own rights—are often put forth in expansive terms. The designation of matters that are ''fit for negotia-

The Decline in Private Sector Unionism

More and more private sector unions are targeting public employees for unionization. This is due in large part to the decline in private sector union membership. Here are some of the factors contributing to this decline:

- Changing values of American workers—Young workers are not knowledgeable about the history of unionism, in particular the oppression of workers, which led to unionization. Young workers are also more interested in upward mobility, aspiring to be part of "management," than solidarity and collective action for the good of all workers.
- Economic conditions—The U.S. has experienced declining business activities and relatively little economic growth in the past several years.
- Foreign competition—The importation of foreign goods and services has led to the loss of jobs for Americans and a decline in union membership.
- Wage/benefit spillover—Economic spillovers from union to nonunion establishments keep the interests of nonunion workers satisfied.
- Union avoidance/busting—Various strategies and tactics (e.g., locating a business in nonunion geographic regions) employed by management to keep unions out.
- Promanagement inclination in government—The current and immediate past federal administrations have been hostile to labor interests.
- Effectiveness of strikes declining—The use of the strike has been weakened by several factors, including (1) economics; that is, where workers cannot afford to be on strike, thereby making them more willing to cross picket lines; (2) public apathy, which in turn permits (3) tougher business attitudes toward striking workers; that is, the "social norm" pressuring organizations not to hire "scabs" or replace striking workers is virtually gone—now, organizations will permanently replace striking workers, and this is perfectly legal; and, (4) automation, which makes strikers replaceable.

tion'' and the definition of what can be submitted to arbitration, if anything, are often exceedingly narrow. For instance, for most of the federal government service, items on which bargaining is prohibited include wages, hours, agencies' missions, budgets, organization; their right to hire, assign, direct, lay off, retain, suspend, remove, demote, or discipline employees; agencies' right to assign work, contract out, and fill positions; and their right to take action in emergencies. Although it is an old-fashioned term, in essence the relatively narrow scope of bargaining found in many public sector jurisdictions is an outgrowth of the concept of governmental ''sovereignty.'' Sovereignty in turn is a reflection of the fundamental legal inequality of the parties. (The concept of sovereignty will be further addressed later in this chapter.) The government is hardly a neutral third party to its own negotiating process.

2. The market is a more remote constraint on public sector collective bargaining. Government revenues are raised primarily through taxation and the provision of monopoly services for user fees. The demand for their services may not fluctuate much. A government whose taxes are too high and services too sparse or poorly performed may become uncompetitive with neighboring jurisdictions. Some of its residents and potential new residents may move to these jurisdictions. Nevertheless, unlike the private sector firm, the uncompetitive government is not likely to disappear. Some of its services may be stopped and others may be curtailed, but its essential functions are likely to be maintained on at least a minimal level. Nor can the ''uncompetitive'' government move to another region or country in search of lower labor costs. Labor's demands for compensation are consequently muted most when a government is on the verge of bankruptcy—but this is a very high price to pay for effective labor relations. Governments may respond to this situation through residency requirements that impede labor mobility and tie the welfare of public employees to the jurisdictions for which they work.

3. Economic issues are not truly distributive, at least among the parties to the collective bargaining negotiations. If rank-and-file workers are paid more, it does not mean that public managers and political officials will necessarily be paid relatively less. Indeed, they may be paid *more* in order to maintain the status imputed by traditional pay ratios. Since those signing labor agreements on behalf of the public employer are dealing with ''other people's money'' (the taxpayers'), the economic relationship of the parties to the bargaining does not have the same direct adversary quality as is typically found in the private sector.

4. The nature of government services and the sources of its revenues are such that society finds it desirable to prohibit strikes and lockouts as

Do Unions Make a Difference?

Illustrated below is a comparison of the weekly median earnings for 1997 of government workers who are unionized and nonunionized.

Category or government worker	Union	Nonunion
Federal	$689	$678
State	$628	$540
Local	$697	$479
Total	$681	$530

Source: U.S. Department of Labor, Bureau of Labor Statistics. *Employment and Earnings*, January 1998; Website: ⟨http://stats.bls.gov/cpsaatab.htm#weekearn⟩.

a means of resolving impasses. The majority of states prohibit strikes altogether; several allow the strike, but only under certain conditions, and generally not when a governmental body determines that it threatens the public health, safety, or welfare. The strike, of course, is an integral and essential aspect of the private sector model. Its absence makes it difficult for public employees to levy severe sanctions on management. Consequently, public managers may fail to take labor's demands seriously and unionized public employees may work for extended periods without a current contract—a situation that is unusual in the private sector.

ADJUSTING THE MODEL

The modification of the fundamental assumptions of the private sector model upon its transfer to the public sector promotes certain changes. Many of these, including procedures for unit determination, recognition, certification, contract and election bars, the union shop, and administrative oversight of the collective bargaining process are important (and will be discussed at a later point), but they are not critical to the operation of the collective bargaining model. Three, however, have a very fundamental impact on how public sector collective bargaining operates differently from private sector practices. One is the fragmented character of the public employer. It is often characterized by a separation of powers that requires labor to present its demands to different units of government. Compensation may require legislative approval; the judiciary is involved in the definition of public employees' rights and obligations and in the determination of which issues are arbitral; the executive is responsible for day-to-day personnel matters, including job design, position classification, assignment, promotion, and adverse actions. Even where bargaining is with a unified employer, such as a special district or school board, the public—as taxpayers, as consumers of a service, and as the electorate—is often deeply involved. Although it may be extending the concept of the fragmented or "multilateral" employer too far, the electorate is clearly perceived by elective political authorities as a direct participant in government. Private firms also pay attention to their customers, of course, but their executives cannot be appointed or recalled by them.

Second, the absence of the right to strike or its highly regulated character requires that the public sector develop substitute procedures for resolving intractable disagreements (i.e., "impasses"). To date, a host of mechanisms has been tried, including mediation; fact-finding with or without recommendation; interest arbitration, be it voluntary, compulsory, binding, or nonbinding; final offer of the whole package or issue-by-issue varieties or with the option of making the award on the basis of the fact finder's report; mediation or arbitration; and super-conciliation. Several of these approaches have no parallel in the private sector.

Third, the relatively limited scope of bargaining found in the federal government and in some state and local jurisdictions forces unionized employees to seek elsewhere what cannot be discussed at the negotiating table, hence public sector unions often concentrate a good deal of their efforts on lobbying and electoral politics. Unions representing private employees also engage in these political activities. In many municipalities, however, public sector unions are such a major force that it becomes difficult to disentangle collective bargaining from political action.

A LOSS OF COHERENCE

These deviations seriously violate the systematic and coherent quality of the private sector model. The fragmented character of the employer and the limited scope of bargaining require that a great deal of labor relations takes place both away from the collective bargaining table and outside the realm of grievance procedures. Unions necessarily have to seek their demands in forums in which the collective bargaining model is irrelevant. Lobbying is appropriate for the legislative forum. Electioneering and contributing to campaigns is useful where elective officials hold the key to what labor wants. The judiciary is the forum for asserting legal and constitutional rights. The latter go well beyond noneconomic matters, as the adjudication of "comparable worth" at the initiation of organized public sector labor illustrates. The multilateral character of public employers also makes coordination of labor relations difficult for governments and detracts from the development of a comprehensive, well-thought-out response to labor's demands. It further complicates the problem of developing proactive approaches to effective labor–management relations.

The impasse procedures used in the public sector have some virtues, but they are characterized by two serious flaws. First, they are not a true substitute for the exercise of economic power that is associated with the strike in the private sector. This is precisely why the private sector has almost no equivalent to the reliance placed on the arbitration of economic matters in the public sector. Even where standards for arbitration include "acceptability" or "ability to pay," such impasse resolution procedures fall far short of approximating the use of economic force. (Indeed, the core problem is that even the *strike* in the public sector may not do this, as it may leave governments better off financially by virtue of taxes collected but not expended on the wages of strikers or the provision of struck services.) Second, many have observed that these impasse procedures tend to suppress the vigor of negotiations by creating "ritual," "chilling," and "narcotic" effects, which will be discussed in the next chapter. In the private sector, however, vigorous bilateral negotiations are considered the heart of the process, and seriously reducing their vitality is viewed as a violation of the collective bargaining model itself.

As a result of these differences, the public sector model is less systematic and coherent than the private. It is open-ended in terms of participants, much activity takes place away from the bargaining table, and it does not have a mechanism, such as a strike or lockout, to force the parties to take each other's position seriously and to bring the contest to a logical closure.

DYSFUNCTION

In the past there has been a tendency to argue that the failures of public sector collective bargaining were due to its relative immaturity. Among its common dysfunctional aspects have been illegal strikes, unfair refusal to grant unions recognition, incomprehensible parity agreements, governmental inability to pay for agreements, employees working for extended periods without a current contract, arbitrators' awards that are set aside through litigation, and a wide range of unfair practices on both sides. Nowadays, however, some practitioners and students of public sector labor relations are questioning whether or not there are serious problems with the public sector collective bargaining model itself. Primary among these are the narrow scope of bargaining and the fragmented character of the public employer, which have the following consequences:

1. They encourage employees to organize, but leave their expectations frustrated because there is not enough to talk about at the bargaining table. Unions therefore turn to *lobbying* and to *prohibited* concerted

activity, such as strikes, in an effort to compel government to respond to their demands. Alternatively, unions are seeking to place more and more in labor–management committees, which address in a cooperative fashion issues of mutual concern to labor and management. (Issues such as wages, however, are never addressed by labor–management committees.)

2. Impasse resolution not only suffers from the effects noted previously, it also ''judicializes'' the collective bargaining process and takes decision making out of the hands of the parties. This frequently gives private individuals de facto authority over aspects of governmental budgets and matters of public policy. As such, important qualities of representative government can be compromised, which is precisely why some governments prefer to have a narrow scope of bargaining and to avoid binding arbitration of economic matters.

3. The collective bargaining model turns labor into the adversary of both management and the taxpaying or service fee-paying public. Public employees, once commonly called ''public servants'' and once thought to exercise a ''public trust,'' are still charged with carrying out the public interest. So are public managers. Neither is paid out of profits; neither should claim to have a monopoly on defining the public interest. So where is the conflict between them? Perhaps it is over the authority imputed by hierarchical relationships, but then the problem is likely to be more inherent in the character of traditional public management than in the absence of effective means for collective bargaining. Today all leading efforts to modernize public management call for employee empowerment. Any institutionalized process that routinely forces public employees to present themselves as adversaries of the community for which they work is inherently polarizing and often an obstacle to achieving the benefits of ''community.''

One could probably point to other dysfunctions that arise from the kind of public sector collective bargaining model that has emerged. At this point, however, the more appropriate question may be whether or not we can develop another approach, such as partnerships. For more than forty years change has been a constant feature of public sector labor relations.

EARLY HISTORY

Perhaps the first major labor dispute affecting the operations of the federal government occurred in 1839, when workers in a Philadelphia naval shipyard went out on strike. It was not until the end of the nineteenth century, however, that any significant group of federal employees tried to organize for collective bargaining.

As has often been true in federal labor relations, postal employees were at the forefront of change. In the late 1880s they began to organize in affiliation with the Knights of Labor. Their first national organization, the National Association of Letter Carriers—which still operates—was established in 1890. The National Federation of Postal Clerks followed shortly thereafter and received its charter from the American Federation of Labor (AFL) in 1906.

These moves were met with hostility from the executive branch. It issued a gag order intended to prevent the postal unions from petitioning Congress for wage increases and better working conditions. The unions responded by calling for statutory protection of their right to organize and to lobby Congress. It came in the form of the Lloyd–LaFollette Act of 1912, which guaranteed federal employees the right to join unions that did authorize the use of strikes. It also granted the right to petition Congress either individually or through an organization. The act remained the only general statutory basis for the organization of federal employees until enactment of the Civil Service Reform Act of 1978. (See Table 12.1 for a summary of the major federal laws and executive orders for labor relations.)

The rights conveyed by the Lloyd–LaFollette Act notwithstanding, the next half century witnessed very little collective bargaining in the federal service. The Government Printing Office, the Tennessee Valley Authority (TVA), and the Department of the Interior were the main exceptions. For the most part, the reasons why collective bargaining was considered inappropriate for the federal government were plain enough.

1. Political executives and career managers were unwilling to share their authority with organized employees. The concept of sovereignty demanded that working conditions be dictated by the government, not negotiated. Public sector bargaining agreements will have budgetary ramifications, but political appointees or career employees are not authorized to obligate federal funds. The taxpayers, who will ultimately foot the bill, cannot sit at the bargaining table.

2. Collective bargaining was viewed as inappropriate for government services. Such services are often essential or directly related to the protection of the public's health or safety. Government is responsible for formulating and implementing public policies aimed at improving the nation's defense, economy, and social welfare. It does not typically sell goods and services in an effort to make a profit. Because government often has a monopoly on what it does, labor shutdowns or slowdowns would leave the public with nowhere to turn for the programs and benefits it provides and they need.

3. The federal workforce comprises a huge number of occupations. Since occupation was traditionally the basis for organizing bargaining units,

TABLE 12.1   Major Labor Relations Policies Covering Federal Workers

Law policy	Major provisions	Employees covered
Lloyd-LaFollette Act (1912)	Gave federal employees the right to join unions that did not authorize strikes; guaranteed federal employees the right to petition Congress for redress of their grievances.	Technically postal workers, but interpreted to cover all federal workers.
Taft–Hartley Act (1947)	Section 305 prohibits federal employees from striking.	Federal, including postal.
Executive Order 10988 (1962)	Gave federal employees the right to form and join unions and to engage in collective bargaining over noneconomic issues. Wages and fringe benefits would continue to be determined by Congress. Allowed for use of advisory arbitration over grievances.	Federal employees except for those in the FBI and CIA, and certain managerial and supervisory employees.
Executive Order 11491 (1969)[a]	Expanded scope of bargaining, provided for secret ballot elections, restricted certain internal affairs (e.g., financial) of unions, created the Federal Labor Relations Commission to administer 11491, created the Federal Mediation and Conciliation Service (FMCS) and Federal Service Impasses Panel (FSIP) to settle labor disputes and resolve impasses.	Same as those covered under executive order 10988.

TABLE 12.1   Continued

Law policy	Major provisions	Employees covered
Postal Reorganization Act (1970)	Incorporates most of the provisions of the National Labor Relations Act (NLRA) of 1935, which covers private sector employees, but striking is prohibited, as is any form of union security other than voluntary checkoff of union dues. Empowers the National Labor Relations Board (NLRB), which oversees the NLRA, to oversee labor relations in the postal service.	Postal workers.
Civil Service Reform Act, Title VII (1978)	Labor rights of covered federal workers now guaranteed by federal law. Solidified provisions incorporated in previous executive orders. FLRC replaced by the Federal Labor Relations Authority (FLRA), the FSIP now a separate entity within the FLRA. Scope of bargaining clarified. Provides for binding arbitration over grievances.	All federal workers except for supervisory personnel, members of the armed services, and employees in the postal service, foreign service, FBI, CIA, GAO, NSA, and TVA.
Executive Order 12871 (1993; National Performance Review)	Creation of National Partnership Council (NPC), comprising union and management officials to oversee the cooperative partnership between labor and government for the purpose of improving the state of labor relations in the federal government.	Nonpostal federal employees covered by a bargaining unit.

[a] Executive Orders 11616 (1971) and 11838 (1975) further modified and strengthened the labor relations program in the federal government.

What Is the Postal Alliance?

In 1913, the National Alliance of Postal Employees was formed, because of the Railway Mail Association's policy of barring African-American clerks. The Postal Alliance was composed mainly of African-American railway mail clerks, but other postal employees were also welcomed. In fact, a faction of the National Association of Letter Carriers (NALC) sought for years to require African-American letter carriers to join the Postal Alliance in order to rid the NALC of African-American carriers. A resolution at the NALC's 1927 convention stated the following:

> Whereas the conditions in the south, as well as the entire Association of the United States, in respect to the colored members of the National Association of Letter Carriers, in that in many of the Branches the colored members have come to majority, and, therefore, places them in authority, causing a disruption in the ranks of the membership. . . .
>
> Whereas their strength in voting has proved without question in these Branches that white letter carriers have been compelled to either withdraw their membership or take the embarrassment of being defeated to positions of local officers and representation in our National Conventions, and
>
> Whereas the higher-minded and considerate colored carriers have recognized these conditions, and desiring to avoid any future trouble have instituted an organization for the colored civil service employees, which is known as the Postal Alliance, its purposes are for the protection of the colored employees and improvement of the service; therefore be it
>
> Resolved, That this convention goes on record as endorsing this organization, and appeals to all colored carriers to avail themselves in its membership in order that peace may be preserved in the service. (*The Postal Record*, 1927, p. 408).

The postal alliance still exists today as the National Alliance of Postal and Federal Employees. The alliance no longer has collective bargaining rights with the postal service, but it does with other federal agencies.

Source: Adapted from Riccucci, Norma M. *Women, Minorities and Unions in the Public Sector*. Westport, Conn.: Greenwood Press, 1990.

allowing collective bargaining in federal agencies would require negotiating with hundreds or thousands of groups of unionized employees. Such labor relations would be very expensive and time-consuming.

4. Only about 10% of all federal employees are in the Washington, D.C., area. The rest are dispersed throughout the country and the world. Allowing bargaining to include "local issues," as it does in the private sector, would undercut standardized personnel practices and perhaps put the scientifically developed personnel system in disarray.

5. Collective bargaining was unnecessary to protect employees' rights because the merit system guaranteed fair treatment, and the Lloyd–LaFollette Act allowed them to lobby Congress for what they wanted. These arguments seemed convincing to several generations of public managers, but in the early 1960s they began to lose their effectiveness.

EARLY CHANGE

The second half of the 1940s witnessed a great deal of labor unrest in the United States. Like other unions, those representing federal employees wanted more for their members. In 1949 they began a campaign to win formalized legal recognition and a greater role in determining working conditions in the federal government. In 1956 they succeeded in obtaining the Democratic Party's commitment to the "recognition by law of the right of employee organizations to represent their members and participate in the formulation and improvement of personnel policies and practices." John F. Kennedy specifically reaffirmed this commitment, helping him prevail over the Republican candidate, Richard M. Nixon.

Kennedy made good on this campaign promise by issuing Executive Order 10988 (January 17, 1962). Its purpose was to promote "employee–management cooperation in the federal service." Ironically, the order was at once a major step toward legitimizing public sector collective bargaining nationwide and yet an open admission that private sector practices were not appropriate in the federal government. It swept away decades of opposition to collective bargaining in the civil service by declaring that "participation of employees in the formulation and implementation of personnel policies affecting them contributes to the effective conduct of the public business," but it also contained an expansive management rights clause, a limited scope of bargaining that did not extend to wages and hours, and prohibitions against strikes. No special means for resolving impasses were developed. Union recognition was complex and provided for "meeting and conferring" as well as the stronger right to engage in collective bargaining.

In 1969, President Nixon tried to modernize federal collective bargaining through Executive Order 11491. Events overtook planning, however, and Nixon's effort was superseded by two statutes that continue to define much of the federal labor relations program.

What Is Labor–Management Cooperation?

Mutual concerns by labor and management over such issues as productivity, poor morale, unsafe working conditions, and cutback management have led to the formation of labor–management committees (LMCs). Such cooperative endeavors allow labor and management to address a common need to tackle a mutual problem that cannot be addressed in an adversarial way at the bargaining table.

One of the earliest and best-known cooperative efforts in the public sector was undertaken during the early days of the Tennessee Valley Authority (TVA), the government corporation formed in the 1930s for controlling flooding and for generating electric power. The TVA and the Tennessee Valley Trades and Labor Council formed a cooperative committee to address such issues as productivity, improving the quality of work and services, and increasing morale.

Today, joint labor–management cooperation is virtually a staple of public sector labor relations. It exists at every level of government and for a variety of purposes.

Source: Adapted from Riccucci, Norma M. *Women, Minorities and Unions in the Public Sector*. Westport, Conn.: Greenwood Press, 1990.

THE FEDERAL PROGRAM MATURES

Collective bargaining practices in the postal service are important because it is so large—some 70,000 employees—and because historically it has been a trend-setter for the rest of the federal service. Its current collective bargaining is based on the Postal Reorganization Act of 1970. The act followed on the heels of the chaotic and disastrous postal strike of 1970, which some 200,000 workers joined. It models postal collective bargaining along private sector lines to a substantial, though not complete, extent. It empowers the National Labor Relations Board to resolve questions of representation and charges of unfair labor practices. It extends the scope of negotiations by allowing postal unions with exclusive recognition to bargain over wages, hours, and other conditions and terms of employment. Moreover, unlike the Kennedy and Nixon executive orders, the act does not contain a management rights clause, which implies that the scope of negotiations should be very similar to that found in private sector labor relations. The major departure from private sector practice is that the act prohibits strikes and requires fact-finding, or when necessary binding arbitration, to overcome impasses. In the view of some, the act tended to make the rest of the federal labor relations program somewhat obsolete because there is little logic in treating the postal service as a unique case. The Civil Service Reform Act of 1978, the next significant development in federal labor relations, did not follow its lead, however.

The Civil Service Reform Act of 1978

The enactment of Title VII of the Civil Service Reform Act of 1978, sometimes called the Federal Service Labor–Management Relations Statute, represented the achievement of a goal sought by organized labor since the 1940s. At long last federal labor relations were made to rest upon a comprehensive statute rather than a series of executive orders. The AFL-CIO was especially supportive of the change, which can be interpreted as creating a relatively permanent framework for federal collective bargaining. Future changes will have to be brought about through legislation rather than by more easily proclaimed executive orders, and labor's strength in Congress, espeically to block change, can be formidable.

Although the act solidified the gains won by labor over the years, it did not fundamentally change the federal labor relations process. It does not apply to supervisors, members of the armed forces or foreign service, and employees of the General Accounting Office (GAO), the Federal Bureau of Investigation, the Central Intelligence Agency, the National Security Agency, the TVA, or the Postal Service. Among its most important features are the following:

1. The establishment of the Federal Labor Relations Authority (FLRA). The new agency is substantially divorced from federal personnel management and is intended to act as a neutral entity. It is headed by a chair and two additional members selected on a bipartisan basis and holding their terms for five years. They are removable only for cause. A general counsel to the FLRA is also appointed for a five-year term. The FLRA is authorized to make determinations concerning appropriate bargaining units, supervise elections and certify exclusive bargaining agents, decide appeals from agency determinations that issues are nonnegotiable, and hold hearings and resolve complaints concerning unfair labor practices (ULPs). In addition, the general counsel has independent investigatory authority. The Federal Service Impasses Panel (FSIP), a separate entity within the FLRA, continues to resolve impasses when appropriate.
2. The act clarifies some aspects of the scope of bargaining. The following working conditions are *nonnegotiable*: (1) matters established by law, such as position classifications, Hatch act enforcement, and pay; (2) governmentwide rules and regulations; (3) rules and regulations of an agency or primary national subdivision, unless the FLRA has determined that there is no compelling need to prohibit negotiations or that a union represents a majority of the affected employees (who make

up a single bargaining unit); (4) management rights, including interpretation of the agency's mission, determination of its budget, organization, number of employees, and internal security, and the right to
take personnel actions involving the assignment of work, contracting
out, promotions, and emergency actions. Management may elect to
negotiate over the following, however, which are deemed *permissive*
subjects of bargaining: (1) the numbers, types, and grades of employees
or positions assigned to an organizational subdivision, work project,
or tour of duty; and (2) technology—the means or the methods of
performing work. *Mandatory* bargaining subjects include: (1) conditions of employment that do not fall into either of the above categories;
(2) procedures for implementing actions within management's preserved rights; (3) appropriate arrangements for employees adversely
affected by management's exercise of its reserved rights; and (4) a
grievance procedure, which must allow for conclusion by binding arbitration.

The FLRA has confronted the tension between the substantive nonnegotiability of management's rights and the mandatory negotiability of
procedures for implementing exercise of these rights by adopting the
doctrine that if a union proposal regarding procedures would prevent
the agency from "acting at all," then the proposal is nonnegotiable. The
theoretical underpinnings of the acting at all doctrine have been sharply
criticized, and it is uncertain whether it will continue to be sustained in
the future. It allows, however, for more vigorous bargaining, within an
already crimped framework, than the management-favored alternative
of prohibiting bargaining if the proposal would create an "unreasonable
delay" in the exercise of reserved rights.

There is also a tension between the nonnegotiability of management
rights and the mandatory negotiability of arrangements for employees
adversely affected by the exercise of such rights. Here, by contrast, the
FLRA adopted a standard that was found too narrow by the courts. It
sought to prohibit the negotiation of proposals that "directly interfered"
with management's rights. The judiciary overturned this standard in favor of one requiring bargaining unless the proposal impinged on management's rights to an "excessive degree," however.

3.   Contract enforcement is to be largely through grievance procedures.
Negotiated grievance procedures must be fair and simple, provide for
expeditious processing, allow the union or an aggrieved employee to
present and process cases, and as noted earlier, provide for binding
arbitration. Grievances cannot pertain to disputes involving prohibited
political activities, retirement, health or life insurance, suspensions and
removals for national security reasons, examinations, certifications, ap-

pointments, and classifications that do not result in an employee's reduction in grade or pay. The grievance procedure may cover or exclude ''appealable actions,'' such as breaches of equal employment opportunity (EEO) regulations or adverse actions that fall within the jurisdiction of the Equal Employment Opportunity Commission (EEOC) and/ or the Merit Systems Protection Board (MSPB). Literally tens of thousands of grievances have gone to binding arbitration. These are summarized in OPM's Labor Agreement Information Retrieval System (LAIRS). Awards can include back pay and other make-whole remedies. Exceptions to interest arbitration or grievance awards (not involving adverse actions) may be filed with the FLRA. The agency will overturn awards when it finds them contrary to federal laws, rules, or regulations or if they are considered defective on some ground that the federal courts have used to reject similar arbitration awards under regulations pertaining to the private sector.

4. Impasses can be brought to the FSIP upon the request of either party. When the FSIP agrees, arbitration can be used to resolve impasses.

5. Exclusive recognition continues as the major basis of collective bargaining. The act continues a policy first established by President Ford in 1975 that encourages the use of larger bargaining units by allowing units to consolidate without elections, providing the unions and agencies involved agree and the FLRA grants approval. As a result of this policy, the average size of bargaining units has risen. In 1980, there were more than 2,600 bargaining relationships. Throughout the postreform period, roughly 60% of the workforce covered by the statute has been organized in bargaining units represented by an exclusive agent.

6. The act includes a number of miscellaneous provisions that are important to collective bargaining. It allows federal workers to engage in informational picketing. Unions are granted the right to have represented employees' dues withheld from their paychecks (dues checkoff) at no cost, but each employee is free to either authorize or refuse to authorize such withholding. Official time is authorized for employees in labor negotiations to the same extent that management time is authorized, thus labor negotiators are now paid for the time they spend in negotiations. Agencies such as OPM, the General Services Administration, and the State Department (excluding the Foreign Service), which issue personnel regulations having applicability to their workforces governmentwide, must consult with unions representing their employees prior to making substantive changes.

The Civil Service Reform Act led to several incremental improvements. Especially important has been the negotiation of grievance procedures, which

Department of Treasury, *IRS* v. *Federal Labor Relations Authority*, 110 S. Ct. 1623 (1990)

Facts—During a round of contract negotiations with the Internal Revenue Service (IRS), the National Treasury Employees Union (NTEU) proposed that if employees wished to raise objections to the contracting out of work by the IRS, they could do so through the grievance and arbitration provisions of the negotiated contract. The IRS refused to bargain over the proposal on the grounds that it was not negotiable under Title VII of the Civil Service Reform Act of 1978. The NTEU challenged the IRS before the Federal Labor Relations Authority (FLRA), which ruled that the IRS was required to negotiate over the proposal.

Issue—Are federal agencies required to bargain over proposals that could directly or indirectly affect their ability to contract government work out to the private sector (a practice often referred to as privatization)?

Decision—The U.S. Supreme Court ruled against the FLRA (and hence the union). Referring to section 7016 of the Civil Service Reform Act of 1978 (which defines "management rights"), the Court said that "nothing in the entire Act . . . shall affect the authority of agency officials to make contracting out determinations."

has reduced the need to rely on adverse action appeals systems. The latter are expensive for the government, which bears the entire cost. According to the OPM, currently over 90% of negotiated grievance procedures provide that the costs of arbitration, if necessary, will be split between the union and the agency.

Never free of criticism, many complaints about the federal relations program remain. Clinton, Gore, and other "reinventers" believe it is modeled on industrial era practices that do not fit today's decentralized personnel management, employee empowerment, and emphasis on results rather than procedures. Unions find it defective, because even though they are legally obligated to represent all bargaining unit employees fairly—both union members and nonmembers alike—there is no procedure for collecting "counterpart" or "fair share" fees from the nonmembers. Only about one-quarter to one-third of all represented employees outside the postal service actually pay dues. Unions also complain that the scope of bargaining is too narrow and agencies do not really believe in collective bargaining. Consequently, unions are still prone to arguing their cases in Congress and the White House. Managers, who are also employees, are concerned that the bargaining between unions and political executives may ignore their interests in being able to manage effectively. When relations in an agency turn hostile, it is very difficult to repair them. Since they have few real weapons, unions may bring a host of grievances or ULPs to try to win concessions from management, but this practice is an abuse of those systems that often deepens distrust.

LABOR–MANAGEMENT PARTNERSHIPS

As noted at the beginning of this chapter, the most recent effort to revamp labor relations at the federal level is the partnering of labor and management to improve the quality of relations between both and to better serve the American people. To this end, the Clinton administration, as part of its broader reinvention program, created the NPC, comprising labor and management representatives.

Some labor analysts and researchers have viewed partnerships as being no different from labor–management committees (LMCs). Labor–management committees, which have existed in the United States since the early nineteenth century, have become increasingly popular in recent years in both the public and private sectors. Initially relied upon during periods of economic austerity and hardship, LMCs are formed to address a host of workplace issues, such as productivity improvement, quality of work life, unsafe or unhealthy working conditions, and even cutback management. The most important feature of cooperative efforts is the willingness of labor and management to address a common need or to tackle mutual problems for the ultimate benefit of both as well as the public.

One of the earliest and best-known cooperative efforts in the public sector was undertaken during the early days of the TVA, the government corporation formed in the 1930s for controlling flooding and for generating electric power. The TVA and the Tennessee Valley Trades and Labor Council formed a cooperative committee to address such issues as improving productivity, improving the quality of work and services, and increasing morale.

The Clinton administration clearly views partnerships as being different from cooperation and LMCs, trumpeting the labor–management partnership at the federal level as a partnership of equals rather than as a struggle between adversaries. To ensure partnering in the true spirit of the term, labor was promised the right to bargain over personnel matters such as agency shop and performance appraisals, issues heretofore excluded from the scope of bargaining at the federal level. Also, partnerships were to be created throughout various federal agencies to further ensure labor's participation in matters affecting their members.

Initially leery of the federal government's notion of partnering, labor was induced to participate with promises to have a voice in perhaps the sine qua non of the NPR's reinvention efforts: downsizing the federal bureaucracy. Specifically, unions were promised that

> Many job cuts would accrue not though layoffs, but through buyouts and attrition.

Many of the jobs targeted for elimination would be held by persons in positions not represented by labor unions (e.g., midlevel managers and personnelists).

Legislation would be sought requiring management to negotiate over issues that were previously not mandatory (e.g., agency shop, classification and performance appraisal).

Partnerships would extend throughout civilian federal agencies, from top to bottom.

It was also understood that Clinton would back the agency shop—a dream that died with the election of a Republican Congress in 1994.

The NPC, however, has not only failed to redefine the role of labor unions in the federal government, but none of these promises made by the Clinton Administration to federal unions as a condition for their partnering with management has been honored.

A number of labor analysts have concluded from the experiences thus far that labor–management partnering, at least at the federal level of government, has already proven unrealistic for the following reasons:

1. Past experience with LMCs at the federal level has often undermined the role of unions.
2. Many members of federal bargaining units are not union members and do not recognize unions as their representatives.
3. Midlevel managers and supervisors are not perceived as partner participants.
4. By helping managers decide which federal workers will lose their jobs under downsizing, unions are betraying their members.

WHY EMPLOYEES UNIONIZE

Even our brief review of the development of collective bargaining in the federal government suggests that barriers to unionization of public employees and the institution of productive labor relations may sometimes seem insuperable, yet today public employees are far more organized than those in the private sector. (See Table 12.2.) Why? What accounted for the tremendous growth of unionization and collective bargaining—especially from the 1960s to the 1980s—in the face of so many obstacles? Several factors can be identified.

1. The Kennedy executive order was a watershed in public sector labor relations. Coming just before the 1960s witnessed tremendous agitation for change in society's ''power structures'' to empower African Americans, other minorities, women, the poor, and younger Americans, it provided a broad endorsement by a popular and subsequently

Requirements for Successful Labor–Management Partnerships

- *Employment security.* Management must assure employees that they will not be adversely affected because of their own efforts to improve productivity.
- *Joint effort.* Management must accept the union as a full and equal partner in the change effort. It must not be a preconceived management program in which the union is asked to participate.
- *Open communication.* Both sides must willingly share information they previously may have regarded as proprietary, sensitive, or irrelevant.
- *Delegate authority/share power.* Decision making must be delegated to lower levels in the organization, consistent with the information and ability to make such decisions.
- *Commitment.* Support from all levels, particularly the highest ranks of management and unions, must be constant and real. It must be conveyed in actions as well as words.
- *Training.* Management must be willing to provide necessary training opportunities and work release time. It must be willing to allow the union an equal voice in these activities.
- *Patience.* Both sides must view the effort as long-term; it is not a quick cure for endemic problems.
- *Faith.* Management must accept the notion that cost-effectiveness will be improved by focusing attention on other aspects of work and the work environment.

Source: Excellence in Public Service. Washington, D.C.: Public Employee Department, AFL-CIO, 1994, p. 3.

TABLE 12.2 Union Membership in Public and Private Sectors (1987–1997)

Employment sector	1987	1997
Public	36.0%	37.2%
Private	17.0%	14.1%

Note: Expressed as percentage of employed workers.
Source: U.S. Bureau of Labor Statistics, Website: http://stats.bls.gov.

martyred president for a basic reorientation of the way public sector
hierarchies treated their employees.

2. The Kennedy order only applied to parts of the federal government,
   but public officials and managers who clung to traditional claims of
   authority while their employees, like many others in the country, were
   demanding change, ended up exacerbating those demands. As the former director of the Federal Advisory Commission on Intergovernmental Relations, Carl Steinberg, once noted, '' 'the head-in-the-sand' attitude of many public employers, rooted in the traditional concept of the
   prerogatives of the sovereign authority and distrust of the economic,
   political, and social objectives of unions . . . has made questions of
   whether employee organizations will be recognized for the purposes
   of discussing grievances and the conditions of work the second most
   frequent cause of strikes.''

3. A growing awareness by the labor movement that unionization and
   union strength in the private sector was diminishing. These organizations sought to unionize unorganized sectors of the economy, including
   public employment, which at the time was growing very rapidly. Many
   unions representing public employees are ''mixed unions'' because
   they also represent private sector workers. The Service Employees International Union (SEIU) and the Teamsters Union are examples.

4. The financial resources and skill that national unions could bring to
   bear on their efforts to organize public employees.

5. The stifling impact of position classification and pay systems on the
   upward mobility of employees in large public bureaucracies.

6. A general sense among clerical employees that their earning power could
   be enhanced and their rights protected through collective bargaining.

7. A growing sense among professional employees such as teachers that
   professionalism and unionization could go hand in hand. In other words,
   collective bargaining could be used to achieve professional goals.

8. The spillover effect of union organizational drives on more placid employee associations. In order to protect their appeal and organizational
   base, many of the latter became more aggressive in demanding a right
   to bargain collectively.

These factors were extremely important in the growth of public sector
unionization during the 1960s and 1970s. Moreover, once unions were able to
organize public employees and negotiate contracts, they had the opportunity to
demonstrate their desirability to those workers who remained unorganized. To
some extent this enabled public sector unions to enroll members of groups that
had traditionally been skeptical of unionization, such as African Americans and

women. Nevertheless, unionization has hardly been uniform. We have already noted that public employee unionization varies with occupation or function. It has also varied with geographic region. For the most part, the southeastern and sunbelt states have been more resistant to public employee and private sector unionization than other states, especially those in the Northeast and Great Lakes regions.

Having discussed some general considerations about public sector unionization and collective bargaining, we now turn our attention to where most of today's action is—at the state and local levels.

STATE AND LOCAL ARRANGEMENTS

The development of the federal labor relations program indicates the general direction that has been taken in the whole area of public sector collective bargaining. The major emphasis has been on the creation of a right to organize and to gain recognition and a process for negotiating and resolving impasses. Once the programs got underway, earlier fears for sovereignty and public order were somewhat alleviated. As unions representing federal employees gained strength in terms of numbers, experience, resources, and legitimacy, they began demanding a more comprehensive role in the determination of personnel matters affecting federal employees. One major result of the federal experience so far has been a movement toward making federal labor relations practices closer to those found in the private sphere. This is especially evident with regard to postal employees. At the state and local level there have been similar developments. There is a good deal more variation, however, and some state programs are far more developed than others.

State and local employees have come up against certain constraints that never affected the federal government, since federal employees were granted the right to organize as early as 1912. Prior to 1968 it was generally believed that the First Amendment did not protect the right of public employees to organize labor unions; therefore, states were free to prohibit them. This position was reversed later that year, however, when a U.S. court of appeals, in *McLaughlin* v. *Tilendis,* held that regulations prohibiting public employees from organizing were unconstitutional. Although laws that forbade unionization, such as those in North Carolina and Alabama, were not specifically involved in the case, the decision cast grave doubt on their constitutionality. The decision did not require that governments engage in collective bargaining, and so a host of options remained open to state lawmakers. In addition, in the early 1960s several courts held that in the absence of specific legislation authorizing collective bargaining, government officials did not have the right to engage in such activity. Subsequently, though, the dominant trend in court decisions shifted to a more permissive position allowing collective bargaining unless it was specifically outlawed. For the most part, then, even in the absence of specific statutory authorization, governmental jurisdictions may establish programs for labor relations and collective bargaining.

Since 1959, when Wisconsin became the first state to enact a comprehensive law governing public sector labor relations, well over half of the states have followed suit. By 1982, 40 states had relatively well-developed public sector labor relations policies—a remarkable change that had occurred during the previous two decades. The specific scope and nature of the states' policies and programs continue to vary widely, however (Table 12.3). There has been some tendency to distinguish between state and local employees and to differentiate among occupations in the various state regulations, thus firefighters, police, teachers, and other employees in a given state may face disparate conditions when seeking to collectively bargain. Moreover, a teacher, firefighter, or other employee who moves from one state to another may find that the available collective bargaining process varies substantially. While there are a number of advantages in this situation, including the flexibility for each state

TABLE 12.3 State Collective Bargaining Provisions Established by Legislation or Administrative Fiat

State	Employees covered				
	State	Local	Police	Firefighters	Teachers
Alabama	—	—	—	Y	Y
Alaska	X	X	X	X	X
Arizona	Y	Y	Y	Y	Y
Arkansas	—	—	—	—	X
California	X	X	X	X	X
Colorado	—	—	—	—	—
Connecticut	X	X	X	X	X
Delaware	X	X	X	X	X
Florida	X	X	X	X	X
Georgia	—	—a	—	X	—
Hawaii	X	X	X	X	X
Idaho	—	X	—	X	X
Illinois	X	X	X	X	X
Indiana	X	X	X	X	X
Iowa	X	X	X	X	X
Kansas	Y	Y	Y	Y	X
Kentucky	—	—	X	X	—
Louisiana	—	Xa	—	—	—

TABLE 12.3 Continued

State	Employees covered				
	State	Local	Police	Firefighters	Teachers
Maine	X	X	X	X	X/Y
Maryland	—	X	—	—	X
Massachusetts	X	X	X	X	X
Michigan	X	X	X	X	X
Minnesota	X/Y	X/Y	X/Y	X/Y	X/Y
Mississippi	—	—	—	—	—
Missouri	Y	Y	—	Y	—
Montana	X	X	X	X	X
Nebraska	X	X	X	X	Y
Nevada	—	X	X	X	X
New Hampshire	X	X	X	X	X
New Jersey	X	X	X	X	X
New Mexico	X	X	X	X	X
New York	X	X	X	X	X
North Carolina	—	—	—	—	—
North Dakota	Y	Y	Y	Y	X
Ohio	X	X	X	X	X
Oklahoma	—	X	X	X	X
Oregon	X	X	X	X	X
Pennsylvania	X/Y	X/Y	X	X	X/Y
Rhode Island	X	X	X	X	X
South Carolina	—	—	—	—	—
South Dakota	X	X	X	X	X
Tennessee	—	—	—	—	X
Texas	—	—	X	X	—
Utah	—	—	—	—	—
Vermont	X	X	X	X	X
Virginia	—	—	—	—	—
Washington	X	X	X	X	X
West Virginia	Y	Y	Y	Y	Y
Wisconsin	X	X	X	X	X
Wyoming	—	—	—	X	—

X: collective bargaining provisions; Y: meet and confer provisions; X/Y: collective bargaining on some issues, meet and confer on others.

Note: Administrative fiat includes, for example, civil service regulation, executive order, or attorney general opinion.

[a] Public transit workers only.

Source: Adapted from Kearney, Richard C. *Labor Relations in the Public Sector*, 2nd ed. New York: Marcel Dekker, 1992; updated from "State Labor Laws," *Labor Relations Reporter.* Washington, D.C.: BNA, 1990).

From *Abood* v. *Detroit* to *Lehnert* v. *Ferris Faculty Assn.*

In 1977, the U.S. Supreme Court issued a ruling in *Abood* v. *Detroit Board of Education* stating that public employees can be constitutionally required to pay a fee (fair share) to unions representing them in collective bargaining even though they are not members of these organizations. The purpose of such a fee, the Court opined, is to promote the government's interest in labor peace and also to prevent free ridership on the part of nonmembers.

Almost 15 years later, the Court's *Lehnert* v. *Ferris Faculty Assn.* (1991) decision again reaffirmed the High Court's supsport for the fair share arrangement. One of the most important aspects of the case turned on the appropriate use of nonmembers' dues. The Court ruled that "a local bargaining representative may charge objecting employees for their pro rata share of the costs associated with otherwise chargeable activities of its state and national affiliates, even if those activities were not performed for the direct benefit of the objecting employees' bargaining unit."

to adopt labor relations practices that are especially tailored to its particular political, economic, and employment conditions, there has occasionally been interest in the possibility of a federal statute to guarantee uniform collective bargaining for state and local employees. If it were constitutional, such a law would make life easier for organized labor and enable the judicial and administrative rulings concerning labor relations in one state to be applied in another. There seems to be little or no enthusiasm for such a statute today, however. Federal policy favors devolution, as in the case of welfare reform, and many states and local governments are busy reinventing their human resource management programs. There is also a good chance that the Supreme Court would find such a law in violation of the Tenth Amendment (e.g., see *Printz* v. *United States*, 1997).

State labor relations could once be divided into "meet and confer" and "negotiations" approaches. The former is premised on notions of sovereignty and the inequality of the parties involved in collective bargaining. Management retains many rights, including the final authority it is able to retain in the face of collective agreements; relationships are premised on equality between the parties engaged in the bargaining process. To the extent that meet and confer is still used, it is likely to be replaced by negotiations or some form of partnering in the future.

What Are the Typical Criteria for Bargaining Unit Determination?

1. A clear and identifiable community of interest among the employees
2. Effective dealings with the unit and efficient operations
3. A history of representation
4. The level of authority of the employees and the officials with whom they might bargain
5. Agreement between the parties
6. The convenience of the employer
7. Politics

For the most part, state legislation is similar to federal statutes and regulations prohibiting strikes by public employees. There is, of course, a long-standing common law prohibition against such strikes and they are therefore illegal even where no explicit statutes exist. Nevertheless, several states have addressed the issue and allow strikes for some categories of public servants. Where states have outlawed strikes, the penalties for striking generally include some form of injunctive relief obtained through judicial action or the issuance of cease-and-desist orders by the administrative agency responsible for the labor relations program (often called a public employment relations board or PERB). Statutes may also provide for the discipline of violating unions and employees. Here, New York State's Taylor Act continues to stand out for its practicality. In the event of what appears to be an illegal strike, the chief legal officer of the employer involved is required to seek an injunction against the union in the state supreme court. The public employer is directed to deduct two days' pay for each day an employee was out on strike in violation of the act. Such employees are also to be placed on probation for a year, thereby jeopardizing their civil service status. Other disciplinary measures and even dismissal are permitted. The act further provides for fines against unions engaging in strikes in violation of injunctions and for the suspension of certain beneficial procedures such as dues check-offs.

To understand the modern complexities of public sector labor relations, however, one must discuss the process, participants, tactics, and politics of public sector labor relations. We begin with a thorough analysis of the process, from which much of the rest follows.

SUPERVISORS

Although once widely denied, the right to join and form unions is now secure for most public employees. The position of supervisors remains problematic, however. Here is a clear case of the difficulty of trying to transfer the private sector model to the public sector. In private corporations, managers are not unionized. Whatever the legal basis of the organization, they are considered part of the employer. The Taft–Hartley Act (1947) excludes private sector supervisors from membership in bargaining units. In the public sector, however, a markedly different situation prevails. The employer is the public or its representative (i.e., the government). Supervisors do not make decisions related to profits and losses and do not have an economic situation vis-á-vis their employer that differs much if at all from rank-and-file employees. They are not paid out of company profits. Moreover, public personnel law often treats supervisors no differently from other employees, as in the case of both political neutrality and residency regulations. As a result of prevailing civil service law, public sector supervisors also tend to have a narrower scope of authority over rank-and-file personnel than do private managers. Do public supervisors have interests or positions sufficiently different from those of other public employees to limit their right to join and form unions?

Which arrangement is best? It all depends on the character of the collective bargaining process in the particular jurisdiction. In general, though, it appears that mixed supervisory–nonsupervisory units are most likely to militate against effective supervision and management for productivity and efficiency. At the same time, the total exclusion of supervisors from the labor relations process makes sense only insofar as employees who are defined as supervisory are distinct in their duties and relationship to the employer. Even then, the meet-and-confer approach would seem to be sensible.

A second problem under the heading of joining and forming unions is that the employer, though interested in the outcome of such efforts, must scrupulously avoid becoming involved in unionizing activities. Among other things, the employer cannot make any effort to dominate a union, show favoritism toward a particular union, or prohibit employees from soliciting membership, distributing literature, or displaying support for a union during nonwork time at the place of employment. Surveillance and interrogation of employees or threats or promises to them have also been ruled unfair labor practices.

ORGANIZING AND UNIT DETERMINATION

Federal, state, and local regulations concerning the collective bargaining process vary widely. Where collective bargaining is sanctioned by law, practice, or judicial interpretation, a process for showing interest and holding elections is generally necessary. Often a showing of interest requires that a union have the support of at least 30% of the employees in the proposed bargaining unit. (The bargaining unit is the jurisdiction over which the union has bargaining rights.) This support can be demonstrated through the use of membership cards, authorization cards to have dues checked off or deducted by the employer, or some form of petition. An election will ordinarily be held when such a showing is made. For a union to become the exclusive representative of the employees in the unit, it must generally receive a majority of the ballots cast. (See Figure 12.3.)

If there are more than two options on the ballot and none gets a majority, either no union will be certified or a runoff election will be held. If no union is elected, an "election bar" takes effect where, depending upon the jurisdiction, union electoral activity would be barred anywhere from one to two years. Unions can also be decertified or replaced by others. This process may be initiated by employees, who may have to demonstrate a 30% showing of interest in decertification. Provisions requiring the employer's right to begin a decertification vary. If a decertification election is held, the union must again muster majority support or lose its status as exclusive representative.

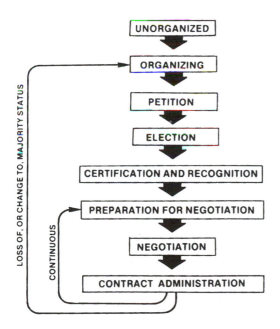

FIGURE 12.3 Typical sequence of organizing events. *Source*: U.S. Office of Personnel Management, *Manager's Handbook*. (Washington, D.C.: U.S. Government Printing Office, 1979, p. 137.

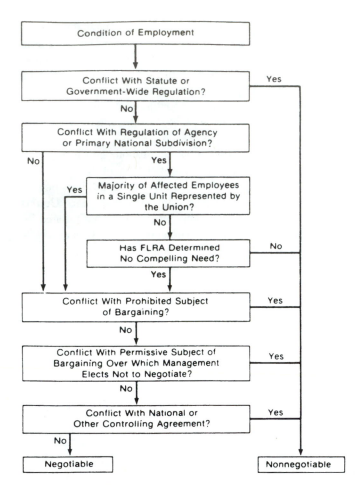

FIGURE 12.4 Determining the scope of bargaining in federal employment. *Source: The Federal Labor–Management Consultant.* Washington, D.C.: U.S. Office of Personnel Management, November 2, 1979.

THE SCOPE OF BARGAINING

Once a collective bargaining relationship is established, the nature of the scope of bargaining becomes of crucial importance (Figure 12.4). It is possible to classify issues concerning the scope of bargaining into three categories: (1) items upon which bargaining is mandatory, (2) items upon which it is permitted, and (3) items upon which it is prohibited. Where specific items will fall varies widely with the regulations of various jurisdictions, however. For example, most federal employees cannot bargain over wages and hours, but this is very much what collective bargaining in municipalities is generally about. In the private sector, bargaining refers to "wages, hours, and other terms and conditions of employment." In the public sector, however, it is common to exclude matters controlled by civil service legislation and to specify a set of management rights that are beyond the scope of bargaining. Matters that fall within the scope of any agency's "mission" are also commonly outside the scope of bargaining. Today the tendency is to consider other matters to be within the scope of bargaining unless specifically excluded by statute, court decision, or PERB ruling. This is especially true of matters having a primary impact on the welfare of the employee rather than upon the operating effectiveness of the government as a whole. Sometimes an even weaker test is used—the subject will be within the scope of bargaining if it bears a "significant relation" to working conditions defined within the mandatory or permitted bargaining categories.

The importance of the scope of bargaining exceeds mere delineation of what the parties can seek to negotiate. It places very serious constraints on management and is related to the use of impasse procedures. In general, management cannot unilaterally alter a working condition that has been defined within the scope of mandatory bargaining. This may be true even if the collective bargaining contract has expired but labor negotiations are underway. Failure to reach agreement on a mandatory item triggers impasse resolution procedures at the appropriate time.

IMPASSE RESOLUTION

If an agreement between a union and an employer cannot be reached on matters within the scope of mandatory bargaining, some method of impasse resolution may be used. In some cases the choice of method, if any, is left to the parties to the negotiations. In others, impasse procedures are mandated by the labor relations statute. In states having comprehensive public sector labor relations programs, the PERB or equivalent agency must generally be notified that the parties are at an impasse before impasse resolution procedures are undertaken. Typically, three kinds of procedures are used as mechanisms for resolving impasses and thereby avoiding breakdowns of the collective bargaining process to the point at which illegal strikes occur or employees are forced to work without a contract. These are mediation, fact-finding, and arbitration.

Mediation involves efforts of a third-party neutral participant to persuade those involved in the dispute to reach a settlement. Mediation cannot work if all of the concerned parties do not support it; it is by nature a voluntary process. Where there is an aura of distrust between the disputants, each side may be unwilling to make compromises lest these become the basis upon which bargaining takes place if the mediator's efforts ultimately fail. Mediation may also represent an effort by the disputants to avoid difficult and prolonged bargaining, although mediators may simply recommend further direct negotiations. Mediators can be private individuals, but in most cases they are supplied by a government agency, such as the Federal Mediation and Conciliation Service. Most state labor laws provide for mediation, and over half of the states offer mediation services.

Mediation is a highly informal process, and much of the information about it is anecdotal. Generally, one supposes, the mediator meets jointly and individually with the disputants. He or she tries to keep them talking to each other and at the bargaining table. Part of the mediator's work is to develop a better climate for negotiations and to try to make the parties more skillful at bargaining. Another part is to try to help the parties to reach a substantive agreement. This may involve determining what each side will agree to and then formulating an acceptable package to which the two sides can subscribe. Sometimes agreement can be facilitated merely by the choice of the right words in proposals and counterproposals.

Mediation is prized for its flexibility. It also has some drawbacks, however. There is no finality to it. Moreover, skillful mediators, who may be difficult to find in any case, may forge agreements by using language that has somewhat different meanings to management and labor. In this event, disputes may resurface in the form of grievances after the contract has been signed. According to Richard Kearney, a leading public sector labor relations authority, mediation is *least* successful (1) in large jurisdictions, (2) where the parties have gone to impasse frequently, (3) where the basic dispute involves the employer's ability to pay, and (4) where the parties face strong external pressures to avoid compromise. Conversely, successful mediation appears to depend very heavily upon timing and trust. It must begin after an impasse has been reached but before positions have hardened so much that compromise is unlikely. If the mediator loses the trust of one side and is viewed as an ally of the other, the process is bound to fail.

Fact-finding involves a third party in more of an investigatory and judicial role. The objective is for a neutral observer to review the key aspects of a dispute and issue a report. The report may simply state the fact-finder's view of the facts or it may include recommendations for a resolution of the dispute. The report may be public or reserved to the parties and any appropriate governmental agencies. Actually, the term fact-finding may be something of a misnomer. According to the Jerry Wurf, who was a powerful leader of the American Federation of State, County, and Municipal Employees (AFSCME), "the parties usually know and understand the facts. The problem is that these facts are interpreted from positions of self-interest and therefore lead rational people to conflicting conclusions." In a sense, fact-finding really amounts to a form of voluntary arbitration. There will be pressure on the parties to accept the fact finder's report and recommendations, if any, but they are not bound by it and are free to seek a different resolution. More than 30 states provide for fact finding in public sector disputes. It tends to work well in part because there is often considerable pressure on the parties to accept a fact-finder's "neutral" or "fair" recommendation. Like mediation, fact-finding depends heavily upon the trust of the two sides in the impartiality of the third party.

Arbitration is another kind of third-party intervention. It can take several forms, but it is always primarily judicial in character. The arbitrator or panel of arbitrators holds hearings, receives evidence, hears the perspectives of the parties to the dispute, and makes recommendations (often called "awards") as to how the impasse should be resolved. Arbitration abandons the hope that the parties to a dispute can reach an agreement themselves; rather, its purpose is to formulate a contract per se. Since arbitration moves away from self-determination in the workplace by imposing conditions, it is seldom used to resolve impasses over economic interests (as opposed to grievances) in the private sector.

There are several forms of arbitration. It can be voluntary or compulsory, depending upon how the parties enter into it. Compulsory arbitration is frequently found in states with comprehensive labor legislation and is used where other impasse procedures have failed or are deemed inappropriate. Arbitration can also be binding or nonbinding, depending on whether the parties are required to adhere to the arbitrator's award. Nonbinding arbitration is similar to fact-finding and suffers from a lack of finality. Arbitration can also take a form called "final offer" or "last best offer." This requires the parties to the impasse to submit their final offers for resolution to the arbitrator.

In "whole-package" final offer arbitration, the arbitrator is required to choose the complete final offer of one side or the other without modification as his of her award. In "issue-by-issue" final offer arbitration, the arbitrator still cannot modify the proposals of the two sides, but he or she can choose the final offer of one on an issue, such as wages, and the final offer of the other on another issue, such as fringe benefits. The efficacy of final offer arbitration is that it prods the parties to put forward reasonable demands. If the union or the employer puts forth unreasonable proposals, the other's will almost certainly be chosen, thus the best way of attaining demands is to make only those that are reasonable. There has, however, been enough irrationality in public sector labor relations in the past to at least raise the specter of both parties putting forward unreasonable demands, in which case final offer arbitration compels the arbitrator to choose an unsatisfactory solution. This possibility highlights the danger of such arbitration and some argue that final offer arbitration should only follow fact-finding and should give the arbitrator the option of using the fact finder's recommendations as the binding award. This practice has been used in some states, most notably Iowa.

In theory, arbitration can take any of these forms since they speak to different aspects of the process. It can be voluntary or compulsory, binding or nonbinding, conventional or final offer. It can also be combined with mediation (med-arb) in an effort to reduce the scope of the dispute. In practice, however, the public sector has tended to opt for the compulsory/binding approach, with increasing attention paid to the final offer format. This approach to impasse resolution is not without potential difficulties, however.

Arbitrators must consider several standards in making awards or in choosing between final offers. *Acceptability* is crucial, especially in nonbinding arbitration. The parties must be willing to live with the award and willing to work in the public interest under it. Acceptability generally depends on getting the two parties to agree that the award reflects the balance of economic power between them. Since arbitration is viewed as a substitute for strikes and lockouts (i.e., the use of economic force), acceptability seeks to substitute the result that would have most likely occurred had the parties been free to use economic weapons.

Equity refers to the fairness of the resolution. Here economic strength is not the main concern; rather, such matters as comparability become important. One of the problems however, is, comparable to whom? Should pay scales and fringe benefits for police in Detroit be compared to (1) firefighters in Detroit, (2) police in New York City, (3) police in Los Angeles, Cleveland, or Buffalo, or (4) police in the suburbs of Detroit? Trying to establish comparable wages for dissimilar occupations is even more difficult than establishing true pay comparability between different public jurisdictions or between public employees and their closest private sector counterparts.

Ability to pay is another standard. It is obvious that arbitration awards must be concerned with the employer's ability to pay. There are some serious complications with this standard, however. How can one determine a public employer's ability to pay? What will happen to the tax base if taxes are raised? Is the budget "padded" enough to sustain an increase in employee compensation? These questions may have no undisputed answers. From an arbitrator's point of view, however, it may be unreasonable for the public employer to ask its employees to work for less than the going market rate. The same employer could not, for example, go to a pencil company and say, "You have very fine pencils and our bureaucrats need many of them, but we'll have to pay you less than the going price because that price is simply more than we can afford." If it is absurd for a city to plead poverty in buying other supplies, why would it be reasonable in buying labor? Faced with this question, some arbitrators are inclined to downgrade the importance of ability to pay except in cases in which the employer is obviously in very dire financial straits. Remember, unless arbitrators protect employees against unreal inability-to-pay claims, civil servants, who are constrained by residency requirements and prohibitions on political activity and strikes, may be easily victimized.

The *public interest* is another standard that arbitrators should take into account in the public sector. As taxpayers, citizens, and recipients of public services and regulations, the public has a strong interest in the outcome of public sector labor negotiations and impasses, but how is the public interest to be ascertained

TABLE 12.4 Public Employees with the Right to Strike, as of 1998

State	Employees covered
Alaska	All public employees except for police and firefighters
California	All but police and firefighters, *providing* a court or California PERB does not rule that striking is illegal[a]
Hawaii	All public employees
Idaho	Firefighters and teachers
Illinois	All public employees except for police, firefighters, and paramedics
Minnesota	All public employees except for police and firefighters
Montana	All public employees
Ohio	All public employees except for police and firefighters
Oregon	All public employees except for police, firefighters, and correctional officers, emergency telephone workers, guards of mental hospitals
Pennsylvania	All public employees except for police, firefighters, prison guards, guards at mental hospitalsf, and court employees
Rhode Island	All state employees
Vermont	All public employees except for correctional officers, court employees, and state employees
Wisconsin	All public employees except for police, firefighters, and state employees

[a] The California State Supreme Court, in *County Sanitation District* v. *L.A. County Employees Association* (699 P.2d 835, 1985), said that unless expressly prohibited by statute—or case law—striking by public employees is not illegal. Firefighters are prohibited by statutory law, police by case law.
Source: Adapted from Kearney, Richard C. *Labor Relations in the Public Sector.* New York: Marcel Dekker, 1984; updated by "State Labor Laws," *Labor Relations Reporter.* Washington, D.C.: BNA, 1998.

in any particular dispute? This is another question without a clear answer. It has led many to consider, however, whether or not arbitrators in the public sector should receive special training and whether or not public sector labor relations statutes should provide more explicit definitions of the public interest.

STRIKES

A strike may occur if an impasse is not resolved. This represents the ultimate breakdown of the collective negotiations process, and in theory, at least, should be the last resort. Although strikes are now legal for some public employees under certain circumstances in several states (see Table 12.4), the strike question continues to loom large in public sector labor relations. Here again we see the problematic nature of trying to adapt private sector practices to the public sector. The strike is a fundamental feature of the private sector process; denying it in the public sector, while nevertheless roughly paralleling other private sector practices, tends to create an imbalance between the parties. This may dictate the use of the strike, even though illegal, for essentially political purposes. Indeed, analysts of the causes of strikes in the public sector have sometimes come to the conclusion that most public sector strikes are unpredictable, perhaps because predicting their political use remains elusive. Moreover, public sector strikes often seem tied as much to the personalities of union leaders and government officials as to prevailing economic conditions.

Collective bargaining in the public sector can be a highly politicized process. Agreements are not necessarily hammered out solely on the basis of rationality and compromise; they are often dictated almost entirely by political muscle. This is perhaps the main reason why labor leaders and unionists so strongly support the right to strike and engage in strikes even when contrary to law. The strike is the ultimate weapon in labor's arsenal. Many labor leaders and sympathizers believe that the prohibition of the right to strike is a denial of a fundamental and inherent right. Moreover, they are wont to claim that collective bargaining can never be more than a charade in the absence of the right to strike. It is felt that management will not take labor negotiations seriously unless the worker has some sanction available. In the absence of the right to strike, management may be patronizing at best, or at worst obstructionist, yet in the view of many labor leaders, collective bargaining depends upon the rough equality of the parties. As a process it "transforms pleading to negotiation." In theoretical consequence, a strike or the threat of one is an essential part of labor–management negotiations.

What about the society as a whole, however? Clearly the state performs vital functions. While some of these are analogous or identical to those that are performed by the private sector, some are uniquely governmental, hence society may pay a very heavy price for strikes in the public sector, not just in terms of lost work days, but in terms of the disruption of essential functions. This is exacerbated by the fact that in many cases the state has a monopoly over services which, if disrupted, cannot be obtained in another fashion. At a given moment, the cost of a strike by strategically placed public employees is likely to appear greater than the cost of reaching a settlement. The public's inconvenience and the elected officials' quest for reelection may make it difficult for the government to take a hard-line stance even if states and cities are in hard times. Public employees are then in a strong position to make gains that they otherwise would not make, and the gains go beyond economic matters to include the right to participate in policy making over such issues as classroom size and the number of police officers assigned to a patrol car.

Each side in the strike controversy raises valid questions. Sam Zagoria, as director of the Labor–Management Relations Service established by the National

The Professional Air Traffic Controller Organization (PATCO) Strike of 1981

On July 29, 1981, 95% of PATCO's 13,000 members, the traffic "cops" at the nation's airports, voted to reject the federal government's final offer. They insisted upon getting twice-a-year cost-of-living increases that would be 1 1/2 times greater than inflation, a 4-day, 32-hour work week without a compensating salary cut, and retirement after 20 years at 75% of base salary. One striking controller stated the feelings of thousands: "Where are they going to get 13,000 controllers and train them before the economy sinks? The reality is, we are it. They have to deal with us."

But the Reagan administration was equally determined in its resolve to keep the planes flying. First, it cut back on many scheduled flights and reduced the staff at some of the smallest airports. Then it put air traffic control supervisors (who were not members of the union) and some retired controllers back into service and ordered as many military controllers as could be spared to civilian duty stations. Finally, President Reagan addressed the entire nation on television. After reminding the American public that it is illegal for federal government employees to strike against their employer and that each controller signed an oath asserting that he or she would never strike, he proclaimed: "They are in violation of the law, and if they do not report for work within 48 hours, they have forfeited their jobs and will be terminated." About 1,000 controllers took the president at his word and reported back to work. Most of the rest thought that he was just bluffing.

The strike continued and the president showed that he wasn't bluffing after all. Over 11,000 controllers received formal letters of dismissal. PATCO's assets were frozen by court order, some PATCO leaders were literally taken away to jail in chains, and the Department of Transportation started formal proceedings to decertify the union.

With its members fired, with practically no public support, and with the fill-in system working better every day, PATCO—the union that had broken ranks with labor to support Republican presidential candidate Reagan—called for labor solidarity. The response was minimal. The major labor leaders verbally supported the strike and deplored the president's efforts at "union busting," but did nothing else. United Auto Workers President Douglas Fraser said that the strike "could do massive damage to the labor movement. That's why PATCO should have talked to the AFL-CIO council"—before they struck. Had any of the major airline unions joined in the strike, the system would surely have been shut down. But none of these unions felt that they had any obligation to support the controllers in any way that mattered.

In late October the Federal Labor Relations Authority formally decertified PATCO—the first time that it had ever done so to any union of federal government workers. In December, PATCO was forced to file for bankruptcy. In the end over 11,000 of the controllers who stayed on strike lost their jobs permanently.

The PATCO episode illustrates several aspects of public sector labor relations. First, it exemplified the passing of labor relations from a period in which unions were relatively secure to one in which they were increasingly vulnerable. Public opinion in favor of containing the cost of government by adopting labor-saving technologies and contracting out to private firms became a major force in many local governments. Unions found themselves doing the unthinkable: bargaining over pay freezes, reductions, givebacks, subcontracting, cutbacks, and more authority for management. Second, once again the symbolic importance of federal labor relations was made clear. Just as the Kennedy executive order helped legitimize public sector collective bargaining in state and local governments, Reagan's union busting showed the public and governments throughout the nation that strikes could be broken and that a determined government could find a way to cope with work stoppages. Third, Reagan's handling of PATCO demonstrated the importance of the legal procedures that govern public sector collective bargaining. Collective bargaining can sometimes be lawless and chaotic, but it is always fundamentally rooted in a legal framework. Governmental employers, like their employees, may choose to overlook the law regulation collective bargaining when they deem it necessary or desirable, but they can also invoke it when it is to their advantage. Illegal strikes were frequently tolerated in the 1960s and early 1970s, but Reagan's message to PATCO was as clear as Coolidge's to Boston's finest—flaunt the law at your own peril.

League of Cities, the U.S. Conference of Mayors, and the National Association of Counties, distilled the arguments of both sides of the strike question.

In his view, the proponents of strikes have to deal with the following challenges:

1. There is no need to legalize strikes because most contracts are negotiated without the threat of a strike.
2. Granting the right to strike would considerably enhance the political power and lobbying abilities of unions. Given the voting power of organized public sector labor and its already formidable political strength, a grant of strike rights would place management in an unenvi-

able position in collective bargaining. This situation might be different if unions were willing to accept restrictions on their political activities.

3. The strike, at least on a prolonged basis, is a weapon of doubtful might. The employer stands to gain financially, at least in the short run, as taxes and other revenues come in even though services are not rendered. In addition, prolonged or exceedingly disruptive strikes may cause sentiment to shift away from the unions, thereby strengthening management's position at the bargaining table.

4. When strikes are called by such vital services as police and fire, the strike may take on an overkill character. The lost services cannot be purchased from a competitor. The whole community becomes a "hostage" for the union.

5. The strike is labor's counterpart to the lockout, but since the latter is inappropriate in the public sector, the former is also unnecessary and undesirable.

On the other hand, those who support prohibitions on the right to strike must also face some serious difficulties.

1. The right of workers in the private sector to strike has long been guaranteed. Those public workers who perform similar functions, such as selling liquor, driving buses, teaching, collecting garbage, and providing nursing, cannot justifiably or logically be treated differently and in a discriminatory fashion.

2. Prohibitions against strikes and court orders forcing public workers to stay on the job are not effective mechanisms for dealing with labor disputes. Fines and the imprisonment of labor leaders may solidify their tenure.

3. In the absence of a strike potential, what assurances will labor have that management will bargain in good faith?

4. Strikes already occur and they do not tend to create the destruction claimed by opponents of the strike.

5. By legalizing the strike, fewer resources will be spent by management in attempting to prevent them; more time and effort will then be placed on substantive issues.

6. Many states have already legalized the strike, even for such vital service employees as police and fire.

The logical path in dealing with strikes, whether legal or illegal, is to make them the least desirable alternative and one that is undertaken only after other possible means of settling disputes have been tried and found unsatisfactory. Experience (with PATCO as a leading example) has shown that strikes are no longer inevitably successful.

Once the contract has been put into effect, the parties must learn to live with it. This may be easier said than done because contract language is often complex and ambiguous. Some contracts run as long as 100 pages or more and present an awesome barrier to being understood fully by any public manager. Inevitably, contracts will use such ambiguous terms as *reasonable notice* of overtime assignments, *just and sufficient cause* for discipline, or *equitable distribution* of overtime, and what's reasonable, just, or equitable in the eyes of the manager may appear arbitrary or unfair to the employee. Somehow disputes over the meaning of the contract must be resolved. Typically this is accomplished through the creation of a grievance procedure.

Grievances generally arise within the realm of the contingent provisions of a contract. These are personnel provisions in which it is expected that change will commonly occur during the life of the contract. For example, discharges, layoffs, reductions in force, promotions, discipline, and transfers are among a contract's contingent provisions. The grievance occurs when the employee and/ or the union reasonably believe that the contract is being violated in a personnel action of this type.

Most public and private sector labor contracts now provide for a mechanism to resolve such grievances. Although there is considerable variation, at least three steps are common. First, the employee and a union steward bring the complaint to the attention of the supervisor. This step is informal and oral. It is hoped that the matter will be quickly resolved. If the grievance is not resolved, a second step may be taken. A formal written complaint is forwarded to the next highest management level. If there is still no resolution, the grievance may be advanced to the third stage, which is arbitration by a neutral third party. Since the collective bargaining contract exists between the employer and the union (not the individual employees), the union's agreement may be necessary before the employee can pursue a grievance. This is especially likely for steps 2 and 3. It should also be noted that in some cases there will be several levels of managerial review prior to permitting the grievance to go to binding arbitration.

Some grievances involve the rights of the union as an organization and the public employer. For example, these might arise in the context of granting released time to union stewards, union security arrangements, and the right of unions to disseminate information at the workplace. Such grievances are generally brought to management's attention and then, if not resolved, submitted to binding arbitration.

In passing, it should be noted that sometimes the grievance system is but one of several channels an employee can pursue in protesting a personnel action. In addition, there are typically statutorily based adverse action appeals systems and EEO complaint systems. Under some procedures the employee is given the choice of pursuing one of these to the exclusion of the others. In other cases, however, they may be used serially or even simultaneously. One of the reasons

Union Security Arrangements

1. *The union shop*—All employees must join and maintain membership in the union. New employees are given a period in which to join, usually 30 days. A number of states, including Alaska, Maine, Kentucky, Washington, and Vermont, have authorized the union shop for some categories of public employees. However, under the U.S. Supreme Court's reasoning in *Abood* v. *Detroit Board of Education* (1977), the constitutionality of this arrangement is dubious since it uses governmental authority to compel individuals to join an organization and can consequently be seen as an abridgement of freedom of association.

2. *The agency shop and fair share*—These arrangements do not require employees to join unions, but they do require them to pay "counterpart" or "fair-share" fees. These fees may be equivalent to the union dues or they may be smaller and intended to cover only those union activities *directly* related to collective bargaining and representing the employee. Such arrangements are not considered to violate the constitutional right of freedom of association. The District of Columbia, Washington, Michigan, Montana, Rhode Island, Connecticut, Vermont, New York, Oregon, North Dakota, Hawaii, Massachusetts, Minnesota, and California are some of the states that use one of these arrangements for certain categories of public employees.

3. *Maintenance of membership*—All employees who are members of a union must maintain their membership in it, but others need not join. States such as Pennsylvania and California use this arrangement for some employees.

4. *The dues checkoff*—This is normally a way of facilitating any of the above arrangements. The employer is authorized to deduct union dues or counterpart or fair-share fees from the employee's paycheck and remit them to the union. Unions value the checkoff highly because it assures them a steady flow of revenue and makes it much easier to collect fees. The union may be required to pay the employer for the checkoff service, but like the checkoff itself this is generally a subject for collective bargaining. Since the checkoff is so valued by unions, there are some jurisdictions that retaliate against unions for illegal strikes by eliminating the service.

for this is that the same personnel action may have several components. For instance, a minority employee may be demoted in violation of a labor contract's seniority clause (a grievance), but also due to prohibited discrimination (an EEO matter) and in violation of civil service rules (an adverse action appeal).

CONCLUSION

Collective bargaining is fundamentally different from most aspects of public personnel administration. It creates a format for determining what much of the content of personnel policy will be, especially at the state and local levels of government, where many unions have a relatively wide scope of bargaining. Much of that which was once established by personnel agencies, such as civil service commissions, is now subject to collective bargaining. In some jurisdictions, this is true of pay, position classification, and probation. Aspects bargaining is an alternative system and forum for setting personnel policy and establishing personnel procedures. It has thus led to claims—unsubstantiated at best—that it has undermined the merit system, yet these contentions continue to illustrate the policies that surround and dominate the field of labor relations in the public sector.

One last thing seems certain, however. A new era of labor relations has been ushered in under such new leaders as John Sweeney, current president of the AFL-CIO, who are determined to breathe new life into the union movement in this country. If successful, unions, both public and private, will become even more critical to human resources management and government performance.

APPENDIX: GLOSSARY OF FEDERAL SECTOR LABOR–MANAGEMENT RELATIONS TERMS*

ABROGATION TEST.   A test the **Federal Labor Relations Authority** applies in determining whether an arbitration award enforcing a contract provision affecting rights reserved to management is deficient. If the provision at issue is an "arrangement" for employees adversely affected by the exercise of those rights, an award enforcing such a provision will not be set aside unless it "abrogates" those rights—i.e., unless it leaves management no discretion at all.

ACCRETION.   When some employees are transferred to another employing entity whose employees are already represented by a union, the FLRA will often find that those employees have "accredit" to (i.e., become part of) the existing **unit** of the new employer, with the result that the transferred employees have a new **exclusive representative** along with a new employer.

---

* Taken from the U.S. Office of Personnel Management, Center for Partnership and Labor–Management Relations, in August 1998.

AGENCY SHOP. A requirement that all employees in the **unit** pay dues or fees to the union to defray the costs of providing representation.

AGREEMENT, NEGOTIATED. A collective bargaining agreement between the employer and the exclusive representative. A collective bargaining agreement must contain a negotiated grievance procedure.

AMENDMENT OF CERTIFICATION PETITION. That portion of the FLRA's multipurpose petition not involving a **question concerning representation** that may be filed at any time in which the petitioner asks the FLRA to amend the certification or recognition to, e.g., reflect changes in the names of the employer or the union.

APPROPRIATE ARRANGEMENT. One of three exceptions to management's rights. Under title 5, United States Code, section 7106(b)(3), a proposal that interferes with management's rights can nonetheless be negotiable if the proposal constitutes an ''arrangement'' for employees adversely affected by the exercise of a management right and if the interference with the mangement right isn't ''excessive'' (as determined by an ''**excessive interference**'' balancing test).

APPROPRIATE UNIT (BARGAINING UNIT). A grouping of employees that a union represents or seeks to represent and that the FLRA finds appropriate for **collective bargaining** purposes.

ARBITRATOR. An impartial third party to whom the parties to an agreement refer their disputes for resolution.
    Grievance arbitration. When the arbitrator interprets and applies the terms of the collective bargaining agreement—and/or, in the Federal sector, laws and regulations determining conditions of employment.
    Interest arbitration. When the arbitrator resolves bargaining impasses by dictating some of the terms of the collective bargaining agreement.

ASSIGN EMPLOYEES. A management right relating to the assignment of employees to positions, shifts, and locations. This right includes discretion to determine ''the personnel requirements of the work of the position, i.e., the qualifications and skills needed to do the work, as well as such job-related individual characteristics as judgment and reliability.'' It also includes discretion to determine the duration of the assignment.

ASSIGN WORK. A management right relating to the assignment of work to employees or positions. The right to assign work includes discretion to determine who is to perform the work; the kind; the amount of work to be performed; the manner in which it is to be performed, as well as when it is to be performed. It also includes ''[t]he right to determine the particular qualifications and skills needed to perform the work and to make judgments as to whether a particular employee meets those qualifications.''

AUTOMATIC RENEWAL CLAUSE.   Many, perhaps most, collective bargaining agreements in the Federal sector have a provision, usually located at the end of the agreement, stating that if neither party gives notice during the agreement's 15–60 day **open period** of its intent to reopen and renegotiate the agreement, the agreement will automatically renew itself for a period of x number of years.

BACK PAY.   Py awarded an employee for compensation lost due to an unjustified personnel action are governed by the requirements of the Back Pay Act, title 5, United States Code, section 5596.

BARGAINING (NEGOTIATING).   A ubiquitous process—sometimes informal and spontaneous, sometimes formal and deliberate—of offer and counteroffer whereby parties to the bargaining process try to reach agreement on the terms of exchange. Formal bargaining processes with associated rituals and bargaining routines vary, depending on their political, economic, and social context.

BARGAINING AGENT.   The union holding exclusive recognition for an **appropriate unit**.

BARGAINING IMPASSE (IMPASSE).   When the parties have reached a deadlock in negotiations they are said to have reached an impasse. The statute provides for assistance by **Federal Mediation and Conciliation Service** mediators and the **Federal Service Impasses Panel** to help the parties settle impasses.

BINDING ARBITRATION.   The law requires that collective bargaining agreements contain a negotiated grievance procedure that terminates in binding arbitration of unresolved grievances.

BUDGET.   A right reserved to management. The Authority has fashioned a two-prong test that it uses to determine whether a proposal interferes with an agency's right to determine its budget: namely, the proposal either has to prescribe particular programs, operations or amounts to be included in an agency's budget, or the agency can substantially demonstrate that the proposal would result in significant and unavoidable cost increases that are not offset by compensating benefits.

BYPASS.   Dealing directly with employees rather than with the **exclusive representative** regarding negotiable **conditions of employment** of bargaining **unit** employees. A bypass is a violation of the **Federal Service Labor–Management Relations Statute**.

CARVEOUT.   An attempt, usually unsuccessful under the **Federal Service**

Labor–Management Relations Statute because it fosters unit fragmentation, to carve out (or sever)—usually along occupational lines (firefighters, nurses)—a subgroup of employees in an existing bargaining **unit** in order to establish a separate, more homogenous unit with a different union as **exclusive representative**.

CERTIFICATION. The FLRA's determination of the results of an election or the status of a union as the **exclusive representative** of all the employees in an appropriate unit.

CERTIFICATION BAR. One-year period after a union is certified as the **exclusive representative** for a unit during which petitions by rival unions or employees seeking to replace or remove the incumbent union will be considered untimely. The bar is designed to give the certified union an opportunity to negotiate a substantive agreement, after which the contract can become a bar, except during the contract's 15–60 day **open period**, to a representation petition.

CHIEF STEWARD. A union official who assists and guides shop stewards. The roles he or she plays within the union are determined by the union. The roles he or she plays in administering the contract are determined by the contract. For example, the **negotiated grievance procedure** may provide that the chief steward becomes the union representative if the grievance reaches a certain step in the grievance procedure.

CLARIFICATION OF UNIT PETITION. That portion of the FLRA's multi-purpose petition *not* involving a **question concerning representation** that may be filed at any time in which the petitioner (union or management) asks the FLRA to determine the bargianing unit status of various employees—i.e., to determine whether they are management officials, supervisors, employees engaged in non-clerical personnel work, or confidential employees, and therefore excluded from the unit (and from the coverage of the collective bargaining agreement applicable to the unit and its negotiated grievance procedure).

COLLECTIVE BARGAINING. Literally, bargaining between and/or among representatives of collectivities (thus involving internal as well as external bargaining); but by custom the expression refers to bargaining between labor organizations and employers.

CIVIL SERVICE REFORM ACT OF 1978 (CSRA). Legislation enacted in October 1978 for the purpose of improving the civil service. It includes the **Federal Service Labor–Management Relations Statute** (FSLMRS), Chapter 71 of title 5 of the United States Code.

CLASSIFICATION ACT EMPLOYEES. Federal employees—typically professional, administrative, technical, and clerical employees (i.e., ''white collar'' employees)—sometimes referred to as ''General Schedule'' employees, to distinguish them from Federal Wage System (blue collar, Wage Grade) employees.

COMPELLING NEED. Test used to determine whether a discretionary agency regulation that doesn't involve the exercise of management's is a valid limitation on the **scope of bargaining**. There are three ''illustrative criteria'' of compelling need: (1) the regulation is essential to the effective and efficient accomplishment of the mission of the agency, (2) the regulation is necessary to insure the maintenance of basic merit principles, and (3) the regulation implements a mandate of law or other authority (e.g., a regulation) in an essentially nondiscretionary manner.

CONFIDENTIAL EMPLOYEE. An employee who acts in a confidential capacity with respect to an individual who formulates or effectuates management policies in the field of labor–management relations. Confidential employees must be excluded from bargaining units.

CONDITIONS OF EMPLOYMENT (COE). Under title 5, United States Code, section 7103(a)(14), conditions of employment ''means personnel policies, practices, and matters, whether established by rule, regulation, or otherwise [e.g., by custom or practice], affecting working conditions, except that such term does not include policies, practices, and matters—(A) relating to political activities prohibited under subchapter III of chapter 73 of this title; (B) relating to the classification of any positions; or (C) to the extent such matters are *specifically provided for by Federal statute*.'' [Emphasis added.]

CONSULTATION. To be distinguished from **negotiation**. The FSLMRS provides for two types of consultation: between qualifying unions and agencies concerning agency-wide regulations and qualifying unions and those agencies issuing Governmentwide regulations.

CONTRACT BAR. The incumbent union is protected from challenge by a rival union if there is an agreement in effect having a term of not more than three years, except during the agreement's **open period**''—i.e., 15 to 60 days prior to the expiration of the agreement.

CONTRACTING OUT. A right reserved to management that includes the right to determine what criteria management will use to determine whether or not to contract out agency work.

''COVERED BY'' DOCTRINE. A doctrine under which an agency does not have to engage in **midterm bargaining** on particular matters because those matters are already ''covered by'' the existing agreement.

DECERTIFICATION. The FLRA's withdrawal of a union's **exclusive recog-**

nition because the union no longer qualifies for such recognition, usually because it has lost a representational election.

DECERTIFICATION PETITION. A petition filed by employees in an existing unit (or an individual acting on their behalf) asking that an election be held to give unit employees an opportunity to end the incumbent union's exclusive recognition. Such a petition must be accompanied by a 30 per cent showing of interest and be timely filed (i.e., not barred by election, certification or contact bars).

DIRECT EMPLOYEES. The Authority has defined this right to include discretion "to supervise and guide [employees] . . . in the performance of their duties on the job." The right to direct, *by itself*, rarely is used as the basis for finding a proposal nonnegotiable. However, when combined with the right to assign work, it is the basis for finding proposals establishing performance standards nonnegotiable.

DISCIPLINE. A right reserved to management that the FLRA has said includes the right "to investigate to determine whether discipline is justified." It also "encompasses the use of the evidence obtained during the investigation."

DUES WITHHOLDING (CHECKOFF). Dues withholding services provided by the agency to unions that win exclusive recognition or dues withholding recognition. If the former, the services must be provided without charge to the union. Employee dues assignments must be voluntary (no union or agency shop arrangements permitted under the **Federal Service Labor–Management Relations Statute**) and may not be revoked except at yearly intervals, but must be terminated when the agreement ceases to be applicable to the employee or when the employee is expelled from membership in the union.

DUES WITHHOLDING RECOGNITION. A very limited form of recognition, under which a union that can show that it has 10 per cent of employees in an appropriate unit as members can qualify for the right only to negotiate a dues deduction arrangement. Such recognition becomes null and void as soon as a union is certified as the **exclusive representative** of the unit.

DUTY TO BARGAIN. Broadly conceived, it refers to both (1) the *circumstances* under which there is a duty to give notice and, upon request, engage in bargaining and (2) the *negotiability* of specific proposals. Disputes over the former usually are processed through the Authority's **unfair labor practice procedure** and frequently involve make-whole and *status quo ante* remedies. Disputes over the latter usually are processed through the Authority's no-fault **negotiability** procedure in which the Authority determines whether or not there is a duty to bargain on the proposal at issue.

ELECTION AGREEMENT.   Agreement entered into by the agency and the union(s) competing for exclusive recognition dealing with campaign procedures, election observers, date and hours of election, challenge ballot procedures, mail balloting (if used), position on the ballot, payroll period for voter eligibility, and the like. Such an agreement is subject to approval by the appropriate FLRA Regional Director.

ELECTION AGREEMENT.   Agreement entered into by the agency and the union(s) competing for exclusive recognition dealing with campaign procedures, election observers, date and hours of election, challenge ballot procedures, mail balloting (if used), position on the ballot, payroll period for voter eligibility, and the like. Such an agreement is subject to approval by the appropriate FLRA Regional Director.

ELECTION BAR.   One-year period after the FLRA has conducted a secret-ballot election for a unit of employees, where the election did not lead to the certification of a union as exclusive representative. During this one-year period the FLRA will not consider any representation petitions for that unit or any subdivisions thereof.

EMPLOYEE.   The term "employee includes an individual "employed in an agency" or "whose employment in an agency has ceased because of any unfair labor practice," but does not include supervisors and management officials or anyone who participates in a strike or members of the uniformed services or employees in the Foreign Service or aliens occupying positions outside the United States.

EQUIVALENT STATUS.   Status given a union challenging the incumbent union that entitles it to roughly equivalent access during the period preceding an election to facilities and services (bulletin boards, internal mail services, etc.) as that enjoyed by the incumbent union.

EXCEPTIONS TO ARBITRATION AWARDS.   A claim that an arbitration award is deficient "on . . . grounds similar to those applied by Federal courts in private sector labor–management relations," or because it violates law, rule or regulation. Some of the "grounds similar to those applied by Federal courts" are: the award doesn't draw its essence from the agreement, the award is based on a nonfact, the arbitrator didn't conduct a fair hearing, or the arbitrator exceeded his/her authority.

EXCLUSIVE RECOGNITION.   Under the **Federal Service Labor–Management Relations Statute**, exclusive recognition is normally obtained by a union as a result of receiving a majority of votes cast in a representational election. The rights a union is accorded as a result of being certified as the **exclusive representative** of the employees in a bargaining unit include, among other things, the right to *negotiate* bargainable aspects of the conditions of employment of bargaining unit employees, to be afforded an opportunity to be present at *formal discussions*, to free *checkoff* arrangements and, at the request of the employee, to be present at *Weingarten* examinations.

EXCLUSIVE REPRESENTATIVE. The union that is certified as the exclusive representative of a unit of employees either by virtue of having won a representation election or because it had been recognized as the exclusive representative before passage of the CSRA. . . . A union holding exclusive recognition is sometimes referred to as the exclusive bargaining agent of the unit.

EXTERNAL LIMITATIONS ON THE EXERCISE OF MANAGEMENT'S RIGHTS. Discretion reserved to management isn't unfettered. Quite apart from any limitations that may be found in the collective bargaining agreement (such as an **appropriate arrangement** provision), its discretion must also be exercised in accordance with the laws and regulations that set limitations on management discretion. Only those external limitations on the exercise of certain rights can be enforced by the union under the **negotiated grievance procedure**.

FAIR REPRESENTATION, DUTY OF. The union's duty to represent the interests of all unit employees without regard to union membership.

FEDERAL LABOR RELATIONS AUTHORITY (FLRA, AUTHORITY). The independent agency responsible for administering the **Federal Service Labor–Management Relations Statute** (FSLMRS). As such, it decides, among other things, representation issues (e.g., the bargaining **unit** status of certain employees), **unfair labor practices** (violations of any of the provisions of the FSLMRS), **negotiability disputes** (i.e., **scope of bargaining** issues), **exceptions to arbitration awards**, as well as resolve disputes over consultation rights regarding agency-wide and Governmentwide regulations.
For more information on the FLRA, see its webpage at http://www.flra.gov/

FEDERAL MEDIATION AND CONCILIATION SERVICE (FMCS). An independent agency that provides mediators to assist the parties in negotiations. Although the bulk of its work is in the private sector, it also provides it services to the Federal sector. FMCS also maintains a roster of qualified private arbitrators, panels of which are referred to the parties upon joint request. See **MEDIATION**.
For more information on the FMCS, see http://www.flra.gov/

FEDERAL SERVICE IMPASSES PANEL (FSIP or Panel). An entity within the FLRA that resolves bargaining impasses, chiefly by ordering the parties to adopt certain contractual provisions relating to the conditions of employment of unit employees. The Panel uses many procedures for resolving impasses, including factfinding, med-arb, final-offer interest arbitration, either by the Panel, individual members of the Panel, the Panel's staff, or by ordering the parties to refer their impasse to an agreed-upon private arbitrator who is to provide services. The Panel is empowered to "take whatever action is necessary and not inconsistent with [the Federal Service Labor–Management Relations Statute] to resolve the impasse."

For more information on FSIP, see www.flra.gov/20.html

FEDERAL SERVICE LABOR-MANAGEMENT RELATIONS STATUTE (FSLMRS). Title 5, United States Code, sections 7101–7135. The statute can be downloaded from http://www.law.cornell.edu/uscode/5/ch71.html.

FINAL-OFFER INTEREST ARBITRATION. A technique for resolving bargaining impasses in which the arbitrator is forced to choose among the final positions of the parties—rather than order adoption of some intermediate position (i.e., "split the difference"). It can apply to individual items or "packages" of items. The theory is that each party, expecting that the interest arbitrator will pick the most reasonable of the two final offers, will have an incentive to move closer to the position of the other party in order to increase the odds that the arbitrator will select its final offer as the more reasonable of the two. This in turn narrows the gap between the parties. If the gap is narrow enough, it can be bridged by the parties themselves (by, e.g., splitting the difference).

FORMAL DISCUSSION. Under title 5, United States Code, section 7114(a)(2)(A), the **exclusive representative** must be given an opportunity to be represented at "any formal discussion between one or more representatives of the agency and one or more employees in the unit or their representatives concerning any *grievance* or any personnel policy or practices or other *general condition of employment*." [Italics added.]

FREE SPEECH. Under title 5, United States Code, section 7116(e), the expression of personal views or opinions, even if critical of the union, is not an **unfair labor practice** if such expression is not made in the context of a representational election and if it "contains no threat of reprisal or force or promise of benefit or was not made under coercive conditions." During the conduct of an election, however, management officials must be neutral. This limited right of free speech applies to agency representatives.

GENERAL COUNSEL. The General Counsel of the **Federal Labor Relations Authority** investigates **unfair labor practice** (ULP) *charges* and files and prosecutes ULP *complaints*. He/she also supervises the Authority's Regional Directors who, in turn, have been delegated authority by the FLRA to process representation petitioners.

GOOD FAITH BARGAINING. A statutory duty to approach negotiations with a sincere resolve to reach a collective bargaining agreement, to be represented by properly authorized representatives who are prepared to discuss and negotiate on any **condition of employment**, to meet at reasonable times and places as frequently as may be necessary and to avoid unnecessary delays, and, in the case of the agency, to furnish upon request data necessary to negotiation.

GRIEVANCE. Under title 5, United States Code, section 7103(a)(9), a grievance "means any complaint—(A) by an employee concerning any matter relating to the employment of the employee; (B) by any labor organization concerning any matter relating to the employment of any employee; or (C) by an employee, labor organization, or agency concerning—(i) the effect or interpretation, or a claim of breach, of a collective bargaining agreement; or (ii) any claimed violation, misinterpretation, or misapplication of any law, rule, or regulation affecting conditions of employment."

GRIEVANCE PROCEDURE. A systematic procedure, devised by the parties to the agreement, by which a grievance moves from one level of authority to the next higher level until it is settled, withdrawn, or referred to arbitration. Under title 5, United States Code, section 7121, a collective bargaining agreement must contain a grievance procedure terminating in final and binding arbitration. Apart from matters that must by statute be excluded (such as grievances relating to retirement, health and life insurance and the classification of positions), the scope of the grievance procedure is to be negotiated by deciding what matters are to be excluded from an otherwise "full scope" procedure—i.e., a procedure that covers all the matters mentioned in the statutory definition of "grievance."

HIRE EMPLOYEES. A right reserved to management. The Authority has said that "the probationary period, including summary termination, constitutes an essential element of an agency's right to hire under [title 5, United States Code,] section 7106(a)(2)(A)."
See **SELECT** for a discussion of the much more frequently utilized right of management, in filling positions, to make selections for appointments from any appropriate source. The relationship between the right to hire and the right to select is still unclear.

I&I (IMPACT AND IMPLEMENTATION) BARGAINING. Even where the decision to change conditions of employment of unit employees is protected by management's rights, there is a duty to notify the union and, upon request, bargain on **procedures** that management will follow in implementing its protected decision as well as on **appropriate arrangements** for employees expected to be adversely affected by the decision. Such bargaining is commonly referred to as "impact and implementation," or "I&I" bargaining, which is the commonest variety of **midterm bargaining**.

INTEREST.   In **interest-based bargaining**, the concerns, needs, or desires behind an issue: *why* the issue is being raised.

INTEREST ARBITRATION.   The arbitrator, instead of interpreting and applying the terms of an agreement to decide a grievance, determines what provisions the parties are to have in their collective bargaining agreement.

INTEREST-BASED BARGAINING (IBB).   A bargaining technique in which the parties start with (or at least focus on) interests rather than proposals; agree on criteria of acceptability that will be used to evaluate alternatives; generate several alternatives that are consistent with their interests; and apply the agreed-upon acceptability criteria to the alternatives so generated in order to arrive at mutually acceptable contract provisions. The success of the technique depends, in large measure, on mutual trust and a willingness to share information. But even where this is lacking, the technique, with its focus on interests and on developing alternatives, tends to make the parties more flexible and open to alternative solutions and thus increases the likelihood of agreement.

INTERVENTION/INTERVENOR.   The action taken by a competing labor organization (intervenor) to place itself as a contender on the ballot for a recognition election originally initiated by another union (petitioner). Non-incumbent intervenors need only produce a 10 per cent showing of interest to be included on the ballot.

INVESTIGATORY EXAMINATION.   See **WEINGARTEN RIGHT**.

LABOR ORGANIZATION.   A uniont—i.e., an organization composed in whole or in part of employees, in which employees participate and pay dues, and which has as a purpose the dealing with an agency concerning grievances and conditions of employment.

LAYOFF EMPLOYEES.   Right reserved to management by title 5, United States Code, section 7106(a)(2)(A).

MANAGEMENT OFFICIAL.   An individual who formulates, determines, or influences the policies of the agency. Such individuals are excluded from **appropriate units**.

MANAGEMENT RIGHTS.   Refers to types of discretion reserved to management officials by statute.

- **Core rights**.   Consists of the rights ''to determine the mission, budget, organization, number of employees, and internal security practices of the agency.''
- **Operational rights**.   Consists of the rights to hire, assign, direct, layoff, and retain employees in the agency, or to suspend, remove, reduce

in grade or pay, or take other disciplinary action against such employees; to assign work, to make determinations with respect to contracting out, and to determine the personnel by which agency operations shall be conducted; with respect to filling positions, to make selections for appointments from among properly ranked and certified candidates for promotion; or any other appropriate source; and to take whatever actions may be necessary to carry out the agency mission during emergencies.

- **Three exceptions.** The three title 5, United States Code, section 7106(b) exceptions to the above involve (1) **title 5, United States Code, section 7106(b)(1) permissive subjects** of bargaining (e.g., staffing patterns, technology) on which, under the statute, agencies can elect to bargain, (2) **procedures** management will follow in exercising its reserved rights, and (C) **appropriate arrangements** for employees adversely affected by the exercise of management rights.

  1. **"Permissive" subjects exception.** This exemption to management's rights "staffing patterns"—i.e., with "the numbers, types, and grades of employees or positions assigned to any organizational subdivision, work project, or tour of duty" and with "the technology, methods, and means of performing work." Under the statute such matters are, moreover, negotiable "at the election of the agency" even if the proposal also directly interferes with the exercise of a title 5, United States Code, section 7106(a) right.
  2. **Procedural "exception."** Title 5, United States Code, section 7106(b)(2), dealing with procedures, really isn't an exception to management's rights as the Authority has held that a proposed "procedure" that "directly interferes" with a management right is not a procedure within the meaning of title 5, United States Code, section 7106(b)(2).
  3. **Appropriate arrangement exception.** Title 5, United States Code, section 7106(b)(3) applies only if the proposal is intended to ameliorate the adverse effects of the exercise of a management right. Where such is the interest of the proposal, the Authority applies a balancing test in which it weighs the extent to which it interferes with the management right and determines whether or not the specific proposal "excessively" interferes with management rights. If the interference is "excessive," the proposal isn't an "appropriate arrangement" and therefore is nonnegotiable. If otherwise, the proposal is a negotiable appropriate arrangement, even though it interferes with management's rights.

  To qualify as an "arrangement" to which it would be proper to apply the excessive interference balancing test, the proposal has to be "tailored" so that it applies only to those employees who would be adversely affected by the proposed management decision.

MEDIATION.   Use of a third party, usually a neutral without authority to impose a settlement, to assist the parties to reach agreement. Mediation techniques vary, but one common practice is for the labor mediator to separate the parties (in order to control communications) and meet with them separately and, in effect, engage in interest-based bargaining with them. Because the mediator usually is a neutral who cannot impose a settlement and because he or she is expected to keep confidences, each party is more willing to be open with the mediator than with the other party (or with an interest arbitrator). Because of this greater openness, the mediator often is able to see areas of possible agreement that the parties are unable to see in direct, unmediated, negotiations.

MED-ARB (mediation followed by interest arbitration).   A process in which a neutral with authority to impose (or to recommend the imposition of) a settlement, first resorts to mediation techniques in an attempt to get the parties to voluntarily agree on unsettled matters, but who can later impose a settlement if mediation fails. The theory behind it is that the parties will be more receptive to the med-arb's suggestions for settlement if they know that the med-arb has authority to impose a settlement.

MIDTERM BARGAINING.   Literally, all bargaining that takes place during the life of the contract. Usually contrasted with term bargaining—i.e., with the renegotiation of an expired (or expiring) contract. Midterm bargaining includes **I&I bargaining, union-initiated midterm bargaining on new matters**; and bargaining pursuant to a **reopener** clause. It excludes matters that are already "**covered by**" the term agreement.

MISSION OF THE AGENCY.   A right reserved to management by title 5, United States Code, section 7106(a)(1). Although illustrative case law on this particular right is meager, it is generally recognized that the right encompasses the determination of the products and services of an agency.

NATIONAL CONSULTATION RIGHTS (NCR).   A union accorded national consultation rights is entitled to be consulted on *agency-wide* regulations before they are promulgated. NCR is to be distinguished from consultation rights with respect to *Governmentwide* regulations, under which a union accorded such recognition must be consulted on proposed Governmentwide regulations before they are promulgated.

NEGOTIABILITY DISPUTES.   Disputes over whether a proposal is nonnegotiable because (a) it is inconsistent with laws, rules, and regulations establishing conditions of employment and/or (b) it interferes with the exercise of rights reserved to management. Negotiability disputes normally are processed under the FLRA's "no fault" negotiability procedures.

NEGOTIATED GRIEVANCE PROCEDURE (NGP). A collective bargaining agreement (CBA) must contain a grievance procedure terminating in final and binding arbitration. The NGP, with a few exceptions involving statutory alternatives (e.g., adverse and performance-based actions), is the exclusive administrative procedure for grievances falling within its coverage. Apart from the matters excluded from the coverage of the NGP by statute—e.g., retirement, life and health insurance, classification of positions—the NGP covers those matters specified in the definition of grievance in title 5, United States Code, section 7103(a)(9), minus any of those matters that teh parties agree to exclude from the NGP.

NUMBER OF EMPLOYEES OF AN AGENCY. A right reserved to management by title 5, United States Code, section 7106(a)(1). There have been no FLRA decisions in which a proposal has been found nonnegotiable because it interfered with this right.

OFFICIAL TIME. At one time treated as a term of art created by title 5, United States Code, section 7131, involving paid time for employees serving as union representatives. However, the Authority has said that section 7131(d) does not preclude parties to a collective bargaining agreement from agreeing to provide official time for other matters; that is, matters other than those relating to labor–management relations activities.

Union negotiators (no more than the number of management negotiators) who also are unit employees are statutorily entitled to official time to negotiate agreements. Official time may not, however, be used to perform internal union business. Title 5, United States Code, section 7131(d) allows the parties to negotiate the amount of official time that shall be granted to specified union representatives for the performance of specified representational functions.

OPEN PERIOD. The 45-day period (15–60 days prior to expiration of agreement) when the union holding exclusive recognition is subject to challenge by a rival union or by unit employees who no longer want to be represented by the union. The open period is an exception to the **contract bar** rule.

ORGANIZATION. A right reserved to management. According to the FLRA, this right encompasses an agency's authority to determine its administrative and functional structure, including the relationship of personnel through lines of control and the distribution of responsibilities for delegated and assigned duties. That is, the right includes the authority to determine how the agency will structure itself to accomplish its mission and functions.

PARTICULARIZED NEED. The Authority's analytical approach in dealing with union requests for information under title 5, United States Code, section 7114(b)(4). Under this approach, the union must establish a "particularized need" for the information and the agency must assert any countervailing interests. The Authority then balances teh one against the other to determine whether a refusal to provide information is a **unfair labor practice**.

PARTNERSHIP.   A form of employee participation established pursuant to Executive Order 12871 in which the parties are expected to deal with matters relating to improving *the performance of the agency* in a non-adversarial, non-litigious manner. The scope of partnership deliberations are broader than those of collective bargaining in that they usually include, e.g., deliberations over the conditions of employment of non-bargaining unit employees. Partnership deliberations also include deliberations over staffing patterns, technology, methods and means—matters integral to improving *agency* performance, which is the overriding purpose of the Order.

PAST PRACTICE (ESTABLISHED PRACTICE).   Existing practices sanctioned by use and acceptance, that are not specifically included in the collective bargaining agreement. Arbitrators use evidence of past practices to interpret ambiguous contract language. In addition, past practices can be enforced under the **negotiated grievance procedure** because they are considered part of the agreement. To qualify as an enforceable established practice, the practice has to be legal, in effect for a certain period, and known and sanctioned by management.

PERMISSIVE SUBJECTS OF BARGAINING.   There are two types of proposals dealing with so-called "permissive subjects of bargaining": proposals dealing with (1) matters covered by title 5, United States Code, section 7106(b)(1)—i.e., with staffing patterns, technology, and methods and means of performing the agency's work, and (2) matters that are not conditions of employment of bargaining unit employees. Regarding the former, it should be noted that although an agency can "elect" not to bargain on a (b)(1) matter, the President has directed heads of agencies to instruct agency management to bargain on such matters in section 2(d) of Executive Order 12871. Regarding the latter, it should be kept in mind that, apart from the statutory exclusions from the definition of **condition of employment** found in title 5, United States Code, section 7103(a)(14), a matter may be found not be a condition of employment because (1) it deals with the conditions of employment of *nonunit employees* (e.g., a proposed procedure for filling supervisory vacancies) or (2) there is no direct connection between the matter dealt with by the proposal and the work situation or employment relationship of bargaining unit employees (e.g., a proposal authorizing unit employees to hunt on a military base when off duty). Regardless of type, once agreement is reached on a permissive subject of bargaining, that agreement cannot be disapproved by the agency head, and is enforceable under the negotiated grievance procedure.

QUESTION CONCERNING REPRESENTATION (QCR). Refers to a petition in which a union seeks to be the **exclusive representative** of an **appropriate unit** of employees, or in which employees in an existing unit want to decertify the incumbent union. The filing of such a petition is said to raise a question concerning representation—i.e., whether, and by whom, unit employees are to be represented. Such petitions are distinguished from petitions seeking to clarify the composition of existing units (e.g., whether certain individuals are in or out of the unit) or to amend the names of the parties to the exclusive bargaining relationship.

REOPENER CLAUSE. Provisions in the CBA specifying the conditions under which one or either party can reopen for renegotiation the agreement or designated parts of the agreement. Although some agreements provide for mutual consent reopeners, such reopeners are unnecessary as the parties can of course agree to reopen and renegotiate their agreement at any time, notwithstanding the contents of the agreement. The purpose of a reopener is to enable one party to *compel* the other party to renegotiate the provisions covered by the reopener.

REPRESENTATION ELECTION. Secret-ballot election to determine whether the employees in an appropriate unit shall have a union as their **EXCLUSIVE REPRESENTATIVE**.

REPRESENTATIONAL FUNCTIONS. Activities performed by union representatives on behalf of the employees for whom the union is the **exclusive representative** regarding their conditions of employment. It includes, among other things, negotiating and policing the terms of the agreement, attending partnership council meetings, being present at **formal discussions** and, upon employee request, *Weingarten* **examinations**.

REPRESENTATION ISSUES. Issues related to how a union gains or loses **exclusive recognition** for a bargaining unit, determining whether a proposed unit of employees is appropriate for the purposes of exclusive recognition, and determining the unit status of various employees.

REPUDIATION OF AGREEMENT. Framework developed by the FLRA to determine whether (1) the breach of the agreement was clear and patent and (2) the provision breached went to the heart of the agreement.

RETAIN EMPLOYEES. A right reserved to management. Although the rights to layoff and retain appear to be opposite sides of the same coin, the FLRA rarely mentions the right to retain when invoking the right to layoff to find nonnegotiable proposals dealing with RIFs and furloughs.

SCOPE OF BARGAINING.   Matters about which the parties can negotiate.

SELECT (WITH RESPECT TO FILLING POSITIONS).   The statute reserves to management the right to make selections for appointments from any appropriate source. The right to select includes discretion to determine what knowledge, skills and abilities are necessary for successful performance in the position to be filled, as well as to determine which candidates possess these qualifications.

SHOWING OF INTEREST (SOI).   The required evidence of employee interest supporting a representation petition. The SOI is 30 per cent for a petition seeking exclusive recognition; 10 per cent to intervene in the selection; and 10 per cent when petitioning for dues allotment recognition. Evidence of such a showing can consist of, e.g., signed and dated authorization cards or petitions.

STAFFING PATTERNS.   A short-hand expression used to refer to title 5, United States Code, section 7106(b)(1)'s long-winded reference to "the numbers, types, and grades of employees or positions assigned to any organizational subdivision, work project, or tour of duty." Under the statute, agencies can elect not to bargain on such matters. However, under Executive Order 12871, the President has directed agencies to bargain on such matters.

STANDARDS OF CONDUCT FOR LABOR ORGANIZATIONS.   Standards regarding internal democratic practices, fiscal responsibility, and procedures to which a union must adhere to qualify for recognition. The Department of Labor has responsibility for making known and enforcing standards of conduct for unions in the Federal and private sectors.

STEWARD.   Union representative to whom the union assigns various representational functions, such as investigating and processing grievances.

SUCCESSORSHIP.   Where, as the result of a reorganization, a portion of an existing unit is transferred to a gaining employer, the latter will be found to be the successor employer (thus inheriting, along with the employees, the **exclusive representative** of those employees and the collective bargaining agreement that applied to those employees) if: (a) the post-transfer unit is appropriate, (b) the transferred bargaining unit employees are a majority in the post-transfer unit, (c) the gaining employer has "substantially" the same mission as the losing employer, (d) the transferred employees perform "substantially" the same duties under "substantially" similar working conditions in the gaining entity, and (e) it is not demonstrated that an election is necessary to determine representation.

SUPERVISOR.   Under title 5, United States Code, section 7103(a)(1), a supervisor is "an individual employed by an agency having authority in the interest of the agency to hire, direct, assign, promote, reward, transfer, furlough, layoff, recall, suspend, discipline, or remove employees, to adjust their grievances, or to effectively recommend such action, if the exercise of the authority is not merely routine or clerical in nature but requires the consistent exercise of independent judgment, except that, with respect to any unit which includes firefighters or nurses, the term 'supervisor' includes only those individuals who devote a preponderance of their employment time to exercising such authority.'' The individual need exercise only one of the indicia of supervisory authority, not a majority of them, to qualify as a supervisor for the purposes of the statute, provided it involves the consistent exercise of independent judgment.

UNFAIR LABOR PRACTICE (ULP). A violation of any of the provisions of the Federal Service Labor–Management Relations Statute. It is a term of art that is narrower in scope than the misleading adjective ''unfair'' suggests. ULP *charges* are filed with the Authority by an individual, a union, or an employer. They are investigated by the General Counsel who issues a ULP *complaint* if the General Counsel concludes the charge(s) have merit, and who prosecutes the matter before an Administrative Law Judge in a factfinding hearing and before the Authority, which decides the matter.

The most common agency ULPs are **duty-to-bargain** ULPs (usually a failure to give the union notice of proposed changes in conditions of employment and/or engage in impact and implementation bargaining), **formal discussion** ULPs, *Weingarten* ULPs, and failure-to-provide-**information** ULPs. The most common ULP committed by a union is a failure to fairly represent (see **fair representation**) all unit members without regard to union membership.

UNION. A labor organization ''composed in whole or in part of employees, in which employees participate and pay dues, and which has as a purpose the dealing with an agency concerning grievances and conditions of employment.''

UNION-INITIATED MIDTERM BARGAINING ON NEW MATTERS. Absent a bargaining waiver, the union has the right to initiate, during the life of the existing agreement, bargaining on matters not **''covered by''** the agreement. There is a split in the circuits, which the Supreme Court has agreed to resolve, regarding this statutory right, with the D.C. Circuit holding that the union has such a right (see **NTEU v. FLRA**, 810 F.2d 295 (D.C. Cir. 1987), and the Fourth Circuit holding that it does not (see *SSA v. FLRA*, 956 F.2d 1280 (4th Cir. 1992). Also see *Dept. of Energy v. FLRA*, Nos. 95-2949 and -3113 (4th Cir. Feb. 13, 1997), where the 4th Circuit went further and held that the FSLMRS *prohibits* such bargaining: consequently, such a right could not be established by collective bargaining agreement.

UNIT DETERMINATION ELECTION. When (a) several petitioners seek to represent different parts of an agency, (b) the proposed units overlap, and (c) the FLRA finds that more than one of the proposed units are appropriate, it lets the employees vote for units as well as unions.

WEINGARTEN **RIGHT**. Under title 5, United States Code, section 7114(a)(2)(B), an employee being examined in an investigation (an investigatory examination or interview) is entitled to union representation if the examination is conducted by a representative of the agency, the employee reasonably believes that the examination may result in disciplinary action, and the employees asks for representation. Such examinations are called *Weingarten* examinations because Congress, in establishing this right, specifically referred to the private sector case establishing such a right.

BIBLIOGRAPHY

Abood v. *Detroit Board of Education*, 431 U.S. 209 (1977).

Ban, Carolyn. "Unions, Management and the NPR," in Donald F. Kettl and John DiIulio Jr. (eds.), *Inside the Reinvention Machine: Appraising Governmental Reform*. Washington, D.C.: Brookings Institution, 1995.

Douglas, Joel M. "Public Sector Unionism: New Approaches—New Strategies," in Carolyn Ban and Norma Riccucci (eds.), *Public Personnel Management—Current Concerns, Future Challenges*. White Plains, N.Y.: Longman Press, 1991.

Excellence in Public Service. Washington, D.C.: Public Employee Department, AFL-CIO, 1994.

Gore, Al. The Report of the National Performance Review. *Creating a Government That Works Better and Costs Less*. Washington, D.C.: U.S. Government Printing Office, 1993.

Hill, Herbert. *Black Labor and the American Legal System*. Madison: University of Wisconsin Press, 1985.

Kearney, Richard C. "Unions in Government: Where Do They Go From Here?" in Steven W. Hays and Richard C. Kearney (eds.), *Public Personnel Administration: Problems and Prospects*, 3rd ed. Englewood Cliffs, N.J.: Prentice-Hall, 1995.

Kearney, Richard C., ed. "Public Sector Labor Relations," symposium, *Review of Public Personnel Administration* (summer 1993).

Kearney, Richard C. *Labor Relations in the Public Sector*, 2nd ed. New York: Marcel Dekker, 1992.

Kearney, Richard C. and Steven W. Hays. "Labor–Management Relations and Participative Decision Making: Toward a New Paradigm," *Public Administration Review*, vol. 54 (January/February 1994), pp. 44–51.

Klinger, Donald E. "Public Sector Collective Bargaining: Is the Glass Half-Full, Half Empty, or Broke?" *Review of Public Personnel Administration* (summer 1993), pp. 19–28.

Lehnert v. *Ferris Faculty Assn.*, 500 U.S. 507 (1991).

Masters, Marick F. and Robert Atkin. "Bargaining, Financial and Political Bases of Federal Sector Unions," *Review of Public Personnel Administration*, vol. 15 (winter 1995), pp. 5–23.

Printz v. *United States*, 138 L Ed. 2d 914 (1997).

Reeves, T. Zane. "Labor–Management Partnership in the Public Sector," in Carolyn Ban and Norma M. Riccucci (eds.), *Public Personnel Management: Current Concerns, Future Challenges*. New York: Longman, 1997, pp. 173–186.

Riccucci, Norma M. *Women, Minorities and Unions in the Public Sector*. Westport, Conn.: Greenwood Press, 1990.

Rosenbloom, David H. and Jay M. Shafritz. *Essentials of Labor Relations*. Englewood Cliffs, N.J.: Reston/Prentice Hall, 1985.

Steiber, Jack. *Public Employee Unionism: Structure, Growth Policy*. Washington, D.C.: Brookings Institution, 1973.

Sulzner, George T. "New Roles, New Strategies: Reinventing the Public Union," in Carolyn Ban and Norma M. Riccucci (eds.), *Public Personnel Management: Current Concerns, Future Challenges*. New York: Longman, 1997, pp. 157–172.

Tobias, Robert M. "Federal Employee Unions and the Human Resource Management Function," in Stephen E. Condrey (ed.), *Handbook of Human Resource Management in Government*. San Francisco: Jossey-Bass, 1998, pp. 258–275.

Working Together for Public Service. Washington, D.C.: U.S. Department of Labor, May 1996.

13

Employee Relations

PROLOGUE: ARE PUBLIC SECTOR EMPLOYEES AT RISK?

In December 1997 a former employee of Caltrans, the California state department of transportation, opened fire with an assault rifle at a maintenance facility in Orange County where he had worked. Before being killed in a gun battle with police, he had killed four male office workers and wounded a police officer. Newspaper accounts indicated that the gunman had been fired recently from his job and had lost an appeal at an administrative hearing.

In March 1998 an administrative employee of the Connecticut state lottery went to his workplace outside Hartford and shot, stabbed, and killed four co-workers before killing himself. Newspaper accounts indicated that the gunman had recently filed a grievance asking that he be paid at a different job rate than his accountant job base, which would amount to an average of $2 more per hour. He had previously taken a four-month stress-related leave and was reportedly very frustrated about his perceived lack of opportunities for advancement.

In April 1998 an inspector with the U.S. Department of Agriculture's plant protection and quarantine programs shot and killed two supervisors during an afternoon meeting before killing himself. Newspaper accounts indicated that the gunman was attending a meeting as the president of a local union to discuss work schedule and shift changes. Officials confirmed the gunman had previously filed a complaint with the federal EEOC, but there was no information about what the complaint involved.

The incidents described above are not normal events in the workplace, but there has been great concern since the 1980s about violence in the workplace. According to the Center for Disease Control & Prevention, by the mid-1990s, homicide emerged as the second leading cause of death in the workplace, ranking only behind motor vehicle accidents.

Violence is dramatic, especially when it occurs in the workplace. As the very short media accounts in this prologue attest, workplace violence is gripping and causes everyone to stop and think about what is happening and why. Were there warning signs that should not have been missed? What steps should be taken to reduce the risks and lower the chance of workplace violence happening?

Actual statistics portray a different story. Murder in the workplace, according to the American Psychological Association, is only a small percentage of all acts of workplace violence and is the lowest among forms of homicide. The studies show 1 in 650 acts of workplace violence involve murder, and workplace homicide is only 4% of all homicides. Also, as the national averages for crime and murder decline, the rates of workplace violence are also declining.

The public sector employee faces two sets of challenges that show disproportionate effects, however. While public sector employees comprise about 18% of the nation's workforce, they account for almost 30% of all workplace homicides. An even larger problem (in terms of frequency, obviously not severity) is work-related physical assault. In a study of workplace assault data using the state of Minnesota, public administration led all occupational categories in the assault/injury rates. The industry average using this 1992 data set for assault/injury rates per 100,000 full-time employees is 47, but the government worker rate was 133 per 100,000 compared to all organizations in the services sector, which was 109. Rates for all other occupational groups were just 22 or lower. Clearly, among the more than 2 million reported physical assaults that occur at job sites annually, public sector employees have a much higher probability of being assaulted than someone in the private sector.

What about the U. S. Postal Service (USPS) and that 1990s expression of "going postal?" The question can be asked—Are employees at USPS in greater danger of being victims of violence from their co-workers? The American Psychological Association study specifically examined that risk and concluded that the workplace homicide rate for USPS from 1983 to 1993 was 0.63 per 100,000 employees, just below the 0.7 national average. Also, while there is a higher incidence of co-workers responsible for workplace homicide in the postal service, the majority of the 20 out of 35 deaths in the 1980 to 1990 period caused by a co-worker came from one single incident, in which 14 persons were killed.

Workplace violence in whatever form requires that organizations take significant steps to establish safer work environments and design preventative strategies. Organizations must begin as many corporate and some government agency leaders have already done, by establishing a series of policies, procedures, and guidelines that form an effective process for communicating what must be done to prevent violence at the job site. It begins with a careful reconsideration of the work space design in terms of security and protecting the identity and safety of those at work. A critical part of the process will include training for supervisors and team leaders in conflict management, in what their roles and responsibilities are in ensuring a zero tolerance policy in the work site toward violence, and in how they should handle confrontational or violent incidents. One state, New Jersey, has responded to the mounting workforce violence problem with an executive order signed by the governor and a mandatory two-day training program for all senior government managers.

Another series of steps requires reviewing personnel policies involving disputes, grievances, disciplinary actions, and especially terminations for both fairness and stress impact. It is also suggested that it is just as important to provide counseling and employee assistance services for terminated employees or those facing some form of adverse action as for those voluntarily seeking help for substance abuse, work stress management or personal financial problems. Providing counseling after workplace violence has occurred is even more critical for all of those affected. An effective policy will plan for helping survivors cope with posttraumatic stress and grief as well as cope with the attending media coverage and getting back to work. Finally, organizations must stress the need for paying closer attention to all forms of communications. Any type of threat, boastful remark about weapons, or strange behaviors must be taken seriously.

WAVE: One State's War Against Workplace Violence

Workers Against Violence Efforts: The Wave Project

As a result of a 1996 New Jersey Department of Personnel study on workplace violence, Governor Christine Todd Whitman signed Executive Order number 49. This order established a ''zero tolerance'' policy for any acts of workplace violence by or against employees, property, or installations in New Jersey government. As part of this project, the state's Human Resource Development Institute (in cooperation with the Communications Workers of America) developed a workplace violence prevention and response training program. The program is now being implemented in all state government agencies and is available to all municipalities and counties.

A major goal of the project is to establish an attitude of concern and
open lines of communication among all state employees, as well as to provide
training about prevention and response strategies to workplace violence.

What Does WAVE Consist of?

- Publication and wide distribution of a booklet entitled "Working
  Toward a Secure Workplace."
- A kickoff teleconference for over 1040 managers in August 1997
  (which was also telecast to the state of Pennsylvania's governor's
  office).
- Development of two basic training courses—a two-day course for
  managers entitled "Prevention and Response Strategies to Workplace Violence," and a one-day course for employees. Using a
  train-the-trainer methodology, over 400 persons were trained in
  presenting the basic courses once an overview of the entire training
  project had been given to every New Jersey state department senior
  staff member. This group of trainers will be responsible for carrying the training to every supervisor and employee in the state.
  Also, CD-ROM and video-workbook versions of the basic course
  for employees are being made available. The training courses include a wide variety of information and guidance about workplace
  violence and current policies. The courses include videos and discussions of situations and perspectives on workplace violence prevention and response to include (1) recognizing signs of distress
  and intimidating behaviors, (2) dealing with threats and threatening behaviors, (3) using internal and external resources to resolve
  conflicts, (4) using training to lower risks and improve employee
  relationships, (5) hiring and firing employees in ways that the
  lower risk of violence, and (6) responding to emergency situations,
  crisis intervention, de-escalating behaviors.
- Two specialty courses—"Crises Management Team Leader" and
  "Human Resource Specialist Role in Workplace Violence"—designed and presented by the National Safe Work Place Institute.
- Presentations to each department on how to develop their "crisis
  management plans" with follow-up guidelines. All state departments must submit for review a crisis management plan as well
  as provide regular reports on workplace violence incidents.

Source: Kay, Elizabeth. State of New Jersey, Department of Personnel, 1998.

DEFINING EMPLOYEE RELATIONS

Employee relations mean more than dealing with workplace violence. This very important area of human resources management covers a wide range of related issues that deal essentially with employee well-being and a supportive work environment. Today the term employee relations covers dispute resolution, grievances, all aspects of employee discipline, stress management and wellness programs, employee safety, and health and environment programs, along with worker compensation and disability policies and substance abuse and employee counseling, or what are usually called employee assistance programs'' (EAPs).

Much of this territory was once considered to be the main purview of unions. Indeed, employee relations was often a term used to denote labor relations. In the public sector, where there has been a long history of limitations and restrictions on what can be bargained over, work conditions became the focal point of bargaining when pay and job tenure were off limits. Of course unions are still greatly concerned with all aspects of work conditions, but today's issues of employee relations are too complex and too critical to be left to the bargaining table. As the partnership between public sector labor unions and managers evolves, employee relations have become a true centerpiece for new initiatives involving the public worker and the workplace across many fronts. Working conditions, dispute resolution, job safety, stress, and health are just a few issues or concerns that constitute employees relations, the topic of this chapter.

FORMAL DISPUTE RESOLUTION MECHANISMS

Conflict reduction and resolution are central to effective human resources management. Traditional civil service systems seek to limit interpersonal conflict by standardizing the treatment of employees. For instance, they provide for pay by grade and step level. Work assignments are regulated by position classification systems and rules for overtime. Promotions and training may be based largely on seniority. In such systems, employees do not compete with one another, and personnel rules are intended to ensure that they are not treated arbitrarily,

Contemporary managerial thinking holds that the traditional civil service approach achieves fairness (in the sense of procedural regularity) at the expense of employee and organizational performance. It seeks to reward high performers with merit pay and bonuses. It also tries to develop and promote employees according to their performance and potential to contribute to the organization. The trade-off here is that employees who are not highly rewarded for their performance may feel they have been treated unfairly.

In both traditional systems and those that are more performance-based, intersocial group relations are a chronic source of perceived unfairness and conflict. As discussed in Chapter 9 (on equal employment opportunity), human resources management systems devote considerable attention to combating prohibited racial, ethnic, and gender discrimination. Nevertheless, many employees consider their work environments to be unfair. For instance, in 1996 the U.S. Merit Systems Protection Board (MSPB) found that a minority of all federal employees agreed that their agencies "have no problem, or a minor one, in providing fair and equitable treatment." Only 21% of African-American employees could say that about their agencies. Among the other groups surveyed, only about 30% of Hispanic, Asian/Pacific Americans, and Native Americans agreed with the statement. Even among non-Hispanic whites, less than half—43%—subscribed to it.

Competition for jobs and promotions is another aspect of human resources management that generates a sense of unfairness. For example, in 1996, 18% of all federal employees claimed to have been "deliberately misled by an agency official about my right to compete," and 25% claimed to have been "denied a job or a promotion because a selecting official gave an unfair advantage to another applicant." About one-third of all federal employees believe that promotions are not based on the candidates' relative ability, knowledge, and skills. An equal proportion claim competition is not fair and open.

Perceptions of unfairness in the workplace inevitably generate conflictual interpersonal relationships. These may seriously detract from organizational performance. In egregious cases, they may also endanger employees' health and lead to violence. The unfortunate expression, going postal refers to the type of aggressive behavior in the workplace that grew out of the very poor human relations in the USPS during the earlier part of the 1990s.

To avoid such deleterious conditions, any well-designed human resources management system will try to assure fairness in the first place and provide formal mechanisms for resolving disputes as a backup. These are always guided by four values that are often in tension with one another: impact on the organization; efficiency or timeliness; fairness to the parties involved; and competent decision making, as measured by the ability to command deference from the individuals directly affected and reviewing bodies, such as courts.

Traditional Adjudicatory Systems

The basic elements of all traditional personnel adjudicatory systems seek to ensure procedural due process. In adverse actions they require notice to the employee; an opportunity to respond; at least one level of appeal within the agency (and often an appeal beyond it to an agency such the MSPB); an opportunity for judicial review after all administrative processes and appeals have been exhausted; separation of investigators from actual decision makers; impartial decision making; a written record to facilitate review; decisions based on a specific standard of proof, such as "clear and convincing evidence" (highly likely), the "preponderance of evidence" (more likely than not), or "substantial evidence" (reasonable); and fair procedures, often including the right to be represented by counsel and to confrontation and cross-examination of adverse witnesses.

Many of the same features are present in EEO and other cases that begin when an employee files a complaint alleging that he or she was subject to a prohibited practice. In these instances, however, the employee has the burden of producing enough evidence to make an initial showing that a violation occurred (*prima facie case*). Because many employees will lack the resources to underwrite an investigation and summon evidence, fairness requires that some governmental unit investigate the employee's claim. If the investigation is done by the agency itself, the investigatory unit must have substantial independence. In some situations in which it appears that there is a serious conflict of interest in allowing an agency to investigate itself, such as alleged reprisals for whistle-blowing, the task may be turned over to a special counsel. Table 13.1 shows the steps taken once a federal employee appeals an agency's action to the MSPB. Figure 13.1 outlines the federal system for handling employee complaints of prohibited discrimination.

Many traditional adjudicatory systems work well on one or more of the four dimensions noted above (impact on organization, efficiency, fairness, and competence). In large agencies or governments, however, developing a system that performs well on each dimension is very difficult, if not impossible. For instance, the federal MSPB gets high ratings for handling adverse action appeals efficiently, fairly, and competently, but the availability of adjudication at the agency level and the opportunity to appeal to the MSPB seriously dampen supervisors' willingness to take action against poor performers. The MSPB data show that in 1996 28% of federal supervisors were unwilling to take adverse actions, even though they considered them warranted. The prime reasons were the time involved in going through the adverse action process (mentioned by 67%); lack of support by upper management (62%); impact on the work group (48%); prospect of facing an EEO complaint (40%); lack of familiarity with procedures (25%); and cost to the agency if the employee appealed (18%). In the same year, a majority of supervisors (59%) and employees (51%) agreed that "their agencies have a major problem separating employees who cannot or will not improve their performance to meet required standards."

Efficiency in particular can be elusive. The federal EEO complaint system is illustrative. As the number of complaints increased from about 17,700 in 1991 to 27,600 in 1997, timeliness fell by the wayside. In 1991, only 3% of the cases appealed to the EEOC remained in its inventory for more than 200 days, but by 1997 the figure had risen dramatically, to 58%. On average it was taking the EEOC over 250 days to process hearings and over 350 to resolve appeals. In 1994, it took agencies an average of 356 days to close complaints, but on average it took the EEOC 707 days to close complaints from its own workforce!

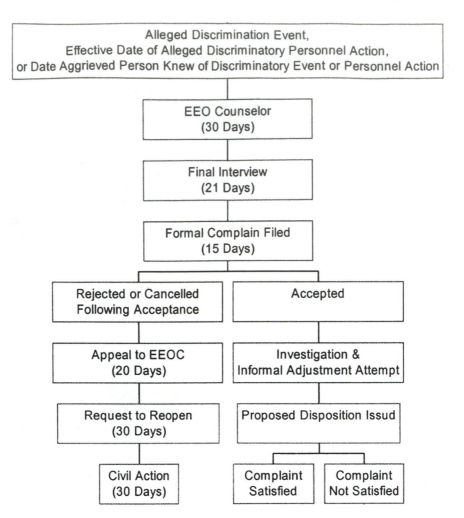

FIGURE 13.1 Procedures for processing individual complaints of discrimination based on race, color, religion, sec, national origin, age, or physical or mental handicap. (a) Informal and formal stages for disposition of complaint; (b) complainant not satisfied with proposed disposition.

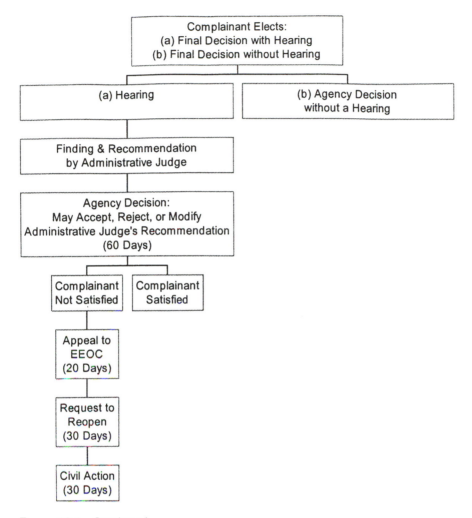

FIGURE 13.1 Continued

The perception of fairness may also be problematic. Of the thousands of federal EEO complaints filed annually, only a few hundred (or even less) typically result in clear findings of discrimination. About 40% of the federal employees who discuss their concerns with federal EEO counselors never file formal complaints. No one knows why—perhaps because those who operate the EEO adjudicatory system do not want the reasons known. The issues may be resolved or the complainants may be dissuaded—both for good and bad reasons. According

TABLE 13.1 Steps in Processing Initial Appeals and Petitions for Review

MSPB Regional Office Steps	
Filing of appeal by appellant.	Within 20 days of effective date of agency personnel action
Appeal received. Appeal acknowledged and entered in Case Tracking System. Case file requested from agency. Appeal assigned to administrative judge.	1–3 days from receipt of appeal
Agency response and case file received. Discovery begins. Prehearing conference scheduled. Notice of hearing issued.	1–26 days from receipt of appeal
Prehearing motions filed and rulings issued. Attempts to achieve settlement (various methods). Discovery completed. Prehearing conferences held. Witnesses identified (if no hearing, close of record set).	10–60 days from receipt of appeal
Hearing held. Record closed.	60–75 days from receipt of appeal
Initial decision issued.	Within 120 days from receipt of initial appeal

Board Headquarters	
Filing of Petition for Review (PFR) by appellant or agency (or OSC or OPM as intervenor).	Within 35 days of date of initial decision
PFR received, acknowledged, and entered in case tracking system. Case file requested from regional office.	1–3 days from receipt of PFR
Response to PFR filed or cross-PFR filed. Case file received.	Within 25 days of date of service of PFR
If cross-petition for review received.	Additional 25 days from date of service of PFR
If extention of time (EOT) request received and granted.	Additional time specified in order granting EOT
Final decision issued.	Board time standard for issuance of final decisions is 110 days
Filing of appeal with U.S. Court of Appeals for the Federal circuit (or in discrimination cases, with the appropriate U.S. District Court of EEOC).	Within 30 days of party's receipt of MSPB's final decision

to the American Federation of Government Employees, agency investigations are a sham—"almost a complete waste of time."

There are better data regarding sexual harassment in the federal workplace. In 1994, 44% of all women in the federal civilian workforce surveyed by the MSPB claimed to have been sexually harassed during the past two years, as did 19% of the male employees. Both figures were up somewhat from a 1987 survey. Only 6% of victims took any kind of formal action, although all were entitled to protection. This tiny minority took one or more of the following steps to vindicate their rights: requested an investigation (42%); filed a discrimination complaint or suit (30%); filed a grievance or adverse action appeal (25%); requested an investigation by an outside organization (14%); or took another unspecified action (17%).

The plurality of the 94% who avoided formal action ignored the harassment or did nothing about it (44%). Thirty-five percent asked or told the harasser to stop, while 28% avoided the harasser. Only 7% went along with the behavior. The victims gave multiple reasons why they were reluctant to take formal action. The top 10 were as follows:

1. Did not think it was serious enough (50%).
2. Other actions resolved the situation (40%).
3. Thought it would make her or his work situation unpleasant (29%).
4. Did not think anything would be done (20%).
5. Thought the situation would not be kept confidential (19%).
6. Thought it would adversely affect her or his career (17%).
7. Did not want to hurt the harasser (17%).
8. Was too embarrassed (11%).
9. Though she or he would be blamed (8%).
10. Did not think she or he would be believed (8%).

Reasons 3 through 6 go directly to a perception that the formal adjudicatory system will not result in fair outcomes. So do 9 and 10, although a much smaller percentage of victims mentioned them. Reason 8, indicates that a significant number of victims find the formal system inhospitable or inaccessible.

Finally, competence varies. The MSPB has a stellar record. In 1997, the U.S. Circuit Court of Appeals for the Federal Circuit heard 444 appeals of MSPB decisions and left 96% of them unchanged. By contrast, during the first nine years of its existence, the Federal Labor Relations Authority was unable to command judicial deference. In fact, it was about as likely to be overruled in federal court as to be upheld! Federal supervisors also had mixed views of the main federal personnel adjudicatory agencies. Figure 13.2 shows their levels of satisfaction and dissatisfaction with each.

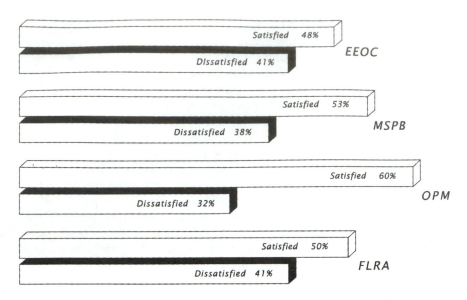

FIGURE 13.2 Level of satisfaction with the handling of the case. Note: Survey participants who responded "neither satisfied nor dissatisfied" are not included in these figures. Source: U.S. MSPB, *Issues of Merit*, August 1997.

Alternative Dispute Resolution Approaches

The costs and limitations of traditional adjudicatory systems have prompted increasing interest in alternative dispute resolution (ADR). Although ADR takes many forms, its key objective is always to substitute resolution for adjudication. Emphasis is placed on settling conflicts before the parties' positions harden, as they often do in formal adjudication. Alternate Dispute Resolution relies on counseling, conciliation, negotiation, mediation, minitrials, and/or arbitration. Agencies may employ full- or part-time dispute resolution specialists to engage in and manage ADR.

In unionized work environments, arbitration is typically used to resolve grievances over the application of work rules, assignments, and so forth. Counseling is also commonly used to resolve workplace disputes. Counselors try to defuse conflicts before they are exacerbated by the need to bolster cases for adjudication. Sometimes employees are bothered by relatively minor concerns; sometimes they are incorrect in believing they were subject to differential or unfair treatment. An explanation or apology may resolve the situation. So may a promise that the behavior in question will never reoccur. Not every slight or injury is intentional. Once an employee explains his or her concerns, a supervisor may be able to correct the situation. It may have been a simple mistake. Once an employee hears a supervisor's explanation, he or she may be satisfied that the action at issue was reasonable. Counselors also advise employees of their rights, the ADR and adjudicatory options, and what the next steps might be.

Face-to-face negotiation or conciliation may be used in conjunction with counseling. If the dispute is serious enough, mediation may also be used. Alternate Dispute Resolution is generally considered effective, but it is not a panacea. It takes expertise in conflict resolution and often involves hard work. It is a key component of the "reinventing government" or new public management movement, which views it as more efficient and flexible than traditional adjudication. It is also more suitable than adjudication for handling disputes in a workforce that transitions in and out of government.

JOB SAFETY AND HEALTH

Personal injuries, illnesses, and even death arising out of work situations are strongly correlated with the pace of industrialization in our society. Rapid progress in any industry has sometimes resulted in individual as well as mass injuries and sometimes fatalities to the workers. We have all heard the horror stories arising out of the experiences in the coal mines (e.g., black lung disease), steel industry, garment and fabric industries, and a host of others. Even today, sweatshops that exploit and pose serious health and safety problems for cheap (often illegal) immigrant labor continue to thrive in this country. Early legislation to regulate and monitor unhealthy and unsafe working conditions (e.g., the Walsh–Healey Public Contracts Act of 1936, the Service Contract Act of 1965) were found to be much too narrow in scope.

In 1970, however, in an effort to seriously address the problems of unsafe, unhealthy working conditions, at least in the private sector, Congress passed the Occupation Safety and Health Act (Public Law 91–596). Parenthetically, Congress's concern may have been less for the workers as compared to the employers. Section 2 (a) of the 1970 act reads: "The Congress finds that personal injuries and illnesses arising out of work situations impose a substantial burden upon, and are a hindrance to, interstate commerce in terms of lost production, wage loss, medical expenses, and disability compensation payments."

The stated purpose of the act is to "assure safe and healthful working conditions for working men and women" and "to encourage the States in their efforts to assure safe and healthful working conditions." The law is administered by the U.S. secretary of labor through the Occupational Safety and Health Administration (OSHA).

One of OSHA's major functions is to conduct on-site safety and health inspections, particularly when any of the following occur or are likely to occur:

1. *Imminent danger.* This refers to an employment situation or environment that is likely to cause death or a serious injury if allowed to continue.

2. *Employee complaints.* Employees can complain to OSHA about safety violations or about unsafe or unhealthy working conditions.
3. *Catastrophes and fatalities.* Deaths or catastrophes and accidents resulting in the hospitalization of five or more employees.
4. *Programmed high-hazard inspections.* Occupations, industries or substances that lead to a high degree of accidents or illnesses. Asbestos and lead are examples of hazardous health substances, and sheet metal and meat cutting are examples of industries prone to high-hazard situations.
5. *Follow-up inspections.* Employers cited for violations are always targeted for reinspection.

Amended in 1990, the Occupational Safety and Health Act, as noted, primarily covers private sector employees; however, there are provisions for the federal government as well as the states. Section 18 of the act reads that

Nothing in this Act shall prevent any State agency or court from asserting jurisdiction under State law over any occupational safety or health issue with respect to which no standard is in effect under section 6. Any State which, at any time, desires to assume responsibility for development and enforcement therein of occupational safety and health standards relating to any occupational safety or health issue with respect to which a Federal standard has been promulgated under section 6 shall submit a State plan for the development of such standards and their enforcement.

Section 19 of the act requires the head of each federal agency to establish and maintain an effective and comprehensive occupational safety and heath program consistent with those standards pertaining to private sector employers. The safety and health program for federal employees is overseen by the Office of Federal Agency Programs (OFAP), operating much like a "mini-OSHA." The OFAP carries out compliance assistance activities, but it also has "line" responsibility for oversight of each federal agency's safety and health programs. The OFAP covers all the regular functions of OSHA, including inspections, data gathering, abatement issues, allegations of reprisal, and employee complaints. It also evaluates how well agencies are complying with their safety and health responsibilities.

A joint labor–management committee, the Federal Safety and Health Advisory Committee (FACOSH), consisting of eight federal employee unions presidents and high-level officials and eight federal-agency assistant secretaries and deputy assistant secretaries, assists the OFAP in carrying out its functions. The FACOSH is chaired by the assistant secretary for the OSHA.

Feds Forge Ahead on Safety

The Occupational Safety and Health Administration, which has been touting its reinvented partnership approach to private industry for several years, now wants to collaborate with the federal sector. The agency's goal: to boost safety and health awareness among federal managers to help reduce accident rates and worker's compensation costs.

Former Labor Secretary Robert Reich initiated the plan back in 1995 after noting that federal injury and illness rates were at a 10-year high. OSHA later surveyed agencies and found that safety and health generally were not considered priorities. "We were concerned," recalls Richard Fairfax, OSHA deputy director of compliance. "For that reason, we are trying to establish a presidential initiative to refocus attention on safety and health."

That initiative, called Fed 2000, was launched in October. Originally slated to start in 1997, the program will use workers' compensation and employment data to identify the 200 federal work sites with the highest lost workday rates—standard measures showing the average number of days per 100 workers that employees had to be put on restricted work duty or could not report to work at all because of an occupational injury or illness in a given year. OSHA then will offer those facilities the chance to work cooperatively to improve safety and health or face inspections and possible citations.

A similar program for private sector employers called the Cooperative Compliance Program, started in 1997, is on hold. Last February, an appeals court judge issued a stay on the program in response to charges from business groups that it coerces participants. The court is scheduled to decide on the meritsdd of the case in December. As of late September, agencies had not raised similar arguments against the Fed 2000 program.

In fact, officials at the National Park Service welcomed the opportunity to join forces with OSHA. "Safety has not been taken too awfully seriously in the history of this organization," admits Richard Powell, risk management program manager for the park service. The agency had an average lost workday rate in fiscal 1997 of 7.15, with some parks experiencing rates greater than 20, Powell says. The federal agency average for that year was 2.51.

OSHA and the Park Service first agreed to partner last February after an inspection at Yellowstone National Park found more than 600 violations, many of which were things OSHA had warned the park of in previous years. During the inspection, which was triggered after a peark mechanic died in a snowmobile accident, OSHA found that the park had an injury and illness rate more than four times the average for all industries.

"They had a safety and health program, but it wasn't working," Fairfax says.

Now the issue is a priority for Park Service Director Robert Stanton. "It's at last on the screen of management," Powell says. The agency has included reducing accidents and workers' compensation costs as performance goals under its Government Performance and Results Act strategic plan. They also are rewriting the safety and health program, converting it from a guideline to a director's order.

Under the Fed 2000 agreement signed in October, OSHA will help 10 Park Service sites evaluate their safety and health problems, and train staff to recognize and fix hazards. Though the agency has a long way to go to improve things, Powell is optimistic. "We recognize our moral as well as our legal responsibility to employee health and safety," he says. "To make that culture shift is a slow process. But I think we're going to get there."

Source: *Government Executive* (November 1998).

Despite these procedural advances, much concern has been expressed about safety and health in the public sector workplace. In 1995 the Department of Labor found that federal injury and illness rates over the past decade had reached record high levels. In a follow-up survey by then secretary of labor Robert Reich, it was determined that many agencies had programs on paper that were not being implemented throughout the agency, and that safety efforts were not real priorities for management.

As federal agencies have begun to reconsider how they might make health and safety core values for workplace management, one issue that immediately comes to the surface is to allow OSHA to fine federal agencies that are cited for violating safety regulations. Indeed, the USPS, which has been cited by OSHA at nearly 6000 work sites for more than 24,000 violations since 1993, is now subject to OSHA's full enforcement authority under provisions of the Postal Safety Enhancement Law of 1998. The Post Office is now subject to the same fines as its competitors in the private sector for workplace safety violations. Incidentally, the precedent that a federal agency should be subject to regulation and fines by another federal agency is not new. The Environmental Protection Agency (EPA) has had such legal authority over federal agencies for environmental legal transgressions since the early 1990s.

Will other federal agencies be added to OSHA's jurisdiction over time? Would monetary fines help or hinder federal agencies in their pursuit of safety and health improvements? Workforce safety statistics certainly show the need

Section 19 of the Occupational Safety and Health Act

(a) it shall be the responsibility of the head of each Federal lagency to establish and maintain an effective and comprehensive occupational safety and health program which is consistent with the standards promulgated under section 6. The head of each agency shall (after consultation with representatives of the employees thereof)—

   (1) provide safe and healthful places and conditions of employment, consistent with the standards set under section 6;

   (2) acquire, maintain, and require the use of safety equipment, personal protective equipment, and devices reasonably necessary to protect employees;

   (3) keep adequate records of all occupational accidents and illnesses for proper evaluation and necessary corrective action;

   (4) consult with the Secretary with regard to the adequacy as to form and content of records kept pursuant to subsection (a)(3) of this section, and

   (5) make an annual report to the Secretary with respect to occupational accidents and injuries and the agency's program under this section. Such report shall include any report submitted under section 7902(e)(2) of title 5, United States Code.

(b) The Secretary shall report to the President a summary or digest of reports submitted to him under subsection (a)(5) of this section, together with his evaluations of and recommendations derived from such reports.

(c) Section 7902(c)(1) of title 5, United States Code, is amended by inserting after ''agencies'' the following: ''and of labor organizations representing employees.''

(d) The Secretary shall have access to records and reports kept and filed by Federal agencies pursuant to subsections (a)(3) and (5) of this section unless those records and reports are specifically required by Executive order to be kept secret in the interest of the national defense or foreign policy, in which case the Secretary shall have access to such information as will not jeopardize national defense or foreign policy.

Source: OSHA Website: ⟨http://www.osha-slc.gov/oshAct-data/OSH-ACT19.html⟩.

for some motivation. A recent sampling in *Government Executive* of annual work-force lost time rates due to work accident or illness clearly shows the need for lots of improvement. (See Table 13.2.)

While it is often the case that employers tend to be more reactive as opposed to proactive (i.e., management waits until OSHA or OFAP have cited a violation and then responds), OSHA has heightened management's awareness of work-place safety and health hazards. For instance, we all now know about the dangers posed by such carcinogenic substances as vinyl chloride, PCBs, cotton dust, and asbestos. As a number of analysts have pointed out, management has been more willing in the post-OSHA era to rectify workplace hazards before being cited, and to improve such vital environmental conditions as noise levels, ventilation, dust- and asbestos-free work spaces, and even stress.

One of the ways employers have become more proactive has been by estab-lishing safety and health policies or programs, often operated or overseen by joint labor–management health and safety committees. Such committees (e.g., FACOSH, discussed earlier), seek to minimize, curtail, or eradicate health and safety threats in the workplace.

Another way in which employers have responded is through EAPs. These programs are designed more to address some of the health and safety threats that are posed by employee behaviors or personal problems, such as smoking, alcohol

TABLE 13.2 Sizing Up Safety: How Lost Workday Rates at Federal Agencies Stacked up Against the Private Sector Average

Architect of the Capitol	10.36
Government Printing Office	7.28
Bureau of Engraving and Printing	7.07
Food Safety Inspection Service	6.82
U.S. Mint	6.21
National Park Service	5.89
Mine Safety and Health Administration	5.25
Defense Commissary Agency	4.52
Immigration and Naturalization Service	4.47
U.S. Postal Service	3.39
Federal agency	2.51
Private industry average	3.4

Note: The standard measure for lost workdays is the average number of days per 100 work-ers that employees had to be put on restricted duty or could not report to work at all because of an occupational injury or illness in a given year.
Source: Occupational Safety and Health Administration (federal figures for fiscal 1997), Bu-reau of Labor Statistics' Annual Survey of Occupational Injuries and Illnesses (private indus-try figures for fiscal 1996).

consumption, or drug use. Employee Assistance Programs will be addressed in greater detail later in this chapter.

Substance Abuse in the Workplace

One of the areas that has received growing attention because of EAPs is the treatment of drug use by employees. Drug abuse cuts across all job levels and all types of organizations, and it costs the nation billions of dollars each year in lost productivity, greater use of medical benefits and drug-related accidents. Employers have hence been very vigilant about monitoring the effects of drug use on the job.

It should be noted that while the Americans with Disabilities Act (ADA) does not consider an employee or job applicant who is currently engaging in the illegal use of drugs to be a "qualified individual with a disability," it does protect individuals who have completed or are participating in supervised drug rehabilitation (e.g., in the form of EAPs) and who are no longer using drugs.

Also, the ADA states that a test for illegal drugs is not considered a medical examination, and therefore employers may conduct drug tests on job applicants or employees and make employment decisions based on the results. The ADA does not encourage, prohibit, or authorize drug testing. In short, an employer may have an EAP to help employees with drug problems, but it may also have a drug-testing policy or program to determine whether or not employees are using illegal drugs. The following section addresses the legality of such programs and policies.

Drug Testing

One of the most controversial areas of personnel policy in the 1980s and 1990s was employee drug testing. In 1986, the President's Commission on Organized Crime recommended drug testing in the workplace as one method for ending the use of illegal drugs, and in that same year President Reagan issued Executive Order 12564 to stop the use of drugs in the federal workplace. Reagan's "war on drugs" culminated in 1988 with passage of the Drug-Free Workplace Act, which was intended to combat employees' use of drugs nationwide.

While the issue of drug testing continues to raise political and social questions, many of the legal concerns were addressed in 1989 by the U.S. Supreme Court, which upheld the constitutionality of employer drug-testing programs under the Fourth Amendment in two landmark cases. In *National Treasury Employees Union* v. *Von Raab* (1989), the Court upheld drug testing in the Customs Service for those employees who both engage in drug interdiction and drug law enforcement and carry firearms. The Court majority first noted that the process of drug testing infringed on the employees' privacy interests. (The employee was taken to a toilet and required to provide a urine sample while a monitor stood by and listened.) The Court reasoned that due to the sensitive nature of their jobs, however, the employees had a diminished expectation of privacy under the Fourth Amendment and that the tests were constitutionally permissible insofar as they were reasonable. The key point in this decision was that the tests were reasonable even though there was no suspicion that any individual employee had been using illegal drugs because of the sensitive nature of these particular Customs Service jobs.

In the second case, *Skinner* v. Railway Labor Executives' Association (1989), the Court upheld a mandatory drug-testing program instituted by the Federal Railroad Administration (FRA) for employees involved in certain types of train accidents. The *Skinner* Court ruled that the government's interest in regulating the railway industry to ensure safety outweighs the Fourth Amendment's guarantee of privacy rights and its warrant and probable-cause requirements.

The framework established in *Von Raab* relies heavily on the public service model's concern that the public be well served by the terms of the public employment relationship. There is a clear and strong public interest in assuring that customs agents charged with drug enforcement are not themselves users of illegal drugs, and as *Skinner* suggests, workers upon whose performance the public safety depends are another category of public employees who might constitutionally be subject to drug testing.

There are also millions of public employees whose functions are such that their performance poses no serious risk to public safety, however. For all practical purposes, the Fourth and Fourteenth Amendments protect such employees from drug tests. If there is a strong individualized suspicion that a particular employee is using illegal substances, however, the government employer may be able to require a drug test, regardless of the employee's position.

More recently, the U.S. Supreme Court further polarized the drug-testing debate in this country by addressing the question of reasonable or individualized suspicion. In *Vernonia School District 47J* v. *Acton* (1995), the Court upheld the suspicionless drug testing of student athletes under the Fourth and Fourteenth Amendments to the U.S. Constitution. The drug-testing policy was implemented in an effort to combat what the school district perceived as a drug epidemic among students, particularly student athletes. In upholding the drug-testing policy, the Court reasoned that students who are minors are not entitled to the same degree of constitutional protections around privacy as adults are. The Court further noted that student athletes have an even lesser expectation of privacy due to their involvement in athletics. Student athletes, the Court opined, are already required to submit to physicals, including urinalysis, before participating in interscholastic athletics, thus drug testing possess no additional burden to student athletes. Although *Vernonia* applies only to student athletes, the decision may have widespread implications, in that the Court based its finding on the reasonableness of a search (for the purposes of drug testing) on factors wholly independent of the constitutional guidelines around the warrant and probable-cause requirement.

Discover the Secret . . . to Beating Drug Tests

The Testclean.Com Website provides valuable tips on how to pass your drug test. Here are some of the "drug-testing solution" products, as advertised on the Web, that can be ordered online.

For Urinalysis

KLEAR is clearly the best product available if you are not subject to supervised testing. **KLEAR** was perfected after thousands of hours of lab work. It is the smallest, most potent, urine purifier sold today. In addition, **KLEAR** does not require any special timing unlike many of the herbal teas. Many National Organization for the Reform of Marijuana Laws (NORML) organizations around the United States recognize this additive as an effective means in defeating the Urine Test. **KLEAR** is easier to use and is more accurate than the teas.

Detoxify Brand **CARBO CLEAN** is formulated with ingredients known to assist the body's natural cleaning system. Using **CARBO CLEAN** as part of a complete detoxification program will ensure that you will be clean when you need to be clean! **CARBO CLEAN** is unique because it employs carbohydrates to cleanse the system.

WHIZZIES are manufactured by Smoke Screen Laboratories. If a piss test might be awaiting you when you report to work tomorrow or tonight, you need a plan. When you cannot substitute a clean sample you might need **WHIZZIES.** Pour one vial of **WHIZZIES** powder into your urine, and you are sure to pass.

For Hair Analysis

Hair Testing is becoming more popular now and many now have struck back with a superior product in CLEAR CHOICE. CLEAR CHOICE includes a special formulated shampoo, conditioner, and protective rinse. This Product is Guaranteed to remove medications, chemical buildup and other impurities from within the hair shaft.

Source: Testclean.com, http://www.testclean.com/default.asp.

In the most recent drug-testing ruling to date, *Chandler* v. *Miller* (1997), the Supreme Court, in a surprising move, struck down the drug testing of political candidates. The Court ruled that a Georgia law requiring political candidates to submit to urine tests for illegal drugs as a condition of appearing on the ballot was unconstitutional under the Fourth and Fourteenth Amendments. The Court

Global Drug Testing Services

Global Drug Testing Services, based in central California, provides employers with a variety of drug tests, including hair analysis and urinalysis. Here's how it advertises for hair analysis on the Web.

> Global Drug Testing Services has the ability to analyze hair samples for drug presence. This method can detect drug use for the previous 90 days. Ingested drugs circulate in a person's bloodstream, which nourishes the developing hair follicle. Trace amounts of the drugs become entrapped in the core of the hair shaft in amounts roughly proportional to those ingested.
>
> These drug residues cannot be washed, bleached, or flushed out and are stable over time. Thus, a drug history can be obtained from the hair of any individual.

Source: http://gdtsrv.com/testing.cfm.

majority found that the drug test was an exercise in political symbolism, and that it unconstitutionally "diminishes personal privacy for a symbol's sake."

Closely coupled with the legal aspects of drug testing, a pressing controversy that arises over drug testing or urinalysis is reliability and validity. By now we are all familiar with the stories of employees eating poppy-seed bagels in the morning and testing positive for drug use that afternoon. Poppy seeds are derived from the poppy plant, which contains traces of opium, thus resulting in an otherwise guileless bagel junkie testing positive for heroin.

What about the occasional smoker of pot who lights up a single weed on the weekend—off duty—and is forced to pee in a cup on Monday? (Executive Order 12564 prohibits federal employees from using drugs off duty as well as while at work). What about the fact that certain drugs can remain in the bloodstream for many days following ingestion? Consider the fact that the federal government spends thousands of dollars each year to "catch people" using drugs, yet the overall hit rate (i.e., the proportion of those tested who are positive) for employees and job applicants has been extraordinarily low—roughly half a percent each. In addition, the estimates of the costs to employers of drug abuse have been overstated. While there is a relationship between drug use and costly employee behavior, this correlation has been shown to be very small.

Some researchers have suggested that drug testing in the workplace has more of a symbolic as opposed to instrumental value—that President Reagan's war on drugs was more a theatrical production to reassure the citizenry that the government could resolve the problem of pervasive drug use in our society than a legitimate effort to actually detect drug users in the workplace and punish them. In other words, while drug testing may promote public confidence, it does not necessarily advance the managerial values of efficiency and effectiveness in work settings. Whatever motives lie behind drug testing, it continues to occur in the public and private sectors; but public personnel managers and public administrators in general need to recognize that symbolic gestures cannot always serve as a justification for administrative actions.

EMPLOYEE ASSISTANCE PROGRAMS

Employee assistance programs are employer-financed programs designed to help workers with problems that may stem from work-related or personal concerns, ranging from alcoholism and drug abuse to marital, family, and financial problems. What exactly is an EAP? The definition provided by the U.S. Employee Assistance Professionals Association shows the full focus and objectives.

> An employee assistance program (EAP) is a worksite-based program designed to assist in the identification and resolution of productivity problems associated with employees impaired by personal concerns including, but not limited to: health, marital, family, financial, alcohol, drug, legal, emotional, stress, or other personal concerns which may adversely affect employee job performance. The specific core activities of EAPs include:
>
> expert consultation and training to appropriate persons in the identification and resolution of job performance issues and
>
> confidential, appropriate, and timely problem assessment services, referrals, treatment and assistance and formation of linkages between workplace and community resources that provide such services.

There are, of course, compelling reasons for public organizations to use some form of institutional counseling in the workplace. All governments have a genuine interest in retaining their employees who are, after all, their intellectual capital. That interest extends to maintaining a positive workforce climate and having programs that assist employees when their personal problems affect their work performance. Such programs recognize that a valued and productive employee can become just as troubled (and nonproductive) because of work or non-work-related factors, or personal, marital, or family-related causes.

In helping employees, organizations are also seeking to reduce the burden on supervisors and managers who often are ill-trained and hard-pressed in terms of time availability to deal with employees' personal problems. Finally, there are major legal and economic liabilities that organizations must consider to ensure they are affording due process to their employees and providing health, insurance, and disability coverage for the workforce. All of these factors have resulted in the trend among public and private sector organizations to establish EAPs to help employees with problems, regardless of cause.

While EAPs have become the dominant form of institutionalized workplace counseling today, their roots go back to early the 1900s. By the time Henry Ford had developed the assembly line, the Ford Motor Company had created a counseling program for its employees in 1914. By the early 1920s Metropolitan Life Insurance and R. H. Macy had hired full-time staff psychiatrists. A study by the Engineering Foundation in New York in 1920 concluded that over 60% of employee dismissals were because of social rather than occupational incompetence. Indeed, throughout the first half of the century in the United States, there were numerous efforts on the part of the human relations movement and the developing industrial psychology movement to provide for some form of counseling services for employees.

Interestingly, the advent of the first stage of structured employee assistance programs came with the occupational alcoholism movement in the 1930s. The founding of Alcoholics Anonymous in 1935 would provide a model for corporations and unions to assist workers with alcoholism problems. Dupont and Eastman Kodak were two of the first major corporations in the early 1940s to create workplace programs that provided for supervisory referral and counseling assistance. The major role of American unions in this movement should be highlighted. In the 1940s and 1950s unions pressed for EAPs that would both treat substance abuse and include a broader mental health basis. By the 1960s the concept of the EAP was well established. Studies now show that the federal government, all state governments, the majority of large city governments, and over 80% of all large corporation (those with over 1000 employees) have EAPs.

Employee assistance programs have broadened both the range of problems they have been willing to address and their methods. The EAP model based originally on the Alcoholics Anonymous concept uses primarily a constructive confrontation approach with the employee seeking help. By the 1960s, EAPs were taking on work stress, family medical issues, financial problems, career concerns, work role conflicts, and a range of other personal problems that would require new models and new methods for assistance.

While the rationale and the basic concept for providing EAPs are fairly straightforward, there are a number of models for constructing and operating an EAP. These models vary depending upon location (Is the EAP on-site or off-site?), control (Is the EAP staffed by internal personnel or external contractors?), range (Does the EAP treat the employee or refer employees to others?), scope (What types of emotional and social employee problems are handled?), and duration of service (Is the EAP a short-term or long-term service provider?)

While there are a wide variety of models using the above design criteria, recent studies show that the majority of EAPs are located off-site and are staffed externally. The larger the organization, however, the more likely that the EAP is staffed with some combination of internal volunteers (such as recovering individuals, union or peer counselors, self-help groups in the workplace) or internal professionals (counselors, social workers, occupational health professionals, and human resources staff). When organizations use external staff arrangements, these are normally contracts with individual professionals (psychologists, psychiatrists, social workers) or with some form of health care-providing organization or facility. A final external option for small organizations growing in usage is to combine as some form of consortia acting as a partnership for contracting with external care providers.

The numerous options listed above for establishing an EAP illustrate some of the difficulty that is encountered in evaluating the effectiveness of EAPs and why it is so hard to assess cost levels, much less benefit, in any comparative way. Compounding this problem of who provides the service, there are various models for categorizing the services provided by EAPs. They can operate very differently in providing a multitude of services, such as consultation with supervisors, constructive confrontatio with employees, short-term counseling, assessment and referral, involvement with health promotion activities, and follow-up and contact with service providers and supervisors during and after treatments.

The task of evaluating how well EAPs work will be an important job for human resource management as it seeks to improve employee relations. It must begin first by dealing with when the EAP service is provided, since employee participation is traditionally thought of as being purely voluntary. That line itself is being crossed more and more as some organizations, notably law enforcement agencies, use referral to an EAP for counseling as part of employee behavior evaluations as a condition for continued work. Nonetheless, as EAP researchers and professionals have noted, the first problem is that EAPs primarily serve high-risk individuals (people who are in crisis and in need of professional intervention), and this represents only a fraction of the workforce.

A second evaluation issue is understanding who uses EAPs and who doesn't. Here again there is a decided bias in what type of employee is referred to an EAP. Numerous studies indicate that upper-level employees were the least likely to participate in an EAP, and that the typical EAP user is younger (under 50), female (single or divorced, as opposed to married), an hourly employee (as opposed to salaried), and actually less likely to be suffering from higher levels of job stress. Some have concluded that a serious weakness of the EAP model is that higher-level professionals and managers are unlikely to use an EAP but would rely on their own health insurance policy (possibly because of their greater concerned about potential adverse career impact). A third evaluation issue is the core concept of self-referral. Again the EAP concept places extensive reliance on supervisory referral (i.e., the superior identifying potential work problems and sending the employee to the EAP for help). Several studies have demonstrated, in fact, that the majority of EAP clients are self-referrals. In three studies done in the 1990s the majority (54%, 96%, and 70%) of all the EAP clients of three different EAP programs were participating on a voluntary basis at their initiative.

This suggests and is confirmed by other research that when the employee knows he or she is in trouble (and has reasonable confidence in the agency's EAP) he or she will seek help and be receptive to that assistance. This is most obvious in the use of EAPs in substance abuse treatment. Employee assistance programs have enjoyed a solid record in helping employees who have admitted alcoholism and substance abuse problems, but a significant factor in the EAP referral process is that when an employee gets to an EAP for alcohol and substance abuse, he or she is accepting the fact that he or she has a problem. The difficulty is that there are very few studies demonstrating the effectiveness of EAPs in reducing alcoholism or substance abuse in the workplace. Indeed, EAPs are relearning the research lessons of a decade ago that concluded that substance abuse by workers is due not as much to conditions of the workplace as to the attributes of the workforce.

In the final analysis, proponents of EAPs may have to concede that as effective as EAPs are, they may not be addressing the majority of employees at risk or reaching an entire range of employees because of their work level who are professionally incapable of seeking help from an EAP before they are in crisis. Clearly, a major future task of human resources management in the employee relations arena will be to determine the cost benefit of EAPs and how they fit in the future drive to create healthier work cultures for all workers.

Employee assistance programs are certainly here to stay. Their growing number is an indication of both the demand for their services and their value. The issue is more what EAPs don't do and who they aren't able to reach. Human resource managers especially know that the pressures in the workplace are accelerating, not lessening. The problems of tomorrow in the workplace may have much less to do with absenteeism or employees being late for work, and much more to being there physically but being overwhelmed mentally—what might be called "presenteeism." In his book *Workplace Counseling*, Michael Carroll provides an apt summary of stress levels in the modern workplace and a definition of this concept: "The modern workplace seems to demand more employee time than ever before, there are fewer resources with which to do the work and more and more employees are suffering from 'presenteeism' (needed to be seen at work while overstressed doing the job)."

Joe Cayer, a eminent public personnel scholar, has pointed out that EAPs are often an overlooked benefit that the organization makes available to its employees, and stressing the importance of EAPs to an employer's overall strategic management plan he notes that

The contemporary organization concerns itself with the personal needs of the employee to an extent never contemplated in the traditional organization. Recognizing that the performance of the employee is affected by many things in the employee's life, employers now attempt to deal with the whole person rather than just his or her organizational role. The stresses in the rest of an employee's life affect how well the employee can perform on the job. The employee benefits by finding ways to resolve problems, and the employer benefits by having an employee who is able to focus on the work. Additionally, the employer is able to retain a valuable resource and does not have to bear the costs of replacing loyal employees and training new personnel.

The point is that EAPs are an important component in the employer's benefits package and overall strategic-planning efforts, and to the extent that they are effective programs, public employers can attract and retain quality employees, which is a chief concern as we move into the next century.

BIBLIOGRAPHY

Berridge, J., C. L. Cooper, and C. Highley-Marchington. *Employee Assistance Programs and Workplace Counseling*. Chichester, U.K.: John Wiley. 1997.

Blum, T. C., and Roman P. M. *Cost-Effectiveness and Preventive Implications of Employee Assistance Programs*. Rockville, Md.: U.S. Public Health Service, 1995.

Bowman, James S. "State Government Response to Workplace Violence," *Public Personnel Management*, vol. 26, no. 2 (summer 1997), pp. 289–301.

Bray, J. W., M. T. French, B. J. Bowland, and L. J. Dunlap. "The Cost of Employee Assistance Programs (EAPs): Findings from Seven Case Studies," *Employee Assistance Quarterly*, vol. 11, no. 4 (1996), pp. 1–19.

Campbell, R. L., and R. E. Langford. *Substance Abuse in the Workplace*. Boca Raton, Fla: CRC Press, 1995.

Carroll, M. *Workplace Counseling*. London: Sage, 1996.

Cascio, Wayne F. *Managing Human Resources*. New York: McGraw-Hill, 1989.

Cayer, N. Joseph. "Employee Benefits: From Health Care to Pensions," in Stephen E. Condrey (ed.), *Handbook of Human Resource Management in Government*. San Francisco: Jossey Bass, 1998, pp. 658–675.

Cayer, N. Joseph. "Privacy and Integrity Testing for Public Employees: Searches, Drug Testing, Polygraphs, and Medical Examinations," in Phillip J. Cooper and Chester A. Newland (eds.), *Handbook of Public Law and Administration*. San Francisco: Jossey-Bass, 1997, pp. 287–298.

Chandler v. *Miller*, 117 S.Ct. 1295 (1997).

Condrey, Stephen E., ed. *Handbook of Human Resource Management in Government*. San Francisco: Jossey-Bass, 1998.

Cooper, C. L., and S. Williams, eds. *Creating Healthy Work Organizations*. Chichester U.K.: John Wiley, 1994.

Csiemik, R. "Employee Assistance Consortia: Developing a Research Agenda," *Employee Assistance Quarterly*, vol. 10, no. 2 (1994), pp. 19–35.

Federal Times (December 22, 1997), p. 15.

Figura, Susanna. "Seeking Safety," *Government Executive* (November 1998), pp. 29–34.

Floyd, Charles Neil. "Searches in the Absence of Individualized Suspicion," *Arkansas Law Review,* vol. 50 (1997), pp. 335–362.

"Workplace Violence Affects Millions of Workers Each Year," *Government Employee Relations Report*, vol. 32, no. 1576 (August 8, 1994), pp. 961–962.

"Gunman Kills 4, Dies in Shootout in Orange," *Los Angeles Times* (December 19, 1997), part A, P. 1.

Harris, M. M., and L. L. Heft. "Alcohol and Drug Use in the Workplace: Issues, Controversies, and Directions for Future Research," *Journal of Management*, vol. 18 (1992), pp. 239–266.

Heskett, Sandra. *Workplace Violence: Before, During, and After*. Boston: Butterworth–Heinemann, 1996.

Johnson, A. "Employee Assistance Programs and Employer Downsizing," *Employee Assistance Quarterly*, vol. 10, no. 4 (1995), pp. 17–29.

Johnson, Pamela R. "Stress and Workplace Violence: It Takes Two to Tango," *Journal of Managerial Psychology*, vol. 11, no. 6 (September 1996), pp. 18–27.

Kotschessa, B. "EAP Research: The State of the Art," *Employee Assistance Quarterly*, vol. 10, no. 2, (1994), pp. 63–72.

LaMar, Wanda, Susan Gererich, William Lohman, and Brad Zaidman. "Work-Related Physical Assault," *Journal of Occupational and Environmental Medicine*, vol. 40, no. 4 (April 1998), pp. 317–324.

Luthans, F. and R. Waldersee. "What Do We Really Know About EAPs?" *Human Resources Management*, vol. 28, no. 3 (1989), pp. 3985–401.

Merit Systems Protection Board. *Issues of Merit*. Washington, D.C., February 1998.
    "Adherence to the Merit Principles in the Workplace: Federal Employees' Views." Washington, D.C., December 1997, p. 90.
    Sexual Harassment in the Federal Workplace. Washington, D.C., 1995, Figure 1, Tables 7, 10, 11.

National Treasury Employees Union v. *Von Raab*, 489 U.S. 656 (1989).

Nigro, Lloyd G. and William L. Waugh. "Violence in the American Workplace: Challenges to the Public Employer," *Public Administration Review*, vol. 56, no. 4 (July–August 1996), pp. 326–333.

Norman, J., R. O. Lempert, and C. P. O'Brien, eds. *Under the Influence: Drugs and the American Workforce*. Washington, D.C.: National Academy Press, 1994.

Perlstein, Linda. "Their Offices Are the Pits, but These Workers Don't Mind," *Washington Post* (August 4, 1998), p. A13.

Riccucci, Norma M. "Constitutions, Statutes, Regulations, and Labor Relations: Dispute Resolution in a Complex Authority Mix," in Phillip J. Cooper and Chester Newland (eds.), *Handbook of Public Law and Administration*. San Francisco: Jossey-Bass, 1997, pp. 274–286.

Riccucci, Norma M. "Drug Testing in the Public Sector: A Legal Analysis," *American Review of Public Administration*, vol. 20 (June 1990), pp. 95–106.

Rivenbark, Leigh. "Cases Swamp EEOC," *Federal Times* (August 10, 1998), p. 3.

Rosenbloom, David H. *Public Administration: Understanding Management, Politics and Law in the Public Sector.* New York: McGraw-Hill, 1998.

"Routine Turns to Tragedy: Shootings," *Los Angeles Times* (April 24, 1998).

Skinner v. *Railway Labor Executives' Association*, 489 U.S. 602 (1989).

Stevenson, Jerry G. and Roger Williamson. "Testing for Drugs: Bathrooms or Barbershops," *Public Personnel Management*, vol. 24 (winter 1995), pp. 467–474.

Vernonia School District 47J v. *Acton*, 115 S.Ct. 2386 (1995).

VandenBos, Gary and Elizabeth Q. Bulatao, eds. *Violence on the Job.* Washington, D.C.: American Psychological Association, 1996.

Wilkinson, Roger W. "Special Needs Exception for Suspicionless Searches Does Not Extend to Candidate Drug Testing," *Suffolk University Law Review*, vol. 31 (1997), pp. 237–247.

Werther, William Jr. and Keith Davis. *Human Resources and Personnel Management*, 3rd ed. New York: McGraw-Hill, 1989.

"Workplace Violence: When a Job Becomes the Only Meaningful Thing in a Person's Life," *Hartford Courant* (March 8, 1998), p. A-14.

Index

Ability to pay, 502
Abood v. *Detroit Board of Education*
    (1977), 115, 116, 494, 504
Acceptability, in nonbinding arbitration,
    502
Access American: Reengineering
    Through Information Technol-
    ogy, 352
Adarand Constructors Inc. v. *Pena*
    (1995), 119, 229, 236, 380
Adjudicatory systems, for handling un-
    fairness charges in the work-
    place, 535–541
Adjustment projections (in workforce
    skills planning), 149
Administrative Careers with America
    (ACWA), 389
  examination system of, 254–256
Adult learning, 312
Advanced-level jobs, 179
Adverse effect, 395
Adverse impact, 226, 395
Adverse-inference rule, 395
Affected class, 395
Affirmative action, 119–120
  from *Bakke* to *Hopwood*, 375–378

[Affirmative action]
  chronology of legal actions affecting,
    379–380
  comparison of equal employment op-
    portunity, diversity and, 422
  defined by EEO, 395–396
  difference between equal employment
    opportunity and, 378
  future of, 415–416
  legal actions affecting, 379–380
  managerial aspects of, 393–408
    developing a plan, 393–400
    monitoring the plan, 400–403
    sexual harassment, 403–408
  See also Equal employment opportunity
AFL-CIO, 461, 483
  new era of labor-management rela-
    tions in public sector and, 510
  See also American Federation of La-
    bor (AFL)
African-Americans:
  ACWA examination system and,
    254–256
  culturally fair tests and, 253
  development of *Uniform Guidelines*
    and, 230–236

[African-Americans]
  inequities in employment in federal
    government, 438–439
  legal decisions about public sector re-
    cruitment and selection affecting,
    224–229
  PACE exam and, 252
  postal alliance and, 480
  racial discrimination cases and, 120
  representation in grade groupings in
    federal government (1997), 390,
    391
  representation in the population, civil-
    ian, and federal workforces
    (1997), 429, 430
  stereotyping of, 449
  subjective discrimination in today's
    workforce, 432–434, 439
  Workforce 2020 report on increase in
    employment of, 425
  See also Affirmative action; Equal
    Employment Opportunity
AFSCME v. *State of Washington*
  (1985), 413
Age discrimination, 413–414
Age Discrimination in Employment Act
  (ADEA) of 1967, 103, 413–
  414
Agriculture, Department of, workplace
  violence in, 531
AIDS/HIV, employment discrimination
  based on, 414–415
Alabama:
  collective bargaining provisions for,
    492
  job classifications in (1986–1998),
    204
Alaska:
  collective bargaining provisions for,
    492
  job classifications in (1986–1998),
    204
  public employees right to strike in
    (1998), 504
Albermarle Paper Company v. *Moody*
  (1975), 230

Alcoholic Anonymous, as model for
  EAPs, 554
Alternative dispute resolution (ADR),
  541–542
American Customer Satisfaction Index,
  348, 349
American Federation of Government
  Employees (AFGE), 461
American Federation of Labor (AFL),
  477
  Boston police strike of 1919 and,
    467
American Federation of State, County,
  and Municipal Employees (AFS-
  CME), 501
American Psychological Association,
  study of workplace violence by,
  532
American Society for Quality Control,
  quality defined by, 344
American Society for Training and Development (ASTD), guidelines
  for "professionalization" of
  training, 309–310
Americans with Disabilities Act (ADA)
  of 1990, 103–104, 414, 415
  substance abuse in the workplace
    and, 549
Arbitration, 501–502
Arizona:
  collective bargaining provisions for,
    492
  job classifications in (1986–1998),
    204
Arkansas:
  collective bargaining provisions for,
    492
  job classifications in (1986–1998),
    204
Art of the Long View, The (Schwartz),
  157–159
Arthur administration, civil service reform and, 11–12
Asian-Americans:
  inequities in employment in federal
    government, 438

[Asian-Americans]
representation in federal workforce (1997), 427–428
representation in grade groupings in federal government, 390, 391
representation in the population, civilian, and federal workforces (1997), 429, 430
stereotyping in the workplace for, 435
subjective discrimination in today's workforce, 432, 434, 439
Workforce 2020 report on increase in employment of, 425
Assembled examinations, 247
Assessment centers, 293–298
typical exercises used by, 295
Atlanta, Georgia, GS and SES salary rages for (2000), 210
Attrition projections (in workforce skills planning), 149
Australia, public-private competitions in, 142
Awards for quality, 340

Balanced scorecard (BSC), 360–361
Baltimore–Washington, GS and SES salary ranges for (2000), 210
Bargaining:
criteria for 495
in federal employment, 498, 499
impasse resolution and, 499–503
Baruch report (1942 report on position classification), 180–183
Baselining, 347
Behavior:
behavioral focus on performance appraisal, 277–281
as level of measuring training evaluation, 330
Behavioralism (learning theory), 312
Behavioralist critique of the position classification system, 185–188
Behaviorally anchored rating scales (BARS), 277
Bell Laboratories, 337

Benchmarking, 347–348
Bill of Rights (as legal framework for public employment), 107–108
Bishop v. *Wood* (1976), 121–122
Black Intelligence Tests of Cultural Homogeneity (BITCH), 283
Board of Regents v. *Roth* (1972), 121
Bona fide occupational qualification (BFOQ), 396, 414
Boston police strike of 1919, 466, 467–468
Boston, Mass., GS and SES salary ranges for (2000), 210
Bottom-line concept, 396
Branti v. *Frankel* (1980), 95
British Civil Service, American civil service reform system and, 243
Broadbanding, 197–201
in the states, 202–205
Brownlow Committee, 19–22, 24
Budget Enforcement Act of 1990, 57
Bureaucracy, representative, 425–427
Bureau of Labor Statistics (BLS), employment predictions for federal and state governments (1986–2006), 151–152
Bureau of Programs and Standards report on public service grade escalation (1963), 184–185
Burlington Industries v. *Ellerth* (1998), 408
Bush administration:
civil service reform and, 56–57
federal pay reform and, 209
Business necessity, 396
Business process reengineering (BPR), 348–355
Business Process Reengineering Assessment Guide (GAO guide to BPR), 351–352

California:
affirmative action and, 416
collective bargaining provisions for, 492

[California]
  fastest growing and declining state
      jobs in (1993 and 1997), 136,
      137
  job classifications in (1986–1998),
      204
  Proposition 209 in, 378
  public employees right to strike in
      (1998), 504
  workplace violence in the public sec-
      tor, 531
Career development, 313–321
Carter administration:
  civil service reform and, 24–29
  EEO program and, 388
Catastrophes, 544
Center for Disease Control & Preven-
      tion, workplace violence re-
      ported by, 532
Center for Women in Government,
      438
Central personnel agency, development
      of, 15–33
  phase I (policing), 16
  phase II (scientific management), 16–
      19
  phase III (centralization), 19–20
  phase IV (decentralization of person-
      nel operations), 20–22
  phase V (demise of civil service com-
      mission), 22–24
  phase VI (reform), 24–32
Chalk v. *U.S. District Court* (1998),
      414–415
Chandler v. *Miller* (1997), 551–552
Changing Federal Workplace, The
      (1996 MSPB merit principles sur-
      vey), 273
Charlotte, North Carolina:
  BSC and, 360
  public–private competitions in, 142
Chicago, Illinois:
  GS and SES salary ranges for (2000),
      210
  positive classification program for
      (1912), 177

Chicago Teachers Union v. *Hudson*
      (1986), 116
Chief Operating Officer (COO) of the
      POB, 74
Chilling effect, 396
City of Richmond v. *Croson* (1989),
      119, 228, 379
Civil Right Act of 1964, 103, 225, 228,
      375, 385
  equal protection and, 119
  gender discrimination and, 386
  pregnancy discrimination amendment
      to, 410, 412, 413
Chicago Teachers Union v. *Hudson*
      (1986), 116
Civil Rights Act of 1991, 103, 228, 387
  sexual harassment and, 404
Civil Service 2000 (Hudson Institute
      1988 report for OPM), 207, 424,
      447
Civil Service Act of 1883. *see* Pendle-
      ton Act
Civil Service Assembly of 1937, 180
Civil Service Commission (CSC), 114
  demise of, 22–24
  early recruiting efforts of (1891), 244
  EEO and, 385, 386, 387, 390
  formation of (1883), 2, 11, 13–15
  job evaluation system of the 1970s
      and, 188–197
  racial discrimination action of, 382
Civil Service Commission of 1912,
      177
Civil Service Improvement Act of 1998,
      77
Civil service reform:
  in the postreform era (1979 to 2000),
      45–92
    aftermath of CSRA of 1978, 48–
      53
    civil service improvements (1999),
      82–90
    civil service reform at state and lo-
      cal level, 77–81
    civil service reform in Clinton's
      second term, 72–77

[Civil service reform]
Clinton administration "transition", 57–60
death of the merit system in Georgia, 45–48
NPR and federal workforce restructuring, 60–67
reinvention of the OPM, 67–72
the Volcker Commission, 53–57
See also First century of civil service reform
Civil Service Reform Act (CSRA) of 1978, 24–32, 289–290, 477, 479, 483–487
aftermath of, 48–53
changes in performance appraisal and, 281
federal merit principles stated in, 97–103
merit principles established by, 26
representative bureaucracy and, 426
WPA amendment to (1989), 32
Civil Service Reform Association (1880), 12
Civil Service Retirement Spouse Equity Act of 1987, 290
Class (defined), 178–179
Classification Act of 1923, 19, 177–178, 288, 382
principles established in, 180
Classification Act of 1949, 22, 183–185
Classification and compensation, 171–220
behavioralist critique, 185–186
classification in the states, 202–208
classification (or staffing) in public sector organization, 176–177
evolution of position classification (scientific management), 177–183
factor evaluation in the 1970s, 188–197
federal pay reform: 1990, 208–212
living wages, 215–217
pay administration in government, 206–208

[Classification and compensation]
reform initiative of the 1990s, 197–201
state and local compensation developments, 212–215
transformation of New York VBA regional office (1993–1997), 171–176
after World War II (Classification Act of 1948), 183–185
Classification method (major category of job evaluation planning), 191, 192
Classroom instructions (training method), 311
Class series (defined), 179
Claus v. *Duquesne Light Company* (1995), 380
Clay–Marcy Senate debate of 1832, 5
Cleveland Board of Education v. *LaFleur* (1974), 116
Cleveland Board of Education v. *Loudermill* (1985), 122
Clinton administration:
Civil Service Reform Act of 1978 and, 486–487
civil service reform and, 31, 57–60, 72–77
reinvention of OPM, 67–72
collective bargaining in the public sector and, 461–463, 466–470
creation of NPC, 461–463
effect of downsizing on government hiring and, 256
federal pay reform and, 209
federal workforce restructuring and, 60–67
labor–management partnership and, 463–466, 497–498
quality management and, 346, 371
revision of affirmative action programs and, 416
sexual harassment and, 404, 407
Coaching (training method), 311
Codd v. *Velger* (1977), 122
Cognitive theory, 312

Cohen v. *Chesterfield County School Board* (1974), 116
Collective bargaining (in the public sector), 104, 466–476
adjusting the private sector model for, 473–474
development of, 466–470
dysfunction in, 475–476
early history of, 476–481
loss of coherence, 474–475
modifications for, 470–473
in the postal service, 482–483
state provisions for, 492–493
Colorado:
collective bargaining provisions for, 492
job classifications in (1986–1998), 204
Commission form of government, decline of, 37–39
Commission on the Status of Women, 385
Communication and feedback, importance in the workplace of, 440–441
Comparable worth, 408–411
Compensation, quality and, 366–367
Competing for Federal Jobs and Restoring Merit to Federal Hiring (MSPB 1990 report), 257–260
Complaints of discrimination, procedure for processing individual complaints, 401–402
Complexity (factor in federal job evaluation system), 191
Compulsory arbitration, 501
Computer networks, 331
Concurrent validity, 250
Congressional Budget Office (CBO), federal compensation and, 208
Congressional Joint Commission on Reclassification of Salaries (1919), 177
Connecticut:
collective bargaining provisions for, 492

[Connecticut]
job classifications in (1986–1998), 204
workplace violence in the public sector, 531
Connick v. *Meyers* (1983), 111
Consent decree, 397
Constitutional law of public employment, 106–109
Construct validity, 251
Content validity, 249, 250
Continuous (or integer) rating scale, 274–275
Contracting out training, 309
Contractor cooperation, 343
Cornerstones of quality management, 342–343
Corpus Christi army depot (CCAD), 360-degree performance appraisal at, 265–265, 268–269
Corruption in post-Civil War era, 12
Costing Human Resources (Cascio), 137
Counseling in the workplace. *see* Employee Assistance Programs (EAPs)
County of Washington, Oregon v. *Gunther* (1981), 413
Crisis management plans, 534
Criterion-related validity, 249, 250–251
Cross-functional teams (CFTs), 369
Culturally fair tests, 283
Current recruitment projections (in workforce skills planning), 149
Customer feedback, 342

Dallas v. *Dallas Fire Fighters Association* (1990), 229
Data collection, diversity awareness and, 447–449
Death and Life of the American Quality Movement, The (Cole), 345
Decision analysis forecasting, 150, 157
Defense, Department of (DOD):
commitment to diversity by, 450–451

[Defense, Department of (DOD)]
Quadrennial Defense Review (QDR)
for, 352
quality management and, 335, 339,
343, 361
Delaware:
collective bargaining provisions for,
492
job classifications in (1986–1998), 204
Delphi Group, report on knowledge
management of, 302
Delphi techniques, 150, 157, 158
Deming Prize, 340
Deming, W. Edwards, 337, 338
Demographic changes in the workforce,
implications for training and development), 326
Disability discrimination, 414
Discontinuous (discrete-unit) rating
scale, 274
Discrimination, 397
disability discrimination, 414
procedure for handling employee complaints of, 537, 539–540
proving, 454–455
subjective, 432–434
Disparate effect, 397
Dispute resolution mechanisms, in managing employee relations, 535–
543
alternative dispute resolution approaches, 541–543
traditional adjudicatory systems, 536–
541
Diversity, management of, 421–459
challenge of ensuring equal opportunities, 423–431
comparison of EEO, affirmative action, and diversity, 422
managing diversity in Seattle, 421–
423
proving discrimination, 454–455
society and the individual share responsibility, 453–454
strategies for greater inclusion, 439–
453

[Diversity, management of]
changing organizational structure
and work processes, 452–453
data collection and training, 447–
449
ensuring effective communication
and feedback, 440–441
leadership and accountability, 450–
452
reorienting personnel policies and
processes, 441–447
unequal treatment in today's workplace, 431–439
glass ceilings, 436–438
other disparities, 438–439
power of subtle differences, 439
stereotypes, 434–435
subjective discrimination, 432–434
Doctrine of privilege, 106–109
Downsizing
BPR and, 348–350
human resource planning and, 139–147
Robert Reich on downsizing, 146
unintended consequences of downsizing, 144–145
Downsizing of America, The, 142
Drug-Free Workplace Act of 1988, 549
Drugs:
Global Drug Testing Services, 552
substance abuse in the workplace,
549
testing for, 549–553
tips on beating the test, 551
Duke Power Company, Dan River Station, 224–226
Du Pont, quality and labor relation is-
sues at, 371

Early phase (of career development),
313
E-commerce scenarios, use by EPA for
human resources planning needs,
160–164
Education, Department of, changes in
general schedule employees
(1982 to 1992), 59

Elrod v. *Burns* (1976), 93–95, 115, 125
Employee assistance programs (EAPs),
   535, 548–549, 553–557
   treatment of employee substance
      abuse by, 549
Employee relations, 531–559
   defining employee relations, 535
   employee assistance programs, 553–
      557
   formal dispute resolution mecha-
      nisms, 535–543
      alternative dispute resolution ap-
         proaches, 541–543
      traditional adjudicatory systems,
         536–541
   job safety and health, 543–553
      drug testing, 549–553
      substance abuse in the workplace,
         549
   workplace violence in the public sec-
      tor, 531–534
Employee surveys, 323
Employment practice, 397
Employment process, essentials of,
   242–246
"Empowerment: The Emperor's New
   Clothes" (Argyris), 362
Environment Protection Agency (EPA),
   scenario-planning work for human resources needs, 160–164
Equal employment opportunity (EEO),
   375–419
   abuses of the past, 378–383
   age discrimination, 413–414
   from *Bakke* to *Hopwood*, 375–378
   challenge of ensuring equal opportuni-
      ties, 423–431
   civil service reform efforts and, 50–
      51
   comparable worth and pay equity,
      408–411
   comparison of affirmative action, di-
      versity and, 422
   comparison of managing diversity
      with, 422
   definition of, 397

[Equal employment opportunity (EEO)]
   development of, 383–390
   difference between affirmative action
      and, 378
   disability discrimination, 414
   discrimination based on HIV/AIDS,
      414–415
   federal employee complaint system
      of, 537–541
   female–male pay gap, 411–412
   future of, 415–516
   language of, 395–399
   legal and judicial developments, 412–
      413
   organization of, 390–393
Equal Employment Opportunity Act of
   1972, 103–104, 226, 386–387
Equal Employment Opportunity Commission (EEOC), 385, 386, 387
   Civil Service Reform Act of 1978
      and, 485
   CSC and, 25–26
   EEO responsibilities transferred to,
      388
   representative bureaucracy issue and,
      427–429
   Uniform Guidelines issued by, 230
Equal employment opportunity coun-
   selor, 397
Equal employment opportunity officer,
   397
Equal Pay Act of 1963, 103, 412, 413
Equal protection, 119–120
Equity, 502
Ethics law, 104
Ethnic quotas, proving discrimination in
   SFUSD and, 454–455
Evaluation:
   systematic approach to, 329
   of training and development, 325–
      330
Examinations:
   ACWA examination system, 254–256
   Churchill on, 248
   as essential of employment process,
      242–243, 246–251

[Examinations]
   FSEE exam, 252
   PACE examination, 252–254, 255,
      388
Exchange programs (training method),
   312
Executive Core Qualifications (ECQs),
   for federal senior executive ser-
   vices, 316–320
Executive Order 8802 of 1941, 384
Executive Order 10988 of 1962, 478,
   481
Executive Order 11491 of 1969, 478,
   481
Exit interview, 154
Experienced level (position classifica-
   tion), 179
Expert individual approach to job analy-
   sis, 278–279

Face validity, 249, 251
Factor comparison method (major category of job evaluation planning),
   191, 192
Factor evaluation system (1970s), 188–
   197
   comparison with other job evaluation
      systems, 194
   five groupings in, 189
   nine factors on which the system is
      based, 190–191
Factors (defined), 178
"Facts and Fallacies in Position Classi-
   fication," (Baruch), 182
Fair Employment Practice Commission
   (FEPC), 398
Fair Employment Practice Committee,
   384
Fair employment practice laws, 398
Fair Employment Practices Board
   (1948), 384
Faragher v. *City of Boca Raton* (1998),
   408
Fatalities, 544
Fed 2000 (OSHA safety and health ini-
   tiative), 545–546

Federal Activities Inventory Reform Act
   (FAIR), 141
Federal Aviation Administration (FAA):
   BSC and, 360
   diversity awareness training at, 447,
      448
Federal compensation, 206–208
   1990 pay reform, 208–212
Federal Employees Pay Council, 206
Federal Equal Opportunity Recruitment
   Program (FEORP), 426
Federal Glass Ceiling Commission, 427,
   435, 436
Federal Human Resource Management
   Reinvention Act of 1995, 72–73
Federal Labor Relations Authority
   (FLRA), 29, 30, 483, 484
   civil service reform efforts and, 50
Federal land management, decline in
   fire-fighting workforce, 131–
   134
Federal Medication and Conciliation Ser-
   vice, 500
Federal Pay Comparability Act of 1970,
   major revision to, 206
Federal Pay Comparability Act of 1990,
   56–57
Federal Pay Reform Act of 1990, 208–
   209
Federal Political Personnel Manual
   (Malek Manual), 38–39
Federal Quality Institute (FQI), 336–
   337, 340, 343
Federal Safety and Health Advisory
   Committee (FACOSH), 544, 548
Federal Salary Act of 1967, 206
Federal Service Entrance Examination
   (FSEE exam), 252
Federal Wildfire Activities (GAO re-
   port), 131–132, 133
Federal Women's Program, 392
Federal workforce, Clinton transition
   team recommendations for, 58–
   60
Federal Workforce Restructuring Act of
   1994, 68–69

Feedback, importance in the workplace
of, 440–441
Feigenbaum, Arnold, 337, 338
Fifth Amendment, doctrine of privilege
and, 108
Final offer arbitration, 501–502
*Firefighters Local Union and Memphis
Fire Department* v. *Stotts*
(1984), 379
First Amendment, doctrine of privilege
and, 108
First century of civil service reform, 1–
42
civil service reform and decline of
the commission format, 37–39
development of central personnel
agency, 15–32
phase I (policing), 16
phase II (scientific management),
16–19
phase III (centralization), 19–20
phase IV (decentralization of personnel operations), 20–22
phase V (demise of civil service
commission), 22–24
phase VI (reform), 24–32
impetus for reform, 8–13
merits of reform, 39–40
motivation for civil service reform,
6–7
origins of the merit system, 1–2
the Pendleton Act of 1883, 13–15
the spoils system, 2–6
state and local institutional arrangements, 33–37
Florida:
collective bargaining provisions for,
492
job classifications in (1986–1998),
204
Foley v. *Connelle* (1978), 117
Follow-up inspection, 544
Formal training, 311
Format for training, 310–312
Fourth Amendment, privacy rights and,
123–125

Fowler v. *New York City Department of
Sanitation* (1989), 125
France, merit system in, 2
Freedom of Association, 115–116
*From Red Tape to Results: Creating a
Government That Works Bet-
ter & Costs Less* (1993 Gore Re-
port), 60
FSEE exam (Federal Service Entrance
Examination), 252
Fullivove v. *Klutznick* (1980), 379
Functional job analysis, 323, 324

Gender differential, 398
Gender discrimination, 398
in employment, 386
equal protection in gender discrimination cases, 120
General Accounting Office (GAO):
broadbanding and, 199
on federal compensation, 207
quality management and, 346, 351–
352
report on decline in fire-fighting workforce, 131–132, 133
General Electric, quality management
program of, 357–358, 361
General Electric Co. v. *Gilbert* (1976),
410
Generalist/team leader phase (of career
development), 313
General scheduled (GS) pay plan, 183
Georgia:
collective bargaining provisions for,
492
job classifications in (1986–1998), 203,
204
merit system in, 45–48
Gilbert v. *Homar* (1997), 122
Glass Ceiling Commission, 387
Glass ceilings, 436–438
Global Drug Testing Services, 552
Glossary of federal sector labor-management relations terms, 510–
528

Glover v. *Eastern Nebraska Community Office of Retardation* (1989), 124–125
"Going postal," 532
Gore Report (1993), 60
Governing, on size and importance of public sector employers, 236–239
Government (magazine), on merit system in Georgia, 45, 46, 48
Government Employees' Training Act of 1958, 288
Grace commission, 62
Grant administration, civil service reform and, 6–7, 9–11
Grievances, 508–510
Griggs v. *Duke Power Company* (1971), 224, 226, 227, 228, 230, 243
Group approach to job analysis, 278–279
Group (or external) ratings, 275
Guide for Improving Performance Appraisal (1978 OPM study), 277–278
Guidelines (factor in federal job evaluation system), 190
Guidelines on Affirmative Action, 400

Harassment in the Federal Workplace (MSPB study), 405
Harley v. *Schuylkill County* (1979), 125
Harris v. *Forklift Systems, Inc.* (1993), 407
Harvard Business Review, 348, 362
Hatch Act of 1939, 114
Hatch Act of 1940, 114
Hawaii:
    collective bargaining provisions for, 492
    job classifications in (1986–1998), 204
    public employees right to strike in (1998), 504
Hayes administration, civil service reform and, 12–13

Health and Human Services, Department of (HHS), change in general schedule employees (1982 to 1992), 59
Hewlett-Packard, 335, 338, 361
Hill-Thomas hearings (1991), 403–404
Hispanic Employment Program, 386, 387, 392
Hispanics:
    inequities in employment in federal government, 438
    subjective discrimination in today's workforce, 432, 434, 439
    Workforce 2020 report on increase in employment of, 425
    See also Affirmative action, Equal employment opportunity (EEO), and Latinos
History of human resources planning, 147–148
HIV/AIDS, employment discrimination based on, 414–415
Hopwood v. *State of Texas* (1996), 376–378
Hostile environment (as sexual harassment), 406–407
Housing and Urban Development, Department of (HUD):
    change in general schedule employees (1982 to 1992), 59
    commitment to diversity by, 450–451
Houston, Texas, GS and SES salary ranges for (2000), 210
How Do Public Managers Manage? (Ban), 96, 128
Hudson Institute, *Workforce 2000* and *Workforce 2020* issued by, 424–425
Human resources information system (HRIS), 323, 324
Human resources management:
    1999 civil service improvements in, 89–90
    objectives of performance appraisal by, 270
    quality and, 364–366

Human resources (HR) planning, 131–
170
environment for, 134–139
forecasting human resources supply,
155–156
forecasting organizational demands,
156–164
historical overview of, 147–148
HR planning in an era of downsizing,
139–147
Robert Reich on downsizing, 146
unintended consequences of downsizing, 144–145
strategic HR planning, 164–168
workforce planning, 149–153

Idaho:
collective bargaining provisions for,
492
job classifications in (1986–1998),
204
public employees right to strike in
(1998), 504
"Ideal type" bureaucratic model, 2
Illinois:
collective bargaining provisions for,
492
job classifications in (1986–1998),
204
public employees right to strike in
(1998), 504
state-wide positive classification program for (1912), 177
Imminent danger, 543
Incentive Award Act of 1954, 288
Indiana:
collective bargaining provisions for,
492
job classifications in (1986–1998),
204
Indianapolis, Indiana, public-private
competitions in, 142
Individual achievement record (IAR),
254
Individualized rights approach to public
employment, 109–110

Informal training (classroom instruc-
tions), 311
Information technology, 331–332
Information Technology Management
Reform Act of 1996, 351–352
Information technology reengineering,
353–354
In re Birmingham Revenue Discrimination Employment Litigation
(1995), 380
Intellectual capital. see Knowledge management (KM) movement
Intergovernmental Personnel Act (IPA)
of 1970, 35–37
Interior, Department of (DOI), downsizing of workforce (1993 and
1998), 132
Internal computer networks, 331
Internal Revenue Service (IRS):
quality management and, 343
reengineering and, 354
Internet, 331
effect of Internet economy on federal
recruitment and selection, 257–
260
Interviews of employees, supervisors, or
work experts, 323–324
Iowa:
collective bargaining provisions for,
492
job classifications in (1986–1998),
204
IRS v. Federal Labor Relations Authority (1990), 486
ISO 9000, 362
ISO 14000, 362

Jackson administration:
civil service reform and, 3–5
spoils doctrine of, 4
Japan, approach to quality management
in, 337, 338, 339
Jefferson administration, civil service reform and, 3
Job (defined), 178
Job analysis (defined), 178

Job evaluation (defined), 178
Job Evaluation and Pay Review Task Force (of the CSC), 188–189
Job Evaluation and Ranking in the Federal Government (1968 report), 198
Job Evaluation Policy Act of 1970, 188
Job evaluation systems (nonsupervisory positions), comparison of, 193, 194
Job rotation programs, 311
Job safety and health, 543–553
  drug testing, 549–553
  substance abuse in the workplace, 549
Jobs in the federal government, fastest growing and declining jobs (1993 and 1997), 136, 137
Johnson (Andrew) administration, civil service reform and, 8–9
Johnson (Lyndon) administration, creation of the EEO, 385, 386
Johnson & Johnson, 335
Johnson v. Santa Clara County Transportation Agency (1987), 227, 229, 443
Journal of Higher Education, on applications of information technology, 331
Juran, Joseph, 337, 338
Justice, Department of, changes in general schedule employees (1982 to 1992), 59

Kansas:
  collective bargaining provisions for, 492
  job classifications in (1986–1998), 204
Kennedy administration:
  collective bargaining and, 481
  EEO programs and, 384–385
Kentucky:
  collective bargaining provisions for, 492

[Kentucky]
  job classifications in (1986–1998), 204
Knights of Labor, 477
Knowledge management (KM) movement, 301–304, 330
Knowledge required by the position (factor in federal job evaluation system), 190

"Labeling" in diversity awareness training, 449
Labor, Department of:
  changes in general schedule employees (1982 to 1992), 69
  guidelines for responsible restructuring, 140
Labor relations, 104
Labor-management relations, 461–529
  collective bargaining, 466–476
  early history, 476–481
    major labor relation policies covering federal workers, 478–479
  federal program matures, 482–487
  glossary of federal sector labor-management relation terms, 510–528
  impasse resolution, 499–503
  organizing and unit determination, 497–498
  origin of federal labor-management partnership, 463–466
  partnerships of labor and management, 487–488
  quality and labor-management cooperation, 370–372
  scope of bargaining, 498, 499
  state and local arrangements, 491–496
  strikes, 503–510
  supervisors, 496
  why employees unionize, 488–491
LaChance v. Erickson (1998), 123
Ladies and Gentlemen of the Civil Service (Sondik Aron), 382
Language of the EEO, 395–399

Latinos:
representation in grade groupings in
federal government (1997), 390,
391
representation in population, civilian,
and federal workforces (1997),
429, 430
See also Affirmative action; Equal
Employment Opportunity, and
Hispanics
Leadership, 315
commitment to diversity by, 450–
452
Leadership for America (Volcker Commission report), 207
Learning (level of measuring training
evaluation), 330
Lebron v. *National Railroad Passenger
Corporation* (1995), 127
Legal actions affecting affirmative action, 379–380
Legal framework, 93–130
comparing legal and managerial
frameworks of government, 96–
97
constitutional law of public employment, 106–109
Elrod v . *Burns* (1976), 93–96
importance of knowing your law, 128
individualized rights approach, 109–
110
merit principles and civil service, 97–
105
civil rights and equal opportunity
law, 103–104
enforcement, 104–105
ethics law, 104
labor relations, 104
for public sector employment, 224–
229
public service model, 110–128
equal protection, 119–120
Fourth Amendment privacy, 123–
125
freedom of association, 115–116
freedom of expression, 110–113

[Legal framework]
liberty, 116–118
political neutrality, 113–115
privatization, 125–128
right to disobey, 125
right to a hearing, 120–123
Lehnert v. *Ferris Faculty Assn.* (1991),
494
Lewinsky affair, 404
Lincoln administration:
patronage appointments and, 15
spoils system and, 6
Living wages, 215–217
Lloyd-LaFollette Act of 1912, 477,
478
Local government:
civil service reform and, 77–81
compensation developments for, 212–
215
diversity in traditionally male occupations (1985 and 1995), 426
EAPs and, 554
federal EEO program and, 387
labor-management relations and,
491–496
merit system and, 33–37
minimum (living) wages and, 215–
217
union vs. nonunion wages for work
in (1998), 473
Los Angeles, California, GS and SES
salary ranges for (2000), 210
Louisiana:
collective bargaining provisions for,
492
job classifications in (1986–1998),
204
Luevano v. *Campbell* (1980), 252
Luevano v. *Devine* (1980), 252

McCarthy v. *Philadelphia Civil Service
Commission* (1976), 118
Mcdonnel Douglas, quality and training
issues at, 369
McLaughlin v. *Tilendis* (1912), 491

Maine:
collective bargaining provisions for, 493
job classifications in (1986–1998), 204
Major functions of performance appraisal, 267–269
Make whole, 398
Malcolm Baldrige Award, 340, 343, 356, 359
Malek Manual, 38–39
Management/executive phase (of career development), 313
Management by objective (MBO), 280
Managerial framework of government, comparing legal framework with, 96–97
Martin v. *Wilks* (1989), 120, 179
Maryland:
collective bargaining provisions for, 493
job classifications in (1986–1998), 204
Massachusetts:
collective bargaining provisions for, 493
job classifications in (1986–1998), 204
Mediation, bargaining and, 499–503
Merit system (pay for performance), 29, 52
basic principles of, 26
civil service reform and, 97–105
civil rights and equal opportunity law, 103–104
enforcement, 104–105
ethics law, 104
labor relations, 104
discrimination practices due to, 389–390
in Georgia, 45–48
history of, 281–286, 287
as impetus for reform, 8–13
1999 civil service improvement in, 82–85
origins of, 13

[Merit system (pay for performance)]
state and local government arrangements of, 33–37
statutory basis for state and local systems, 36–37
Merit System Protection Board (MSPB), 28–29
broadbanding and, 199
civil service reform efforts and, 450
exit survey developed by, 154
federal compensation and, 208
glass ceiling study of, 436–437
merit principles and, 105
performance appraisals survey by, 271, 272, 273, 276
personal liberty and, 118
report on federal recruitment and hiring methods (1999), 257–260
report on inequities in minority employment in federal government, 438–439
study of sexual harassment in the federal government, 405, 541, 542
subjective discrimination survey by, 432–433
supervisory vs. employee ratings of performance (1999 survey), 271, 272
surveys on performance appraisal and merit pay, 283, 285–287
unfair workplace charges and, 536, 537, 538
Merit System Standards (1979), 23
Meritor Savings Bank v. *Vinson* (1986), 406
Metro Broadcasting v. *F. C. C.* (1990), 379
Mexican-Americans. *see* Hispanics; Latinos
Michigan:
civil service executive recruitment in, 221–224
collective bargaining provisions for, 493
job classifications in (1986–1998), 204

Minimum wages, 215–217
Minnesota:
  collective bargaining provisions for,
    493
  job classifications in (1986–1998),
    204
  public employees right to strike in
    (1998), 504
  strategic human resources staffing
    model from, 166–167
Minorities:
  ACWA examination system and,
    254–256
  culturally fair tests and, 253
  development of *Uniform Guidelines*
    and, 230–236
  inequities in employment in federal
    government for, 438–439
  legal decisions about public sector re-
    cruitment and selection affecting,
    224–229
  PACE exam and, 252
  See also Affirmative action, catego-
    ries of minorities, and Equal Em-
    ployment Opportunity (EEO)
Mississippi:
  collective bargaining provisions for,
    493
  job classifications in (1986–1998),
    205
Missouri:
  collective bargaining provisions for,
    493
  job classifications in (1986–1998),
    205
Mitchell in Civil Service Commission v.
    *National Association of Letter
    Carriers* (1973), 114–115
Model career planning, 323, 324
Modeling (training method), 311–312
Model Public Personnel Administration
    Law of National Civil Service
    Reform League (1970), 39
Montana:
  collective bargaining provisions for,
    493

[Montana]
  job classifications in (1986–1998), 205
  public employees right to strike in
    (1998), 504
Motivation for civil service reform, 6–7
Motorola, 335, 361
  quality management program of,
    357–358
*Mt. Healthy City School District Board
    of Education* v. *Doyle* (1977),
    122–123
Multisource appraisals, 293–298

NAACP, ethnic quotas in San Francisco
    Unified School District and,
    454–455
NASA:
  application of QCs at, 339
  quality management and, 335, 339,
    343, 361
National Academy of Public Administra-
    tion (NAPA):
  report of broadbanding, 197, 200–201
  study of federal recruitment, 256
National Academy of Science, 284–285
National Association of Letter Carriers
    (NALC), 477, 480
  postal strike of 1970 and, 469–470
National Civil Service Reform League,
    12
  Model Public Personnel Administra-
    tion Law (1970) of, 39
National Commission on the Public Ser-
    vice. *see* Volcker Commission
National Commission on the State and
    Local Public Service (1991). *see*
    Winter Commission
National Federation of Federal Employ-
    ees (NFFE), 461
National Federation of Postal Clerks,
    477
National Fire and Aviation Management
    Workforce, needs analysis report
    of (1997), 132
National Institute of Standards and Tech-
    nology, 197

National Labor Review Board (NLRB), 371

National Park Service, OSHA and, 545–546

National Partnership Council (NPC), 461–463, 488

National Performance Review (NPR), 31, 346–348, 461, 463, 479
  federal workforce restructuring and, 60–67
  recommendations for reinventing human resources management, 65–67
  recommendations for reinventing OPM, 69–70

National Safe Work Place Institute, 534

National Treasury Employees Union (NTEU), 461

National Treasury Employees Union v. *Von Raab* (1989), 549–550

Native Americans:
  inequities in employment in federal government, 438
  representation in grade groupings in the federal government, 390, 391
  representation in the population, civilian, and federal workforces, 429, 430
  stereotyping in the workplace for, 435
  subjective discrimination in today's workforce, 432, 434, 439
  See also Affirmative action and Equal employment opportunity (EEO)

Nature and Meaning of Grade Escalation Under the Classification Act, The (1963 report), 184–185

Naval Aviation Supply Office, quality and compensation issues for, 367

Naval Ocean Systems Center (California), experiments in broadbanding at, 197–199

Naval Weapon Center (California), experiments in broadbanding at, 197–199

Nebraska:
  collective bargaining provisions for, 493
  job classifications in (1986–1998), 205

Needs assessment training, 321–325
  established techniques for, 322–325

Negro in Federal Employment, The (Krislov), 425–426

Nevada:
  collective bargaining provisions for, 493
  job classifications in (1986–1998), 205

New Hampshire:
  collective bargaining provisions for, 493
  job classifications in (1986–1998), 205

New Jersey:
  collective bargaining provisions for, 493
  job classifications in (1986–1998), 205
  WAVE project in, 533–534

New Leader, The (Morrison), 444–445

New Mexico:
  collective bargaining provisions for, 493
  job classifications in (1986–1998), 205

New York City, GS and SES salary ranges for (2000), 210

New York Civil Service Reform Association (1877), 12–13

New York Customhouse, corruption in, 12

New York State Center for Women in Government, reevaluation of class and comp systems, 195

New York State:
  civil service reform in, 48
  collective bargaining provisions for, 493
  job classifications in (1986–1998), 205

[New York State]
merit system in, 33
Veteran Benefits Administration regional office, changes in staffing
classification, and compensation
systems (1993–1997), 171–176
New York Times, 243–244
"Nexus" test of the MSPB, 118
Nixon administration:
collective bargaining and, 481
EEO programs and, 385–386
Nonbinding arbitration, 501
Nonpartisan speech, 110–113
Norfolk Naval Shipyards, application of
QCs at, 339
North Carolina:
collective bargaining provisions for,
493
job classifications in (1986–1998),
205
North Dakota:
collective bargaining provisions for,
493
job classifications in (1986–1998),
205

O'Connor v. Ortega (1087), 123–124
O'Hare v. *City of Northlake* (1996),
127
Oakland, California, study of personnel
policies and politics in, 186–188
Objectives of performance appraisal,
267, 270
Occupational group (defined), 179
Occupational Safety and Health Admin-
istration (OSHA), 543–549
federal safety and health initiative
(Fed 2000) of, 545–546
Occupation Safety and Health Act of
1970, 543–544
section 19 of, 547
Office of Affirmative Employment Pro-
grams, 387
Office of Federal Agency Programs
(OFAP), 544

Office of Federal Contract Compliance
Programs (OFCCP), 400–403
Office of Personnel Management
(OPM):
ACWA examination system of, 254–
256
broadbanding and, 199
Civil Service Reform Act of 1978
and, 485
civil service reform efforts and, 49
classification system reforms issued
by (1986), 195–197
Clinton transition team recommendations for, 57–60
CSC replaced by, 26–27
decision analysis forecasting technique of, 157
EEO program and, 387
federal compensation, 207
FQI as part of, 336
leadership role in improving human
resources management, 90
1978 guide for improving performance appraisal, 277–278
organizational chart for (1999), 27,
71
PACE exam and, 252–253
partnership agreements in the federal
government (1997), 462
PMRS terminated by, 285
proposal for reforming SES, 75–77
reinvention of, 67–72
report on inequities in minority employment in federal government,
438–439
representative bureaucracy issue and,
427–429
survey of employee's attitude toward
performance appraisal, 271
Volcker Commission and, 54, 55
Office of Strategic Services (OSS), assessment center concept and, 294
Ohio:
collective bargaining provisions for,
493

[Ohio]
job classifications in (1986–1998), 205
public employees right to strike in (1998), 504
Oklahoma:
collective bargaining provisions for, 493
job classifications in (1986–1998), 205
Omaha, Nebraska, 360-degree appraisal system for, 297–298
Oncale v. *Sundowner Offshore Services* (1998), 408
Online educational course series, 331
On-the-job training (coaching), 311
Oral examinations, 247–248
Oral interviews, 324
Oregon:
collective bargaining provisions for, 493
job classifications in (1986–1998), 205
public employees right to strike in (1998), 504
Organizational objectives and strategies for achieving diversity in workplace, 451
Organizational requirements for human resources planning, 149, 150, 151–153
OSC, civil service reform efforts and, 50

Participate management, 342
Participative methods (approach to performance appraisal), 279–281
"Passive representation," 427
PATCOB, 428–429
Patrician reformer, 10
Patronage, 8
curbs on power of, 8–9
Elrod v. *Burns* case, 93–95
Pay administration in government, 206–208

Pay equity, 408–411
female-male pay gap, 411–412
Pay for Performance (National Academy of Science report on appraisal and merit pay), 284–285
Pay reform, the Volcker Commission and, 56–57
Peer ratings, 275
Pendleton Act of 1883, 1, 2, 7, 9, 11, 13–15, 24, 33, 39, 97, 114, 243, 288
Pennsylvania:
collective bargaining provisions for, 493
job classifications in (1986–1998), 205
public employees right to strike in (1998), 504
Performance appraisal, 265–300
assessment centers, 293–298
assessment of multisource appraisals, 293–298
behavioral focus on, 277–281
changes to reflect workforce diversity, 444–446
chronology of employee performance management in federal government, 288–292
history of merit pay, 281–286, 287
problem of, 267–273
quality management and, 364–366
review of performance evaluation reports, 323, 324
state government perspectives on merit pay, 287–293
360 degree appraisal, 265–267, 268–269
traditional approach to, 273–276
Performance-based organizations (PBOs), 73, 74
Performance examinations, 247
Performance Management and Recognition System (1987 MSPB report), 283

Performance Management and Recognition System (PMRS) of 1984, 52, 281–283, 284, 285
  legislation extends (1989 and 1991), 291
  termination of (1993), 285, 291
Performance Rating Act of 1950, 288
Personal contacts (factor in federal job evaluation system), 191
Personal liberty, 116–118
Personnel Administrator v. Feeney (1979), 38
Personnel policies and processes:
  changes to reflect workforce diversity, 441–447
    performance appraisals, awards, and development, 444–446
    recruitment and selection practices, 441–444
    work arrangements and benefits, 446–447
  management and training, 306–310
  quality management and personnel management policies, 363–372
PEST projections, 160
Philadelphia, Pennsylvania:
  naval shipyard strike of 1839, 476
  public–private competitions in, 142
Phoenix, Arizona, public–private competitions in, 142
Physical demands (factor in federal job evaluation system), 191
Pickering v. Board of Education (1968), 111
Placement (essential of employment process), 242–243
Point-rating method (major category of job evaluation planning), 191, 192
Political neutrality, 113–115
Polygraph test, for pre-employment screening, 126
Position:
  as defined by the Baruch report, 181–182
  definition of, 178

[Position]
  evolution of position classification, 177–183
Positive classification, language of, 178–179
Position Classification: A Behavioral Analysis for the Public Service (Shafritz), 185–188
Position Classification: A Guide for City and County Managers, 178–179
Position classifiers, 187
Position description method (approach to performance appraisal), 278
Postal alliance, 480
Postal Reorganization Act of 1970, 470, 479, 482–483
Postal Safety Enhancement Law of 1998, 546
Postal strike of 1970, 466, 469–470
Predictive validity, 250
Pregnancy Discrimination Act of 1978, 410
President's Award for Quality, 340, 343, 359
President's Committee on Administrative Management (1937). see Brownlow Committee
President's Committee on Equal Employment Opportunity, 385
President's Committee on Government Employment Policy (1995), 384
President's Task Force on Federal Training Technology (1999), 332
Printz v. United States (1997), 494
Privacy rights of public employees, 123–125
Private sector models:
  of collective bargaining, 466–468
  of employment, 106–109
Privatization, 125–128
Problem-solving teams, training and development of, 369–370
Process metrics, 342
Process redesign teams (PRTs), 369, 370

Professional Air Traffic Controllers Organization (PATCO), strike of 1961, 506–507
Professional and Administrative Career Examination (PACE), 252–254, 255
  discontinuation of, 388
Programmed high-hazard inspections, 544
Proposed Framework for Improving the Senior Executive Service (OPM proposal), 75–77
Proposition 209 in California, 378
Protected class, 398
Prussia, merit system in, 2
Public Administration Review, 253–254
Public interest in arbitration, 503
Public Personnel Administration (Mosher and Kingsley), 6
Public sector employment, increasing size of, 236–241
Public service model, 110–128
  equal protection, 119–120
  Fourth Amendment privacy, 123–125
  freedom of association, 115–116
  freedom of expression, 110–113
  liberty, 116–118
  political neutrality, 113–115
  privatization, 125–128
  right to disobey, 125
  right to a hearing, 120–123
Purpose of personal contracts (factor in federal job evaluation system), 191

Quadrennial Defense Review (QDR) for the DOD, 352
Quality assurance, 337
Quality circles (QCs), 339, 370
Quality improvement teams (QITs), 369
Quality management and reengineering, 335–373
  advent of TQM, 341–344
  cornerstones of quality management, 342–343

(Quality management and reengineering)
  "demise" of TQM and the BPR challenge in the 1990s, 345–350
  gulf between quality haves and have nots, 361–366
  origins of quality management, 337–341
  personnel management policies vs. quality management premises, 363–372
    quality and compensation issues, 366–367
    quality and labor relation issues, 370–372
    quality and personnel policy, 364–366
    quality and training and development, 367–370
  quality on the edge, 356–361
  understanding reengineering as change management, 350–355
Quality of work life (QWL) movement, 370
Quid pro quo sexual harassment, 406

Race, Gender, and Rhetoric (Fernandez), 450
Race differential, 398
Race discrimination cases, equal protection and, 120
Ramspeck Act of 1940, 288
Rankin v. *McPherson* (1987), 110–113
Ranking method (major category of job evaluation planning), 191, 192
Rank-in-person system, 241–242
Rank-in-position system, 241–242
Rating scales for performance appraisal, 274–275
Reaction (level of measuring training evaluation), 330
Reading assistant, 398
Reagan administration:
  civil service reform and, 49–53
  PATCO strike of 1961 and, 506–507

[Reagan administration]
  quality management and, 343
  war-on-drugs program of, 549–550,
    552–553
Reasonable accommodation, 398
Recruitment, changes to reflect work-
    force diversity, 441–444
Recruitment and selection, 221–263
  civil service executive recruitment in
    Michigan, 221–224
  development (and decline) of uniform
    guidelines, 230–236
  essentials of employment process,
    242–246
  examination and validation, 246–251
  federal case history from PACE to
    ACWA, 251–256
  hiring in the 1990s, 236, 237
  human capital in government, 256–
    260
  importance of public employment,
    236–241
  legal environment of public sector se-
    lection, 224–229
  personal rank versus position rank,
    241–242
Reengineering. see Quality management
    and reengineering
Reengineering the Corporation (Ham-
    mer and Champy), 348
Regents of the University of California
    v. Bakke (1978), 375–376, 379
Rehabilitation Act of 1973, 103
  Title V of, 388
Reich, Robert, on effects of downsizing,
    146
Reinventing Government (Osborne and
    Gaebler), 61–62, 346
Reinventing Human Resources Manage-
    ment, 63
Religious discrimination, 398–399
Representative bureaucracy, 399, 425–
    427
Restrictive credentialism, 399
Results (level of measuring training eval-
    uation), 330

"Retaining Quality Federal Employees:
    Life After PACE," 253–254
Retroactive seniority, 399
Reverse discrimination, 375
Rhode Island:
  collective bargaining provisions for,
    493
  job classifications in (1986–1998),
    205
  public employees right to strike in
    (1998), 504
Richardson v. McKnight (1997), 128
Right to a hearing, 121-123
Right to disobey, 125
Rightful place, 399
Role playing (training method), 311
Roosevelt (Franklin) administration:
  civil service reform and, 20–21
  Executive Order 8802 of, 384
Rutan v. Republican Party of Illinois
    (1990), 14, 95

Sabbatical programs (training method),
    312
Safety on the job, 543–553
  drug testing, 549–553
  substance abuse in the workplace,
    549
Salary Reform Act of 1962, 206, 288
Same-sex harassment, 408
San Francisco, California, GS and SES
    salary ranges for (2000), 210
San Francisco Unified School District
    (SFUSD), desegregation system
    in, 454–455
Sara Lee Company, 446
Scenario planning, 157–164
  EPA planning for human resources
    needs, 160–164
  PEST projections, 160
Schedule "B" appointment authority of
    the OPM, 252–253
Schultz v. Wheaton Glass Co. (1970)
    408
Scientific management, 16–19, 177–
    183, 337

Scope and effect (factor in federal job evaluation system), 191
Seattle, Washington, managing diversity in, 421–423
Second generation human resources planning technique, 150, 151
Selection (essential of employment process), 242–243
  changes to reflect workforce diversity, 441–444
Self-appraisal, 275
Self-paced learning training, 311–312
Semiautonomous work teams (SAWTs), 369
Senior executive service (SES), 29
  civil service reform and, 51–52, 73–77
  ECQs for, 316–320
  member profile (Sept. 1998), 75
Sensitivity training, 311
Service Contract Act of 1965, 543
706 agency, 399
Sexual harassment, 382, 403–408
  MSPB survey of harassment in the federal workplace (1994), 541, 542
Sheet Metal Workers' International Association v. *EEOC* (1986), 379
Shelton v. *Tucker* (1960), 115
Simulation (training method), 311–312
Six sigma black belts, 357–358
Skills training or demonstration, 310
Skinner v. *Railway Labor Executive's Association* (1989), 550
"Sleazegate," 404
Social learning (learning theory), 312
Social Life of Information, The (Brown and Duguid), 332
Social Security Administration (SSA), reengineering and, 353–354
Society, cultivating a multicultural workplace as responsibility of, 453–454
Society for Industrial and Organization Psychology, 235

South Carolina:
  civil service reform and, 80–81
  collective bargaining provisions for, 493
  job classifications in (1986–1998), 205
South Dakota:
  collective bargaining provisions for, 493
  job classifications in (1986–1998), 205
Special conferences and seminars (training method), 311
Specialist/professional phase (of career development), 313
Speech, freedom of, 110–113
Spoils system, 2–6, 93
Staffing flexibilities, 1999 civil service improvements in, 86–88
State, Department of, changes in general schedule employees (1982 to 1992), 59
State government:
  BLS employment predictions for (1986–2006), 151–152
  civil service reform and, 77–81
  compensation developments for, 212–215
  diversity in traditionally male occupations (1985 and 1995), 426
  EAPs and, 554
  fastest growing and declining jobs in (1993 and 1997), 136, 137
  federal EEO program and, 387
  job classifications in (1986–1998), 204–205
  labor-management relations and, 491–496
  merit pay system and, 33–37, 287–293
  minimum (living) wages and, 215–217
  union vs. nonunion wages for works in (1998), 473
Stereotyping in the workplace, 434–435
  "labeling" and, 449

Strict scrutiny test, 376
Strikes, 503–510
Subjective discrimination, 432–434
Subordinate ratings, 275
Substance abuse in the workplace, 549
Supervisors, 496
Supervisory controls (factor in federal
    job evaluation system), 190
Supervisory-level jobs, 179
Supply and demand aspects of human re-
    sources planning, 153–164
Sweatshops, 543
Systemic discrimination, 399

Taft administration:
    patronage appointments and, 15
    racial discrimination during, 381
Taft-Hartley Act of 1947, 478, 496
Tailhook scandal, 404
*Taxman v. Piscataway Town Board of
    Education* (1997), 380
Taylor, Frederick, 337
    development of "scientific manage-
    ment", 16
"Tear It Down," (Hornestay), 209
Technology-based training (TBT):
    federal government use of, 332
    impact on training and development,
    331–332
Tennessee Valley Authority (TVA),
    labor-management cooperation
    and, 482, 487
Tennessee Valley Trades and Labor
    Council, 482, 487
Tennessee:
    collective bargaining provisions for,
    493
    job classifications in (1986–1998),
    205
Tenure of Office Act of 1867, 9
Texas:
    collective bargaining provisions for,
    493
    job classifications in (1986–1998),
    205

Third generation human resources plan-
    ning technique, 151–153
360-degree performance appraisal sys-
    tems, 265–267, 268–269, 297–
    298
Total quality management (TQM), 335,
    336, 339–341, 362
    advent of, 341–344
    definition of, 344
    demise of, 345–350
*Toward Effective Performance in the
    Federal Government* (1988
    MSPB report), 283
Traditional personnel management, ap-
    proach to performance appraisal
    of, 270, 273–276
Training and development, 301–334
    assessing training: the evaluation is-
    sue, 325–330
    career development and the em-
    ployee, 313–321
    diversity awareness in, 447–449
    evolution of, 304–306
    "knowledge management" move-
    ment, 301–304
    methods of training, 310–313
    on planning training: the strategy is-
    sue, 321–325
    quality and, 367–370
    systems approach to, 323
    technology and, 331–332
    training and personnel relationship,
    306–310
Transportation, Department of, changes
    in general schedule employees
    (1982 to 1992), 59
Treasury, Department of, changes in
    general schedule employees
    (1982 to 1992), 59
Truman administration:
    civil service reform and, 21–22
    EEO program and, 384

Unequal treatment in today's workforce,
    431–439
    glass ceilings, 436–438

[Unequal treatment in today's workforce]
other disparities, 438–439
power of subtle differences, 439
stereotypes, 434–435
subjective discrimination, 432–434
Unfair labor practice charges (1986–
1995), 464
Unfairness in the workplace, dispute resolution mechanisms for prevention of, 535–543
alternative dispute resolution approaches, 541–543
traditional adjudicatory systems, 536–
541
Uniform efficiency rating system
(1935), 288
*Uniform Guidelines on Employee Selec-
tion Procedures*, 230–236
Union of Japanese Scientists and Engineers, the Deming Prize and,
340
Unions:
decline in private sector unionism,
471
unionization in public and private sectors (1987 and 1997), 488, 489
unionization of public employees,
488–491
United Kingdom, public–private competitions in, 142
United Public Workers v. *Mitchell*
(1947), 114
United States (U.S.), job classifications
by state government (1986–
1998), 204–205
U.S. Customs Service, application of
QCs for, 339
U.S. Employee Assistance Professionals
Association, 553
U.S. Postal Service (USPS):
health and safety violations of, 546
workplace violence and, 532
U.S. Supreme Court:
employer drug-testing programs and,
549–552
labor–management relations and, 494

[U.S. Supreme Court]
legal decisions re employment selection, 224, 225–226, 227, 228,
229, 230
ruling on recruitment and selection
practices, 443
ruling on sexual harassment, 406,
407, 408
United States. v. *Georgia Power Company* (1973), 230
United States v. *National Treasury Employee Union* (1995), 118–119
United States v. *Paradise* (1987), 119,
379
United States v. *South Carolina* (1978),
235
United Steelworkers of America v. *Weber* (1979), 379
University of California at Davis, 375
University of Texas School of Law, 376
Utah:
collective bargaining provisions for,
493
job classifications in (1986–1998),
205

Validation, 246–251
Validity of the training and development evaluation, 328
Vermont:
collective bargaining provisions for,
493
job classifications in (1986–1998),
205
public employees right to strike in
(1998), 504
Vernonia School District 471 v. *Acton*
(1995), 550
Veterans Administration (VA):
New York regional office changes in
staffing, classification, and compensation systems (1993–1997),
171–176
quality management and, 343
Veterans preference, 383

Violence in the public sector workplace,
    531–534
Virginia:
    collective bargaining provisions for,
        493
    job classifications in (1986–1998),
        205
Virtual learning, 312–313
Vocational Rehabilitation Act of 1973,
    414
Volcker Commission, 53–57, 207
Voluntary arbitration, 501

Walsh–Healy Public Contracts Act of
    1936, 543
Wards Cove v. *Atonio* (1989), 226–228
Washington:
    broadbanding in, 202
    collective bargaining provisions for,
        493
    job classifications in (1986–1998),
        205
Washington–Baltimore, GS and SES sal-
    ary ranges for (2000), 210
Washington Management System, 202
Washington v. *Davis* (1976), 234–235
Waters v. *Churchill* (1994), 110
Weber, Max, bureaucratic model of, 2
West v. *Atkins* (1988), 127
West Virginia:
    collective bargaining provisions for,
        493
    job classifications in (1986–1998),
        203, 205
Whistleblower Protection Act (WPA) of
    1989, 32
Wilson administration, racial discrimina-
    tion during, 381–382
Winter Commission, 78–80, 426–427
Wisconsin:
    collective bargaining provisions for,
        493
    job classifications in (1986–1998),
        205
    public employees right to strike in
        (1998), 504

Women:
    comparable worth and pay equity for,
        408–411
    employment in traditionally male oc-
        cupations (1985 and 1996), 426–
        427
    female–male pay gap, 411–412
    glass ceilings for, 436–438
    increase in the workforce (1950–
        1997), 424–425
    past treatment in the federal services
        of, 382–383
    representation in grade groupings in
        federal government (1997), 390,
        391
    representation in the population, civil-
        ian, and federal workforces
        (1997), 429, 430
    sexual harassment and, 403–408
    stereotyping in the workplace for,
        435
    subjective discrimination in today's
        workforce, 429, 432, 433, 434
    work arrangements and benefits for
        working mothers, 446–447
Woodland v. *City of Houston* (1990),
    126
Work arrangements, changes to reflect
    workforce diversity, 444–446
Work environment (factor in federal job
    evaluation system), 191
Worker benefits, changes to reflect work-
    force diversity, 444–446
Workers Against Violence Efforts
    (WAVE), 533–534
Workforce planning, 149–153
Workforce 2000 (Hudson Institute
    study), 424, 427
Workforce 2020 (Hudson Institute
    study), 424–425, 454
Work groups, training and development
    of, 369–370
Working for America (1989 MSPB re-
    port), 271, 276
Working mothers, work arrangements
    and benefits for, 446–447

Workplace Counseling (Carroll), 556
Workplace violence in the public sector, 531–534
Work planning and review (WPR) system, 280
Written examinations, 247
Written performance evaluation, 273–276
Wygant v. *Jackson Bd. of Ed.* (1986), 379

Wyoming:
collective bargaining provisions for, 493
job classifications in (1986–1998), 205

Xerox, 335, 338, 361